36: *British Novelists, 1890-1929: Modernists,* edited by Thomas F. Staley (1985)

37: *American Writers of the Early Republic,* edited by Emory Elliott (1985)

38: *Afro-American Writers After 1955: Dramatists and Prose Writers,* edited by Thadious M. Davis and Trudier Harris (1985)

39: *British Novelists, 1660-1800,* 2 parts, edited by Martin C. Battestin (1985)

40: *Poets of Great Britain and Ireland Since 1960,* 2 parts, edited by Vincent B. Sherry, Jr. (1985)

41: *Afro-American Poets Since 1955,* edited by Trudier Harris and Thadious M. Davis (1985)

42: *American Writers for Children Before 1900,* edited by Glenn E. Estes (1985)

43: *American Newspaper Journalists, 1690-1872,* edited by Perry J. Ashley (1986)

44: *American Screenwriters,* Second Series, edited by Randall Clark, Robert E. Morsberger, and Stephen O. Lesser (1986)

45: *American Poets, 1880-1945,* First Series, edited by Peter Quartermain (1986)

46: *American Literary Publishing Houses, 1900-1980: Trade and Paperback,* edited by Peter Dzwonkoski (1986)

47: *American Historians, 1866-1912,* edited by Clyde N. Wilson (1986)

48: *American Poets, 1880-1945,* Second Series, edited by Peter Quartermain (1986)

49: *American Literary Publishing Houses, 1638-1899,* 2 parts, edited by Peter Dzwonkoski (1986)

50: *Afro-American Writers Before the Harlem Renaissance,* edited by Trudier Harris (1986)

51: *Afro-American Writers from the Harlem Renaissance to 1940,* edited by Trudier Harris (1987)

52: *American Writers for Children Since 1960: Fiction,* edited by Glenn E. Estes (1986)

53: *Canadian Writers Since 1960,* First Series, edited by W. H. New (1986)

54: *American Poets, 1880-1945,* Third Series, 2 parts, edited by Peter Quartermain (1987)

55: *Victorian Prose Writers Before 1867,* edited by William B. Thesing (1987)

56: *German Fiction Writers, 1914-1945,* edited by James Hardin (1987)

57: *Victorian Prose Writers After 1867,* edited by William B. Thesing (1987)

58: *Jacobean and Caroline Dramatists,* edited by Fredson Bowers (1987)

59: *American Literary Critics and Scholars, 1800-1850,* edited by John W. Rathbun and Monica M. Grecu (1987)

60: *Canadian Writers Since 1960,* Second Series, edited by W. H. New (1987)

61: *American Writers for Children Since 1960: Poets, Illustrators, and Nonfiction Authors,* edited by Glenn E. Estes (1987)

62: *Elizabethan Dramatists,* edited by Fredson Bowers (1987)

63: *Modern American Critics, 1920-1955,* edited by Gregory S. Jay (1988)

64: *American Literary Critics and Scholars, 1850-1880,* edited by John W. Rathbun and Monica M. Grecu (1988)

65: *French Novelists, 1900-1930,* edited by Catharine Savage Brosman (1988)

66: *German Fiction Writers, 1885-1913,* 2 parts, edited by James Hardin (1988)

67: *Modern American Critics Since 1955,* edited by Gregory S. Jay (1988)

68: *Canadian Writers, 1920-1959,* First Series, edited by W. H. New (1988)

69: *Contemporary German Fiction Writers,* First Series, edited by Wolfgang D. Elfe and James Hardin (1988)

70: *British Mystery Writers, 1860-1919,* edited by Bernard Benstock and Thomas F. Staley (1988)

(Continued on back endsheets)

Dictionary of Literary Biography • Volume Eighty-five

Austrian Fiction Writers
After 1914

Dictionary of Literary Biography • Volume Eighty-five

Austrian Fiction Writers After 1914

Edited by
James Hardin
University of South Carolina

and

Donald G. Daviau
University of California, Riverside

8080

A Bruccoli Clark Layman Book
Gale Research Inc.
Detroit, New York, Fort Lauderdale, London

Manufactured by Edwards Brothers, Inc.
Ann Arbor, Michigan
Printed in the United States of America

Library of Congress Cataloging-in-Publication Data

Austrian fiction writers after 1914 / edited by James
    Hardin and Donald G. Daviau.
    "A Bruccoli Clark Layman book."
    Includes index.
    ISBN 0-8103-4563-3
    1. German fiction–Austrian authors–Bio-bibliography.
2. German fiction–20th century–Bio-bibliography. 3. Novelists, Austrian–20th century–Biography–Dictionaries. I.
Hardin, James N. II. Daviau, Donald G. III. Series.
PT3814.A98 1989
833'.9109–dc20
[B]
                                                89-7890P
                                                     CIP

Contents

Plan of the Series...vii

Foreword...ix

Acknowledgments...xi

Ilse Aichinger (1921-   ).......................................3
  Dagmar C. G. Lorenz

H. C. Artmann (1921-   ).......................................14
  Peter Pabisch

Ingeborg Bachmann (1926-1973).....................24
  Karen Achberger

Vicki Baum (1888-1960) 40
  Lynda J. King

Konrad Bayer (1932-1964)...............................55
  Joseph G. McVeigh

Thomas Bernhard (1931-1989) 62
  Steve Dowden

Imma von Bodmershof (1895-1982) 78
  Jorun B. Johns

Hermann Broch (1886-1951)............................82
  Paul Michael Lützeler and John Carson Pettey

Elias Canetti (1905-   )....................................103
  Thomas H. Falk

Heimito von Doderer (1896-1966) 111
  Andrew W. Barker

Milo Dor (1923-   )..130
  Jerry Glenn

Albert Drach (1902-   )...................................138
  Ernestine Schlant

Jeannie Ebner (1918-   )..................................148
  August Obermayer

Herbert Eisenreich (1925-1986) 153
  Renate Latimer

Erich Fried (1921-1988) 158
  Jerry Glenn

Barbara Frischmuth (1941-   )........................166
  Donald G. Daviau

Peter Handke (1942-   )...................................173
  Stephanie Barbé Hammer

Peter Henisch (1943-   )..................................188
  Ludwig Fischer

Ödön von Horváth (1901-1938) 193
  Horst Jarka

Franz Innerhofer (1944-   ).............................211
  Gerald A. Fetz

Elfriede Jelinek (1946-   )................................217
  Frank W. Young

Gert F. Jonke (1946-   )...................................224
  Johannes W. Vazulik

Alfred Kolleritsch (1931-   )............................233
  Beth Bjorklund

Alexander Lernet-Holenia (1897-1976)..........238
  Hugo Schmidt

Friederike Mayröcker (1924-   ).......................247
  Beth Bjorklund

Erika Mitterer (1906-   )..................................252
  Catherine Hutter

Peter Rosei (1946-   ).......................................258
  Robert Acker

Gerhard Roth (1942-   )...................................263
  Sigrid Bauschinger

Joseph Roth (1894-1939)................................270
  Sidney Rosenfeld

George Saiko (1892-1962)...............................288
  Friedrich Achberger

Friedrich Torberg (1908-1979).......................293
  Cornelius Schnauber

Johannes Urzidil (1896-1970) 301
  Wolfgang D. Elfe

Martina Wied (1882-1957)..............................311
  Sylvia M. Patsch

Herbert Zand (1923-1970)..............................316
  Pamela S. Saur

Checklist of Further Readings........................323

Contributors...327

Cumulative Index..331

Plan of the Series

The advisory board, the editors, and the publisher of the *Dictionary of Literary Biography* are joined in endorsing Mark Twain's declaration. The literature of a nation provides an inexhaustible resource of permanent worth. We intend to make literature and its creators better understood and more accessible to students and the reading public, while satisfying the standards of teachers and scholars.

To meet these requirements, *literary biography* has been construed in terms of the author's achievement. The most important thing about a writer is his writing. Accordingly, the entries in *DLB* are career biographies, tracing the development of the author's canon and the evolution of his reputation.

The purpose of *DLB* is not only to provide reliable information in a convenient format but also to place the figures in the larger perspective of literary history and to offer appraisals of their accomplishments by qualified scholars.

The publication plan for *DLB* resulted from two years of preparation. The project was proposed to Bruccoli Clark by Frederick G. Ruffner, president of the Gale Research Company, in November 1975. After specimen entries were prepared and typeset, an advisory board was formed to refine the entry format and develop the series rationale. In meetings held during 1976, the publisher, series editors, and advisory board approved the scheme for a comprehensive biographical dictionary of persons who contributed to North American literature. Editorial work on the first volume began in January 1977, and it was published in 1978. In order to make *DLB* more than a reference tool and to compile volumes that individually have claim to status as literary history, it was decided to organize volumes by topic, period, or genre. Each of these freestanding volumes provides a biographical-bibliographical guide and overview for a particular area of literature. We are convinced that this organization—as opposed to a single alphabet method—constitutes a valuable innovation in the presentation of reference material. The volume plan necessarily requires many decisions for the placement and treatment of authors who might properly be included in two or three volumes. In some instances a major figure will be included in separate volumes, but with different entries emphasizing the aspect of his career appropriate to each volume. Ernest Hemingway, for example, is represented in *American Writers in Paris, 1920-1939* by an entry focusing on his expatriate apprenticeship; he is also in *American Novelists, 1910-1945* with an entry surveying his entire career. Each volume includes a cumulative index of subject authors and articles. Comprehensive indexes to the entire series are planned.

With volume ten in 1982 it was decided to enlarge the scope of *DLB*. By the end of 1986 twenty-one volumes treating British literature had been published, and volumes for Commonwealth and Modern European literature were in progress. The series has been further augmented by the *DLB Yearbooks* (since 1981) which update published entries and add new entries to keep the *DLB* current with contemporary activity. There have also been *DLB Documentary Series* volumes which provide biographical and critical source materials for figures whose work is judged to have particular interest for students. One of these companion volumes is entirely devoted to Tennessee Williams.

We define literature as the *intellectual commerce of a nation:* not merely as belles lettres but as that ample and complex process by which ideas are generated, shaped, and transmitted. *DLB* entries are not limited to "creative writers" but extend to other figures who in their time and in their way influenced the mind of a people. Thus the series encompasses historians, journalists, publishers, and screenwriters. By this means readers of *DLB* may be aided to perceive litera-

---

ture not as cult scripture in the keeping of intellectual high priests but firmly positioned at the center of a nation's life.

DLB includes the major writers appropriate to each volume and those standing in the ranks immediately behind them. Scholarly and critical counsel has been sought in deciding which minor figures to include and how full their entries should be. Wherever possible, useful references are made to figures who do not warrant separate entries.

Each *DLB* volume has a volume editor responsible for planning the volume, selecting the figures for inclusion, and assigning the entries. Volume editors are also responsible for preparing, where appropriate, appendices surveying the major periodicals and literary and intellectual movements for their volumes, as well as lists of further readings. Work on the series as a whole is coordinated at the Bruccoli Clark Layman editorial center in Columbia, South Carolina, where the editorial staff is responsible for accuracy of the published volumes.

One feature that distinguishes *DLB* is the illustration policy–its concern with the iconography of literature. Just as an author is influenced by his surroundings, so is the reader's understanding of the author enhanced by a knowledge of his environment. Therefore *DLB* volumes include not only drawings, paintings, and photographs of authors, often depicting them at various stages in their careers, but also illustrations of their families and places where they lived. Title pages are regularly reproduced in facsimile along with dust jackets for modern authors. The dust jackets are a special feature of *DLB* because they often document better than anything else the way in which an author's work was perceived in its own time. Specimens of the writers' manuscripts are included when feasible.

Samuel Johnson rightly decreed that "The chief glory of every people arises from its authors." The purpose of the *Dictionary of Literary Biography* is to compile literary history in the surest way available to us–by accurate and comprehensive treatment of the lives and work of those who contributed to it.

The *DLB* Advisory Board

Foreword

DLB 85: Austrian Fiction Writers After 1914 deals with Austrian writers whose first published works appeared after the outbreak of World War I–an event that, especially for Austria, marked the close of an era: by the end of the war the vast, powerful, and diverse Austro-Hungarian Empire of some fifty million people had been reduced to a "torso" of fewer than eight million. Writers of the early postwar period tended to be nostalgic for Austria's former imperial greatness. The old idea of unification of Austria and Germany was revived; it was finally carried out in 1938 by Hitler, driving many Austrian writers into exile. After World War II Austria rose from defeat to become a prosperous nonaligned nation, but some of its younger writers have refused to allow their countrymen to forget their Nazi past.

Although some of the writers treated in this volume are better known as poets (Friederike Mayröcker and Erika Mitterer, for example) or dramatists (Ödön von Horváth) than as writers of fiction, the principle followed was to include such figures but to concentrate on their fiction, touching on other genres insofar as they are relevant either to the fiction or to the general development of the writer in question. Some of these authors will reappear in a subsequent DLB volume on German-language dramatists.

As in previous DLB volumes on German and Austrian authors, we have included not only writers of unquestioned literary significance and lesser talents who are especially typical of a given movement or tendency but also unjustly neglected writers. Among writers of the first magnitude covered in this volume are Ingeborg Bachmann, Thomas Bernhard, Hermann Broch, Elias Canetti, Peter Handke, and Joseph Roth. Writers whose place in the literary canon is still being debated include Milo Dor, Jeannie Ebner, Barbara Frischmuth, Alexander Lernet-Holenia, Friedrich Torberg, and Herbert Zand. Vicki Baum was a writer of Trivialliteratur (popular literature) whose novels have historical and sociological importance. A writer whose works have only recently begun to attract the critical attention they deserve is Albert Drach, whose first book appeared in 1919. There are many other contemporary Austrian writers who deserve inclusion but had to be left out because of limitations of space; it is hoped that a subsequent volume will include these emerging talents.

The contributors to this volume attempted to look at their subjects with fresh eyes, to examine the authors' works as well as the secondary literature. The bibliography at the beginning of each entry lists all first editions of the subject's books in chronological order; if an English translation exists, the first American and British editions of the translation are listed. The bibliography also lists translations into German, forewords, contributions to collections, and books edited by the subject, as well as selected periodical publications. We trust that even the specialist will find bibliographical information in some entries that was previously unavailable in English or German reference works.

Assuming that many readers will have little or no knowledge of German, the entries include translations of German titles, quotations, and terms. Important secondary literature is listed at the end of each entry. The location of the letters and other papers (Nachlaß) has been provided in all cases where it is known.

DLB 85: Austrian Fiction Writers After 1914 continues the coverage of DLB 81: Austrian Fiction Writers, 1875-1913 and parallels DLB 56: German Fiction Writers, 1914-1945. It is part of a series of DLB volumes treating German-language literature, including DLB 66: German Fiction Writers, 1885-1913; DLB 69: Contemporary German Fiction Writers, First Series; and DLB 75: Contemporary German Fiction Writers, Second Series. Future DLB volumes will treat the writers of the "Age of Goethe"; twentieth-century German, Austrian, and Swiss dramatists; and seventeenth-century German writers.

–James Hardin and Donald G. Daviau

Acknowledgments

This book was produced by Bruccoli Clark Layman, Inc. Karen L. Rood is senior editor for the *Dictionary of Literary Biography* series. Philip B. Dematteis was the in-house editor.

Production coordinator is James W. Hipp. Systems manager is Charles D. Brower. Art supervisor is Susan Todd. Penney L. Haughton is responsible for layout and graphics. Copyediting supervisor is Joan M. Prince. Typesetting supervisor is Kathleen M. Flanagan. William Adams, Laura Ingram, and Michael D. Senecal are editorial associates. The production staff includes Rowena Betts, Nancy Brevard-Bracey, Joseph M. Bruccoli, Teresa Chaney, Patricia Coate, Marie Creed, Allison Deal, Holly Deal, Sarah A. Estes, Brian A. Glassman, Cynthia Hallman, Susan C. Heath, Mary Long, Kathy S. Merlette, Laura Garren Moore, and Sheri Beckett Neal. Jean W. Ross is permissions editor.

Walter W. Ross and Jennifer Toth did the library research with the assistance of the reference staff at the Thomas Cooper Library of the University of South Carolina: Lisa Antley, Daniel Boice, Faye Chadwell, Cathy Eckman, Gary Geer, Cathie Gottlieb, David L. Haggard, Jens Holley, Jackie Kinder, Marcia Martin, Jean Rhyne, Beverly Steele, Ellen Tillett, Carol Tobin, and Virginia Weathers.

The editors express their warm gratitude to Ms. Friederike Zeitlhofer of the Austrian Institute, New York, for her invaluable assitance in securing illustrations and information for this volume.

Dictionary of Literary Biography • Volume Eighty-five

Austrian Fiction Writers
After 1914

Dictionary of Literary Biography

Ilse Aichinger

(1 November 1921-   )

Dagmar C. G. Lorenz
Ohio State University

BOOKS: *Die größere Hoffnung: Roman* (Vienna &
Amsterdam: Bermann-Fischer, 1948); translated by Cornelia Schaeffer as *Herod's Children* (New York: Atheneum, 1963);
Rede unter dem Galgen: Erzählungen (Vienna: Jungbrunnen, 1952); republished as *Der Gefesselte: Erzählungen* (Frankfurt am Main: Fischer, 1953); translated by Eric Mosbacher
as *The Bound Man and Other Stories* (London:
Secker & Warburg, 1955; New York: Noonday Press, 1956);
Zu keiner Stunde (Frankfurt am Main: Fischer,
1957)–"Zu keiner Stunde," "Belvedere," "Er-
stes Semester," "Sonntagsdienst," translated
by James C. Alldridge as "Never at Any
Time," "Belvedere," "First Term," "Sunday
Duty," respectively, in his *Ilse Aichinger* (Che-
ster Springs, Pa.: Dufour Editions, 1969;
London: Wolff, 1969); "Tauben und Wölfe,"
translated by Allen H. Chappel as "Doves
and Wolves," in Chappel, ed., *Ilse Aichinger:
Selected Poetry and Prose* (Durango, Colo.:
Logbridge-Rhodes, 1983);
Besuch im Pfarrhaus: Ein Hörspiel; Drei Dialoge
(Frankfurt am Main: Fischer, 1961); "Weiße
Chrysanthemen," translated by Chappel as
"White Chrysanthemums," in *Ilse Aichinger:
Selected Poetry and Prose;*
Wo ich wohne: Erzählungen, Gedichte, Dialoge (Frank-
furt am Main: Fischer, 1963);
Eliza, Eliza: Erzählungen (Frankfurt am Main: Fi-
scher, 1965)–"Mein grüner Esel," "Die
Maus," translated by Alldridge as "My
Green Donkey," "The Mouse," respectively,

*Ilse Aichinger in 1951 (Photo: S. Fischer Verlag, Frankfurt
am Main)*

in *Ilse Aichinger;* "Eliza, Eliza," "Fünf Vor-
schläge," "Mein grüner Esel," "Die Puppe,"
translated by Chappel as "Eliza, Eliza," "Five

3

Proposals," "My Green Donkey," "The Doll," respectively, in *Ilse Aichinger: Selected Poetry and Prose;*

Ilse Aichinger: Selected Short Stories and Dialogue, edited and translated by Alldridge (Oxford & New York: Pergamon Press, 1966);

Auckland: 4 Hörspiele (Frankfurt am Main: Fischer, 1969)–"Die Schwestern Jouet," translated by Chappel as "The Jouet Sisters," in *Ilse Aichinger: Selected Poetry and Prose;*

Nachricht vom Tag: Erzählungen (Frankfurt am Main: Fischer, 1970)–"Die Rampenmaler," translated by Brian L. Harris as "Platforms," *Dimension,* 2 (1969): 142-150;

Dialoge, Erzählungen, Gedichte, edited by Heinz F. Schafroth (Stuttgart: Reclam, 1971);

Schlechte Wörter (Frankfurt am Main: Fischer, 1976) –"Schlechte Wörter," "Wisconsin und Apfelreis," "Dover," "Der Gast," translated by Chappel as "Inferior Words," "Wisconsin and Apple-Rice," "Dover," "The Guest," respectively, in *Ilse Aichinger: Selected Poetry and Prose;*

Verschenkter Rat: Gedichte (Frankfurt am Main: Fischer, 1978);

Meine Sprache und ich: Erzählungen (Frankfurt am Main: Fischer, 1978)–"Meine Sprache und ich," translated by Richard Mills as "My Language and I," *Dimension,* 8 (1975): 20-26;

Spiegelgeschichte: Erzählungen und Dialoge (Leipzig & Weimar: Kiepenheuer, 1979);

Knöpfe: Hörspiel (Düsseldorf: Eremiten-Presse, 1980);

Kleist, Moos, Fasane: Erinnerungen, Notate, Reden (Frankfurt am Main: Fischer, 1987).

OTHER: "Knöpfe," in *Hörspiele,* edited by Ernst Schnabel (Frankfurt am Main: Fischer, 1961), pp. 43-79;

"Kleist, Moos, Fasane," in *Atlas: Zusammengestellt von deutschen Autoren* (Berlin: Wagenbach, 1965), pp. 273-280;

"Unser Kaminkehrer," in *Portraits: 28 Erzählungen über ein Thema,* edited by Walther Karsch (Berlin: Herbig, 1967), pp. 155-158;

"Wien 1945," in *Städte 1945,* edited by Ingeborg Drewitz (Düsseldorf & Cologne: Diederichs, 1970), pp. 175-176;

"Der letzte Tag," by Aichinger and Günter Eich, in Eich, *Gesammelte Werke,* volume 3 (Frankfurt am Main: Suhrkamp, 1973), pp. 851-896;

Eich, *Gedichte,* edited by Aichinger (Frankfurt am Main: Suhrkamp, 1973);

"Zum Gegenstand," in *Glückliches Österreich,* edited by Jochen Jung (Salzburg & Vienna: Residenz, 1978), pp. 12-16;

"Sich nicht anpassen lassen . . ." in *Das kurze Leben der Sophie Scholl,* by Hermann Vinke (Ravensburg, 1980), pp. 179-186.

PERIODICAL PUBLICATIONS: "Aufruf zum Mißtrauen," *Plan,* 7 (July 1946): 588;

"Die Vögel beginnen zu singen, wenn es noch finster ist," *Freude an Büchern,* 3-4 (1952): 39-40;

"Über das Erzählen in dieser Zeit," *Blätter für Literatur, Funk und Bühne,* 1 (1952): 1;

"Plätze und Straßen," *Jahresring* (1954): 19-24;

"Adalbert Stifter: Erzählungen," *Adalbert Stifter Institut Vierteljahresschrift,* 28 (1979): 93-94;

"Die Zumutung des Atmens: Zu Franz Kafka," *Neue Rundschau,* 94 (1983): 59-63.

In the aftermath of Nazism, Ilse Aichinger produced works with a personal yet politically and socially sensitive vision of reality. Her prose and poetry offer conceptual alternatives that the Nazi use of language had all but erased through propaganda, media manipulation, and bureaucratization. Aichinger's writing is profoundly antifascist. Persecution, the loss of loved ones, and the threat of death shaped a gentle, pacifistic, but relentless poetic voice which insists on commemoration of the dead and on honesty as the basis for forgiveness. Aichinger has an affinity with the great Jewish poetesses of the German language–Else Lasker-Schüler, Gertrud Kolmar, and Nelly Sachs–and the most clear-sighted of Jewish children, Anne Frank.

Aichinger was born in Vienna in 1921 to Leopold Aichinger, a Jewish doctor, and Berta Kremer Aichinger, a gentile teacher, and grew up in Vienna and Linz. She graduated from high school in 1939. Classified as a "Half Jew," she was barred from entering medical school. During the war she performed forced labor in a pharmacy. Many of her Jewish relatives, among them her grandmother, who had raised her while her mother worked, died in concentration camps. Aichinger's father got a divorce for the sake of his career. Her twin sister Helga (Mitchie) immigrated to England while Aichinger stayed with her mother, who had been unable to secure a visa. From 1942 until 1945 she participated in antifascist activities. During this time she began to take notes for a novel.

The German poet Günter Eich, whom Aichinger married in 1953

Immediately after the war she visited her sister and took a liking to British culture which is reflected in her use of English names for characters in many of her works. She enrolled in medical school at the University of Vienna in 1947 but devoted most of her time to writing. After five semesters she discontinued her studies, joining the Fischer publishing company as a reader. Her novel *Die größere Hoffnung* (The Greater Hope; translated as *Herod's Children*, 1963) was published in 1948.

In 1949 Aichinger worked with Inge Scholl, the sister of the executed German student resistance fighters Hans and Sophie Scholl, and other intellectuals to establish the Hochschule für Gestaltung (Academy for Arts and Designs) in

Ulm, West Germany. At the 1951 meeting of the writers' association Gruppe (Group) 47 she read her short story "Der Gefesselte" (1953; translated as "The Bound Man," 1955). She created a sensation; her florid style seemed baroque compared to the terse prose of the young West German authors who had proclaimed 1945 a time for a new beginning after what they perceived as the collapse of German culture. Aichinger never broke with tradition. She wrote to remember, to make connections, while most other postwar German and Austrian authors, at least at first, wanted to reject and forget the past.

In 1953 she married the poet Günter Eich; the couple had two children, Clemens and Mirjam. Aichinger and Eich lived in various vil-

Dust jacket by Rudolf Müller-Hofmann for Aichinger's novel about a Viennese girl who identifies with her Jewish friends during Nazi rule in Austria (Deutsches Literaturarchiv, Marbach am Neckar)

lages in Austria and southern Germany, close to the border between the two countries, and traveled extensively. The two writers collaborated to such an extent that Aichinger herself is not sure as to her contribution to some of her husband's works. There is an affinity between their poetic styles. Aichinger's work, however, is unmistakable. For example, although the radio play "Der letzte Tag" (The Last Day, 1973) was published under Eich's name, it is obvious which aspects of the text are hers. Eich died in 1972; Aichinger continued to live in the village of Groß-Gmain, near Salzburg, for several years after his death. She currently lives in Frankfurt am Main.

Aichinger's work evolved from the Holocaust and the war. While for the majority of German writers the end of the war represented the de-

struction of German culture, for her it was a liberation. Aichinger resisted the trends set by World War II veterans, as well as influences from the United States, above all Ernest Hemingway's machismo, as too authoritarian. She remained an outsider, rejecting the heritage of the Vaterland (fatherland). Her spiritual home is the Mutterland (motherland), a term also used by Lasker-Schüler, Kolmar, and Sachs. It signifies her birthright–according to Jewish tradition the child of a Jewish mother is Jewish–and the preeminence of the wife and mother in Judaism.

The returning exiles Hans Weigel and Hermann Hakel took the leadership role in Austria's postwar culture. There was a rebirth of the fantastic and of surrealism in painting and sculpture, and Otto Basil's journal *Plan* made an

Dust jacket designed by Otl Aicher for Aichinger's 1965 collection of thematically related stories (S. Fischer-Archiv, Frankfurt am Main)

effort to come to terms with Austria's Nazi heritage. Basil published Aichinger's essay "Aufruf zum Mißtrauen" (A Call for Distrust, 1946), which warned against too much self-confidence too early.

Conservatism and economic depression impaired these trends. In search of a national identity Austrian writers created a new nationalistic diction. Progressive authors were published in West Germany, some in East Germany; Aichinger's publisher is Fischer in Frankfurt am Main. Women writers, particularly those more ambitious than the traditional family authors—let alone Holocaust authors—were not favorites of the critics. Aichinger had no reason to deny her heritage and, unlike other postwar authors, no reason to fabricate apologetic stories of the "little man" who was but a pawn in the Nazis' game. Her perspective is that of the victims; her topics are alienation from the German-Austrian public and survival on the fringe.

Aichinger's musical, sensual language is rich in imagery; it is a language of prophecy reminiscent of the Old Testament. At times it echoes romanticism and expressionism. She combines elements from legends, dreams, tales, superstition, and folklore. Her approach is similar to that of Elias Canetti, who uses psychology, sociology, anthropology, myth, and poetry to try to understand the twentieth century. A disbeliever in authority, she ridicules principles such as law and order, good and evil, as simplistic. She exposes the limitations of pseudoscientific systems.

Aichinger's concept of character is not developmental in the sense of the bildungsroman, with its protagonist's societal integration. The societies she portrays do not seem to be ones into which it is worth being accepted. Female experience is expressed in positive terms. The woman's realm—the home, housework, needlework, and games—offer alternatives to domination by males. From this sheltered sphere a "naive" look is taken at the forces which shape society but touch the average woman's life only marginally. Seen through the eyes of Aichinger's women or children figures, the activities from which men derive status seem absurd. Her protagonists are mostly female but have an asexual quality, indicating that biology is a secondary factor. Fathers and lovers are depicted as helpless, incompetent, or destructive. Only as platonic friends do male figures assume positive roles. Aichinger's skepticism toward passion is based on fear of irrationality.

Aichinger's works follow a creative logic; they are certainly not the result of automatic writing, as has been suggested. By transposing intellectual patterns into unexpected contexts, as in dreams, commonly acknowledged assumptions are made to appear grotesquely alien and are exposed to criticism.

In the mid 1950s, when Germany rearmed, the economy was booming, and Austria became independent, Aichinger abandoned topical themes. Her stories convey suspicion of the spotless towns under a government with ostentatiously philo-Semitic policies and repeatedly desecrated Jewish cemeteries. She began to eliminate empirical reality in favor of "antirealities" and to adopt avant-garde techniques such as abstraction, hermetic discourse, black humor, and elements from the theater of the absurd. Gradually her work be-

Dust jacket designed by Aicher for Aichinger's 1976 collection of short stories. The title story deals with the abuse of language (S. Fischer-Archiv, Frankfurt am Main).

came a dialogue with the dead. She is fascinated with the unknown realm before birth and after death, between which life is an interlude. In the 1950s and 1960s Aichinger wrote radio plays which captured the eeriness of life in a country recovering from a nearly total demise and already celebrating its material success. The plays reflect the insecurity of the first generation living with the atomic bomb and repressing that insecurity as they repress memories of the Holocaust. Voices from the past and the present blend, suggesting that nothing is ever lost. The beyond is crowded with ghosts and visions of suffering, the here and now with figures no less ghostly. The present does not know how much it is in the grip of the past. There is a struggle to integrate the past, to catch a glimpse of the beyond.

Die größere Hoffnung remains Aichinger's most straightforward work. It is divided into short chapters with rapidly changing scenes of action. The protagonist, Ellen, the daughter of a Nazi father and a Jewish mother, is not required to wear the yellow star but chooses to do so to demonstrate solidarity with her friends. The friends, a group of persecuted Jewish children, assume a choruslike function. By sharing the fate of the Jews, Ellen places herself on the side of the victims. Yet she refuses to play the victim's role: relying on her inner resources she develops a mystical way of life. She seems limited by her youth and lack of outside support, but she copes more successfully than the adults. While her environment is grotesque, Ellen's reactions are surprisingly sane. Away from the staid ways of the adults, she attains an inner balance. Nazi doctrine does not affect her as it does some of her friends, who begin to hate themselves. The Star of David, once a people's pride, is used to brand its wearer. Being refused service in a store teaches Ellen about discrimination. Ellen's grandmother commits suicide when she mistakes the footsteps of a deserter for those of the Gestapo; Ellen's father is a terrified agent of a system of terror. Rarely do adults succeed in their plans. They operate under the illusion that they control their destinies. They lack the flexibility to reorient themselves amid chaos. No presuppositions burden Ellen's mind; her opinions are formed for the moment.

Some episodes are intensely realistic, such as when Ellen and her friends are found sitting on a park bench in violation of the law. The confrontation is dramatic: the officer is Ellen's father. Bitter irony prevails as the Jewish children sit by the river hoping for a child to fall into the water so that they can prove their worth by saving it. They do not understand that no good deed redeems those whose crime is having been born. To close the circle of absurdity, Ellen, who needs no rehabilitation, passes by and saves a child while her friends indulge themselves in a moment of joy illegally offered them by the owner of a merry-go-round. Other episodes such as Ellen's narrow escape from arrest, the children playing in the Jewish cemetery for lack of any other place to go, and their attempts at leaving the country could have occurred in just this way. But figures such as Augustine (a folk hero who survived a drunken fall into a pit of plague victims), Christopher Columbus, and a persecuted King David who resembles Jesus are superimposed on the "realistic" segments in a dream sequence. *Die größere Hoffnung* is told from the per-

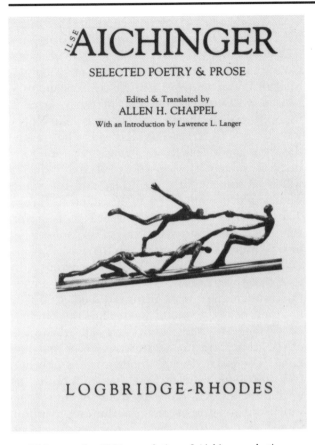

Title page for 1983 translation of Aichinger selections

spective of children; sociopolitical aspects are outside its scope. The novel deals with integrity and the will to live. In the end, Ellen is killed by an exploding shell during the Allied siege of Vienna; the moment of her liberation is the moment of her death.

Aichinger states in the introduction to the story collection *Der Gefesselte* (1953; translated as *The Bound Man and Other Stories*, 1955) that postwar narrators are not in danger of being long-winded but of being discreet to the point of silence. Scenes, gestures, and images take the place of explanations. The stories, written between 1948 and 1951, describe both external reality and psychological states, keeping them independent so that they may run counter to one another. In "Spiegelgeschichte" (translated as "Story in a Mirror") the external action–a woman dying after an abortion–is introduced almost as an afterthought while the reader becomes involved with the protagonist's memories of her unhappy childhood and the insignificant love affair that led to her pregnancy. "Das Plakat" (translated as "The Advertisement"), "Mondgeschichte" (translated as "Moon Story"), "Die geöffnete

Order" (translated as "The Opened Order"), "Der Hauslehrer" (translated as "The Private Tutor"), "Engel in der Nacht" (translated as "Angels in the Night"), and "Das Fenstertheater" (translated as "Window Entertainment") thematize the discrepancy between an individual's perceptions, on the one hand, and reality, taken as a majority consensus, on the other. The protagonists' intense perceptions remain valid. Aichinger suggests that what is termed reality is the result of indoctrination. Only by transcending this reality does the protagonist in "Mondgeschichte" gain her intellectual and emotional freedom. The sober, dull, adult worldview can even kill, as in "Engel in der Nacht."

"Rede unter dem Galgen" (translated as "Speech under the Gallows") is an exalted monologue reminiscent of the choric passages in *Die größere Hoffnung* and Nietzsche's *Also sprach Zarathustra* (1892; translated as *Thus Spake Zarathustra*, 1896). A delinquent addresses the crowds before and after an unexpected pardon. The situation evokes Germany's fate before and after 1945 as well as that of the Holocaust survivors; it is the archetypal situation of doom and grace. While impending death lends the speaker certainty and an attitude of defiance, since he has nothing to lose, liberation reopens the future and puts an end to his grimly heroic stance. Reduced to being merely human again, he faces resocialization and the tasks of everyday life. Here Aichinger's disdain of heroes comes to the fore. The shock of unexpected freedom also figures in "Der Gefesselte," whose protagonist is freed by a woman who does not realize how much he depends on his shackles: he has made living in bondage his livelihood. After his liberation he panics; lacking any other coping mechanism, he resorts to violence.

"Plätze und Straßen" (Squares and Streets, 1954) consists of meditations on Viennese locations. The wind blows through the deserted Judengasse (Jews' Alley) where businesses fail because there are no customers. The buildings look at the passersby as if they had eyes. The grass growing in the street indicates that after the Holocaust there is no traffic here; it also evokes the biblical image of fleeting human life. The Judengasse has become a monument to its murdered inhabitants. Horror and sadness set the mood of almost every location in the inner city. There is the terror of the girls who return from a dance to find their father dead in the section titled "Verbindungsbahn" (Connecting Train or

Railroad). The mass exodus in "Philippshof" is particularly shocking because of the indirect portrayal: events, not their agents, are mentioned, just as Nazi bureaucrats envisioned processes without considering people. Instead of stating that people are leaving or being taken away by force, the narrator observes that the rooms are growing.

Zu keiner Stunde (At No Hour, 1957) contains dialogues which contrast different positions, resulting in the consolidation of opposites, compromise, or submission. Frequently it is not the better argument but the more ruthless rhetoric which decides victory. In the surrealistic settings appear dwarfs, herds of white bulls in the Belvedere gardens, and ghosts. The unfamiliar elements are intended to produce a liberating, objectifying effect: in weighing the merits of an argument, self-interest on the part of the reader is excluded. "Französische Botschaft" (French Message or French Embassy), the best known of the dialogues, combines a debate about change and stagnation with a humorous comment on the Annunciation. Marie does not submit to the command of authority; she rejects the policeman who promises her eternity by offering to transform her into a statue on a church pillar. The angelic message becomes "French," frivolous, an act of corruption: a representative of the law makes a pass at a young girl. The German word *Botschaft* means both message and embassy; the French embassy in Vienna, a palace built as if meant to last for eternity, inspired the work. Its golden ornaments lend a ludicrous credibility to the prophet Elias's appearance: since Marie has refused the policeman's offer, Elias, in Christian interpretation considered a prefiguration of Christ and a prophet of his coming, passes by in his flaming wagon. Marie prefers her humanity to immortality. The dialogue ridicules any belief which devalues life on earth so that death and killing are taken lightly. There is an underlying Jewish message as well: the announcer of the Messiah passes by because the Messiah has not come, leaving mankind to hope for his arrival.

In the radio play "Knöpfe" (Buttons, 1961), the exploitation of people brings Nazi practices to mind: female workers in a button factory are themselves made into buttons. The victims' refusal to believe the unbelievable or to take action for fear of reprisal make the murderers' job easy. Only Ann escapes because of her lover's unrelenting questioning. The play exposes such ideals as doing one's job and being a dutiful citizen as shams.

Besuch im Pfarrhaus (Visit at the Parsonage, 1961) contains a radio play and three dialogues. The devastation of war and the dangers of militarism are central themes. The ghosts in "Nicht vor Mailand" (Not before Milan) are civilians and military men, leftovers from the war who hover in the windows of a burned-out house. " 'Ein Knabe war ich nie' " ("I have never been a boy"), says the young soldier. The colonel, on the other hand, has memories of a normal youth during which he was taught the courage and the manly virtues which culminated in his military career. The most vividly depicted character is a girl whose life was destroyed through no fault of her own. "Weiße Chrysanthemen" (translated as "White Chrysanthemums," 1983) confronts the idea that love, beauty, brutality, murder, adventure, and heroism can be intertwined. Coupling love and death, love and war, seems the ultimate perversion. In "Besuch im Pfarrhaus" the voices of children activate associations in a parson's mind. The isolated man's inner world is ugly and confused. The "man of God" has no serenity, no wisdom to impart, and knows only of those ways which did not work–yet he is the one to whom those in spiritual need must turn. "Paßüberquerung" (Crossing the Pass) is a tribute to Sachs, whose works, like Aichinger's, focus on the suffering of the weak, children, and old people. In "Paßüberquerung" a group of children prepares for a dangerous exodus. An old woman mentor, an invisible presence, watches over them. "Chrigina" is also dominated by a female figure. There could be no greater contrast between the spirit guide based on the fragile Sachs and Frau Holle, the energetic heavenly housekeeper who is denied credit for her work in this supernatural story about a playful runaway girl. "Paßüberquerung" and "Chrigina" suggest different, equally valid female leadership models.

"Kleist, Moos, Fasane" (1965)–the title alludes to three streets in Vienna's Third District–deals with childhood memories. Nostalgia evokes a world which even to the adult is mysterious. Peace and joyful expectation emanate from the grandmother's middle-class home with its intellectual, emotional, and financial limitations. The old woman inspires love and security and instills in her granddaughter a desire for learning. The atmosphere is reminiscent of *Die größere Hoffnung*, in which Judaism is associated with an insistence on culture and education.

The collection *Eliza, Eliza* (1965) is carefully structured; its three parts are thematically connected. The story "Mein Vater aus Stroh" (My Father Made of Straw) introduces the first section, "Mein grüner Esel" (translated as "My Green Donkey," 1969) the second, and "Der Engel" (The Angel) the third. Relationships, above all love, are explored. "Mein grüner Esel" suggests tolerance and a distant affection as the right kind of love: the green donkey is a mediator between the known and the unknown, an angel who inspires the earthbound onlooker with tenderness as a catalyst for spiritual growth. The stories following "Mein Vater aus Stroh" deal with the problems of those shaped by ideologies of the past: stagnation or uprootedness. The former applies to the father made of straw. He is reduced to a state of powerlessness. His services have been ill rewarded. He is left isolated and vulnerable, to be pitied and cared for; his child displays the same tender concern for him as does the student in "Der Bastard" (The Bastard) for his teacher. The stories show the superficiality of social change: only the actors, not the patterns, have changed. The new era means little more than new oppressors and new victims. In "Alte Liebe" (Old Love) an aimlessly wandering old couple is rejected by people living in comfortable homes; a young woman who claims not to know them has appropriated their possessions. Only the horse acknowledges its former owners. In the end a group of transients forms, outsiders bound together by their marginality. "Eliza, Eliza" also contrasts gentle vagrants with compassionless, firmly situated individuals. An upper-class woman recognizes that the transients are her relatives. Leaving her possessions opens her to love. "Port Sing" tells of an extermination of rabbits that has gone unrecorded, since rabbits do not write history. (Rabbits are symbols of the fulfillment of the commandment to be fruitful and multiply; they are occasionally depicted on Jewish tombstones.) In "Wiegenfest" (Cradle Celebration) a baby's first impression is of cones of two different colors, representing the polarization of the sexes and the division of body and soul. The impact of religion is the theme of "Mit den Hirten" (With the Shepherds), which suggests the limitations of Christian doctrine. The prose in *Eliza, Eliza* demands participation, riddle solving, and the weighing of arguments.

Auckland (1969) contains three new radio plays, as well as a republication of "Besuch im Pfarrhaus." "Nachmittag in Ostende" (Afternoon in Ostend) establishes a panorama of historical simultaneity through characters from different periods: the Thirty Years War, the eighteenth century, and Greek antiquity are mixed up as they would be in the course of an afternoon of television viewing. Common to all three eras are the overpowering of the weak, women, and children. "Nachmittag in Ostende" suggests that Nazism is the logical consequence of patriarchy. While Oakland, California, provided the immediate inspiration for "Auckland," the title also alludes to the poet Karl Wolfskehl's last refuge in exile. Aichinger's Auckland is bad taste, misogyny, and racism. The characters are insensitive, self-centered, crude braggarts. Under the guise of frankness one person bullies another. Auckland represents the chaos of a "late capitalist" society as envisioned in Marx and Engels's *Communist Manifesto* (1848); it is a murderous place like Bertolt Brecht's Mahagonny. Woman is outside the public sphere; her place is under the hair dryer. The counterpart to the masculine spirit is the world of "Die Schwestern Jouet" (translated as "The Jouet Sisters," 1983), a creation myth with a woman creator. Rosalie creates, destroys, and tortures at will; she is neither all-good nor all-knowing. The play appears to be a reaction to overidealistic feminist views of women.

The title story of the collection *Schlechte Wörter* (1976; story translated as "Inferior Words," 1983) declares that it is time to stop hiding behind language to avoid communication and that it is that which lies closest to the heart that resists communication the most. To one as practiced in the language of silence as the narrator in "Rahels Kleider" (Rahel's Clothes), speaking means concealing. The texts convey no "positive" message. Seemingly harmless phenomena such as rain can become catastrophic; the world seems a frightful place. Only a dishonest view of life can turn hideous reality into a lullaby. Minor events such as the spilling of milk in "Flecken" (Spots) show that even at home no one has power over the minutest detail. Repeated mention of dead fathers evokes the past which shaped the present. The seemingly insignificant milk spots suggest sperm, thus procreation and contraception—events with unfathomable consequences. In "Zweifel an Balkonen" (Doubts about Balconies) Aichinger tries to show that the separation of one's own property from everyone else's, of the private sector from the public sphere, is the mentality that creates wars. "Liebhaber der Westsäulen" (Lovers of the Western Columns) shows peaceful people as outsiders who love rare things. The majority–disdainfully termed "die

Frohgemuten" (the merry-hearted ones)–those in favor of building highways, the supposedly young at heart, are suspicious of them. Aichinger targets the values of those who, like Hitler's crowds and the Führer himself, loved highways and–ostensibly–young people. "Der Gast" (translated as "The Guest," 1983) criticizes the evaluation of a person on the grounds of manners and correct speech; while these attributes are prerequisites for success, they are no evidence of integrity. "Ambros" takes place at a moment of historical and philosophical change: while the majority of his contemporaries accept the new religion of resurrection, Ambros rejects it since he has never observed anyone returning from the grave. Moreover, he is taken aback by the aggressiveness of the new sect. "Dover" describes a spiritual place where being and appearance coincide. The stark, exposed cliffs make no pretense, allow for no illusions. That which lies inside is directly visible. "Privas" explores the same theme in a lunatic asylum: the characters expose themselves in the most elemental, childish way, having been stripped of their language and civilized behavior. In "Rahels Kleider" the narrator describes how she keeps from discussing matters she would rather keep silent about. She rehearses conversations in which she might become involved concerning Rahel, who left her clothes behind when she departed suddenly. Clearly the narrator is not afraid to discuss suffering, poverty, and death, as she openly addresses these topics. Rahel's story seems to involve more gruesome events. The narrator considers making small talk and a fast escape by any available means the best strategy to keep her secret. The shift from Jewish to Christian imagery suggests the Holocaust as the context of Rahel's disappearance. "Wisconsin und Apfelreis" (translated as "Wisconsin and Apple-Rice," 1983) questions the domination of the Western world by the United States. Behind the sentimentality of motherhood and apple pie lurks sadomasochism. The text incorporates English vocabulary to signal the linguistic and cultural invasion.

In the radio play "Gare Maritime" (Maritime Station) the protagonists are puppets who are more alive than those who are ostensibly human. Joe and Joan are on display at a place reminiscent of the Auschwitz camp museum or the museum planned at Prague by the Nazis to document the soon-to-be extinct Jewish culture. They are characterized in the language of the camp masters, who ordered workers in burial details not to

refer to the dead Jews as "victims" or "people" but as "puppets" or "dirt." Being inconspicuous is their survival technique; thus they keep changing appearance and material form. Joan, as a female, is more advanced in this art; she teaches Joe how to stop breathing. "Gare Maritime" conveys the terror of being at the mercy of persecutors but also shows the power of individual, nonviolent resistance. The nobility of the puppets is contrasted with the moral decay of the perpetrators and their children. The youthful museum visitors brutalize not only their victims but also each other. When Joe and Joan no longer fit into the exhibit they are mangled and thrown out. The play, however, ends on a faintly hopeful note: as the two broken bodies mingle into one big mess, Joe and Joan conclude that they are making progress.

Aichinger received the Advancement Prize of the Federal Ministry for Instruction and Culture in 1952; the Bremen Prize in 1955; the Immermann Prize of the City of Düsseldorf in 1957; the Literature Prize of the Bavarian Academy of Fine Arts in 1961; the Anton Wildgans Prize of Austrian Industry in 1968; the Nelly Sachs Prize of the City of Dortmund in 1971; the Prize of the City of Vienna and the Appreciation Prize of the Federal Minister for Instruction and Art in 1974; the Great Austrian State Prize and the Roswitha Memorial Medal of the City of Bad Gandersheim in 1975; the Georg Trakl Prize for Poetry of the City of Salzburg, the Franz Nabl Prize of the City of Graz, and the Petrarca Prize of the City of Munich in 1979; and the Franz Kafka Prize of the City of Klosterneuburg in 1983. She is a member of the Academy of the Arts of West Berlin, the P.E.N. Club of the Federal Republic of Germany, and the Academy of Sciences and Literature of Mainz.

Letters:

Gertrud Fußenegger, "Briefwechsel," *Frankfurter Anthologie*, 5 (1980): 231-233.

References:

James C. Alldridge, *Ilse Aichinger* (Chester Springs, Pa.: Dufour Editions, 1969; London: Wolff, 1969);

Carol Bedwell, "The Ambivalent Image in Aichinger's 'Spiegelgeschichte,'" *Révue des langues vivantes*, 33 (1967): 362-368;

Bedwell, "Who Is the Bound Man?: Towards an Interpretation of Ilse Aichinger's "Der Gefesselte," *German Quarterly*, 38 (January 1965): 30-37;

Anne-Marie Bouisson, "Ilse Aichinger: Approche d'une évolution," *Austriaca*, 7 (1978): 13-22;

Alan Corkhill, "Ilse Aichingers 'Seegeister' und Christa Reinigs 'Drei Schiffe,' " *Colloquia Germanica*, 15 (1982): 122-132;

Monika Frommelt Coruba, "Zum frühen Werk Ilse Aichingers," in *Romantik und Moderne: Festschrift für Helmut Motekat*, edited by Erich Huber-Thoma und Ghemela Adler (Frankfurt am Main & New York: Lang, 1986), pp. 529-541;

Sabine Döhler, "Ilse Aichinger," in *Österreichische Autoren des 20. Jahrhunderts*, edited by Hannelore Prosche (Berlin: Volk und Wissen, 1988), pp. 540-562;

Werner Eggers, "Ilse Aichinger," in *Deutsche Literatur seit 1945*, edited by Dietrich Weber (Stuttgart: Kröner, 1970), pp. 252-270;

Marianna E. Fleming, "Ilse Aichinger: 'Die Sicht der Entfremdung'–ein Versuch, die Symbolik ihres Werkes von dessen Gesamtstruktur her zu erschließen," Ph.D. dissertation, University of Maryland, 1974;

Erich Fried, "Über Gedichte Ilse Aichingers," *Neue Rundschau*, 91 (1981): 25-38;

Antje Friedrichs, "Untersuchungen zur Prosa Ilse Aichingers," Ph.D. dissertation, University of Münster, 1970;

Helga-Maleen Gerresheim, "Ilse Aichinger," in *Deutsche Dichter der Gegenwart*, edited by Benno von Wiese (Berlin: Schmidt, 1973), pp. 481-496;

Alexander Hildebrand, "Zu Ilse Aichingers Gedichten," *Literatur und Kritik*, 23 (1968): 161-167;

Wolfgang Hildesheimer, "Das absurde Ich," in his *Interpretationen: James Joyce, Georg Büchner. Zwei Frankfurter Vorlesungen* (Frankfurt am Main: Suhrkamp, 1969), pp. 84-110;

Hildesheimer, "Ilse Aichinger: 'Der Querbalken,' " *Merkur*, 12 (1963): 1179-1185;

Hellmuth Himmel, "Ilse Aichingers Prosastück 'Der Querbalken': Vier Interpretationsversuche," *Sprachkunst*, 5 (1974): 280-300;

Kurt Kersten, *Ein Kinderroman aus der Nazizeit: Ilse Aichingers "Die größere Hoffnung"* (Berlin: Aufbau, n.d.);

Lawrence Langer, *The Holocaust and the Literary Imagination* (New Haven & London: Yale University Press, 1975), pp. 134-165;

Wayne Lautenschlager, "Images and Narrative Techniques in the Prose of Ilse Aichinger," Ph.D. dissertation, Washington University, 1976;

Gisela Lindemann, *Ilse Aichinger* (Munich: Beck, 1988);

Rodney Livingstone, "German Literature from 1945," in *Periods in German Literature*, edited by J. M. Ritchie (London: Wolff, 1966), pp. 283-303;

Ruth Lorbe, "Die deutsche Kurzgeschichte der Jahrhundertmitte," *Der Deutschunterricht*, 9 (1957): 36-54;

Dagmar C. G. Lorenz, *Ilse Aichinger* (Königstein: Athenäum, 1981);

Rainer Lübbren, "Die Sprache der Bilder: Zu Ilse Aichingers Erzählung 'Eliza, Eliza,' " *Neue Rundschau*, 76 (1965): 626-636;

Patricia Haas Stanley, "Ilse Aichinger's Absurd I," *German Studies Review*, 2 (1979): 331-350.

H. C. Artmann

(12 June 1921-   )

Peter Pabisch
University of New Mexico

BOOKS: *med ana schwoazzn dintn* (Salzburg: Müller, 1958);

Von denen Husaren und anderen Seil-Tänzern (Munich: Piper, 1959);

hosn rosn baa, by Artmann, Gerhard Rühm, and Friedrich Achleitner (Vienna: Frick, 1959);

Das Suchen nach dem gestrigen Tag oder Schnee auf einem heißen Brotwecken: Eintragungen eines bizarren Liebhabers (Olten & Freiburg im Breisgau: Walter, 1964);

verbarium: gedichte (Olten & Freiburg im Breisgau: Walter, 1966);

Drakula, Drakula: Ein transsylvanisches Abenteuer (Berlin: Rainer, 1966);

allerleirausch: neue schöne kinderreime (Berlin: Rainer, 1967);

Fleiß und Industrie (Frankfurt am Main: Suhrkamp, 1967);

Persische Quatrainen (Stuttgart: Collispress, 1967);

Grünverschlossene Botschaft: 90 Träume (Salzburg: Residenz, 1967); translated by Derk Wynand as "Green-Sealed Message" in *Under the Cover of a Hat & Green-Sealed Message* (New York & London: Quartet, 1985);

tök ph'rong süleng (Munich: Hartmann, 1967);

Der handkolorierte Menschenfresser (Stuttgart: Collispresse, 1968);

Überall wo Hamlet hinkam (Stuttgart: Collispresse, 1969);

Kleinere Taschenkünste, fast eine Chinoiserie (Vienna: Universal, 1969);

Frankenstein in Sussex; Fleiß und Industrie (Frankfurt am Main: Suhrkamp, 1969);

Die Anfangsbuchstaben der Flagge: Geschichten für Kajüten, Kamine und Kinositze (Salzburg: Residenz, 1969);

die fahrt zur insel nantucket: theater, edited by Peter O. Chotjewitz (Neuwied: Luchterhand, 1969);

Ein lilienweißer brief aus lincolnshire: Gedichte aus 21 jahren, edited by Gerald Bisinger (Frankfurt am Main: Suhrkamp, 1969);

Das im Walde verlorene Totem: Prosadichtungen 1949-1953 (Salzburg: Residenz, 1970);

H. C. Artmann in 1984 (Gabriela Brandenstein, Vienna)

The Best of H. C. Artmann, edited by Klaus Reichert (Frankfurt am Main: Suhrkamp, 1970);

Yeti oder John, ich reise . . . , by Artmann, Rainer Pichler, and Hannes Schneider (Munich: Willing, 1970);

Walter Schmögners böse Bilder: Brave Worte (Vienna & Munich: Jugend und Volk, 1970);

how much, schatzi? (Frankfurt am Main: Suhrkamp, 1971);

Der aeronautische Sindtbart oder Seltsame Luftreise von Niedercalifornien nach Crain: Ein Fragment, von dem Autor selbst aus dem Yucatekischen anno 1958 ins Teutsche gebracht, edited by Reichert (Salzburg: Residenz, 1971);

Artmann's father, 1915 (S. Weitzmann, Vienna)

Märchen, as H. C. Artmannsen (Frankfurt am Main: Suhrkamp, 1972);

Von der Wiener Seite (Berlin: Literarisches Colloquium, 1972);

Ompül (Zurich & Munich: Artemis, 1974); translated by Olive Jones as *Angus* (London: Methuen, 1974);

Unter der Bedeckung eines Hutes: Montagen und Sequenzen (Salzburg: Residenz, 1974); translated by Wynand as "Under the Cover of a Hat," in *Under the Cover of a Hat & Green-Sealed Message*;

Aus meiner Botanisiertrommel: Balladen und Naturgedichte (Salzburg: Residenz, 1975);

Gedichte über die Liebe und über die Lasterhaftigkeit, edited by Elisabeth Borchers (Frankfurt am Main: Suhrkamp, 1975);

1. Rixdorfer Laboratorium zur Erstellung von literarischen und bildnerischen Simultan-Kunststücken in der Fachwerkstatt Rixdorfer Drucke auf Schloß Gümse vom 8.-18. Juni 1975, by Artmann and others (Hamburg: Merlin, 1975);

Christopher und Peregrin und was weiter geschah: Ein Bären-Roman in drei Kapiteln, by Artmann and Barbara Wehr (Frankfurt am Main: Insel, 1975);

Die Jagd nach Dr. U. oder Ein einsamer Spiegel, in dem sich der Tag reflektiert (Salzburg: Residenz, 1977);

Artmann's mother, 1912 (S. Weitzmann, Vienna)

Nachrichten aus Nord und Süd (Salzburg: Residenz, 1978);

Grammatik der Rosen: Gesammelte Prosa, edited by Reichert, 3 volumes (Salzburg & Vienna: Residenz, 1979);

Die Wanderer (Erlangen & Munich: Renner, 1979);

Kein Pfeffer für Czermak: Ein Votivsäulchen für das goldene Wiener Gemüt (Vienna & Munich: Sessler, 1980);

Triumph des Herzens (Munich: Galerie Klewan, 1982);

Die Sonne war ein grünes Ei: Von der Erschaffung der Welt und ihren Dingen (Salzburg: Residenz, 1982);

Im Schatten der Burenwurst: Skizzen aus Wien (Salzburg: Residenz, 1983);

Das prahlen des urwaldes im dschungel (Berlin: Rainer, 1983);

Verzaubert, verwunschen: Das Waldviertel (Vienna: Brandstätter, 1984);

Artmann, H. C., Dichter (Salzburg: Residenz, 1986);

Under the Cover of a Hat & Green-Sealed Message, translated by Wynand (New York: Quartet, 1986);

Wer dichten kann ist Dichtersmann: Eine Auswahl aus dem Werk, edited by Christina Weiß and Karl Riha (Stuttgart: Reclam, 1986).

OTHER: *Mein Erbteil von Vater und Mutter: Überlieferungen und Mythen aus Lappland,* compiled by Artmann (Hamburg: Merlin, 1969);

Karlheinz Pilcz, *Grotesken: Zeichnungen, Radierungen,* contributions by Artmann (Baden: Weilburg, 1970);

Detective Magazine der 13, edited by Artmann (Salzburg: Residenz, 1971);

Gottfried Helnwein, contributions by Artmann (Vienna: Orac, 1981);

Franz Stelzhamer, *Lieder und Gedichte,* edited by Artmann (Schärding: Heindl, 1981).

TRANSLATIONS: *Der Schlüssel des Heiligen Patrick: Religiöse Dichtungen der Kelten,* selected and translated by Artmann (Salzburg: Müller, 1959);

Francisco de Quevido y Villegas, *Der abenteuerliche Buscón oder Leben und Taten des weitbeschrieenen Glücksritters Don Pablos aus Segovia: Eine kurzweilige Geschichte in spanischer Sprache* (Frankfurt am Main: Insel, 1963);

Carl von Linné, *Lappländische Reise,* translated by Artmann and Helli Clervall (Frankfurt am Main: Insel, 1964);

Edward Lear, *Nonsense Verse* (Frankfurt am Main: Insel, 1964);

Hanan J. Ayalti, ed., *Je länger ein Blinder lebt, desto mehr sieht er: Jiddische Sprichwörter* (Frankfurt am Main: Insel, 1965);

Tage Aurell, *Martina* (Frankfurt am Main: Suhrkamp, 1965);

Daisy Ashford, Junge Gäste oder Mr. Salteenas Plan: Ein Liebes-und Gesellschaftsroman um 1900 geschrieben von Daisy Ashford in Alter von 9 Jahren (Olten & Freiburg im Breisgau: Walter, 1965);

Daisy and Angela Ashford, *Liebe und Ehe: Drei Geschichten* (Frankfurt am Main: Insel, 1967);

François Villon, *Baladen: In Wiener Mundart* (Frankfurt am Main: Insel, 1968);

H. P. Lovecraft, *Cthulhu: Geistergeschichten* (Frankfurt am Main: Suhrkamp, 1968);

Harry Graham, *Herzlose Reime für herzlose Heime* (Zurich: Diogenes, 1968);

Pedro Calderón de la Barca, *Dame Kobold: Komödie in drei Akten* (Vienna: Sessler, 1969);

Daisy Ashford, *Wo Lieb am tiefsten liegt* (Frankfurt am Main: Insel, 1969);

Eugène-Marin Labiche, *Die Jagd nach dem Raben: Komödie in fünf Akten*, translated by Artmann and Barbara Wehr (Vienna: Sessler, 1970);

Labiche, *Der Prix Martin: Komödie in drei Akten*, translated by Artmann and Wehr (Vienna: Sessler, 1971);

Cyril Tourneur, *Tragödie der Rächer* (Vienna: Sessler, 1971);

Lars Gustafsson, *Die nächtliche Huldigung: Schauspiel in drei Akten* (Neuwied & Berlin: Luchterhand, 1971);

Molière, *Arzt wider Willen* (Vienna: Sessler, 1972);

Alfred de Musset, *Die Wette* (Vienna: Sessler, 1972);

Lope de Vega, *Der Kavalier vom Mirakel* (Vienna: Sessler, 1972);

Tirso de Molina, *Don Gil von den grünen Hosen* (Vienna: Sessler, 1972);

Ludvig Holberg, *Henrik und Pernilla* (Vienna: Sessler, 1972);

Labiche, *Celimar: Comédie-Vaudeville in drei Akten* (Vienna: Sessler, 1973);

Augustin Moreto y Cavana, *Der unwiderstehliche Don Diego* (Vienna: Sessler, 1973);

Molière, *Die Streiche des Scapin* (Vienna: Sessler, 1973);

Pierre Augustin Caron de Beaumarchais, *Der tolle Tag* (Vienna: Sessler, 1973);

Pierre Carlet de Chamblain de Marivaux, *Liebe und Zufall* (Vienna: Sessler, 1973);

Labiche, *Die Reise des Herrn Perrichon: Lustspiel in vier Akten* (Vienna: Sessler, 1973);

Carlo Goldoni, *Der Lügner: Komödie in drei Akten* (Vienna & Munich: Sessler, 1974);

Molière, *George Dandin oder Der genasführte Ehemann* (Vienna & Munich: Sessler, 1974);

Carl Michael Bellman, *Der Lieb zu gefallen: Eine Auswahl aus seiner Lieder*, translated by Artmann and Michael Korth, music by Johannes Heimrath (Munich: Heimeran, 1976);

Ludwig Holberg, *Der Konfuse*, translated by Artmann and Herbert Wochinz (Vienna & Munich: Sessler, 1976);

Terence Hanburg White, *Der König auf Camelot*, translated by Rudolf Rocholl, verse translated by Artmann, 2 volumes (Stuttgart: Klett, 1976).

Known by his friends as "da H. C." (pronounced "hah-tseh") or "da Artmann," H. C. Artmann enjoys great popularity and an ever-growing number of admirers. Unlike most of his colleagues, this self-made poet had little formal education. He has led a carefree life which continues to be rich in adventure. Artmann's opposition to the values of the establishment is reflected in his personal life: he has fathered a half-dozen children in and out of wedlock.

Artmann's gypsylike life-style contrasts sharply with his working-class upbringing: the son of a showmaker, Hans Carl Laertes Artmann was born in St. Achatz am Walde, Lower Austria, on 12 June 1921 and raised in Vienna. Artmann holds his mother, who is still alive, in high esteem and has included her in several lecture tours, readings, and literary conferences. He attended only eight years of school. After being wounded on the eastern front during World War II, he served as an interpreter with the American army from 1945 to 1949. His personality is colorful and unpredictable. He has lived and traveled in many European countries, favoring the Federal Republic of Germany, Sweden, England, Spain, and Ireland. His talent for learning languages is prodigious, at least as far as reading and listening are concerned, and he has translated works by authors such as François Villon, Pedro Calderón de la Barca, Carlo Goldoni, Edward Lear, Molière, and Linnaeus (Carl von Linné).

Most of his translations are more interpretative than literal because Artmann brings his own creative personality to bear on the translated work. His 1968 translation of Villon's ballads into Viennese dialect received rave reviews. He is similar to Bertolt Brecht in his readiness to borrow from many literary sources for his own work. He will, for example, use a "baroque" style or eighteenth-century iambic verse to parody his own era; he uses Japanese haiku and Spanish *greguerías* in a similar improvisational way. He plays with literary language to such an extent that the meaning and plot of a work are sometimes submerged in a verbal masquerade. Artmann appears in costumes and masks when reading his works, assuming the roles of an Arab sheik, a poet laureate in a baroque wig, or a scruffy, unshaven Alpine peasant. In a spirit of alcoholic buffoonery he delights audiences with impromptu bons mots and puns. His popularity has made him one of the most noticed representatives of contemporary German-language literature. Artmann's work has developed out of his interest in the formal and abstract aspects of language; the word rather than the object is the

Artmann (right) with his brother Erwin, 1928 (photo: Kunstsalon, Vienna)

focal point of this interest. Artmann is intrigued by the elements of individual words–their syllables and vowels–and the phonetic qualities of words.

As a leading figure in the Austrian movement called the "Wild Fifties," Artmann rejected traditional literature and used it in a satirical manner. The 1950s were years of experiment, and the revolutionary members of the "Wild Fifties" considered themselves the spiritual heirs of the artists and writers of the first decades of the twentieth century. They missed no opportunity to demonstrate their opposition to the fascist period of the 1930s and 1940s. They idolized expressionism and dadaism from George Grosz to Kurt Schwitters but also supported Brechtian engagement. They took as their models artists and writers such as Gertrude Stein, Ernest Hemingway, Ezra Pound, Pablo Picasso, the French symbolists and surrealists, and the Italian futurist Filippo Tommaso Marinetti. Artmann fought in the forefront of those who wanted a breakthrough to a new era.

He began his career by writing symbolistic poetry. Only a few of these poems have been preserved; they can be found in *Ein lilienweißer brief aus lincolnshire* (A Lilywhite Letter from Lincoln-

shire, 1969). The book summarizes the first twenty-one years of Artmann's achievement as a poet and includes the period of his experimentation with haiku and *greguerías*.

In 1953 Artmann and Gerhard Rühm, Friedrich Achleitner, Ossi Wiener, and Konrad Bayer formed the literary "Wiener Gruppe" (Vienna Group), which existed until Bayer committed suicide in 1964. Under Artmann's leadership the group began an investigation of the German language: they studied the history of the language by reading older literature in Vienna's National Library and observed the language used in the streets, cafés, and pubs. They also studied nonverbal forms of communication such as gesture and mimicry. By 1958 they had gathered the materials that formed the basis for the writings in dialect with which they were to score their greatest successes.

Their products were disparate. Artmann wrote baroque verse and prose epigrams in the manner of Andreas Gryphius and adventure stories in the fashion of Hans Grimmelshausen. He translated and rewrote Irish church poetry in *Der Schlüssel des Heiligen Patrick* (The Key of St. Patrick, 1959), which contains prayers mixed with pagan lore. Most important, he published his best-

Artmann in Ireland, 1960

selling book of dialect poetry, *med ana schwoazzn dintn* (With Black Ink, 1958). If cockney were elevated to the level of a literary language, English would have something parallel to what Artmann achieved in his works of dialect poetry in German. *Med ana schwoazzn dintn* received widespread acclaim, but this praise was based on a misunderstanding: poems offered in a spirit of sarcasm and satire, as a criticism of what Artmann judged to be ugly language, were received as tender, loving folklore. *Med ana schwoazzn dintn* is a convincing mask of folklore meant to unmask an insensitive and brutal society that had refused to recognize the horrors of World War II as a heritage of its character. The book unmasked the proverbial "Wiener Gemütlichkeit" (Viennese charm) as false and hollow. It revealed a layer of societal emotions that should have shocked the very audience it delighted. This misunderstanding occurred because the exaggeration employed by Artmann to express moral criticism was laughed off as harmless cartoonlike joking.

In his dialect poetry Artmann uses archetypal figures of Viennese life and lore. Some of these figures are more helpless and pathetic than

sinister–for example, the lover who has been deserted by his sweetheart in the poem "Ohne dich" (Without You). The key phrase in this poem is "den gschdis gem," an expression from the card game Tarock which means to play one's trump card, to reject or even annihilate another player. No standard German idiom can convey a similar image of complete devastation. The trump card or Gschdis depicts a handsome officer or torero, against whom all competition must be in vain. The card is usually thrown onto the table with a strong downward motion of the player's arm, banning any chance for an opponent to win the game–a gesture of the utmost cold-bloodedness. The example indicates how Artmann uses colorful folkloristic terms to evoke a particular understanding in his readers; critics have pointed to Artmann's use of literary elements accessible to all educational levels in Viennese society. While Artmann's other poetry was known in the 1950s only to a small audience of artists and literati, the dialect poetry drew the attention of the *Times Literary Supplement* in 1963 and inspired a global wave of dialect poetry. In recognition of Artmann's success the city of Vienna provided him a subsidized apartment.

Artmann, Rühm, and Achleitner collaborated on another book of dialect poetry, with the morbid title *hosn rosn baa* (Pants Roses Bones, 1959). Although it was not a best-seller like *med ana schwoazzn dintn*, it was one of the major publications of a new literary era that would reach its apex in the works of Thomas Bernhard and Peter Handke in the late 1960s. During this phase language was analyzed without consideration for content. In a cleansing process, German was to be freed of terms which used Hitler's phraseology or the language of any previous authoritarian era.

Although Artmann established his literary reputation with dialect poetry, he later abandoned the form. His popularity and privileges ended abruptly in 1960, when he left Austria to escape an alimony suit. He went to Berlin, then moved to Malmö, Sweden; he did not return to his home country until 1970, when he settled in Salzburg. During this period he had to make a living from translations, but he reentered the literary scene with the diarylike *Das Suchen nach dem gestrigen Tag* (In Search of Yesterday) in 1964. Some autobiographical lines from the volume illustrate his state of mind at this time:

Meine heimat ist Österreich, mein vaterland Europa, mein wohnort Malmö, meine hautfarbe weiß, meine augen blau, mein mut verschieden, meine laune launisch, mein räusche richtig, meine ausdauer stark, meine anliegen sprunghaft, meine sehnsüchte wie die windrose, im handumdrehen zufrieden, im handumdrehen verdrossen, ein freund der fröhlichkeit, im grunde traurig, den mädchen gewogen, ein großer kinogeher, ein liebhaber des twist. . . . ciao gestammelt, fortgegangen, a gesagt, b gemacht, c gedacht, d geworden.

Alles was man sich vornimmt, wird anders als man sichs erhofft. . . .

(My home country is Austria, my fatherland is Europe, my place of residence Malmö, the color of my skin is white, my eyes are blue, my courage variable, my moods moody, I am often thoroughly drunk, my endurance is stern, my requests are inconsistent, my longings are comparable to the windrose, one minute I am satisfied, the next minute I am miserable, I like good times, am basically sad, with the girls handy, a great moviegoer, a connoisseur of the twist. . . . I stammered ciao and left, then I said "a," did "b," thought "c," became "d."

Everything we have planned turns out differently than we hoped for. . . .)

A group of Artmann's friends published a "festschrift" in celebration of his forty-fifth birthday in 1966. This book initiated a second wave of production on Artmann's part. These publications offer considerable stylistic variety and are tied together only by the reappearance of Artmann's name throughout the texts. In *Drakula* (1966) he revels in the gruesome details of the bloodsucking monster's appetites. He reworks the Babylonian *Book of Dreams* in *Grünverschlossene Botschaft* (1967; translated as "Green-Sealed Message," 1985), revealing the mythical quality of the human mind in a series of fantasies, visions, and nightmares. His book of stories *Mein Erbteil von Vater und Mutter* (My Heritage from Father and Mother, 1969) draws on the mythology of Lapland. Artmann is one of several authors writing about the legendary abominable snowman in the volume *Yeti oder John, ich reise* (Yeti; or, John, I'm Traveling, 1970), giving his stories the adventurous scenes and exotic settings made popular in the Tarzan films. In 1969 Peter O. Chotjewitz edited a collection of Artmann's short dramas, *die fahrt zur insel nantucket: theater* (The Journey to the Island of Nantucket: Theater Plays). One of these plays, *Kein Pfeffer für Czermak* (No Pepper for Czermak, 1954), juxtaposes the world of the artist, represented by Czermak, to the narrow-minded world of daily life, represented by the grocer Gschweidl. The latter refuses to sell pepper to the former because he considers Czermak a "worthless" artist; in addition, Czermak has had the audacity to court Gschweidl's niece. The despotic, self-righteous local tyrant Gschweidl was adopted by the cabaretists Carl Merz and Helmut Qualtinger as the model for the title character in their *Der Herr Karl* (1962), a Viennese opportunist with Hitlerian characteristics. Television productions throughout the world featured characters modeled on Herr Karl; the figure of Archie Bunker in the American television series "All in the Family" finds its original sources in Herr Karl and Gschweidl. Klaus Reichert brought out *The Best of H. C. Artmann* (1970), a collection of prose and poetry which, in spite of its English title, is entirely in German. Gerald Bisinger edited the collection of poems *Ein lilienweißer brief aus lincolnshire* as well as the first scholarly book on Artmann, *Über H. C. Artmann* (About H. C. Artmann, 1972).

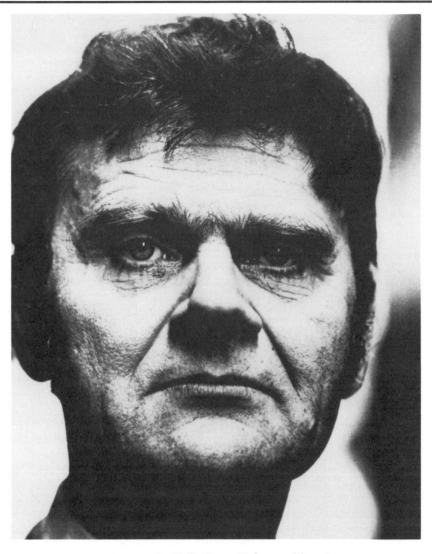

Artmann in 1967 (Franz Hubmann, Vienna)

By the early 1970s a return to more conventional literary forms had begun in German literature. Artmann adapted to the change in his own way. He published a book of poetry, *Aus meiner Botanisiertrommel* (From My Botanical Box, 1975), and a novella, *Nachrichten aus Nord und Süd* (News from North and South, 1978). Typically for Artmann, the two works are poles apart in style. In the former volume Artmann returns to rhyme and iambic meter, in obvious opposition to the prose poetry of the 1970s. In *Nachrichten aus Nord und Süd* he assesses his status within Austrian and German literature. There is no punctuation and no capitalization; one thought flows into the next, and each thought is charged with multiple meanings from the previous and following thoughts. There is no plot. In 1979 Artmann's prose work was collected by Reichert in the three-

volume anthology *Grammatik der Rosen* (Grammar of Roses). His latest publications, especially *Die Sonne war ein grünes Ei* (The Sun Was a Green Egg, 1982) and *Im Schatten der Burenwurst* (In the Shade of the Polish Sausage, 1983), are reworked versions of his stories from the 1950s and early 1960s dealing with Viennese episodes. These stories can be seen as extentions of themes he treated in his dialect poetry.

In three decades of writing Artmann has revealed a series of archetypal images buried in the human subconscious: cannibals, sex murderers, brutal and braggart soldiers, apelike beings, vampires, and animalistic lovers. He is skeptical of all cultural achievement because he believes that man is plagued by the primitive side of his nature. Artmann adopts a clownish humor to make his point, and his humorous style often obscures

Illustration by "Ironimus" for Artmann's 1983 collection of stories Im Schatten der Burenwurst

a serious message. The nonpolitical nature of his work has opened doors for him in East Germany. He appeared before students from East Berlin in 1985 and is as celebrated there as in West Berlin or Salzburg. He received the Austrian State Prize for Literature in 1960 and 1974, the Prize for Literature of the City of Vienna in 1977, and a special prize for his achievements in Austrian literature in 1981.

References:

James C. Alldridge, "H. C. Artmann and the English Nonsense Tradition," in *Affinities: Essays in German and English Literature,* edited by R. W. Last (London: Wolff, 1971), pp. 168-183;

Konrad Bayer, "hans carl artmann und die wiener dichtergruppe," in Artmann's *Ein lilienweißer brief aus lincolnshire: Gedichte aus 21 jahren* (Frankfurt am Main: Suhrkamp, 1969), pp. 7-16;

Gerald Bisinger, ed., *Über H. C. Artmann* (Frankfurt am Main: Suhrkamp, 1972);

Bisinger and Peter O. Chotjewitz, eds., *Der Landgraf zu Camprodon: Festschrift für den Husar am Münster Hieronymus Caspar Laertes Artmann* (Hamburg: Ramsegar, 1966);

Chotjewitz, "Sechzehn Jahre Artmann," *Literatur und Kritik,* 3 (1966): 18-32;

Josef Donnenberg, ed., *Pose, Possen, Poesie: Zum Werk H. C. Artmanns* (Stuttgart: Akademischer Verlag, 1981);

Walter Höllerer, ed., *Artmann: Biographie* (Berlin: Literarisches Colloquium, 1967);

Peter Pabisch, *H. C. Artmann: Ein Versuch über die literarische Alogik* (Vienna: Schendl, 1978);

Pabisch, "Sensitivität und Kalkül in der jüngsten Prosa H. C. Artmanns," *Modern Austrian Literature,* 13, no. 1 (1980): 129-147;

Artmann in 1986 (Werner Schnelle, Salzburg)

Pabisch and Alfred Rodríguez, "Hans Carl Artmann's Adaptation of Ramón Gómez de la Serna's Greguería," *World Literature Today*, 53 (Spring 1979): 231-234;

Karl Riha, *Cross-reading und Cross-talking: Zitat-Collagen als poetische und satirische Technik* (Stuttgart: Metzler, 1971), pp. 63-69;

Riha, *Moritat, Song, Bänkelsang: Zur Geschichte der modernen Ballade* (Göttingen: Sachse & Pohl, 1965), pp. 137-148;

Gerhard Rühm, ed., *Die Wiener Gruppe: Achleitner, Artmann, Bayer, Rühm, Wiener* (Reinbek: Rowohlt, 1967);

Hilde Schmölzer, *Das böse Wien: 16 Gespräche mit österreichischen Künstlern* (Munich: Nymphenburger Verlagshandlung, 1973);

Hannes Schneider, "Artmanns frühe Werke," in Artmann's *Das im Walde verlorene Totem* (Salzburg: Residenz, 1970), pp. 103-110;

Werner Welzig, "Die Regel des Gegensatzes in H. C. Artmanns Dialektgedichten," *Mundart und Geschichte*, 4 (1967): 175-180.

Ingeborg Bachmann

(25 June 1926-17 October 1973)

Karen Achberger
St. Olaf College

BOOKS: *Die gestundete Zeit: Gedichte* (Frankfurt am Main: Frankfurter Verlagsanstalt, 1953);

Der Idiot: Ballett-Pantomime nach F. M. Dostojewski von Tatjana Gsovski, music by Hans Werner Henze (Mainz: Schott, 1955);

Anrufung des Großen Bären (Munich: Piper, 1956);

Der gute Gott von Manhattan: Hörspiel (Munich: Piper, 1958);

Nachtstücke und Arien nach Gedichten von Ingeborg Bachmann für Sopran und großes Orchester: Studien-Partitur, music by Henze (Mainz: Schott, 1958);

Der Prinz von Homburg: Oper in drei Akten nach dem Schauspiel von Heinrich von Kleist, music by Henze (Mainz: Schott, 1960);

Jugend in einer österreichischen Stadt (Wülfrath: Heiderhoff, 1961);

Gedichte: Eine Auswahl (Berlin & Weimar: Aufbau, 1961);

Das dreißigste Jahr: Erzählungen (Munich: Piper, 1961); translated by Michael Bullock as *The Thirtieth Year* (New York: Knopf, 1964; London: Deutsch, 1964);

Der gute Gott von Manhattan; Die Zikaden: Zwei Hörspiele (Munich: Deutscher Taschenbuch Verlag, 1963);

Gedichte, Erzählungen, Hörspiel, Essays (Munich: Piper, 1964);

Chorfantasie über die "Lieder von einer Insel" von Ingeborg Bachmann für gemischten Chor, Posaune, zwei Violoncelli, Kontrabaß, Portativ, Pauken und Schlagwerk: Partitur, music by Henze (Mainz: Schott, 1964);

Der junge Lord: Komische Oper in zwei Akten von Ingeborg Bachmann nach einer Parabel aus "Der Scheik von Alessandria und seine Sklaven" von Wilhelm Hauff, music by Henze (Mainz: Schott, 1965); translated as *The Young Milord: Comic Opera* (Mainz & New York: Schott, 1967);

Ein Ort für Zufälle (Berlin: Wagenbach, 1965);

Malina: Roman (Frankfurt am Main: Suhrkamp, 1971); translated by Philip Boehm as *Malina* (New York: Holmes & Meier, 1989);

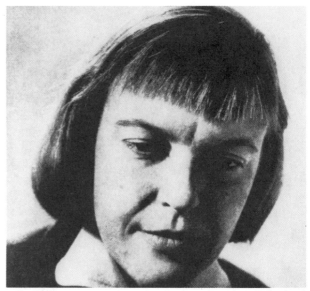

(Photo: Wolkensinger)

Simultan: Neue Erzählungen (Munich: Piper, 1972); translated by Mary Fran Gilbert as *Three Paths to the Lake* (New York: Holmes & Meier, 1989);

Undine geht: Erzählungen (Leipzig: Reclam, 1973; enlarged, 1976);

Die Hörspiele (Munich: Piper, 1976)—comprises "Ein Geschäft mit Träumen," "Die Zikaden," "Der gute Gott von Manhattan";

Werke, edited by Christine Koschel, Inge von Weidenbaum, and Clemens Münster, 4 volumes (Munich: Piper, 1978);

Der Fall Franza; Requiem für Fanny Goldmann (Munich: Piper, 1979);

Sämtliche Erzählungen (Munich: Piper, 1980);

Frankfurter Vorlesungen: Probleme zeitgenössischer Dichtung (Munich: Piper, 1980);

Die Gedichte (Leipzig: Insel, 1981);

Die Wahrheit ist dem Menschen zumutbar: Essays, Reden, Kleinere Schriften (Munich: Piper, 1981);

Die Fähre: Erzählungen (Munich: Deutscher Ta-
    schenbuch Verlag, 1982);
Sämtliche Gedichte (Munich: Piper, 1983);
Das Honditschkreuz (Munich: Piper, 1983);
*Wir müssen wahre Sätze finden: Gespräche und Inter-
    views*, edited by Koschel and Weidenbaum
    (Munich: Piper, 1983);
*Ingeborg Bachmann: Bilder aus ihrem Leben. Mit Tex-
    ten aus ihrem Werk*, edited by Andreas Hapke-
    meyer (Munich: Piper, 1983);
*Liebe: Dunkler Erdteil. Gedichte aus den Jahren
    1942-1967* (Munich: Piper, 1984);
*Undine geht; Das Gebell; Ein Wildermuth: Drei Erzäh-
    lungen* (Stuttgart: Reclam, 1984);
*Die kritische Aufnahme der Existentialphilosophie Mar-
    tin Heideggers*, edited by Robert Pichl (Mu-
    nich: Piper, 1985);
In the Storm of Roses: Selected Poems, translated and
    edited by Mark Anderson (Princeton: Prince-
    ton University Press, 1986).

OTHER: Ludwig Wittgenstein, *Schriften*, contribu-
    tions by Bachmann (Frankfurt am Main:
    Suhrkamp, 1960);
Giuseppe Ungaretti, *Gedichte: Italienisch und
    deutsch*, translated by Bachmann (Frankfurt
    am Main: Suhrkamp, 1961);
Italienische Lyrik des 20. Jahrhunderts, edited by
    Christine Wolter, translated by Bachmann
    and others (Berlin & Weimar: Aufbau,
    1971);
Ungaretti, *Freude der Schiffbrüche*, edited by Wol-
    ter, translated by Bachmann and others (Ber-
    lin: Volk und Welt, 1977);
"Gier," edited by Robert Pichl, in *Der dunkle Schat-
    ten, dem ich schon seit Anfang folge*, edited by
    Hans Höller (Vienna: Löcker, 1982), pp.
    17-61;
Klagenfurt, edited by Hans G. Trenkwelder, contri-
    butions by Bachmann (Klagenfurt: Carin-
    thia, 1982).

PERIODICAL PUBLICATION: "Entfremdung,"
    Lynkeus: Dichtung, Kunst, Kritik, 1 (December
    1948 / January 1949): 31.

Ingeborg Bachmann ranks with Robert
Musil, Hermann Broch, and Peter Handke as
one of the most distinguished Austrian prose writers of the twentieth century and is recognized,
along with Günter Eich and Paul Celan, as the
most prominent German-language lyrical voice of
the early post-World War II period. Her influence on contemporary German-language authors

is comparable to that of Virginia Woolf on modern English writers; it can be seen in the works
of the East German writer Christa Wolf, the West
German Günter Grass, the Swiss Max Frisch, and
the major Austrian writers Thomas Bernhard,
Erich Fried, and Handke. The city of Klagenfurt
has established a Bachmann museum and in
1977 began awarding an annual Ingeborg
Bachmann Literary Prize for young writers. Several documentary films have been made on her
life, and five of her stories have been made into
films. Poems by Bachmann have been set to
music by Luigi Nono, Franz Bernhardt, and
Hans Werner Henze, and her novel *Malina*
(1971; translated, 1989) has been made into a
chamber opera for radio by the Austrian composer Otto Brusatti. In 1959-1960 she was the
first writer to deliver the Frankfurt Lectures on Poetics. Her writing received wide acclaim from the
beginning: in 1953, while still in her twenties,
she received the annual prize of the avant-garde
circle of writers known as the Gruppe 47; she
also received the Literature Prize of the Culture
Circle of German Industry in 1955; the Bremen
Prize in 1957; the literary prize of the Association of German Critics, a distinction comparable
to the Pulitzer Prize in the United States, in
1961; the Georg Büchner Prize in 1964; the
Great Austrian State Prize in 1968; and the
Anton Wildgans Prize in 1971. In academic circles, Bachmann was acclaimed in the 1950s for
her poetry, then ignored when she became too
popular a personality in the 1960s and 1970s.
The 1980s brought international critical attention
to Bachmann as one of the major writers of the
century, not only for her poetry but increasingly
for her prose. Several volumes of scholarship devoted to her have appeared since 1980 in West
Germany, Austria, and the United States, and
scholarly symposia on Bachmann have been held
in Istanbul; Ljubljana, Yugoslavia; Bad Segeberg,
West Germany; Rome; Warsaw; Basel; Nantes,
France; Brussels; and Pavia, Italy.

Beyond the critical reception of her works,
Bachmann the woman was and is a legend. From
her first appearance in 1952 before the Gruppe
47 and the cover story on her in the German
news magazine *Der Spiegel* in 1954 to her sensational death in 1973, it was the blond, fairy-tale
princess from Austria, fragile and girlish in appearance yet proud and wise, the shy, awkward,
"great" poet, the intelligent woman in largely
male circles, the "First Lady of the Group 47"
who fascinated German, and especially Austrian,

Bachmann in 1962 (Ingeborg Bachmann: Eine Einführung, *1963*)

tial outsider as the intellectual, suffering woman.

Born in Klagenfurt in the southern Austrian province of Carinthia, Bachmann belongs to that generation of Germans and Austrians who experienced National Socialism and World War II at an early age and who in the following decades had to deal with their devastating effects. The oldest of three children of Mathias Bachmann, a high school teacher, and Olga Haas Bachmann, she attended a coeducational high school until 1938; under the Nazis she was moved to a girls' school until her graduation in 1944. Her initial course of postsecondary study at a pedagogical institute in Klagenfurt was interrupted at the end of the war, after which she began her study of philosophy at the Universities of Innsbruck, Graz, and Vienna, completing a doctoral thesis at the University of Vienna in 1949 on the critical reception of Martin Heidegger's philosophy of existentialism. During the early 1950s she lived for the most part in Vienna and Munich, working for Austrian radio and Bavarian television; from 1953 to 1957 she lived as a freelance writer in Ischia, Naples, Rome, and Munich, traveling to the United States in 1955 at the invitation of Harvard University; between 1958 and 1962 she alternated between Rome and Zurich; she lived in West Berlin from 1963 to 1965 and in Rome from the end of 1965 until her death. She lived with Henze from 1953 to 1956 and with Frisch from 1958 to 1962.

Bachmann's literary production is divided into an early and a late period; after 1956 there is a shift in genre and thematic focus. Despite this division, one theme runs throughout Bachmann's oeuvre: the constant state of war. One of her first published poems, "Entfremdung" (Alienation, 1948), ends with an image of nature fleeing in the face of the permanent state of war: the sun drums a death roll on empty pails lying in a village while a swarm of bees escapes to the wilderness after stinging the last human, who is too numb to feel anything. One of her best-known poems, "Alle Tage" (Every Day) in the collection *Die gestundete Zeit* (Borrowed Time, 1953), begins: "Der Krieg wird nicht mehr erklärt, sondern fortgesetzt" (War is no longer declared, only continued). While the theme is gender-neutral in her poetry, it becomes increasingly gender-specific in Bachmann's prose. She makes the connection between war and love and shows in her later writing, beginning with the radio play *Der gute Gott von Manhattan* (The Good God of Manhattan, 1958), the de-

readers. A focus on Bachmann's life and personality left her literary works, especially the later prose works, largely ignored in the German-language press. Reviews of her readings and of her Frankfurt lectures focused on her appearance and demeanor; reviews of her books made connections between her writing and her life. The blurring of distinctions between her work and her life was most profound after she accidentally set fire to herself in her Rome apartment in 1973; her death after weeks of suffering seemed like something out of one of her stories. The observation of the tenth anniversary of her death in 1983 and of her sixtieth birthday in 1986, as well as the publication of the four-volume collected edition of her works in 1978, have again evoked in the German press the image of the timid, existen-

structive nature of love for women. The warlike aspect of the relationship between the sexes is most prominent in the novels of her "Todesarten" (Ways of Death) cycle, the major project of her final years, where she began to survey the forms of death women suffer in patriarchal society. In "Der Fall Franza" (The Case of Franza, 1979) she refers to "einen stummen Ehekrieg" (a silent marriage-war), and in *Malina* the narrator closes the central chapter by saying: "Es ist immer Krieg. Hier ist immer Gewalt. Hier ist immer Kampf. Es ist der ewige Krieg" (It is always war. Here is always force. Here is always battle. It is the eternal war).

Bachmann's first volume of poetry, *Die gestundete Zeit*, consists of twenty-three poems on the theme of running out of time. The title poem begins and ends with the line "Es kommen härtere Tage" (Harder days are coming). In the face of the onset of a new age, often suggested in the poems by the image of departure on a journey, a sense of urgency and of hope prevails; the impending catastrophe, frequently indicated by a nature metaphor, requires immediate action. Warnings, directions, and orders to the reader imply a belief in self-reliance and the redemptive value of courageous individual action. The poem "Ausfahrt" (Leaving Port), which opens the volume, is typical of the collection and of early postwar Austrian literature in general. It describes a ship embarking on a voyage as the sun sinks and the water darkens. In contrast to the traditional images of heading out to sea at daybreak and returning to dock at sunset, the beginning of a journey here is linked to the ending of the day. Amid increasing obscurity, the reader is cautioned to watch carefully and to strive to keep the ever darker and more distant coastline clearly in view. The mood is one of urgency, signaling the threatening character of running out of time. Yet a belief in the value of courageous self-assertion–careful watching and standing firm–prevails: "Die kleine Fischerhütte behält im Aug" (Keep the little fishing cottage in view), "und wenn das Schiff hart stampft und einen unsicheren Schritt tut, steh ruhig auf Deck" (and when the ship pitches hard and takes a faltering step, stand firmly on deck). The poem is informed by a tension between the irresistible forces of nature and the appeal to the reader to resist: "gegen den unverrückbaren Himmel zu stehen, der ungangbaren Wasser nicht zu achten und das Schiff über die Wellen zu heben, auf das immerwiederkehrende Sonnenufer zu" (to stand against the immovable sky, to pay no heed to the impassable waters and to lift your ship over the waves toward the ever reappearing sun shore). The futility of such resistance is disregarded in this early poem, and Bachmann held throughout her life a belief in a better world while at the same time questioning its feasibility. In an interview in the year of her death, she confessed: "Ich glaube wirklich an etwas, und das nenne ich 'ein Tag wird kommen.' . . . Es wird nicht kommen, und trotzdem glaube ich daran. Denn wenn ich nicht mehr daran glauben kann, kann ich auch nicht mehr schreiben" (I really believe in something and I call it "a day shall come." . . . It won't come and I believe in it anyway. For if I can't believe in it anymore, I am also unable to go on writing).

Bachmann's second and final volume of poetry, *Anrufung des Großen Bären* (Invocation of the Great Bear, 1956) opens with the poem "Das Spiel ist aus" (The Game Is Over). Ship and water metaphors continue to dominate, but the message they carry has drastically changed from the previous volume. While the adult reader was called to social positions and actions in the earlier poems, "Das Spiel ist aus" offers an imaginary dialogue of a child talking to her little brother in an intimate family setting. The moral call to vigilance and upright posture in "Ausfahrt" is now the invitation to go to bed; the socially responsible adult is now the child playing in the private world of family and fantasy. "Wir müssen schlafen gehen, Liebster, das Spiel ist aus" (We must go to sleep, dearest, the game is over). The journey has become a voyage into the world of daydreams and fantasy, an imaginary trip "den Himmel hinunter" (down the sky). The hope implicit in the earlier collection has yielded to resignation: "wir gehen unter" (we will go under). In its regression into the private world of the child's imagination, this poem is typical of the volume and of the spirit of the times. The approaching night of the earlier collection has arrived: the constellation of the title is visible only at night, and another poem of this collection, "Curriculum Vitae," says explicitly: "Immer die Nacht. Und kein Tag" (Always night. And no day). In the face of this night, Bachmann offers a mythical layer of meaning, a second level of reference, in which other truths can be told. In turning to mythical images, Bachmann begins a direction which becomes prominent in her prose writing, where a hopeless reality is frequently countered by a utopian world of mythic fantasy.

Drawing of Bachmann by Gerda von Stengel, 1965

The second collection of poems also introduces themes which become increasingly important in Bachmann's later writing: death and destruction, opposing parts of the self, the painful dualism of thinking and sensuality. The title poem opens with an exchange between shepherds and the Great Bear. The humans challenge the bear to come down to earth and appear before them. The bear answers that they are of no significance, likening them to the scales of a pine cone. In the ancient symbol of the celestial Great Bear rests that threat of destruction and the consciousness of downfall, a fear of distant and uncanny supernatural forces which are indifferent toward humans at the same time they gratuitously break into human lives.

Bachmann, who worked in Vienna at the radio station Rot-Weiß-Rot (Red-White-Red, the colors of the Austrian flag) from 1951 to 1953, first as a script writer and then as an editor, wrote three radio plays. The subject of the plays is flight from reality. The first play, "Ein Geschäft mit Träumen" (A Business with Dreams, 1976), was written during 1952 at a time when the work of the writer in postwar Austria and Germany was exactly the business referred to in the title and when the radio play was the literary genre which seemed best suited to carry the writers' dreams to the public. In the face of the postwar reality and the recent National Socialist past, both of which most Germans and Austrians found difficult to confront, a literature which offered dreams and fantasy was a popular commodity. At a time when most of the theaters, concert halls, opera houses, and libraries destroyed in the war had not yet been rebuilt, the wounded German and Austrian nations found solace in an art form which was readily accessible and could offer an entertaining escape from reality. "Ein Geschäft mit Träumen" depicts an office worker who leaves work one evening, takes a walk through the streets of Vienna, and passes over into an unreal realm in which he finds a dark little shop selling dreams–not for money, but in exchange for time. He is shown three dreams: a nightmare, a power fantasy, and one which culminates in his underwater encounter amid the songs of sirens with a secretary from his office who has been shipwrecked in a storm. He wants to buy the third dream but cannot afford the month it would cost him. As the dream ends, the final words of the lovers are repeated over and over, "als ob eine Platte immer wieder abliefe" (as if the record had gotten stuck), a reminder of the technical packaging of these escapes from the real world which Bachmann, like the keeper of the dream shop, is offering through her art.

In her second radio play, "Die Zikaden" (The Cicadas, 1976), written in 1954 and first broadcast in 1955, Bachmann places the theme of escape from reality even more sharply in focus. The action takes place on a remote island, where the creatures of the title can be heard singing each day at noon; the final lines of the play reveal that the cicadas were humans who lost their humanness when they stopped eating, drinking, and loving and escaped into song. This metaphor is a warning of the dehumanization that results from attempting to flee from reality through a preoccupation with art.

Six of the island inhabitants, fugitives from the outside world who are psychically shipwrecked and thus well on their way to becoming cicadas, enter into a series of duets with the beautiful-voiced Antonio, the only native islander—who, as his name suggests, is essentially *Ton* (tone). While they remain "hooked" on the island and will éventually degenerate into cicadas, Robinson, who "consumes" Antonio in moderation—he stays distant and merely admits to pleasure at hearing the sound of Antonio's voice—returns to civilization. Bachmann is showing here that art as mere entertainment will only serve to further dehumanize society by preventing the absolutely necessary work of coming to terms with the past. In the final moments of the play the narrator explicitly cautions the listener to remember as a means of staying human: "Such nicht zu vergessen! Erinnere dich! Und der dürre Gesang deiner Sehnsucht wird Fleisch" (Seek not to forget! Remember! And the dry song of your longing will become flesh). Art must provide an understanding of present and past reality, not an escape from reality. This artistic credo of Bachmann's has been misunderstood, especially in the early 1970s when she was criticized for a lack of social or political engagement in her writing. The danger of art due to its potentially narcotic effect also received attention in Bachmann's Frankfurt lectures and was a factor contributing to her turn from poetry to prose after 1956.

In Bachmann's last and best-known radio play, "Der gute Gott von Manhattan," which was first broadcast in 1958, two levels of action alternate: the love story of the American student, Jennifer, and the European, Jan, and the trial of the "Good God of Manhattan" for Jennifer's murder; the love story is revealed in flashbacks narrated by the Good God and the judge in the courtroom. The theme, the impossibility of love in contemporary society, is a central one in Bachmann's oeuvre. Here love is undermined not from within but from without: the Good God is the agent of those vague and undefined forces in the world which condemn love and destroy it whenever it dares to exist. What starts, for Jan at least, as a passing fling begins to show signs of becoming a more lasting and committed relationship. This development, however, necessitates the intervention of the Good God and his lieutenants, Billie and Frankie, leaders of a corps of several hundred chipmunks who assist him in assassinating lovers throughout the city. The increasing isolation of Jennifer and Jan from the rest of society is symbolized in the upward movement of their place of intimacy from a cheap, dirty ground-floor hotel room to rooms on the seventh, thirtieth, and finally fifty-seventh floor of the Atlantic Hotel. They are not only physically more and more remote from society but spiritually and emotionally less "down to earth" as they soar higher and higher into the heavens. Jan is saved from the explosion of the bomb which the Good God planted in their room by his desire to distance himself from the relationship, first by running an errand and then by sitting in a bar for a moment before returning to their room.

The woman is the sole victim of love; the murderer, judge, and survivor are all male. Whether one views Jennifer's death as victimization or as transcendence—as a modern "love-death"—the theme of woman's destruction in patriarchal society becomes increasingly important in Bachmann's later works. Society's refusal to allow love affects the two partners differently: the male returns to that society unscathed, while the female is consumed alone in the volatile heat of the space they had shared. The relationship between Jan and Jennifer is shown not only as a withdrawal from the social order but also as an escape from the past. After the lovers move to their room on the thirtieth floor, Jennifer begins to inquire about Jan's past. Jan admits to having several prefabricated versions of his past, asks Jennifer to excuse his not sharing them with her, and argues for a relationship based on their present knowledge of one another. He advocates communication based on common experiences of the-

Manuscript for a poem by Bachmann (Albert Soergel and Curt Hohoff, Dichtung und Dichter der Zeit, *volume 2 [Düsseldorf: Bagel, 1963])*

ater, music, art, and film—that is, not a direct communication based on their real lives but an understanding mediated through the arts. Thus the theme of art as a substitute for life, which is central to "Die Zikaden," is also sounded here.

In her acceptance speech for the Radio Play Prize of the Blind War Veterans, which she was awarded for *Der gute Gott von Manhattan*, Bachmann emphasized the need for retaining a vision of the ideal: "Es ist auch mir gewiß, daß wir in der Ordnung bleiben müssen. Innerhalb der Grenzen aber haben wir den Blick gerichtet auf das Vollkommene, das Unmögliche, Unerreichbare, sei es der Liebe, der Freiheit oder jeder reinen Größe. Im Widerspiel des Unmöglichen mit dem Möglichen erweitern wir unsere Möglichkeiten" (I too am certain that we must remain within the given order. Within limits, however, we have our sights aimed at the perfect, the impos-

sible, unattainable, be it of love, of freedom or of every pure value. In the interplay between the impossible and the possible we expand our possibilities).

The ethical and aesthetic issues which concerned Bachmann as a writer—such questions as the role of the writer and of literature, the problem of saying "I" and of naming, and the modernist skepticism about language—are discussed in her main theoretical work, the five lectures on poetics which she gave at the University of Frankfurt between November 1959 and February 1960. In the first lecture, "Fragen und Scheinfragen" (Questions and Pseudoquestions), Bachmann focuses on the role of the writer and the literary work in the modern world and lists the essential questions, which she terms "zerstörerische, furchtbare . . . in ihrer Einfachheit" (destructive, frightening . . . in their simplicity): Why write?

What do we mean by change and why do we want it through art? What are the limitations of the writer who wants to bring about change? Although she does not answer these questions directly, Bachmann views the great literary accomplishments of the twentieth century as expressions of a moral and intellectual renewal in the individual writers; the writers' new thinking and experiencing forms the core of their literary works. She also associates literary renewal with writers who are on the verge of silence due to self-doubt and despair over the impotence of language and cites Hugo von Hofmannsthal's "Chandos Letter" ("Ein Brief" [1905; translated as "The Letter," 1942]) as the first articulation of this dilemma.

In her second lecture on poetry Bachmann points out that each poem has a new and unique grasp on reality and that this uniqueness is inherent in the idiom in which it is written. A poem cannot, therefore, be translated without losing some of its power to capture reality. A novel or a play, on the other hand, *can* be translated adequately, since its grasp on reality manifests itself beyond the level of words in the story, perspective, structure, and characters of the work. She also distinguishes between poets of the contemporary generation, such as Günter Eich, who see the world from a new perspective and feel called to pass on their insights, and poets of Stefan George's generation, who passed on ever more refined aesthetic intricacies as amoral distractions (*l'art pour l'art*).

Bachmann's third lecture, "Das schreibende Ich" (The Writing I), on first-person narration, clearly situates her within the modernist tradition, which questions the accountability and authenticity of the narrative voice. She begins with the simplest and least problematic narrative situation, that of memoirs, where the I of a statesman such as Winston Churchill or Charles de Gaulle is treated "naively," that is, as an established public identity. She distinguishes several variations of the I in novels, which in contrast to the I in letters and diaries take on form as three-dimensional figures in the texts. Henry Miller and Céline, in placing their personal experiences directly at the center of their novels, create an identity of author and protagonist and thereby renounce the invention of a fictional first-person narrator. Two types of double first-person narrative involve the creation of a second narrator who either narrates the inner story directly, as in Tolstoy's *The Kreutzer Sonata* (1889), or has left be-

hind a written text which narrates the inner story, as in Dostoyevski's *The House of the Dead* (1861-1862). The talents or idiosyncrasies of the work's narrator can allow for a new treatment of time (Italo Svevo), of material (Marcel Proust), or of space (Hans Henny Jahnn). In the modern novel the narrator no longer lives in the story; rather, the story exists in the narrator. The I proves indestructible, even in the face of the inability to narrate: in Samuel Beckett's last novel, *L'Innommable* (1953; translated as *The Unnameable*, 1958), all content has been liquidated and the "Ich ohne Gewähr" (I without guarantees) continues to exist only as a "Platzhalter der menschlichen Stimme" (place saver for the human voice). The modernist "Platzhalter" function is depicted in Bachmann's *Malina*, in which the nameless female narrator at the end of the novel literally disappears into a crack in the wall.

In her fourth lecture, "Der Umgang mit Namen" (Close Association with Names), Bachmann cites examples which mark the end of the age of "vertrauensvolle Namensgebung" (confident naming): "Namensverweigerung" (denied names), in Kafka's *Das Schloß* (1926; translated as *The Castle*, 1930); "Namensironisierung" (ironic naming) in Thomas Mann, whom she terms "der letzte große Namenserfinder, ein Namenzauberer" (the last great name inventor, a name magician); "Namensspiel, mit und ohne Bedeutung, die Erschütterung des Namens" (name games, with and without meaning, shaken names) in James Joyce's *Ulysses* (1922), and an even more radical treatment in William Faulkner's *The Sound and the Fury* (1929), where the identity of characters is not secured by names at all but suggested by context. Proust's *A la recherche du temps perdu* (1913-1927; translated as *Remembrance of Times Past*, 1922-1931), more than any other work draws attention to the nature, handling, and functioning of names.

In her last lecture, "Literatur als Utopie" (Literature as Utopia), Bachmann discusses the prerequisites for a literature which is to be utopian. Literature makes the readers aware of the "Mangel" (lack) both in the work and in their own world. The readers remove this lack, the withered aspect of every great work, by giving the work a chance. Each work of literature is "ein nach vorn geöffnetes Reich von unbekannten Grenzen" (a realm which reaches ahead and has unknown limits). The utopian quality of literature is that it remains "ungeschlossen" (unclosed), that it has the force of all times pressing

Bachmann in Rome in the fall of 1968 (photo copyright © by Leonore Mau)

against it, that it is open to interaction with readers in all times. It resists being pigeonholed and entombed, it is not given to being rendered harmless and dated, and it moves toward a new language or "Utopie der Sprache" (utopia of language). Its strength lies in its state of "verzweiflungsvollen Unterwegsseins zu dieser Sprache" (being despairingly en route to this language). For Bachmann, utopia is not a place but a direction. Literature as utopia is moving toward and never attaining a language which can transcend the usual limits of "die schlechte Sprache" (the wretched language) which is all that we

have. Literature offers a fragmentary glimpse, in a line or a scene, of that language which governs our imagination, which we struggle to imitate, and in which we can comprehend ourselves and glimpse the possibility of peace.

Her belief in the power of literature to humanize the world and her conviction of its duty to do so, attested to in the Frankfurt lectures, led to a shift in focus for Bachmann. In the year following the lectures she turned from poetry to fiction. In a few last poems written in the 1960s she expressed her refusal "eine Metapher aus[zu]staffieren mit einer Mandelblüte" (to dress

Bachmann in 1971 (Piper Verlag, Munich)

a metaphor with an almond blossom) or "die Syntax [zu kreuzigen] auf einen Lichteffekt . . . " (to crucify syntax on a trick of light)–that is, to produce literary "Delikatessen" (delicacies).

A year after the Frankfurt lectures Bachmann's first volume of stories, *Das dreißigste Jahr* (1961; translated as *The Thirtieth Year*, 1964), appeared. The seven stories in the collection are not narratives in the conventional sense but moments of reflection, lyrical impressions, monologues, and tightly composed images which suggest a radical rebellion against that "worst of all possible worlds" in which the protagonists find themselves. After a prelude, "Jugend in einer österreichischen Stadt" (translated as "Youth in an Austrian Town"), in which a childhood of fear-

ful obedience is recalled with quiet, dispassionate aversion, the six following stories break open to life's moments of crisis, of coming of age, for which the year thirty is symbolic. In all the stories there is a yearning for renewal, for another order, for salvation, which at times takes on mythic proportions and which, though glimpsed for a moment, is unattainable. These clashes of utopian vision with real limitations are moments of breakthrough and breakdown, moments of truth in what have otherwise been lives of illusion. In the parabolic "Alles" (Everything) a thirty-year-old father who wants to create the world anew through his son must face the reality that the son is like everyone else and has appropriated all the traditions he was meant to destroy;

the father accepts his son's ordinariness, loses interest in the boy, and the son falls to his death on a school field trip. After an automobile accident the thirty-year-old man of the title story is forced to take stock of his rather ordinary life up to that point and falls apart. Likewise, the presiding judge in "Ein Wildermuth" (translated as "A Wildermuth"), whose life has centered around knowing the truth, comes to the realization that there is no truth and suffers a nervous breakdown as a result. A confrontation with a stranger in a Viennese pub and the man's death at the hands of reunited war veterans whom he had offended cause a Viennese Jew in "Unter Mördern und Irren" (translated as "Among Murderers and Madmen") to view his life and companions in a new light. After a momentary glimpse of another life outside of her patriarchal marriage, Charlotte in "Ein Schritt nach Gomorrha" (translated as "A Step toward Gomorrah") sets her alarm clock and prepares to pick up her husband at the depot the next morning. And in "Undine geht" (translated as "Undine Goes") the water nymph Undine sees the inhumanity of the world of humans and breaks with it but longs for reunion with her human lover. The protagonists have expanded their awareness and understanding of human existence; they have glimpsed the impossible while remaining grounded firmly in reality. They have, in Bachmann's words, expanded their possibilities "in the interplay between the impossible and the possible." Her central figures are shaken into new awareness; they are given a vision of a new reality together with the knowledge that it is unattainable, and in this respect they are totally modern protagonists.

Their powerlessness and shock when they discover that the world is not as they had envisaged it lend Bachmann's characters a Kafkaesque quality. The themes of crime, guilt, and trial as well as the parabolic nature of the stories are also reminiscent of Kafka. Another striking similarity is the frequent splitting of the central characters into two persons to represent different aspects of the same individual. In "Alles" the son is that part of the father which is young and offers hope for the future; when the father gives up that part of himself in resignation, the son dies. In "Ein Wildermuth" both the judge and the defendant have the same surname, suggesting an identification of the two. The judge's world is shaken when he is confronted with the repressed part of himself, a part whose actions defy ordering into his previously understood world. After

all her guests have left the party, Charlotte finds in her smoke-filled apartment a girl in black and red offering her a life beyond the confines of her marriage. The girl responds to Charlotte's unuttered thoughts, suggesting that she is not the separate, external being she appears to be; and at the end of the story the two women lie down side by side in similar if not identical white undergarments. In "Unter Mördern und Irren," an "Unbekanter" (unknown man) appears in the pub on an evening when fewer than the usual number of Jews are present, tells unsettling stories about the war and his murderous role in it, then ends up dead in the street after apparently provoking a group of soldiers celebrating in the basement. The narrator returns home and notices blood on his hand from touching the body. He feels that the blood is a kind of protection, like the dragon's blood that made Achilles and Siegfried invulnerable. Putting the "unknown one" out of circulation restores order and composure to the narrator's world.

Unlike Kafka, Bachmann shows suffering and breakdown not merely in vague existential terms but in their specific social contexts. The nightmare of growing up in an Austrian city depicted in the opening story of the collection is not the timeless and placeless experience of Kafka's world: clearly, the city is Klagenfurt and the time is that of the Third Reich. Fascism in her stories is the historical experience of her generation; in "Jugend in einer österreichischen Stadt" the reality of a fascist political system is recalled through childhood impressions, and in "Unter Mördern und Irren" the depiction of Austrian men recalling their war experiences in a Viennese pub shows how little attitudes and values have changed since the National Socialist period. In the two stories with female narrators, however, it is the oppressiveness of the relationship between the sexes which is thematized: Charlotte, whom Bachmann characterizes with allusions to the Old Testament Lot, faces for a moment the evil of her marriage before returning to it; and Undine rejects the inhumane world of men, albeit with ambivalence.

The crimes against women in contemporary society, the subtle and common ways in which they are murdered in total compliance with the law is the subject of Bachmann's "Todesarten" cycle. The first novel, *Malina*, appeared in 1971; the other two, "Der Fall Franza" and "Requiem für Fanny Goldmann," appeared in her *Werke* (Works, 1978) as fragments. Like the three fe-

Advertisement by the Piper publishing house for Bachmann's works

male protagonists of the cycle, the five women in Bachmann's other collection of stories, *Simultan* (Simultaneous, 1972; translated as *Three Paths to the Lake*, 1989), can be seen as victims of a subtle and ubiquitous kind of fascism. In an interview a few months before her death Bachmann dis-cussed the origins of fascism: "Er fängt nicht an mit den ersten Bomben, die geworfen werden, er fängt nicht an mit dem Terror, über den man lesen kann, in jeder Zeitung. Er fängt an in Beziehungen zwischen Menschen. Der Faschismus ist das erste in der Beziehung zwischen einem Mann und einer Frau, und ich habe versucht zu sagen ... hier in dieser Gesellschaft ist immer Krieg. Es gibt nicht Krieg und Frieden, es gibt nur den Krieg" (It doesn't start with the first bombs that are dropped; it doesn't start with the terror which one can read about, in every newspaper. It starts in relation-ships between people. Fascism is the first thing in the relationship between a man and a woman, and I attempted to say ... that here in this soci-ety there is always war. There isn't war and peace, there's only war).

The stories in *Simultan* explore the possibility of survival as a woman in the Austrian society of the 1960s. Each of the five female protagonists, like the three women in the "Todesarten" cycle, is destroyed; but in contrast to the novel and fragments, in which the women actually die, the destruction in the stories is symbolic: one woman's coiffure and makeup are ruined by rain and tears; another is full of blood and cuts after walking into a revolving door; an old woman living alone is plagued by the imaginary barking of a dog; even the two successful professional women in the stories which frame the collection–an interpreter and a war correspondent–function in typically female roles as mediators of the thoughts and actions of men. While the two professional women–Nadja in "Simultan" (Simultaneous) and Elisabeth in "Drei Wege zum See" (Three Paths to the Lake)–seem to function well professionally, socially, and sexually, the other protagonists are clearly sensually reduced women: Frau Jordan in "Das Gebell" (The Barking) hears the imaginary dog barking more and more loudly, Miranda in "Ihr glücklichen Augen" (You Wondrous Eyes) refuses to wear her glasses as she grows increasingly nearsighted, and Beatrix in "Probleme, Probleme" (Problems, Problems) needs more and more sleep while facing the world only from behind an expensive, carefully constructed mask of cosmetics. While the two professional women move about freely in the world of men, flying from city to city in their work, the other three retreat more and more from a world which has become unbearable. Yet they all share the same existential situation: each of the women protects the men in her life from the unpleasant reality of her situation, and each pays with her own life. While surviving in "reality," the women in Bachmann's stories symbolically self-destruct as an expression of the rage they do not even know exists.

Since the publication in 1978 of the two fragmentary novels in the four-volume edition of Bachmann's works, scholars have focused increasingly on her fiction. Bachmann intended the cycle to show the "ways of death" resulting from the continuation of fascist behavior and thought in postwar Austria, to expose the crimes which are totally legal and commonplace and go unnoticed and unpunished. *Malina*, like most of Bachmann's narratives, has little action. It consists largely of a nameless narrator's thoughts, conversations, letters, and dreams, and ends with her slipping into a crack in the wall. As a counter-point to her destruction, Bachmann interweaves throughout the first chapter a utopian legend, "Die Geheimnisse der Prinzessin von Kagran" (The Secrets of the Princess of Kagran), set off by italics, and twice cites a motif from Arnold Schönberg's "Pierrot lunaire" song cycle in musical notation. Despite the glimpse of transcendence offered by these countertexts, the novel's focus is the destruction of its narrator, which Bachmann exposes as an act of violence. The novel begins with the sentences "Mord oder Selbstmord? Es gibt keine Zeugen" (Murder or suicide? There are no witnesses) and ends with the statement, "Es war Mord" (It was murder). Thus the first and last word of the novel is *Mord*, pointing to the criminal nature of the commonplace destruction of the female voice. Each of the three chapters exposes a destructive relationship the narrator has had with a man: her blind infatuation with her Hungarian lover in the first chapter, "Glücklich mit Ivan" (Happy with Ivan); her abuse at the hands of her father, which is revealed to her in nightmares in the second chapter, "Der dritte Mann" (The Third Man); and her replacement by her male alter ego, Malina, in the final chapter, "Von letzten Dingen" (Of Last Things).

In "Der Fall Franza," Franza is psychologically destroyed by her husband, the well-known Viennese psychiatrist Leopold Jordan (the son of Frau Jordan in "Das Gebell"), who has made her into a case study in connection with his book on female concentration camp survivors who had been used for experiments by Nazi doctors. After a nervous breakdown Franza journeys with her brother to Egypt, where she is able to connect her own exploitation to that of other victims–a butchered camel; a bound woman said to be insane; a cretin; Queen Hatshepsut, whose son tried to eradicate every trace of her from the temple–and where she dies after being raped at a pyramid and beating her head against the stone wall in protest. In "Requiem für Fanny Goldmann" the actress Fanny Goldmann is exploited as the subject of a book by her lover, the opportunistic playwright Anton Marek. After the book appears and the details of her private life are exposed, Fanny is consumed by hatred and alcoholism and dies from a lung infection.

That these novels were intended to connect ways of thinking and acting prevalent in contemporary Germany and Austria with the National Socialist past is clear from Bachmann's introductory comments to "Der Fall Franza": "Es ist mir, und wahrscheinlich auch Ihnen oft durch den Kopf gegangen, wohin das Virus Verbrechen gegangen ist–es kann doch nicht vor zwanzig Jahren plötzlich aus unserer Welt verschwunden sein, bloß weil hier Mord nicht mehr ausgezeichnet, verlangt, mit Orden bedacht und unterstützt wird. Die Massaker sind zwar vorbei, die Mörder noch unter uns . . ." (I have often wondered, and you probably have, too, where the virus crime has gone–it can't simply have suddenly disappeared from our world twenty years ago just because murder is no longer distinguished, demanded, and supported by the awarding of medals. While the massacres are past, the murderers are still among us . . .).

Bachmann had planned the "Todesarten" cycle to include more than three novels, but on 18 September 1973 she suffered second- and third-degree burns over more than one-third of her body in a fire in her Rome apartment. Her death on 17 October resulted from the burns, complicated by withdrawal from drugs she had been taking. A seven-month police investigation concluded that the fire was accidental. Although she had expressed the wish to be buried in the Protestant cemetery in Rome, her family had her interred in the Annabichl cemetery in Klagenfurt.

Bibliographies:

Otto Bareiss and Frauke Ohloff, *Ingeborg Bachmann: Eine Bibliographie* (Munich: Piper, 1978);

Bareiss, "Ingeborg-Bachmann-Bibliographie 1977/78-1981/82: Nachträge und Ergänzungen. Zum 10. Todestag von Ingeborg Bachmann (17. Oktober 1983)," *Jahrbuch der Grillparzer-Gesellschaft*, 15 (1983): 173-217;

Bareiss, "Ingeborg Bachmann-Bibliographie 1981/1982-Sommer 1985. Nachträge und Ergänzungen. Teil II," *Jahrbuch der Grillparzer-Gesellschaft*, 16 (1986): 201-275.

References:

Karen Achberger, "Art as a Force for Change: Bachmann and Brecht," in *Fictions of Culture: Studies in Honor of Walter H. Sokel*, edited by Steven Taubeneck (Detroit: Wayne State University Press, 1989), pp. 289-303;

Achberger, "Ingeborg Bachmann's 'Homburg' Libretto: Kleist Between Humanism and Existentialism," *Modern Austrian Literature*, 12, nos. 3/4 (1979): 305-315;

Achberger, "Musik und 'Komposition' in Ingeborg Bachmanns *Zikaden* und *Malina*," *German Quarterly*, 61 (Spring 1988): 193-212;

Acta Neophilologica, special Bachmann issue, edited by Janez Stanonik, 17 (1984);

Acta Universitatis Lodziensis, special Bachmann issue, edited by Krzysztof A. Kuczynski, 11 (1984);

Beatrice Angst-Hürlimann, *Im Widerspiel des Unmöglichen mit dem Möglichen: Zum Problem der Sprache bei Ingeborg Bachmann* (Zurich: Juris, 1971);

Elke Atzler, "Geschichte und Geschichten gegen den Strich: Ingeborg Bachmanns 'Todesartenzyklus,'" *Zeitgeschichte*, 11 (May 1984): 267-276;

Atzler, "Ingeborg Bachmanns Roman 'Malina' im Spiegel der literarischen Kritik," *Jahrbuch der Grillparzer-Gesellschaft*, 15 (1983): 155-171;

Kurt Bartsch, "Die Hörspiele von Ingeborg Bachmann," *Die andere Welt: Aspekte der österreichischen Literatur des 19. und 20. Jahrhunderts. Festschrift für H. Himmel*, edited by Bartsch and others (Bern & Munich: Francke, 1979), pp. 311-334;

Bartsch, *Ingeborg Bachmann* (Stuttgart: Metzler, 1988);

Bartsch, "Ein nach vorn geöffnetes Reich von unbekannten Grenzen: Zur Bedeutung Musils für Ingeborg Bachmanns Literaturauffassung," in *Robert Musil: Untersuchungen*, edited by Uwe Baur and Elisabeth Castex (Königstein: Athenäum, 1980), pp. 162-169;

Peter Beicken, *Ingeborg Bachmann* (Munich: Beck, 1988);

Beth Bjorklund, "Ingeborg Bachmann," in *Major Figures of Modern Austrian Literature*, edited by Donald G. Daviau (Riverside, Cal.: Ariadne Press, 1988), pp. 49-82;

Peter Brinkemper, "Liebe als Fragment: Affinitäten und Differenzen zwischen Bachmann und Barthes," *Jahrbuch der Grillparzer-Gesellschaft*, 16 (1986): 189-199;

Dinah Dodds, "The Lesbian Relationship in Bachmann's 'Ein Schritt nach Gomorrha,'" *Monatshefte*, 72 (Winter 1980): 431-438;

Ria Endres, " 'Die Wahrheit ist dem Menschen zumutbar': Zur Dichtung der Ingeborg Bachmann," *Neue Rundschau*, 92, no. 4 (1981): 71-97;

Inta Ezergailis, *Women Writers–The Divided Self: Analysis of Novels by Christa Wolf, Ingeborg Bachmann, Doris Lessing and Others* (Bonn: Bouvier, 1982);

Erich Fried, *"Ich grenz noch an ein Wort und an ein andres Land": Über Ingeborg Bachmann. Erinnerung, einige Anmerkungen zu ihrem Gedicht "Böhmen liegt am Meer" und ein Nachruf* (Berlin: Friedenauer Presse, 1983);

Sandra Frieden, "Bachmann's 'Malina' and 'Todesarten': Subliminal Crimes," *German Quarterly*, 56 (January 1983): 61-73;

Christa Gürtler, *Schreiben Frauen anders? Untersuchungen zu Ingeborg Bachmann und Barbara Frischmuth* (Stuttgart: Heinz, 1983);

Ortrud Gutjahr, *Fragmente unwiderstehlicher Liebe: Zur Dialogstruktur literarischer Subjektentgrenzung in Ingeborg Bachmanns "Der Fall Franza"* (Würzburg: Königshausen & Neumann, 1988);

Andreas Hapkemeyer, "Die Funktion der Personennamen in Ingeborg Bachmanns später Prosa," *Literatur und Kritik*, 19 (September/October 1984): 352-363;

Hapkemeyer, *Die Sprachthematik in der Prosa Ingeborg Bachmanns: Todesarten und Sprachformen* (Frankfurt am Main: Lang, 1982);

Hans Höller, *Ingeborg Bachmann: Das Werk. Von den frühesten Gedichten bis zum "Todesarten"-Zyklus* (Frankfurt am Main: Athenäum, 1987);

Höller, "Der 'Todesarten Zyklus' des 19. Jahrhunderts: Ingeborg Bachmann und Franz Grillparzer," *Jahrbuch der Grillparzer-Gesellschaft*, 15 (1983): 141-153;

Höller, ed., *Der dunkle Schatten, dem ich schon seit Anfang folge* (Vienna: Löcker, 1982);

Irene Holeschofsky, "Bewußtseinsdarstellung und Ironie in Ingeborg Bachmanns Erzählung 'Simultan,' " *Sprachkunst*, 11 (1980): 63-70;

Ingeborg Bachmann: Eine Einführung (Munich: Piper, 1963);

Interpretationen zu Ingeborg Bachmann (Munich: Oldenbourg, 1976);

Elfriede Jelinek, "Der Krieg mit anderen Mitteln: Über Ingeborg Bachmann," *Die schwarze Botin*, 21 (December 1983): 149-153;

Uwe Johnson, *Eine Reise nach Klagenfurt* (Frankfurt am Main: Suhrkamp, 1974);

Annette Klaubert, *Symbolische Strukturen bei Ingeborg Bachmann: Malina im Kontext der Kurzgeschichten* (Frankfurt am Main: Lang, 1983);

Kurt Klinger, "Hofmannsthal und Ingeborg Bachmann: Beispiel einer Nachwirkung," in his *Theater und Tabus: Essays, Berichte, Reden* (Eisenstadt: Edition Roetzer, 1984), pp. 215-246;

Sara Lennox, "Bachmann Reading / Reading Bachmann: Wilkie Collins's *The Woman in White* in the *Todesarten*," *German Quarterly*, 61 (Spring 1988): 183-192;

Lennox, "In the Cemetery of the Murdered Daughters: Ingeborg Bachmann's 'Malina,' " *Studies of Twentieth Century Literature*, 5 (Fall 1980): 75-105;

Irmele von der Lühe, " 'Ich ohne Gewähr': Ingeborg Bachmanns Frankfurter Vorlesungen zur Poetik," *Entwürfe von Frauen in der Literatur des 20. Jahrhunderts*, edited by Lühe (Berlin: Argument, 1982), pp. 106-131; translated as " 'I without guarantees': Ingeborg Bachmann's Frankfurt Lectures on Poetics," *New German Critique*, 27 (1982): 31-56;

Lühe, "Schreiben und Leben: Der Fall Ingeborg Bachmann," in *Feministische Literaturwissenschaft: Dokumentation der Tagung in Hamburg vom Mai 1983*, edited by Inge Stephan and Sigrid Weigel (Berlin: Argument, 1984), pp. 43-53;

Gudrun B. Mauch, "Ingeborg Bachmanns Erzählband 'Simultan,' " *Modern Austrian Literature*, 12, nos. 3/4 (1979): 273-304;

Theo Mechtenberg, *Utopie als ästhetische Kategorie: Eine Untersuchung der Lyrik Ingeborg Bachmanns* (Stuttgart: Heinz, 1978);

Modern Austrian Literature, special Bachmann issue, 18, no. 3/4 (1985);

Irena Omelaniuk, "Ingeborg Bachmann's 'Drei Wege zum See': A Legacy of Joseph Roth," *Seminar*, 19 (November 1983): 246-264;

Holger Pausch, *Ingeborg Bachmann* (Berlin: Colloquium, 1975);

Robert Pichl, "Dr. phil. Ingeborg Bachmann: Prolegomena zur kritischen Edition einer Doktorarbeit," *Jahrbuch der Grillparzer-Gesellschaft*, 16 (1986): 167-188;

Pichl, "Flucht, Grenzüberschreitung und Landnahme als Schlüsselmotive in Ingeborg Bachmanns später Prosa," *Sprachkunst*, 16, no. 2 (1985): 221-230;

Pichl, "Voraussetzungen und Problemhorizont der gegenwärtigen Ingeborg Bachmann-Forschung," *Jahrbuch der Grillparzer-Gesellschaft*, 14 (1980): 77-93;

Claus Reinert, *Unzumutbare Wahrheiten? Einführung in Ingeborg Bachmanns Hörspiel "Der gute Gott von Manhattan"* (Bonn: Bouvier, 1983);

Hanna Schnedl-Bubeniček, "Die andere Wirklichkeit: Traumsprache und Sprachkörper bei Ingeborg Bachmann," in *eine frau ist eine frau ist eine frau . . . Autorinnen über Autorin-*

nen, edited by Elfriede Gerstl (Vienna: Promedia, 1985), pp. 124-143;

George C. Schoolfield, "Ingeborg Bachmann," in *Essays on Contemporary German Literature*, edited by Brian Keith-Smith (London: Wolff, 1966), pp. 187-212;

Ellen Summerfield, *Ingeborg Bachmann: Die Auflösung der Figur in ihrem Roman "Malina"* (Bonn: Bouvier, 1976);

Zbigniew Swiatlowski, "Auf der Suche nach dem Land Utopia: Zur poetologischen Position von Ingeborg Bachmann und Christa Wolf," *Weimarer Beiträge*, 30, no. 6 (1984): 2011-2027;

text + kritik, special Bachmann issue, 6 (1964);

text + kritik, special Bachmann issue, edited by Heinz Ludwig Arnold and Sigrid Weigel (1984);

Bärbel Thau, *Gesellschaftsbild und Utopie im Spätwerk Ingeborg Bachmanns: Untersuchungen zum "Todesarten"-Zyklus und zu "Simultan"* (Bern, Frankfurt am Main & New York: Lang, 1986);

Klaus Wagner, "Bachmann: Stenogramm der Zeit," *Der Spiegel*, 8 (18 August 1954): 26-29;

Sigrid Weigel, "Ingeborg Bachmann—Was folgt auf das Schweigen? Zu ihrem 10. Todestag am 17. Oktober," *Frankfurter Rundschau*, 15 October 1983, feuilleton section, p. 3;

Weigel, "Das Schreiben des Mangels als Produktion von Utopie," *Die Horen*, 28 (1983): 149-155;

Weigel, *Die Stimme der Medusa* (Frankfurt am Main: Tende, 1987);

Bernd Witte, "Ingeborg Bachmann," in *Kritisches Lexikon zur deutschen Gegenwartsliteratur*, volume 1, edited by Heinz Ludwig Arnold (Munich: Edition text + kritik, 1978-1980);

Witte, "Ingeborg Bachmann," in *Neue Literatur der Frauen: Deutschsprachige Autorinnen der Gegenwart*, edited by Heinz Puknus (Munich: Beck, 1980), pp. 37-43;

Witte, "Schmerzton: Ingeborg Bachmann. Perspektiven einer feministischen Literatur," *Die Horen*, 28, no. 4 (1983): 76-82;

Christa Wolf, "Die zumutbare Wahrheit: Prosa der Ingeborg Bachmann," in her *Lesen und Schreiben: Aufsätze und Prosastücke* (Neuwied: Luchterhand, 1972), pp. 121-134;

Eva Christina Zeller, *Ingeborg Bachmann: Der Fall Franza* (Frankfurt am Main, Bern, New York & Paris: Lang, 1988).

Papers:

The Ingeborg Bachmann collection, which encompasses more than six thousand pages of typescript and handwritten documents, is at the Austrian National Library in Vienna.

Vicki Baum

(24 January 1888-29 August 1960)

Lynda J. King
Oregon State University

BOOKS: *Frühe Schatten: Das Ende einer Kindheit. Roman* (Berlin: Reiß, 1914);

Der Eingang zur Bühne: Roman (Berlin: Ullstein, 1920); translated by Felice and Alan Martin Harvey as *Once in Vienna* (London: Bles, 1943; New York: Didier, 1945);

Schloßtheater: Novellen (Berlin & Stuttgart: Deutsche Verlags-Anstalt, 1921);

Die Tänze der Ina Raffay: Ein Leben. Roman (Berlin: Ullstein, 1921); republished as *Kein Platz für Tränen* (Bayreuth: Hestia, 1982);

Die andern Tage: Novellen (Stuttgart: Deutsche Verlags-Anstalt, 1922);

Bubenreise: Eine Erzählung für junge Menschen (Berlin: Ullstein, 1923);

Die Welt ohne Sünde: Roman einer Minute (Stuttgart: Deutsche Verlags-Anstalt, 1923);

Ulle, der Zwerg: Roman (Stuttgart: Deutsche Verlags-Anstalt, 1924);

Der Weg: Novelle (Berlin: Deutsche Verlags-Anstalt, 1925; edited by Erwin T. Mohme, New York: Crofts, 1931);

Miniaturen (Berlin: Weltgeist-Bücher, 1926);

Tanzpause (Stuttgart: Fleischhauer & Spohn, 1926);

Feme: Bußfahrt einer verirrten Jugend. Roman (Berlin: Ullstein, 1927); translated by Erich Sutton as *Secret Sentence* (Garden City, N.Y.: Doubleday, Doran, 1932; London: Bles, 1932);

Hell in Frauensee: Ein heiterer Roman von Liebe und Hunger (Berlin: Ullstein, 1927); translated by Basil Creighton as *Martin's Summer* (New York: Cosmopolitan, 1931; London: Bles, 1933);

stud. chem. Helene Willfüer: Roman (Berlin: Ullstein, 1928); translated by Félice Bashford as *Helene* (London: Bles, 1932); translated by Ida Zeitlin as *Helene* (Garden City, N.Y.: Doubleday, Doran, 1933);

Halloh, wer fängt Flip und Flap? Oder: Das große Abenteuer von Bastelhans und Quasselgrete. Ein Kinderstück in 6 Bildern (Berlin: Arcadia, 1929);

Vicki Baum (photo courtesy of Wolfgang Lert)

Menschen im Hotel: Ein Kolportageroman mit Hintergründen (Berlin: Ullstein, 1929); translated by Creighton as *Grand Hotel* (London: Bles, 1930; Garden City, N.Y.: Doubleday, Doran, 1931);

Zwischenfall in Lohwinckel: Roman (Berlin: Ullstein, 1930); translated by Margaret Goldsmith as *Results of an Accident* (London: Bles, 1931); translation republished as *... And Life Goes On* (Garden City, N.Y.: Doubleday, Doran, 1931);

Pariser Platz 13: Komödie in 3 Akten (Vienna & Berlin: Marton, 1930);

Das Leben ohne Geheimnis: Roman (Berlin: Ullstein, 1932); translated by Zeitlin as *Falling Star* (Garden City, N.Y.: Doubleday, Doran, 1934; London: Bles, 1934);

Divine Drudge: A Play in Three Acts, by Baum and John Golden (New York, Los Angeles & London: French, 1934);

Das große Einmaleins: Roman (Amsterdam: Querido, 1935); translated by Creighton as *Men Never Know* (Garden City, N.Y.: Doubleday, Doran, 1935; London: Bles, 1935); German version republished as *Rendez-vous in Paris: Roman* (Cologne: Kiepenheuer & Witsch, 1951);

Die Karriere der Doris Hart: Roman (Amsterdam: Querido, 1936); translated by Creighton as *Sing, Sister, Sing* (Garden City, N.Y.: Doubleday, Doran, 1936); translation republished as *Career* (London: Bles, 1936);

Liebe und Tod auf Bali: Roman (Amsterdam: Querido, 1937); translated by Creighton as *Tale of Bali* (Garden City, N.Y.: Doubleday, Doran, 1937); translation republished as *A Tale from Bali* (London: Bles, 1937);

Der große Ausverkauf: Roman (Amsterdam: Querido, 1937); translated by Paul Selver as *Central Stores* (London: Bles, 1940);

Hotel Shanghai: Roman (Amsterdam: Querido, 1939); translated by Creighton as *Shanghai '37* (Garden City, N.Y.: Doubleday, Doran, 1939); translation republished as *Nanking Road* (London: Bles, 1939);

Die große Pause: Roman (Stockholm: Bermann-Fischer, 1941); translated as *Grand Opera* (London: Bles, 1942);

The Christmas Carp (Garden City, N.Y.: Doubleday, Doran, 1941);

The Ship and the Shore (Garden City, N.Y.: Doubleday, Doran, 1941); translated into German by Justinian Frisch as *Die fremde Nacht: Roman* (Vienna: Novitas, 1951); German translation republished as *Es begann an Bord: Roman* (Munich: Heyne, 1963);

Marion Alive (Garden City, N.Y.: Doubleday, Doran, 1942; London: Joseph, 1943); translated into German by Fritz and Li Zielesch as *Marion lebt: Ein Roman* (Stockholm: Bermann-Fischer, 1943); German translation republished as *Marion* (Frankfurt am Main: Büchergilde Gutenberg, 1954);

The Weeping Wood (Garden City, N.Y.: Doubleday, Doran, 1943; London: Joseph, 1945); translated into German by Fritz and Li Zielesch as *Kautschuk: Roman in fünfzehn Erzählungen* (Stockholm: Bermann-Fischer, 1945); German translation republished as *Cahuchu: Strom der Tränen. Roman* (Cologne: Kiepenheuer & Witsch, 1952);

Hotel Berlin '43 (Garden City, N.Y.: Doubleday, Doran, 1944); republished as *Berlin Hotel* (London: Joseph, 1944); translated into German by Grete Dupont as *Hier stand ein Hotel* (Zurich: Büchergilde Gutenberg, 1947);

Mortgage on Life (Garden City, N.Y.: Doubleday, Doran, 1946; London: Joseph, 1946); translated into German as *Verpfändetes Leben* (Hamburg: Blüchert, 1963);

Schicksalsflug: Roman, translated into German by Dupont (Amsterdam: Querido, 1947); English version published as *Flight of Fate* (London: Joseph, 1965);

Headless Angel (Garden City, N.Y.: Doubleday, 1948; London: Joseph, 1948); translated into German as *Clarinda: Roman* (Amsterdam: Querido, 1949);

Danger from Deer (Garden City, N.Y.: Doubleday, 1951; London: Joseph, 1951); translated into German as *Vor Rehen wird gewarnt: Roman* (Cologne: Kiepenheuer & Witsch, 1953);

The Mustard Seed (New York: Dial, 1953; London: Joseph, 1953); translated by Fritz and Li Zielesch as *Kristall im Lehm: Roman* (Cologne: Kiepenheuer & Witsch, 1953);

Die Strandwache: Novellen (Cologne: Kiepenheuer & Witsch, 1953);

Written on Water: A Novel (Garden City, N.Y.: Doubleday, 1956; London: Joseph, 1957); translated into German by Werner Krauss as *Flut und Flamme: Roman* (Cologne & Berlin: Kiepenheuer & Witsch, 1956); English version republished as *Blood on the Sea* (London: Landsborough, 1960);

Tiburon: A Novel (Hollywood, Cal., 1956);

Theme for Ballet (Garden City, N.Y.: Doubleday, 1958); republished as *Ballerina* (London: Joseph, 1958); translated into German as *Die goldenen Schuhe: Roman einer Primaballerina* (Cologne: Kiepenheuer & Witsch, 1959);

Es war alles ganz anders: Erinnerungen (Berlin: Ullstein, 1962); English version published as *It Was All Quite Different: The Memoirs of Vicki Baum* (New York: Funk & Wagnalls, 1964); English version republished as *I Know What I'm Worth* (London: Joseph, 1964).

PERIODICAL PUBLICATIONS: "Nächte," *Erdgeist*, 3, no. 17 (1908): 652;

Baum endorsing a wristwatch in a 1929 advertisement in the Berliner Illustrirte Zeitung *(courtesy of the Deutsche Schillergesellschaft / Literaturarchiv, Marbach am Neckar, Federal Republic of Germany)*

"Einsamkeit," *Erdgeist*, 3, no. 19 (1908): 733;

"Das Tor des Friedens," *Der Merker*, 1, no. 16 (1910): 666;

"Glockenspiel," *Der Merker*, 1, no. 20-21 (1910): 825;

"Der kleine Page," *Jugend*, 4 (1910): 78-79;

"Alter Schloßpark," *Licht und Schatten*, 1, no. 7 (1911);

"Schloßtheater," *Licht und Schatten*, 2, no. 8 (1912);

Review of L. Andro, *Der Klimenole*, *Das literarische Echo*, 25 (1922-1923): 934;

"Begegnung," *Uhu*, 1 (November 1924): 52-67, 127-132;

Review of Paula Busch, *Aus dem Tagebuch der kleinen Lisinka vom Zirkus*, *Die Literatur*, 27 (1924-1925): 301;

"Panik: Die Geschichte einer Entgleisung," *Uhu*, 2 (July 1926): 21-32, 122-128;

"Das Auto im Film," *Die Dame*, 54 (October 1926): 32, 34, 38, 40;

"Rahal Sanzara, eine neue Dichterin und ihr Roman 'Das verlorene Kind,'" *Berliner Illustrirte Zeitung* (21 November 1926): 1573, 1582;

"Die Ballettstunde: Bilder aus der Schule der Berliner Staatsoper," *Berliner Illustrirte Zeitung* (21 November 1926): 1587-1589;

"Entlarvte Liebe: Die Chemie der Gefühle," *Uhu*, 3 (November 1926): 86-91;

"Die Sterne sprechen: Bildwerke aus deutschen Domen," *Die Dame*, 54 (December 1926): 12-14, 51-52;

"Blick aus dem Fenster," *Uhu*, 3 (January 1927): 16;

"Omuna geht auf den Maskenball: Eine Faschingsgeschichte," *Uhu*, 3 (February 1927): 18-28, 125-128;

"Früher Frühling," *Die Dame*, 54 (March 1927): 4;

"Der Herr im andern Auto: Eine Frühlingsgeschichte," *Die Dame*, 54 (April 1927): 2, 4-7;

Baum in her office at her home in Berlin, late 1920s (photo courtesy of Wolfgang Lert)

Review of K. Hielscher, *Jugoslawien*, *Uhu*, 3 (April 1927): 125;

Review of Alexander Castel, *Der Unfug der Liebe*, *Uhu*, 3 (June 1927): 116-118;

"Reisebücher," *Uhu*, 3 (July 1927): 121-124;

Review of Robert Scheu, *Der Weg des Lebenskünstlers*, *Uhu*, 3 (August 1927): 114;

"O, diese Eltern: Die Kluft zwischen den Generationen," *Berliner Illustrirte Zeitung* (28 August 1927): 1389-1390;

Review of Wilhelm Speyer, *Charlotte etwas verrückt*, *Uhu*, 3 (September 1927): 112;

"Leute von heute," *Die Dame*, 55 (November 1927): 17-19, 32;

"Erfahrungen mit der Verjüngung: Ein Rundgang durch die Laboratorien einer neuen Wissenschaft," *Uhu*, 4 (December 1927): 32-40;

Review of Georg Fröschel, *Hochzeitsreise wie noch nie*, *Uhu*, 4 (August 1928): 113;

"Die langweilige Erotik," *Wiener Allgemeine Zeitung*, 19 September 1928, p. 5;

"24. Dezember geschlossen . . . ," *Uhu*, 5 (December 1928): 29-42;

"Die Mütter von morgen–die Backfische von heute," *Uhu*, 5 (February 1929): 46-53;

"Karriere in der Holzmarktstraße: Eine wahre Geschichte aus dem Glashaus," *Uhu*, 5 (August 1929): 74-88;

"Vergessenes Parfüm: Eine ungeschriebene Geschichte," *Die Dame*, 56 (August 1929): 15-16, 30-38;

"Geschenke für Mama," *Die Dame*, 57 (December 1929): 6, 43-44, 47-48;

"Zwei neue Kleider und ein Mann," *Die Dame*, 57 (January 1930): 6, 8, 9-11, 38, 46;

"Apropos Alter," *Die Dame*, 57 (February 1930): 18;

"Welche Frau ist am begehrtesten?," *Uhu*, 7 (October 1930): 65-74;

"Lippenstift, Parfüm und Spitzenwäsche in Sowjetrußland," *Die Dame*, 58 (January 1931): 21;

"Ich wundere mich," *Die Dame*, 58 (February 1931): 8-10;

"Angst vor Kitsch," *Uhu*, 7 (July 1931): 104-105;

"Ein bißchen New York: Vom guten Aussehen," *Die Dame*, 58 (August 1931): 2, 28;

"Das Vier-Dollar Paradies," *Die Dame*, 58 (September 1931): 2;

"Unglücklich in Hollywood: Das Leben der großen und kleinen Sterne," *Uhu*, 8 (May 1932): 105-108;

"I Discover America," *Good Housekeeping*, 95 (July 1932): 30-31, 196-199;

"Film Face," *Ladies' Home Journal*, 49 (November 1932): 100-101;

"December 24th–Closed: A Short Story," *Good Housekeeping*, 95 (December 1932): 16-19, 149-152;

"Silver Fox," *Pictorial Review*, 34 (April 1933): 12-13;

"Masked Ball," *Pictorial Review*, 34 (July 1933): 10-11;

"Once I Wore Ermine," *Pictorial Review*, 35 (December 1933): 14-15;

"Game of Life," *Pictorial Review*, 36 (November 1934): 12-13;

"Big Shot," *Collier's*, 98 (19 September 1936): 7-9, 69-71;

"Lessons of the Old Sock," *Reader's Digest*, 39 (September 1941): 37-39;

"Size 12 Tantrum: Story," *Woman's Home Companion*, 76 (August 1949): 18-19;

"Backstairs Bachelor," *Saturday Evening Post*, 227 (17 July 1954): 26-27, 68, 70, 73;

"Rückblick einer geborenen Realistin: Ein Selbstporträt," *Welt und Wort*, 17 (1962): 343-344;

"Kringelein kam aus Lundenburg," *Arbeiter Zeitung* (Vienna), 21 January 1968, p. 68.

On 4 January 1929 a front-page caricature in the liberal literary magazine *Literarische Welt* satirized the "Vorarbeiten einiger Prominenter" (preliminary work of some prominent people): Thomas Mann, Emil Ludwig, Jakob Wassermann, and Vicki Baum. Baum was shown gazing resolutely at an abacus, her picture captioned: "Vicky [*sic*] Baum beschäftigt sich mit Relativitätstheorie für ihren neuen Ullsteinroman" (Vicky Baum occupies herself with the theory of relativity for her new Ullstein novel). On 8 September of that year the advertising section of the enormously popular *Berliner Illustrirte Zeitung* featured a half-page testimonial by Baum on the excellence of Alpina watches. From the widely varying audiences targeted by these two periodicals, the name Vicki Baum was sure to elicit the same response: she was a star, a recognizable personality associated with financial success who rose to fame in late Weimar Germany, then went on to international stardom of a magnitude seldom achieved by German-language writers. Her works continue to sell around the world, and in the Federal Republic of Germany several of her stories and a documentary about her have been filmed for television.

Baum's reception by the scholarly community has been rocky. By the mid to late 1950s a consensus had been established that her works were substandard, superseding more positive evaluations set forth in the immediate postwar years. One factor involved in the critical shift was the forms of distribution chosen to reintroduce Baum into Germany: book club editions and magazine serializations in the 1950s made her works popular but were not likely to establish her credentials as a serious writer among German scholars traditionally suspicious of mass success. Baum's works were ignored or were dismissed as Trivialliteratur.

More recently, the claim that her works are mere potboilers has been challenged; this development can be seen as part of the expansion of research into Weimar Republic literature, but it is also related to the enlargement of the boundaries of literary scholarship. Aside from the question of her critical reputation, Baum's rise to fame in late Weimar Germany represents a fascinating example of the interrelationship of literature, the publishing and book industry, and reader response.

The main source of information about her life and career is Baum's posthumously published autobiography *Es war alles ganz anders* (1962; trans-

Olga Tschechowa as Helene in the 1929 film version of Baum's novel stud. chem. Helene Willfüer *(courtesy of the Deutsche Schillergesellschaft / Literaturarchiv, Marbach am Neckar, Federal Republic of Germany)*

lated as *It Was All Quite Different*, 1964), a highly subjective chronicle designed in part to counter her negative critical image. Born in 1888 into a middle-class Jewish family in Vienna, Hedwig (Vicki) Baum was the only child of a tyrannical father, Hermann Baum, and a chronically ailing mother, Mathilde Donat Baum, who was finally institutionalized for manic depression. Her mother insisted that Baum have a career–an unusual idea at that time–and the child began studying the harp at age eight, attended the Vienna Conservatory from 1904 until 1910, and performed as a teenager with leading Viennese orchestras. Even though music was her primary vocation, she had always written stories "for her drawer"; according to Baum, her first husband, Max Prels, whom she married in 1906, put his name on several of these stories and sold them to a German magazine.

After divorcing Prels, she left Vienna in 1912 to take a position in the Darmstadt city orchestra, marrying the conductor, Richard Lert, on 17 July 1916. She also taught at the musical high school in Darmstadt. A novel, *Frühe Schatten*

(Early Shadows, 1914), had no significant impact on reviewers or the general public. Moving with Lert to Kiel, Baum gave up her music career to bear two sons, Wolfgang and Peter, during World War I. At that time she decided to try earning money as a writer because of her family's precarious financial situation. Her first novel written specifically for that purpose, *Der Eingang zur Bühne* (translated as *Once in Vienna*, 1943), was accepted by the Ullstein publishing house for its inexpensive popular book series around 1916 but did not appear until 1920. After she wrote a second book for Ullstein–it was probably *Die Tänze der Ina Raffay* (The Dances of Ina Raffay, 1921), but she does not name it in her memoirs–the company wanted to sign her to an exclusive contract; she refused the offer but agreed to write two more novels for the firm. She had ambitions to write works of higher literary quality than those that appeared in the Ullstein series, and between 1920 and 1926 she wrote more books for other publishers than for Ullstein.

Since their first printings, Baum's pre-1926 works have not been the subject of critical scrutiny; but contemporary reviewers generally shared Baum's judgment that several of them had literary merit, especially *Der Weg* (The Way, 1925), which won a literary contest sponsored by the *Kölnische Zeitung* and was judged by Thomas Mann. Her shorter pre-1926 pieces come across today as readable and insightful character portraits of social outsiders, while with *Ulle, der Zwerg* (Ulle, the Dwarf, 1924) Baum transparently tried to be "deep" and to write "good literature."

A turning point in Baum's career came in 1926, when she decided to dedicate her talents exclusively to writing for the mass market. She signed a contract with Ullstein in which she agreed to supply suitable works, and Ullstein agreed to use its many resources to sell them and to promote Baum as a writer of best-sellers. Emulating American business techniques, Ullstein's owners had molded the company into an efficient enterprise; it was able to expand despite an economic crisis in the publishing trade and became the largest publishing house in Europe by 1929. The firm's books were designed, promoted, and distributed to ensure the highest possible sales.

By the end of the decade Baum had become one of Ullstein's most successful ventures; her novel *stud. chem. Helene Willfüer* (Chemistry Student Helene Willfüer, 1928; translated as

Advertisement in the Vossische Zeitung *for the serialization of Baum's "hotel novel" in the* Berliner Illustrirte Zeitung *(courtesy of the Deutsche Schillergesellschaft / Literaturarchiv, Marbach am Neckar, Federal Republic of Germany)*

Helene, 1932) raised the circulation of the firm's *Berliner Illustrirte Zeitung* by an estimated two hundred thousand during its serialization. Baum contributed stories, reports, poems, and reviews for the company's periodicals, and her novels sold well in book form, but the *Berliner Illustrirte Zeitung*, with a circulation of almost two million, was the cornerstone of her fame. Five of her novels were serialized in the weekly between 1926 and 1932.

Once Baum had decided to produce commercial works, she began writing in a manner akin to the Neue Sachlichkeit (New Objectivity), a literary trend of the mid to late 1920s in Germany. Although there was no New Objectivist program per se, those associated with the trend conceived of their work as antimetaphysical and nonspeculative, communicating the exact image of the here and now to a broad audience through the touchable, visible, and experiential. Writers were regarded as craftsmen (Baum's favorite term for her work was "good craftsmanship") creating products that should be judged by how well they met consumers' needs; and since their consumers were supposed to be a broad audience, they wrote in a style accessible to a cross section of the reading public. Content was to take precedence over form; a favorite theme was the individual in mass society. Baum's natural style was at its best when she was telling a story by relating what appeared to be authentic surface details; her thematic focus on the individual in modern society and her decision to write for the market also dovetailed with the New Objectivity. Weimar-era reviews of Baum's works repeatedly used the vocabulary of New Objectivity, especially when critiquing *stud. chem. Helene Willfüer*. The reviews of that novel also concentrated on her choice of the much-debated topic of the New Woman, the 1920s label for the liberated woman, as a theme.

Stud. chem. Helene Willfüer depicts a woman's struggle to control her life, but the novel's melodramatic elements and affirmation of traditional male-female relationships conflict with its depiction of a strong and determined woman. The chemistry student and later professional chemist Helene overcomes many crises, but she realizes at the end of the novel that she has always loved a man who was introduced in the book's first pages and decides to abandon her work for his career.

A strong, sensible, goal-oriented person, Helene must have her strength tested before she truly gains control of her life. The greatest test is her pregnancy: believing that society will not ac-

Dust jacket for the English translation of Menschen im Hotel *(Humanities Research Center, University of Texas at Austin)*

cept her single motherhood and fearing that she will have to give up her chosen career, Helene seeks an abortion. Sharing waiting rooms with other women in similar circumstances, Helene responds with strong sisterly emotion in some of the novel's most genuine scenes. (Baum was not a feminist, nor did she ever advocate abortion, but her portrayal of Helene's desperate search for a doctor powerfully and sympathetically dramatizes the fundamental importance of the abortion question for many women.) When respectable doctors are unwilling to break the strict antiabortion laws, Helene turns to a seedy illegal abortionist; but the operation is foiled when a police raid closes the "clinic."

The desperate Helene uncharacteristically puts her life into the hands of the baby's father, a weak figure named Rainer, and accepts his "solution" of double suicide. But after Rainer dies she changes her mind, and she eventually realizes that her life can include both child and career. Her sudden weakness and the necessity of seeing Rainer die before she can awaken are poorly motivated; it seems as if Baum needed to do away with the main competitor so that the true love could reenter the scene uncontested. In any case, Helene finishes her doctorate, bears a son, and achieves professional success. But she is dissatisfied: she lacks a relationship with a man. Chance rejoins Helene with her true love, and they decide to try a relationship based on traditional roles. The fact that the love interest was introduced in the first pages suggests that Helene has not developed at all. Baum asks why her heroine cannot have both love and her own career; her

only answer to the questions she poses about women's changing position in society is a retreat into conventional roles.

Despite its weaknesses, many contemporary reviewers who advocated women's emancipation praised *stud. chem. Helene Willfüer*, so pleased were they that a popular novel depicted the topic at all and granted positive qualities to the New Woman. *Stud. chem. Helene Willfüer* was indeed one of the most widely circulated versions of the New Woman theme in 1920s German-language literature; one reviewer noted that the novel caused "a great uproar," and another said that this "young girl of our times" was being discussed in all social circles.

The thematic focus of Baum's novel *Menschen im Hotel* (People in the Hotel, 1929; translated as *Grand Hotel*, 1930) is modern urban society. In Great Britain it was lauded by established critics: in a 20 August 1930 letter to Mary Leonard, Hugh Walpole praised its contribution to understanding contemporary life; on the dust jacket for the 1932 American edition J. B. Priestley called it "a sort of motion picture of modern life"; Hermon Ould related its cinematic technique to experiments by other contemporary German writers who were trying to translate into written form the possibilities of the new medium of film. At the same time, reviewers in Germany attacked her Ullstein image rather than assessing the text or its value for a specific audience.

Instrumental in introducing the "hotel novel"–in which the hotel functions structurally as a central location where unrelated persons of all classes and social groups come together, inter-

Advertisement for the theatrical version of Baum's novel in the 19 January 1930 issue of the Berliner Illustrirte Zeitung *(courtesy of the Deutsche Schillergesellschaft / Literaturarchiv, Marbach am Neckar, Federal Republic of Germany)*

act, then go their separate ways—*Menschen im Hotel* depicts events in the lives of six guests during their stay at the fictitious Grand Hotel in Berlin. With no chapters and few major divisions, *Menschen im Hotel* is made up of short scenes or episodes, each of which revolves around one figure; sometimes the same scene is repeated from the perspective of another character. The characters are obvious stereotypes designed by Baum to communicate her vision of life in modern society, which is symbolized by the hotel. Baum believed that the new society of the 1920s held both promise and despair for the people who lived in it,

and the experiences of the characters in the hotel are both positive and negative. For the disillusioned war casualty Dr. Otternschlag and the overstressed industrialist Preysing, the modern world is atomized and lacking in values, a place where alienated people rarely communicate. Conversely, for Kringelein, Preysing's bookkeeper who is fleeing provincial narrowness; for the gentleman confidence man and thief Baron Gaigern; and for Flämmchen, the New Woman as stenographer, the hotel opens exciting possibilities for a new form of existence. The Pavlovian dancer Grusinskaya hints that the woman artist could

Baum on the set of the M-G-M film version of Grand Hotel
in 1931 (photo courtesy of Wolfgang Lert)

unite the two sides, but this suggestion is never
fully developed. Kringelein is perhaps the novel's
most fascinating figure. Upon learning that he is
terminally ill, the bookkeeper summarily abandons his job and his wife, takes his life savings,
and goes to Berlin. The character is one of many
contemporary portraits of the "little man," a lower-
middle-class white-collar worker who longs to
break out of alienation and loneliness to experience a different, more exotic and exciting life in
Berlin, the big city he was fascinated by in films
and illustrated magazines. This little man is confronted with the author's version of the two sides
of life in modern society as represented by the disillusioned Dr. Otternschlag and the prototypical
urban man, Baron Gaigern. Since for Dr.
Otternschlag modern life is an empty shell, he
tries to convince Kringelein that impersonal modern Berlin is a horrible place; he then guides the
bookkeeper on the standard tour of Berlin's
sights, which symbolize the past the doctor longs
for. Kringelein then meets Baron Gaigern, for
whom modern life is exciting and liberating. He in-

troduces Kringelein to boxing, fast cars, air-
planes, gambling casinos, and fashionable clothes,
allowing the bookkeeper to taste all the thrills he
expected in modern Berlin. Despite being drawn
to Gaigern's life, Kringelein finally rejects both
versions of the modern world: having gained a
new self-image and new vitality in Berlin, he decides to trust in the traditional values of love and
friendship and leaves the hotel with Flämmchen.

The framing device of the hotel suggests
a different message than the positive one of
Kringelein's discovery of a meaningful life. It is a
giant, impersonal, efficiently run enterprise controlled by no named person and represented
only by professionally friendly employees; no
matter what the individuals do or think in it, the
hotel remains. This point is driven home
through various stylistic and narrative devices, including portraying the action from the hotel's perspective and switching into present tense to describe its mechanisms. The individual's
importance is reduced and relativized, while the
seeming permanence of the symbolic hotel is underscored. The criticism can be leveled against
Baum, as it was against many writers of the New
Objectivity, that by depicting the modern world
as unchanging and unchangeable she showed a society whose mechanisms were so overwhelming
and impersonal that readers might believe that
they had no choice but to resign to the inevitabil-
ity of the social and political order.

Another turning point in Baum's career was
the Berlin premiere of the dramatic version of
Menschen im Hotel in January 1930 and the translation of both the novel and the play into English.
The novel was an overnight sensation in Great
Britain, and the Broadway adaptation, which
premiered in November 1930, was hailed as the
hit of the season. Doubleday, Doran, which had
turned down the novel several years earlier, published it in the United States in February 1931; it
shot to the top of the best-seller list, and by 1936
it had been translated into at least sixteen languages.

In April 1931 Baum went to the United
States, where she helped with Doubleday's massive promotional campaign, negotiated with the
firm for future novels, and worked for the Paramount and Metro-Goldwyn-Mayer studios. She returned briefly to Germany late in the year; in
early 1932 she and her family left Germany per-
manently. She said later that her early emigration was motivated both by the ominous political
developments in Germany and by her attraction

Baum with her American publisher, Nelson Doubleday, in 1931 (photo courtesy of Wolfgang Lert)

to the United States. Although she preferred the cultural climate of New York, she decided to live in California because of her contacts with the film industry. She lived at several addresses in the Los Angeles area, including Pasadena, where her husband became the conductor of the city orchestra. Until 1949 she was involved in writing projects for the film industry: she had a long-term contract with M-G-M but also worked for Paramount, Republic, Universal, RKO, 20th Century-Fox, and Warner Bros. She also traveled to research exotic locations for such novels as *Liebe*

und Tod auf Bali (Love and Death on Bali, 1937; translated as *Tale of Bali*, 1937), which depicts life on Bali and a violent incident between the natives and the Dutch colonial administration between 1904 and 1906. While working for M-G-M she wrote an adaptation of *Menschen im Hotel*; but her screenplay was not used for the studio's 1932 classic *Grand Hotel*, starring Greta Garbo, John and Lionel Barrymore, and Joan Crawford. Nevertheless, Baum's name became even more well known because of the movie, and her fate was sealed: she was to remain for the rest of her life the "woman who wrote *Grand Hotel*."

Baum at Mount Rainier with her husband Richard Lert and their sons, Wolfgang and Peter (photo courtesy of Wolfgang Lert)

Baum continued to write in German for several years after her emigration, but her career in Germany was interrupted when the National Socialists banned her works. Until she switched to writing exclusively in English in the early 1940s, her works often appeared first in English translation, then in German in exile publishing houses; afterward she was increasingly identified as an American writer of German background, and in July 1938 she became a United States citizen. She decided to learn to write in English because of problems with the translations of several of her novels, especially *Zwischenfall in Lohwinckel* (Incident in Lohwinckel, 1930; translated as . . . *And Life Goes On*, 1931) and *Das Leben ohne Geheimnis* (Life without Secrets, 1932; translated as *Falling Star*, 1934). Accounts vary as to how well she spoke English when she first arrived in the United States, but she was fluent enough by 1941

to compose a complete novel, *The Ship and the Shore*. It is impossible to ascertain how much help she got from the editors at Doubleday with this novel, but her letters to the firm in the 1930s and 1940s are written in idiomatic American English. British and American reviews of the series of poorly translated books, up to *Die Karriere der Doris Hart* (The Career of Doris Hart, 1936; translated as *Sing, Sister, Sing*, 1936) were predominantly negative. With *Liebe und Tod auf Bali* her fortunes among the critics began to improve; but Baum was in fact using the same basic formula in both the "better" and the "worse" books, a formula she continued to count on—with modifications—for most of her novels. Based on her two earlier successes, the formula had two variations. The *stud. chem. Helene Willfüer* variation revolves around a long-suffering heroine who interacts with a group of secondary figures. The

Menschen im Hotel variation, which was generally better received by critics, features an ensemble of characters who spend a dramatic twenty-four hours in one central location; the characters' past lives are described and then their fortunes are intertwined. In both variations, sensationalism and melodrama are combined with fatalistic endings that imply that the characters were destined to act as they did. In both variations, also, Baum constructs seemingly accurate and authentic backdrops; her ability to do so often earned her praise—for example, for *Liebe und Tod auf Bali* and for *Hotel Shanghai* (Hotel Shanghai, 1939; translated as *Shanghai '37*, 1939). As these examples suggest, Baum modified the formula in the late 1930s by writing about more exotic locations and enriching the novels with a historical perspective. Part of the basic formula was a traditional narrative structure, but at times she used more complicated narrative techniques, as she had in *Menschen im Hotel*. Such techniques as shifting perspectives, a modified stream-of-consciousness narrative, montages, and similar techniques can challenge readers to free themselves from the dictates of a narrator and think for themselves; but in popular fiction challenges can go only so far before many readers put down the book—and close their pocketbooks. At her best, Baum was a master at knowing exactly how far to go before returning to a comforting, all-knowing narrator.

During the 1930s and 1940s Baum was busy turning out scripts, writing for magazines, making publicity tours, checking translations, writing novels, and traveling around the world. Feeling increasing pressure to turn out too much too quickly, she complained to her Doubleday editors that they were forcing her to produce texts of inferior quality. Actually, however, the problem lay as much in Baum herself as in Doubleday's demands. She had always had two conflicting attitudes toward herself as a writer: she wanted and needed to earn money by writing, but she also wanted to be taken seriously by writing "good" literature. Her feeling that her true gifts were being limited by constraints of commercial literature increased as she grew older. Adding to this feeling was Baum's growing uneasiness with the label "the woman who wrote *Grand Hotel*." Eventually she came to believe that even if she wrote a great novel, it would never be recognized as such because critics expected her to write the same type of novel she had written before. To an extent, Baum was justified in this view. Unlike their counterparts in Germany, British and American

critics did not pan Baum's works *because* they were potential best-sellers; but they did have certain expectations: Baum was supposed to produce—to paraphrase her own words—first-rate novels of the second rank, and they scrutinized every new book to see whether Baum recombined the elements of her formula in a different and interesting way.

In 1939 critics decided that *Hotel Shanghai* was a successful modification of the *Menschen im Hotel* variation of the formula. The lives of nine guests at the Shanghai Hotel are traced from birth; then the characters are bound together as they move inexorably toward the climax, in which they are killed during the bombing of the hotel in the 1937 Japanese attack on Shanghai. Critics praised Baum's ability to give readers a vivid picture of Shanghai, just as they had praised her two years earlier for her depiction of Balinese life in *Tale of Bali*. Some questioned how authentic the backdrops actually were, since it was difficult for readers unfamiliar with the exotic location to separate fact from fiction; but Baum did try to become as familiar as possible with her subjects in the time allotted to her. In the case of *The Weeping Wood* (1943), her zeal to provide her story with an authentic backdrop backfired with some critics: the reviewer for the *New Yorker*, for example, complained that readers might just as well look up the article on rubber in an encyclopedia as read the book. *The Weeping Wood* is a series of loosely connected stories dealing with people whose lives were influenced by rubber. Its panoramic plot begins in Brazil in the 1740s; moves to Boston and London in the nineteenth century; to Sumatra before World War I; to Germany under the Nazis; to Akron, Ohio; and finally to New York and Washington, D.C. Again Baum conducted much of her research on location, and she had to get special permission from the War Department to inspect the Goodyear rubber plant in Akron. The section of the novel located in Nazi Germany deals with the production of synthetic rubber, a German invention, at a chemical plant modeled on the I. G. Farben concern. To make this section as authentic as possible she spoke with chemists who had worked at Farben before fleeing to the United States and with other exiles who had experienced the bombing raids on the Farben plant. Richard Ziegfeld contends that the novel only needs a "sympathetic audience" to be recognized as having all the "elements of first-class fiction: a soundly-woven, compelling narrative structure, a serious

Baum at her desk in Hollywood during World War II (Vicki Baum, Es war alles ganz anders: Erinnerungen, *1962)*

social issue, and remarkably rich, accurate detail. . . ."

After a series of novels reusing elements of the basic formula, including *Marion Alive* (1942), *Hotel Berlin '43* (1944), and *Mortgage on Life* (1946), Baum's dissatisfaction with her career reached a crisis during her work on *Headless Angel* (1948). She complained bitterly about deadlines and the extensive cuts suggested by her editor at Doubleday, but she was also distressed by the firm's promotional campaign, which she linked to the overall climate in the postwar United States—an attitude which evaluated people and countries on the basis of "what are they trying to sell us?" She believed that the result was a "progressive lowering of the spiritual standards of the U.S." She decided to express her opinions about these issues in a work of "good literature." Baum planned to write the book under a pseudonym and have it published by a different company, hoping that she would finally rid herself of the "woman who wrote *Grand Hotel*" straitjacket.

But the ruse did not work: Dial Press published *The Mustard Seed* in 1953 under her own name, and the dust jacket even stated that the author had written *Grand Hotel.*

The Mustard Seed is the story of Giano Benedetto, a faith healer and exponent of a back-to-nature life-style who can be seen as either a Christ figure or a Hitler figure. Giano is brought from his remote mountain region in Italy to Los Angeles by a wealthy American to rehabilitate his brother, who has grave psychological problems. Baum's two goals, criticizing contemporary American society and proving that she could write a "good" novel, are clear in the content and form of *The Mustard Seed.* The contrast between Giano and decadent Los Angeles provides Baum ample opportunity for social criticism, but her "solution" to the problems she depicts recalls earlier novels: she does not suggest changing specific social, economic, or political structures but implies that a person can only escape by returning to nature or retreating into a private, inner sphere.

The form of *The Mustard Seed* is far more complex than that of any of her earlier novels; but although she shows virtuosity in her use of sophisticated techniques, once again the omniscient narrator returns to tell readers how to interpret the novel. Critics generally praised the novel but noted nothing especially different in it, a conclusion shared by Johann Holzner in his 1984 analysis of the work.

For the 1956 publication of *Written on Water* Baum returned to Doubleday, which also published her last novel, *Theme for Ballet*, in 1958. Her memoirs, written around this time, are filled with justifications for her choices in life, especially the decision to write commercial literature. Baum died on 29 August 1960 in Los Angeles, and her obituaries all mentioned that she was "the woman who wrote *Grand Hotel*."

Bibliographies:

Robert Bell, "Vicki Baum," in *Deutsche Exilliteratur seit 1933*, volume 1, *Kalifornien*, part 2, edited by John M. Spalek, Joseph Strelka, and Sandra H. Hawrylchak (Bern & Munich: Francke, 1976), pp. 6-13;

Spalek, *Guide to the Archival Materials of the German-Speaking Emigration to the United States after 1933* (Charlottesville: University Press of Virginia, 1978), pp. 51-55.

References:

Dorothee Bayer, *Der triviale Familien-und Liebesroman im 20. Jahrhundert* (Tübingen: Tübinger Vereinigung für Volkskunde, 1963);

Robert Bell, "Vicki Baum," in *Deutsche Exilliteratur seit 1933*, volume 1, *Kalifornien*, part 1, edited by John M. Spalek and Joseph Strelka (Bern & Munich: Francke, 1976), pp. 247-258;

Gisela Berglund, *Deutsche Opposition gegen Hitler in Presse und Roman des Exils: Eine Darstellung und ein Vergleich mit der historischen Wirklichkeit* (Stockholm: Almquist & Wiksell, 1972), pp. 255-263;

Renny Harrigan, "Die emanzipierte Frau im deutschen Roman der Weimarer Republik," in *Stereotyp und Vorurteil in der Literatur*, edited

by James Elliot, Jürgen Pelzer, and Carole Poore (Göttingen: Vandenhoeck & Ruprecht, 1978), pp. 65-83;

Johann Holzner, "Literarische Verfahrensweisen und Botschaften der Vicki Baum," in *Erzählgattungen der Trivialliteratur*, edited by Zdenko Skreb and Uwe Baur (Innsbruck: Institut für Germanistik, University of Innsbruck, 1984), pp. 233-250;

Martha Katz, "Österreichische Frauendichtung der Gegenwart: Ein Beitrag zur Psychologie der weiblichen Kunst," Ph.D. dissertation, University of Vienna, 1937;

Lynda J. King, *Best-Sellers by Design: Vicki Baum and the House of Ullstein* (Detroit: Wayne State University Press, 1988);

King, "The Image of Fame: Vicki Baum in Weimar Germany," *German Quarterly*, 58, no. 3 (1985): 375-393;

King, "The Woman Question and Politics in Austrian Interwar Literature," *German Studies Review*, 6, no. 1 (1983): 75-100;

Hermon Ould, "Experiments in Technique: Vicki Baum and Arnold Zweig," *Bookman*, 79 (November 1930): 132;

Franz Trescher, "Vicki Baum oder Talent und Betrieb: Der Kleinbürger und die Illusion," *Bildungsarbeit* (Vienna), 19 (December 1932): 1;

Richard E. Ziegfeld, "The Exile Writer and His Publisher: Vicki Baum and Doubleday," in *Deutsche Exilliteratur: Literatur der Nachkriegszeit. Akten des dritten Exilliteratur-Symposiums der University of South Carolina*, edited by Wolfgang Elfe, James Hardin, and Günther Holst (Bern, Frankfurt am Main & Las Vegas: Lang, 1981), pp. 144-153;

Ernestine Zottleder, "Das Bild der zeitgenössischen Frau im deutschen Frauenroman vom Naturalismus bis zur Gegenwart," Ph.D. dissertation, University of Vienna, 1932.

Papers:

Letters concerning Baum's association with Doubleday and Company are in the Vicki Baum collection at the State University of New York at Albany.

Konrad Bayer

(17 December 1932-10 October 1964)

Joseph G. McVeigh
Smith College

BOOKS: *starker toback: kleine fibel für den ratlosen,* by Bayer and Oswald Wiener (Paris: Dead language press, 1962);

der stein der weisen (Berlin: Fietkau, 1963);

montagen 1956, by Bayer, H. C. Artmann, and Gerhard Rühm (Bleiburg: Kulturer, 1964);

der kopf des vitus bering (Olten & Freiburg im Breisgau: Walter, 1965); translated by Walter Billeter as *The Head of Vitus Bering: A Portrait in Prose* (Melbourne: Rigmarole of the Hours, 1979);

der sechste sinn: texte von konrad bayer, edited by Rühm (Reinbek: Rowohlt, 1966); "der sechste sinn" revised by Rühm as *der sechste sinn: roman* (Reinbek: Rowohlt, 1969);

Das Gesamtwerk, edited by Rühm (Reinbek: Rowohlt, 1977);

Sämtliche Werke, edited by Rühm, 2 volumes (Stuttgart: Klett-Cotta, 1985);

Selected Works of Konrad Bayer, translated by M. Green (London: Atlas, 1986).

OTHER: Gerhard Rühm, ed., *Die Wiener Gruppe: Achleitner, Artmann, Bayer, Rühm, Wiener. Texte, Gemeinschaftsarbeiten, Aktionen,* contributions by Bayer (Reinbek: Rowohlt, 1967);

H. C. Artmann, *Ein lilienweißer brief aus lincolnshire: gedichte aus 21 jähren,* edited by Gerald Bisinger, portrait of Artmann by Bayer (Frankfurt am Main: Suhrkamp, 1969);

"konrad bayer zeitung: tagebuch 63," in *wien: bildkompendium wiener aktionismus und film,* edited by Peter Weibel (Frankfurt am Main: Kohlkunstverlag, 1970), n. pag.

PERIODICAL PUBLICATIONS: "gestern heute morgen," "der neunertz specken klaster," *publikationen,* no. 1 (1957);

"triumph," *publikationen,* no. 2 (1957);

"kinderlied," *Neue Wege,* no. 132 (1957/1958);

"signal," *edition 62,* no. 1 (1962);

"die birne," *edition 62,* no. 2 (1962);

"bissen brot," by Bayer and Gerhard Rühm, *manuskripte,* no. 2 (1962);

Konrad Bayer (photo: Otto Breicha, Vienna)

"karl ein karl," *manuskripte,* no. 5 (1962);

"die begabten zuschauer," *Blätter,* no. 2 (1962);

"bräutigall & anonymphe," *Eröffnungen,* no. 8/9 (1963);

"franz," *texturen,* no. 7 (1963);

"flucht," *manuskripte,* no. 8 (1963);

"lapidares museum," "die elektrische hierarchie," *Neue Wege*, no. 194 (1964);

"die tänzer trommeln und springen," "balsader binsam," "stadt," *werkstatt aspekt*, no. 1 (1964);

"kriminelle ansätze," *Wort in der Zeit*, no. 2 (1964);

"ferdinandlein," "georg, der läufer," "nkole," "thorstein," *Wort in der Zeit*, no. 9 (1964);

"der gefliddderte rosengarten," *neues bilderreiches poetarium*, no. 2 (1964);

"hans carl artmann und die wiener dichter-gruppe," *werkstatt aspekt*, no. 1 (1964);

"The Vienna Group," *Times Literary Supplement*, 3 September 1964, p. 784;

"der verspätete geburtstag," *manuskripte*, no. 10 (1964);

"gertruds ohr," *Eröffnungen*, no. 13 (1964);

"der kohlenhändler und sein feind," *Wort in der Zeit*, no. 1/2 (1965);

"wie das zepter der menschen," "die kleider eines russigen nach einer bergwerks-besichtigung," *manuskripte*, no. 21 (1967);

die boxer, Protokolle, no. 1 (1970);

"Brief an Ida," *manuskripte*, no. 37/38 (1973);

"der schwarze prinz," *Nervenkritik*, no. 1 (1976);

"prosa," "(invention 1954)," *neue texte*, no. 25 (1981).

The literary output of Konrad Bayer is by no means extensive. Between 1955, when he wrote what he called his "erste halbwegs brauchbare geschichte" (first halfway useful story), "der capitän" (the captain, 1966), until his suicide in 1964, Bayer produced only two major works, the "portrait in prose" *der kopf des vitus bering* (1965; translated as *The Head of Vitus Bering*, 1979) and the incomplete novel "der sechste sinn" (the sixth sense, 1966), both of which appeared posthumously. The remainder and by far the largest part of his work consists of shorter experimental pieces, many of which were not published until his collected works came out in 1977.

Bayer saw only a few of his writings appear in print during his lifetime: two collaborative works with fellow members of the "Wiener Gruppe" (Vienna Group), *starker toback: kleine fibel für den ratlosen* (strong tobacco: little primer for the perplexed, 1962), with Oswald Wiener, and *montagen 1956* (assembly lines 1956, 1964), with Hans Carl Artmann and Gerhard Rühm; *der stein der weisen* (the stone of wisdom, 1963); and pieces in various periodicals. Bayer did, however, read and perform many of his avant-garde

works in a series of literary cabarets with other members of the Wiener Gruppe in 1958 and 1959. In addition, several of his short dramatic texts were staged by student and experimental theaters in Vienna in the early 1960s: *die begabten zuschauer* (the talented spectators, 1962); *der fliegende holländer / kosmologie / ein kriminal stück* (the flying dutchman / cosmology / a criminal play, published in *Die Wiener Gruppe*, edited by Rühm, 1967) by Bayer and Rühm; *bräutigall & anonymphe* (unpublished; performed, 1963); and *kinderoper* (children's opera, published in *Die Wiener Gruppe*, 1967) by Bayer, Friedrich Achleitner, Rühm, and Wiener. Two of his better-known plays were first staged after his death: *kasperl am elektrischen stuhl* (kasperl in the electric chair, 1966), which premiered during the Vienna Festival of 1968, and the fragment *die boxer* (the boxers, 1970), which was first performed in Zurich in 1971. His consistent refusal to use capitalization in his works–a stylistic trait he shared with his fellow avant-garde writers in the Wiener Gruppe–was based on the belief that modern German, like most living languages, is undergoing a process of reduction and simplification. The lack of capital letters was not only a rational continuation of this development but also provided a wider basis for syntactic and semantic experimentation.

Bayer was born in Vienna on 17 December 1932. His early interest in the poet Georg Trakl, surrealism, and Dada brought him in 1951 to Albert Paris Gütersloh's Artclub in Vienna, the focal point of modernist culture in Austria in the early 1950s, where he met Artmann, Rühm, Wiener, and Achleitner. In 1954 Bayer, Artmann, and Rühm formed the literary club Exil–a name that reflects the isolation of modernist literature in Austria at that time–and organized readings and group literary projects. With the addition of Wiener and Achleitner they became known as the Wiener Gruppe, first appearing together under this collective name in June 1958. In 1957 Bayer resigned his position at a bank, made a short-lived attempt to study psychology at the University of Vienna, then briefly managed the art gallery of his friend Ernst Fuchs before leaving to pursue his career as a writer. He was married in 1960. He collaborated extensively with other members of the Wiener Gruppe until it was dissolved in 1964. In 1962 the group established an avant-garde literary journal, *edition 62*, with Bayer as editor; the publication died after two issues. He was a contributing editor of the journal *Eröffnungen*

Bayer (extreme left) at the Café Hawelka in 1958 with other members of the Wiener Gruppe: (from left) H. C. Artmann, Gerhard Rühm, Friedrich Achleitner (Franz Hubmann, Vienna)

in 1964. Bayer wrote and acted in several experimental films: *Mosaik im Vertrauen* (Mosaic in Trust, 1955) by Peter Kubelka, and *Sonne halt!* (Sun Halt!, three versions, 1959-1962) and *Am Rand* (On the Edge, three versions, 1961-1963) by Ferry Radax. Radax directed the filming of *der kopf des vitus bering* in 1970 and *Berg, Berg* (Mountain, Mountain), based on Bayer's "thorstein" (1964), in 1972.

In 1963 Bayer spent several months in France. That year provided the first major breakthrough in his career as a writer; his work began to achieve recognition outside of Vienna with the publication of *der stein der weisen* in Berlin and his discovery at the annual meeting of the Gruppe 47 in Saulgau, near Ulm. In January 1964 *der kopf des vitus bering* was produced as a radio play by the Norddeutscher Rundfunk and Sender Freies Berlin; soon thereafter Bayer had commitments to publish *der kopf des vitus bering* and "der sechste sinn." When he and fellow members of the Wiener Gruppe were recognized by the offi-

cial Austrian literary journal *Wort in der Zeit* in 1964, Bayer's star appeared to be rising. But when the members of the group went their separate ways later that year, Bayer chose not to leave Austria for the larger literary market of Germany, as had many writers of his generation. Instead, he withdrew to a castle, Schloß Hagenberg, in Lower Austria to work on "der sechste sinn," which is colored throughout by a growing sense of resignation and finality. Drawn from his diary of 1962, the work contains many comments which presage his suicide on 10 October before completion of the novel: "man muß sich umbringen, um die hoffnung zu begraben. . . . es gibt nichts was zu erreichen wäre außer dem tod" (to bury hope, you must kill yourself. . . . there is nothing to accomplish except death).

Bayer's experimental works do not easily lend themselves to interpretation, partly because most of them underwent constant revision but also because his work is an expression of what Rühm called his "extremen individual-an-

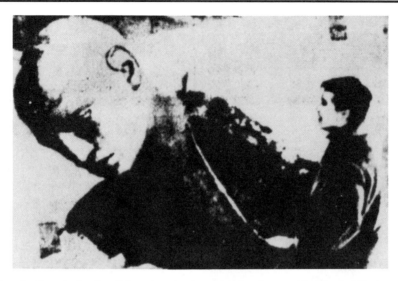

Frontispiece for Bayer's der kopf des vitus bering, *showing Bayer with a bust of Bering on a leash*

archismus" (extreme individual anarchism). His experimental writings can be divided into two categories: those focusing on lexical and those concentrating on semantic innovation. The texts of the former category owe much to the sound poems of the dadaists: individual words are not bound together by a syntactical context. No longer a vehicle of meaning, each syllable assumes the function of a raw material of sound which, when woven together with others, creates an impression based solely on acoustical value. These texts, which are typical of Bayer's earlier writings, often revolve around sound groups such as *ammel, ummel* or *enz, anz, erz*, as in the poems "balsader binsam" (1964) and "der neunertz specken klaster" (1957), both written in 1954. The montage of sounds usually retains the rhythm of spoken language, giving the illusion of contextual order. In fact, however, Bayer structured these and similar works according to mathematical formulae. This style of writing, called "methodical inventionism," can be applied to series of words or sentences as well as syllables and sounds, evoking absurd images as in the poem "der kutscher sitzt auf dem tanzmeister" (the coachman sits on the dancing instructor, 1966). Bayer's most ambitious attempt to make literary creation into a mechanical process is the poem "der vogel singt" (the bird sings, 1966), which is subtitled "eine dichtungsmaschine in 571 bestandteilen" (a poetry machine in 571 component parts). Bayer explains the poem as "ein versuch einer nachbildung. nachgebaut wurden natürliche funktionen auf grund von naturbeobachtung und menschl[icher] schluß-

folgerung" (an attempt at replication. natural functions were replicated on the basis of observations of nature and human reasoning). The work is divided into six major segments centered on combinations of the elements air, earth, water, and fire; subdivisions within each section incorporate permutations of images and component words. In *der stein der weisen* Bayer similarly views language as an "elektrische hierarchie" (electrical hierarchy) in which the meaning of a word or phrase is determined by preceding words and sentences: "jeder satz betritt die situation, die alle vorhergehenden geschaffen haben. / diese neutralen sätze laden sich mit der situation auf . . . / die situation ist eine elektrische spannung" (each sentence steps into the situation that all the preceding ones have created. / these neutral sentences charge themselves with the situation . . . / the situation is an electrical potential). Language is fluid, he says: "alles kann dies und jenes heißen. / alles mag auch etwas anderes heißen" (everything can be called this or that. / everything may also be called something else). But despite this fluidity language can create the illusion of bridging the gap between subject and object, mind and external reality: "es gibt nichts gemeinsames. nur die sprache schafft gemeinschaften" (there is no common ground. only language creates groupings). The conventions of language result in the uniformity of everyday communication: "alle meine vorfahren und auch alle anderen haben die sprache zusammengebosselt . . . und so wurde . . . alles gleich gemacht und nun ist alles das gleiche und keiner merkt es" (all my ancestors, and all others too, pieced together language

... and thus was ... everything made the same and now it's all the same and nobody notices).

Many of the poems and chansons which Bayer wrote for the literary cabarets of the Wiener Gruppe–he often accompanied himself on the banjo–were more conventional in style. Poems such as "niemand hilft mir" (no one helps me, 1966), "moritat vom tätowierten mädchen" (ballad of the tattooed girl, 1966), "schöne welt" (beautiful world, 1966), or "marie dein liebster wartet" (marie your beloved is waiting, 1966) combine somber themes of death and despair with contrastingly lively rhythms and rhymes reminiscent of Bertolt Brecht and Christian Morgenstern. Although they are not among his more avant-garde writings, some of the cabaret songs do share a common feature with the second category of experimental works, those focusing on semantic elements and examining the banalities and contradictions of everyday language. The primary stylistic methods here are the juxtaposition of clichés or common phrases with contrasting sentences, as in the fragment of conversation "guten morgen" (good morning, 1966), or the montage of news reporting and marketing language in "17. jänner 1962" (17 January 1962, 1966). The problem of verbal communication is a common theme throughout Bayer's work. The struggle of the individual to confront and understand reality through language is depicted in the dramatic fragment *die boxer* as involving physical pain. The pugilists in this play–only three of a projected eighteen rounds were completed–intersperse their blows with trite phrases and snatches of everyday conversation. The bout begins with an exchange of polite greetings, but the alternation of words and punches quickly degenerates into brutality. The play focuses on the conventions of language which feign meaningful communication where in reality none exists. The impasse results in a violent assertion of the individual will. Bayer did not plan to show either boxer as the victor, since in such a struggle there can be none.

One of the few longer works to be completed before Bayer's death, *der kopf des vitus bering* presents in seventy-eight loosely connected segments a series of images and thought fragments concerning the eighteenth-century Russian Arctic explorer Vitus Bering. A detailed appendix provides historical data and sources. There is no continuity of time, place, or action; Bayer is concerned with Bering's consciousness and perception of the world around him. A series of associative images ties together the external and inter-nal reality of the explorer and parallels his discovery of new Arctic territories with his transcendence of the sensual limits of consciousness. The image of the bear that occurs throughout the work–and which is evoked by the name Bering itself (the German word *Bär* is pronounced almost the same as the English word *bear*)–is tied both to the polar regions and to reflections on levels of consciousness: the picture of Bayer holding a bust of Bering on a leash which precedes the title page and the reference in the text to a dancing bear on a leash clearly associate this image with the bear in Heinrich von Kleist's essay "Über das Marionettentheater" (On the Marionette Theater, 1810). The recurring motifs of coldness, ice, and the color blue signify not only the Arctic conditions but silence and death. Of Bering's death Bayer says: "sein gesicht wurde langsam BLAU" (his face slowly turned BLUE). Bering's epilepsy–his forename, Vitus, is that of the patron saint of epileptics–represents for Bayer a means of crossing beyond normal consciousness to the "idealer sinn" (ideal sense). The belief of Arctic peoples that epileptic seizures were a form of divine ecstasy and thus of a higher consciousness is cited in the appendix.

Bering's deeds and accomplishments do not constitute for Bayer the true identity of the man; identity is rather a function of self-consciousness. Thus, the title of the work refers to the head of the main character, since the head represents the seat of consciousness. In other works, such as *der stein der weisen* and the poem "ich und mein körper" (I and my body, 1966), the independence of body and identity is expressed as physical separation. Bering's inner search for a clearer view of his identity in the chilling wastes of the Arctic is a metaphor for Bayer's own search for the "ideal sense" concealed beneath social and linguistic conventions.

This search serves as the basis of his last major work, the unfinished novel *der sechste sinn*, which consists of a mosaic of thoughts and experiences mostly drawn from Bayer's Berlin diary of 1962. Bayer speaks through the figure of Franz Goldenberg, the central character of the novel; other characters are modeled after friends and fellow writers such as Artmann (called Neuwerk in the novel). The "sixth sense" of the title is identical with the "ideal sense" which characterizes Bering's extrasensual perception of the world; both Bering and Goldenberg attempt to arrive at a self-identity not determined by social conventions or sensual experience. The motifs of cold-

Page from the manuscript for Bayer's unfinished novel der sechste sinn *(Konrad Bayer,* Sämtliche Werke, *edited by Gerhard Rühm, volume 2, 1985)*

ness and ice which were associated with the expanded perception of Bering contrast with a similar use of the motif of fire in "der sechste sinn." While Goldenberg claims to have the sixth sense, he is struck by the meaninglessness of what he sees, a world of phenomena without causes: "es gibt keine ursachen . . . es gibt nur erscheinungen" (there are no causes . . . there are only phenomena). The stark tone of hopelessness in the "Nachtrag" (postscript)–the last fragments of the novel written before Bayer's death– was absent from *der kopf des vitus bering*. The frustration inherent in language and communication plays a more central role in "der sechste sinn" than in the earlier work. Goldenberg's maxim is "du darfst nicht zuhören, dann wirst du alles besser verstehen" (you must not listen, then you will better understand everything); ignoring the world around him, he records over and over again in his notebooks the same meaningless information. In his attempt to dispel the repetitive cycle of his existence Goldenberg deliberately forgets what he has written on the slips of paper he keeps in his pockets so that he can enjoy reading them anew. The monotony he hopes to overcome in this fashion is inflicted on the reader by the repetition of whole passages with only minor variations. The continuity of the work is broken by two completely unreadable segments.

These last two major works contain all the basic themes and motifs of Bayer's writings, which Rühm identifies as paradox, force, rebellion, freezing, paralysis, death, and the random nature of things. Since the publication of *Das Gesamtwerk* in 1977 Bayer's writings have enjoyed renewed critical interest, including a major symposium on the author in Vienna in 1979 and a special issue of the journal *Protokolle* in 1983.

Letters:

"Briefe an Ida," *manuskripte*, no. 37/38 (1973): 53-60;

"Konrad Bayer: Briefe an seine Verleger," edited by Ulrich Janetzki, *Sondern*, no. 4 (1979): n. pag.

References:

Michael Butler, "From the 'Wiener Gruppe' to Ernst Jandl," in *Modern Austrian Writing: Literature and Society after 1945*, edited by Alan

Best and Hans Wolfschütz (London & Totowa, N.J.: Barnes & Noble, 1980), pp. 236-251;

Adolf Haslinger, "Konrad Bayers *der sechste sinn*: Literarische Montage im österreichischen Gegenwartsroman," in *Festschrift für Adalbert Schmidt*, edited by Gerlinde Weiss and Gerd Dieter Stein (Stuttgart: Heinz, 1976), pp. 389-409;

Ulrich Janetzki, *Alphabet und Welt: Über Konrad Bayer* (Königstein: Hain, 1982);

Janetzki, "Versuch, das Unsagbare zu zeigen: Konrad Bayer, *der stein der weisen*," *Sprache im technischen Zeitalter*, 17, no. 68 (1978): 330-344;

Janetzki, "Die Welt als sprachbewirkte Illusion: Überlegungen zu Konrad Bayer," *Sprache im technischen Zeitalter*, 20, no. 80 (1981): 335-352;

Johannes Mager, "Konrad Bayer: 'Der Kopf des Vitus Bering: Ein Porträt in Prosa,'" *Austriaca*, no. 7 (1978): 131-140;

Protokolle: Zeitschrift für Literatur und Kunst, special Bayer issue, no. 1 (1983);

Gerhard Rühm, ed., *Konrad Bayer: Symposion Wien 1979* (Linz: Edition neue texte, 1981);

Franz Schuh, "Protest ohne protestieren: Zur Widersetzlichkeit von Konrad Bayers Literatur," *Protokolle*, no. 4 (1981): 31-43;

Gisela Steinwachs, "konzept der dichtungsmaschine," *Sprache im technischen Zeitalter*, 14, no. 55 (1975): 204-208;

Kurt Strasser, *Experimentelle Literaturansätze im Nachkriegs-Wien: Am Beispiel von Konrad Bayer* (Stuttgart: Heinz, 1986);

Michael Töteberg, "Konrad Bayer," in *Kritisches Lexikon zur deutschsprachigen Gegenwartsliteratur*, edited by Heinz Ludwig Arnold (Munich: Edition text + kritik, 1979), pp. 1-10, A-C;

Oswald Wiener, "Einiges über Konrad Bayer," *Die Zeit*, 17 February 1978;

Senta Ziegler, "'ich hab ein schloß in der bretagne': Konrad Bayer in Hagenberg," *das pult*, no. 54 (1979): 52-60;

Dieter E. Zimmer, "Erinnerung an Konrad Bayer," *Die Zeit*, 23 October 1964.

Papers:

Konrad Bayer's papers are in the possession of his widow, Traudl Bayer, in Vienna.

Thomas Bernhard

(9 February 1931-12 February 1989)

Steve Dowden
Yale University

BOOKS: *Auf der Erde und in der Hölle: Gedichte* (Salzburg: Müller, 1957);

In hora mortis (Salzburg: Müller, 1958);

Unter dem Eisen des Mondes: Gedichte (Cologne & Berlin: Kiepenheuer & Witsch, 1958);

die rosen der einöde: fünf sätze für ballett, stimmen, und orchester (Frankfurt am Main: Fischer, 1959);

Frost (Frankfurt am Main: Insel, 1963);

Amras (Frankfurt am Main: Insel, 1964);

Prosa (Frankfurt am Main: Suhrkamp, 1967);

Verstörung: Roman (Frankfurt am Main: Insel, 1967); translated by Richard and Clara Winston as *Gargoyles* (New York: Knopf, 1970);

Ungenach: Erzählung (Frankfurt am Main: Suhrkamp, 1968);

Ein Fest für Boris (Frankfurt am Main: Suhrkamp, 1968);

An der Baumgrenze: Erzählungen (Salzburg: Residenz, 1969);

Ereignisse (Berlin: Literarisches Colloquium, 1969);

Watten: Ein Nachlaß (Frankfurt am Main: Suhrkamp, 1969);

Das Kalkwerk (Frankfurt am Main: Suhrkamp, 1970); translated by Sophie Wilkins as *The Lime Works* (New York: Knopf, 1973):

Der Italiener (Salzburg: Residenz, 1971);

Midland in Stilfs: Drei Erzählungen (Frankfurt am Main: Suhrkamp, 1971);

Gehen (Frankfurt am Main: Suhrkamp, 1971);

Der Ignorant und der Wahnsinnige (Frankfurt am Main: Suhrkamp, 1972);

Die Jagdgesellschaft (Frankfurt am Main: Suhrkamp, 1974); translated by Gitta Honegger as "The Hunting Party," *Performing Arts Journal*, 5 (1980): 101-131;

Die Macht der Gewohnheit: Komödie (Frankfurt am Main: Suhrkamp, 1974); translated by Neville and Stephen Plaice as *The Force of Habit: A Comedy* (London: Heinemann, 1976);

Der Kulterer: Eine Filmgeschichte (Salzburg: Residenz, 1974);

Thomas Bernhard

Der Präsident (Frankfurt am Main: Suhrkamp, 1975); translated by Honegger as *The President*, in *The President & Eve of Retirement* (New York: Performing Arts Journal Publications, 1982), pp. 17-114;

Die Ursache: Eine Andeutung (Salzburg: Residenz, 1975); translated by David McLintock as "An Indication of the Cause," in *Gathering Evidence: A Memoir* (New York: Knopf, 1985), pp. 75-141;

Korrektur: Roman (Frankfurt am Main: Suhrkamp, 1975); translated by Wilkins as *Correction* (New York: Knopf, 1979);

Der Wetterfleck: Erzählungen (Stuttgart: Reclam, 1976);

Die Berühmten (Frankfurt am Main: Suhrkamp, 1976);

Minetti: Ein Portrait des Künstlers als alter Mann (Frankfurt am Main: Suhrkamp, 1976);

Der Keller: Eine Entziehung (Salzburg: Residenz, 1976); translated by McLintock as "The Cellar: An Escape," in *Gathering Evidence: A Memoir*, pp. 142-213;

Der Atem: Eine Entscheidung (Salzburg & Vienna: Residenz, 1978); translated by McLintock as "Breath: A Decision," in *Gathering Evidence: A Memoir*, pp. 215-275;

Die Kälte: Eine Isolation (Salzburg: Residenz, 1978); translated by McLintock as "In the Cold," in *Gathering Evidence: A Memoir*, pp. 277-340;

Ja (Frankfurt am Main: Suhrkamp, 1978);

Der Stimmenimitator (Frankfurt am Main: Suhrkamp, 1978);

Immanuel Kant: Komödie (Frankfurt am Main: Suhrkamp, 1978);

Die Erzählungen (Frankfurt am Main: Suhrkamp, 1979);

Vor dem Ruhestand: Eine Komödie von deutscher Seele (Frankfurt am Main: Suhrkamp, 1979); translated by Honegger as *Eve of Retirement*, in *The President & Eve of Retirement*, pp. 115-207;

Der Weltverbesserer (Frankfurt am Main: Suhrkamp, 1979);

Die Billigesser (Frankfurt am Main: Suhrkamp, 1980);

Über allen Gipfeln ist Ruh: Ein deutscher Dichtertag um 1980. Komödie (Frankfurt am Main: Suhrkamp, 1981);

Am Ziel (Frankfurt am Main: Suhrkamp, 1981);

Ave Vergil: Gedicht (Frankfurt am Main: Suhrkamp, 1981);

Wittgensteins Neffe: Eine Freundschaft (Frankfurt am Main: Suhrkamp, 1982); translated by McLintock as *Wittgenstein's Nephew: A Friendship* (New York: Knopf, 1989);

Ein Kind (Salzburg: Residenz, 1982); translated by McLintock as "A Child," in *Gathering Evidence: A Memoir*, pp. 1-73;

Beton (Frankfurt am Main: Suhrkamp, 1982); translated by McLintock as *Concrete* (New York: Knopf, 1984; London: Dent, 1984);

Der Schein trügt (Frankfurt am Main: Suhrkamp, 1983); translated by Honegger as *Appearances Are Deceiving*, Theater, 15 (1983): 13-51;

Der Untergeher (Frankfurt am Main: Suhrkamp, 1983);

Bernhard in 1964 (photo: Otto Breicha, Vienna; Bildarchiv der Österreichischen Nationalbibliothek)

Der Theatermacher (Frankfurt am Main: Suhrkamp, 1984);

Holzfällen: Eine Erregung (Frankfurt am Main: Suhrkamp, 1984); translated by McLintock as *Woodcutters* (New York: Knopf, 1987);

Ritter, Dene, Voss (Frankfurt am Main: Suhrkamp, 1984);

Alte Meister: Komödie (Frankfurt am Main: Suhrkamp, 1985); translated by Ewald Osers as *Old Masters* (London: Quartet, 1989);

Einfach kompliziert (Frankfurt am Main: Suhrkamp, 1986);

Auslöschung: Ein Zerfall (Frankfurt am Main: Suhrkamp, 1986);

Elisabeth II. (Frankfurt am Main: Suhrkamp, 1987);

Der deutsche Mittagstisch: Dramolette (Frankfurt am Main: Suhrkamp, 1988);

Stücke, 4 volumes (Frankfurt am Main: Suhrkamp, 1988);

Heldenplatz (Frankfurt am Main: Suhrkamp, 1988);

Die Irren; Die Häftlinge (Frankfurt am Main: Insel, 1988);

In der Höhe: Rettungsversuch, Unsinn (Salzburg: Residenz, 1989).

OTHER: "Großer, unbegreiflicher Hunger," in *Stimmen der Gegenwart 1954,* edited by Hans Weigel (Vienna: Dürer, 1954), pp. 138-143;

"Der Schweinehüter," in *Stimmen der Gegenwart 1956* (Vienna & Munich: Herold, 1956), pp. 158-179;

"Ein Frühling," in *Spektrum des Geistes 1964: Literaturkalender* (Ebenhausen: Voss, 1963), p. 36;

"Der Italiener," in *Insel-Almanach auf das Jahr 1965* (Frankfurt am Main: Insel, 1964);

"Mit der Klarheit nimmt die Kälte zu," in *Jahresring 65/66* (Stuttgart: DVA, 1965), pp. 243-245;

"Nie und mit nichts fertig werden," in *Deutsche Akademie für Sprache und Dichtung: Jahrbuch 1970* (Heidelberg & Darmstadt: Schneider, 1971), pp. 83-84.

PERIODICAL PUBLICATIONS: "Ein Zeugenaussage," *Wort in der Zeit* (1964): 38-43;

"Ein junger Schriftsteller," *Wort in der Zeit* (1965): 56-59;

"Politische Morgenandacht," *Wort in der Zeit* (1966): 11-13;

"Unsterblichkeit ist unmöglich: Landschaft der Kindheit," *Neues Forum,* 169-170 (1968): 95-97;

"Der Wahrheit und dem Tod auf der Spur: Zwei Reden," *Neues Forum,* 173 (1968): 347-349;

"Der Berg," *Literatur und Kritik,* 46 (1970): 330-352;

"Vor der Akademie," *Frankfurter Allgemeine Zeitung,* 19 October 1970, p. 22;

"Als Verwalter in Asyl: Fragment," *Merkur,* 24 (1970): 1163-1164;

"Die Komödie der Eitelkeit," *Die Zeit,* 27 February 1976, p. 55;

"Was Österreich nicht lesen soll: Die Kleinbürger auf der Heuchelleiter," *Die Zeit,* 17 February 1978, p. 40;

"Der doppelte Herr Bernhard," *Die Zeit,* 31 August 1979, pp. 43-44;

"Zu meinem Austritt," *Frankfurter Allgemeine Zeitung,* 7 December 1979, p. 25;

"Der pensionierte Salonsozialist," *profil* (Vienna), 26 January 1981, pp. 52-53;

"Goethe schtirbt," *Die Zeit,* 19 March 1982, pp. 41-42;

"Montaigne: Eine Erzählung in 22 Fortsetzungen," *Die Zeit,* 8 October 1982, literature section, pp. 1-22;

"Mein glückliches Österreich," *Die Zeit,* 11 March 1988, p. 75;

"Zwei Briefe an Klaus Peymann," *Die Zeit,* 3 March 1989, p. 14.

Thomas Bernhard, one of postwar Austria's most original prose stylists, was also one of its most prolific writers. Between the 1950s and his death in 1989 Bernhard wrote fifteen novels and long narratives, eighteen stage plays, six book-length autobiographical pieces, and a few volumes of lyric poetry. His popular reputation rests partly on the high quality of his unusual prose with its philosophical pessimism, partly on his combative personal style. A loner both in art and in life, he cultivated the image of an intellectual curmudgeon; he was known for his irascible attacks on cultural and political figures, from the Nobel Prize winner Elias Canetti to Austrian chancellor Bruno Kreisky. In his work Bernhard ponders death, madness, and disease; above all, he concerns himself with modern Austria, a theme that merges seamlessly with the motifs of decay and death.

The details of Bernhard's life are recorded in his various memoirs, most of which have been collected and translated into English in one volume under the title *Gathering Evidence* (1985). Though Bernhard's mother and father both were Austrian, he was not born there: Hertha Bernhard gave birth to him in a Dutch home for unwed mothers. His father, a carpenter named Alois Zuckerstätter, not only deserted them but never acknowledged the child as his son; Bernhard never knew him. Zuckerstätter was killed in Germany under ambiguous circumstances during World War II; Hertha later married Emil Fabjan, whom she met in Vienna in 1935.

Bernhard spent his childhood in Austria and southeastern Bavaria, always in the vicinity of Salzburg, with his mother, stepfather, half-siblings, and his mother's parents; sometimes other relatives or boarders shared their already crowded living space. It was the era of the Great Depression, exacerbated in Austria by the aftermath of World War I, and Bernhard's parents worked at menial jobs. The brightest lights in Bernhard's family life were his maternal grandparents, Johannes Freumbichler and Anna Bernhard. (He shared his grandmother's maiden

Cover of a paperback edition of the English translation of Bernhard's 1967 novel Verstörung, *about the horrors witnessed by a country doctor's son as he accompanies his father on his rounds*

name because his mother, too, was born out of wedlock; only after thirty-two years did the eccentric Freumbichler marry Anna Bernhard.) Freumbichler, a modestly successful though impoverished novelist, introduced Bernhard to the life of the mind. On long walks Freumbichler lectured to Bernhard on a great variety of themes. From his grandfather the future novelist absorbed a pessimistic outlook that owed much to Freumbichler's reading of Michel Montaigne, Arthur Schopenhauer, Blaise Pascal, and Friedrich Nietzsche.

Bernhard's schooling took place in Salzburg in a Nazi-run institution that continued under Catholic administration after the war. The experience was useless and miserable; he could discern no difference between the two authoritarian regimes. His emancipation came at the age of sixteen when a grocer in one of Salzburg's shabbier postwar housing projects accepted him as an apprentice. Bernhard cheerfully recalled his time there as an education in life and as a fitting complement to the philosophical education he had received from his grandfather. During these happy times Bernhard developed a serious interest in singing.

At the age of eighteen Bernhard became seriously ill; in the hospital his condition was diagnosed as terminal. In his characteristically uncooperative way, however, Bernhard refused to die, though he did go on to contract tuberculosis in Austria's less-than-wholesome public health system. Lung disease confined him to hospitals and clinics during his late teens and early twenties, ending his hopes for a singing career. Bernhard later emphasized the centrality of disease as an intellectually productive force in his life. The experience of grave illness kept him in touch with the human condition, from which honors, prosperity, and flattery might otherwise have estranged him. Indeed, Bernhard was notorious for the contempt he showered on those who awarded him literary prizes.

Against all expectation Bernhard recovered from his illnesses and went on to study music and acting in Vienna in 1951. In 1952 he returned to Salzburg to attend the Mozarteum, from which he was graduated in 1956 with a thesis on Artaud and Brecht. During the late 1950s he worked as a courtroom reporter, beer-truck driver, laborer, and free-lance journalist while honing his writing skills. He published three slim volumes of melancholy poetry and some short narratives.

"Der Schweinehüter" (The Swineherd), a brief tale published in 1956, early demonstrates the young writer's considerable narrative talent; but the typically Bernhardian concerns–misery, isolation, suicide–are dealt with in a way that is not characteristic of him. The protagonist, an unpleasant man driven to the brink of suicide by years of degradation and humiliation, brutally mistreats and kills the pig he and his wife have raised; the pig's rotting carcass symbolizes the state of the pig's innermost self. As he is preparing to hang himself from a tree in the forest, he is saved at the last minute by a vision of Christ crucified. Bernhard was aware of his debt to the fiction of Austria's Catholic tradition, such as Adalbert Stifter's "Bergkristall" (1853; translated as "Rock Crystal," 1945). The later Bernhard, an outspoken critic of religion in general and of Austrian Catholicism in particular, never offers any hope of rescue to his foundering protagonists. On the contrary, Bernhard's fiction is known best for its pitiless intensity; as he says in his memoirs, "Das Leben spricht eine kürzere, vernichtendere Sprache, die wir selbst heute sprechen, wir sind nicht mehr so sentimental, daß wir noch Hoffnung hätten. Die Hoffnungslosigkeit hat uns die Klarheit verschafft über Menschen, Gegenstände, Verhältnisse, Vergangenheit, Zukunft und so fort" (Life speaks a shorter, more annihilating language that we speak even today; we are no longer so sentimental as to foster hope. Lack of hope has brought clarity to our view of people, objects, situations, the past, the future, and so forth). With unswerving "clarity" Bernhard presses human misery to the direst consequences, to personal calamities that cannot be escaped. Religious, aesthetic, and political transcendence are largely absent from Bernhard's imaginary worlds; detached "clarity" of vision overthrows the illusion of redemption.

With the appearance of *Frost* in 1963 Bernhard rose suddenly to literary prominence. A medical resident has been asked by the surgeon under whom he works to travel to a small Styrian town to observe and report on the mental state of the aging and cynical artist Strauch. The novel portrays the young doctor's observations on Strauch's existence in the backwaters of contemporary Austria, mostly in the form of entries in his journal. Gradually the superior strength of the old man's philosophical pessimism saps the inner resolve of the young man, and he, too, is devoured by the frost: "Der Frost frißt alles auf," says the old artist, "Bäume, Menschen, das Vieh und was in den Bäumen ist, und in den Menschen und im Vieh" (The frost eats up everything, trees, people, animals and what's in the trees and in the people and in the animals). In *Frost*, as elsewhere, Bernhard proceeds from the assumption that modern life has fallen into a state of ineluctable decline. The image of gradually deepening frost suggests an annihilation that is slow, deadening, and absolute. There can be no escape or redemption.

In *Frost*, Strauch speculates on the possibility of an "innere Erbfolgekrankheit" (congenital inner defect) in the Austrian national spirit. In *Amras* (1964) Bernhard uses inherited disease and incestuous homoeroticism as metaphors for the sterile spirit of postwar Austria, transmuting Austrian national identity into a form of epilepsy that is supposed to be congenital among inhabitants of the Tirol. Two brothers unexpectedly survive a suicide pact they had formed with their parents. The younger brother is a musically gifted epileptic; the elder, who is the narrator, is a scientific researcher. After their unexpected and undesired recovery they retire to a lonely tower at Amras, near Innsbruck. They are oppressed by

Thomas Bernhard (photo: Otto Breicha, Vienna)

fear of the "Tirolean Epilepsy" that has debilitated not only their lives but also those of many other families in the region. By the end of the long monologue the younger brother has committed suicide, and the narrator is losing his grip on life.

Amras sets a pattern that recurs throughout Bernhard's fiction. First, his favorite stylistic device, the extended monologue, makes its debut here. *Frost* had been largely epistolary, whereas in *Amras* the narrator alone spins out the memories and observations that constitute the story. No other speaker intrudes into the verbal solipsism of his world. Bernhard's later works enlarge and elaborate on the monologue technique that he begins to explore in *Amras*. Second, the suicidal

brothers are typical of the artists, scientists, and intellectuals whom Bernhard favors as protagonists. Their fates are paradigmatic: the artist is too sensitive to survive in the toxic Austrian atmosphere; after his brother's death, the scientific narrator leads a solitary existence among ignorant woodcutters with whom he cannot communicate. Art cannot survive in Austria, and the life of the mind leads no more than a marginal and precarious existence there. Third, the setting of *Amras* is a tower, an image that has an allegorical significance for Bernhard. Its features are typical: it belongs to the narrator's family and is of considerable antiquity; the protagonists have retreated into its narrow and oppressive confines; once splendid, it has fallen into ruin. This tower is the

Cover of a paperback edition of the English translation of Bernhard's 1970 novel, Das Kalkwerk, *about a man who kills his invalid wife*

first in a series of castles and estates that symbolize the isolation, fallen grandeur, and barren decay of modern Austria.

Though Bernhard's open contempt for Austria was expressed not only in his fiction but also in speeches and interviews, he chose to live there for the whole of his writing career. In 1965 he bought a farmstead near Gmunden in Upper Austria, where he remained all his adult life. He traveled to England, eastern Europe, the Balkans, and the Mediterranean countries, yet he inevitably returned to Austria. When asked about his own place in Austrian literature, Bernhard responded: "N'oubliez pas non plus le poids de l'histoire. Le passé de l'empire des Habsbourg est incrusté dans notre chair. Chez moi, c'est peut-être plus visible que chez les autres. Cela se manifeste sous la forme d'un véritable amour-haine pour l'Autriche, que constitue finalement la clef de tout ce que j'écrits" (You mustn't forget the weight of history. The past of the Hapsburg empire inheres in our very flesh. Perhaps it is more visible with me than with others. It is expressed as a veritable love-hate toward Austria that is ultimately the key to everything I write). The assertion is odd, considering that the contemporary Austria of Bernhard's fiction is the merest shadow of the empire that disappeared forever in 1918. He refers to the empire only obliquely, in the image of ancient estates that have fallen into decline and ruin, perhaps also as the ruined bodies of the old men whom he favors as protagonists. Disease and decline have all but obliterated the once-vigorous spirit.

Bernhard regards his homeland as something like a disease from which no recovery is possible. He dwells especially on lingering illnesses that slowly debilitate their victims. There is no glamour in sickness for him, but his fascination with the degradation of body and soul has a nearly voyeuristic quality, akin to the photography of Diane Arbus. In *Verstörung* (Derangement, 1967; translated as *Gargoyles*, 1970) the rounds of a country doctor provide Bernhard with the premise for a harrowing glimpse of the depravity of body and spirit in a backward part of rural Styria. The narrator is a mining student, the son of the physician, who accompanies his father through a chamber of horrors. The young man comes face to face for the first time in his life with abject misery: neglected old people, insanity, congenital feeblemindedness, invalids, deformity, and disease. The young man's descent into his Austrian inferno of disease and madness builds to a spectacular verbal climax. The doctor's final patient is Prince Saurau, a garrulous old misanthrope who lives in a grand but decaying ancestral castle that commands a view for hundreds of miles in all directions. The final portion of the book is an enormous monologue spoken by Saurau, whose powerful but unstable mind annihilates all values in a verbal storm of solipsistic spleen. Bernhard demonstrates how inward-directed consciousness, traditionally the seat of reasoned critique and detached observation, can reach a state of total alienation. Only the rational, observing presence of the young mining student keeps Saurau's condition from representing a general judgment on the fate of reason and autonomy in the modern era. But the overwhelming strength of Bernhard's pathologically introspective protagonists—artists, musicians, scholars, scientists, and thinkers of every sort—suggests that the Enlightenment's autonomous self may at last have careened out of reason's orbit.

Bernhard's mature prose style is achieved in Saurau's insane monologue. The text dispenses with paragraph breaks; sentences pour forth their venom in long rivers of rhythmic prose that swirl with eddies of bile and gall. Yet this bitter prose is musical; it is written for the ear. The style seems to owe much to Bernhard's musical training and sensibilities, though the grating dissonance of his language is anything but lyrical. It is a music that embodies not the intellect but the will—as one might expect of a writer well versed in Schopenhauer. Old Saurau's grandiose, insane monologue is a tour de force of narrative technique. Bernhard uses the technique on an even larger scale in his next major novel, *Das Kalkwerk* (1970; translated as *The Lime Works*, 1973).

An extraordinarily oppressive narrative, *Das Kalkwerk* relates the events, trivial and significant alike, that lead to the killing of an invalid woman in a backwater Austrian community. Konrad, an eccentric autodidact in his fifties, has withdrawn with his crippled wife to the isolated lime works so that he can work undisturbed on a scientific book, a study of hearing. After years the project has come to nothing. On Christmas Eve he shoots and kills his wife. The narrator, a nameless insurance salesman, tells all he has heard about the Konrads in local inns and taverns. Gossip, supposition, and hearsay are the substance of his report: "Und ich habe zwanzig Jahre an dieses Hirngespinst geglaubt!, soll sie mehrere Male noch am Vorabend der sogenannten Bluttat (wie im Laska gesagt wird) ausgerufen haben, möglicherweise, sagt Fro, habe ihn, Konrad, das seine Frau erschießen lassen. Andererseits soll er, Konrad, gerade am Vorabend der Tat nach langer Zeit wieder zärtlich zu ihr gewesen sein (heißt es im Lanner). Im Gmachl ist davon die Rede, daß Konrad die Bluttat *von langer Hand* vorbereitet habe, im Stiegler sprechen sie aber heute noch von einer *Kurzschlußhandlung*, wie, wenn es, wie es im Lanner auch heißt, *gemeiner vorsätzlicher Mord*, wenn es, wie im Gmachl, *eine Wahnsinnstat* gewesen sei, im Laska wird auch vermutet, Konrad habe seine Frau gar nicht erschießen wollen, nach längerer Zeit habe er versucht, den Mannlicher-Karabiner zu putzen. . . . Konrad selbst soll ja bis heute zu der Tat nicht die geringste vorwärtsbringende Aussage gemacht haben, angeblich hockt er völlig gebrochen in der Welser Kreisgerichtszelle und beantwortet keine der Hunderte und wahrscheinlich Tausende von Fragen, die an ihn gestellt werden" (And I have believed in this figment of your imagination for twenty years! she is supposed to have shouted several times on the evening before the bloody deed [as they put it at Laska's], possibly, says Fro, that made him, Konrad, shoot his wife. On the other hand, he,

Bernhard circa 1988

Konrad, is supposed to have been tender toward his wife again for the first time in ages just on the evening before he shot her [so they say at the Lanner]. Word has it in the Gmachl that Konrad *took his own sweet time* in planning the bloody deed, in the Stiegler they are still talking today about a *sudden impulse,* no matter whether, as they also say at Lanner's, it was *cold-blooded premeditated murder,* or, as at the Gmachl, *an insane act,* at Laska's they also suspect that Konrad did not want to shoot his wife at all, that he was trying to clean his Mannlicher carbine for the first time after a long while. . . . To this day Konrad, supposedly, has not furthered matters with even the least comment about the deed, he purportedly just sits in jail at Wels, an utterly broken man, without answering any of the hundreds and probably thousands of questions being put to him). Turning on clichés and formulas, the language of this passage calls attention to the circuitous and tentative link between talk and truth. Likewise, the novel's governing metaphor, the lime works, symbolizes the ambiguity of knowing. The reader never learns exactly what the played-out quarry looks like and is never told how the Konrads' house is situated with regard to it; he only knows that they live "at" the derelict lime works, an old stone labyrinth long in the possession of Konrad's family.

All of the reader's knowledge about the lime works and Konrad's doings there comes via the narrator, whose commentary is as labyrinthine as the lime works themselves. Only one point of view, the perspective of a single consciousness, is permitted; all else is rumor, conjecture, and reportage. The novel's carefully framed point of view imposes significant limits on Bernhard's inquiry into the nature of his protagonist, Konrad.

Like *Verstörung, Das Kalkwerk* turns out to be a tale of hypertrophied intellect. On his ruthless journey inward, Konrad discovers only an empty, decaying house and exhausted mine. This symbolic inner citadel of Konrad's self, the lime works, turns out to be incapable of supporting his spiritual life. His wife–the female alter ego who is also his half-sister–would like nothing better than to return to friends and family, but Konrad's stubborn obsession with his work leads him to immure himself and his unlucky wife in a void. This habitation is, because abandoned and derelict, no real place at all. It does not do the work of an ancestral home, for Konrad derives no sense of identity from it. It holds no memories, no family, not even any furniture. Contemptuous of actual places and things, Konrad has retreated into the mere abstraction of the inner man. The victim of this retreat is his murdered wife-sister, the image of his suppressed, more humane self.

Bernhard's most celebrated novel has much in common with *Das Kalkwerk*. Roithamer, the protagonist of *Korrektur* (1975; translated as *Correction*, 1979), is modeled on the philosopher Ludwig Wittgenstein, but he crucially resembles Konrad in his monomaniacal obsession with a single intellectual project. Konrad's study of hearing is transformed into Roithamer's preoccupation with architecture; the lame wife becomes a sister crippled and finally killed by her brother's selfish love; and the isolated lime works recurs as a unique architectural project: a house designed in the form of a cone, located in a wilderness, and intended to be the perfect home for the beloved sister. Like many Bernhard protagonists, Roithamer is a wealthy intellectual who is heir to an ancient Austrian estate. When his inheritance comes through he will dissolve the estate, for, characteristically, he despises both it and his venal family. Completion of the cone project, like Konrad's retreat into the lime works, seemingly represents a utopian alternative to family, home, and Austria. But his self-absorbed genius dwells in a morbid fantasy, symbolized by the taxidermy projects of his noncommunicative friend Höller: though Roithamer does not intentionally kill his sister, he brings about her death by entombing her in his monstrous cone like an ancient Egyptian sister-queen mummified in a pyramid. Roithamer hangs himself in a forest clearing; suicide is the ultimate "correction" of life's failure to live up to intellectual and philosophical perfection.

The narration of *Korrektur* begins shortly after Roithamer's suicide. The nameless narrator, an Austrian mathematician and longtime colleague of Roithamer at Cambridge University, has come to stay in the tiny garret where the philosopher lived and worked. The garret is in the home of the Höller family, perched high over a roaring mountain torrent in Upper Austria. The mathematician immerses himself in Roithamer's papers and tells the story of his friend's life in prose of daunting strength and originality. In the end it is not Roithamer's suicide that "corrects" his failure in life but the compassionate attempt of his biographer, through the medium of narrative art, to understand that life.

With *Korrektur* Bernhard integrated the basic ideas and motifs that he had been experimenting with since his earliest work. In the late 1970s he turned more and more in the direction of autobiography. Beginning with the publication of *Die Ursache: Eine Andeutung* (translated as "An Indication of the Cause," 1985) in 1975, his memoirs began to appear in quick succession. *Die Ursache*, which describes his life from age thirteen to sixteen at boarding school in Salzburg, sets the tone for the rest. Bernhard describes Salzburg as a "Todeskrankheit, in welche ihre Bewohner hineingeboren und hineingezogen werden, und gehen sie nicht in dem entscheidenden Zeitpunkt weg, machen sie direkt oder indirekt früher oder später unter allen diesen entsetzlichen Umständen entweder urplötzlich Selbstmord oder gehen direkt oder indirekt langsam und elendig auf diesem im Grunde durch und durch menschenfeindlichen architektonisch-erzbischöflich-stumpfsinnig-nationalsozialistisch-katholischen Todesboden zugrunde. Die Stadt ist für den, der sie und ihre Bewohner kennt, ein auf der Oberfläche schöner, aber unter dieser Oberfläche tatsächlich fürchterlicher Friedhof der Phantasien und Wünsche" (terminal disease that its inhabitants contract through heredity or contamination, and if they do not escape at the decisive moment, they sooner or later directly or indirectly under all these dreadful circumstances either kill themselves suddenly, or they perish slowly and wretchedly, directly or indirectly, on this at bottom thoroughly and murderously misanthropic architectonic-archdiocesal-feebleminded-National-Socialist-Catholic soil. For anyone who knows the city and its dwellers, Salzburg is superficially beautiful, but beneath the surface it is in fact a loathsome cemetery of dreams and desires). Bernhard notes that the school's authoritarian Nazi control and the postwar Catholic administration's "Schreckensregiment" (reign of terror) were merely two expressions of the same Austrian spirit. *Der Keller: Eine Entziehung* (1976; translated as "The Cellar: An Escape," 1985) recounts his flight from school into an apprenticeship in a grocery located in a cellar in Salzburg's "Scherzhauserfeld" settlement, a postwar housing development inhabited by the poor and the outcast. *Der Atem: Eine Entscheidung* (1978; translated as "Breath: A Decision," 1985) and *Die Kälte: Eine Isolation* (The Cold: An Isolation, 1978; translated as "In the Cold," 1985) recount Bernhard's battle against lung disease and the Austrian public health system. His experiences of dismal clinics, disease, and other patients gave body to the pessimism his grandfather had instilled in him; that he survived at all Bernhard attributes to his contempt for doctors, to willpower, and to total self-reliance. In the end, he believes, it is futility that carries the day; yet his pessimism is paradoxically accompanied by a spirit of revolt, expressed most vividly in his passion for music and writing. The contradiction between what Bernhard claims as his outlook on life and the relentless fervor of his literary creativity informs all his fiction.

In *Ein Kind* (1982; translated as "A Child," 1985) Bernhard jumps back in time to his earliest childhood. Poverty and a crowded home life generated tension, and, though the bond of love between Bernhard and his mother remained strong, pitched battles erupted between them. Bernhard recalls bouts of frenzied verbal abuse: "Da mich die körperliche Züchtigung letztenendes unbeeindruckt gelassen hat, versuchte sie, mich mit den fürchterlichsten Sätzen in die Kniee zu zwingen, sie verletzte jedesmal meine Seele zutiefst, wenn sie *Du hast mir noch gefehlt!* oder *Du bist mein ganzes Unglück, Dich soll der Teufel holen! Du hast mein Leben zerstört! Du bist an allem schuld! Du bist mein Tod! Du bist ein Nichts, ich schäme mich deiner! Du bist ein Nichtsnutz wie dein Vater! Du bist nichts wert! Du Unfriedenstifter! Du Lügner!* sagte" (Because physical punishment in the end left me unimpressed, she tried to bring

me to my knees with the most terrible sentences; she wounded me deeply every time she said things like *You're all I needed!* or *You're the cause of all my unhappiness, to hell with you! You've ruined my life! You're to blame for everything! You're the death of me! You're a nothing, I'm ashamed of you! You're a bum like your father! You're worthless! You troublemaker! You liar!*). Bernhard perhaps inherited from her his affinity for the hailstorm of abuse; in later life he practically raised it to the level of a literary genre. Bernhard was also a chronic bedwetter, and his mother made certain that his shame was a matter of public record: "Der ganze Taubenmarkt und die ganze Schaumburgerstraße wußten, daß ich ein Bettnässer war. Meine Mutter hatte ja jeden Tag diese meine Schreckensfahne gehißt. Mit eingezogenem Kopf kam ich von der Schule nachhause, da flatterte im Wind, was allen anzeigte, was ich war" (Everybody at the Tauben Market and everybody in Schaumburger Street knew I was a bedwetter. My mother hoisted daily the banner of my disgrace. When I would come home from school, shoulders hunched, it would be flapping in the wind, showing everyone what I was). Small wonder that Bernhard's family eventually placed him in a boarding school for maladjusted children.

With his autobiographical project completed, Bernhard turned again to fiction. In *Der Stimmenimitator* (The Voice Mimic, 1978) he abandons his usual expansive prose style for an anecdotal and aphoristic mode he had used only once before, in *Ereignisse* (Events, 1969). Cruel and senseless events are counterbalanced by the plainspoken ease of his language, by sentences so sharply honed and gracefully balanced that entire scenes are suffused with a razor-sharp irony. The miniature "Die Magd" (The Milkmaid) is typical: "Wir haben es vorige Woche erlebt, daß fünf Kühe nacheinander in unseren Schnellzug gelaufen sind, mit welchem wir nach Wien zurückfahren mußten, und völlig zerstückelt wurden. Nachdem die Geleise freigemacht worden waren, von den Zugbegleitern und selbst von dem mit einer Spitzhacke herbeigelaufenen Lokomotivführer, war der Zug nach etwa vierzig Minuten Aufenthalt wieder weiter gefahren. Aus dem Fenster schauend, hatte ich die Magd sehen können, die schreiend gegen einen in der Dämmerung gelegenen Hof gelaufen ist" (A week ago we witnessed five cows running one after another into the express train we had taken back to Vienna, so that they were totally mangled. After the tracks had been cleared by the train crew and even by the engineer, who came running with a pickax, the locomotive was once again underway after a forty-minute delay. Looking out of the window, I was able to see the milkmaid as she ran screaming toward a farmhouse that lay in the twilight).

Like his poor milkmaid, part of Bernhard flees in stunned grief from the sheer cruelty of death. He is a writer divided against himself: fascinated and delighted by the power of art to transform life into poetry but also transfixed by mute terror at the certainty of death. In a world of brutality and certain destruction, Bernhard seeks refuge in denouncing the powers that will annihilate him. His art toils against death even as it assures the reader that there is no hope. Bernhard's fiction usually divides the world between two perspectives: that of the protagonist marked for death and that of a second figure, like the man on the train, who functions as a witness. The act of witnessing–writing–is for Bernhard the perpetual renewal of the self's minor victories in its skirmishes with death.

In the autobiographical novel *Wittgensteins Neffe: Eine Freundschaft* (1982; translated as *Wittgenstein's Nephew: A Friendship*, 1989) Bernhard is once again hospitalized, this time convalescing after cancer surgery in 1967. Paul Wittgenstein, the aging nephew of the Viennese philosopher, is dying in the hospital's mental ward. Bernhard ponders his friendship with Paul Wittgenstein, an intellectual nonconformist from a distinguished Austrian family: "Ein Jahrhundert haben die Wittgenstein Waffen und Maschinen erzeugt, bis sie schließlich und endlich den Ludwig und den Paul erzeugt haben, den berühmten und epochemachenden Philosophen und den, wenigstens in Wien nicht weniger berühmten oder gerade dort noch berühmteren Verrückten, der im Grunde genauso philosophisch war wie sein Onkel Ludwig, wie umgekehrt der philosophische Ludwig so verrückt wie sein Neffe Paul..." (For a whole century the Wittgensteins had produced weapons and machines, until finally they produced Ludwig and Paul, the famous, epoch-making philosopher and the madman who, in Vienna at least, or especially in Vienna, was equally famous and possibly more so, a madman who was basically as philosophical as his uncle Ludwig, the philosophical Ludwig who was basically as mad as his nephew Paul...). The motif of the family renegade is familiar, but this painfully honest "novel" lacks the humorless venom of his earlier works. Though

Bernhard's pessimism remains intact, its bitterness is tempered by irony, compassion, and self-criticism. Bernhard's feelings of guilt over his friend's lonely death are central to the work: "Wir meiden die vom Tod Gezeichneten und auch ich hatte dieser Niedrigkeit nachgegeben. Ich mied in den letzten Monaten seines Lebens meinen Freund ganz bewußt aus dem niedrigen Selbsterhaltungstrieb, was ich mir nicht verzeihe" (We shun those marked by death, and even I surrendered to this shabby attitude. Quite deliberately, out of a base instinct for self-preservation, I shunned my friend in the last months of his life, something for which I cannot forgive myself). But the novel, if this engrossing hodgepodge of observations and anecdotes really is a novel, also has a comic spirit that marks a new emphasis in Bernhard's writing. He indulges his considerable gift for malediction against a host of his favorite outrages: the folly of literary prizes, the opportunism of Austrian artists, the dictatorship of the Burgtheater's underhanded personnel, and the Viennese "Kaffeehausaufsuchkrankheit" (coffeehouse-seeking disease) from which he suffers. When Bernhard and Wittgenstein one day fail to obtain a Swiss newspaper they want to read, Bernhard's narrative voice breaks into a seriocomic aria of rage "gegen dieses rückständige, hinterwäldlerische, gleichzeitig geradezu abstoßend größenwahnsinnige Land" (against this backward, bigoted, backwoods country that simultaneously contrives to uphold its revolting delusions of grandeur).

Rudolf, the self-obsessed musicologist of *Beton* (1982; translated as *Concrete*, 1984), fails to help a Bavarian woman he meets in the dismal vacation "paradise" of Majorca. Locked in futile combat with his work and against his sister, he is traveling to escape his inner failures. In Palma, among the seven-tier concrete tombs which are common in Mediterranean countries, he meets the luckless Anna Härdtl, a young mother whose husband, because of reversals in their small business, has committed suicide while they were on a depressing package tour of the island. Comically absorbed in his delicate nervous system and in his endless procrastinations, Rudolf has little to offer Frau Härdtl. In fact, the irascible recluse is an exploiter of human suffering: her misery helps him pull himself together. When he returns two years later, a sudden urge prompts him to visit the grave of Anna Härdtl's husband. When he arrives he finds Anna's name next to her husband's, along with the word *suicido*.

Der Untergeher (Going Under, 1983) tells the story of the pianist Glenn Gould and two fictional colleagues–a failed concert pianist named Wertheimer and the narrator, who has given up the piano to write a book titled *On Glenn Gould*. After Gould collapses in the midst of his legendary performance of Bach's "Goldberg Variations" and dies of heart failure, the others must come to terms with their lesser gifts. Wertheimer hangs himself, and the narrator escapes into writing, reflection, and travel. Above all, the surviving member of the trio must deal with his failure to aid his friend Wertheimer, whom Gould had dubbed an "Untergeher," a man destined for decline.

In *Holzfällen: Eine Erregung* (Felling Timber: An Excitation, 1984; translated as *Woodcutters*, 1987) Bernhard singles out Austria's cultural elite for special defamation. The nameless narrator, a successful writer visiting old Viennese haunts, settles into a wingback chair at a late-night dinner party. While waiting for the guest of honor, a famous actor, to join the group after his evening performance, the writer mulls over the lives of his former friends, most of whom he has not seen for twenty years. They have fallen prey to vanity, alcohol, ambition, and venal dissipations of every demeaning sort. The host, a composer named Auersberger, has wasted his life in pursuit of the Viennese beau monde; Jeannie, the writer's former lover, has sold herself to the Austrian ministry of culture for the sake of literary prizes and state subventions; and the honored guest is "der Prototypus der durch und durch phantasielosen und also völlig geistlosen Poltermimen" (the prototype of the unimaginative and therefore also totally mindless ham actor) from the Burgtheater. Casting a shadow over the already grim proceedings is the memory of another old friend who had hanged herself and whose funeral had been held earlier in the day. His evening with former friends and colleagues is a confrontation with the past, with himself, and with death. Bernhard applies the satirical edge of his verbal blade to the milieu from which he emerged, and he does not spare himself: his contempt for these people includes frank self-contempt, at least to the extent that he is identical with the narrator. But certain of Bernhard's former friends were ill disposed to take a philosophical perspective on the book. A composer named Gerhard Lampersberg, for whom Bernhard had composed a libretto in the late 1950s, not unreasonably believed himself slandered in the figure of Auersberger. He managed to have sales of the book stopped for a time in Austria and started a scandal that generated commotion in the Austrian and German press for many weeks.

The central figure of *Alte Meister* (1985; translated as *Old Masters*, 1989) is the eighty-two-year-old Reger, the Austrian music critic for the London *Times*. Since the death of his wife thirty-two years earlier, Reger has come every other day to Vienna's Museum of Art History to look at the paintings of the old masters, in particular Tintoretto's "Man with a White Beard." The narrative begins on the day Reger has broken his habit of decades by appearing two days in a row. He has summoned the narrator to join him in front of the Tintoretto painting, where he inveighs, in a long comic passage, against the public toilets of Vienna's cafés. He rages no less satirically against Stifter and Martin Heidegger as spoilers of literature and philosophy, only to reveal that he is related to them by blood. His main obsession–reminiscent of Wertheimer's Glenn Gould complex, Roithamer's compulsion to perfect his cone, or Konrad's rage to complete the ultimate work on the faculty of hearing–is to find the hidden flaw in the paintings he studies, the flaw that will release him from the utopian claims of perfection: "Das Vollkommene droht uns nicht nur ununterbrochen mit unserer Vernichtung, es vernichtet uns auch, alles, das hier unter dem Kennwort *Meisterwerk* an den Wänden hängt, sagte er. . . . Erst wenn wir immer wieder darauf gekommen sind, daß es das Ganze und das Vollkommene nicht gibt, haben wir die Möglichkeit des Weiterlebens. Wir halten das Ganze und das Vollkommene nicht aus" (Perfection not only continually threatens us with our annihilation, it also annihilates us, everything that hangs on the walls here with the appellation *masterpiece*, he said. . . . Only when we repeatedly discover, have discovered, that wholeness and perfection do not exist do we have the possibility of living on. We can't endure wholeness and perfection). The theme of *Alte Meister* is the place of aesthetic perfection in an era of rampant decline. Reger measures great art against the loss of his wife. Since her death, only his visits to the old masters have sustained him, even though he despises them and the museum that contains them. For thirty years he has studied the "Man with a White Beard," which embodies for him all that is false and cynical about high culture. Yet he also understands that art, especially music, continually restores his grip on life. His story ends ironically with a redemptive visit to the detested Burgtheater for a performance of Heinrich von Kleist's comic masterpiece *Der zerbrochene Krug* (The Broken Pitcher, 1811). The narrator's closing remark encapsulates Reger's philosophy of living among the works of the old masters: "Die Vorstellung war entsetzlich" (The performance was horrific). Great art, even when it is flawed, has a redemptive quality.

Auslöschung (Obliteration, 1986) is Bernhard's longest prose work and his final major piece of fiction. It is a great synthesis of his interests and concerns: music, Nazism, family, Catholicism, selfishness, death, and Austria's squandered history. The protagonist is Franz-Josef Murau, an Austrian intellectual who lives a solitary existence in Rome. The pattern is familiar: the son of a wealthy and ancient family, Murau has rejected his parents–the morally depraved generation of Austrian Nazidom–and fled from the ancestral estate, Wolfsegg, into a self-imposed exile. His vast monologue, which is reported in a peculiarly useful grammatical feature of German, the subjunctive of indirect discourse, begins with a telegram that informs him of an automobile accident in which his parents and elder brother have been killed. He is now the unwilling heir to an estate and an existence he has despised all his life. There is no escape from his identity as an Austrian or from the historical burdens which encumber that identity. The novel consists of Murau's labyrinthine ruminations on his family and his past: "Mein Bericht ist nichts anderes als meine Auslöschung.... Wir tragen alle einen Wolfsegg mit uns herum und haben den Willen, es auszulöschen zu unserer Errettung, es, indem wir es aufschreiben wollen, vernichten wollen, auslöschen" (My report is nothing other than my obliteration.... We all carry a Wolfsegg around with us and have the aim of obliterating it for the sake of our salvation, to obliterate it by wanting to write about it, by wanting to annihilate it). Murau's aim of obliterating his past by writing about it points to the underlying motive for Bernhard's own autobiography and fiction: in naming the horror around and within him, in giving to it the objective form of a written text, Bernhard frees himself from the claims of the ghosts that haunt him, even if the liberation lasts only momentarily. "Man muß das Ungeheuerliche, und jeder hat in seinem Leben so ein Ungeheuerliches, angehen und verwirklichen und vollenden," affirms the narrator of *Korrektur*, "oder sich von diesem Ungeheuerlichen vernichten las-

sen, bevor man noch in ein solches Ungeheuerliches hineingegangen ist" (You have to approach and realize and complete the monstrousness–everyone has some kind of monstrousness in his life–or else be destroyed by this monstrousness even before you have entered into it). Like Roithamer, Murau also wishes to "correct" history, insofar as such a thing is possible. Each writes his personal reckoning with family and self, and each hurries toward death. But in Murau's case the ultimate correction is not suicide; the reader does not learn what causes his untimely death. Decisive instead is the quixotic gesture of "correction" expressed in his will: Murau turns over the family estate to the Jewish community of Vienna.

Although Bernhard despised literary awards, he was the recipient of many: the Julius Campe Prize in 1964; the Bremen Prize in 1965; the Presentation of the Culture Circle of the Federated League of German Industry in 1967; the Austrian State Prize for Literature and the Anton Wildgans Prize of Austrian Industry in 1968; the Georg Büchner Prize in 1970; the Franz Theodor Csokor Prize, the Adolf Grimme Prize, and the Grillparzer Prize in 1972; the Hannover Dramatist's Prize and the Prix Séguier in 1974; the Literature Prize of the Austrian Chamber of Commerce in 1976; and the Premio Modello in 1983.

When Bernhard succumbed to years of heart and lung disease in 1989 at his home in Gmunden, three days after his fifty-eighth birthday, his death went unannounced–in accordance with his wishes–until after the funeral. When the terms of his will became known, Austria's most scurrilous writer precipitated the last of the many scandals that swirled around him during his career. The will entailed that none of his works may be published in Austria and that none of his stage plays may be performed there for seventy years, the duration of his copyright. The interdict precipitated a run on his works in Austrian bookstores. Bernhard's account of his young manhood, *In der Höhe: Rettungsversuch, Unsinn* (Up High: Rescue Attempt, Nonsense, 1989), which had been completed in 1959, was published in time to escape the ban.

Interviews:

"Thomas Bernhard," in Andre Müller, *Entblößungen* (Munich: Goldmann, 1979), pp. 59-102;

"Ich könnte auf dem Papier jemand umbringen," *Der Spiegel*, 26 (23 June 1980): 172-182;

"Aveux et paradoxes de Thomas Bernhard," *Le Monde*, 7 January 1983, p. 15;

"Ich behaupte nicht, mit der Welt gehe es schlechter: Aus einem Gespräch mit Thomas Bernhard," *Frankfurter Allgemeine Zeitung*, 24 February 1983, p. 23;

"Von einer Katastrophe in die Andere," *Süddeutsche Zeitung*, 17 / 18 January 1987, pp. 169-170;

Kurt Hofmann, *Aus Gesprächen mit Thomas Bernhard* (Vienna: Löcker, 1988).

Bibliographies:

Bernhard Sorg and Michael Töteberg, "Thomas Bernhard," in *Kritisches Lexikon zur deutschsprachigen Gegenwartsliteratur*, edited by Heinz Ludwig Arnold (Munich: Edition text + kritik, 1978), n. pag.;

Jens Dittmar, *Thomas Bernhard Werkgeschichte* (Frankfurt am Main: Suhrkamp, 1981).

References:

Mark Anderson, "Notes on Thomas Bernhard," *Raritan*, 7 (1987): 81-96;

Arnold Barthofer, "Vorliebe für die Kömodie: Todesangst; Anmerkungen zum Kömodienbegriff bei Thomas Bernhard," *Vierteljahresschrift des Adalbert-Stifter-Instituts* (1982): 77-100;

Günter Blöcker, "Wie Existenznot durch Sprachnot glaubwürdig wird," *Merkur*, 24 (1970): 1181-1187;

Alexander von Bormann, ed., *Sehnsuchtsangst: Zur österreichischen Literatur der Gegenwart* (Amsterdam: Rodopi, 1987);

Anneliese Botond, ed., *Über Thomas Bernhard* (Frankfurt am Main: Suhrkamp, 1970);

Gudrun Brokoph-Mauch, "Thomas Bernhard," in *Major Figures of Contemporary Austrian Literature*, edited by Donald G. Daviau (Bern: Lang, 1987), pp. 89-115;

Urs Bugmann, *Bewältigungsversuch: Thomas Bernhards autobiographische Schriften* (Bern & Las Vegas: Lang, 1981);

D. A. Craig, "The Novels of Thomas Bernhard: A Report," *German Life and Letters*, 25 (July 1972): 343-353;

Carl Dahlhaus, "Lauter Untergeher: Der Anti-Psycholog Thomas Bernhard," *Die Zeit*, 13 January 1984, p. 36;

Peter Demetz, "Thomas Bernhard: The Dark Side of Life," in his *After the Fires: Recent Writing in the Germanies, Switzerland, and Austria* (New York: Harcourt Brace Jovanovich, 1986), pp. 199-212;

A. P. Dierick, "Thomas Bernhard's Austrian Neurosis: Symbol or Expedient?," *Modern Austrian Literature*, 12, no. 1 (1979): 73-93;

Stephen Dowden, *Understanding Thomas Bernhard* (Columbia, S.C.: University of South Carolina Press, forthcoming);

Michael C. Eben, "Thomas Bernhard's *Frost*: Early Indications of an Austrian Demise," *Neophilologus*, 69 (October 1985): 590-603;

Gerald Fetz, "Thomas Bernhard and the 'Modern Novel,'" in *The Modern German Novel*, edited by Keith Bullivant (Leamington Spa, U.K.: Berg, 1987);

Bernd Fischer, *"Gehen" von Thomas Bernhard: Eine Studie zum Problem der Moderne* (Bonn: Bouvier, 1985);

Thomas Fraund, *Bewegung-Korrektur-Utopie: Studien zum Verhältnis von Melancholie und Ästhetik im Erzählwerk Thomas Bernhards* (Frankfurt am Main: Lang, 1986);

Herbert Gamper, *Thomas Bernhard* (Munich: Deutscher Taschenbuch Verlag, 1977);

Robert Godwin-Jones, "The Terrible Idyll: Thomas Bernhard's *Das Kalkwerk*," *Germanic Notes*, 13, no. 1 (1982): 8-10;

Andreas Gössling, *Thomas Bernhards frühe Prosakunst* (Berlin: De Gruyter, 1987);

Gerhard vom Hofe and Peter Pfaff, *Das Elend des Polyphem: Zum Thema der Subjecktivität bei Thomas Bernhard, Peter Handke, Wolfgang Koeppen, und Botho Strauss* (Königstein: Athenäum, 1980);

Ferdinand van Ingen, "Denk-Übungen: Zum Prosawerk Thomas Bernhards," in *Studien zur österreichischen Erzählliteratur der Gegenwart*, edited by Herbert Zeman (Amsterdam: Rodopi, 1982), pp. 37-86;

Manfred Jurgensen, ed., *Bernhard: Annäherungen* (Bern & Munich: Francke, 1981);

Margarete Kohlenbach, *Das Ende der Vollkommenheit: Zum Verständnis von Thomas Bernhards "Korrektur"* (Tübingen: Narr, 1986);

Josef König, *"Nichts als ein Totenmaskenball": Studien zum Verständnis der ästhetischen Intentionen im Werk Thomas Bernhards* (Frankfurt am Main: Lang, 1983);

Wolfgang Kralicek, "Sein Wille geschehe: Thomas Bernhards letzter Text sorgt posthum für Erregung," *Wochenpresse* (Vienna), 24 February 1989, pp. 42-43;

Martin Lüdke, "Ein 'Ich' in der Bewegung: stillgestellt—Wegmarken der Bernhardschen

Autobiographie," *Merkur*, 35 (1981): 1175-1183;

Caroline Markolin, *Die Großväter sind die Lehrer: Johannes Freumbichler und sein Enkel Thomas Bernhard* (Salzburg: Müller, 1988);

David McLintock, "Tense and Narrative Perspective in Two Works by Thomas Bernhard," *Oxford German Studies*, 11 (1980): 1-26;

Nicholas J. Meyerhofer, *Thomas Bernhard* (Berlin: Colloquium, 1985);

Modern Austrian Literature, special Bernhard issue, 21, no. 314 (1988);

Michael P. Olsen, "Misogynist Exposed? The Sister Figure in Thomas Bernhard's *Beton* and *Der Untergeher*," *New German Review*, 3 (1980): 30-40;

Claus Peymann, "Die Unvernünftigen sterben nicht aus," *Theater heute*, 8 (1979): 4-10;

Alfred Pittertschatscher, ed., *Literarisches Kolloquium Linz '84 Thomas Bernhard* (Linz: Land Oberösterreich, 1985);

Karlheinz Rossbacher, "Thomas Bernhard: *Das Kalkwerk*," in *Deutsche Romane des 20. Jahrhunderts*, edited by Paul Michael Lützeler (Königstein: Athenäum, 1983);

Wendelin Schmidt-Dengler and Martin Huber, eds., *Statt Bernhard: Über Misanthropie im Werk Thomas Bernhards* (Vienna: Edition S, 1987);

Walter Schönau, "Thomas Bernhards *Ereignisse* oder Die Wiederkehr des Verdrängten: Eine psychoanalytische Interpretation," *Wissen und Erfahrung: Ein Festschrift für Hermann Meyer* (Tübingen: Niemeyer, 1976), pp. 829-844;

W. G. Sebald, *Die Beschreibung des Unglücks: Zur österreichischen Literatur von Stifter bis Handke* (Salzburg: Residenz, 1985);

Bernd Seydel, *Die Vernunft der Winterkälte: Gleichgültigkeit als Equilibrismus im Werk Thomas Bernhards* (Würzburg: Königshausen Neumann, 1986);

Bernhard Sorg, *Thomas Bernhard* (Munich: Beck, 1977);

text + kritik, special Bernhard issue, 43 (1974);

Kathleen Thorpe, "The Autobiographical Works of Thomas Bernhard," *Acta Germanica*, 13 (1980): 189-200;

John Updike, "Ungreat Lives," *New Yorker* (4 February 1985): 97-101;

Hans Wolfschütz, "Thomas Bernhard: The Mask of Death," in *Modern Austrian Writing*, edited by A. Best and H. Wolfschütz (Totowa, N.J.: Barnes & Noble, 1980), pp. 214-235.

Papers:
The terms of Thomas Bernhard's will prohibit the use or publication of his papers. He went so far as to prohibit the republication, recitation, or performance in Austria of his *published* works for the duration of his copyright (seventy years).

Imma von Bodmershof
(10 August 1895-26 August 1982)

Jorun B. Johns
California State University, San Bernardino

BOOKS: *Der zweite Sommer: Roman* (Berlin: Fischer, 1937);

Die Stadt in Flandern (Berlin: Fischer, 1939); revised as *Das verlorene Meer* (Vienna: Herold, 1952);

Die Rosse des Urban Roithner (Innsbruck: Österreichische Verlagsanstalt, 1950);

Solange es Tag ist (Innsbruck: Österreichische Verlagsanstalt, 1953)—comprises "Solange es Tag ist," "Milch auf Gestein," "Der Tanz," "Theres Piernagl";

Sieben Handvoll Salz (Gütersloh: Bertelsmann, 1958);

Unter acht Winden, edited by Hajo Jappe (Graz & Vienna: Stiasny, 1962);

Haiku (Munich: Langen-Müller, 1962);

Die Bartabnahme (Vienna: Österreichische Verlagsanstalt, 1966);

Sonnenuhr: Haiku (Salzburg: Stifterbibliothek, 1970);

Mohn und Granit vom Waldviertel (St. Pölten: Niederösterreichisches Pressehaus, 1976);

Im fremden Garten: 99 Haiku (Zurich: Arche, 1980);

Gesammelte Werke in Einzelausgaben, 4 volumes (Karlsruhe: Von Loeper/St. Pölten: Niederösterreichisches Pressehaus, 1982-1986).

OTHER: *Die Jahreszeiten: Fünfundzwanzig Meisterwerke alter Buchmalerei,* contributions by Bodmershof (Berlin: Krüger, 1942);

Haiku, contributions by Bodmershof (Vienna: Holzhausen, 1975).

PERIODICAL PUBLICATIONS: "Cäsar Trübswasser: Das erste Kapitel eines unvollendeten Romans," *Wort in der Zeit,* 2, no. 6 (1956): 27-33;

"Haiku und Tanka," *Wort in der Zeit,* 5, no. 4 (1959): 26-27;

"Christian von Ehrenfels: Eine biographische Skizze," *Wort in der Zeit,* 5, no. 8 (1959): 21-24;

"Sonnenblumen," *Die Furche* (Vienna), 21 August 1965, literature section, pp. 1-2.

Imma von Bodmershof, whose work represents a continuation of the Austrian narrative tradition in the manner of the nineteenth-century writer Adalbert Stifter, achieved belated recognition after World War II. Her fiction owes much of its appeal to her close observation of nature and to her psychological insights. Its metaphysical content is expressed in images and symbols from nature, depicted in vivid language that often takes on poetic rhythms and could be considered poetry in prose. She became a member of the P.E.N. Club in 1950 and received her first major official distinction with the awarding of the Great Austrian State Prize for Literature in 1958. Further honors include the Culture Prize of Lower Austria in 1965 and the Prize of the City of Vienna and the Cross of Honor for Art and Science (First Class) in 1969.

Imma von Ehrenfels was born on 10 August 1895 in Graz, but she always felt that her real home was the Waldviertel, the wooded hills and mountains north of Melk in Lower Austria; she spent most of her childhood there on her father's estate at Schloß Lichtenau. She studied art history and philosophy at the Universities of Prague and Munich but never received a degree. Of the influences on her development she felt that her father, the philosopher and psychologist Christian von Ehrenfels, whose essay "Über Gestaltqualitäten" (Concerning Gestalt Qualities, 1890) laid the foundation for Gestalt psychology, was the most important, followed by the philologist and Hölderlin scholar Norbert von Hellingrath. She became engaged to the latter in 1913, but he was killed in World War I in 1916. Through her father and her fiancé she met many scholars, scientists, and writers, including Rainer Maria Rilke and the poets of the Stefan George circle. After her marriage in 1924 to the political scientist Wilhelm von Bodmershof she divided her time between Vienna and Schloß

Imma von Bodmershof in 1941 (pencil sketch by Robert Fuchs; courtesy of the Bildarchiv der Österreichischen Nationalbibliothek)

Rastbach in the Waldviertel, where she died on 26 August 1982.

Bodmershof sets her works in a variety of locations, including foreign countries familiar to her from her travels, but she is at her best in describing Austrian provincials from peasants to aristocrats. She rarely sets the action in a city, and when she does so it is only to establish contrast with the countryside. The wide diversity of settings in her works has caused some critics to overlook the underlying unity of their themes and ideas. Almost all of Bodmershof's main characters are on a quest, a search for their inner selves. They are placed between two worlds, the real and the transcendental, which they try to reconcile; the force of chaos must be overcome by a will to create order. This idea derives from her father's theory in his *Kosmogonie* (1916) that the world originated from the interaction of the principles of chaotic disorder and psychoid unity of gestalt. Bodmershof illustrates this concept in her first novel, *Der zweite Sommer* (The Second Summer, 1937), through the image of steam, which moves the pistons of an engine only when it is confined. The destructive powers that confront Bodmershof's characters take on differing shapes, but her protagonists are always called upon to fight against chaos and follow inner laws that bring them closer to an understanding of their existence. Some characters follow their inner law blindly, without rational understanding; others, especially girls on the threshold of womanhood, arrive at a point of self-realization intuitively; still others do so through cognitive understanding.

The consequences of disturbing a preexisting order forms the theme of *Der zweite Sommer*, which describes the conflict between the conservative values of the young aristocrat Karin, who personally manages her estate in the Waldviertel, and her architect husband Johannes's urge for innovation. Johannes soon realizes that creative freedom in architecture can only be attained by following certain laws; similarly, personal freedom also has limitations that must be observed. He achieves the insight that one must carefully determine whether preserving the old does not outweigh the value of the new. He writes to Karin hoping that their second summer will provide another chance for their marriage. The symbolism of the novel points to the possibility of reconciliation: the pivotal events take place on St. John's Eve (23 June) connoting a sense of purification and regeneration.

The difficulty of self-realization is the theme of Bodmershof's most poetic and symbolic novel, *Die Stadt in Flandern* (The City in Flanders, 1939). A German historian, Cornelius, who has reached an impasse in his life, comes to work in the archives of Bruges, to which he has felt drawn since his childhood. As he studies the history of the city—its beginnings, its rise to become one of the most important ports in northern Europe, and its decline because of the silting of its canals—he feels that the real secret of the past remains hidden from him. A wound inflicted by a young girl results in blood poisoning; as Cornelius lies in his room he realizes that he is the city and that his veins are like the choked canals. He summons all his strength and ascends the belfry which dates from the time when the water flowed freely in the canals. In the pale light of dawn he has the feeling that invisible waters fill the depths beneath him and that the return of the sea is possible. This event is the beginning of his recovery. He can now approach the second half of his life with a new understanding of the relationship between essence and appearance. He had previously looked at a row of houses reflected in the water and had been perplexed because the reflection seemed more vivid and, in its gentle movement, more alive than the houses above it. But the girl had intuitively grasped the meaning and said: "Ja, beides zusammen nur ist das Ganze" (Yes, only both together make up the whole).

The novel *Die Rosse des Urban Roithner* (The Horses of Urban Roithner) was Bodmershof's greatest popular success; while in production the book was destroyed twice by fires and air raids in 1943 and was not printed and distributed until 1950. Urban Roithner is a farmhand who conceives the ambition of becoming a horse farmer after he sees a pair of extraordinary black steeds which seem to pull their load as if it were weightless. He and his wife build up a run-down farm. His passion for horses involves him in some profitable but shady dealings. In spite of his rising fortunes, he has a feeling of futility. He wants to be able to live contentedly like those around him but is constantly driven by his obsession with the black horses. One day after pursuing them in a storm he returns home to find his wife dead in childbirth. He leaves the house and is never seen again. Some say that Roithner and the horses fell into a ravine, but a turf digger reports seeing his wagon disappear into the high forest just as the morning star was rising over the horizon. The star, the forest, and the black horses assume symbolic significance in connection with Urban's quest. Urban is a Faust figure who feels compelled to strive toward an indefinable goal; when he believes that he has reached his aim he realizes that it does not correspond to the ideal he had envisioned; he continues his search, even though he senses that he will have to make a sacrifice to attain it. His elusive goal is symbolized by the black horses, which are at the same time magnificent and terrible. Although the ending is left ambiguous, positive symbols predominate; thus it is impossible to associate Roithner's disappearance with the forces of evil, even though his quest, like that of Faust, of necessity involved him in a struggle with chaos.

A quest for one's inner self is described in the novel *Sieben Handvoll Salz* (Seven Handfuls of Salt, 1958). Roberto, a young German veteran, inherits property at the foot of Mt. Aetna in Sicily. He has to overcome physical difficulties, psychological obstacles, and make a spiritual commitment before he can take possession of his inheritance. He is told that a person must eat seven handfuls of salt before he can feel integrated into Sicilian society, and by the end of the novel he is well on the way to this goal. He comes to understand the symbolic meaning of an ancient stone depicting the cult of Mithras, showing the sacrifice of an ox flanked by two men carrying torches; one man holds his torch high and the other points his torch downward. He realizes that the sacrifice demanded is the victory over oneself. The volcano, which both physically and symbolically overshadows the action of the novel, represents fire that can be put into the hand of a person as a torch to be held upward or downward; the decision about the direction has to be made by each individual. Roberto receives spiritual guidance from the beautiful artist Giliola, one of Bodmershof's intuitive women, whose ceramic pieces seem to be an illustration of Ehrenfels's theory of chaos being shaped by will.

In *Die Bartabnahme* (Taking Off the Beard, 1966) a Spanish freedom fighter in exile reconsiders his political theories and atheistic philosophy. While an old comrade from the civil war shaves off his beard, the protagonist reminisces about his son, who became a priest and died for his convictions. He wonders if he has been blinded by his political and religious bias; had he seen only one of the two sides that make up a man?

In the volumes *Haiku* (1962) and *Sonnenuhr* (Sundial, 1970) Bodmershof adapts the strict Japanese form of lyric poetry of seventeen or twenty-one syllables. The poems, like the novels, take their point of departure from images of nature and culminate in the expression of a transcendental feeling or idea.

Bodmershof's last work of fiction, *Mohn und Granit vom Waldviertel* (Poppies and Granite of the Waldviertel, 1976), continues the same view of nature as a union of appearance and essence resulting in a harmonious ordered universe. The book describes the region of Austria with which she felt the greatest kinship.

References:

Ingrid Aichinger, "Beides zusammen nur ist das Ganze: Das Werk der österreichischen Dichterin Imma Bodmershof," *Österreich in Geschichte und Literatur*, 19, no. 7 (1966): 358-379;

Aichinger, "Der Zwang zur Entscheidung vor dem Chaos: Untersuchungen zu Imma Bodmershofs Roman *Sieben Handvoll Salz*," *Modern Austrian Literature*, 12, no. 3/4 (1979): 97-111;

Helmut A. Fiechtner, "Imma Bodmershof," *Wort in der Zeit*, 3, no. 6 (1957): 1-5;

Norbert Langer, "Imma v. Bodmershof," in his *Dichter aus Österreich: Erste Folge* (Vienna & Munich: Österreichischer Bundesverlag, 1963), pp. 11-15.

Hermann Broch

(1 November 1886-30 May 1951)

Paul Michael Lützeler
Washington University
and
John Carson Pettey
University of Nevada, Reno

BOOKS: *Die Schlafwandler: Eine Romantrilogie*, 3 volumes (Munich & Zurich: Rhein, 1931-1932); translated by Willa and Edwin Muir as *The Sleepwalkers: A Trilogy* (New York: Little, Brown, 1932; London: Secker, 1932);

Die Unbekannte Größe: Roman (Berlin: Fischer, 1933); translated by Willa and Edwin Muir as *The Unknown Quantity* (New York: Viking Press, 1935; London: Collins, 1935);

James Joyce und die Gegenwart: Rede zu Joyces 50. Geburtstag (Vienna, Leipzig & Zurich: Reichner, 1936); translated by Maria and Eugène Jolas as "James Joyce and the Present Age," in *A James Joyce Yearbook* (Paris: Transition Press, 1949), pp. 68-108;

The City of Man: A Declaration on World Democracy, by Broch, Herbert Agar, and others (New York: Viking Press, 1940);

Der Tod des Vergil: Roman (New York: Pantheon, 1945); translated by Jean Starr Untermeyer as *The Death of Virgil* (New York: Pantheon, 1945; London: Routledge, 1946);

Die Schuldlosen: Roman in elf Erzählungen (Munich: Weismann, 1950); translated by Ralph Manheim as *The Guiltless* (Boston & Toronto: Little, Brown, 1974);

Gesammelte Werke, 10 volumes (Zurich: Rhein, 1952-1961)—includes volume 1, *Gedichte: Mit 9 Bildern und 2 Handschriftproben des Autors*, edited by Erich Kahler (1953); volume 2, *Die Schlafwandler. Romantrilogie* (1952); volume 3, *Der Tod des Vergil. Epische Dichtung* (1952); volume 4, *Der Versucher: Roman*, edited by Felix Stössinger (1953); republished as *Demeter* (Frankfurt am Main: Suhrkamp, 1967); volume 6, *Dichten und Erkennen: Essays*, edited by Hannah Arendt (1955); volume 7, *Erkennen und Handeln: Essays*, edited by Arendt (1955); volume 8, *Briefe: Von 1929 bis 1951*, edited by Robert Pick (1957); volume 9, *Massenpsychologie: Schriften aus dem*

Nachlaß, edited by Wolfgang Rothe (1959); volume 10, *Die unbekannte Größe und frühe Schriften*, edited by Ernst Schönwiese, and *Mit den Briefen an Willa Muir*, edited by Eric William Herd (1961);

Nur das Herz ist das Wirkliche, edited by Schönwiese (Graz: Stiasny, 1959);

Die Entsühnung: Schauspiel, in der Hörspielfassung, edited by Schönwiese (Zurich: Rhein, 1961);

Die Heimkehr: Prosa und Lyrik. Auswahl aus dem dichterischen Werk ergänzt durch den Vortrag Geist und Zeitgeist, edited by Harald Binde (Frankfurt am Main & Hamburg: Fischer, 1962);

Hermann Broch der Dichter: Eine Auswahl aus dem dichterischen Werk, edited by Binde (Zurich: Rhein, 1964);

Hermann Broch der Denker: Eine Auswahl aus dem essayistischen Werk und aus Briefen, edited by Binde (Zurich: Rhein, 1966);

Short Stories, edited by Herd (London: Oxford University Press, 1966);

Die Idee ist ewig: Essays und Briefe, edited by Binde (Munich: Deutscher Taschenbuch Verlag, 1968);

Zur Universitätsreform, edited by Götz Wienold (Frankfurt am Main: Suhrkamp, 1969);

Bergroman: Die drei Originalfassungen, edited by Frank Kress and Hans Albert Maier, 4 volumes (Frankfurt am Main: Suhrkamp, 1969);

Gedanken zur Politik, edited by Dieter Hildebrandt (Frankfurt am Main: Suhrkamp, 1970);

Barbara und andere Novellen: Eine Auswahl aus dem dichterischen Werk, edited by Paul Michael Lützeler (Frankfurt am Main: Suhrkamp, 1973)—comprises "Eine methodologische Novelle," "Ophelia," "Leutnant Jaretzki," "Hanna Wendling," "Eine leichte Enttäuschung," "Vorüberziehende Wolke," "Ein Abend Angst," "Die Heimkehr," "Der Meeresspiegel," "Esperance," "Barbara," "Die Heim-

Hermann Broch (Bildarchiv der Österreichischen Nationalbibliothek)

kehr des Vergil," "Die vier Reden des Stu-
dienrats Zacharias," "Die Erzählung der
Magd Zerline";

*Völkerbund-Resolution: Das vollständige politische
Pamphlet von 1937 mit Kommentar, Entwurf
und Korrespondenz,* edited by Lützeler (Salzburg: Müller, 1973);

Kommentierte Werkausgabe, edited by Lützeler, 17
volumes (Frankfurt am Main: Suhrkamp,
1974-1981)—includes volume 1, *Die Schlafwandler: Eine Romantrilogie* (1978); volume 2,
Die Unbekannte Größe: Roman (1977); volume
3, *Die Verzauberung* (1976); translated by
H. F. Broch de Rothermann as *The Spell*
(New York: Farrar, Straus & Giroux, 1987);
volume 4, *Der Tod des Vergil: Roman* (1976);
volume 5, *Die Schuldlosen: Roman in elf Erzählungen* (1974); volume 6, *Novellen; Prosa;
Fragmente* (1980); volume 7, *Dramen* (1979),

including *Die Entsühnung,* translated by
George E. Wellwarth and Broch de Rothermann as *The Atonement,* in *German Drama between the Wars,* edited by Wellwarth (New
York: Dutton, 1972); volume 8, *Gedichte*
(1980); volume 9, part 1, *Schriften zur Literatur: Kritik* (1975); "Hugo von Hofmannsthal
und seine Zeit," translated by Michael P.
Steinberg as *Hugo von Hofmannsthal and His
Time: The European Imagination, 1860-1920*
(Chicago & London: University of Chicago
Press, 1984); volume 9, part 2, *Schriften zur Literatur: Theorie* (1975); volume 10, part 1, *Philosophische Schriften: Kritik* (1977); volume 10,
part 2, *Philosophische Schriften: Theorie*
(1977); volume 11, *Politische Schriften* (1979);
volume 12, *Massenwahntheorie. Beiträge zu
Einer Psychologie der Politik* (1979); volume
13, part 1, *Briefe 1913-1938* (1981); volume

Broch's parents, Josef and Johanna Schnabel Broch (Yale Collection of German Literature, Beinecke Library)

13, part 2, *Briefe 1938-1945* (1981); volume 13, part 3, *Briefe 1945-1951* (1981).

OTHER: "Logik einer zerfallenden Welt," in *Wiedergeburt der Liebe: Die unsichtbare Revolution*, edited by Frank Thiess (Berlin: Zsolnay, 1931), pp. 361-380;

"Gedanken zum Problem der Erkenntnis in der Musik," in *Almanach: "Das 48. Jahr"* (Berlin: Fischer, 1934), pp. 53-66;

"Eh ich erwacht," "Über die Felswand," "Helle Sommernacht," "Sommerwiese," "Schon lich-tet der Herbst den Wald," "Die Waldlicht-ung," "Später Herbst," "Nachtgewitter," "Lago Maggiore," "Das Nimmergewesene," in *Patmos: Zwölf Lyriker*, edited by Ernst Schönwiese (Vienna: Johannespresse, 1935), pp. 57-67;

"Mythos und Altersstil," in Rachel Bespaloff, *On the Iliad*, translated by Mary McCarthy (New York: Pantheon, 1947), pp. 9-33;

"Vom Altern," in *Frank Thiess: Werk und Dichter. 32 Beiträge zur Problematik unserer Zeit*, edited by Rolf Italiaander (Hamburg: Krüger, 1950), p. 9.

PERIODICAL PUBLICATIONS: "Philistrosität, Realismus, Idealismus der Kunst," *Der Brenner*, 3 (1 February 1913): 399-415;

"Antwort auf eine Rundfrage über Karl Kraus," *Der Brenner*, 3 (15 June 1913): 849-859;

"Mathematisches Mysterium," *Der Brenner*, 4 (1 November 1913): 136;

"Ethik: Unter Hinweis auf H. St. Chamberlains Buch *Immanuel Kant*," *Der Brenner*, 4 (1 May 1914): 684-690;

"Otto Kaus, Dostojewski: Zur Kritik einer Persönlichkeit. Ein Versuch," *Die Aktion*, 6 (1916): 578-579;

"Zolas Vorurteil," *Summa*, 1, no. 1 (1917): 155-158;

"Morgenstern," *Summa*, 1, no. 2 (1917): 150-154;

"Zum Begriff der Geisteswissenschaften," *Summa*, 1, no. 3 (1917): 199-209;

"Eine methodologische Novelle," *Summa*, 2, no. 3 (1918): 151-159;

"Heinrich von Stein: Gesammelte Dichtungen," *Summa*, 2, no. 3 (1918): 166-169;

"Konstruktion der historischen Wirklichkeit," *Summa*, 2, no. 4 (1918): i-xvi;

"Die Straße (Offener Brief an Franz Blei)," *Die Rettung*, 1 (20 December 1918): 25-26;

"Konstitutionelle Diktatur als demokratisches Rätesystem," *Der Friede*, 3 (11 April 1919): 269-273;

"Wasserkräfte und Abfallenergien im Wiener Überlandnetz," *Der Neue Tag* (Vienna), 31 August 1919, p. 11;

"Der Theaterkritiker Polgar," *Die Neue Rundschau*, 31 (May 1920): 655-656;

"Der Kunstkritiker (Dem Theaterkritiker A. P.)," *Die Rettung*, 2, no. 6 (1920): 78-80;

"Der Schriftsteller Franz Blei (zum fünfzigsten Geburtstag)," *Prager Presse*, 20 April 1921;

"Die erkenntnistheoretische Bedeutung des Begriffes 'Revolution' und die Wiederbelebung der Hegelschen Dialektik: Zu den Büchern Arthur Lieberts," *Prager Presse*, 30 July 1922, "Dichtung und Welt," supplement, pp. iii-iv;

"Max Adler: Marx als Denker, Engels als Denker," *Kantstudien*, 27, no. 1/2 (1922): 184-186;

"Albert Spaier: La pensée et la quantité," *Annalen der Philosophie*, 7 (1928): 112;

"Leben ohne platonische Idee," *Die literarische Welt*, 8 (5 August 1932): 1-4;

"Verwandlung, nach Edwin Muir: 'The Threefold Place,'" *Die literarische Welt*, 8 (2 September 1932): 5;

"Eine leichte Enttäuschung," *Die Neue Rundschau*, 44 (April 1933): 502-517;

"Vorüberziehende Wolke," *Frankfurter Zeitung*, 21 April 1933, p. 9;

"Das Böse im Wertsystem der Kunst," *Die Neue Rundschau*, 44 (August 1933): 157-191;

"Ein Abend Angst," *Berliner Börsen-Courier*, 6 August 1933, second supplement, pp. 9-10;

"Neue religiöse Dichtung?," *Berliner Börsen-Courier*, 3 October 1933, p. 7;

"Die Heimkehr," *Die Neue Rundschau*, 44 (December 1933): 765-795;

"Zwei Bücher von Franz Kafka," *Die Welt im Wort*, 21 December 1933, supplement, p. 2;

"Der Meeresspiegel," *Die Welt im Wort*, 28 December 1933, pp. 3-4;

"Erneuerung des Theaters?" *Wiener Zeitung*, 11 November 1934, p. 3;

"Allein, nach James Joyce 'Alone,'" *das silberboot*, 1 (October 1935): 31;

"Morgen am Fenster, nach T. S. Eliot 'Morning at the Window,'" *das silberboot*, 2 (June 1936): 105;

"Erwägungen zum Problem des Kulturtodes," *das silberboot*, 1 (December 1936): 251-256;

"Alfred Polgar: Handbuch des Kritikers," *Mass und Wert*, 5 (May/June 1938): 817-818;

"Ethische Pflicht," *Saturday Review of Literature*, 22 (19 October 1940): 8;

"Berthold Viertel: Fürchte dich nicht," *Aufbau* (New York), 7 (30 January 1942): 11; (6 February 1942): 25;

"Letzter Ausbruch eines Größenwahnes: Hitlers Abschiedsrede," *Saturday Review*, 27 (21 October 1944): 5-8;

"Robert Pick: The Terhoven File," *Aufbau* (New York), 10 (27 October 1944): 9;

"Hanns Sachs: Freud, Master and Friend," *Aufbau* (New York), 11 (5 January 1945): 273-274;

"Rede über Viertel," *Plan*, 2, no. 5 (1947): 297-301;

"Paul Reiwald: Vom Geist der Massen," *American Journal of International Law*, 41 (January 1947): 358-359;

"Friedrich Torberg: Hier bin ich, mein Vater," *Aufbau* (New York), 14 (2 July 1948): 11-12;

"Erklärung zu Frank Thiess," *Aufbau* (New York), 14 (15 October 1948): 9;

"Werner Richter: Frankreich. Von Gambetta zu Clemenceau," *Schweizer Rundschau*, 48 (March 1949): 1031-1033;

"Elisabeth Langgässer: Das unauslöschliche Siegel," *Literarische Revue*, 4 (1949): 56-59;

Broch's birthplace: 37 Franz-Josefs-Kai, Vienna (Bildarchiv der Österreichischen Nationalbibliothek)

"Geschichte als moralische Anthropologie: Erich Kahlers 'Scienza Nuova,' " *Hamburger Akademische Rundschau*, 3, no. 6 (1949): 406-416;

"Trotzdem: Humane Politik. Verwirklichung einer Utopie," *Die Neue Rundschau*, 61, no. 1 (1950): 1-31.

About a year before his death on 30 May 1951 Hermann Broch received a letter from his son, Hermann Friedrich Broch de Rothermann, in which Broch's reception in postwar Austria and Germany was characterized as that of an "unknown quantity"–a reference to Broch's second novel. Though Broch's name was "in the air" his works remained unknown save to a small and select readership; his reputation in literary circles both inside and outside of German-speaking countries, on the other hand, had been firmly established. Commercial popularity and financial success eluded Broch throughout his career, but this failure did not lessen his importance as a philosopher, experimental novelist, and critic of the intellectual and cultural trends of his day. While it

was perhaps his philosophical concerns and his penchant for nontraditional narrative techniques in his novels that kept him from gaining a larger readership during his lifetime, these same aspects of his fiction and essays constitute his growing significance for scholars today. Undaunted by his lack of fame and pecuniary reward, Broch worked indefatigably on projects ranging from aesthetics to mass psychology, from epistemology to politics, while repeatedly returning to the literary medium to express his theories and perceptions.

Broch's literary interests had no precedent in his family background, which on both sides consisted of Jewish merchants whose gradually accrued wealth had drawn them from the provinces to Vienna, the commercial center of the Austro-Hungarian Empire. With this integration into the economic center came an attempt at social assimilation, a process that was accompanied by deemphasis on Judaic customs and rituals. Broch was born on 1 November 1886 to Josef Broch, a wholesaler of textiles, and Johanna

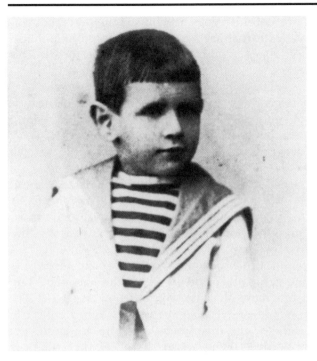

Broch in 1890 (Yale Collection of German Literature, Beinecke Library)

Schnabel Broch. A brother, Friedrich (Fritz), was born in 1889. Josef Broch's economic aspirations were realized in 1906 with the acquisition of a textile factory at Teesdorf. Broch's interests in humanistic studies were stifled by his father's demand that he pursue an educational regimen befitting an up-and-coming businessman. While his father fostered only feelings of resentment and fear in him, Broch's relationship with his mother was marked by a dutiful affection which was rebuffed by her greater attachment to his younger brother. These family tensions are depicted in the story of the Pasenows in the first novel of his trilogy *Die Schlafwandler* (1931-1932; translated as *The Sleepwalkers*, 1932). In 1906-1907, on the instructions of his father, Broch studied textile engineering at Mülhausen (now Mulhouse, France) in Alsace. In October 1907 he went to the United States to investigate advances in cotton production, about which, he later admitted, he learned little. At the end of the year he became assistant director in charge of administrative affairs at the Teesdorf factory.

At about that time he fell in love with Franziska von Rothermann, the daughter of a well-to-do sugar manufacturer; her family's concern for social position initially stood in the way of the courtship between the two young lovers. But his conversion to Catholicism in May 1909 and his

rise in the Teesdorf administration made possible his marriage to Franziska on 11 December 1909. On 4 October 1910 their only child, Hermann Friedrich Maria, affectionately called "Pitz," was born. (In later years the son became estranged from his father, even changing his surname; but most of their differences were resolved by the time of Broch's death.) Broch's increasing dissatisfaction with his unchosen profession drove him to spend most of his free time in the autodidactic study of philosophy. With her growing resentment of the provincial life at Teesdorf, Franziska's affections for her husband grew colder, and after seven years of marriage the relationship had become irreparable; but the prevailing Catholic influence in Austria prevented a divorce until 1923.

When Fritz Broch enlisted in the Austrian air force at the outbreak of World War I, Broch was compelled to take charge of all administrative duties at Teesdorf. Under his skillful managerial hand the family business prospered, reaching its financial apex in 1915-1916. To escape from the factory he began frequenting the café scene of Vienna, where he came into contact with such prominent literary figures as Willy Haas, Paul Schrecker, Robert Musil, and Franz Blei. In 1918 he published in Blei's journal *Summa* his first fictional piece, "Eine methodologische Novelle" (A Methodological Novella), which Sidonie Cassirer has characterized as a "whimsical satire on bourgeois mediocrity, on philosophical determinism, and, indirectly, on the formal rules governing the *Novelle* itself." The novella describes the love affair between Antigonus, a young teacher of mathematics at a small-town gymnasium, and Philaminthe, the daughter of a petit bourgeois widow. The lovers meet when Antigonus rents a room in the widow's house; they talk, fall in love, and decide to marry. What makes the novella unique is the narrator's invitation to the reader to construct the plausible elements of personality, time, and situation that would allow such love to reach consummation. The novella is intended as a counterargument to the determinism of the naturalists. In his reviews for *Summa* Broch commended Émile Zola for his style and his humanity but criticized his materialism; he attacked Heinrich von Stein as a positivist, linking his ideas with those of Richard Wagner and the philistinism of the previous generation; although he discovered a "gravitätischen Leichtsinn" (grave levity) in Christian Morgenstern's humorous poetry, he felt Morgenstern lacked precision in the formulation of his ideas. These reviews serve as what Cassirer calls a "rough draft" for his subsequent fictional critiques of his time.

In 1925 Broch began five years of study at the University of Vienna, where he attended lectures by Moritz Schlick and Rudolf Carnap of the Wiener Kreis (Vienna Circle) and participated in seminars on mathematics. In 1927 he sold the textile factory and also began a course of psychoanalysis with Hedwig Schaxel, a student of Freud, that would continue until 1935. Gradually Broch became disillusioned with the logical positivist leanings of his professors; he began to feel the members of the Wiener Kreis were ignoring ethics and metaphysics. These subjects, he decided, could more properly be investigated in literature than in philosophy.

Broch's literary career can be said to have begun when he met Frank Thiess in the winter of 1928-1929. Broch and Thiess became close friends despite the differences in their literary leanings: Broch found his paradigm in James Joyce, while Thiess wrote popular novels reminiscent of the realistic style of the nineteenth century. Broch read Thiess's novels as a "corrective" for any extremes in his own style. Thiess took Broch under his wing; Broch called his friend the "Schutzengel der Schlafwandler" (guardian angel of *The Sleepwalkers*) for his constant advice on and public approbation of the novel. In 1930 Broch met the publisher Daniel Brody, whose firm, the Rhein Verlag, had published the German translation of Joyce's *Ulysses* (1922) in 1927. On 26 March 1930 Broch and Brody discussed the first draft of *Die Schlafwandler*. Six weeks later they negotiated the publishing contract for *Pasenow oder die Romantik, 1888* (translated as "The Romantic, [1888]"), the first part of the trilogy. During the summer Broch's confidence in the financial success of his novel grew as he worked on the second draft; but he later felt the need to correct the material, delaying its publication until November 1930 (dated 1931). Part two, *Esch oder die Anarchie 1903* (translated as "The Anarchist [1903]"), arrived at the publishers in April 1931, six months later than originally planned. Brody had wanted the entire trilogy on the market in time for the Christmas shopping season, but Broch's continual reworkings postponed the final novel, *Huguenau oder die Sachlichkeit 1918* (translated as "The Realist [1918]"), until April 1932. Though his desire to perfect his narratives enhanced their literary quality, it proved less beneficial in financial terms as the second and third novels of the trilogy also missed the potentially lucrative Christmas market. Bad timing of publication dates would become the rule for Broch's works.

The tripartite structure of *Die Schlafwandler* reflects three critical stages in the recent historical and cultural development of Germany. Falling back on ideas first espoused in his 1911 essay first published in volume 10, part 1, of the *Kommentierte Werkausgabe* (1977), "Ornamente (Der Fall Loos)" (Ornaments [The Loos Case]), Broch characterizes each period according to its dominant intellectual style: romantic, anarchistic, and objective. Structurally and stylistically the first two novels are conventional, while in *Huguenau* Broch includes lyrical, dramatic, essayistic, and aphoristic elements within the narrative. The protagonists–Joachim von Pasenow, August Esch, and Wilhelm Huguenau–are differentiated as the aesthetic, the unaesthetic, and the anti-aesthetic, respectively. The actual "hero" of the trilogy is the iconoclastic cotton importer Eduard von Bertrand, whose thoughts and perceptions permeate each novel despite his absence from the third one. The protagonist of the first novel, Joachim von Pasenow, is an officer of noble birth who attempts to render his life meaningful through hopelessly impractical actions, such as confrontations with his father and a defiant love affair with a bar dancer named Ruzena. He is attracted by the cynicism of his friend Bertrand, but is ultimately unable to break with conventional familial duties. His lack of emotional progress exemplifies the degeneration of the Prussian nobility in the face of the modern world. His eventual marriage to Elisabeth Baddensen, a baron's daughter who is his ideal of chastity, underscores in a humorous final scene his lack of harmony with the world around him.

The revolt against convention which Joachim fails to accomplish is achieved in part by the fired bookkeeper August Esch in the second novel; but his attempts at revolution are as ill fated as Pasenow's emotional longings. Irrationally, he connects all of the world's injustice and evil with the industrialist Bertrand, whom he denounces to the police as a homosexual. Bertrand's subsequent suicide does not end Esch's inner turmoil. Escaping into erotic excesses in his marriage to Mutter Hentjen, the owner of a bar in the working-class section of Cologne, Esch dreams of going to America but finally returns to his work with the new status of chief bookkeeper. His violent, anarchistic rages

Broch in 1905 (Hermann Broch Museum, Teesdorf) and Franziska von Rotherman in 1906 (photo property of Hermann Friedrich Broch de Rothermann, New York). The two were married in 1909.

eventually subside, as reflected in his lessening aggression toward his wife: "Manchmal schlug er sie noch, aber immer weniger und schließlich gar nicht mehr" (Sometimes he still hit her, but less and less and finally not at all).

The protagonist of the third novel, Wilhelm Huguenau, is an entrepreneur. His unbridled egocentrism is symbolized by his extreme myopia; the world exists only as an extension of his "Privattheologie" (private theology) of exploitation. After deserting from the army he settles in a small town on the Mosel, where he becomes a partner in a newspaper owned by Esch. He socializes with the town's leading citizens, among them the aging Pasenow. The fates of the three main figures illustrate the "Wertzerfall" (disintegration of values) precipitated by World War I: Pasenow gradually succumbs to his illusions and goes insane; Esch is murdered by his ruthless partner; Huguenau rapes Esch's widow, marries for the sake of social convention, and becomes complacently wealthy. *Huguenau* is by far the most complex of the three novels in that it incorporates multiple subplots, such as that of the doomed love affair of the Salvation Army girl Marie and the Jew Nuchem in Berlin, and essayistic chapters on the decay of values.

The reception of *Die Schlafwandler* by the intelligentsia was most positive. Thomas Mann noted in his diary that the novels were "intellectually rich and stimulating"; Hermann Hesse rated

them among the best of contemporary fiction; Hans A. Joachim's review in the *Neue Rundschau* compared Broch's creation to that of God in Genesis. Edwin and Willa Muir's translation of the trilogy, *The Sleepwalkers,* came to the attention of Aldous Huxley, T. S. Eliot, Stephen Spender, and Thornton Wilder. Edwin Muir's review in the *Bookman* described the work as a "masterpiece" because of its experimental form and Broch's "extremely comprehensive, profound, and exact knowledge of the human heart and mind." Writing to Martin Secker, the English publisher of the Muirs' translation of the trilogy, Aldous Huxley was equally impressed by the inventiveness of Broch's style: "I read the trilogy with steadily increasing admiration. It is the work of a mind of extraordinary power and depth, and at the same time of extraordinary subtlety and sensitivity–of a philosopher who is also an artist of exceptional refinement and purity. It is a difficult book that makes great demands of the reader–nothing less than his whole mind at the highest pitch of attention. Not at all a book for tired business men! But I hope, all the same, that it will be widely read; for it is manifestly a work of first-rate importance." Despite such reviews the novels' readers were limited to a group of writers who themselves were part of the literary vanguard; in addition, the political climate of Germany had been so radically altered by the time of their publication that their financial failure

Broch (left) and his younger brother Friedrich (Fritz) in 1908

was assured. Broch remarked, paraphrasing a German proverb, that "der Verleger denkt, und Hitler lenkt" (the publisher proposes and Hitler disposes). The lack of popular response to the trilogy is an example of the sociopolitical and cultural somnambulance attacked in the work itself.

Throughout the early 1930s, as Broch's reputation increased among the international literary avant-garde, his financial situation grew more precarious. On 22 April 1932 he read his essay *James Joyce und die Gegenwart* (James Joyce and the Present Age, 1936) at the Ottakring Adult Education Center in Vienna, where Heinrich and Thomas Mann, Arnold Schönberg, Franz Werfel, and C. G. Jung had previously spoken. Broch held that Joyce had achieved in *Ulysses* what Goethe had attempted to do in *Wilhelm Meisters Wanderjahre* (1829): to capture through a radical narra-

tive mode the "Totalität" (totality) of an epoch within a single work of art. Four days after his speech, Broch himself was the subject of a lecture by Ernst Schönwiese, who discussed the merits of the recently published trilogy. During the next two years Broch became a regular speaker at the center. There he read his examination of the novel form, "Das Weltbild des Romans" (The Novel's World Image, published in volume 9, part 2 of the *Kommentierte Werkausgabe*, 1975), which again advocated that totality through which the novel could reveal the ethical failings of contemporary society. Broch criticized the anti-intellectual climate promulgated by the National Socialists as fundamentally false in "Leben ohne platonische Idee" (Life without Platonic Form), published in the journal *Die Literarische Welt* in 1932. In April 1934 he approached Brody with the request that

Broch and his wife with their son, Hermann Friedrich Maria ("Pitz"), in 1911 (Hermann Broch Museum, Teesdorf)

these essays be published in a single volume for the general public, but the publisher felt that such a volume would bring little reward for either himself or its author.

In the years 1932 to 1934 Broch began working in the dramatic medium. His first play, *Die Entsühnung* (published in volume 7 of the *Kommentierte Werkausgabe*, 1979; translated as *The Atonement*, 1972), concerns the labor disputes at the Filsmann family factories in the waning days of the Weimar Republic; the picture presented is pessimistic and quasi-tragic. Broch portrays the social strata of the Weimar Republic and its inevitably catastrophic confrontations uncompromisingly and exactly. *Die Entsühnung* also provides evidence of Broch's wrestling with questions of literary tradition and form; he said in a letter to the Muirs that he tried to combine naturalistic with abstract techniques but admitted that the

combination was only partially successful. No German theater would perform the unpublished play. It finally had its premiere in Zurich on 15 March 1934, but the producer felt that it needed to be shortened. He therefore excised the elegiac epilogue, the "Totenklage" (lament for the dead) of the mothers, which Broch considered the most essential scene. The play, which was performed under the title *Denn sie wissen nicht, was sie tun* (For They Know Not What They Do), drew small audiences and was canceled after a short run. (The German premiere took place on 3 June 1981 in Osnabrück, almost fifty years after the play's composition). During 1934 Broch wrote the comedy *Aus der Luft gegriffen* (Pure Invention; published in volume 7 of the *Kommentierte Werkausgabe*), but Otto Preminger, the director of the Theater in der Josefstadt in Vienna, considered it "too cold and too literary" to stage.

Broch in 1926 (drawing by Georg Kirsta)

Broch completed his next novel in only six months. *Die Unbekannte Größe* (1933; translated as *The Unknown Quantity,* 1935) tells the story of the young mathematician Richard Hieck's attempts to counter life's irrational forces through scientific rationality. His love for the lab assistant Ilse and the death of his younger brother Otto bring disorder into the academician's otherwise orderly world. Slowly, through discussions with friends and family, Richard constructs a theory of the "unknown quantity," an underlying religiosity in human perception that connects reason and irrationality in the soul. The novel is too short to deal adequately with such difficult issues, however, and even Broch found his protagonist's resolution unsatisfactory and unconvincing. The nov-

el's poor showing in the German and American marketplace (Broch referred to it as a "worst seller") confirmed his doubts.

At about the same time Broch wrote five novellas, which he attempted in vain to have published in one volume, and some poetry. Ernst Schönwiese included twelve of the poems in his anthology *Patmos: Zwölf Lyriker* (1935). In 1934 Broch was asked to write the screenplay for a film to be directed by Berthold Viertel, a leftist Austrian emigré living in England, but the combination of an antifascist writer and a Marxist director had little chance of success in Austria in the 1930s. Broch wrote a film version of *Die unbekannte Größe* titled "Das unbekannte X: Der Film einer physikalischen Theorie" (X, the Unknown: The Film of a Physical Theory), but nothing came of the venture. Metro-Goldwyn-Mayer approached him about filming *The Sleepwalkers*, but that project was also dropped.

Although Broch had established his name in European literature, his works of the early 1930s were artistic compromises for the sake of barely adequate financial gains. Broch finally decided to leave these compromises behind and to concentrate his efforts on a new novel, *Die Verzauberung* (1976; translated as *The Spell*, 1987). For this novel Broch broke with his model, Joyce, feeling that the radical subjectivity of *Ulysses* bordered on the asocial; he was also determined to avoid what he considered the realist approach of Thomas Mann. Broch wanted to expose the sociopolitical climate that had led to National Socialism, the nadir of European culture. Broch studied some French provincial novels and the contemporary Austrian popular novel. With the rise of nationalism in Austria and Germany there had been an increase in the popularity of "Heimatromane" (provincial novels), and it was in part against this often insipid type of writing that Broch aimed his work. To assure himself of the quiet needed to complete the novel Broch moved to a farm near Mösern in the Tirol; but his work on *Die Verzauberung* was interrupted in late 1935 by the writing of his assessment of cultural decay, "Erwägungen zum Problem des Kulturtodes" (Considerations on the Problem of Cultural Death), which was published the following year in Schönwiese's journal *das silberboot*. Although the essay expressed skepticism about the function of literature in the era of National Socialism, Broch was determined to complete his novel, and in January 1936 he sent Brody the first draft.

Die Verzauberung was originally planned as the first part of another trilogy, to be titled "Bergroman" (Mountain Novel), but the subsequent parts were never written. The novel remains a fragment; the third version, which was never completed, was published after Broch's death. Unlike his other novels, *Die Verzauberung* has a first-person narrator, a country doctor who has fled his urban practice for the serenity of a small mountain village. His dreams of a peaceful existence are disrupted by the arrival of a stranger, Marius Ratti, a demagogue based on Hitler. Ratti uses eloquent turns of phrase to convince the villagers that their salvation lies in recapturing the golden age of preindustrial times; taking his meaning literally, the community reopens its gold mine. The intoxication of this poten-

tial new greatness metastasizes into mass hysteria: the gruesome outcome is the ritualistic blood sacrifice of Irmgard, a girl who is in love with Ratti. The counterpoint to Ratti is Mutter (Mother) Gisson, Irmgard's grandmother, who represents an older, more natural order than Ratti's brutal atavism. The doctor realizes the danger inherent in Ratti's demonic magic and is even susceptible to it, but he remains unable to achieve the natural power of self-redemption achieved by the aged Mutter Gisson. The symbolic interplay of nature and politics in this novel is an unusually successful response to the "Blut-und-Boden" (blood and soil) literature endorsed by the National Socialists.

Broch's work on his fiction was also interrupted by his growing interest in the international peace movement. He sent his "Völkerbund-Resolution" (League of Nations Resolution) to Thomas Mann for publication in Mann's journal *Mass und Wert*, but Mann declined it. The article called for a new declaration of human rights and called on the League of Nations to enforce control of those rights and to oversee the armaments industry. The resolution was finally published in 1973.

Since the death of his father in October 1933 there had been a dispute over the estate between Broch and his brother Fritz. Broch had been named executor of the will upon their mother's refusal of those duties, but almost immediately Fritz had filed suit against him. Their mother had been left forty thousand Austrian schillings and two houses; the interest on the money and the rent from the houses were given to Broch, who divided the income into monthly allowances for his mother, his son, and himself. In late December 1936 Broch learned that Fritz was again seeking to wrest his inheritance from him; on receiving the news he had a heart attack. On recovering, Broch, who was thirty-five hundred Swiss francs in debt to Brody, felt compelled to fight his brother in court for the security of his family. These trials consumed a great deal of his time and energy; referring to *Die Verzauberung*, he commented later that they constituted a "Mord an dem Buch" (murder of the book).

While revising *Die Verzauberung* Broch had read Theodor Haecker's *Vergil: Vater des Abendlandes* (Virgil: Father of the West, 1931) after hearing the philosopher speak at the Ottakring Adult Education Center. With his interest in Virgil aroused, he set about studying the *Aeneid* and the *Eclogues*. In Virgil Broch saw a liter-

Broch in 1939, portrait by Rudolf von Ripper (Yale Collection of German Literature, Beinecke Library)

ary figure who stood at the end of a cultural epoch and whose aversion to the political changes of his day caused him to want to burn his magnum opus, the *Aeneid*, which glorified the Roman state. Broch's skepticism about literature in an era of "cultural death" is paralleled in the thoughts and actions of the dying poet in his novella "Die Heimkehr des Vergil" (Virgil's Return, 1973), which rendered into fiction ideas he had stated in essay form two years earlier. On 11 December 1937 Broch read selections from the novella at the Institute Anderl-Rogge in Graz. He then retired to the rural atmosphere of Alt-Aussee in Styria to revise the work, but the novel which grew from the novella would not be published for another eight years and then not in Europe.

On 13 March 1938, the day following the march of German troops into Austria, Broch was arrested and imprisoned in Alt-Aussee after his postman reported to the authorities that he subscribed to *Das Wort*, the leading organ of literary exiles in the Soviet Union. Because of this subscription Broch was considered a Marxist; the Nazis seemed unaware of his Jewish heritage. In prison his correspondence was limited to postcards, the chronic stomach ailment he had suffered since the 1920s was exacerbated by the stress, and he became increasingly convinced that he faced a death sentence. He worked daily on his Virgil novel, which became more of a diary than a literary project. At Broch's trial in Bad Aussee the judge released him with the stipulation that Broch travel immediately to Vienna and register with the police. In Vienna Broch hid with friends. The necessity of emigration became increasingly apparent to Broch, who, fearing the worst, gave Thiess the typescript of *Die Ver-*

Broch in 1942 (photo: Trude Geiringer)

zauberung; Thiess sent it to Edwin Muir in Scotland for safekeeping.

In April 1938 Paul Schrecker, a friend from Broch's early days in Vienna, persuaded Anna Herzog, another longtime friend residing in Paris, to seek assistance for Broch from James Joyce. When he heard of Broch's predicament, Joyce immediately interceded to help him secure an exit visa. In May Edwin Muir, Stephen Hudson, and Aldous Huxley began trying to obtain a British visa for Broch. The papers were finally processed, but with bureaucratic delays in both England and Austria they did not reach Broch until 20 July 1938. Unable to dissuade his mother from remaining in her homeland (she would die in the Theresienstadt concentration camp in 1942), he flew from Vienna to London via Rotterdam, boarding the plane with only twenty Reichsmark in his pocket. In London Broch met Hudson and Stefan Zweig; he was soon invited by the Muirs to stay with them in St. Andrews. There Broch began again to work on his League of Na-

tions resolution; this renewed political activity aroused the consternation of Brody, who wrote Broch that his main task was the completion of his Virgil novel. Brody likened the author to Dante, emphasizing that the Italian poet's contribution to the world came from his poetry and not from his politics. Despite these admonitions Broch continued revising the resolution.

On 21 September Broch received an American visa through the United States consulate in Glasgow, and the following week he booked passage for New York. Arriving on 9 October, Broch met with the writers Richard Bermann and Erich von Kahler; they worked with the American Guild for German Cultural Freedom, an organization established for dealing with the problems facing exiles from National Socialism. Broch traveled to Princeton to thank Albert Einstein for his letter of recommendation in the matter of Broch's visa. He also met with Henry Seidel Canby, the editor of the *Saturday Review of Literature* and professor of English and American litera-

Manuscript page for Der Tod des Vergil *(Yale Collection of German Literature, Beinecke Library, and Hermann Broch literary estate)*

1947 caricature of Broch by Derso

tures at Yale University; through Canby Broch hoped to obtain a position at an American university, but he lacked the necessary academic credentials. Canby was a member of the American Guild, which had been founded by Prince Hubertus zu Löwenstein to preserve German culture in exile; Broch received fifty dollars per month from the guild for a short time to cover his living expenses. Canby procured a six-weeks residency for Broch at the artists' colony Yaddo in Saratoga Springs, New York, beginning in June 1939. At Yaddo Broch became acquainted with the poet Jean Starr Untermeyer, whose translation of the "Schicksals-Elegien" (fate-elegies) in the manuscript of his Virgil novel so impressed him that he chose her to become the translator of the entire work.

During 1939 Broch began work on his studies of mass psychology, even though he had been given a stipend by the Carl Schurz Memorial Association to continue working on his fiction. In September 1939 he was the guest of Thomas Mann in Princeton; Mann helped Broch receive a Guggenheim Fellowship stipend of twenty-five hundred dollars for the fiscal year 1940. The stipend was extended until December 1941 to allow Broch to complete his study of mass psychology. In Princeton Broch met Giuseppe Antonio Borgese, the Italian historian and author of *Goliath: The March of Fascism* (1937), and with him organized other authors for the compilation of a

book favoring democracy. *The City of Man: A Declaration on World Democracy* was published in November 1940 by the Viking Press.

The City of Man describes the cataclysmic situation facing the world, argues against the appeasement policy of the past and in favor of America as the last stronghold of democracy, and advocates a peace established and preserved by a universal state with universal representation. *The City of Man* is somewhat utopian; nevertheless, it is an important document representing one of the rare instances of American and European intellectual teamwork. Broch's participation in the project heightened his visibility in the American academic community, and in early 1942 Hadley Cantril of the Office of Public Opinion Research applied to the Rockefeller Foundation for a stipend of two thousand dollars from May 1942 to April 1943 to make possible Broch's study of mass psychology. Broch was unable to complete the essay in the allotted time and turned to the Bollingen Foundation for further support in late 1944. Even though later he requested an extension of this second funding, he left the study unfinished. Some of the manuscripts and notes, edited by Wolfgang Rothe, were published in 1959 as volume 9 of his collected works.

The Virgil novel had been occupying more and more of his attention since early 1940. At that time he had sent copies to Brody, Muir, and other friends, most of whom urged him not to leave the novel unpublished. On 22 April 1942 Broch received a literary prize from the American Academy of Arts and Sciences for the fourth version of the novel. With that money he was finally able to pay back the debts he had incurred through his assistance to other refugees. Broch then applied himself diligently to the task of completing the novel, while Untermeyer worked on the English translation. *Der Tod des Vergil* (translated as *The Death of Virgil*) was published by Pantheon Books in June 1945 in both German and English editions, reflecting the status of its newly naturalized Austrian-American author.

The novel is divided into four parts, each of which is named for one of the four elements of antiquity. The opening section, "Wasser" (Water), describes the dying poet's return by ship to Italy and his abhorrence at the sight of the jubilant throngs attending the emperor's triumphal procession. The mass hysteria aroused by Augustus makes Virgil conscious of the animal nature of man and leads him to decide to destroy his masterpiece. "Feuer" (Fire) depicts the dying poet's fever-

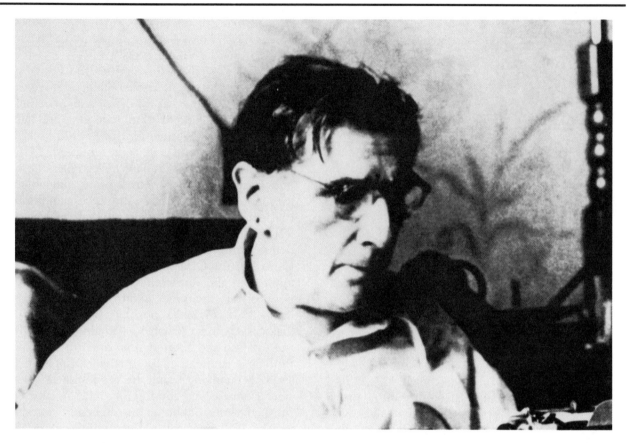

Broch in the hospital at Princeton, October 1948 (photo: Anne Marie M. G. Broch)

ish final night, during which images from his past are resurrected in his mind. "Erde" (Earth) brings the novel back to more solid ground: Virgil, epitomizing Roman intellectual life, argues against his antithesis, the emperor, that most political personage, that he has the right to destroy his own work as he deems fit. Augustus, supporting the rights of the state over the individual, tries to dissuade what he considers the rash action of the dying poet. In the final section, "Äther" (Ether), antithetical positions and divergent elements coalesce into a unity with the eternal as Virgil slips into death. Each element suggests the events of the last day of Virgil's life and his respective moods through its associative quality. Perhaps the most striking stylistic invention of the novel is the lyrical passages embedded within the prose; these "eclogues" are especially effective in the long interior monologue sequences. *Der Tod des Vergil* is reminiscent of Joyce in its presentation of the totality of an epoch within a single day; yet there the similarity ends, since, unlike his former model, Broch blends the lyrical and prose genres. *Der Tod des Vergil* deals with the death of the "Wertsystem" (value system) of the

Roman Empire and the first glimmerings of the new Wertsystem of Christianity. Broch links the disintegration of the pagan world with that of the modern world, revealing–more clearly than in any of his other works–his cultural pessimism.

Between 1946 and 1948 there were only nine reviews of *Der Tod des Vergil* in German, indicating that Broch's importance had diminished in Germany and Austria. In contrast, in the United States the book elicited some thirty reviews. Aldous Huxley found *The Death of Virgil* stylistically inferior to Broch's trilogy. Günther Anders, who wrote an even less complimentary review for the *Austro-American Tribune*, reiterated some earlier critical assessments of "Joyce imitation" and "themeless mass." Hannah Arendt, on the other hand, wrote in the *Nation* that the book placed Broch firmly in the avant-garde of the twentieth-century novel with Proust and Kafka. In the reviews Broch was compared to such disparate writers as Kafka, Proust, Thomas Wolfe, Hermann Hesse, Thomas Mann, Martin Heidegger, Richard Wagner, and Joyce. Hermann Weigand's suggestion that the idea for the novel had come from Broch's reading of Dante so disturbed

Broch that he protested against it in a letter to Weigand and in a sonnet titled "Dantes Schatten" (Dante's Shadow, published in volume 8 of the *Kommentierte Werkausgabe*, 1980). As usual, Broch received little financial gain from his novel.

In November 1948 the Friedrich Schiller University in Jena, East Germany, offered Broch a post in psychology and literature, but Broch rejected the offer. Although Broch was not a Marxist, his work was held in esteem by the leadership of the eastern zone. Beginning in July 1947 Broch received a monthly allowance of fifty dollars from Wilhelm Roth, a wealthy German expatriate. On 17 June 1948 Broch suffered a broken leg and was hospitalized in Princeton. Ironically, with health and accident insurance, he was financially better off in the hospital. Broch said that his convalescence made him a "Kombination von Hiob und Lazarus" (combination of Job and Lazarus)–a remark that might appropriately be applied to the whole of his exile experience since 1938. While in the hospital he began work on a study of Hugo von Hofmannsthal which had originally been planned as an introduction to Hofmannsthal's *Selected Prose* (1952). Broch felt that a mere accounting of his compatriot's literary achievements in vacuo would oversimplify the measure of his works; therefore he felt it necessary to include an analysis of the cultural phenomena surrounding Hofmannsthal's literary production. His discussion centered on the social class he best understood and to which his subject belonged–the bourgeoisie. The middle class had dictated tastes in Austria and Germany in the latter half of the nineteenth century; its leading artist was Richard Wagner, in whose operas the desires of the bourgeoisie were collected and articulated. Despite his praise for much of Hofmannsthal's work Broch's study ends by taking a position in favor of the ethics of Karl Kraus over the purely aesthetic predilections of the poet. Such a preference is not surprising, since Hofmannsthal had no influence on Broch's works, whereas the satirical tone of both *Die Schlafwandler* and *Die Schuldlosen* (1950; translated as *The Guiltless*, 1974) resembles Kraus's polemical essays and aphorisms. The Hofmannsthal study was published posthumously as "Hugo von Hofmannsthal und seine Zeit" (1975; translated as *Hugo von Hofmannsthal and His Time*, 1984).

In 1948 Willi Weismann, whose monthly *Die Fähre* had published an entire issue on Broch on the occasion of his sixtieth birthday in 1946, proposed the publication of a collection of his novellas and short stories. Broch sent him five stories, and a few months later Weismann returned the galley proofs. In correcting the proofs Broch decided that the stories–four of which he had written in the early 1930s–could not be printed in their present form. In June 1949 he began work on other stories to supplement the original five, and a month later he had a tentative form for the book: "Elf Novellen und drei Gedichte, beinahe ein Roman" (Eleven novellas and three poems, practically a novel). The novel, *Die Schuldlosen*, was published in mid December 1950–once again too late for the Christmas market.

Die Schuldlosen is introduced with a parable which has its roots in the Hassidic narrative tradition of the *tsadi'kim* (saintly men), reminiscent of much of Martin Buber's work. This enigmatic, paradoxical tale relates the attempts of some shtetl members to comprehend the meaning of the voice of God in Genesis. The rabbi, in accordance with the practices of that tradition, provokes his students to rethink their questions by recasting them as counterquestions; but those seeking a single definitive answer so convolute the essential question that they lose sight of the original purpose. Finally, after loudly laughing at their muddled theological thinking, the rabbi tells them that it is time, the remembered past, which contains both the Lord's voice and silence in one undifferentiated state. This Talmudic paradox is left unresolved for both the students and the reader. God's creation of the world remains ineffable in human discourse.

Each of the three story sections–the "Vor-Geschichten" (prestories), the "Geschichten" (stories), and the "Nach-Geschichten" (poststories)–is preceded by a poetry section. Recalling the opening parable, these sections are called "Stimmen" (voices) and are assigned the dates 1913, 1923, and 1933, corresponding to the stages of political decay that culminated in Hitler's assumption of power. Each set of poems is a mixture of various lyrical forms, some traditional–the emblem, the ballad, the folk song, the elegy, and the sonnet–and some free verse forms of Broch's own invention. Thematically, *Die Schuldlosen*–the title is ironic–centers on the question of collective German guilt. Andreas, a Dutch diamond dealer, arrives in a small German town and takes up lodging with the Baroness von W. and her daughter Hildegard. Like Huguenau, he cleverly exploits the economic disaster of the post-World War I period, amassing a considerable sum of money

Broch's friend Erich von Kahler tending Broch's grave in the Union District Cemetery, Killingworth, Connecticut, in 1961 (photo property of Alice von Kahler, Princeton, N.J.)

through currency fluctuations and real estate investments. After attending a meeting of some local Socialists, Andreas spends a drunken evening with the schoolmaster Zacharias, who gives long diatribes on the future greatness of the German nation. Zacharias's language foreshadows the political rhetoric adopted by the German nationalists who supported Hitler's bid for political control. In a dreamlike episode the young businessman meets Melitta, a poor laundress. Their love affair is thwarted by Hildegard, who tells Melitta that she and Andreas are to be married. Believing this lie, Melitta commits suicide. Hildegard seduces Andreas, but her aggressiveness renders him impotent. Andreas takes the baroness and her chambermaid Zerline to a secluded hunting lodge. Melitta's grandfather, an old beekeeper, confronts Andreas toward the novel's end with his complacency and failure to accept responsibility, and Andreas's depraved desire for the "Nicht-Seiende" (nonbeing) is finally realized with his suicide. Without focusing on actual historical events, Broch has critically de-

picted the indifference and inertia of Germans of all classes that allowed the National Socialists to rise to power.

Weismann's reaction to the unique form of *Die Schuldlosen* was rather negative; he especially felt that the poetry impaired the rhythm of the narrative. Broch, however, felt that the novel might have been his masterpiece because of the cohesion achieved through the poems; he referred to *Die Schuldlosen* as a "Seiltänzerkunststück" (tightrope walker's work of art). Critical reaction was varied. The *Times Literary Supplement* of 29 March 1953 characterized the poetry as "some of those homemade verses that German writers for the past century have been so ready to turn out on their sewing machines." Karl August Horst's review in *Merkur* praised the experimental nature of the novel but expressed doubts as to whether Broch had succeeded in achieving his goal. Perhaps the most positive view of *Die Schuldlosen* came from Broch's friend Erich von Kahler, who felt that the importance of examining the phenomenon of guilt and its origins should not be overlooked.

On 5 December 1949 Broch had married Anne Marie Meier-Graefe, whom he had met in Vienna in 1937. On 1 April 1951 he suffered a heart attack while once again reworking *Die Verzauberung*. While convalescing in New Haven, he wrote to an editor at the Alfred A. Knopf publishing house that "the irony of fate sometimes hits the racing horse just going through the goal: that is I." On 30 May 1951 he had another heart attack; this one was fatal.

Broch received only limited recognition for his literary and critical achievements. In spite of efforts by the Austrian P.E.N. Club, he failed to receive the Nobel Prize for Literature in 1950; financially, his efforts were disastrous. Broch's recalcitrant commitment to novelistic experiment and his uncompromising analysis of contemporary issues combined to deny him accolades in his lifetime; but because of these very qualities his place in German letters of the twentieth century has been irrevocably established.

Letters:

Hermann Broch–Daniel Brody: Briefwechsel 1930-1951, edited by Bertold Hack and Marietta Kleiss (Frankfurt am Main: Buchhändler-Vereinigung, 1971);

Hermann Broch. Briefe über Deutschland: Die Korrespondenz mit Volkmar von Zühlsdorff, edited by Paul Michael Lützeler (Frankfurt am Main: Suhrkamp, 1986).

Biography:

Paul Michael Lützeler, *Hermann Broch: Eine Biographie* (Frankfurt am Main: Suhrkamp, 1985); translated by Janice Furness as *Hermann Broch: A Biography* (London: Quartet, 1987).

References:

Günther Anders, "Der Tod des Vergil ... und die Diagnose seiner Krankheit (Zu Brochs neuem Werk)," *Austro-American Tribune,* 4, no. 2 (1945): 9, 12;

Hannah Arendt, "No Longer and Not Yet," *Nation,* 163 (14 June 1946): 300-302;

Jean-Paul Bier, "Hermann Broch et *La Mort de Virgile*" (Paris: Larousse, 1974);

Gisela Brude-Firnau, ed., *Materialien zu Hermann Brochs "Die Schlafwandler"* (Frankfurt am Main: Suhrkamp, 1972);

Sidonie Cassirer, "Hermann Broch's Early Writings," *PMLA,* 75 (1965): 453-462;

Dorrit Claire Cohn, *The Sleepwalkers: Elucidations of Hermann Broch's Trilogy* (The Hague & Paris: Mouton, 1966);

Timm Collmann, *Zeit und Geschichte in Hermann Brochs Roman "Der Tod des Vergil"* (Bonn: Bouvier, 1967);

Sverre Dahl, *Relativität und Absolutheit: Studien zur Geschichtsphilosophie Hermann Brochs (bis 1932)* (Bern: Lang, 1980);

Stephen D. Dowden, ed., *Hermann Broch: Literature, Philosophy, Politics. The Yale Broch Symposium* (Columbia, S.C.: Camden House, 1988);

Manfred Durzak, *Hermann Broch: Der Dichter und seine Zeit* (Stuttgart: Kohlhammer, 1968);

Durzak, *Hermann Broch: Dichtung und Erkenntnis* (Stuttgart: Kohlhammer, 1978);

Durzak, *Hermann Broch in Selbstzeugnissen und Bilddokumenten* (Reinbek: Rowohlt, 1966);

Durzak, ed., *Hermann Broch: Perspektiven der Forschung* (Munich: Fink, 1972);

Die Fähre, special Broch issue, 8 (November 1946);

Waldo Frank, "The Novel as Poem," *New Republic,* 113 (20 August 1945): 226-228;

James Hardin, "Das Thema der Erlösung in den Romanen Hermann Brochs," *Schweizer Monatshefte,* 52 (July 1972): 257-261;

Hermann Hesse, "Beim Malen," *Dresdener Neueste Nachrichten,* 29 May 1932;

Hesse, "Die Schlafwandler," *Neue Zürcher Zeitung,* 15 June 1932;

Aldous Huxley, "Why Virgil Offered a Sacrifice," *New York Herald Tribune Weekly Book Review,* 8 July 1945, p. 5;

Hans A. Joachim, "Ausgewählte Romane," *Neue Rundschau,* 44 (January 1933): 129-131;

Erich Kahler, *Die Philosophie von Hermann Broch* (Tübingen: Mohr, 1962);

Kahler, ed., *Dichter wider Willen: Einführung in das Werk von Hermann Broch* (Zurich: Rhein, 1958);

Thomas Koebner, *Hermann Broch: Leben und Werk* (Bern & Munich: Francke, 1965);

Hermann Krapoth, *Dichtung und Philosophie: Eine Studie zum Werk Hermann Brochs* (Bonn: Bouvier, 1971);

Leo Kreutzer, *Erkenntnistheorie und Prophetie: Hermann Brochs Romantrilogie "Die Schlafwandler"* (Tübingen: Niemeyer, 1966);

Paul Michael Lützeler, *Hermann Broch–Ethik und Politik: Studien zum Frühwerk und zur Romantrilogie "Die Schlafwandler"* (Munich: Winkler, 1973);

Lützeler, ed., *Brochs Verzauberung* (Frankfurt am Main: Suhrkamp, 1983);

Lützeler, ed., *Hermann Broch* (Frankfurt am Main: Suhrkamp, 1986);

Lützeler, ed., *Materialien zu Hermann Brochs "Der Tod des Vergil"* (Frankfurt am Main: Suhrkamp, 1976);

Karin Mack and Wolfgang Hofer, eds., *Spiegelungen: Denkbilder zur Biographie Brochs* (Vienna: Sonderzahl, 1984);

Karl Robert Mandelkow, *Hermann Brochs Romantrilogie "Die Schlafwandler": Gestaltung und Reflexion im modernen deutschen Roman* (Heidelberg: Winter, 1962);

D. Meinert, *Die Darstellung der Dimensionen menschlicher Existenz in Brochs "Tod des Vergil"* (Bern & Munich: Francke, 1962);

Karl Menges, *Kritische Studien zur Wertphilosophie Hermann Brochs* (Tübingen: Niemeyer, 1970);

Modern Austrian Literature, special Broch issue, 13, no. 4 (1980);

Edwin Muir, "Hermann Broch," *Bookman,* 75 (1932): 664-668;

Hartmut Reinhardt, *Erweiterter Naturalismus: Untersuchungen zum Konstruktionsverfahren in Hermann Brochs Romantrilogie "Die Schlafwandler"* (Cologne & Vienna: Böhlau, 1972);

Renato Saviane, *Apocalissi e Messianismo nei Romanzi di Hermann Broch* (Padua: Università di Padova, 1971);

Ernestine Schlant, *Hermann Broch* (Boston: Twayne, 1978);

Schlant, *Die Philosophie Hermann Brochs* (Bern & Munich: Francke, 1971);

Grover Smith, ed., *Letters of Aldous Huxley* (New York & Evanston, Ill.: Harper & Row, 1969), pp. 364-365;

Hartmut Steinecke, *Hermann Broch und der polyhistorische Roman: Studien zur Theorie und Technik eines Romantyps der Moderne* (Bonn: Bouvier, 1968);

Joseph Strelka, ed., *Broch heute* (Bern & Munich: Francke, 1978);

Richard Thieberger, ed., *Hermann Broch und seine Zeit* (Bern: Lang, 1980);

Peter Bruce Waldeck, *Die Kindheitsproblematik bei Hermann Broch* (Munich: Fink, 1968);

Hermann J. Weigand, "Broch's Death of Virgil: Program Notes," *PMLA,* 62 (June 1947): 525-554;

Theodore Ziolkowski, *Hermann Broch* (New York & London: Columbia University Press, 1964).

Papers:

Hermann Broch's papers are at the Beinecke Rare Book Library, Yale University. His correspondence with his publisher, Daniel Brody, is in the Deutsches Literaturarchiv, Marbach, Federal Republic of Germany.

Elias Canetti
(25 July 1905-   )

Thomas H. Falk
Michigan State University

BOOKS: *Die Blendung: Roman* (Vienna, Leipzig & Zurich: Reichner, 1936); translated by C. V. Wedgwood as *Auto-da-Fé* (London: Cape, 1946); republished as *The Tower of Babel* (New York: Knopf, 1947);

Komödie der Eitelkeit: Drama (Munich: Weismann, 1950); translated by Gitta Honegger as *Comedy of Vanity* (New York: Performing Arts Journal Publications, 1983);

Fritz Wotruba (Vienna: Rosenbaum, 1955);

Masse und Macht (Hamburg: Claassen, 1960); translated by Carol Stewart as *Crowds and Power* (London: Gollancz, 1962; New York: Viking, 1962);

Welt im Kopf, edited by Erich Fried (Graz & Vienna: Stiasny, 1962);

Hochzeit: Drama (Munich: Hanser, 1964); translated by Honegger as *The Wedding* (New York: Performing Arts Journal Publications, 1986);

Die Befristeten: Drama (Munich: Hanser, 1964); translated by Honegger as *Life-Terms* (New York: Performing Arts Journal Publications, 1983); translated by Stewart as *The Numbered* (London: Calder & Boyars, 1984);

Dramen (Munich: Hanser, 1964)–comprises *Hochzeit, Komödie der Eitelkeit, Die Befristeten*;

Aufzeichnungen 1942-1948 (Munich: Hanser, 1965);

Die Stimmen von Marrakesch: Aufzeichnungen nach einer Reise (Munich: Hanser, 1967); translated by J. A. Underwood as *The Voices of Marrakesh: A Record of a Visit* (London: Calder & Boyars, 1978; New York: Seabury Press, 1978);

Der andere Prozeß: Kafkas Briefe an Felice (Munich: Hanser, 1969); translated by Christopher Middleton as *Kafka's Other Trial: The Letters to Felice* (London: Calder & Boyars, 1974; New York: Schocken, 1974);

Alle vergeudete Verehrung: Aufzeichnungen 1949-1960 (Munich: Hanser, 1970);

Die gespaltene Zukunft: Aufsätze und Gespräche (Munich: Hanser, 1972);

Elias Canetti (photo copyright © by Isolde Ohlbaum, Munich)

Macht und Überleben: Drei Essays (Berlin: Literarisches Colloquium, 1972);

Die Provinz des Menschen: Aufzeichnungen 1942-1972 (Munich: Hanser, 1973); translated by Joachim Neugroschel as *The Human Province* (New York: Seabury Press, 1978);

Der Ohrenzeuge: Fünfzig Charaktere (Munich: Hanser, 1974); translated by Neugroschel as *Earwitness: Fifty Characters* (New York: Seabury Press, 1979);

103

Das Gewissen der Worte (Munich: Hanser, 1975; en-
larged, 1976); translated by Neugroschel as
The Conscience of Words (New York: Seabury
Press, 1979);

Der Überlebende (Frankfurt am Main: Suhrkamp,
1975);

Der Beruf des Dichters (Munich: Hanser, 1976);

Die gerettete Zunge: Geschichte einer Jugend (Munich: Hanser, 1977); translated by Neugroschel as *The Tongue Set Free: Remembrance of
a European Childhood* (New York: Conti-
nuum, 1979);

Die Fackel im Ohr: Lebensgeschichte 1921-1931 (Munich: Hanser, 1980); translated by Neugroschel as *The Torch in My Ear* (New York: Farrar, Straus & Giroux, 1982);

Das Augenspiel: Lebensgeschichte 1931-1937 (Mu-
nich: Hanser, 1985); translated by Ralph
Manheim as *The Play of the Eyes* (New York:
Farrar, Straus & Giroux, 1986);

Das Geheimherz der Uhr: Aufzeichnungen 1973-1985
(Munich: Hanser, 1987).

TRANSLATIONS: Upton Sinclair, *Leidweg der
Liebe* (Berlin: Malik, 1930);

Sinclair, *Das Geld schreibt. Eine Studie über die ameri-
kanische Literatur* (Berlin: Malik, 1930);

Sinclair, *Alkohol* (Berlin: Malik, 1932).

Elias Canetti's oeuvre is not extensive, but
he has written with style and wit in all major
genres except poetry. When Canetti won the
Nobel Prize for Literature in 1981, Dr. Johannes
Edfelt said in a speech at the ceremony that the
laureate's major concern in his fiction and nonfiction has been to identify "the threat exercised by
the 'massman' within ourselves." His one novel,
Die Blendung (The Deception, 1936; translated as
Auto-da-Fé, 1946), was identified by the Swedish
Academy as a metaphor representing this major
problem of modern man. The academy also
praised his theoretical study *Masse und Macht*
(1960; translated as *Crowds and Power*, 1962) as "a
magisterial work" on the origin and nature of
the crowd. Canetti has been awarded the highest
literary prizes but has enjoyed only a small and select readership of writers and scholars. Susan
Sontag has quoted Canetti as saying that he set
out to "grab this century by the throat," and he
has done so with power and grace. His comment
on Kafka can be applied to Canetti's own work
with equal validity: "Man wird gut, während man
ihn liest, aber ohne stolz darauf zu sein" (One

*Canetti with his cousin, Mathilde Camhi, in Vienna in 1930
(photo property of Raphael Sorin, Paris)*

turns good while reading him but without being
proud of it).

The oldest of three sons, Canetti was born
on 25 July 1905 in Rutschuk (now Ruse), Bulgaria. His father's family belonged to that group
of Sephardic Jews who had been driven out of
Spain at the time of the Inquisition. They had settled in Andrianople, Turkey, for several centuries
prior to relocating in Rutschuk, a trading center
on the Danube River. His father, Jacques
Canetti, always retained his Turkish citizenship;
consequently, his children were also Turkish citizens. Canetti's mother, Mathilde Arditti Canetti,
belonged to one of Rutschuk's old and distinguished families of Sephardic Jews. Both parents
had studied in Vienna, adopting the cosmo-
politanism of the old imperial city and becoming
totally engrossed in and enamored of the classical German and European theater tradition. If
the family had not insisted that Jacques Canetti
enter the family's wholesale grocery business, he
might have become an actor. The mother used

her interest in dramatic literature as the most important educational device during Canetti's early years.

The language the family spoke at home was Ladino, a mixed Spanish and Hebrew dialect spoken by the Jews of Spanish extraction living in the Balkan states. Canetti was also exposed to Bulgarian, Hebrew, Turkish, Greek, Albanian, Armenian, Romanian, and Russian. The parents spoke German when they did not want their children to understand what they were saying. This experience with so many languages undoubtedly led to Canetti's highly sensitive acoustic perception. In later years he would say that each individual has a specific "acoustic mask," a fingerprint of speech. Everything Canetti experienced, even in the earliest years, seemed to find its way into his writings. His earliest memory, the fear of having his tongue cut off if he revealed the truth of his nanny's amorous activities, is integrated into an episode in his novel.

When Canetti was six years old his father escaped the oppressive atmosphere of working in a family business in a small eastern European town by joining his brothers-in-law's business in Manchester, England. There Canetti learned English and started school. But even more important, it was there that his father introduced him to literature and the life of the imagination. After reading a book Canetti would discuss it with his father and would then receive another. He read *The Arabian Nights*, Grimm's fairy tales, *Robinson Crusoe*, *Gulliver's Travels*, *Tales from Shakespeare*, *Don Quixote*, Dante, and *William Tell* and later said that he was most grateful to his father for never telling him that fairy tales were untrue. This life of youthful joy was shattered in October 1912 with the sudden death of his father from a heart attack. Since Canetti's mother had always been nostalgic for Vienna, she decided in May 1913 to move there. During a three-month sojourn in Lausanne, Switzerland, she intensively taught her son German so that he would be ready to enter the third grade in Vienna. Much to the surprise of everyone but his mother, Canetti was fluent in the language when the family arrived in Vienna in the fall. This experience gave him a language that he would use for all of his major writings; it also provided him with a lifelong cultural identity.

In 1916 the family moved to Zurich to escape the ravages of World War I. The Swiss city was a paradise for Canetti during his formative years. At age fourteen he completed his first liter-

Canetti circa 1968, sketch by Rudolf Schönwald (Bildarchiv der Österreichischen Nationalbibliothek)

ary work, a historical tragedy in five acts of 2,290 lines of blank verse titled "Junius Brutus." He dedicated the unpublished play to his mother, his strictest and most important teacher. Years later Canetti noted that this play, for all its faults, was his first work that confronted the horror of the death penalty, an issue of lifelong concern.

Much to Canetti's dismay, in 1921 the family moved to Frankfurt am Main. If the previous half decade was lived in a dream world, the years in Frankfurt introduced Canetti to the harshness of reality. Although he was not personally affected by the German inflation, he experienced its manifestations when he saw an old woman collapse and die of hunger in the street. On another occasion Canetti had his first experience with the power of a crowd when he saw a mass demonstration against the murder of the Jewish industrialist Walter Rathenau in 1922. For decades thereafter Canetti devoted great energy to gaining an understanding of crowds and power.

In 1924 Canetti matriculated at the University of Vienna as a student of chemistry. He received a doctorate in 1929 but never worked as a chemist. Perhaps the most important experience of these years was his encounter with Vienna's master polemicist, Karl Kraus. Canetti said at the time he received the Nobel Prize that Kraus taught him to hear the sounds that make up the "acoustic masks" of different individuals; more important, Kraus "gegen Krieg geimpft" (inoculated [him] against war).

In 1929 Canetti began writing *Die Blendung*. Originally he planned this work to be one in a series of eight novels which were to make up a "Comédie Humaine an Irren" (Human Comedy of Madmen). Each novel would have as its protagonist a character who lived a life dedicated to the extreme pursuit of a concept or ideal–the man of truth, the visionary who wants to live in outer space, the religious fanatic, the collector, the spendthrift, the enemy of death, the actor, and the bookman. The bookman (Büchermensch), Dr. Peter Kien, is the protagonist of *Die Blendung*. Kien, at age forty, is the greatest living authority on sinology. He has been offered chairs of oriental philology at several major universities but has declined each invitation. He no longer even gives papers at conferences, even though the entire scholarly community relies on his final judgment. He has withdrawn to his personal library of twenty-five thousand volumes on the top floor of an apartment house at No. 24 Ehrlich Straße. (Even though it is never stated specifically, the reader can assume that the locale of the novel is Vienna.) Eight years ago Kien hired Therese Krumbholz, who was then fifty-six, as a housekeeper. Each day she dusts one of the four rooms of the library from floor to ceiling and prepares Kien's meals, which he takes at his desk. Kien, having severed all contact with the world and withdrawn to scholarly activities in his library, is leading the life of "Ein Kopf ohne Welt" (A Head without a World), as the first part of the novel is titled. The reader soon realizes that Kien has a pathological relationship with his books: he speaks to them, he scolds them as one would a recalcitrant child, and on occasion he suspects them of harboring ill will toward him. On other occasions Kien's views seem much more rational: for example, his suggestion that a novel can help the reader to think himself into another person's place seems an acceptable account of what takes place in the reading process.

To assure the continued care of his library, Kien decides to marry his loyal housekeeper; Therese agrees to the marriage because it will provide her with material security in her advancing years. Kien allows Therese to speak to him for only a few minutes during the noon meal, and at that time he concentrates on not listening to her. While Kien remains totally devoted to his scholarly work, Therese sets about securing her future. She assumes that Kien must be rich because he was overgenerous in paying her prior to their marriage and now seems to pay no attention to money matters. When she asks for money to buy furniture, for instance, he gives her a large amount. What she does not understand is that he is just trying to get rid of her so that he will not be bothered at his work. From this misunderstanding begins Therese's great search for Kien's bankbook and his will. Not finding either, she assumes that Kien deceived her about his finances. She sets out to get revenge by invading the solitude of Kien's library, making it impossible for him to work. Kien flees from the house.

Homeless and separated from his library, the helpless misogynist and hermit becomes the easy prey of a ruthless exploiter, the dwarf Fischerle, in the section of the novel titled "Kopflose Welt" (Headless World). To continue his sinological studies Kien imagines that he is carrying his library in his head. Each day he adds more imaginary books to his head library, and each evening he imagines himself taking them out and stacking them on the floor of his hotel room. As he accumulates more and more imaginary books, he needs ever larger rooms. When the task becomes too great he hires Fischerle, who introduces himself as the World Chess Champion Siegfried Fischer and plays along with the head-library game. Through a variety of tricks he swindles Kien out of most of his money.

One source Kien uses to build his head library is the municipal pawnshop, the Theresianum (based on the Dorotheum in Vienna). But rather than buying books, he pays would-be customers not to pawn their books. Fischerle enlists four friends who pretend to want to pawn books but just take Kien's money. One day while Kien is standing in the hallway of the Theresianum his wife and the caretaker of his apartment house come to pawn Kien's books. A row breaks out, the police come, and Kien is accused of theft for preventing the sale of his own books. Although he sees Therese, in his disordered mind he believes that she did not throw him out of his apartment but that he locked her in the apartment and that she has died of starvation. When the police tell him that he is accused,

Canetti

he admits that he is his wife's murderer. The caretaker, a retired policeman named Benedikt Pfaff, realizes that he can profit from the situation. He vouches for Kien at the police station and takes him home to his basement apartment. Forcing Kien to live in a totally dark room, Pfaff ensconces himself with Therese in the top-floor apartment.

At this point Kien's brother Georg, a psychiatrist, arrives from Paris. In the third section of the novel, "Welt im Kopf" (World in the Head), a divorce is arranged, and Therese is established as the owner of a dairy store on the other side of town. She and Pfaff will receive generous sums of money from Georg Kien provided that they stay away from the sinologist. Peter Kien's apartment is refurbished, and his library is reclaimed

from the pawnshop. By the time Georg returns to Paris he even seems to have cured Peter's psychosis. But suddenly Kien is attacked by his mania. He places all his beloved books in a pile in the center of the room, sets them on fire, and perishes.

Although Canetti never wrote the other seven novels of the "Human Comedy of Madmen," some of the protagonists of those planned works appear in *Die Blendung* in slightly different guises. Peter Kien's extreme pursuit of his sinological studies differs little from the man who would pursue a certain truth, or the visionary, or even the religious fanatic; likewise, Kien represents the collector and the spendthrift. The most fascinating aspect of the book is the meticulous development of the psychological imbalance of the

Drawing of Canetti by Alfred Hrdlicka, 1980 (courtesy of Gerald Stieg, with permission of the artist)

major characters. Kien, Therese, Fischerle, Pfaff, and even Georg Kien each suffers from his or her own brand of madness, and the exposition of each form of madness is finely crafted. In his only major work of fiction, written at the age of twenty-five, Canetti exhibits a mastery of storytelling that his later works, both fiction and nonfiction, confirm.

It took Canetti a long time to convince himself that the book was worthy of publication. Finally, almost five years after he completed the manuscript, Canetti's friend, the writer Stefan Zweig, found a publisher for it. It was well received by some critics and was praised by Hermann Broch, Alban Berg, Thomas Mann, Robert Musil, and Hermann Hesse. But with Hitler in power and the March 1938 annexation of Austria by Germany, Canetti, a Jew, was unable to have his book distributed in most of the German-speaking market. When the novel was translated into English after World War II, many

critics and reviewers labeled the work "too difficult." Little effort was made to promote the translation, and it soon went out of print. After Canetti won the Nobel Prize he showed his bitterness for the years of neglect by withholding permission to have his works printed in England until 1985.

In 1932, shortly after completing *Die Blendung*, Canetti wrote his first play, *Hochzeit* (1964; translated as *The Wedding*, 1986). After World War II he wrote two other plays, *Komödie der Eitelkeit* (1950; translated as *Comedy of Vanity*, 1983) and *Die Befristeten* (1964; translated as *Life-Terms*, 1983). When the first two of these plays premiered in Braunschweig in the Federal Republic of Germany in 1965, they were received with outrage and disapproval; but productions prepared by the director Hans Hollmann in the late 1970s and early 1980s in Vienna and Basel were highly successful. Hollmann understood these plays of the theater of the absurd and the concept of the "acoustic masks" which Canetti had created.

In February 1934 Canetti married Venetia Toubner-Calderon, whom he had met at Kraus's lectures. In November 1938 they were among the last Jews to flee from Vienna to Paris following the annexation of Austria to Germany. The next year they moved to London.

While in exile Canetti wrote his major nonfiction work, *Masse und Macht*. The impetus for this study can be traced back to 15 July 1927, when Canetti observed firsthand the dynamics of the crowd that set fire to the Palace of Justice in Vienna. (The same event forms the core of Heimito von Doderer's novel *Die Dämonen* [1956; translated as *The Demons*, 1961].) Canetti's further experiences with mob behavior and the inexplicable power of Hitler to incite mass hysteria compelled him to examine the origins, makeup, and behavior of crowds in a vast array of societies from the earliest times to the present.

His wife died in May 1963, and Canetti married Hera Buschor in 1971; their daughter, Johanna, was born in 1972. In recent years Canetti has divided his residence between Hampstead, England, and Zurich, Switzerland.

During the war Canetti had begun setting aside an hour or two each day for writing "Aufzeichnungen" (Notes); they eventually covered the years from 1942 to 1985 and were published in four volumes between 1965 and 1987. These aphoristic writings on a host of topics from the myths of various cultures, languages, war and revolutions, the fate of the Jews, to crowds and power are extraordinary miniature essays which, according to some scholars, may someday be regarded as Canetti's most significant contribution to German literature.

Some of Canetti's longer essays were collected in *Das Gewissen der Worte* (1975; enlarged, 1976; translated as *The Conscience of Words*, 1979). These essays deal with people who had a major impact on Canetti's writing and thinking during the decades devoted to the study of crowds and power: Broch, Musil, Kraus, Stendhal, Tolstoy, and Aristophanes. The most important essay in the collection is Canetti's study of the tortured relationship of Franz Kafka and his fiancée Felice Bauer, as it can be read in the letters he sent her while writing *Der Prozeß* (1925; translated as *The Trial*, 1937); the essay had appeared separately in 1969 as *Der andere Prozeß* (translated as *Kafka's Other Trial*, 1974).

The three volumes of Canetti's autobiography, *Die gerettete Zunge: Geschichte einer Jugend* (1977; translated as *The Tongue Set Free: Remem-* brance of a European Childhood, 1979), *Die Fackel im Ohr: Lebensgeschichte 1921-1931* (1980; translated as *The Torch in My Ear*, 1982), and *Das Augenspiel: Lebensgeschichte 1931-1937* (1985; translated as *The Play of the Eyes*, 1986), serve not only as a chronicle of the author's life but also as an important contribution to historical writing.

Although Canetti was recognized for his work only late in life, he has been awarded some of the most distinguished literary prizes: the Grand Prix International du Club Française du Livre in 1949, the Writer's Prize of the City of Vienna in 1966, the Great Austrian State Prize in 1967, the Georg Büchner Prize in 1972, the Franz Nabl Prize of the City of Graz in 1975, the Orden Pour le Mérite in 1980, the Nobel Prize for Literature and the Franz Kafka Prize in 1981, and the Great Service Cross of the Federal Republic of Germany in 1983. He received honorary doctoral degrees from the University of Manchester in 1975 and the University of Munich in 1976.

When Canetti was awarded the Nobel Prize there was a curious reaction in the press. The *New York Times* noted that Canetti was "the first native of Bulgaria to win the prize." The *Times* of London identified Canetti as "the first British citizen to win the literature prize since Winston Churchill" and said, "most unusually of all for a British laureate, Dr. Canetti writes, and has always written, in German." At the same time the Austrian literary journal *Literatur und Kritik* wrote that "Canetti ist nicht österreichischer Staatsbürger, aber dank seiner Bekenntnisse dürfen wir ihn unserer Literatur zurechnen. Er ist der erste Autor österreichischen Wesens, der den Nobelpreis erhält" (Canetti is not an Austrian citizen, but in recognition of his acknowledgment we may include him in our literature. He is the first author of truly Austrian spirit who has received the Nobel Prize). It is perhaps understandable that so many countries and language groups wanted to share the honor of the laureate, if only by spurious association. At the Nobel Prize ceremony Edfelt called him an "exiled and cosmopolitan author" who "has one native land, and that is the German language. He has never abandoned it, and he has often avowed his love of the highest manifestations of the classical German culture.... With your versatile writings, which attack sick tendencies in our age, you wish to serve the cause of humanity. Intellectual passion is combined in you with the moral responsibility that—in your own words—'is nourished by mercy.' "

References:

Friedbert Aspetsberger and Gerald Stieg, eds., *Elias Canetti: Blendung als Lebensform* (Königsberg: Athenäum, 1985);

Dagmar Barnouw, *Elias Canetti* (Stuttgart: Metzler, 1979);

Barnouw, "Elias Canetti–Poet and Intellectual," in *Major Figures of Contemporary Austrian Literature*, edited by Donald G. Daviau (New York: Lang, 1987), pp. 117-141;

Kurt Bartsch and Gerhard Melzer, eds., *Elias Canetti: Experte der Macht* (Graz: Droschl, 1985);

Russell A. Berman, "The Charismatic Novel: Robert Musil, Hermann Hesse, and Elias Canetti," in his *The Rise of the Modern German Novel* (Cambridge, Mass.: Harvard University Press, 1986), pp. 179-204;

Alfons-M. Bischoff, *Elias Canetti: Stationen zum Werk* (Bern & Frankfurt am Main: Lang, 1973);

Mechthild Curtius, *Kritik der Verdinglichung in Canettis Roman "Die Blendung" Eine Sozialpsychologische Literaturanalyse* (Bonn: Bouvier, 1973);

Festschrift, Hüter der Verwandlung: Beiträge zum Werk von Elias Canetti (Munich: Hanser, 1985); translated by Michael Hulse as *Essays in Honor of Elias Canetti* (New York: Farrar, Straus & Giroux, 1987);

Leslie Fiedler, "The Tower of Babel," *Partisan Review*, 3 (May / June 1947): 316-320;

Herbert G. Göpfert, ed., *Canetti lesen: Erfahrungen mit seinen Büchern* (Munich: Hanser, 1975);

Gitta Honegger, "Acoustic Masks: Strategies of Language in the Theater of Canetti, Bernhard, and Handke," *Modern Austrian Literature*, 18, no. 2 (1985): 57-66;

Detlef Krumme, *Lesemodelle: Canetti, Grass, Höllerer* (Munich: Hanser, 1983), pp. 31-84;

J. W. McFarlane, "The Tiresian Vision," *Durham University Journal*, 49, no. 3 (1957): 109-115;

Modern Austrian Literature, special Canetti issue, 16, no. 3 / 4 (1983);

Idris Parry, "Elias Canetti's Novel *Die Blendung*," in *Essays in German Literature*, edited by F. Norman, volume 1 (London: London University Press, 1965), pp. 145-166;

Edgar Piel, "Herr seines Schicksals ist der Mensch allein: Elias Canettis *Blendung* als eine andere *Comédie humain*," *Literatur und Kritik*, no. 157 / 158 (August / September 1981): 444-461;

David Roberts, *Kopf und Welt: Elias Canettis Roman "Die Blendung"* (Munich: Hanser, 1975);

Sidney Rosenfeld, "1981 Nobel Laureate Elias Canetti: A Writer Apart," *World Literature Today*, 56, no. 1 (1982): 5-9;

Peter Russell, "The Vision of Man in Elias Canetti's *Die Blendung*," *German Life and Letters*, 28 (October 1974): 24-35;

Ingo Seidler, "Who Is Elias Canetti," in *Cross Currents: A Yearbook of Central European Culture, 1982*, edited by Ladislav Matejka and Benjamin Stolz (Ann Arbor: University of Michigan Press, 1982), pp. 107-123;

Walter H. Sokel, "The Ambiguity of Madness: Elias Canetti's Novel *Die Blendung*," in *Views and Reviews of Modern German Literature: Festschrift for A. D. Klarmann*, edited by Karl S. Weimar (Munich: Delp, 1974), pp. 181-187;

Susan Sontag, "Mind as Passion," in her *Under the Sign of Saturn* (New York: Farrar, Straus & Giroux, 1980), pp. 181-204;

Edward A. Thomson, "Elias Canetti's *Die Blendung* and the Changing Image of Madness," *German Life and Letters*, 26 (October 1972): 38-47;

David Turner, "The Intellectual as King Canute," in *Modern Austrian Writing: Literature and Society after 1945*, edited by Alan Best and Hans Wolfschütz (London: Wolff, 1980), pp. 79-96;

Marion E. Wiley, "Elias Canetti's Reflective Prose," *Modern Austrian Literature*, 12, no. 2 (1979): 129-139.

Heimito von Doderer

(5 September 1896-23 December 1966)

Andrew W. Barker
University of Edinburgh

BOOKS: *Gassen und Landschaft* (Vienna: Haybach, 1923);

Die Bresche: Ein Vorgang in vierundzwanzig Stunden (Vienna: Haybach, 1924);

Das Geheimnis des Reichs: Roman aus dem russischen Bürgerkrieg (Vienna: Saturn, 1930);

Der Fall Gütersloh: Ein Schicksal und seine Deutung (Vienna: Haybach, 1930);

Ein Mord den jeder begeht (Munich: Beck, 1938); translated by Richard and Clara Winston as *Every Man a Murderer* (New York: Knopf, 1964);

Ein Umweg: Roman (Munich: Beck, 1940);

Die erleuchteten Fenster oder Die Menschwerdung des Amtsrates Julius Zihal: Roman (Munich: Biederstein, 1950);

Die Strudlhofstiege oder Melzer und die Tiefe der Jahre (Munich: Biederstein, 1951); extracts translated by Vincent Kling as "The Strudlhof Steps," *Chicago Review*, 26, no. 2 (1974): 107-138;

Das letzte Abenteuer: Erzählung (Munich: Biederstein, 1953);

Die Dämonen: Roman. Nach der Chronik des Sektionsrates Geyrenhoff (Munich: Biederstein, 1956); translated by Richard and Clara Winston as *The Demons*, 2 volumes (New York: Knopf, 1961; London: Weidenfeld, 1962);

Ein Weg im Dunkeln: Gedichte und epigrammatische Verse (Munich: Biederstein, 1957);

Die Posaunen von Jericho: Neues Divertimento (Zurich: Arche, 1958); translated by Kling as "The Trumpets of Jericho," *Chicago Review*, 26, no. 2 (1974): 5-35;

Grundlagen und Funktion des Romans (Nuremberg: Glock & Lutz, 1959); translated as "Principles and Function of the Novel," in *30th International Congress of the P.E.N. Clubs, Frankfurt 1959* (Frankfurt am Main: Propyläen, 1960), pp. 56-68;

Die Peinigung der Lederbeutelchen: Erzählungen (Munich: Biederstein, 1959); title story translated by Robert S. Rosen as "The Torment of the Leather Pouches," *Odyssey Review*, 3

Heimito von Doderer (Austrian Institute)

(March 1963): 219-232; "Ein anderer Kratki-Baschik," translated by Astrid Ivask as "The Magician's Art," *Literary Review*, 5 (Autumn 1961): 5-15; "Zwei Lügen oder Eine antikische Tragödie auf dem Dorfe," translated by Kling as "Two Lies; or, Classical Tragedy in a Village," *Chicago Review*, 26, no. 2 (1974): 97-106; "Eine Person von Porzellan," translated by Kling as "A Person Made of Porcelain," *Chicago Review*, 26, no. 2 (1974): 70-73; "Die Amputation," translated as "The Amputation," *Ciba Symposium* (Amsterdam), 12, no. 1 (1964): 42-46;

Wege und Umwege, edited by Herbert Eisenreich (Graz & Vienna: Stiasny, 1960);

Die Merowinger oder Die totale Familie: Roman (Munich: Biederstein, 1962);

Albert Paris Gütersloh: Autor und Werk, by Doderer and others (Munich: Piper, 1962);

Roman No. 7, Erster Teil: Die Wasserfälle von Slunj (Munich: Biederstein, 1963); translated by Eithne Wilkins and Ernst Kaiser as *The Waterfalls of Slunj* (New York: Harcourt, Brace & World, 1966);

Tangenten: Tagebuch eines Schriftstellers (Munich: Biederstein, 1964);

Meine neunzehn Lebensläufe und neun andere Geschichten (Munich: Biederstein, 1966); title story translated by Kling as "My 19 Curricula Vitae," *Chicago Review,* 26, no. 2 (1974): 79-85; "Trethofen" and "Sonatine," translated by Ivask as "Two Short Stories," *Literary Review,* 6 (Winter 1962/1963): 176-180;

Unter schwarzen Sternen: Erzählungen (Munich: Biederstein, 1966); title story translated by Kling as "Under Black Stars," *Chicago Review,* 26, no. 2 (1974): 36-54;

Roman No. 7, Zweiter Teil: Der Grenzwald. Fragment (Munich: Biederstein, 1967);

Frühe Prosa: Die Bresche; Jutta Bamberger; Das Geheimnis des Reichs, by Hans Flesch-Brunningen (Munich: Biederstein, 1968);

Repertorium: Ein Begreifbuch von höheren und niederen Lebens-Sachen, edited by Dietrich Weber (Munich: Biederstein, 1969);

Die Wiederkehr der Drachen: Aufsätze, Traktate, Reden, edited by Wendelin Schmidt-Dengler (Munich: Biederstein, 1972); "Roman und Leser," translated by Kling as "The Novel and the Reader," *Chicago Review,* 26, no. 2 (1974): 74-77;

Die Erzählungen, edited by Schmidt-Dengler (Munich: Biederstein, 1972);

Commentarii: Tagebücher aus dem Nachlaß, edited by Schmidt-Dengler (Munich: Biederstein, 1976);

Das Doderer-Buch: Eine Auswahl aus dem Werk Heimito von Doderers, edited by Karl Heinz Kramberg (Munich: Biederstein, 1976);

Begegnung mit Heimito von Doderer, edited by Michael Horowitz (Vienna & Munich: Amalthea, 1983);

Commentarii 1957-1966, edited by Schmidt-Dengler (Munich: Biederstein, 1985).

OTHER: Albert Paris Gütersloh, *Gewaltig staunt der Mensch,* edited by Doderer (Graz: Stiasny, 1963);

Robert Löbl, *Wien in Farben: Ein Farbbildbuch nach Aufnahmen von Robert Löbl,* texts by Doderer and others (Innsbruck, Vienna & Munich: Tyrolia, 1967);

Herbert Eisenreich, *Die Freunde meiner Frau und neunzehn andere Kurzgeschichten,* foreword by Doderer (Zurich: Diogenes, 1978).

PERIODICAL PUBLICATION: "Divertimento No. V.," *Merkur,* 8 (1954): 647-659.

The last of six children, Heimito von Doderer was born in a small eighteenth-century chateau in Weidlingau, on the rural fringes of Vienna, to Wilhelm Ritter von Doderer, an architect and civil engineer, and his German-born wife Luise Wilhelmine von Hügel von Doderer. The writer, whose striking Christian name is a diminutive of the Spanish Jaime, grew up in a family not only of some affluence but also one with literary connections: through his paternal grandmother he was related to the romantic poet Nikolaus Lenau. The family was Protestant, although Doderer himself eventually converted to the dominant Catholicism of his homeland. His birthplace, the Laudonsche Forsthaus, erected for the Empress Maria Theresa's Field Marshal Gideon von Laudon, had been rented by Doderer's father so that his family could be closer to him while he was at work regulating the flow of the unpredictable Wien river. The Doderers normally lived at 12 Stammgasse in Vienna's Third District, not far from the spot where the Wien flows into the Danube Canal, but they had also had a villa at Prein in the Raxgebiet, at the eastern extremity of the Alpine chain, two hours' train ride to the south of Vienna. Doderer retained a lasting love for this area of childhood idylls and reproduces it with affectionate detail in the historical novel *Ein Umweg* (A Diversion, 1940), set in the seventeenth century, and in *Die Strudlhofstiege* (The Strudlhof Steps, 1951), set between 1911 and 1925. The ambience of Doderer's Viennese childhood near the Danube with its then-marshy borders and quiet inlets figures memorably in the early scenes depicting Conrad Castiletz's childhood in *Ein Mord den jeder begeht* (1938; translated as *Every Man a Murderer,* 1964). This novel, like *Die Strudlhofstiege,* portrays the tense relationship between a despotic father and an uncertain son, which Doderer experienced in real life.

As a pupil at the Landstraßer Gymnasium Doderer was not outstanding, but he graduated without too great a struggle in July 1914 and went on the study law at the University of Vienna. In the last novel he was able to complete, *Die Wasserfälle von Slunj* (1963; translated as *The Waterfalls of Slunj*, 1966), there are scenes calling upon the distant days of his gymnasium education; there even appears, marginally, a schoolboy by the name of Doderer. Such references are unusual in the work of an author who, though drawing heavily on the experiences of an often turbulent life, tried to avoid the directly autobiographical. His reticence was such that when he was requested by his publisher to provide an account of his life on the occasion of his seventieth birthday, he replied with a parody bordering on evasion. In the introduction to the work in which this piece appears, *Meine neunzehn Lebensläufe und neun andere Geschichten* (My Nineteen Curricula Vitae and Nine Other Stories, 1966), Doderer writes: "Das Direkt-Autobiographische ist nichts anders als das Schreiben des Nicht-Schriftstellers. . . . Ein Schriftsteller hat keine Biographie" (The directly autobiographical is nothing but the writing of a nonwriter. . . . A writer has no biography). Such details as did emerge about him in the fifteen years of literary celebrity he enjoyed from the publication of *Die Strudlhofstiege* until his death in 1966 were strictly edited by the author in the interests of an image which did not always correspond to the realities of his life.

In 1915 he was called up for military service in the Third Dragoons, the most exclusive Viennese regiment, whose officers were forbidden to use public transport because they all had their own horses. After taking part in the Battle of Oleszy, one of the last to include a full-scale cavalry charge, he was taken prisoner by Czarist troops on 12 July 1916. During his four years of captivity he started to write fiction, but only fragments survive. For the officers, if not for the men, a life of some cultural vitality, diversity, and even a measure of liberty seems to have evolved in the prison camps, and Doderer was able to spend long hours indulging his passion for soccer. During this enforced absence from home he grew to love "Mother Russia" in a way typical of many conservatively inclined Austro-German writers in the earlier part of the century. In the novel *Das Geheimnis des Reichs* (The Secret of the Kingdom, 1930) and in his last, fragmentary work, *Der Grenzwald* (The Forest Boundary,

1967), Doderer calls on the experiences of his time in Russia.

Doderer's final return to freedom did not come until 1920, after an epic trek across the Asian steppes, where he was an eyewitness to the turbulence of civil war and revolution. When he got back to Vienna, wearing an English soldier's tunic, his sense of returning to a strange world, so different from the late Hapsburg glow of his privileged childhood, can only have been heightened by the refusal of a recently engaged concierge to permit him to enter his own home. This incident could have been the seed from which the later novelist's famously and sometimes hilariously bitter hatred of the "concierge clan" grew.

His resolve to become a writer was already firm by the start of the 1920s, but his wish took years to come true. He noted in his diary that he felt that he had no choice but to become a writer; on the other hand, he was plagued by feelings of inadequacy on many fronts. He was anguished by his sexuality, which manifested itself in sadomasochistic urges; by his deficient education; and by his need for independence while remaining financially reliant on his family. At this time he developed his interest in serious music, and the analogy of music to the epic came to form the basis for both his literary theory and, ostensibly, his practice. He read widely, and it is clear from his early diaries that the works of Albert Paris Gütersloh and Otto Weininger, writers who remained points of reference for him for decades, were already known to him. He also knew Oswald Spengler's *Der Untergang des Abendlandes* (1918-1922; translated as *The Decline of the West*, 1926). His urge to write, however, was countered by pecuniary uncertainty and familial disapproval; he took to journalism to offset the former and resumed his studies to alleviate the latter, knowing that such a course would both placate his parents and help to plug the gaps in his knowledge. He thus became a student again at the University of Vienna, studying history and psychology in the belief that these disciplines would most further his writing career. He was increasingly alienated by the methodology of history as practiced at the university, however, especially what he felt to be the outmoded positivism of his professors.

Despite his assertions of sloth, Doderer's capacity for hard work can be seen in the fact that while writing newspaper feuilletons and studying he also managed to have two books published before receiving his doctorate in 1925. In 1923 his first work appeared, a book of verse titled *Gassen und Landschaft* (Streets and Landscapes), a good deal of which had been composed while Doderer was in captivity. His talent was not primarily a lyric one, even though his prose contains passages of considerable lyric beauty; but he continued to write verse for much of his life. A second poetry volume, *Ein Weg im Dunkeln* (A Path in the Darkness), appeared in 1957. The verse is of no special distinction, and it is not hard to regard this publication as the commercial exploitation of a name made famous through *Die Strudlhofstiege* and *Die Dämonen* (1956; translated as *The Demons*, 1961).

The first of Doderer's narratives to appear was *Die Bresche* (The Breach, 1924); it was published by his friend Rudolf Haybach, whom he had met in the camps in Russia. Like so many a narrative debut, *Die Bresche* has strong autobiographical features, reflecting to a considerable extent the author's concern about his sexuality. Completed by 1921 and rejected by at least one publisher before being taken on by Haybach, *Die Bresche* reveals many of the hallmarks of expressionist prose: extreme characterization, rhapsodic interludes, experiments in narrative technique, and examination of how an individual attains his "true self." Jan Herzka, the apparently respectable bourgeois hero of the tale, admits the truth about himself when he gives in to his sadomasochistic urges in defiance of his everyday obsession with orderliness. But the price of his liberation, the "breach" from which his real self emerges, is the humiliation and physical degradation of his unsuspecting lover, Magdalena Güllich. He takes her to the circus before returning to a shabby rented room, where, incited to fever pitch by the ringmaster's whip, he subjects her to a crude physical assault. The high-flown rhetoric cannot conceal that Herzka only comes to a true assessment of himself at the price of another's misery. The novel has a certain power and vitality, and it marks the first appearance of the theme of "Menschwerdung" (humanization), which would be central to Doderer's conception of the self for the rest of his career. Primarily a religious term denoting the Incarnation, it is used by Doderer in a secular sense to denote self-realization and the liberation of individual perception from the shackles imposed by upbringing, environment, and societal expectations. As Michael Bachem comments, " 'humanization' involves deep insight into oneself, acceptance of the world as it is, complete avoidance of all ideologies."

Die Bresche also offers the first instance in Doderer's work of a father figure, an authority who validates the life of the protagonist. The Russian composer Slobedeff makes sense of things for Herzka and points to a way out of the confusion he feels after the assault on Magdalena. Throughout most of his life Doderer needed figures of authority he could look up to: Thomas Aquinas; Gütersloh; and Weininger, the Jewish Viennese philosopher cum psychologist notorious for *Geschlecht und Charakter* (Sex and Character), a misogynistic and anti-Semitic diatribe published in 1903. Like Spengler, Weininger stressed the importance of physiognomy in the appraisal of character; both were presumably echoing their reading of Arthur Schopenhauer ("For the face of a man says straight out *what he is*"). Physiognomical characterization became fundamental to Doderer's writing technique. It is not hard to see fascistic elements in the "science" of physiognomy, and Doderer's espousal of this outlook is a further indication of his place among culturally conservative writers in the decades before World War II.

During the six years between the appearance of *Die Bresche* and *Das Geheimnis des Reichs* Doderer developed his notion of the relationship between the prose epic and music. He also worked on a series of experimental stories he called "Divertimenti," most of which were unpublished until they were collected in *Die Erzählungen* (The Tales, 1972). The performing aspect of these stories was particularly strong; Doderer memorized them and delivered at least one of them complete at an oral recitation. Inordinately proud of his remarkable memory, he was fond of quoting from the ancient classics and in later years claimed that a prerequisite for entry into his intimate circle was the ability to recite by heart at least one Latin poem. *Die Bresche* itself had started life as a Divertimento but had soon outgrown the bounds of what could feasibly be remembered and recited.

The importance of the Divertimenti to Doderer may be gauged from the fact that in 1954, thirty years after its composition, he saw fit to publish "Divertimento No. V." That Doderer should have chosen this of all his juvenilia for publication at the height of his fame is a token of its significance for him and shows the strong links that exist, thematically if not always stylistically, between his apprentice works and those of his maturity. Like Jan Herzka in *Die Bresche*, Georg, the main character of "Divertimento No. V" is a stickler for order. He does everything in his power to put his life into a neat and tidy shape, but the more he tries the less he succeeds. In the first of the four sections Georg's carefully arranged world seems to be coming apart, inducing in him something approaching panic as he tries to reintroduce order to things. In a state of utter confusion he rushes out of his office and is hit by a passing bus, which, oblivious as he is to the external world, he fails to spot in time. In the second section he wakes up in the hospital, where he is unable to concern himself directly with the chaos of his life outside. Meanwhile, as the third section demonstrates, all the problems that have driven Georg to the point of distraction are sorting themselves out of their own accord, without his intervention. In the concluding section Georg happily realizes that if things are left alone, they will assume a natural order independent of human intervention.

"Divertimento No. V" reveals an idea that runs through Doderer's work from start to finish: the notion that when we attempt to impose order on the empirical world, we set up a "zweite Wirklichkeit" (second reality) which blinds us to how things actually are. Doderer's distaste for subjective tinkering would develop into an abhorrence of all ideologies that was tantamount to an ideology itself. His mature outlook, foreshadowed here, displays a passive optimism based on the smug assumption that things are always for the best. People who simply give themselves up to the "Mechanik des Lebens" (mechanism of life) and the equally undefined "Mechanik des Geistes" (mechanism of the mind, a phrase perhaps taken over from Walther Rathenau's work of that title published in 1913) will, in Doderer's view, live in that state of enlightened self-knowledge which is commensurate with being a true "Mensch" (human being). This forsaking of imprisonment in a "second reality" to achieve insight and truth in the "real" world is what Doderer dubs "Menschwerdung."

From the same period as the Divertimenti and *Die Bresche* stems "Jutta Bamberger" (1968), a work which was to occupy its author for many years without ever assuming a completed shape. It is a novel of adolescence, a popular topic in the Freud-inspired ambience of the early twentieth century; but unlike such works as Robert Musil's *Die Verwirrungen des Zöglings Törleß* (1906; translated as *Young Törless*, 1955) and Hermann Hesse's *Unterm Rad* (Under the Wheel, 1906; translated as *The Prodigy*, 1957), it has a female protago-

nist. Like much of Doderer's more mature work it is polycentric rather than unilinear in construction. The turbulence of Jutta's awakening sexuality is compounded by the realization that her orientation is chiefly toward her own sex. On the whole, the delicacy of the subject matter evokes prose of subtlety and empathy from Doderer, leading Bachem to rank it "among the most sensitive portraits of youth, adolescence, and troubled sexuality in conflict with its surroundings."

Just as "Divertimento No. V" displays in paradigmatic fashion the belief that direct action will only end in the negation of one's wishes, "Leon Pujot" (1929; published in *Die Peinigung der Lederbeutelchen* [The Torment of the Leather Pouches, 1959]) demonstrates most concisely the theme of "Menschwerdung." In this story, based on an actual incident reported in the *Neues Wiener Journal* (but also bearing strong resemblance to the railroad heroics so much in vogue on the silent screen of which Doderer was a devotee), the title character stops a runaway train by an act of extraordinary heroism. He thus saves hundreds of lives and also frees himself from the shackles of his former existence, mundanely driving a taxi between Nancy and Paris, in thrall to a girl who failed to respond to his feelings. In taking command of the train Pujot also takes command of his life; he undergoes a "Zweite Geburt" (second birth), sees things for what they are, and goes off into the world as a new man, aware of himself and his environment in a new and fulfilling way. In its indirect way life has presented Pujot with an opportunity to change direction, to put his existence on a different track. (The railway setting of the story is typical of Doderer, who constantly employs metaphors drawn from train travel to illuminate the developments in his characters.)

Compared with anything Doderer had previously published, *Das Geheimnis des Reichs* marks a great advance both in thematic scope and in technical aspects of the narration. The work, whose title is drawn from the final words of Gerhart Hauptmann's *Der Narr in Christo Emanuel Quint* (1910; translated as *The Fool in Christ Emanuel Quint*, 1911), also started as a Divertimento but soon grew into a full-length novel. It represents Doderer's first attempt to distill his experiences in Siberia into a literary format. *Das Geheimnis des Reichs* is also the first of Doderer's "polygraphic" works, that is, a narration on several spatial and temporal planes, built up of short, mosaiclike fragments which eventually combine to present a whole picture. Stylistically, the novel still bears many traces of expressionist prose. One of its chief strands is the personal history of René Stangeler, an autobiographical figure who had appeared in some earlier stories and would play a prominent part in the novels of the 1950s upon which Doderer's reputation rests. Stangeler's story is woven into recollections of the Russian Revolution and of POW escapades and love affairs in Siberia, intermingled with philosophical reflections and discussions of recent Russian history. Although often confusing and stylistically uncertain, the novel captures the turbulence of revolutionary times, when normal constraints go by the board. The brutality of the period finds its most potent expression in the villainous Hugo Blau, a Viennese clothier turned Czech legionnaire turned Legitimist turned Bolshevik who eventually gets his just comeuppance at the hands of the Red Army. It is disturbing to note that this scoundrel, a man of total baseness, bears an obviously Jewish surname. Both White Russians and Bolsheviks stand equally condemned in the narrator's eyes, and the novel ends with Tolstoyan peasants facilitating the escape of Stangeler and his friend Alwersik to the West. The "secret of the kingdom" appears to reside in human fellowship, based on the tenets of Jesus Christ rather than on the precepts of the Soviet Revolution. As Cedric E. Williams has noted, "The narrator reserves his compassion and respect for the Russian people—for their spiritual resources, not their political organization.... He emphasizes that the emancipation of the Russian masses was due in the first instance to a personal religious feeling, to a new consciousness of self. It would be boring to show that such an interpretation is scarcely tenable as a historical explanation. It is redolent of Rilke's mystique of Holy Mother Russia, or of Dostoyevsky's salvation from the East, rather than of political realities of 1917 to 1920. The narrator's distortion cannot be justified as fictional license since it is offered as an objective statement in the context of the novel's interpolations of historical narrative."

In Siberia Doderer had avidly read Güthersloh's *Die tanzende Törin* (The Dancing Fool, 1910) one of the most significant early expressionist prose narratives, and he had met its author in 1924. In 1929 Haybach invited him to write a book on Güthersloh, and while preparing it he read Güthersloh's *Die Bekenntnisse eines modernen Malers* (Confessions of a Modern Painter, 1926). Elizabeth Hesson says that Doderer, whose sense of self was not high at the time, "saw in the work

a confirmation of his own position as a writer, a reinforcement of his belief in his own abilities." Güthersloh's text does not give up its secrets easily, being couched in a virtually impenetrable style for a small, elite group of like-minded readers. He ostensibly grapples with the artist's problem of self-justification in the light of his own antiutilitarian view of art; but as Bachem puts it, the thrust of these "confessions" is "anti-Puritan, anti-Marxist, anti-Gnostic, anti-Hegelian, and occasionally anti-democratic." To that list one might add "latently anti-Semitic." What seems to have attracted Doderer to this work was Güthersloh's insistence on accepting the world as fundamentally good and his belief that "die Tiefe ist außen" (depth is on the surface)—that appearances do not necessarily deceive, either in the phenomenal world or in the psyche. Accordingly, Güthersloh, like Spengler and Weininger, sets great store by physiognomical classification. Doderer also found in Güthersloh's work confirmation of his own view that it is possible, by means of a "second birth," to put one's past behind one, confront the world in a new and fruitful fashion, and emerge as a "real" human being. Güthersloh became the benign father figure to counter the disparagement Doderer suffered from his real father. Hans Joachim Schröder sees strongly fascist tendencies in Güthersloh's work, with its glorification of the irrational, its detestation of the "liberal," and its propagation of the leader principle. Yet Schröder admits that Doderer's *Der Fall Güthersloh* (The Case of Güthersloh, 1930) reveals no such easily identifiable fascistic traits. It is a laborious examination of the relationship between art and morality, which is at least as much about Doderer as it is about Güthersloh. Schröder is probably correct in maintaining, however, that it was Doderer's reading of *Die Bekenntnisse eines modernen Malers* that helped increase his receptivity to National Socialism.

In 1930 Doderer married Gusti Hasterlik, the daughter of a Jewish surgeon, after a tortuous courtship that had begun during World War I. They were separated within two years and were divorced in 1934. In the same year as his marriage Doderer began work on the project that was to concern him for the next quarter of a century—the composition of *Die Dämonen*, one of the boldest and broadest canvases in modern European letters. It originated in the author's esoteric predilection for overweight Jewish women; soon it grew to cover Doderer's increasing obsession with the Jews as the source of all his own and his country's ills. The original working title, "Dicke Damen" (Fat Ladies), was later amended to "Die Dämonen"–probably subsequent to his reading in 1931 of Dostoyevski's *The Possessed* (1871-1872), whose German title is *Die Dämonen*. By 19 July 1933, after Hitler took power in Germany, he had recast the title as "Die Dämonen der Ostmark." ("Ostmark" [Eastern Marches] was the name with which the Führer hoped to submerge the separate identity of the Austrian state; it is ironic that *Die Dämonen* was to be the novel which set the seal on Doderer's reputation as the grand old man of *Austrian* letters.) On 1 April 1933 he joined the Austrian Nazi party, which was banned by Chancellor Dollfuß on 19 June after a terrorist attack by Nazis on a platoon of police auxiliaries.

Doderer found it impossible to publish in Austria *Ein Umweg*, which he had begun in 1931 as a diversion from *Die Dämonen*. He reworked the novel in 1934 and took it with him to the Bavarian town of Dachau, where he took up residence in August 1936. Given Doderer's dislike of social and political conditions in Austria, it was a logical step for him to go and live in the land which he felt had cleaned up the "liberale Schlammflut" (tide of liberal filth) of the postwar years. Yet the country "wo das Irrationale wieder einen seiner großen Einbrüche in die Geschichte vollzogen hat" (where the irrational had again accomplished one of its great breaches in history) was a sore disappointment to the avid Nazi. The reality of Hitlerdom was in total contrast to notions of the rebirth of the medieval empire which Doderer harbored. He also found that, Aryan though he was, his career was not furthered by the bureaucracy surrounding Propaganda Minister Joseph Goebbels's Reichsschriftumskammer, the organization for Nazi writers. Ironically, then, having come home to the Reich, he found himself unable to make progress on *Die Damonen*, the very novel in which he had set out to celebrate the ideals of a "judenfrei" (Jew-free) Greater Germany. Through Haybach, also an unabashed Nazi, he gained entrée to the respected Nazi-sympathizing publishing house of C. H. Beck in Munich, with which he signed a contract in 1937. Doderer gave the seventeen completed chapters of *Die Dämonen* to the firm but then decided that he did not, after all, want the work to be published. The reasons for this diffidence, so at odds with his earlier despair at failing to get work accepted, are difficult to determine; Wendelin Schmidt-Dengler suggests that the

book was not Nazi enough for the publishers. Another reason might be Doderer's realization that his plan to complete the novel in three sections was no longer feasible, if only on grounds of length: part 1 already ran to more than seven hundred typescript pages. At all events, the reasons he gave twenty years later for the deferred appearance of his chef d'oeuvre–in Hesson's words, that "he feared that the political content of the novel would lend itself to polemical misuse and also that in the climate of the times the work would not be a success"–are unconvincing.

For all his exertions, Doderer's published corpus of work remained slender through most of the 1930s: *Ein Umweg* had to wait until 1940 before it was published; in 1936 Doderer recast into final form *Das letzte Abenteuer* (The Last Adventure), a medieval tale of knights, dragons, and fair maidens, whose origins went back to 1917 but which did not come out until 1953. When it did appear, it carried an "autobiographisches Nachwort" (autobiographical postscript) which, while revealing little about Doderer the man, says a lot about his concept of the writer. He stresses the primacy of the memory for the creative author and dismisses fiction that deals with current events as nonliterature, as merely a newspaper between hard covers. The author must not quarry the present for material but must wait until events of the past spontaneously re-present themselves via the unfettered workings of the memory. Probably as a reaction against the subject of *Die Dämonen* he turned to what might broadly be termed "historical fiction" in *Ein Umweg* and *Das letzte Abenteuer*, though Doderer himself rejected the pigeonholing of these works into such a category. For him *Das letzte Abenteuer* was merely a piece of escapism, and it is certainly hard to conceive of anything more different from *Die Dämonen* than this slender tale of courtly derring-do. (Such historically based fiction was, however, a pronounced feature of literary production in the Third Reich.) Ruy de Fanez, a lonely Spanish knight rides out, at the age of forty, to gain a duchess's hand. He knows that this could be his last adventure, not only because he will have to fight a particularly fiery dragon, but also because the age of chivalry is all but dead. He conquers the dragon, but in a mystical encounter with the beast he comes to realize that the prize of the duchess and duchy will provide no fulfillment. More and more he listens to the prompting of his memory and moves away from the preordained strategies of courtly behavior; these had constituted a protective wall around his life, but they had also blinded him to reality. Now he sees; but in his case "Menschwerdung" brings no lasting happiness, for soon after rejecting the duchy he meets his death.

Particularly in the completed works of the 1930s–*Das letzte Abenteuer, Ein Umweg,* and *Ein Mord den jeder begeht*–a deeply pessimistic strand is revealed in Doderer's approach to the question of human self-fulfillment, one quite at odds with Nazi optimism for the future of Aryan man. Gone is the glib patness of "Divertimento No. V"; it is replaced by a gloomy vision of the world as a vale of tears. Increasingly he is obsessed by the indirect nature of valid experience, by the conviction that direct striving negates the nature of the world itself, that to intervene in life, to attempt to impose one's own order is to invite trouble. He comes more and more to believe that the person who "apperceives" will recognize that there is only limited scope for autonomous action and will live in a sane and well-balanced world, which will be guaranteed by the ill-defined "mechanism of life." The novels and stories of the 1930s show the disastrous consequences of what he feels is the almost universal reluctance of people to acknowledge this natural chain of cause and effect; even when they do accept the futility of direct action they still fail to find contentment– indeed, they often lose their lives. As early as 1921 Doderer had noted in his diary that his basic outlook was more passive than active, that he had a "leises Widerstreben in mir gegen das *Handeln*, das Eingreifen, das Verstricktwerden in den Kausalnexus eines Vorganges, das Beeinflussen oder Richtunggeben einer anderen Persönlichkeit gegenüber" (quiet antipathy toward *action*, intervention, getting caught up in the causal nexus of an event, the influencing or directing of another personality). Repeatedly in his novels one finds a clash between the wishes of the individual human character, which is subjective, willful, dynamic, and active, and the workings of an unseen order, which demands passive and tolerant understanding of its processes.

Its very title indicates that *Ein Umweg* portrays life's indirect path. It is a book that has attracted scant attention from Doderer's critics, who, on the whole, have been drawn to the postwar novels dealing with Viennese society in the early decades of the twentieth century; a novel about seventeenth-century Austria provides little of immediate interest to a commentator who sees Doderer first and foremost as a social chronicler.

Yet the very escape into the past, away from the pressing actuality of the years 1931 to 1934 when it was written, sheds light on the preoccupations of a writer who was a more than competent historian–the distinguished Oswald Redlich said that Doderer was the best student he ever had. It is also, however, a novel which, in its preoccupation with a racial outsider in a Germanic society, displays clear affinities with concerns of the 1930s.

Ein Umweg is linked with *Das letzte Abenteuer* in that the Spanish officer Count Manuel Cuendias, one of the later novel's chief figures, assumes the name Ruy de Fanez when enjoying incognito sallies into student life. He, too, has a mystical encounter with an animal; in fact it is a chamois, but it is reckoned by his gillie to be a dragon. Like the other Fanez he fails to kill the beast, and the experience leads to a similar deepening of self-awareness through the stimulus of memory. From this point on Cuendias increasingly rejects the trammels dictated by his status and profession. His life moves in a strange counterpoint to that of Paul Brandter, a mercenary sentenced to die for crimes committed during the Thirty Years' War. According to the convention of the time, if a condemned man can find a woman to marry him, his life will be spared; and in a moment of weakness, Brandter calls out for help as he is about to die. The servant girl Hanna offers herself as his "Galgenbraut" (gallows bride); Cuendias, the presiding officer at the execution, responds to the custom, and Brandter is spared what he knew to be his destiny. He and Hanna go off to a life of frustration and alienation in Styria, while Cuendias realizes that he has fallen in love with Hanna. Brandter, Hanna, and Cuendias have interfered with the preordained "mechanism," and Doderer shows how the natural process, which in its workings neatly mirrors the intention of the established judicial order, reasserts itself. Several years later Cuendias finds himself in the Brandters' village, where he stumbles upon Hanna in flagrante delicto with his company bugler. The suspicious Brandter mistakes Cuendias for the bugler and stabs him to death. Realizing his mistake, he kills the bugler and Hanna. In its goriness the denouement is reminiscent of a Jacobean tragedy, with Brandter doing to death those who, with the best of intentions, had helped him in what he now recognizes as a mistaken desire to avert his true destiny. He allows himself to be arrested, tried, and sentenced to death. The novel thus ends where it started, with Brandter on the scaffold, aware of the fittingness of his imminent death; even the language at the end of the novel reproduces that at the beginning.

This move certainly demonstrates its author's belief in the circuitous nature of the life process, but it also raises disturbing ethical issues. In taking revenge on those he considers have deflected him from the true path of his life–judicial execution–Brandter disregards his own responsibility in crying out for succor in the first place. There is also something disconcerting about a vision of life, albeit in the evocation of a past and supposedly more violent age, which endorses the deaths of innocent people because they had helped place another onto the wrong track in life. Whereas Doderer normally disparages the implementation of the will, Brandter's deadly revenge is seemingly justified because it reestablishes the disturbed natural order. In the final analysis, all that appears to matter is that Paul Brandter has once more acknowledged the reality of his own life. Yet, as in *Das letzte Abenteuer* and, later, in *Ein Mord den jeder begeht*, such an insight into reality, the prerequisite for "Menschwerdung," becomes the signal not for new and fulfilled life but for death. Stylistically, this novel comes closer to Doderer's later work than the often expressionistically colored works of the 1920s; not for the last time will the reader be struck by what a reviewer in the *Times Literary Supplement* called Doderer's "unremitting propensity for digression and longwindedness." The author himself had little liking for this novel because he came to reject the sort of linear plotting characteristic of it and its successor, *Ein Mord den jeder begeht;* on the other hand, he did not disown it, recognizing it to be the book that helped him win the publishing contract he so longed for and which was to stand him in good stead for the remainder of his writing career.

Ein Mord den jeder begeht, conceived in 1935, was published by Beck in October 1938. The autobiographical opening chapters dealing with the boyhood of Conrad Castiletz are as impressive as anything he had written up to that point. The psychological security of a publisher's contract seems to have given him a firmer sense of self, which in turn allowed him to release in artistic form many painful childhood memories. Surprisingly for a novel published in Nazi Germany it opens with an arresting, Freud-tinged assertion: "Jeder bekommt seine Kindheit über den Kopf gestülpt wie einen Eimer. Später erst zeigt sich, was darin

Doderer in 1951, photo by Herbert List (Bildarchiv der Österreichischen Nationalbibliothek)

war. Aber ein ganzes Leben lang rinnt das an uns herunter, da mag einer die Kleider oder auch Kostüme wechseln wie er will" (Everyone gets his childhood clapped over his head like a bucket. Only later on do we find out what was in it. But it keeps on running down us for the rest of our lives, no matter how often you have a change of clothes or costume). A quarter of the novel is devoted to Castiletz's childhood, spent catching newts beside the quiet inlets of the old unregulated Danube, playing with toy trains, and being terrified by the vagaries of an upbringing that mixes an unusually high degree of freedom with constant fear of his elderly father's unpredictable, semimaniacal rages. The impact of these adult temper tantrums on the only child is to induce in him the attempt to regulate his life down to the last detail so as to avoid incurring paternal wrath over some trivial incident; later he tries to impose this prophylactic approach upon all aspects of his existence. The chapters bearing on Castiletz's childhood form a long and detailed prelude to a part of the story which bears some superficial similarity to a detective novel, in which the twenty-two-year-old Castiletz tries to solve the mystery of his sister-in-law Louison Veik's death seven years previously. Everything of significance in the unwinding of the narrative, which reveals how Castiletz had himself been the unwitting "murderer," transpires in a manner that is profoundly roundabout and beyond his classifying urges: he knows that Veik died in a Swabian railway tunnel, yet he has to journey to Berlin before discovering that he is her killer. The structural similarity with *Ein Umweg* is clear: the episodic narration reflects Doderer's understanding of the indirect nature of experience. Castiletz's mentor and father figure, Hohenlocher, remarks somewhat arcanely that in discovering his complicity, Castiletz has discovered an eternal law which most people spend a lifetime trying to avoid. In spite of the title, the work does not really explain how this "murder" is universally applicable. Nor is Castiletz permitted a new life as a real "Mensch" after recognizing the interlinked nature of past and present and the futility, indeed the recklessness, of imposing one's own pattern of order upon life; for almost as soon as he has come to self-knowledge, he dies in a gas explosion caused by his drunken landlady. (Doderer loved to point out that on the very day of the novel's publication an identical incident took place in Düsseldorf.)

The novel is both a fascinating and provocative evocation of a troubled and sensitive childhood and, as Vincent Docherty has shown, one of the earliest "anti-detective stories"–a form now best known in German through the work of Friedrich Dürrenmatt. The classical detective story demonstrates the triumph of the logical, sifting intellect over the apparently impenetrable phenomena of the world. In Doderer's novel, however, the opposite obtains: all progress in the search for Veik's killer comes about through apparent chance, spurred on by the promptings of the memory or the senses. The novel thus celebrates irrationalism via the very literary mode that generally features the triumph of the rational mind. The irrationalism of *Ein Mord den jeder begeht* does not, however, make it a National Socialist novel. Indeed, since by 1938 Doderer was becoming disillusioned with National Socialism and was moving toward conversion to Catholicism, it is tempting to look for features in the novel which could be construed as muted criticism of a system he increasingly rejected. One might point to the painful failure in life of Con-

rad Castiletz, an archetypal blond-haired, blue-eyed Teuton, and to the catastrophic effects of imposing an artificial "order" on life. After the war Doderer made no public comment about the possible political implications of this novel, which was the first of his works to come to the attention of a wider-reading public.

By the end of the 1930s Doderer's writing had settled into two distinct though occasionally convergent modes: a prevalent and generally realistic one and one which is grotesque and at times surrealistic. The realistic mode is not particularly political in character and is underpinned by a profoundly irrational concept of the individual's place in the order of things; to the other mode German critics are fond of attaching the label "skurril" (droll). It is mostly in his shorter works that he sallies forth into an absurdist world. In the longer fiction the realistic mode generally prevails, and not until 1962 did he publish a full-scale novel in his most grotesque vein–*Die Merowinger* (The Merovingians). In the short story "Eine Person von Porzellan" (1935; published in *Die Peinigung der Lederbeutelchen;* translated as "A Person Made of Porcelain," 1974) an eminently respectable lady, a habitué of a coffeehouse and the picture of prim gentility, is revealed in her true colors when the narrator follows her home and discovers that she is a covert devourer of human flesh. Her larder is a large room full of corpses which she mutilates and consumes to the accompaniment of grunts and squeaks. The next day the narrator blithely watches the "porcelain lady" daintily take her coffee. Seeing that the "order" of her life is merely the cover for a hideous disorder satisfies the narrator, who no longer finds her interesting. This cynical and unpleasant little story ends flippantly: "Später hab' ich sie dann nie mehr zu Gesicht bekommen. (Ist wohl eingesperrt worden)" (Later, I never came across her again. [Probably been locked away]). If there is humor in such a woman-hating tale, it is of a fairly specialized appeal.

The humor in the last novel Doderer was able to finish before the war is also of a specialized kind, yet it is on the whole palatable. *Die erleuchteten Fenster oder Die Menschwerdung des Amtsrates Julius Zihal* (The Illuminated Windows; or, The Humanization of the Magistrate Julius Zihal, 1950), completed in 1939, is a short satirical novel which Bachem finds "reminiscent of the tone of Sterne or Jean Paul." Yet it too has as the basis for much of its humor the unpleasant theme of voyeurism. Like Conrad Castiletz, Julius Zihal is an obsessive personality, consumed by a desire for orderliness. He has spent his life as a tax inspector in Vienna, and much of the satire relates to the way in which bureaucracy stifles both the bureaucrats and their victims. Cast out into the world by retirement and bereft of the security offered by his tax manuals, statutes, and ordinances, Zihal tries to create a new order in his life by spying on and logging the nocturnal activities of his neighbors: he has been so institutionalized by his service in the bureaucracy that even an activity like furtively watching women disrobe has to succumb to his codifying urge. For the narrator, Zihal is not a real "Mensch"; he is an animal, a worm, a slug, a troglodyte who meets his comeuppance when, engaged in his nightly spying, he notices someone else observing *him* through field glasses. This discovery causes Zihal to fall from the table on which he was perilously balanced; he also falls into an abyss of uncertainty and confusion that releases him from his obsession. In a way typical of the later Doderer the release from Zihal's mania brings with it a revaluation of language itself: for the first time his speech becomes authentic, no longer the preprogrammed mouthings of the civil service manuals. He thus leaves the realm of his "second reality" and in the evening of his life achieves real humanity. To underline his change in status, symbolized by the smashing of his telescope as he fell, Doderer allows Zihal the fulfillment of a warm relationship with the woman of his dreams. Whereas previously "Menschwerdung" had been synonymous with death, here it is compatible with a happy ending. A new optimism entered Doderer's work at the same time he decided no longer to be a Nazi and to convert to Roman Catholicism. The book did not appear until 1950; in the Third Reich a novel with comparatively daring sexual connotations, lacking in anything "völkisch," and one that recalls warmly and humorously the days of the independent Austrian Empire, and which points out the socially and linguistically perverting tendencies of an intrusive state apparatus, had little chance of being published.

Disavowing his allegiance to the Nazi party and publicly joining the Catholic church were courageous acts on Doderer's part. He later believed that he was spared from persecution only because of his military service: in April 1940 he was conscripted into the air force. As a Luftwaffe captain he served as commandant of Orly airport

in Paris before being transferred to the eastern front in 1942. Back in Austria in the summer of 1943, he became an examiner of aspiring Luftwaffe officers in Vienna; this role is recalled in the story "Unter schwarzen Sternen" (1966; translated as "Under Black Stars," 1974), in which an "alttestamentarische Schönheit" (Old Testament beauty) is murdered in the Theresienstadt concentration camp because she hesitated too long before trying to flee Vienna. During the last two years of the war Doderer went to Bohemia, north Germany, and finally to Norway, where he became a POW for the second time when he was captured by the British on 7 May 1945. In January 1946 he was released in Linz, Upper Austria; because of his party membership he was forbidden to publish until 1950. From 1946 to 1948 he was hard at work completing *Die Strudlhofstiege*. In 1948 he also finished the essay "Sexualität und totaler Staat" (Sexuality and Totalitarian State, published in *Die Wiederkehr der Drachen* [The Return of the Dragons, 1972]), which, as Elizabeth Hesson remarks, "deals in theoretical terms with the problem of fascism. Doderer had now taken up an antipolitical position and was also endeavoring to prove that totalitarian regimes find their sustenance in any form of deviant sexual behavior. Doderer makes this rather contentious mode of thought into one of the central themes of *Die Dämonen* and links it to his concept of the 'second reality.' "

Doderer also resumed the rigorous study of history, which had last exercised him over two decades previously. In 1950 he was accepted as a member of the Institute for Research in Austrian History with a dissertation on monastic politics in the later Dark Ages.

Although he had had to wait many years for fame, it now came virtually overnight. Disturbed by postwar modernism, the avant-garde writing of the Gruppe (Group) 47, and the Marxism of Bertolt Brecht, the bourgeois readership in West Germany and Austria responded warmly to the panoramic, erudite, but entertaining vastness of the *Die Strudlhofstiege*, a novel that for all its narrative intricacies still provided a "good read." Its length–nearly nine hundred pages–did nothing to dampen the enthusiastic reception accorded a book which looked back lovingly and reasonably uncritically on a pre-Nazi Austrian past centered in Vienna in 1911 and 1925 and which was resolutely personal in its presentation. Deliberately overlooking the political hiatus caused by the Great War and the collapse of Hapsburg

Passage from the manuscript for Doderer's panoramic novel Die Strudlhofstiege *(Biederstein Verlag, Munich)*

rule, the author sets out to show that individual history is not totally overshadowed by political events, that the First Austrian Republic of 1925 is deeply rooted in events of the last days of the monarchy in 1911. The novel thus attempts to demonstrate an underlying unity in the face of apparently cataclysmic change.

The novel, which was inspired by Doderer's spontaneous memories in Russia and France in 1941-1942, evokes in fond detail the city and social caste which were closest to his heart with a complexity and attempted objectivity grounded in the nineteenth-century novel yet with an intrusive narrative voice which owes much to Jean Paul and to Laurence Sterne's *Tristram Shandy* (1760-1767). Doderer attempts to overcome the potential shapelessness of a novel that tries to reproduce a totality by imposing order upon diversity; he does so by weaving the seemingly disparate and unconnected strands of his polycentric narration into one culminating event which demonstrates the underlying connectedness of apparently unrelated persons and incidents. In *Die Strudlhofstiege*, where the steps of the novel's title serve as a further unifying device, the various diverse events, plots, and subplots coalesce in the accident in which Mary K. is run down by a streetcar and loses a leg. This incident, which forms the climax of the novel, is adumbrated on the first page so that the reader can follow a major strand of the work free from traditional sus-

pense. The many-layered, interwoven nature of the narration means, however, that Doderer's masterful evocation of his society is achieved at the expense of dynamic plotting. At times, too, he seems too indebted to such devices as mistaken identities, criminal intrigues, and the convenient marriage to form the happy ending. If the novel has a main character, it is perhaps the strangely passive and rather colorless Major Melzer. His "Menschwerdung" comes when he, an Aryan, helps save the life of Mary K., his former fiancée rejected for her Jewishness, after her accident. For his efforts he is rewarded with a bride, the fair Thea Rokitzer. The novel's subtitle, *Melzer und die Tiefe der Jahre* (Melzer and the Depth of the Years), reflects the importance of memory in the scheme of the work. A far more active character is the autobiographical René Stangeler, who is involved in a relationship with the Jewish Grete Siebenschein. Yet the enduring impact of the novel lies ultimately in none of these characters but in the evocation of the genius loci of Vienna–especially of the Alsergrund, one of the oldest suburbs of Vienna, the birthplace of Franz Schubert and the location of the Strudlhof Steps. In this novel there emerges in full Doderer's gift for producing what he called "die Anatomie des Augenblicks" (the anatomy of the instant), the condensed yet utterly convincing depiction of mood, of place, or aura, of the everyday, tangible quiddity of the material world. The tremendous sense of solidity of that world juxtaposed against the random fleetingness and unpredictability of human relationships appealed to the sensibilities of many readers in the 1950s, when Doderer virtually became the court poet of the Second Austrian Republic.

Any attempt to summarize this vast canvas is doomed to failure; for allied to its bulk is a fundamental lack of a specific "theme," unless it is the characters' shared problem of achieving apperceptivity and the importance of the memory in the development of the healthy and rounded individual. Melzer ultimately comes to realize that the integration of events from 1911 is vital to his life in 1925; the import of the novel is to reassure the Austrians of the essential unity of their lives over and beyond the events of 1938 to 1945. Despite Doderer's disavowal of all ideologies, the tacit ideological thrust of the novel is not hard to discern.

During his career Doderer collected an anthology of maxims, aphorisms, and aperçus that was published posthumously under the title *Repertorium: Ein Begreifbuch von höheren und niederen Lebens-Sachen* (Reportorium: A Comprehension-Book of Higher and Lower Life-Things, 1969). One of the maxims is: "Ein Werk der Erzählungskunst ist es um so mehr, je weniger man durch eine Inhaltsangabe davon eine Vorstellung geben kann" (A work of literature is all the more artistic, the less a summary of its contents can give us an idea of what it is about). This maxim, written down in 1966, certainly holds true for *Die Strudlhofstiege* and equally so for its successor *Die Dämonen*, a work of even longer provenance and still greater bulk, which finally found its way into the bookseller's window in 1956. In the five years between these two creations Doderer published three shorter works—*Das letzte Abenteuer;* "Divertimento No. V"; and a new piece, written in 1951. This work, the seventh Divertimento, is titled *Die Posaunen von Jericho* (The Trumpets of Jericho) and was first published in the periodical *Merkur* in 1954 and published in book form in 1958. Doderer saw it as his ultimate success in handling the formal problems raised by the Divertimento. Perhaps because of his awareness of the potential formlessness of a "totaler Roman" (total novel) such as *Die Dämonen*, Doderer became preoccupied with the problems of form in the prose narrative. The priority of form over content was axiomatic for him, and in *Die Posaunen von Jericho* he felt that he had achieved his aim: a form which stood in a relation-

ship to life like an empty mold, which, on being held under water, instantly fills up so that form and content become an integrated unit. In its four sections the story chronicles the narrator's perceptions of and reactions to a series of unsavory and absurd encounters. Mixing realism with the grotesque, buffoonery with high seriousness, the work encapsulates the antinomies in Doderer's writing. In his last years he would say that his aim in writing was "mit dem Leben fertig zu werden" (to come to terms with life), and in this last of the Divertimenti an autobiographically drawn writer discovers that through confrontation with the world in all its contradictions the walls of his prejudices are demolished, and he can face the future in a state of apperceptive awareness. The setting is postwar Vienna; the problems confronted include anti-Semitism, child molesting, middle-class adult hooliganism, and the impossibility of simplistic ethical judgments. All of this is filtered through the perceptions of the flawed narrator, Dr. Döblinger, who at the last achieves the state of secular grace Doderer calls "Menschwerdung."

In his diary Doderer concluded that if *Die Dämonen* had a theme it was that of order–the problems which ensue for the self and the world when the desire to impose order corrupts and corrodes God-given reality into a "Pseudo-Konkretion" (pseudo-concretion), a "second reality." At the same time, the novel also presents the problems of order as reflected in the very act of writing a narrative. Fired by his "erotische Liebe" (erotic love) for objective facts and a militant dislike of anything ideological, Doderer uses a variety of narrators, both first-person–for example, Geyrenhoff, who chronicles his inability to relate the novel–and authorial. Of all Doderer's works this novel has called forth the most critical comment, ranging from acceptance of the vast work on the author's own terms as an ideology-free critique of all ideologies to the rejection of it as the work of, at best, an unrepentant archconservative. Bruce Turner has attempted to review the novel in the light of its own paradoxes: as a novel which perversely sees the roots of the rise of fascism in the actions of Social Democrats at the burning of the Palace of Justice on 15 July 1927; as a novel with a demonstrably historical climax, written by a trained historian with a contempt for positivistic historiography; and as a novel about the First Republic designed to cast a rosy glow on the comfortable bourgeois realities of the Second. A novel about a profound politi-

Doderer carrying the manuscript of Die Dämonen, *a novel on which he worked for twenty-five years (copyright © by Biederstein Verlag, Munich)*

cal and human tragedy that ends in a spate of happy marriages, a novel in which Jew is reconciled with German, aristocrat with proletarian, Social Democrat with Christian Socialist, it can be regarded as evading historical reality. Simplistically, the work shifts ultimate blame for the catastrophic events of 15 July 1927 away from all political factions, even from the police, and onto the common criminal element present in any society. Moreover, the poetic justice of the novel, in which the agitator and murderer Meisgeier is shot to death by the police in the Vienna sewers, is problematic: if Meisgeier represents nascent fascism, his death in the bowels of the city in no man-

ner corresponds to the reality of later events, when the Nazis came to guide Greater Germany's destiny for a dozen years. Indeed, the blatantly unjudicial shooting of Meisgeier seems closer in spirit to the fascism it is supposed to dispose of than to a democratic state based on the rule of law. The novel is certainly flawed both ideologically, as Schröder and Anton Reininger have demonstrated, and artistically, as Martin Swales has suggested in his examination of its complex narration. Yet it remains a work of subtlety, complexity, and stature. In its insistence on the primacy of individual history over political history the novel evokes with magisterial sweep the feeling of what life may well have been like, especially for the bourgeoisie, in the troubled early years of the First Republic. Its range is broad–from prince to prostitute, from soothsayer to socialite–and it even tries to confront, if not altogether convincingly, the problem of the concentration camps in an episode placed at the strategic center of the novel: the discovery of a late medieval document concerning religious fanaticism and witch torture. As Turner writes: "The subterranean caverns, sealed off from the outside world, illustrate the secrecy with which the concentration camps were operated," while the "pedantic attention to detail and to the comforts of the chambers devoted to 'simulated' torture approximates the elaborate planning required for decimation in gas chambers disguised as showering facilities." Yet the fact that the torture of innocent women in this medieval dungeon is revealed as simulated rather than actual surely detracts from the parallel of the caverns with Auschwitz. The bathos of this manuscript composed in Early New High German–a linguistic tour de force on Doderer's part–cannot simply be passed off, as Turner tries to pass it off, with the comment that "in the face of ineffable horrors, words can aspire but to gallows humour." Ernst Weiß demonstrated the contrary in his novel about Hitler and Dachau, *Ich, der Augenzeuge* (1963; translated as *The Eyewitness*, 1977).

With *Die Dämonen* Doderer achieved an overwhelming success based not only on the recognition of the book's literary qualities–its rampant vitality, command of detail, and astonishing linguistic range–but also on its appeal to a large part of the German-speaking world that was seeking assurance about its personal and national past from the perspective of a present which, a decade after the nadir of 1945, seemed almost too good to be true. Doderer's stock at this point had risen high indeed. Married since 1952 to Maria Emma Thoma, he divided his time between a bachelor flat in the Währingerstraße, not far from the Strudlhof Steps, and his wife's home at Landshut in Bavaria. In the late 1950s he entered into a long-standing liaison with the writer Dorothea Zeeman, who recalls her days with Doderer in memoirs most notable for their loveless objectivity.

Die Dämonen and *Die Strudlhofstiege*, novels recognizably part of the tradition of European realism, left Doderer's widespread readership utterly unprepared for the grotesqueries of *Die Merowinger*, though some may have been at least partially alerted by the publication in 1959 of the short-story collection *Die Peinigung der Lederbeutelchen* (The Torment of the Leather Pouches). Much of the material in this book is in the same quasi-surrealistic mode found in *Die Merowinger*, a work which Dietrich Weber summarizes as "a world of giants and dwarfs, comical freaks and monstrosities, in a word: a world of figurines . . . a grotesque world." The novel, whose reception fell far short of that accorded to the preceding Viennese works, has at its center the richly bearded midget Childerich von Bartenbruch III, last of the Merovingians and a power-crazed paterfamilias whose motto is "la famille c'est moi." A mixture of high and low farce, the book climaxes with the castration of Childerich, who probably goes farther than any other of Doderer's creations in his mania for imposing a subjectively conceived order on the world around him. His megalomania manifests itself in his obsession with controlling the lives and purses of others on the basis of family authority. He thus marries the widows of his father and grandfather, making him according to his logic, his own father, son, grandson, uncle, cousin, and grandfather. Beneath the novel's knockabout fun there is a serious purpose: Childerich is prey to violent and uncontrollable outbreaks of rage, a condition Doderer regards as "Apperceptions-Verweigerung" (deperception) in one of its most catastrophic manifestations because it blinds the victim completely to the realities of self and world. Doderer demonstrates here the lengths to which a fanatic is prepared to go in his imposition of a personally understood notion of order on the world. Critics have seen in the work a satire directed against the totalitarian state, against the pretensions of the "total novel," even against the psychotherapeutic methods of the Göttinger Aggressionsschule (Göttingen Aggression School). The author himself, at work on the novel throughout the 1950s, found relaxation in giving full rein to a creative urge he normally tried to stem in the interest of "realism."

It was to realism (more or less) that he returned in an unfinished cycle of four novels, titled *Roman No. 7* out of his respect for Beethoven's Seventh Symphony rather than its place in his own output. Only the first volume, *Die Wasserfälle von Slunj*, was completed before he succumbed to cancer. In this work he returns to the world that had so enchanted the readers of the Viennese chronicles. The lucidity and suggestiveness of the narration mark this novel as one

Doderer

of Doderer's finest achievements. Both here and in its fragmentary companion *Der Grenzwald* Doderer returns to southern and central Europe around the turn of the century: Vienna once more looms large, and there are excursions into Slovenia, the Balkans, and Russia. Both novels are dominated by the troublesome nature of relationships between parents and children. *Die Wasserfälle von Slunj* concerns the relationship of Robert Clayton and his son Donald, exiled English entrepreneurs involved in the founding years of Austrian industry; in tones distantly recalling Thomas Mann's *Buddenbrooks* (1901; translated, 1924), the generation of the father is seen to be more vital, energetic, and successful than that of the son. Yet as Bachem points out, the theme of decline so clearly evident within the Clayton family is not repeated in other familial constellations within the novel: "other children rebel, become independent, ignore their parents . . . or rise socially above the position of their parents. The final impression is one of criss-crossing lines of development, a complicated texture of individual fates selected from all levels of society." In a novel notable for its sustained use of water im-

agery, Donald, unable to put his personal stamp on life, meets an untimely end at the waterfalls of Slunj, the very place of his conception; his widowed father has in the meantime married the woman Donald loved. Donald Clayton is another of Doderer's "deperceptive" characters, yet there is nothing demonic about him. His life is a sad chronicle of wasted opportunities, unlike that of his friend Chwostik, a man of humble origins who grasps every opportunity that life offers in his unerring ascent of the social and professional ladder. Unlike Donald, he is also noticeably successful in his sex life; and for Doderer there is a nexus between apperception and sexuality. The novel is further notable for the prominence it gives to Monica Bachler, a liberated woman who makes her mark as an engineer in a male-dominated profession, captivates the repressed Donald, and marries Robert.

That the second novel of the cycle, *Der Grenzwald*, should remain a fragment represents one of the greater losses to modern Austrian fiction. It admittedly retreads old ground–Vienna, World War I, Siberia, the generational conflict–yet with a power, concentration, and spareness which show Doderer's powers increasing, rather than declining through age and ill health. His intention of writing a novel in which, as he put it, "facta loquuntur" (deeds speak), seemed here within his grasp. The intrusive, Sterne-like narrators of past novels have been largely abandoned in favor of the seemingly unnarrated presentation of character, event, and above all mood. Moreover, in the figure of Zienhammer, Doderer comes closer to portraying the reality of evil than he ever did in *Die Dämonen*. There the banality of evil often seems to rob it of its essence; here its appalling and unreflected ordinariness makes a far greater impact. Of the projected development of the rest of the cycle, frustratingly little is known; Dorothea Zeeman, who could probably have told most, prefers instead to reveal the not always edifying intimacies of Doderer's most personal sphere. Heaped with honors–the Novelist's Prize of the Confederation of German Industry in 1954, the Grand Award of the Austrian State in 1957, the Pirkheim Medal of Nuremberg in 1958, and the Wilhelm Raabe Prize and the Ring of Honor of the City of Vienna in 1966–Doderer finally succumbed to his illness in December 1966. His grave is in the beautiful cemetery at Grinzing, not far from Gustav Mahler's.

With his death an era ended. Doderer's years of greatest renown had coincided with the rebuilding of prosperity and confidence in the Second Republic, in the years dominated by the Grand Coalition between the right-wing People's party and the Austrian Socialist party. These had been years of anti-Communist consensus, when Brecht was boycotted at the Vienna Burgtheater; they had also been years when Austrian literature failed to partake in the modernist explosion characteristic of much postwar writing in the Federal Republic of Germany. With the ending of political consensus and the belated entrée of literary experimentalism, Doderer's hard-won preeminence began to wane. In the 1970s doubts were cast on his writing above all from an ideological angle, and the great claims made for his art by conservatively inclined critics in the 1950s began to be questioned. It was felt by many that Doderer's Vienna was not really to be mentioned in the same breath as Dickens's London, Joyce's Dublin, or Balzac's Paris. While Doderer's name is often found alongside those of Musil, Joseph Roth, and Hermann Broch in the canonical listings of the modern Austrian novel, his work has yet to generate the same level of critical interest as theirs. Nevertheless, Doderer has much to offer, even if one accepts fully the powerful ideological arguments that can be raised against aspects of his writing. To be sure, he often accepted uncritically and unquestioningly certain authorities as counters to anarchy–in the postwar period, these authorities could be summed up as the newly founded Republic and the laws of language itself. Yet Doderer was only too aware of a tendency toward anarchy within himself; he noted in his diary in 1951 that given a free choice he would like nothing better than to have money to indulge in a series of sexual debaucheries, mindless drinking bouts, and fisticuffs. In this tension between an inner seething and the obsession with order one can hear distant echoes of his great Austrian precursor Adalbert Stifter. And if the novel is the artistic form best suited to reproduce city life, then Doderer's works respond to that challenge more adequately than do those of any of his successors in Austria. As Georg Schmid has noted, Doderer is not only an urban but also an extremely urbane writer, of whom the erstwhile enfant terrible of Austro-German letters, Peter Handke, could write in his journal in 1977: "Zeichen eines großen Schriftstellers (Doderer): man nimmt von ihm auch praktische Ratschläge für den Alltag an" (Signs of a great writer [Doderer]: you accept practical tips for everyday life from him). Written off by some as an insignificant voice, Doderer's status has certainly undergone revision since his death; but as a reviewer in the *Times Literary Supplement* noted, not to name Doderer's achievement "is to ignore a rare and important epic vision within twentieth-century literature."

Letters:

Heimito von Doderer/Albert Paris Gütersloh: Briefwechsel, 1928-1962, edited by Reinhold Treml (Munich: Biederstein, 1986).

Biographies:

Xaver Schaffgotsch, ed., *Erinnerungen an Heimito von Doderer* (Munich: Biederstein, 1972);

Michael Horowitz, ed., *Begeghung mit Heimito von Doderer* (Vienna & Munich: Amalthea, 1983).

References:

"At Random in Vienna," *Times Literary Supplement,* 20 April 1973, p. 449;

Michael Bachem, *Heimito von Doderer* (Boston: Hall, 1981);

Andrew W. Barker, "Heimito von Doderer and National Socialism," *German Life and Letters*, new series, 41, no. 2 (1988): 145-158;

Barker, "'Kammern der Befängnis'—An Aspect of Thought and Image in the Work of Heimito von Doderer," *Modern Austrian Literature*, 14, no. 1/2 (1981): 25-43;

Alfred Barthofer, "Leonard Kakabsa: Success or Failure? Marginalia to a Key Character in Doderer's Novel *Die Dämonen*," *Forum for Modern Language Studies*, 14, no. 3 (1978): 304-315;

Andrew Boeleskevy, "Spatial Form and Moral Ambiguity: A Note on Heimito von Doderer's Narrative Technique," *German Quarterly*, 47 (January 1974): 55-59;

Peter Dettmering, *Dichtung und Psychoanalyse II: Shakespeare, Goethe, Jean Paul, Doderer* (Munich: Nymphenburger Verlagshandlung, 1974);

Vincent J. Docherty, "The Reception of Heimito von Doderer as Exemplified by the Critics' Response to *Ein Mord den jeder begeht and Die Merowinger*," Ph.D. dissertation, University of Glasgow, 1984;

Wolfgang Düsing, *Erinnerung und Identität: Untersuchungen zu einem Erzählproblem bei Musil, Döblin und Doderer* (Munich: Fink, 1982);

Roswitha Fischer, *Studien zur Entstehungsgeschichte der "Strudlhofstiege" Heimito von Doderers* (Vienna: Wilhelm Braumüller Universitäts-Verlagsbuchhandlung, 1975);

Pierre Grappin and Jean-Pierre Christophe, eds., *L'actualité de Doderer* (Metz: Didier-Erudition, 1986);

Michael Hamburger, *From Prophecy to Exorcism: The Premises of Modern German Literature* (London: Longmans, Green, 1965), pp. 1-28;

Peter Handke, *Das Gewicht der Welt: Ein Journal (November 1975-März 1977)* (Salzburg: Residenz, 1977); translated by Ralph Manheim as *The Weight of the World* (New York: Farrar, Straus & Giroux, 1984; London: Secker & Warburg, 1984);

Henry Hatfield, *Crisis and Continuity in Modern German Fiction* (Ithaca, N.Y. & London: Cornell University Press, 1969), pp. 90-108;

Sylvia Hayward-Jones, "Fate, Guilt and Freedom in Heimito von Doderer's *Ein Mord* and *Ein Umweg*," *German Life and Letters*, 14 (April 1961): 160-164;

Heimito von Doderer (1896-1966): Symposium anläß lich des 80. Geburtstags. Wien 1976 (Salzburg: Neugebaur, 1978);

Elizabeth C. Hesson, "Bibliography of Secondary Material on Heimito von Doderer," *Modern Austrian Literature*, 19, no. 2 (1986): 47-60;

Hesson, *Twentieth Century Odyssey: A Study of Heimito von Doderer's "Die Dämonen"* (Columbia, S. C.: Camden House, 1982);

Ivar Ivask, "Heimito von Doderer: An Introduction," *Wisconsin Studies in Contemporary Literature*, 8 (Autumn 1967): 528-547;

Ivask, ed., "An International Symposium in Memory of Heimito von Doderer (1896-1966)," *Books Abroad*, 42 (Summer 1968): 343-384;

David L. Jones, "Proust and Doderer as Historical Novelists," *Comparative Literature Studies*, 10, no. 1 (1973): 9-23;

Gabriele Kucher, *Thomas Mann und Heimito von Doderer: Mythos und Geschichte. Auflösung als Zusammenfassung im modernen Roman* (Nuremberg: Carl, 1981);

M. Dean Larsen, "Heimito von Doderer: The Elusive Realist," *Chicago Review*, 26, no. 2 (1974): 55-69;

Dieter Liewerscheidt, "Heimito von Doderer: *Die erleuchteten Fenster*," *Wirkendes Wort*, no. 1 (1976): 3-26;

Liewerscheidt, *Satirischer Anspruch und Selbstpersiflage in Heimito von Doderers Roman "Die Merowinger"* (Cologne: Privately printed, 1976);

Malcolm McInnes, "Österreich–Österreicher–Am Österreichischten: Heimito von Doderer and Austria," *Colloquia Germanica*, 18, no. 1 (1985): 18-40;

Peter Pabisch, "The Uniqueness of Austrian Literature: An Introductory Contemplation of Heimito von Doderer," *Chicago Review*, 26, no. 2 (1974): 86-96;

Pabisch and Alan Best, "The 'Total Novel': Heimito von Doderer and Albert Paris Gütersloh," in *Modern Austrian Writing: Literature and Society after 1945*, edited by Best and Hans Wolfschütz (London: Wolff, 1980), pp. 63-78;

Engelbert Pfeiffer, *Heimito von Doderers Alsergrund-Erlebnis* (Vienna: Privately printed, 1983);

Heinz Politzer, "Heimito von Doderer's *Demons* and the Modern Kakanian Novel," in *The Contemporary Novel in German*, edited by Robert H. Heitner (Austin & London: University of Texas Press, 1967), pp. 37-62;

Anton Reininger, *Die Erlösung des Bürgers: Eine ideologiekritische Studie zum Werk Heimito von Doderers* (Bonn: Bouvier, 1975);

Ingrid Werkgartner Ryan, *Zufall und Freiheit in Heimito von Doderers "Dämonen"* (Vienna, Cologne & Graz: Böhlau, 1986);

Georg Schmid, *Doderer lesen: Zu einer historischen Theorie der literarischen Praxis. Essai* (Salzburg: Neugebaur, 1978);

Wendelin Schmidt-Dengler, "Rückzug auf die Sprache," in *Österreichische Literatur der Dreißiger Jahre*, edited by K. Amann & A. Berger (Vienna, Cologne & Graz: Böhlau, 1985), pp. 291-302;

Schmidt-Dengler, " 'Die Strudlhofstiege': Literatur zwischen Anarchie und Ordnung," in *Das größere Österreich*, edited by Kristian Sotriffer (Vienna: Edition Tusch, 1982), pp. 387-392;

Schmidt-Dengler, "Die Thematisierung der Sprache in Heimito von Doderers 'Die Dämonen,' " in *Sprachthematik in der österreichischen Literatur des 20. Jahrhunderts* (Vienna: Hirt, 1974), pp. 119-134;

Hans Joachim Schröder, *Apperzeption und Vorurteil: Untersuchungen zur Reflexion Heimito von Doderers* (Heidelberg: Carl Winter Universitätsverlag, 1976);

Michael Shaw, "Doderer's *Posaunen von Jericho*," *Symposium*, 21 (Summer 1967): 141-154;

Martin Swales, "The Narrator in the Novels of Heimito von Doderer," *Modern Language Review*, 61, no. 1 (1966): 85-95;

Frank Trommler, "Doderer und Gütersloh," in his *Roman und Wirklichkeit: Eine Ortsbestimmung am Beispiel von Musil, Broch, Roth, Doderer und Gütersloh* (Stuttgart: Kohlhammer, 1966), pp. 133-167;

Bruce Irvin Turner, *Doderer and the Politics of Marriage: Personal and Social History in "Die Dämonen"* (Stuttgart: Heinz, 1982);

Roderick H. Watt, " 'Der Einbruch von unten': An Austrian Syndrome of the Inter-War Years?," *German Life and Letters*, 27, no. 4 (1974): 315-324;

Dietrich Weber, *Heimito von Doderer* (Munich: Beck, 1987);

Weber, *Heimito von Doderer: Studien zu seinem Romanwerk* (Munich: Beck, 1963);

Cedric E. Williams, "Heimito von Doderer," in *The Broken Eagle: The Politics of Austrian Literature from Empire to Anschluss* (London: Elek, 1974), pp. 132-145;

Lutz-Werner Wolff, *Wiedereroberte Außenwelt: Studien zur Erzählweise Heimito von Doderers am Beispiel des "Romans No. 7"* (Göppingen: Kümmerle, 1969);

Dorothea Zeeman, *Jungfrau und Reptil: Leben zwischen 1945 und 1972* (Frankfurt am Main: Suhrkamp, 1982).

Papers:

Heimito von Doderer's papers are in the manuscript collection of the Austrian National Library, Vienna.

Milo Dor
(7 March 1923-   )

Jerry Glenn
University of Cincinnati

BOOKS: *Unterwegs* (Vienna: Müller, 1947);

Tote auf Urlaub: Roman (Stuttgart: Deutsche Verlags-Anstalt, 1952); translated by Michael Bullock as *Dead Men on Leave* (London: Barrie & Rockliff, 1962);

Der unterirdische Strom: Träume in der Mitte des Jahrhunderts. Ein Versuch, by Dor and Reinhard Federmann (Frankfurt am Main: Frankfurter Verlagsanstalt, 1953);

Und einer folgt dem andern, by Dor and Federmann (Nuremberg: Nest, 1953);

Internationale Zone: Roman, by Dor and Federmann (Frankfurt am Main & Vienna: Forum, 1953; revised edition, Vienna: Medusa, 1984);

Führer durch Jugoslawien, by Dor and Federmann (Amsterdam: De Lange, 1954);

Romeo und Julia in Wien: Roman, by Dor and Federmann (Bad Wörishofen: Kindler & Schiermeyer, 1954);

Othello von Salerno: Roman, by Dor and Federmann (Munich: Kindler, 1956);

Die Frau auf dem Medaillon, by Dor and Federmann, as Alexander Dormann (Vienna: Buchgemeinschaft Donauland, 1959);

Nichts als Erinnerung: Roman (Stuttgart: Goverts, 1959);

Das Gesicht unseres Jahrhunderts: Sechzig Jahre Zeitgeschehen in mehr als sechshundert Bildern, by Dor and Federmann (Vienna: Forum, 1960);

Salto mortale: Erzählungen (Zurich: Arche, 1960);

Die Abenteuer des Herrn Rafaeljan: Roman, by Dor and Federmann (Gütersloh: Signum, 1963);

Ballade vom menschlichen Körper (Graz: Stiasny, 1966);

Die weiße Stadt: Roman (Hamburg: Hoffmann & Campe, 1969);

Das Pferd auf dem Balkon (Vienna: Jugend und Volk, 1971);

Meine Reisen nach Wien (Eisenstadt: Roetzer, 1974);

Menuett: Farce in 3 Akten (Eisenstadt: Roetzer/ Vienna & Munich: Sessler, 1975);

Alle meine Brüder: Roman (Munich: Bertelsmann, 1978);

Die Raikow Saga (Munich: Langen-Müller, 1979);

Meine Reisen nach Wien und andere Verirrungen: Gesammelte Erzählungen (Munich: Langen-Müller, 1981);

Der letzte Sonntag: Bericht über das Attentat von Sarajewo (Vienna: Amalthea, 1982);

Auf der Suche nach der größeren Heimat (St. Pölten: Niederösterreichisches Pressehaus, 1988);

Auf dem falschen Dampfer: Fragmente einer Biographie (Vienna & Darmstadt: Zsolnay, 1988).

OTHER: Günther Birkenfeld and others, *Sprung in die Freiheit: Berichte über die Ursachen, Begleitumstände und Folgen der Maßenflucht aus der Sowjetischen Besatzungszone Deutschlands*, introduction by Dor and Reinhard Federmann (Ulm: Knorr & Hirth, 1953);

Es ist nicht leicht, ein Mann zu sein: Ein Brevier voll nützlicher und unnützer Ratschläge für den Herrn von heute, edited by Dor (Munich: Heyne, 1955);

Stephen Crane, *Die Flagge des Mutes: Roman*, translated by Dor and Elisabeth Moltkau (Frankfurt am Main & Vienna: Forum, 1955);

Ivo Andrić, *Der verdammte Hof: Erzählung*, translated by Dor and Federmann (Berlin & Frankfurt am Main: Suhrkamp, 1957);

Oskar Davico, *Die Libelle: Roman*, translated by Dor and Federmann, as Wolfgang Dohrmann (Berlin: Aufbau, 1958);

Georges Simenon, *Maigret und der Schatten am Fenster*, translated by Dor and Federmann (Cologne & Berlin: Kiepenheuer & Witsch, 1959);

Mond überm Zigeunerwagen: Zigeunerlieder, translated by Dor and Federmann (Munich: Langen-Müller, 1959);

Andrić, *Die Geliebte des Veli Pascha: Siebzehn Novellen*, translated by Dor, Federmann, and Alois Schmaus (Stuttgart: Steingrüben, 1959);

Milo Dor (photo copyright © by Peter Wurst)

Isaak Babel, *Zwei Welten: Die Geschichten des Isaak Babel,* translated by Dor and Federmann (Munich, Vienna & Basel: Desch, 1960);

Die Verbannten: Eine Anthologie, edited by Dor (Graz: Stiasny, 1962);

Gemordete Literatur: Dichter der russischen Revolution, edited by Dor and Federmann (Salzburg: Müller, 1963);

Genosse Sokrates: Serbische Satiren, edited by Dor (Vienna: Hunna, 1963);

Andrić, *Die Brücke über die Zepa,* translated by Dor, Federmann, and Schmaus (Heidelberg: Furche, 1963);

Tausend Jahre Liebe: Klassiker der erotischen Literatur, edited by Dor and Federmann (Vienna: Deutsch, 1964);

Der politische Witz, edited by Dor and Federmann (Munich: Desch, 1964);

Der Flug des Ikaros: Jugoslawische Autoren von heute. Hörspiele, edited by Dor (Herrenalb: Erdmann, 1964);

Ein Orden für Argil: Jugoslawien in Erzählungen seiner besten zeitgenössischen Autoren, edited by Dor (Herrenalb: Erdmann, 1965);

Der Sohn des Wesirs: Märchen aus Jugoslawien, edited by Dor (Vienna: Jugend und Volk, 1965);

Dor (left) at the beginning of the 1950s with his friend and collaborator Reinhard Federmann

Der galante Witz, edited by Dor and Federmann (Munich: Desch, 1966);

Der groteske Witz, edited by Dor and Federmann (Munich: Desch, 1968);

Popa Vasko, *Nebenhimmel: Gedichte,* translated by Dor and Karl Dedecius (Munich: Hanser, 1969);

Miroslav Krleža, *Galizien: Stück in 3 Akten,* translated by Dor (Vienna: Universal Edition Schauspiel, 1971);

Krleža, *In Agonie: Ein Stück in 2 Akten,* translated by Dor (Vienna: Sessler Neue Edition, 1973);

Die Pestsäule: In memoriam Reinhard Federmann, edited by Dor (Vienna: Löcker & Wögenstein, 1977);

Babel, *Petersburg 1918: Reportagen,* translated and edited by Dor and Federmann (Pfullingen: Neske, 1977);

Leo Zogmayer, *Istrien,* essay by Dor (Vienna: Edition Hilger, 1981);

Schreib wie du schweigst: Serbische Aphorismen, edited by Dor (Vienna, Munich & Zurich: Europa, 1984);

Die Leiche im Keller: Dokumente des Widerstands

gegen Dr. Kurt Waldheim, edited by Dor (Vienna: Picus, 1988).

First recognized as an important writer in 1951, Milo Dor continues to occupy a prominent position in Austrian and German intellectual circles. He is one of those rare examples of an author who does not write in his native language; he was in his twenties when he abandoned his native Serbo-Croatian for German. Also, his participation in the resistance against the Nazis is unusual among German and Austrian writers; originally active in communist resistance groups in Yugoslavia, he was ostracized by his former friends when he began to question their methods and ultimate intentions. His anti-Nazi activities did not cease; he spent part of the war in prisons and detention camps, where he was subjected to extended periods of torture. His autobiographical novel *Tote auf Urlaub* (1952; translated as *Dead Men on Leave,* 1962) was widely hailed as *the* personal and political confession of a lost generation of central European leftists who became disillusioned with Marxism. Dor has continued to produce fiction of high literary merit but has also taken on many other roles: editor, translator (most notably of Yugoslavian literature), author of plays and features for radio and television, and articulate spokesman for various causes.

The son of Milan Doroslovac, a physician, and Alexandra Bajic Doroslovac, Milutin Doroslovac was born in Budapest in 1923. His family moved from town to town in Yugoslavia until 1933, when his father established a practice in Belgrade. Doroslovac's literary career began while he was still in high school, with poems and essays written in Serbo-Croatian in student journals. Soon after the Nazi occupation of Yugoslavia, his political activities led to his expulsion from school, but he earned his diploma in 1941 without attending classes. He joined the resistance movement and was arrested in 1942. After a year in custody he was sent to Vienna, where he worked in a furniture factory and, using false identification papers, enrolled in the university to study theater. In September 1944 he was arrested by the Gestapo, which correctly suspected him of being involved with the resistance, and was not released until Russian troops reached Vienna in April 1945.

Dor decided to remain in Vienna rather than return to Yugoslavia, which faced an uncertain political future. The following decade was marked by a struggle to establish himself as a German-language writer while supporting his family: he married in 1946, and a son, Milan, was born a year later. He established contact with Otto Basil, the editor of the revived progressive journal *Plan,* to which he contributed essays and fiction. His first book, *Unterwegs* (On the Road), appeared in 1947 under the pseudonym Milo Dor. Some of the nine short stories in the book are third-person narratives tending toward realism; others, written in the first person, are characterized by introspection and a turning away from external reality. A mood of uncertainty is reflected in the stories–the political uncertainty of the war years and the first postwar years in occupied Vienna and the existential uncertainty of Dor's generation. Not only does Dor have no answers, he does not even have the proper questions; the search for these questions is a unifying element in the otherwise diverse collection.

In 1951 Dor finished a close second to Heinrich Böll in the balloting for the literary prize of the Gruppe (Group) 47, a loosely organized association of younger German-speaking writers. Several of Dor's supporters were outraged at the outcome; Walter Jens called it a dis-

grace. But the group's acclaim was not yet the ticket to success it would soon become, and it was only with difficulty that Dor was able to find a publisher for his first novel, *Tote auf Urlaub.* The action of this work, which, although it was not planned as such, was to become the middle part of an autobiographical trilogy, is set in wartime Yugoslavia and Vienna but includes flashbacks. One of the central issues is the relationship of Dor's alter ego, Mladen Raikow, to the Communist party. Mladen begins to have doubts about communism at the time of the Hitler-Stalin pact, and as a result of these doubts he is ostracized by the party and by many of his friends.

Two chapters, both set in prison, bring out the principal themes of the novel. In "Ein interessantes Pokerspiel" (An Interesting Game of Poker) Mladen is being tortured by the Nazis, who hope to learn details about the resistance movement. Mladen likens his situation to that of a poker player who, in the absence of a winning hand, must bluff in order to avoid losing the game. His bluff is successful: a halt is called to the torture before Mladen betrays his comrades or is killed by his tormentors. The element of luck or chance–of *Spiel,* which in German means game or play in every sense from the most trivial to the most serious–is important in the novel and in virtually all of Dor's later works. The following chapter, "Ballade vom menschlichen Körper" (Ballad of the Human Body), centers on two other prisoners: former schoolmates with the same first name, Anissie, and similar last names. One is a member of the resistance and the other a Nazi collaborator who was arrested when he accidentally left his identification papers in his room. The collaborator hears a name called that he takes for his own and runs to the door of his cell, thinking that his story has been verified and he is to be released. But the name was that of the other Anissie, and the collaborator is executed in his stead. The surviving Anissie, who assumes the other's identity, reappears later in the novel. Again the element of chance is of paramount importance; so is the question of identity, which runs like a thread throughout the book as political allegiance and personal character are shown to be nebulous concepts.

Tote auf Urlaub is usually viewed as a powerful political statement, and its literary qualities are generally overlooked. One of the principal devices used in the book is heat and cold imagery: as the novel opens, a man who is standing on the street begins "zu frösteln" (to feel cold); at the

Dust jacket for Dor's 1959 novel about a teenager trying to find direction in life

end of the book Mladen is lying in a room looking "in den fahlen Aprilmorgen, der kalt in das Zimmer hereinkroch" (out into the dreary April morning, which was coldly creeping into the room). Throughout the novel the references to coldness are not only realistically descriptive but also symbolic of the problematic nature of the resistance movement and of the uncertainties of the future in postwar Vienna. In keeping with the novel's grim mood, references to warmth, which are typically associated with meaningful though transient human relationships, are infrequent.

In 1954 Dor assumed a leading role in speaking out for the younger generation of writers against the Austrian literary establishment. His first marriage ended in divorce, and on 20 July 1955 he married Elisabeth Prückner-Moltkau. Throughout the 1950s he earned his living as a free-lance writer. He did translations; wrote for

newspapers, radio, and television; and published several popular adventure novels and romances in collaboration with Reinhard Federmann, including *Internationale Zone* (International Zone, 1953), set in the postwar Viennese milieu made familiar by the film *The Third Man* (1949).

His next major work was the novel *Nichts als Erinnerung* (Nothing but Memory, 1959). Mladen Raikow and several other characters from *Tote auf Urlaub* appear in the book, which otherwise has little in common with Dor's first novel. The action is concentrated in a period of six days in October 1936; political topics are introduced only occasionally and ironically, as when one of Mladen's uncles contemplates going to Spain to fight in the civil war without knowing which side he should join. Mladen is portrayed as a fairly typical if somewhat intellectual teenager, who during the first part of the week is preoccupied with thoughts of an older girl with whom he has fallen in love. He sells his stamp collection to buy her a birthday present, only to learn that she is engaged. He then turns his attention to his poetry and decides that his ambition is to become a great writer, only to reverse himself again the following day when he comes to the Faustian conclusion that experience is superior to art and intellect. This lack of direction is shared by most of the characters and emerges as one of the novel's principal themes, reflecting the worldwide political malaise of the 1930s. The most important secondary character is Mladen's grandfather, Slobodan, formerly a prosperous banker but now on the verge of bankruptcy after an unsuccessful business venture. One of the book's most memorable scenes is a card game in which the participants are Slobodan; Marko, a boy Slobodan had taken in and treated as one of the family; and a government official who has come to lay claim to Slobodan's possessions for nonpayment of taxes. The official, a compulsive gambler, loses all his money and goes heavily into debt to Marko. Under the circumstances, Slobodan has no choice but to declare the debt forgiven. Although the official reciprocates by tagging only insignificant household items for confiscation, Slobodan is unable to take advantage of his stroke of luck: a broken old man, he dies soon after. Several of the novel's threads come together in the final chapter as Mladen, his father, and an uncle travel by train to attend Slobodan's funeral. The book's central themes—transience and loss—also come sharply into focus in this final chapter. As in *Tote auf Urlaub*, if under considerably less dramatic circumstances, the uncertainties of life and the absence of meaningful goals are at the heart of the work.

Salto mortale, Dor's second collection of short stories, appeared in 1960. These stories, which Dor later described as "satirische Auseinandersetzungen mit der absurden politischen Situation" (satirical examinations of the absurd political situation), mark a new direction in his work. The title story, which is well known in the United States by virtue of its inclusion in a popular second-year German reader, is Kafkaesque: the narrator, a copy editor for a newspaper in a central European city, awakens one morning to discover that no one—his boss, his landlady, his girlfriend, or his friends in the neighborhood bar—recognizes him. But unlike the typical situation in Kafka, here there is an explanation: the narrator had rewritten an insignificant political story in such a way that it became nonsense, and the party has ordered his systematic ostracism. The end is "happy," if equally absurd: the ostracism ceases when the narrator writes an anonymous letter accusing one of his coworkers of the misdeed. As so often in Dor's fiction, the themes of identity and political choice are central. *Salto mortale* was followed in 1966 by another collection, *Ballade vom menschlichen Körper*, which includes selections from *Unterwegs* and chapters from *Tote auf Urlaub* and *Nichts als Erinnerung* in addition to new stories.

Die weiße Stadt (The White City), the final volume of Dor's autobiographical trilogy, appeared in 1969. The title refers both to the name Belgrade, which means White City in Yugoslavian, and to snow-covered Vienna. The time is the late 1960s, but flashbacks trace Mladen's fortunes since the end of World War II. His existence has remained unsettled, and his career is depicted as a comedy of errors and near misses; the big break in the form of an award, a lucrative job, or an influential contact continues to slip from his grasp as he supplements his meager income from writing by operating a small antique store. He visits Belgrade, where he feels alienated in the postwar political environment; although he lives in Vienna, he feels that he is a stranger there, too. The structure is quite different from that of the preceding novels. The book begins with an ironic "Interview des Autors mit sich selbst" (Interview of the Author with Himself) in which Dor discusses his research on Mladen (he casually mentions his research on Stjepan Zanovich, one of the principal characters in a novel that would not appear until 1978). Other interviews with people who knew Mladen follow, and further interviews are interspersed throughout the novel as Dor pursues his continual search for the proper questions. In the concluding chapter Dor offers some speculations on what the future might hold for Mladen, only to reject each of them.

Dor later remarked that, contrary to the opinions of some critics and readers, he was not identical with Mladen Raikow but only related to him. Although many of the episodes of *Die weiße Stadt* are based on events from the author's life, at the time the novel was published Dor was happily married to his second wife, was earning a decent living through his journalism, and had achieved a certain amount of recognition as a literary artist: in 1962 he had been awarded the Austrian State Prize for literature.

The early 1970s were turbulent times for Austrian writers, as battles raged within the P.E.N. Club between established authors and younger members of the avant-garde. Dor, who received the Anton Wildgans Prize in 1972, found himself defending the values of the establishment against the Young Turks. His primary interest, however, was the free-lance writer's lack of financial security, and he devoted much time and energy working for retirement programs and other benefits for writers. He wrote several important features for television, some in collaboration with his son, who had become a prominent film director. In 1974 he published *Meine Reisen nach Wien* (My Journeys to Vienna), a collection of essays in which the primary theme is his ambivalent attitude toward Vienna. His negative feelings are for the most part based on the difficulty a living writer has in finding acceptance in the city; his reasons for loving Vienna are more difficult to express, and he can say little more than: "Ich brauche ganz einfach diese Stadt, um überhaupt leben und schreiben zu können" (I simply need this city, in order to be able to live and write at all). He is especially fond of the Josefstadt, the section of Vienna in which he lives: "Hier wird das Leben nicht im Sturm genommen, sondern einfach genossen, ohne Lärm, aber in vollen Zügen" (Here life is not tumultuous but is simply enjoyed, without much ado, but to the fullest).

Through most of the 1970s Dor was at work on *Alle meine Brüder* (All My Brothers, 1978). It marks a radical departure for Dor, whose previous novels had dealt with things he had directly experienced. The narrative is ostensibly an account begun in 1820 by Miroslav Zanovich, who attempts to delve into the adventur-

Dor in 1959

ous and mysterious lives of his three older brothers. The focal point of his interest is Stefano (whom he called Stjepan in the "interview" at the beginning of *Die weiße Stadt*): philosopher, poet, ladies' man, self-styled pretender to the Albanian crown, and aspirant to the Polish crown–in short, confidence man par excellence. Another form of brotherhood, Freemasonry, also plays a major role. *Spiel* figures prominently, from the father's profession of gambler to the author's attitude toward his narrative and his characters. The brothers' paths traverse late eighteenth-century Europe, and a historical panorama unfolds. Promising leads prove to be dead ends for the narrator, and his quest for brothers and brotherhood is ultimately futile. Miroslav's premises–most notably his admiration of Stefano, who, betrayed by a brother Freemason, dies in a debtor's prison–were false; the questions he posed were not the right ones. In 1978 Dor received the Prize of the City of Vienna.

In 1979 Dor's trilogy was reprinted in one

volume under the title *Die Raikow Saga*. Two years later the collection *Meine Reisen nach Wien und andere Verirrungen* (My Journeys to Vienna and Other Wrong Turns) was published with the somewhat misleading subtitle *Gesammelte Erzählungen* (Collected Stories). Although the stories of *Unterwegs, Salto mortale,* and *Ballade vom menschlichen Körper* are included, along with previously uncollected fiction, the volume also contains the essays of *Meine Reisen nach Wien;* other essays include Dor's poignant tribute to his friend and collaborator Federmann, who died in 1976.

Dor's novel *Der letzte Sonntag: Bericht über das Attentat von Sarajewo* (The Last Sunday: Report on the Assassination at Sarajewo, 1982) is a carefully researched depiction of the events following the assassination of Archduke Francis Ferdinand as seen from the perspective of Leo Pfeffer, a minor official assigned to investigate the murder. Contrary to the expectations of his superiors, Pfeffer's painstaking interrogation of the youthful killers leads him to the conclusion that the deed was committed without the knowledge of the Serbian government. But truth and objectivity are irrelevant; those in power in Vienna are not interested in conclusions that would avert war but in justifying the war for which all Europe is mobilizing. As in *Alle meine Brüder*, the protagonist's efforts prove to be an exercise in futility.

Milo Dor is a paradoxical figure: a disillusioned Marxist who has found no new god to replace the one that failed; a philosophical pessimist who retains his good humor and ability to enjoy life; an author who writes in a language he mastered only as an adult; a person who has as much bad as good to say about Vienna, where he has resided since 1945; an angry young man who became a grand old man, while losing little of his revolutionary fervor in the process. Though he was once considered the equal of Heinrich Böll, his universally recognized gift as a natural storyteller came to be a liability rather than an asset as literary taste and conventions changed in the 1950s and 1960s, and novels with recognizable plots and fully developed characters fell from favor. Nonetheless, his serious literary works continue to be praised by many critics, and not only by traditionalists. Michael Scharang, one of the leading representatives of the younger generation of Austrian writers, began his review of Dor's trilogy: "So nachhaltig wie bei der Lektüre von Milo Dors *Die Raikow Saga* habe ich mich noch nie darüber geärgert, ein Buch nicht schon längst gelesen zu haben" (I have never before been as sorry that I had not already read a book as I was while reading Milo Dor's *Die Raikow Saga*).

References:

Reinhard Federmann, "Eine Geschichte vom Dank," in *Aufforderung zum Mißtrauen*, edited by Otto Breicha and Gerhard Fritsch (Salzburg: Residenz, 1967), pp. 466-475;

Gerhard Fritsch, Introduction to Dor's *Ballade vom menschlichen Körper* (Graz: Stiasny, 1966);

Für Milo Dor: Das große kleine Dorf aus dem wir stammen, edited by Peter Grünauer (Vienna: Maioli, 1983);

Ruth V. Gross, *Plan and the Austrian Rebirth: Portrait of a Journal* (Columbia, S.C.: Camden House, 1982), pp. 75-78, 87-91;

Hans Werner Richter, "Serbien muß sterben: Milo Dor," in his *Im Etablissement der Schmetterlinge* (Munich: Hanser, 1986), pp. 80-87;

Michael Scharang, "Beruf: Fremder. Zu Milo Dor und seiner Trilogie 'Die Raikow Saga,'" *Die Presse* (Vienna), 5 July 1980;

György Sebestýen, "Hommage à Milo Dor," in his *Studien zur Literatur* (Eisenstadt: Roetzer, 1980), pp. 282-286;

Hans Weigel, "Mitteleuropas heimatlose Linke," *Der Monat*, 43 (1952): 87-91;

Thomas Weyz, "Belgrade and Vienna: A View of Empire," *American-German Review*, 36, no. 1 (1969): 30-32.

Albert Drach

(17 December 1902-   )

Ernestine Schlant
Montclair State College

BOOKS: *Kinder der Träume: Gedichte* (Vienna: Amalthea, 1919);

Gesammelte Werke, volume 1: *Das große Protokoll gegen Zwetschkenbaum: Roman* (Munich & Vienna: Langen-Müller, 1964); volume 2: *Das Spiel vom Meister Siebentot und weitere Verkleidungen* (Munich & Vienna: Langen-Müller, 1965); volume 3: *Die kleinen Protokolle und das Goggelbuch* (Munich & Vienna: Langen-Müller, 1965); volume 4: *Das Aneinandervorbeispiel und die inneren Verkleidungen* (Munich & Vienna: Langen-Müller, 1966); volume 5: *Unsentimentale Reise: Bericht* (Munich & Vienna: Langen-Müller, 1966); volume 6: *"Z.Z.," das ist die Zwischenzeit* (Hamburg & Düsseldorf: Claassen, 1968); volume 8: *Untersuchung an Mädeln: Kriminal-Protokoll* (Hamburg & Düsseldorf: Claassen, 1971); volume 7: *Gottes Tod ein Unfall: Dramen und Gedichte* (Hamburg & Düsseldorf: Claassen, 1972);

In Sachen de Sade: Nach dessen urschriftlichen Texten und denen seiner Kontaktpersonen (Hamburg & Düsseldorf: Claassen, 1974).

OTHER: "Beginn der Emigration," in *Erlebte Zeit*, edited by Manfred Franke (Stuttgart: Goverts, 1968), pp. 55-78;

"Lessing," in *Lessing heute*, edited by Edward Dvoretzky (Stuttgart: Akademischer Verlag, 1981), pp. 52-60.

Albert Drach is one of the major chroniclers of the history of Austrian society from the last days of the Hapsburg monarchy to the present. He is a highly political writer in that he is concerned with the political consequences of social behavior: in his novels and plays he depicts the mentality that permitted the rise and the practices of National Socialism–a mentality that still exists. Drach can be considered an avant-garde writer, since he spearheaded many of the literary movements that became prevalent after World War II; yet he was "discovered" only in the 1960s. After

an initial success with his novel *Das große Protokoll gegen Zwetschkenbaum* (The Large Brief against Zwetschkenbaum, 1964) his reputation has grown only slowly, probably because his criticism is unmitigating, his challenges to the social and political complacency he describes are uncomfortable, his language is consistently and highly ironic, and his style makes no concessions to easy consumption. He received the Cultural Prize of the City of Vienna for poetry in 1972, the Prize of Lower Austria in 1975, the Gold Cross of Lower Austria in 1977, the Franz Theodor Csokor Prize of the P.E.N. Club in 1982, the Georg Büchner Prize of the German Academy for Language and Poetry in 1988, and Austria's Manes Sperber Prize for Literature, also in 1988.

Drach was born in Vienna in 1902, the only child of Wilhelm and Jenny Pater Drach. His father taught mathematics and physics at the Wiedener Oberrealschule in Vienna and later had a career in management at the Österreichische Länderbank; in his spare time he founded and managed the small Wiedener Theater. Drach's grandfather had moved to Vienna from Bukowina, following a pattern that was typical for many Jews of the Hapsburg Empire after the Austrian government granted them equal rights in 1867. Drach's mother came from a well-to-do merchant's family that had moved to Vienna from Nickolsburg in southern Moravia.

Drach grew up in the last two decades of the Hapsburg Empire, at a time when Vienna was rivaled only by Paris as Europe's most brilliant artistic and cultural center. His work first appeared in print in 1914, when some of his poems were published in the *Neues Wiener Journal*. A volume of collected poems, *Kinder der Träume* (Children of Dreams), was published in 1919. But by that time World War I had destroyed the glory of fin-de-siècle Vienna; after the peace treaty of 1919 the city was an oversized capital in a truncated country. In the following years many of its artists and intellectuals left, often for Berlin, where they contributed to the meteoric rise of

Albert Drach (photo copyright © by Hans Heinrich)

that city as an artistic center during the brief and tormented period of the Weimar Republic.

The 1920s were not a good time for a young Austrian artist to establish his reputation as a poet and playwright; Drach realized that he would have to earn a living in a conventional profession. He began the study of law at the University of Vienna in 1921, and in January 1926 he obtained his doctorate of jurisprudence. He became a trial lawyer in Mödling, near Vienna, where his parents had acquired the Drach-Hof, a palatial residence with adjacent gardens. During the 1920s he wrote plays, short stories, and poems. But chances for publication were practically nonexistent, and during the 1930s his production dwindled. Seven months after the Anschluß (annexation of Austria by Nazi Germany) in March 1938, Drach joined the large number of refugees who were desperate to leave the country. His escape route took him to Yugoslavia and from there to relatives in Paris. With the approach of the German troops in 1940 he fled to the south of France. He

was apprehended and sent to various French detention camps, where shipment to the German camps was always a strong possibility. Released through some bureaucratic mistake in 1942, he hid in the mountains above Nice until the arrival of the Allied troops in 1944. In 1947 he returned to Austria and resumed his law practice. Eventually, he regained possession of the Drach-Hof. In 1954 he married a concert singer; they have two children. Until 1964, when the first volume in an eight-volume edition of his collected works was published, Drach was virtually unknown. Even today not all of his work from the 1920s to the 1940s has been published.

Drach stands comparison with the other great analysts of Austria's demise, such as his contemporaries Joseph Roth, Heimito von Doderer, and Elias Canetti, and perhaps even with the luminaries of the older generation, Robert Musil and Hermann Broch. Most of these writers end their probing of Austrian society with the absorption of Austria into the Third Reich in 1938; Drach

Certificate issued by the Vichy government of occupied France in June 1943 attesting that Drach was not Jewish (photo: André Fischer)

alone carries his concern with Austrian society into the postwar era. He serves as a vital link connecting the pre-1938 literature of Austria with that of post-1945. For his social-critical purposes Drach has forged a language reflecting the three major areas of his concerns: the Austrian vernacular, Yiddish, and the language of the law. The long, involuted sentences that mirror, dissect, and indict an all-pervasive confusion of values may be considered the fountainhead of much of the experimental writing, by authors such as Jakov Lind, Thomas Bernhard, Elfriede Jelinek, and Gert F. Jonke, that has characterized Austrian literature since the 1960s.

Drach's four novels were not conceived as a cycle, yet they combine to establish a historical continuity. *Das große Protokoll gegen Zwetschkenbaum* takes place during the last years of the Hapsburg monarchy and the early period after World War I. "Z.Z.," *das ist die Zwischenzeit* ("Z.Z.," That Is, the Intermediate Time, 1968) deals with the years 1935 to 1938. *Unsentimentale Reise* (Unsentimental Journey, 1966), continuing where "Z.Z.," *das ist die Zwischenzeit* leaves off, describes an Aus-

trian Jew's exile in southern France and the Allied invasion and victory in 1944. *Untersuchung an Mädeln* (Investigation of Girls, 1971), subtitled *Kriminal-Protokoll* (Criminal Brief), is set in postwar Austria.

Drach does not want these works to be read as fiction but as depictions of reality as perceived from within the legal system. With the exception of *Unsentimentale Reise* they are written in the style appropriate to legal documents: the language is ponderous; valuable details are crammed together with irrelevancies and lost in labyrinthine sentence structures. Drach uses this bureaucratic language to convey the opaqueness, insensitivity, and leveling effect of the system and to show that there is a feedback relationship between language and those who create and use it. Bureaucratic language becomes a powerful vehicle to standardize behavior and thought; it stresses involuted procedure rather than rationality and subjects the bureaucrat to more stringent dehumanization than any of the offenders with whom he has to deal. The following passage from *Das große Protokoll gegen Zwetschkenbaum* can

Drach circa 1946 (photo: André Fischer)

serve as an example: "Als Chotek nunmehr, ohne Zusammenhang mit dem Vorigen, die Verlegenheitsbemerkung einwarf, ein Richter müsse strenge sein, entschuldigte sich Bampanello mit Gründen der Menschlichkeit, es nicht immer genügend gewesen zu sein. So kam er auf einen Ha-̈usler [Kleinhüttenbesitzer] zu sprechen, der nach fortgesetzten Holzdiebstählen im Walde schließlich bei einem solchen Betreten, mit Rücksicht auf die Versorgung seiner zwei mutterlosen Kinder seitens Bampanello nicht mit der gesetzlichen Höchststrafe von sechs, sondern nur mit einer solchen von fünf Monaten belegt worden sei. Der Mann sei übrigens auf das bloße Gerücht von der Erkrankung eines seiner beiden Kinder ausgebrochen und, wieder in den Arrest zurückgebracht, nach Erhalt der amtlichen Nachricht vom Ableben seines fünfjährigen Sohnes Friedrich abgefahren, indem er während der disziplinarischen Ahndung seines ersten Entweichens in Einzel- und Dunkelhaft sich mit einem vorschriftswidrig eingeschmuggelten Rasiermesser die Halsschlagader zu stark angezapft habe" (When Chotek now, without connection to what had pre-

ceded, made the embarrassed remark that a judge had to be strict, Bampanello excused himself with reasons of humanity for not always having been strict enough. Thus he came to speak of a squatter [owner of a shack] who after repeatedly stealing firewood in the forest was finally apprehended, yet in consideration of his two motherless children had not been sentenced by Bampanello to the maximum punishment of six months in jail but only to five months. Incidentally, the man broke out of jail at the mere rumor that one of his children was sick and, back in jail and having received official notification of the demise of his five-year-old son Friedrich, had croaked by tapping his neck artery too strongly with a razor illegally smuggled into his solitary confinement in a dark cell, into which he was dispatched as a disciplinary measure for his earlier jailbreak).

The story related here is that of a lawbreaker who had been treated not too kindly but too harshly; it is the story of a desperate man who is too poor to buy firewood and must steal it, who has two small children and no wife, who loves his children enough to break out of jail when one of them is sick, and who commits suicide in solitary confinement when he is informed that his child has died. The tragedy of this poor man must be read between the lines of Bampanello's account, for Bampanello is impervious to it. Drach shows in Bampanello's insensitivity the obtuseness of the bureaucrat who totally identifies with a system that operates within the confines of "maximum punishment," "official notification," "disciplinary measures," "solitary confinement," and "illegal smuggling" (smuggling, of course, is always illegal; the redundancy is used by Bampanello to further sensationalize the "criminal" character of the prisoner). One of the horrors of Drach's sketch lies in Bampanello's self-righteousness, which stems from his sense of being part of a system that imposes its standards on others. The legal system, presumably designed to serve mankind, has become its master and executioner. While the victims of the system stand to lose their lives, the "servants" of the system stand to lose their humanity. Bampanello does not notice his contradictory statement on the illness of the child: if the illness was a "mere rumor," why did the child die? On the contrary, the jailbreak only proves to him that he had been too humanitarian. Similarly, it is not necessary for him to consider whether a suicide in jail does not indict the system for its lack of precautionary

The Drach-Hof, Drach's home in the town of Mödling, near Vienna (photo: André Fischer)

measures, nor whether the "illegally smuggled" razor points to sloppy administrative procedures. There is nobody to whom "the system" and its representatives are accountable.

In this episode another dimension is brought into play that runs through all of Drach's work: the dimension of class differences. Bampanello is callous and self-righteous because he is dealing with a poor man. The language reflects these class distinctions clearly, for only in relation to the poor man whose life and death are worth nothing can Bampanello afford to use cynically the terms *abgefahren*, which literally means "departed" but idiomatically means "croaked," or *angezapft*, which means "tapped" (like a barrel of beer). An ironic reference to the same kind of class distinctions occurs with the definition of the word *Häusler* (squatter) as *Kleinhüttenbesitzer* (owner of a shack). The latter term glosses over the fact that the owner of a shack in truth owns nothing; and it suggests that a man who is an "owner" might not be as poor as he appears, thereby making his crime of stealing firewood even less excusable. The word denies the existence of poverty and misery and allows Bampanello to act as if he and the "owner" were equals; it plays havoc with the reality of the situation. Yet the abyss between reality and the language used to describe it does not need to be bridged. On the contrary, Bampanello's skill rests in exploiting this difference. At the same time that he appears to be fair by elevating a squatter to the lofty heights of "ownership," he also appears to be "just" since he is meting out punishment even to "owners." He thereby suggests that where the law is concerned, everybody is equal. Yet Bampanello and everybody listening to his account know that he would never impose this treatment on the owner of substantial possessions. This and similar techniques tear open the fabric of lies that one class of people has fashioned to protect itself from human and civic responsibilities.

The protagonist of *Das große Protokoll gegen Zwetschkenbaum* is the Hassidic Jew Schmul Leib Zwetschkenbaum. One day toward the end of World War I the police find him sitting under a Zwetschkenbaum (plum tree) in a village near Vienna; he does not know how he arrived there. Since there are many prune pits strewn about and he carries neither identification papers nor money, he is charged with vagrancy and theft. His arrest is the beginning of an odyssey that takes him through the bureaucratic machinery, jails, hospitals, and an insane asylum and brings him into contact with a cross section of the Austrian population. Zwetschkenbaum fashions for himself a persona that is part naiveté and part shrewdness and which allows him to survive. After his release from the asylum and a series of mishaps he marries a prostitute. The marriage is meant as a joke by those who maneuvered him into it, but Zwetschkenbaum is oblivious to the seamy aspect of the affair. Eventually he becomes the owner of a second-hand clothing store where, in all ignorance, he sells stolen goods. The police break up the operation; Zwetschkenbaum flees and is again apprehended at the site of his first "crime."

The episodic structure of the narrative; the panoramic presentation of society from the perspective of the hero; the physical mistreatment of the hero, who always survives to bumble into the next adventure; and the hero's innocence and ignorance as a shield against his destruction by a society in turmoil are elements that characterize the picaresque novel. This aspect is further enhanced when Zwetschkenbaum's misadventures are presented as slapstick comedy or farce. Yet the vicious, senseless abuses; the disproportion between the mistreatment and the alleged crime; and the incongruity between overpowering bureaucracy and helpless individual frequently border on the grotesque. Long before the postwar writers of the absurd, Drach expressed the sense of all-pervasive helplessness that is bearable only in the guise of comedy and farce.

The sinister undercurrent of the novel comes from Drach's focus on Zwetschkenbaum as a Jew. After the collapse of the Hapsburg empire chaos, famine, and revolutionary unrest erode social responsibility and breed brutality. Drach shows how in these difficult years gentiles and Jews alike are primarily concerned with their own physical survival and cultivate a readiness to turn on each other for profit. Yet where the Jews' aggressiveness never leaves the economic sphere, that of the gentiles is soon cloaked in the scapegoat ideology of anti-Semitism. Here and in the later novels Drach demonstrates that anti-Semitism is the consequence of deep-rooted fears and frustrations that surface with particular vehemence during turbulent and disastrous times. Small-town shopkeepers, villagers, and lower-echelon bureaucrats act in concert with prison inmates, thieves, rapists, and murderers. Afraid of losing their precarious foothold on the social ladder, respected citizens and law-abiding subalterns join in an unholy alliance with criminals to celebrate an ideology in which they are the masters. The novel ends with a literary conceit: a young clerk is charged with the inquest and asked to title it "Das große Protokoll gegen Zwetschkenbaum." In a vast circular sweep the end of the narrative reverts to its beginning.

"Z.Z.," das ist die Zwischenzeit is structurally similar to *Das große Protokoll gegen Zwetschkenbaum*: it consists of a series of tableaux that are connected by a central character and present a large assortment of social strata. The period covered runs from the middle of the 1930s to the fall of 1938, but for the sake of documenting the continuity of certain behavior patterns the narrative is interrupted by occasional flash-forwards into the Nazi and post-Nazi periods. The picaresque elements of *Das große Protokoll gegen Zwetschkenbaum* have disappeared; factual reportage predominates. The protagonist is a Jewish lawyer in his early thirties. Unlike the picaro he is alert rather than naive and intelligent rather than shrewd. He is never named but is referred to only as "der Sohn" (the son); he chooses to live in a prolonged adolescence, refusing to have a family or any other obligations. Uninterested in pursuing his career because he understands the interim character of the period in which he lives, he whiles his time away in sexual adventures. The detailed, monotonous descriptions of these

Drach reading from his novel Das große Protokoll gegen Zwetschkenbaum, *about a Jewish picaro*

sordid affairs drive home the point that sexual promiscuity, lack of commitment, and indifference characterize an entire society that has grown cynical in every respect. As in *Das große Protokoll gegen Zwetschkenbaum* Drach shows that the Jews are not immune to the general mood; but in distinction to the gentiles they lack the noxious belligerence of a self-serving ideology.

In the nearly twenty years that separate the events of *Das große Protokoll gegen Zwetschkenbaum* from those of "Z.Z.," *das ist die Zwischenzeits* brutality and barbarization have spread through all levels of society. Drach points again to the petit-bourgeois roots of the National Socialist movement, and he includes in this classification the educated and the pseudohumanists whose incredulity at the events in neighboring Germany does not prevent them from secretly enrolling in the Nazi party—a form of insurance that soon pays handsome dividends. He presents case studies of the heady effect sudden superiority has on the gentile petite bourgeoisie, and he provides previously unrevealed information on the acceptance and execution of Nazi policies in Austria.

The practice of law reflects the general cynicism; Drach gives many examples of the ideological manipulation of the legal process in Austria long before the Anschluß. In a gallant gesture toward his mother, who insists that fighting for what is right is not a meaningless undertaking, the son allows himself to be drawn into a few trials in which the insignificance of the cases stands in no reasonable proportion to the bureaucratic efforts invested in making him lose. Justice does prevail, but the victories are short-lived. In the son Drach illustrates the trapped intellectual whose political observations are astute but whose infrequent, sporadic acts of resistance are irrelevant in confrontation with a well-organized mass movement. The novel ends in October 1938, when the son escapes to Yugoslavia; he is ostensibly on his way to Liberia, the only country for which he can still afford the price of a visa.

Unsentimentale Reise is clearly autobiographical. In flashbacks the narrator, who now calls himself Peter Coucou, fills in the gap from 1938 until 1942. From Yugoslavia he had fled to relatives in Paris. At the approach of the German troops he had traveled south until he was apprehended by the police of the Vichy government and sent to various camps. In a series of episodes Drach provides case studies of human behavior under extreme stress. The settings for these episodes, way stations of Peter Coucou's exile, are the internment camps in southern France, the French administration and refugee community in Nice, and the village of Caminflour in the Maritime Alps, where Coucou hides until the arrival of the Allied troops in 1944. Refugee existence, internment, and shipment to the death camps in Germany are controlled by the bureaucracy, and the possession or acquisition of the correct papers becomes a matter of life or death. The desperate urgency of the refugees stands in contrast to the cool, even polite efficiency of the bureaucrats. Even when the deadly machinery seems to break down, reprieve is only momentary. A case in point is Peter Coucou's inexplicable release from the Rives Altes camp; he suspects that the commander liked him and put his name on the list of those to be released, knowing that he would not get very far. Outside of camp Coucou is still not safe: a German-speaking male civilian in France during the war is unavoidably suspect, since all nonimprisoned German males wear uniforms of the military or of the Nazi party.

Sex, an innocuous pastime in "Z.Z.," *das ist die Zwischenzeit,* may now become deadly: it can quickly separate the circumcised Jews from the non-Jews. The bored young girls in Caminflour are suspicious of Coucou and try to seduce him, hoping for some excitement from the game of manhunt and denunciation. In a grotesquely funny scene Coucou must listen to the panicked confession of a French writer who had to be circumcised for medical reasons and now fears that he will be taken for a Jew.

Drach shows an affinity with the writers of the absurd, but he avoids taking refuge in distortions and never allows horror to acquire symbolic meaning. He does not want the grotesque inhumanities to become bearable or acceptable as parables of some ulterior human condition. With few exceptions he fastens his gaze on man's pettiness, ill will, and greed, and he shows how these characteristics transcend any national or so-called racial boundaries. The French mountain villagers help the Jews who escape from the camps; yet they do so not in a sense of outraged humanity but as a common front against the German enemy. In addition, they make money from the refugees, who literally have to buy their lives on indefinite installment plans. When the opportunity arises, these petits bourgeois do not hesitate to pillage the dead. With the arrival of the Allied troops Coucou returns to Nice, where he works as an interpreter

for the Allies and tries to come to terms with the horrors of the past years. *Unsentimentale Reise* concludes with a surreal scene in which Coucou gives in to his despair. Survival into black marketeering and an era of revenge parading as justice has not been worth it. Wishing to join those who died in the gas chambers, he opens the gas valve in his minuscule room and lies down to die.

There are no Jews in *Untersuchung an Mädeln* because there are practically no Jews left in post-Hitler Austria. Never far from farce and the grotesque, yet never permitting them as relief from a nearly unbearable nightmare, Drach describes the trial of two young women accused of killing with a car jack a cattle dealer who had picked them up hitchhiking and had forced them to have intercourse with him. The cattle dealer's body was never found, and evidence that the alleged victim has actually fled the country in an insurance fraud scheme is suppressed.

From a technical point of view this novel is Drach's most ambitious narrative. It relates in the form of a legal brief the experiences of the young women in the contemporary Austrian prison system and their treatment by the representatives of the law. The brief includes the women's depositions and their statements at repeated investigations by the prosecutors, the defending lawyers' reconstructions, and witnesses' opinions. Drach uses these multiple perspectives not to demonstrate the impossibility of ever getting to the truth but to show how simple facts can be obfuscated, how plain statements are deliberately distorted, how bias parades as objective insight, how people can be manipulated by means of language.

The chronological progression of the narrative from the accidental apprehension of the hitchhikers until the day of the verdict is interrupted by frequent flashbacks that provide acute portrayals of present-day Austrian society. Drach introduces the defendants, their friends and relatives, the prosecutors, the lawyers, the judges, the jurors, the witnesses, the prison personnel, and the other inmates with the detached yet concentrated attention of the social scientist. The accumulated evidence drives home the disturbing realization that the military defeat of National Socialism has not eradicated the petit-bourgeois prejudices that allowed the rise of Hitler. The scapegoat ideology is as rampant, as vicious, and as vindictive as ever, although it is now directed against the fabricated sex lives of the two young women. Stella

Blumentrost and Esmeralda Nepalek are prosecuted with such viciousness because they bring into the open the multiple hypocritical standards which society imposes. The irony lies in the fact that they are not social or sexual rebels but rather allow themselves to be used in accordance with the standards they were taught. These standards above all prescribe submission to the inevitably male authorities–father, lover, bureaucrats. When they engage in sex in public places such as a train, a rest room, or the roadside, they are not driven by insatiable sexual urges but by a desire to cooperate with the male's self-image of dominance. In Stella and Esmeralda, Drach draws the portrait of all subjugated people who define themselves according to the view of the dominant group.

Drach is even more explicit in his devastating criticism of the legal bureaucracy and its representatives in this novel than he was in *Das große Protokoll gegen Zwetschkenbaum*. Not irony but rage infuses these portraits in which stupidity and prejudice masquerade as smugly secure knowledge. The two women must be cast as criminals to satisfy the hypocrisy and the desire for sensationalism of the self-righteous: "Sofern nun im folgenden von einem Vorleben der Mädel die Rede ist oder sein kann, so kommt nur ein solches in Betracht, das einschlägig ist, also entweder so beschaffen, daß hieraus eine Eignung zu den begangenen Straftaten aufgeschlüsselt und deren Begehungsart aufgehellt wird oder aber sich sogar der Nährboden für eine andersartige Veranlagung ergeben würde, mithin was voranging mit dem Verbrechensgeschehen in auffallendem Widerspruch stünde. Auch Umstände solcher Art müßten nicht unbedingt für mildernd, schon gar nicht für schuldausschliessend gehalten werden, sie würden vielmehr geradezu gegenteilig ins Gewicht fallen, wenn erzicherisch und vorbildmäßig eine bessere Einsicht und Gesinnung erwartet werden dürfte, und selbst der Umgang mit Schlechtberatern und der Einfluß bereits Schuldiggewordener dürften frühe Führung und gute Vorurteile nicht im Nu umwerfen, verwirren, geschweige denn in deren Widerpart verwandeln. Denn gerade bei Weibspersonen, hinsichtlich welcher Philosophen und Dichter mitunter die unmittelbare Anschauung der Vernunft in Zweifel stellen, ist nach allgemeiner Ansicht rege Verstandesarbeit zum eigenen Nutzen vorauszusetzen und kann daher mit gutem Grund moralische Haltung verlangt und nötigenfalls erzwungen werden" (Insofar as in the following the earlier life of the girls is or could be the subject of discussion, only such a life can be considered as is pertinent, hence either of such a nature that from it one can deduce qualifications for the committed crime and gain clarification as to the manner in which it was committed, or that the nurturing soil for a perverse inclination could be established; hence, what preceded the crime would be in glaring contrast with the commission of the same. Yet circumstances of such a nature would not necessarily have to be considered mitigating and certainly not exonerating; on the contrary, they would actually weigh against them if through education and role models a better insight and attitude could be expected; and even contact with people of bad counsel and the influence of those already on the path of crime should not be capable of overturning at the drop of a hat previous good conduct and good opinions, confuse them, and even less, turn them into their opposite. Since particularly as far as female persons are concerned, with regard to whom philosophers and poets occasionally doubt the immediate faculty of reason, one can presuppose, according to generally accepted opinion, busy mental activities directed to their own advantage, and one can therefore with good reason expect, and, if need be enforce, a moral attitude). The novel ends with the jury returning from their deliberations, ready to pronounce the verdict.

The pervasive absurdist sense of existence in Drach's novels stems from his characters inhabiting a closed universe: none of them can envision a life or society different from his own. The servants of the system have been trained to accept the labyrinthine, corrupt authority of a structure that determines their lives. The bureaucrats and their sympathizers have everything at stake in perpetuating the system, since they draw their identity and their hope of advancement from it. The lack of self-perception on the part of the victims also works against change. Stubborn insistence on their innocence, the only vestige of integrity and dignity the bureaucracy cannot take from them, is not enough to question the system. There are similarities between Drach's protagonists and some of Kafka's, but whereas Kafka has his heroes keep searching for an ultimate answer, which is pushed into ever more metaphysical realms, Drach remains anchored in the here and now. For Kafka the Law is a metaphysical entity, austere in its transcendence, and a symbol of all that is unattainable; for Drach it remains merely the law: formulated, interpreted, used, and misused by man, the product of man's activities and, as such, his reflection. Drach penetrates deeply into the absurdist position of modern man not by confronting an abyss of meaning, by suggesting leaps of faith, or by challenging a *deus absconditus* but by recording in concrete examples what man is capable of doing to his fellowman. If Drach were a dialectical materialist he could draw comfort from the belief that *because* the system is so warped and inhuman it will not remain. But Drach's division of mankind into victims and victimizers seems a permanent accommodation. In 1927, in *Das Satanspiel vom göttlichen Marquis de Sade* (The Satan Play of the Divine Marquis de Sade), published in volume two of his collected works (1965), he had the cynical Marquis de Sade express a point of view that is even more adamantly maintained by the author of *Untersuchung an Mädeln:* "Die Gesetze sind gegen diejenigen, die nicht dabei waren, als sie gemacht wurden. Ob sie sich nun fügen oder auflehnen, sie sind schuldig, in der Ordnung zu bleiben, keinen Platz zu haben und erdrückt zu werden. Entrinnen sie durch ein Loch nach aussen zu denen, die immer dort waren, dann treten sie zu diesen hinzu oder an deren Stelle. Sie machen nun selber Gesetze und sind gut. Böse ist nur der, der zugrundegeht, und auch der ist gut für die Ordung, denn sie wird durch seine Vernichtung bestätigt" (The laws are made against those who were not present when they were made. Whether they abide or revolt, they are guilty of remaining in the order, of not having any place, and of being crushed. If they escape through a hole to the outside and to those who have always been there, they either join them or take over their positions. Now they themselves make laws and are good. Evil is only he who perishes, but even he is good for the order, for it is confirmed through his destruction).

Drach's position is that of an outraged humanist. In showing how bigoted, thoughtless, and mean-spirited man can be, Drach appeals to a vision of humanity that stands in direct opposition to these descriptions. In Drach's universe man is responsible for the actions he commits, the society he creates, and the history that takes shape as a consequence. The burden of history lies squarely on man's shoulders.

References:

Friedrich Lothar Brassloff, "Albert Drach: ein Dichter in ständigem Kriegszustand," *Emuna: Horizonte zur Diskussion über Israel und das Judentum,* 8 (1973): 131-134;

"Die Eintracht des Vergessens: Der Fall Albert Drach oder Die Schnellebigkeit des Literaturmarktes," *Süddeutsche Zeitung,* 11 August 1987, feuilleton section, p. 27;

Ruth V. Gross, "Kaspar/Kasperl: Repetition and Difference in Handke and Drach," *German Quarterly,* 54 (March 1981): 154-165;

Sigrid Löffler, "Eingestürztes Weltvertrauen: Primo Levi und Albert Drach," *Profil,* no. 15 (11 April 1988): 102, 104;

Jürgen Manthey, "Schwejk kommt ins KZ," *Die Zeit,* 27 May 1988, feuilleton section, p. 55;

Annette Papenberg-Weber, "Autoren: Albert Drach," *Börsenblatt für den deutschen Buchhandel* (1-3 January 1989): 22-23;

Ernestine Schlant, "An Introduction to the Prose Narratives of Albert Drach," *Modern Austrian Literature,* 13, no. 3 (1980): 69-85.

Jeannie Ebner
(17 November 1918-   )

August Obermayer
University of Otago

BOOKS: *Gesang an das Heute: Gesichte, Gedichte, Geschichten* (Vienna: Jungbrunnen, 1952);

Sie warten auf Antwort: Roman (Vienna & Munich: Herold, 1954);

Die Wildnis früher Sommer: Roman (Cologne & Berlin: Kiepenheuer & Witsch, 1958; revised edition, Graz, Vienna & Cologne: Styria, 1978);

Der Königstiger: Erzählung (Gütersloh: Mohn, 1959);

Die Götter reden nicht: Erzählungen (Gütersloh: Mohn, 1961);

Im Schatten der Göttin, edited by Walter Buchebner (Graz & Vienna: Stiasny, 1963);

Figuren in Schwarz und Weiß: Roman (Gütersloh: Mohn, 1964);

Gedichte (Gütersloh: Mohn, 1965);

Prosadichtungen (Salzburg: Müller, 1973);

Protokoll aus einem Zwischenreich: Erzählungen (Graz, Vienna & Cologne: Styria, 1975);

Gedichte und Meditationen (Baden: Grasl, 1978);

Sag ich: Gedichte (Cologne: Hermansen, 1978);

Erfrorene Rosen: Tagebucherzählungen (Graz, Vienna & Cologne: Styria, 1979);

Niederösterreich, edited by Christian Brandstätter (Vienna, Munich & Zurich: Molden Edition, 1979);

Drei Flötentöne: Roman (Graz, Vienna & Cologne: Styria, 1981);

Aktäon: Novelle (Graz, Vienna & Cologne: Styria, 1983);

Das Bild der beiden Schwestern: Erzählungen (Leipzig: St. Benno, 1984);

Papierschiffchen treiben: Erlebnisse einer Kindheit (Graz, Vienna & Cologne: Styria, 1987).

TRANSLATIONS: H. V. Morton, *Spanische Reise* (Berlin: Ullstein, 1957);

Nancy Hallinan, *Kleine Lampe im großen Wind* (Frankfurt am Main: Fischer, 1958);

Ludwig Bemelmans, *Die Frau meines Lebens* (Cologne: Kiepenheuer & Witsch, 1958);

Bernard Frizell, *Julie* (Hamburg: Mosaik, 1962);

Walter Macken, *Gott schuf den Sonntag* (Munich: Rex, 1962);

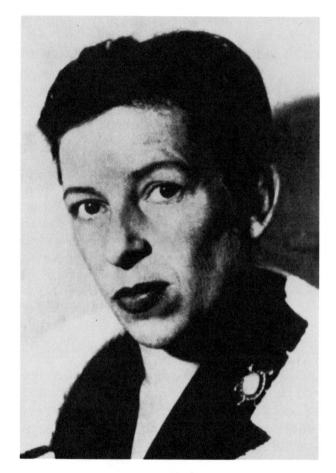

Jeannie Ebner (Bildarchiv der Österreichischen Nationalbibliothek)

Edna O'Brien, *Die Fünfzehnjährigen* (Hamburg: Rütten & Loening, 1963);

Macken, *Wer Augen hat zu sehen . . .* (Munich: Rex, 1963);

Francis MacManus, *Zieh hin, lieber Fluß* (Munich: Rex, 1964);

Peader O'Donnell, *Die Inselleute von Inniscara* (Munich: Rex, 1964);

Miss Read, *Unser kleines Schicksal* (Munich: Rex, 1964);

Read, *Blick über den Zaun* (Munich: Rex, 1965);

Joseph-Émile Muller, *Kleine Enzyklopädie der Kunst: Moderne Malerei*, 5 volumes (Gütersloh: Mohn, 1965);

Michael MacLaverty, *Zu ihren Lebzeiten* (Munich: Rex, 1966);

O'Donnell, *Die großen Fenster* (Munich: Rex, 1966);

MacManus, *Heimkehr nach Watergate* (Munich: Rex, 1966);

Meriol Trevor, *Morgen werden wir leben* (Munich: Rex, 1966);

Salvador de Madariaga, *Über Don Quichote* (Vienna: Moden, 1967);

Yael Dayan, *Der Tod hat zwei Söhne* (Vienna: Molden, 1968);

Dayan, *Spuren im Staub* (Vienna: Molden, 1969);

Derek Lambert, *Engel im Schnee* (Berlin: Ullstein, 1970);

Sarah Gainham, *Die Nymphe* (Vienna: Molden, 1970);

N. Scott Momaday, *Haus aus Dämmerung* (Berlin: Ullstein, 1971);

Lady Cynthia Asquith, *Schrecksekunden* (Tübingen: Wunderlich & Leins, 1971);

Rosemary Harris, *Eine Katze für Noahs Arche* (Vienna: Jugend und Volk, 1972);

Richard Bach, *Die Möwe Jonathan* (Berlin: Ullstein, 1972);

Martin Esslin, *Jenseits des Absurden* (Vienna: Europa, 1972);

J. B. Priestley, *Snoggle von der Milchstraße* (Recklinghausen: Bitter, 1973);

Virginia Hamilton, *Der Planet des Patrick Brown* (Zurich: Benziger, 1973);

Ann Nall Stallworth, *Nächstes Jahr um diese Zeit* (Munich: Ehrenwirth, 1974);

Larry Woiwode, *Ein Stern, ein Stein-Staub* (Berlin: Ullstein, 1980).

When her first novel, *Sie warten auf Antwort* (They Are Waiting for an Answer), appeared in 1954, Jeannie Ebner immediately won critical acclaim and was praised as the representative of a reborn Austrian literature. This accolade did not translate into sales figures, however, and she was forced to earn a living translating books from English into German. Ebner has refused to participate in the deliberate manufacture of publicity in which some young writers have excelled. In a time when the literary sensation was front-page news, Ebner has relied on the merit of her work and the belief that quality and honesty will ultimately prevail.

Jeannie Ebner was born on 17 November 1918 in Sydney, Australia. Her father, Johann Ebner, the black sheep of his family, had been sent to Australia at an early age to spare his middle-class family political embarrassment. His wife went with him, but she soon had to return to Vienna to be institutionalized for mental illness. He tried his luck at many enterprises and accumulated a modest fortune. After more than twenty years of living alone he placed an advertisement in a Viennese newspaper which led to a correspondence with Ida Ganaus. She joined him in Australia and became the mother of his two children, although, as a Catholic, he never divorced his wife. About 1920 the family moved to Wiener Neustadt, Austria, where Johann Ebner invested his money in houses and several businesses, formally adopted his children, and legally arranged for Ida Ganaus to bear his name officially. He died in 1926. During the Great Depression the family lost everything except their shares in a forwarding business.

Jeannie Ebner, who retained her bilingual facility, received all her education in Wiener Neustadt: four years of elementary school, four years in a gymnasium, and two years at a commercial college. She then served an apprenticeship in the family forwarding business, buying out the other partners when she reached the age of twenty-one. In 1941 she enrolled at the Academy of Fine Arts in Vienna to study sculpture, leaving the business in the hands of a manager. Early in 1945 her apartment and business were destroyed in an air raid. She and her mother moved to the Kitzbühler Horn in Tirol, where they lived for a year in a converted mountain cabin. They then moved to Golling, near Salzburg, where Ebner gave English lessons and worked as a painter and a designer of souvenirs. Ebner returned to Vienna in the autumn of 1946 and became a typist for the American military forces. When she lost her typing job in 1949, she was already considering a career as a full-time writer. While writing her first novel she supported herself with part-time office work and by helping the writer Hans Weigel edit the annual anthology *Stimmen der Gegenwart*. Ebner decided to devote her life to writing when the first novel, *Sie warten auf Antwort*, was an immediate success with the critics. In 1964 she married Ernst Allinger, with whom she had had a relationship since 1948. In 1968 she became editor of the journal *Literatur und Kritik*, which she developed into an internationally respected publication. Ebner has always had an affinity for lyric poetry and wrote her first poem at the age of twelve, but it is as a writer of fiction that she became a major figure of contemporary Austrian literature.

Although she cannot recall having read either Franz Kafka or Robert Musil before writing her first novel, her work shows influences of these literary giants. Its mythological style, the creation of a self-contained fictional world functioning in accordance with laws that do not necessarily correspond to those of the everyday world, is reminiscent of Kafka. But Ebner also introduces an emphasis on rationality: there is a highly conscious narrator in control who is not caught up in the events of the novel but narrates with full knowledge of the situation. This narrator is also conscious of the concept of the possible, which Musil made famous, and comes, as Musil did, to the conclusion that what might have happened in the novel is of no less importance than what does happen.

Sie warten auf Antwort is concerned with the phenomenon of helplessness. The original title was "Die Hilflosen" (The Helpless Ones), and it was changed to the present title only at the last moment. The characters all feel that they have lost control over their lives, and their actions can be seen as attempts to overcome this helplessness. The action takes place in the capital city of a country dominated by a large river. This river has its source in a distant land, a peaceful, fertile, paradisiacal country. From this other country the angelic Angelika and the Mephistophelian Muni come to the capital city. They are perceived by the inhabitants of the capital city as messengers from another world, but Angelika and Muni have only a faint recollection of their homeland. Angelika breaks away from her peaceful and carefree existence only to find herself reduced to a state of helplessness and dependence. Muni represents the irresponsible revolutionary principle; but not even he is in control of his life. Angelika inspires other characters to acts of charity; Muni inspires them to revolt. Life in the city is governed by three powerful institutions: das Bauamt (the Building Office), which is the civil authority; die Organisation (the Organization), which is responsible for religion and metaphysics; and die Bande (the Gang), which represents the criminal fraternity. The Building Authority and the Organization derive their authority from the mysterious Baumeister (Masterbuilder), whom no one has ever seen and whose existence is doubted by skeptics.

The ordinary individual is therefore helplessly subjected to the demands of these institutions. Even the educated and active Dr. Fröhlich becomes helpless by the end of the novel, having learned not only that all his life he has asked meaningless questions but also that it was the purpose of his life to ask these questions. He has then achieved all that there is to be achieved: he has learned not to take life too seriously. Consequently, he is no longer suited for life. He dies peacefully, admiring a blue butterfly.

Ebner wrote several short stories in the mythological style of her first novel, but in her second novel, *Die Wildnis früher Sommer* (The Jungle of Early Summer, 1958), a more realistic and psychological style emerges. The protagonist, Pin, constantly thinks and speaks in metaphors; but for her these metaphors reflect reality. She has reached the threshold of adulthood but refuses to cross it; she does not distinguish between dream, fantasy, and reality. Everything Pin perceives is equally real to her. Refusing to grow up, she does not live past the age of sixteen: she perishes before she can be forced to accept the "real" world that she has always despised. One day she does not return from an excursion into the dreamworld. The novel contains a parable titled "Die Chronik der Familie Abouan" (The Chronicle of the Family Abouan) which marks a return to Ebner's original mythological style. This chronicle links the fates of the members of Pin's family with that of all mankind. Since the changeover from the symbolic and mythological mode to a more realistic one had not been fully completed, Ebner thoroughly revised the work for its third edition in 1978 and cut it to two-thirds of its original length.

Ebner's autobiographical third novel, *Figuren in Schwarz und Weiß* (Figures in Black and White, 1964), is set in Vienna between 1925 and 1955. The novel takes its title from the game of chess, in which the two sides are clearly distinguishable; in real life, however, good and evil are not always clearly distinguishable. Ebner analyzes the rise of National Socialism in Germany and the annexation of Austria in 1938 from the perspective of the middle- and upper-middle classes, groups which, through their inactivity, were partly responsible for the disaster. It was a highly sophisticated stratum of society that was also politically naive. It was a social asset to adapt to given situations and not to lower oneself by taking an interest in politics. Hitler was regarded as uneducated and vulgar and was therefore not taken seriously.

Ebner circa 1981

Because of these attitudes the new system took over unopposed. Most people carried on as before, deliberately remaining ignorant of the real situation. One such person is the protagonist, Theres Meinhardt, who is mainly concerned with her personal problems. After the collapse of the Third Reich, documentation of the horrors of the concentration camps shocks Theres into the realization that ignorance is equivalent to guilt. Theres decides to become a writer even though she does not believe that literature influences politics; at the most, she hopes that her writing may help some individuals.

Ebner's fourth novel, *Drei Flötentöne* (Three Sounds of a Flute, 1981), consists of three stories about three women. As the novel proceeds the impression grows that the three women are actually three facets of one person. The writer Gertrud is the only one who succeeds in life: she has a happy marriage, a fulfilling career, and an attitude which enables her to accept the approach of old age gracefully. Jana, a dancer who fails to achieve a successful career on the stage, becomes an alcoholic and commits suicide. The idealistic Tschuptschik also commits suicide when she finds herself pregnant and is unable to bear the

thought of bringing a child into an imperfect world. That Gertrud survives in a state of happiness suggests that Ebner is rejecting the realm of dream which was depicted in her earlier work as the realm of truth.

The novella *Aktäon* (1983) takes its title from the Greek myth of the hunter Actaeon, who, caught spying on the goddess Artemis while she was bathing, was turned into a stag and torn apart by his own dogs. Considering that Artemis would have had more cause for indignation if Actaeon had ignored her, Ebner tells the story of a woman in her sixties who believes that erotic passion is behind her, only to discover to her amazement that she is physically attracted to a man. But since the man is unaware of her feelings, the narrator is able to reflect on this situation in a detached manner; she can observe herself being in love and turn these observations and reflections into literature. *Aktäon*, like *Drei Flötentöne*, stresses the possibilities of happiness that old age has to offer.

In *Papierschiffchen treiben: Erlebnisse einer Kindheit* (Paper Boats Are Floating: Experiences of a Childhood, 1987) Ebner looks back on her childhood. She also reflects critically on the problems a writer faces when trying to convert personal experiences into literature. The narrative is interlaced with observations and judgments that turn the autobiography into a commentary on the general state of affairs of her time. There is in this work a new tone of resignation, without bitterness or regret, as the narrator prepares to deal with the approach of death.

Ebner found her major theme early in her career: the dilemma of trying to justify an ethical existence in an ever-changing world. In her struggle with this subject Ebner changed her mode of presentation from mythological and allegorical abstraction to a realistic and psychologically motivated treatment of her own past. Her novels are documents of their time and works of art that, in the sequence of their appearance, develop from the general to the personal level.

References:

Jorun Johns, "Jeannie Ebner: Eine Bibliographie," *Modern Austrian Literature*, 12, no. 3/4 (1979): 209-236;

Carine Kleiber, *Jeannie Ebner: Eine Einführung* (Bonn, Frankfurt am Main & New York: Lang, 1985);

August Obermayer, "Beiträge zu einer Bewältigung der Hilflosigkeit: Zu Jeannie Ebners Roman *Sie warten auf Antwort*," *Modern Austrian Literature*, 14, no. 1/2 (1981): 62-79;

Obermayer, "Jeannie Ebner," in *Major Figures of Contemporary Austrian Literature*, edited by Donald G. Daviau (New York, Bern & Frankfurt am Main: Lang, 1987), pp. 143-161;

Theodor Sapper, "Jeannie Ebners dichterisches Werk," *Literatur und Kritik*, 130 (1978): 578-599;

Gottfried Stix, "Jeannie Ebners Dichtungen und das Äußerste," *Literatur und Kritik*, 130 (1978): 600-605;

Victor Suchy, "Die Traumhäuptige. Traum und Wirklichkeit im Werk Jeannie Ebners," *Literatur und Kritik*, 227/228 (1988): 335-348.

Herbert Eisenreich
(7 February 1925-6 June 1986)

Renate Latimer
Auburn University

BOOKS: *Einladung, deutlich zu leben* (Vienna: Jungbrunnen, 1952);

Auch in ihrer Sünde: Roman (Hamburg: Schröder, 1953);

Böse schöne Welt: Erzählungen (Stuttgart: Scherz & Goverts, 1957); "Erlebnis wie bei Dostojewski" translated by Renate Latimer as "A Dostoevskian Experience," *New Orleans Review*, 11, no. 2 (1984): 67-72;

Wovon wir leben und woran wir sterben: Ein Hörspiel (Frankfurt am Main: Europäische Verlags-Anstalt, 1958);

Carnuntum: Geist und Fleisch (Vienna: Verlag für Jugend und Volk, 1960);

Große Welt auf kleinen Schienen: Das Entstehen einer Modellanlage (Salzburg: Residenz, 1963);

Der Urgroßvater (Gütersloh: Mohn, 1964);

Reaktionen: Essays zur Literatur (Gütersloh: Mohn, 1964);

Sozusagen Liebesgeschichten (Gütersloh: Mohn, 1965); "Der schwerste Parcours der Welt" translated by Astrid Ivask as "The Toughest Steeplechase in the World," *Literary Review*, 9, no. 4 (1966): 605-611; "Abschied zur Liebe" translated by Latimer as "Farewell to Love," *Short Story International*, 61 (1987): 7-15;

Ich im Auto (Salzburg: Residenz, 1966);

Sebastian; Die Ketzer: Zwei Dialoge (Gütersloh: Mohn, 1966);

Die Freunde meiner Frau und 19 andere Kurzgeschichten (Zurich: Diogenes, 1966);

Das kleine Stifterbuch (Salzburg: Residenz, 1967);

Ein schöner Sieg und 21 andere Mißverständnisse (Graz, Vienna & Cologne: Styria, 1973); "Lob des Handwerks" translated by Peter Hutchinson as "In Praise of Craftsmanship," in *Anthology of Modern Austrian Literature,* edited by Adolf Opel (London: Oswald Wolff, 1981), pp. 184-186; "Ein Freund des Hauses" translated by Latimer as "A Friend of the Family," *Short Story International*, 68 (1988): 7-21;

Die blaue Distel der Romantik: Erzählungen (Graz, Vienna & Cologne: Styria, 1976);

Verlorene Funde: Gedichte 1946-1952 (Graz, Vienna & Cologne: Styria, 1976);

Das Leben als Freizeit (Düsseldorf: Edition Freizeit Verlags-Gesellschaft, 1976);

Groschenweisheiten: Aus dem Zettelkram eines Sophisten (Mühlacker: Stieglitz, 1985);

Der alte Adam: Aus dem Zettelkram eines Sophisten (Mühlacker: Stieglitz, 1985);

Die abgelegte Zeit (Vienna: Herold, 1985);

Memoiren des Kopfes: Aus dem Zettelkram eines Sophisten (Mühlacker: Stieglitz, 1986).

OTHER: Heimito von Doderer, *Wege und Umwege: Eine Auswahl,* edited by Eisenreich (Graz: Stiasny, 1960);

Liebesgeschichten aus Österreich, edited by Eisenreich and Maria Eisenreich (Zurich: Diogenes, 1978).

Although Herbert Eisenreich wrote essays, poetry, radio plays, novels, and criticism, the short story is his principal domain. He regarded the short story as the purest and most lyrical prose genre, as "ein wortgewordener Augenblick" (a moment transformed into words) that needs no explanation, names, dates, or places, that renders insignificant what happened before and what will happen after. It tells of a momentary confrontation with life, love, or death; it does not permit itself a dramatic ending but is a fragment of an unending narration. Eisenreich's artistic virtues are best displayed in his precise and exact observation–often ironic as well as laconic–of the small, even minute, which, he felt, were governed by the same laws as the big, the noisy, and the violent. In Eisenreich's chiseled language every word, every comma is chosen with care; but, like Guy de Maupassant and Gustave Flaubert, he hides this struggle and renders his artistry invisible and his style unaffected.

Eisenreich was born in Linz on 7 February 1925 to Josef and Elisabeth Wurz Eisenreich. His

Herbert Eisenreich

father, a bank clerk, died young, leaving Eisenreich's mother to raise the three children alone. After elementary school Eisenreich was sent to the Bundeserziehungsanstalt (Federal Educational Establishment) in Vienna, which offered free schooling to gifted children. He considered his three years in Vienna to be among his happiest. After the Anschluß (annexation of Austria by Nazi Germany) in 1938 he had to return to the Linz Realgymnasium, where he failed his school-leaving examination–not because he had to support himself by washing glasses in a laboratory and tutoring but simply because he was not interested in school. He preferred to visit courtrooms, and it was there that he learned about life. In 1943 he joined the military, not out of patriotism but because he did not know how to avoid it. He was proud that he did not kill anyone during the war. He was wounded in the shoulder and suffered from the effects of that injury for the rest of his life. After his release from a military hospital and brief captivity in an American POW camp he passed the school-leaving exam with distinction and began to study philology, Germanics,

and dramaturgy at the University of Vienna. He soon broke off his studies to earn a living as a messenger for the Vienna *Kurier* and to write. In 1946 he won the prize of the *Linzer Volksblatt* for a short story about a soldier returning home. Years of travel in Germany, Yugoslavia, and France as a free-lance writer, foreign correspondent, and commentator for newspapers followed. He lived in Hamburg from 1952 to 1954, in Stuttgart from 1954 to 1956, and divided his time between Vienna and Sandl in Upper Austria from 1958 to 1967. His radio play *Wovon wir leben und woran wir sterben* (What We Live on and What We Die of, 1958) was awarded the Prix d'Italia in 1957. His marriages to Ilse Perl, Waltraud Kuhls, and Georgine Varga ended in divorce. He lived in Vienna from 1967 until his death on 6 June 1986. His works have been translated into Dutch, Polish, Czech, Japanese, Russian, Swedish, Hungarian, and Italian, and five of his stories have appeared in English. Other literary awards bestowed upon Eisenreich include the Austrian State Prize in 1958, the Great Art Prize of North Rhine-Westphalia in 1965, the Anton Wildgans

Eisenreich (standing, at right) at the Café Raimund in Vienna at the beginning of the 1950s

Prize in 1970, the Georg Mackensen Prize in 1971, the Peter Altenberg Prize in 1984, and the Franz Theodor Csokor Prize in 1985.

Although Eisenreich's one hundred or so short stories range from the tragic to the grotesque and deal with topics as diverse as the Hungarian revolution, an Adriatic beach, Biedermeier Vienna, and a honeymoon journey, he maintained that his central subject matter is that of misunderstanding, misconstruing, or misconception: a misunderstood gesture, a misinterpreted action, an imprecise word that results in an unintended but not necessarily unpleasant relationship. In his essay "Das schlechte Beispiel des Herbert Eisenreich" (The Bad Example of Herbert Eisenreich), which appears as an epilogue in *Ein schöner Sieg und 21 andere Mißverständnisse* (A Beautiful Victory and 21 Other Misunderstandings, 1973), Eisenreich claims that this motif of misunderstanding can be traced to his gymnasium days in Linz, when his German teacher asked the pupils to expand on an anecdote from the diary of the nineteenth-century dramatist Friedrich Hebbel: "Ein Toter wird von einem Mörder verscharrt, an der selben Stelle, wo ein anderer einen Schatz verborgen hat. Der Mörder findet den Schatz und nimmt ihn mit; wie der andere später sein Gold holen will, wird er beim Graben ertappt und gilt für den Mörder" (A mur-

derer is burying a dead man in the same spot where another person has buried a treasure. The murderer finds the treasure and takes it along; later, when the other person comes to fetch his gold, he is discovered while digging in the earth and is mistaken as the murderer).

In his stories of failed marriages, broken commitments, atrophied souls, and competitive struggles Eisenreich never preaches or teaches, judges or condemns. His often nameless protagonists sin without being sinners, do evil without being criminals, err in a world that is evil and beautiful, repulsive and attractive. He describes his own middle-class milieu of academics, intellectuals, students, and the military; he is primarily a portraitist of the Viennese bourgeoisie. He is interested not in political but in personal events, which he analyzes in a compact, elliptical style that is often acerbic or frivolous and is always elegant.

Eisenreich, a member of the generation whose intellectual and literary development took place during the postwar years, describes the paradoxical nature of that generation in *Reaktionen: Essays zur Literatur* (Reactions: Essays on Literature, 1964): "eine zwar illusionslose, nicht aber eine nihilistische Generation; eine skeptische, nicht aber eine ungläubige; eine autoritätsfeindliche, nicht aber eine anarchistische. . . . Sie lebt

Eisenreich in Amras in the Tirol, 1965 (Bildarchiv der Österreichischen Nationalbibliothek)

durchaus in der Gegenwart, aber sie versucht, ihre gegenwärtige Position in der Vergangenheit zu fundieren. Sie ist nicht konservativ, aber sie besinnt sich auf die Tradition" (a generation without illusions, but not characterized by nihilism; a skeptical generation but not disbelieving; one hostile to authority but not anarchical. . . . Our generation lives absolutely in the present but tries to ground its present position in the past. It is not conservative, but it remembers tradition). In these traditional and conventional literary essays, ranging in subject matter from Marcus Aurelius to Fritz von Herzmanovsky-Orlando, Eisenreich concentrates on Austrian literature; many of the essays show his admiration for Johann Nestroy, Adalbert Stifter, and especially Heimito von Doderer. Like Doderer, Eisenreich is a chronicler of Viennese society; the works of both writers tend to be episodic and aphoristic and to emphasize form over content. Both are fascinated not by historical and political events but by the exploration of the genius loci, the monotony of daily rituals; both depict man's coming to grips with

reality, which results in his renewal or Menschwerdung (humanization).

In the six hundred pages of his novel fragment *Die abgelegte Zeit* (The Discarded Time, 1985) Eisenreich offers a panorama of Austrian society from 1938 to 1953; the protagonists are members of the author's generation. The original title, "Sieger und Besiegte" (Victors and Vanquished), had no political connotation or reference to 1945; it was meant in a metaphorical sense, indicating whether the novel's figures affirm or negate life in war, marriage, captivity, or career. Eisenreich presents a variety of characters and milieus: a general, a common soldier, a half-Jewish family, young intellectuals and artists, an American industrialist, a prostitute, a physician, battlefields, cafés, barracks, the apartment of a Viennese scholar.

Eisenreich did not believe that literature should be ideological or politically engaged. In the 1970s, when engagement rather than art was demanded of writers, when storytelling without strong language was considered reactionary, and when a generation in blue jeans proclaimed non-conformity as the ne plus ultra of morality, Eisenreich was neither published nor noticed. His aesthetic concepts have been rejected by younger Austrian writers. In 1985, however, the year before he died of a brain tumor, he received the Franz Kafka Literature Prize and the Medal of Honor of the City of Vienna. Both pleased him and, according to his fourth wife, Maria Pesti Eisenreich, gave rise to a melancholy smile.

References:

Otto Basil, *Das große Erbe* (Graz: Stiasny, 1962);

Robert Blauhut, *Österreichische Novellistik des 20. Jahrhunderts* (Vienna: Braumüller, 1966), pp. 279-283;

Maria Eisenreich, "Ein Opfer des Konformismus: Gedanken von und zu Herbert Eisenreich," *Zentrum*, 10 (September 1986): 20-23;

Hermann Friedl, "Herbert Eisenreich oder schreiben, um leben zu lernen," *Wort in der Zeit*, 7, no. 8 (1961): 6-12;

Karl August Horst, "Herbert Eisenreich," in *Schriftsteller der Gegenwart*, edited by Klaus Nonnenmann (Olten: Walter, 1963), pp. 98-102;

Reinhold Klemm, "Herbert Eisenreich: Vom morbus sacer in der neueren Romanliteratur," *Wort in der Zeit*, 2, no. 2 (1956): 23-26;

Marcel Reich-Ranicki, *Literatur der kleinen Schritte: Deutsche Schriftsteller heute* (Munich: Piper, 1967), pp. 63-70;

Wendelin Schmidt-Dengler, " 'Erlebnis wie bei Dostojewski' und 'Die ganze Geschichte': Zu zwei Erzählungen von Herbert Eisenreich," *Zeitschrift für deutsche Philologie*, 87 (1968): 591-612;

Schmidt-Dengler, "Herbert Eisenreich," in *Deutsche Literatur der Gegenwart in Einzeldarstellungen*, volume 1, edited by Dietrich Weber (Stuttgart: Kröner, 1976), pp. 260-276;

Johannes Würtz, " 'Ars critica.' Zu Herbert Eisenreich: Der Kritiker, Rang und Amt," *Wort in der Zeit*, 2, no. 9 (1956): 43-47.

Papers:

Herbert Eisenreich's literary estate is in the possession of Christine Fritsch, Vienna.

Erich Fried
(6 May 1921-22 November 1988)

Jerry Glenn
University of Cincinnati

BOOKS: *They Fight in the Dark: The Story of Aus
tria's Youth* (London: Young Austria in Great
Britain, 1944);

Deutschland: Gedichte (London: Austrian P.E.N.,
1944);

Österreich: Gedichte (London & Zurich: Atrium,
1945);

Gedichte (Hamburg: Claassen, 1958);

Ein Soldat und ein Mädchen: Roman (Hamburg:
Claassen, 1960);

Reich der Steine: Zyklische Gedichte (Hamburg: Claassen, 1963);

Georg Eisler, by Fried and Ernst Köller (Vienna:
Grasl, 1964);

Warngedichte (Munich: Hanser, 1964);

Überlegungen: Gedichtzyklus (Munich: Hanser,
1964);

Kinder und Narren: Prosa (Munich: Hanser, 1965);

und Vietnam und: Einundvierzig Gedichte (Berlin:
Wagenbach, 1966);

*Arden muß sterben: Eine Oper vom Tod des reichen
Arden von Faversham,* music by Alexander
Goehr (London: Schott / New York: Associ-
ated Music Publishers, 1967); translated by
Geoffrey Skelton as *Arden Must Die: An
Opera on the Death of the Wealthy Arden of Faver-
sham* (London: Schott / New York: Associ-
ated Music Publishers, 1967);

Anfechtungen: Fünfzig Gedichte (Berlin: Wagenbach, 1967);

Zeitfragen: Gedichte (Munich: Hanser, 1968);

Intellektuelle und Sozialismus, by Fried, Paul A. Ba-
ran, and Gaston Salvatore (Berlin: Wagenbach, 1968);

Befreiung von der Flucht: Gedichte und Gegengedichte
(Hamburg: Claassen, 1968; revised edition,
Düsseldorf: Claassen, 1983);

Last Honours, translated by Georg Rapp (London:
Turret, 1968);

*Die Beine der größeren Lügen: Einundfünfzig Ge-
dichte* (Berlin: Wagenbach, 1969);

Gedichte, edited by Bernd Jentzsch (Berlin: Neues
Leben, 1969);

photo: Hans Bach, Darmstadt

On Pain of Seeing: Poems, translated by Rapp (Chicago: Swallow Press, 1969; London: Rapp &
Whiting, 1969);

Unter Nebenfeinden: Fünfzig Gedichte (Berlin: Wagenbach, 1970);

Aufforderung zur Unruhe: Ausgewählte Gedichte (Munich: Deutscher Taschenbuch Verlag, 1972);

*Die Freiheit den Mund aufzumachen: Achtundvierzig
Gedichte* (Berlin: Wagenbach, 1972);

Gegengift: 49 Gedichte und ein Zyklus (Berlin: Wagenbach, 1974);

Höre, Israel! Gedichte und Fußnoten (Hamburg:
Assoziation, 1974; revised edition, Frankfurt am Main: Syndikat, 1983);

*Fast alles Mögliche: Wahre Geschichten und gültige Lü-
gen* (Berlin: Wagenbach, 1975);

Kampf ohne Engel, edited by Frank Beer (Berlin: Volk und Welt, 1976);

So kam ich unter die Deutschen: Gedichte (Hamburg: Assoziation, 1977);

Die bunten Getüme: Siebzig Gedichte (Berlin: Wagenbach, 1977);

100 Gedichte ohne Vaterland (Berlin: Wagenbach, 1978); translated by Stuart Hood as *100 Poems without a Country* (London: Calder, 1978);

Liebesgedichte (Berlin: Wagenbach, 1979);

Lebensschatten: Gedichte (Berlin: Wagenbach, 1981);

Zur Zeit und zur Unzeit: Gedichte (Cologne: Bund, 1981);

Das Nahe suchen: Gedichte (Berlin: Wagenbach, 1982);

Das Unmaß aller Dinge: Fünfunddreißig Erzählungen (Berlin: Wagenbach, 1982);

Das Mißverständnis (Frankfurt am Main: Ali Baba, 1982);

Es ist was es ist: Liebesgedichte, Angstgedichte, Zorngedichte (Berlin: Wagenbach, 1983);

Angst und Trost: Erzählungen und Gedichte über Juden und Nazis (Frankfurt am Main: Ali Baba, 1983);

Ich grenz noch an ein Wort und an ein andres Land: Über Ingeborg Bachmann–Erinnerung, einige Anmerkungen zu ihrem Gedicht "Böhmen liegt am Meer" und ein Nachruf (Berlin: Friedenauer Presse, 1983);

Immendorf: Neue Bilder und Skulpturen, by Fried and Peter Schneider (Hamburg: Galerie Ascan Crone, 1984);

Beunruhigungen: Gedichte (Berlin: Wagenbach, 1984);

Und nicht taub und stumpf werden: Unrecht, Widerstand und Protest. Reden, Polemiken, Gedichte (Dorsten: Multi-Media, 1984);

. . . und alle seine Mörder . . . : Ein Schauspiel (Vienna: Promedia, 1984);

In die Sinne einradiert: Gedichte (Cologne: Bund, 1985);

Von Bis nach Seit: Gedichte aus den Jahren 1945-1958 (Vienna: Promedia, 1985);

Um Klarheit: Gedichte gegen das Vergessen (Berlin: Wagenbach, 1985);

Die da reden gegen Vernichtung: Psychologie, bildende Kunst und Dichtung gegen den Krieg, by Fried, Alfred Hrdlicka, and Erwin Ringel, edited by Alexander Klauser, Judith Klauser, and Michael Lewin (Vienna: Europa, 1985);

Wächst das Rettende auch? Gedichte für den Frieden (Cologne: Bund, 1986);

Fried at around age six

Frühe Gedichte (Düsseldorf: Claassen, 1986);

Mitunter sogar Lachen: Zwischenfälle und Erinnerungen (Berlin: Wagenbach, 1986);

Vorübungen für Wunder: Gedichte vom Zorn und von der Liebe (Berlin: Wagenbach, 1987);

Gegen das Vergessen (Cologne: Bund, 1987);

Nicht verdrängen nicht gewöhnen: Texte zum Thema Österreich (Vienna: Europa, 1987);

Wo liegt Nicaragua? Gedichte und ein Gespräch, by Fried and Heinrich Albertz (Wuppertal: Nahua, 1987);

Am Rand unserer Lebenszeit: Gedichte (Berlin: Wagenbach, 1987);

Gedanken in und an Deutschland: Essays und Reden, edited by Lewin (Vienna: Europa, 1988);

Von der Nachfolge dieses jungen Menschen, der nie alt wird (Darmstadt: Büchner, 1988).

OTHER: Elias Canetti, *Welt im Kopf,* edited by Fried (Vienna: Stiasny, 1962);

"Ein Versuch, Farbe zu bekennen," in *Ich lebe nicht in der Bundesrepublik*, edited by Hermann Kesten (Munich: List, 1963), pp. 43-48;

Am Beispiel Peter-Paul Zahl: Eine Dokumentation, edited by Fried, Helga M. Novak, and the Initiativgruppe P. P. Zahl (Frankfurt am Main: Sozialistische Verlagsauslieferung, 1976);

Bertolt Brecht Poems, edited by Fried, John Willett, and Ralph Manheim (3 volumes, London: Eyre Methuen, 1976; revised edition, 1 volume, London: Eyre Methuen, 1979; New York: Methuen, 1979);

Agnes Stein, trans., *Four German Poets: Günter Eich, Hilde Domin, Erich Fried, Günter Kunert*, includes translations of poems by Fried (New York: Red Dust, 1979);

Stephanie Vernholz, ed., *Ganz oben leichte Vögel: Gedichte*, includes poems by Fried (Hattingen: Flieter, 1982).

TRANSLATIONS: Dylan Thomas, *Unter dem Milchwald* (Heidelberg: Drei Brücken, 1954);

Thomas, *Am frühen Morgen: Autobiographisches, Radio-Essays, Gedichte und Prosa* (Heidelberg: Drei Brücken, 1957);

Eric Linklater, *Der Teufel in der Gasgone: Bühnenmanuskript* (Berlin: Bloch, 1958);

T. S. Eliot, *Ein verdienter Staatsmann* (Frankfurt am Main: Suhrkamp, 1959);

Thomas, *Der Doktor und die Teufel* (Frankfurt am Main: Fischer, 1959);

Graham Greene, *Der verbindliche Liebhaber* (Hamburg & Vienna: Zsolnay, 1960);

Terence Rattigan, *Ross: Bühnenmanuskript* (Basel: Reiss, 1960);

Euripides, *Die Bacchantinnen: Bühnenmanuskript* (Berlin: Bloch, 1960);

Thomas, *Ein Blick aufs Meer*, translated by Fried and Enzio von Cramon (Heidelberg: Drei Brücken, 1961);

Richard Wright, *Der Mann, der nach Chikago ging: Erzählungen*, translated by Fried and Cramon (Hamburg: Claassen, 1961);

William Shakespeare, *Ein Sommernachtstraum* (Frankfurt am Main: Fischer, 1964);

Edith Sitwell, *Gedichte*, translated by Fried, Christian Enzenberger, and Werner Vordtriebe (Frankfurt am Main: Insel, 1964);

Jakov Lind, *Die Heiden* (Neuwied & Berlin: Luchterhand, 1965);

David Rokeah, *Von Sommer zu Sommer* (Frankfurt am Main: Fischer, 1965);

Der Stern, der tat sie lenken: Alte englische Lieder und Hymnen (Munich: Hanser, 1966);

Thomas, *Ausgewählte Gedichte* (Munich: Hanser, 1967);

Shakespeare, *Shakespeare-Übersetzungen: Romeo und Julia; Julius Cäsar; Hamlet* (Munich: Hanser, 1968);

Shakespeare, *Shakespeare-Übersetzungen: Das Trauerspiel von König Richard dem Zweiten; Das Leben von König Heinrich dem Fünften* (Berlin: Wagenbach, 1969);

Shakespeare, *Shakespeare-Übersetzungen: Viel Getue um Nichts; Die lustigen Weiber von Windsor* (Berlin: Wagenbach, 1970);

Shakespeare, *Shakespeare-Übersetzungen: Antonius und Kleopatra; Perikles, Fürst von Tyrus* (Berlin: Wagenbach, 1970);

Shakespeare, *Shakespeare-Übersetzungen: Ein Sommernachtstraum; Zwölfte Nacht oder Was ihr wollt* (Berlin: Wagenbach, 1970);

Shakespeare, *Shakespeare-Übersetzungen: König Cymbelin; Zwei Herren aus Verona* (Berlin: Wagenbach, 1970);

Rokeah, *Kein anderer Tag*, translated by Fried, Rokeah, and Johanna Renate Döring (Frankfurt am Main: Fischer, 1971);

John Ford, *Schade, daß sie eine Hure war: Bühnenmanuskript* (Berlin: Bloch, 1972);

Shakespeare, *Shakespeare-Übersetzungen: Hamlet; Othello* (Berlin: Wagenbach, 1972);

Arnold Wesker, *Die Küche* (Frankfurt am Main: Suhrkamp, 1972);

Shakespeare, *Shakespeare-Übersetzungen: Maß für Maß; Romeo und Julia* (Berlin: Wagenbach, 1974);

Sylvia Plath, *Ariel: Gedichte, englisch und deutsch* (Frankfurt am Main: Suhrkamp, 1974);

Thomas, *Die Nachgänger* (Schenefeld: Raamin-Presse, 1977);

Shakespeare, *Shakespeare-Übersetzungen: Troilus und Cressida; Timon von Athen* (Berlin: Wagenbach, 1981);

Shakespeare, *Shakespeare-Übersetzungen: Der Kaufmann von Venedig; Der Sturm* (Berlin: Wagenbach, 1984);

Shakespeare, *Shakespeare-Übersetzungen: Titus Andronicus; Julius Cäsar* (Berlin: Wagenbach, 1985);

Aristophanes, *Lysistrata* (Berlin: Wagenbach, 1985).

PERIODICAL PUBLICATIONS: "Abschied von der BBC," *Kürbiskern*, 2 (1968): 283-285;

Fried in the 1950s (photo: Claassen Verlag; property of Teddy Schwarz)

"Ist Antizionismus Antisemitismus?," *Merkur,* 30 (1976): 547-552.

Erich Fried was one of modern Austrian literature's most complex and controversial figures: a Jewish survivor of Nazi persecution who was opposed to the policies of the Israeli government and sympathetic to the Palestinians; a German-language poet who objected to many of the actions of the West German government; a Marxist who disapproved of the practice of Marxism. Primarily known as a lyric poet, Fried published more than twenty-five collections of verse, and from 1963 until his death in 1988 scarcely a year passed without the appearance of at least one volume of poetry. Although not all of his poetry is of high quality, his best work is among the most distinguished contemporary Austrian verse. His linguistic virtuosity, manifested in his mastery of sophisticated wordplay, is unexcelled. But it is his leftist political stance that has attracted the most attention and stirred up the most controversy. Whereas the political messages of his poems often seem simplistic, in his fiction the ambiguity of the moral questions can be more adequately re-

flected. Many critics maintain that his fiction is among the most interesting to have appeared in German since the early 1960s. He received the Schiller Prize in 1965, the Austrian Appreciation Prize for Literature in 1972, the Prix International des Éditeurs in 1977, the Prize of the City of Vienna for Literature in 1980, and the Bremen Literature Prize in 1983.

Born in Vienna in 1921 to Hugo and Nellie Stein Fried, Fried witnessed the political upheavals of the 1920s and the depression and the increase of anti-Semitism during the 1930s. Soon after the German annexation of Austria in 1938 Fried's apolitical father was sent to a concentration camp; later that year Fried fled to London, which remained his home for the rest of his life. He began to write soon after his arrival in England, publishing poems and essays in exile journals in addition to two slender collections of verse, *Deutschland* (Germany, 1944) and *Österreich* (Austria, 1945). These early works are traditional in form and use of language; thematically, however, they anticipate the mature Fried, a nonconformist who felt compelled to question the validity of prevalent clichés. At a time when the world

Fried with his son David, who illustrated some of Fried's books (photo: Catherine Fried)

was bent on revenge against the German nation, Fried insisted in these early poems on distinguishing "zwischen der Vernichtung der feindlichen Idee und der Vernichtung der feindlichen Menschen" (between the destruction of the hostile idea and the destruction of hostile human beings). But poetry was not Fried's primary concern; most of his time not spent earning a living as a chemist in a dairy, a librarian, and a worker in a glass factory was devoted to working with groups involved in helping others–including his mother–escape from the Nazi-controlled Continent. His other relatives and many of his friends perished in concentration camps. During this period he became critical of the difference between Marxist theory and the practices of the Marxist groups with which he was associated.

Fried married Maria Marburg in 1944; a son was born that year and a daughter in 1951. His personal life was far from settled. His first marriage ended in divorce, and he married Nan Spence in 1951. In 1952 he became a commenta-

tor for the BBC, a position he would hold until 1968. A son, David, who was to become an artist and illustrate some of Fried's books, was born in 1958. During the decade following the war Fried was distressed by the oppressive nature of the Stalinist regimes of eastern Europe, the cold war, the rehabilitation of many former Nazis in West Germany, and the increasingly materialistic bent of West German society; his poems of the period rely heavily on wordplay, and their lack of political content reflects his disillusionment. The collection *Gedichte* (Poems, 1958) was not widely acclaimed, although reviewers typically expressed admiration for Fried's linguistic virtuosity. Dissatisfied with the direction his original poetry was taking, Fried turned to literary translation. His German versions of works by Dylan Thomas, T. S. Eliot, and others soon earned him an outstanding reputation in this field. In the early 1960s he began translating Shakespeare's dramas.

Fried had begun writing his first major work of fiction, the novel *Ein Soldat und ein*

Fried's wife, Catherine Fried-Boswell (photo by Graham Kirk, London)

Mädchen (A Soldier and a Girl), in 1946; a first version was completed in 1952, but it was not published until 1960. The narrator retells a story he was told by the soldier of the title, a Jew of German origin serving in the American army. Helga, the girl of the title, had served as a concentration-camp guard and had been condemned to death as a war criminal. Her final request had been that she be allowed to spend the night before her execution with one of her guards, and she had arbitrarily pointed to the Jewish soldier. During the trial the soldier had come to see that she was not an evil person and that she did not deserve the death sentence. After sleeping with her he had made every effort to have her sentence commuted, but without success. The trauma had led to emotional instability and ultimately to his confinement in a mental institution. The soldier's writings—which constitute, along with the narrator's comments, four-fifths of the novel—reflect his inability to come to terms with the situation. *Ein Soldat und ein Mädchen* is a work of considerable complexity. The soldier's stories, some of them realistic accounts of childhood experiences, others Kafkaesque parables, reflect his preoccupa-

tion with questions of guilt, evil, and existential angst.

In 1965 Fried married Catherine Boswell, whose etchings would accompany the poems of *In die Sinne einradiert* (Etched into the Senses, 1985); a daughter was born in 1965 and twin boys in 1969. Encouraged by the de-Stalinization of eastern Europe and incensed by the Vietnam War and the threat of nuclear weapons, Fried again turned to overtly political themes in the poetry collections *Überlegungen* (Reflections, 1964) and *und Vietnam und* (and Vietnam and, 1966). Political involvement characterizes Fried's verse until the late 1970s, most notably in *Höre, Israel!* (Hear, Israel!, 1974), in which the Israeli government's treatment of the Palestinians is subjected to scathing attack, and *So kam ich unter die Deutschen* (Thus I Came among the Germans, 1977), which excoriates what Fried considers the West German government's brutality toward terrorists.

The turn to political subjects was not immediately reflected in Fried's fiction. His first collection of short stories, *Kinder und Narren* (Children and Fools, 1965), is highly eclectic, containing, in the words of one reviewer, "Parabeln, Märchen, Betrachtungen, Satiren" (parables, fairy tales, contemplations, satires). The Kafkaesque first story, "Im Garten" (In the Garden), tells of a child whose playground is a field that consists of grass growing over the roots of a large tree, with nothing underneath except an immense abyss. In the last story in the book, "Der Anlauf" (The Start), Fried comments ironically on the difficulties of writing fiction today–a common theme in contemporary German and Austrian literature–and implies that his brand of moralistic writing is especially hard to produce. The stories are mostly satirical. Several are written in a style reminiscent of Kafka, with realistic narration at odds with the absurdity of the situation described. Others, some of which are heavily laden with puns, consist of the ruminations of a childish narrator. The implied comparison between the childish attitudes of the narrators and a healthy "childlike" attitude toward life is a unifying factor in this otherwise diverse collection.

Fried's next collection of short prose, *Fast alles Mögliche* (Almost Everything Possible, 1975), deals with specific political and social issues–the environment, Vietnam, police brutality, women's rights. Several of the stories are scarcely fiction in the traditional sense; the narrator often merges with the author as the distinction between story and essay virtually ceases to exist. The clearly fictional pieces are for the most part Kafkaesque satires. "Ein aufstrebendes Unternehmen" (A Rising Enterprise) is about a new commercial venture: a "used woman" store. Giving details such as the exact location of the business and the effect its success has had on other establishments in the vicinity, the narrator effusively praises the concept and execution of the enterprise before concluding with an indignant condemnation of a similar store opened by women to dispose of their used men. The next story, "Das Recht auf die Stimme" (The Right to the Voice), about a man whose life is devoted to collecting the death songs of birds, is equally grotesque. This story is followed by a straightforward account of Fried's visit to Auschwitz in 1967. The reader is intended to compare the grotesque fictional absurdity of the two preceding stories with the grotesque historical absurdity of the death camp.

Fried's third collection of short prose, *Das Unmaß aller Dinge* (The Immeasure of All Things, 1982), contains a few parables and satires reminiscent of his earlier work. In one of these, "Theotherapie" (Theotherapy), the narrator advances the proposition that if God were to

Portrait of Fried by David Fried

be examined by a group of psychiatrists, the conclusion would be that He is insane. As in the earlier satires, an absurd situation offering a serious comment on society is presented in a narrative abounding in comically irrelevant details, such as an explanation of the Septuagint and extensive comments on how the work of the psychiatrists might be financed. But on the whole the tone is much more reflective and subdued than in the earlier collections. The narrator is often not a fictional protagonist but Fried himself directly addressing his readers on various moral and political topics.

Angst und Trost: Erzählungen und Gedichte über Juden und Nazis (Fear and Consolation: Stories and Poems about Jews and Nazis, 1983) contains prose and poetry on a single theme. On the surface the stories are accounts of the author's childhood experiences in Vienna, although the content is often so bizarre that the reader familiar with Fried's critical and satirical bent will question their authenticity: Nazi and leftist Jewish students distributing illegal flyers warn each other of the approach of the authorities and trade copies of their propaganda material as if they were baseball cards; a Nazi youth group has difficulty finding a hall in which to hold a farewell party for one of its members who is discovered to have

Jewish ancestry. The simple and direct style, lacking the irrelevant details that characterize Fried's satires, is a hint that the stories are not satiric; and the author removes all doubt in the first sentence of the concluding essay: "Alles, was in diesen Geschichten berichtet ist, habe ich wirklich erlebt" (I have actually experienced everything that is reported in these stories). The Nazis portrayed here are with few exceptions normal and decent—if misguided—people who did not recognize the relationship between their theoretical anti-Semitism and the fate of their Jewish friends until it was too late. These childhood experiences provide an explanation of his lifelong insistence on distinguishing between ideas and the human beings who think them, as well as his penchant for looking beyond clichés to probe the complex, often paradoxical truth of a given issue.

A representative selection of Fried's autobiographical and political essays is included in *Und nicht taub und stumpf werden* (And Not Become Deaf and Dull, 1984). Most of the themes of his fiction are addressed clearly and unambiguously in the essays: the role of the writer in society, war, political oppression in the Federal Republic of Germany, and the oppressive nature of Zionism. That these essays are simultaneously impassioned pleas and clear, rational arguments underscores the complex nature of the writer Erich Fried. Fried died of cancer in Baden-Baden, West Germany, on 22 November 1988.

References:

Jerry Glenn, "Erich Fried," in *Major Figures of Contemporary Austrian Literature*, edited by Donald G. Daviau (New York: Lang, 1987), pp. 163-183;

Ruth V. Gross, Plan *and the Austrian Rebirth: Portrait of a Journal* (Columbia, S.C.: Camden House, 1982), pp. 108-112;

Martin Kane, "From Solipsism to Engagement: The Development of Erich Fried as a Political Poet," *Forum for Modern Language Studies,* 21 (April 1985): 151-169;

Volker Kaukoreit, "Auswahlbibliographie zu Erich Fried," *Freibeuter,* 7 (1981): 27-32;

Kaukoreit, "Erich Fried im Londoner Exil," *Die Horen,* 134 (1984): 59-72;

Kaukoreit, "Der Weg eines bunten Gestüms: Eine vorläufige Biographie des Dichters Erich Fried," *Freibeuter,* 7 (1981): 20-23;

Hanjo Kesting, "Erich Fried," in *Kritisches Lexikon zur deutschsprachigen Gegenwartsliteratur,* edited by H. L. Arnold (Munich: Edition text + kritik, 1980);

Kesting, "Gedichte ohne Vaterland: Der Lyriker Erich Fried," in his *Dichter ohne Vaterland: Gespräche und Aufsätze zur Literatur* (Bonn: Dietz, 1982), pp. 39-51;

Rex Last, "Erich Fried: Poetry and Politics," in *Modern Austrian Writing: Literature and Society after 1945,* edited by Alan Best and Hans Wolfschütz (London: Wolff, 1980; Totowa, N.J.: Barnes & Noble, 1980), pp. 181-196;

text + kritik, special Fried issue, 91 (1986);

Jürgen Wertheimer, "Erich Fried," in *Die deutsche Lyrik 1945-1975,* edited by Klaus Weissenberger (Düsseldorf: Bagel, 1981), pp. 344-352;

Rudolf Wolff, ed., *Erich Fried: Gespräche und Kritiken* (Bonn: Bouvier, 1986);

Michael Zeller, "Im Zeichen des ewigen Juden: Zur Konkretion des politischen Engagements in der Lyrik Erich Frieds," in his *Gedichte haben Zeit: Aufriß einer zeitgenössischen Poetik* (Stuttgart: Klett, 1982), pp. 153-196.

Barbara Frischmuth
(5 July 1941-)

Donald G. Daviau
University of California, Riverside

BOOKS: *Die Klosterschule* (Frankfurt am Main: Suhrkamp, 1968);

Amoralische Kinderklapper (Frankfurt am Main: Suhrkamp, 1969);

Geschichten für Stanek (Berlin: Literarisches Colloquium, 1969);

Der Pluderich (Frankfurt am Main: Insel, 1969);

Philomena Mückenschnabel (Frankfurt am Main: Insel, 1970);

Polsterer (Frankfurt am Main: Insel, 1970);

Tage und Jahre: Sätze zur Situation (Salzburg: Residenz, 1971);

Ida—und ob! (Munich & Vienna: Jugend und Volk, 1972);

Die Prinzessin in der Zwirnspule und andere Puppenspiele für Kinder (Munich: Ellermann, 1972);

Rückkehr zum vorläufigen Ausgangspunkt: Erzählungen (Salzburg: Residenz, 1973);

Das Verschwinden des Schattens in der Sonne: Roman (Frankfurt am Main: Suhrkamp, 1973);

Haschen nach Wind: Erzählungen (Salzburg: Residenz, 1974);

Grizzly Dickbauch und Frau Nuffl (Pfaffenweiler: Pfaffenweiler Presse, 1975);

Die Mystifikationen der Sophie Silber: Roman (Salzburg: Residenz, 1976);

Amy oder Die Metamorphose: Roman (Salzburg: Residenz, 1978);

Kai und die Liebe zu den Modellen: Roman (Salzburg & Vienna: Residenz, 1979);

Entzug—ein Menetekel der zärtlichsten Art (Pfaffenweiler: Pfaffenweiler Presse, 1979);

Bindungen: Erzählung (Salzburg: Residenz, 1980);

Die Ferienfamilie: Roman (Salzburg & Vienna: Residenz, 1981);

Landschaft für Engel (Vienna & New York: Molden, 1981);

Vom Leben des Pierrot: Erzählungen (Pfaffenweiler: Pfaffenweiler Presse, 1982);

Die Frau im Mond: Roman (Salzburg: Residenz, 1982);

Traumgrenze: Erzählungen (Salzburg: Residenz, 1983);

Kopftänzer: Roman (Salzburg: Residenz, 1984);

Herrin der Tiere: Erzählung (Salzburg: Residenz, 1986);

Über die Verhältnisse: Roman (Salzburg: Residenz, 1987).

TRANSLATIONS: Sandor Weöres, *Der von Ungarn: Gedichte und fünf Zeichnungen*, translated by Frischmuth and Robert Stauffer (Frankfurt am Main: Suhrkamp, 1969);

Edward Lear, *Die Jumblies* (Frankfurt am Main: Insel, 1970);

Das elfte Gebot: Moderne ungarische Dramen, translated by Frischmuth, Vera Thies, and Ita Szent-Iványi (Leipzig: Reclam, 1977).

Since she arrived on the Austrian literary scene with her novel *Die Klosterschule* (The Parochial School, 1968), Barbara Frischmuth's reputation has grown in tandem with her literary production in a variety of forms and styles: primarily novels, but also short stories, children's books, essays, and experiments in drama and lyric poetry. Today she is the best-known woman writer in Austria. She received the Austrian Prize for Childrens' Books in 1972, the Literary Prize of Styria in 1973, the Anton Wildgans Prize in 1974, the Prize of the City of Vienna, the Award of the Cultural Circle of German Industry, and Honor Roll of the Hans Christian Andersen Prize in 1975, the Sandoz Prize for Literature in 1977, the Literary Prize of the City of Vienna in 1979, the Gedok Prize for Literature in 1983, and the Ida Dehmel Prize also in 1983.

Frischmuth was born in 1941 in the resort community of Alt-Aussee, Styria, where her parents owned the largest hotel. She graduated from high school in 1958 and moved to Graz. She studied Turkish and Hungarian at the translator's institute of the University of Graz; she also spent 1961 as a student in Erzurum, Turkey, and 1963 in Debrecen, Hungary. She has made translations from both languages into German. She pursued Oriental studies at the University of Vienna from 1964 to 1967. She married young, had a son,

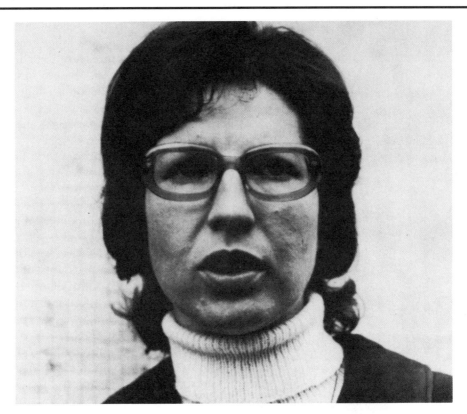

Barbara Frischmuth (photo: Brigitte Friedrich, Cologne)

and was divorced. Much of her work is autobiographical, although she is beginning to expand into new areas. She divides her time between Alt-Aussee and Vienna.

Frischmuth began her literary career as a member of the Graz organization of writers known as the Forum Stadtpark. She was initially influenced by the language skepticism prevalent in the late 1960s. This concern with language as a means used by institutions to inculcate ideas and thus to manipulate people became the theme of *Die Klosterschule*. In an interview she said that the novel made use of ideas gained through her study of eastern languages: "Jedenfalls konnte oder glaubte ich zumindest, mir zwar den Zweifel, nicht aber das Verzweifeln an der Sprache leisten zu können . . . Und langsam spürte ich, wie sich meine Sinne geschärft hatten, wie ich für Phrasen, Redundanzen, Manipulationen hellhörig wurde . . . Und dann versuchte ich mir diese Erfahrung als Methode des Schreibens nutzbar zu machen. Es entstand 'Die Klosterschule' . . . " (In any case I was able or at least I believed that I was able to accept skepticism about language but not despair over language . . . and slowly I perceived how my senses had sharpened, how I had become attuned to

phrases, redundancies, and manipulations . . . And then I tried to make this experience useful as a method of writing. Thus originated *Die Klosterschule* . . .). *Die Klosterschule,* a depiction of a girls' Catholic boarding school, is based on her own experiences at such a school. Frischmuth demonstrates how the impressionable schoolgirls are influenced by the constant repetition of the dogmas that comprise the Catholic philosophy of life for women. The girls are presented with a view of women that is intended to prepare them for their future roles as wives and mothers. Frischmuth demonstrates that it is difficult for women to achieve independence after being educated in old-fashioned ideas about women's subordinate status. Frischmuth went on to re-create children's language in two collections of fairy tales suitable for adults as well as children: *Amoralische Kinderklapper* (Amoral Noisemaker, 1969) and *Geschichten für Stanek* (Stories for Stanek, 1969). She also wrote several books purely for children: *Der Pluderich* (1969), *Philomena Mückenschnabel* (1970), *Polsterer* (1970), *Die Prinzessin in der Zwirnspule* (The Princess in the Spool of Thread, 1972), *Ida—und ob!* (Ida—and How!, 1972), and *Grizzly Dickbauch und Frau Nuffl* (Grizzly Potbelly and Mrs. Nuffl, 1975). These

Barbara Frischmuth (photo: Otto Breicha, Vienna)

works reveal her rich imagination, her empathy with children, her humor, and her ability to create a children's vocabulary. They contain the same blend of reality and the fairy tale that characterizes some of her major novels.

Tage und Jahre: Sätze zur Situation (Days and Years: Sentences on the Situation, 1971) is a collection of statements describing a series of disconnected actions and phenomena. The effect is similar to that achieved by pointillistic painting. Frischmuth provides no transitions nor interpretation, thus forcing the reader to create a unified text out of the given elements. What the protagonist feels is not described but must be inferred from her actions. The entries range from a few lines to several pages. In the first half of the book, subtitled "Tage," the first entry says: "Ich steche Sterne aus. Das Blech bricht, ich habe mich geschnitten. Mein Finger blutet in den Teig" (I press out stars. The tin breaks. I have cut myself. My finger bleeds into the dough). There are passages about the weather, the mail, pets, workers, and television, rendered as objectively as possible to avoid manipulating the read-

ers' reactions. In the second half of the book, "Jahre," the entries are longer, corresponding to the longer time unit. Here Frischmuth deals with her childhood in Alt-Aussee; fantasies are interspersed with recollections. The technique remains the same: the reader is presented with a series of independent passages and must fit them together himself.

In the next three years Frischmuth published two volumes of stories and a novel. The nineteen stories in *Rückkehr zum vorläufigen Ausgangspunkt* (Return to the Preliminary Starting Point, 1973) are all autobiographical; some recall her childhood, others are set in the present. They range from children's stories to tales of horse racing and impressions of Istanbul. Many of the stories are set in Alt-Aussee and describe life in the country without glorifying or condemning it. The novel *Das Verschwinden des Schattens in der Sonne* (The Disappearance of the Shadow in the Sun, 1973) combines Frischmuth's firsthand knowledge of Istanbul, natural gift for fantasy, and talent for vivid description. The anonymous narrator, a Viennese university student, is in Istanbul to trace the history of the Dervish order. Through her association with Aytem, a young Turkish teacher, and Turgut, a university student involved with a radical political group, she is placed between the traditional and the revolutionary. Despite her knowledge of the language, her receptiveness to the culture, and her eagerness to be accepted into Turkish society, she is never regarded as more than a tourist. As long as she has a passport and a ticket home she remains an outsider. After Turgut is killed by the police during a political demonstration she returns home with a newfound wisdom. The title of the novel symbolizes her awakening from a dreamlike state of fascination with exotic Istanbul to the sober, unblinking light of reality. She has learned that life is not the way she had imagined it; in contrast to the women in *Haschen nach Wind,* she has matured through her experiences.

The four tales in *Haschen nach Wind* (Grasping at the Wind, 1974) are concerned with the problems women face in trying to balance family and career. No solutions are provided. None of the stories has a happy ending; as Reinhard Urbach comments: "Es sind Sackgassengeschichten: So kann es nicht mehr weitergehen, denken sich die Frauen, die nicht mehr ein noch aus wissen. Aber es geht so weiter. . . . Diese Geschichten sind zum Nacherleben, zum Wiedererkennen, zum Selbsterkennen. Sie helfen

Cover for Frischmuth's 1979 collection of two stories of erotic longing

those of attendants coming to take her to an institution, end the story on a note of ambiguity. In "Baum des vergessenen Hundes" (Tree of the Forgotten Dog) Sybill flees into the woods to recover from the psychological strain of a joyless marriage. She decides to leave her husband and return to her job in an antique shop, where she can regain a sense of individuality and freedom. At the end of the story her husband buries his head in her lap in confusion, while she thinks of stabbing him in the neck "damit es ein für allemal zu Ende war, und sie sich und ihn nicht länger quälen mußte" (so that it would be over once and for all and she would no longer have to torment herself and him). In the title story a fourteen-year-òld girl has an affair with one of her teachers, believing that he will marry her. When she becomes pregnant he rejects her, and she commits suicide in the woods. The protagonist of the final story, "Unzeit" (Bad Time), is Euridice, a divorced mother. She married in college and dropped out to have her twins while her husband finished his studies; then they separated. At the moment she is at a loss about how to proceed with her life. Temporary love affairs are unsatisfying, but she does not want to marry again. When her former husband spends Christmas with her and the children she briefly lets her guard down, only to end by feeling that he has taken advantage of her again. She resolves never to trust anyone.

Die Mystifikationen der Sophie Silber (The Mystifications of Sophie Silber, 1976) is the first volume of a trilogy dealing with women's liberation. In this realistic fairy tale the exploitation of natural resources by humans has reached such proportions that the spirit world is being threatened. The spirits have come to Alt-Aussee from all over the world to discuss their future. Sophie Silber has been invited to the meeting by Amaryllis Sternwieser, her guardian angel. Sophie, an actress in a wandering troupe of players, has just been engaged at a major theater in Vienna and is ready to begin a new career. In a trance Sophie sees the course of her future life; the episode is then obliterated from her conscious mind, leaving only a memory like that of a faded dream. But as a result of this experience she is invested with new independence and self-confidence. Her decision to reclaim Klemens, the son she has left with foster parents for eighteen years, is a sign that she no longer needs the protection of Amaryllis. Since the spirits cannot halt the devastation of their realm, they decide to transform themselves

nicht heraus aus den Problemen, sie helfen hinein" (They are stories with dead ends: things cannot continue this way any longer, think the women, who no longer know which way to turn. But things do continue this way. . . . These stories are for reliving, for recalling, for self-recognition. They do not help us out of the problems, they help us into them). The first tale, "Bleibenlassen" (Let Things Be), is told from the woman's point of view, as is almost all of Frischmuth's work; the men in her writings are hardly more than foils. The protagonist is a graphic artist who is trying to hold her marriage together while pursuing her career. Finally, her husband's infidelity throws her into a state of shock and confusion, and she begins beating him. Her husband thinks that she has lost her mind. Approaching footsteps, which may be

Illustration by Heinz Treiber for Frischmuth's story "Die Reise ans Ende der Welt" in Entzug–ein Menetekel der zärtlichsten Art

into mortals. By assuming the forms of humans, they can ensure that the humans will no longer represent a danger to the world. This fairy tale presents a feminist program for the future: the humanized female spirits will not become political activists but will simply live well-integrated, happy, successful lives as independent career women and thus serve as role models for other women. When the numbers of such women have grown sufficiently, they will be able to change the course of events.

Amaryllis's life after her transformation into human form is the subject of *Amy oder Die Metamorphose* (Amy; or, The Metamorphosis, 1978). Amaryllis Sternwieser takes over the body of Amy Stern, transforming a sickly, antisocial medical student into a healthy, gregarious, and attractive woman. Amy's revitalization astonishes her friends and the customers at the Café Windrose, where she works during the summer. She inspires confidence, and people willingly talk to her. Amy tries to learn about human life by listening to women's discussions of their relationships

with men. She hears from women who are dominated by their husbands and from others who have pursued careers either with or without marriage; other women tell of their lives with oversexed, impotent, or boring men. With the encouragement of the sculptress Maya, Amy gives up medicine and becomes a writer. She has an affair with Klemens, Sophie Silber's son; when she becomes pregnant, Klemens offers to marry her, but it is clear that he would prefer that she have an abortion. Amy decides to raise the child by herself. The mysterious Altmann, who is actually the fairy Alpinox in human form, offers to subsidize her career; the owner of the Café Windrose also offers to make her a partner and eventual heir. She dismisses both offers. Amy's decision to raise her child alone represents one facet of the new feminist spirit; another contribution will be her writings, by which she hopes to influence society.

Frischmuth concludes the trilogy with a projection of the future in *Kai und die Liebe zu den Modellen* (Kai and the Love of Possibilities, 1979). Five years have passed and Amy is raising her son, Kai, alone. Klemens visits occasionally, but his journalistic career is so demanding that he has no time to be a father. Amy is not certain that she would want Klemens to live with her and Kai, for she fears that his presence would interfere with her unique relationship with her son, whom she treats as an equal. She occasionally dresses him as a girl so that he can grow up naturally with girls without emphasizing the differences between them.

In two tales published together in 1979 under the title *Entzug–ein Menetekel der zärtlichsten Art* (Withdrawal–a Most Tender Warning) Frischmuth departs from her usual objective style and describes erotic longing in sensuous imagery and sexual symbolism. The title story consists of a letter from a woman to her absent lover. Her longing for love is described in a series of metaphors. In the second tale, "Die Reise ans Ende der Welt" (The Journey to the End of the World), a young teacher creates an ideal lover in fantasy. The voice of her imaginary lover, Osman, summons her into the ocean. As she searches for him in the depths, the reader learns about her past and accompanies her on imaginary travels to Alexandria. Suddenly she feels Osman beside her, and her happiness is complete. At this point her dead body rises out of the water, frightening some boaters.

Two short novels return to the themes of the trilogy: the struggles of the career woman,

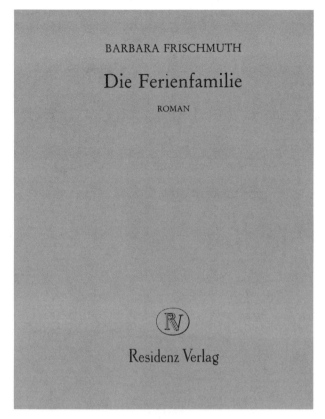

BARBARA FRISCHMUTH

Die Ferienfamilie

ROMAN

Residenz Verlag

Title page for Frischmuth's 1981 novel about parent-child relationships

the possibilities and limitations of personal growth, and the proper methods of child rearing. In *Bindungen* (Unions, 1980) Fanny, an emancipated woman who is studying for a career in archaeology, attempts to regain her balance following the breakup of a love affair. In the soothing atmosphere of nature and the harmonious home life of her sister Malwina's family, Fanny overcomes her grief, and at the end she is ready to resume her studies. In *Die Ferienfamilie* (The Family on Vacation, 1981) Nora, a writer, spends the summer in the country with her son and two other children from broken homes. Nora discusses with the children their feelings toward their absent parents. Prominent in the novel is the notion that all adults should love all children, rather than leaving that responsibility to the actual parents. Nora also defends parents against the children's accusations, explaining how difficult it is to find the time that one should take for children. In the novel *Kopftänzer* (Head Dancers, 1984) the parallel stories of two protagonists are told in alternating fashion until they come together near the end. Dinah is fired from her job as a reporter for overzealousness in her investiga-

tion of a secret organization. She withdraws to a cloister to think things through. Dan, a young man just out of school, is equally disoriented. He joins a group of idealists–the same group Dinah was fired for investigating–who devote their time to fruitless discussions. A splinter group under the leadership of a young radical named Gabriel is tired of the useless talk and ready to bring about revolutionary changes by force. Dinah and Dan find each other at one of the group's meetings, enjoy a night of happiness together, then drift apart. The various strands of the plot are left unresolved. *Kopftänzer* is at its best when Frischmuth displays her talent for description; it falters when she indulges in philosophical discussions of God, faith, evolution, and revolution, citing Plato, the Gnostics, Theresa of Avila, and Martin Buber.

Frischmuth's writings offer a model study of the development of contemporary Austrian literature from an aesthetic preoccupation with language to a concern for social issues. The recent development toward subjectivity and emotionalism is a reaction to the strict logic introduced into literature under the influence of the philosophy of Ludwig Wittgenstein, language skepticism, and sterile and contrived forms of concrete poetry. Frischmuth's characters, even the supernatural ones, stand out vividly; the only apparent weakness is a lack of roundedness and depth, especially in the male characters.

References:

Donald G. Daviau, "Barbara Frischmuth," in *Major Figures of Contemporary Austrian Literature* (New York & Bern: Lang, 1987), pp. 185-206;

Daviau, "Neuere Entwicklungen in der modernen österreichischen Prosa: Die Werke von Barbara Frischmuth," *Modern Austrian Literature,* 13, no. 1 (1980): 177-216;

Franz Fühmann, "Gespräch über Barbara Frischmuth," *Sinn und Form,* 28 (March / April 1976): 423-436;

Dietmar Grieser, "Eine leidige Angelegenheit: Barbara Frischmuth und 'Die Klosterschule': Eine Feedback-Studie," in his *Schauplätze österreichischer Dichtung* (Munich: Langen, 1974), pp. 169-179;

Christa Gürtler, *Schreiben Frauen anders? Untersuchungen zu Ingeborg Bachmann und Barbara Frischmuth* (Stuttgart: Akademischer Verlag, 1983);

Barbara Frischmuth (photo courtesy of Residenz Verlag)

Paul M. Haberland, "The Role of Art in the Writings of Barbara Frischmuth," *Modern Austrian Literature*, 14, no. 1 / 2 (1981): 85-96;

Jorun B. Johns, "Barbara Frischmuth: Eine Bibliographie der Werke und der Sekundärliteratur bis Herbst 1980," *Modern Austrian Literature*, 14, no. 1 (1981): 101-128;

Johns and Ulrich Janetzski, "Barbara Frischmuth," in *Kritisches Lexikon zur deutschsprachigen Gegewartsliteratur*, edited by Heinz Ludwig Arnold (Munich: Edition text + kritik, 1978);

Ulrike Kindl, "Barbara Frischmuth," in *Neue Literatur der Frauen*, edited by Heinz Puknus (Munich: Beck, 1980), pp. 144-148;

Paul Kruntorad, "Prosa in Österreich seit 1945," in *Die zeitgenössische Literatur Österreichs*, edited by Hilde Spiel (Zurich & Munich: Kindler, 1976), pp. 246-269;

Jürgen Serke, "Barbara Frischmuth: Die Macht neu verteilen, so daß sie keine Gefahr mehr für die Welt bedeutet!," in his *Frauen schreiben: Ein Stern-Buch* (Hamburg: Gruner & Jahr, 1979), pp. 150-163, 320-321, 330, 331;

Reinhard Urbach, " 'Haschen nach Wind': Die neuen Erzählungen der Barbara Frischmuth," *Neue Zürcher Zeitung*, 14 December 1974.

Peter Handke

(6 December 1942-   )

Stephanie Barbé Hammer
University of California, Riverside

BOOKS: *Die Hornissen: Roman* (Frankfurt am Main: Suhrkamp, 1966);

Publikumsbeschimpfung und andere Sprechstücke (Frankfurt am Main: Suhrkamp, 1966)—comprises *Publikumsbeschimpfung, Weissagung, Selbstbezichtigung;* partially translated by Michael Roloff as *Offending the Audience; and, Self-Accusation* (London: Methuen, 1971);

Begrüssung des Aufsichtrats: Prosatexte (Salzburg: Residenz, 1967);

Der Hausierer: Roman (Frankfurt am Main: Suhrkamp, 1967);

Hilferufe (Frankfurt am Main: Suhrkamp, 1967);

Kaspar (Frankfurt am Main: Suhrkamp, 1968);

Hörspiel (Cologne: Kiepenheuer & Witsch, 1968);

Hörspiel Nr. 2 (Cologne: Kiepenheuer & Witsch, 1969);

Prosa, Gedichte, Theaterstücke, Hörspiel, Aufsätze (Frankfurt am Main: Suhrkamp, 1969);

Deutsche Gedichte (Frankfurt am Main: Euphorion, 1969);

Die Innenwelt der Aussenwelt der Innenwelt (Frankfurt am Main: Suhrkamp, 1969); translated by Roloff as *The Innerworld of the Outerworld of the Innerworld* (New York: Seabury Press, 1974);

Quodlibet (Frankfurt am Main: Published by the author, 1970);

Die Angst des Tormanns beim Elfmeter (Frankfurt am Main: Suhrkamp, 1970); translated by Roloff as *The Goalie's Anxiety at the Penalty Kick* (New York: Farrar, Straus & Giroux, 1972; London: Eyre Methuen, 1977);

Hörspiel Nr. 2, 3, 4 (Frankfurt am Main: Suhrkamp, 1970);

Wind und Meer: Vier Hörspiele (Frankfurt am Main: Suhrkamp, 1970)—comprises "Wind und Meer," "Geräusch eines Geräusches," "Hörspiel 2";

Chronik der laufenden Ereignisse (Frankfurt am Main: Suhrkamp, 1971);

Der Ritt über den Bodensee (Frankfurt am Main: Suhrkamp, 1971); translated by Roloff as

Peter Handke (photo: Otto Breicha, Vienna)

The Ride across Lake Constance (London: Eyre Methuen, 1973);

Ich bin ein Bewohner des Elfenbeinturms (Frankfurt am Main: Suhrkamp, 1972);

Der kurze Brief zum langen Abschied (Frankfurt am Main: Suhrkamp, 1972); translated by Ralph Manheim as *Short Letter, Long Farewell* (New York: Farrar, Straus & Giroux, 1974; London: Eyre Methuen, 1977);

Stücke (Frankfurt am Main: Suhrkamp, 1972)—comprises *Publikumsbeschimpfung, Weissagung, Selbstbezichtigung, Hilferufe, Kaspar;* translated by Roloff as *Kaspar and Other Plays* (New York: Farrar, Straus & Giroux, 1970)—

comprises *Offending the Audience, Prophecy, Self-Accusation, Calling for Help, Kaspar*;

Wunschloses Unglück: Erzählung (Salzburg: Residenz, 1972); translated by Manheim as *A Sorrow beyond Dreams* (New York: Farrar, Straus & Giroux, 1975; London: Souvenir Press, 1976);

Stücke 2 (Frankfurt am Main: Suhrkamp, 1973)–comprises *Das Mündel will Vormund sein, Quodlibet, Der Ritt über den Bodensee;* translated by Roloff and Karl Weber as *The Ride across Lake Constance and Other Plays* (New York: Farrar, Straus & Giroux, 1976)–comprises *Prophecy, Calling for Help, My Foot My Tutor, Quodlibet, The Ride across Lake Constance, They Are Dying Out*;

Die Unvernünftigen sterben aus (Frankfurt am Main: Suhrkamp, 1973); translated by Roloff and Weber as *They Are Dying Out* (London: Eyre Methuen, 1975);

Als das Wünschen noch geholfen hat (Frankfurt am Main: Suhrkamp, 1974); translated by Roloff as *Nonsense and Happiness* (New York: Urizen, 1976; London: Pluto Press, 1976);

Falsche Bewegung (Frankfurt am Main: Suhrkamp, 1975);

Der Rand der Wörter: Erzählungen, Gedichte, Stücke, edited by Heinz F. Schafroth (Stuttgart: Reclam, 1975);

Die Stunde der wahren Empfindung (Frankfurt am Main: Suhrkamp, 1975); translated by Manheim as *A Moment of True Feeling* (New York: Farrar, Straus & Giroux, 1977);

Das Ende des Flanierens (Vienna: Davidpresse, 1976);

Die linkshändige Frau: Erzählung (Frankfurt am Main: Suhrkamp, 1976); translated by Manheim as *The Left-Handed Woman* (New York: Farrar, Straus & Giroux, 1978; London: Eyre Methuen, 1980);

Das Gewicht der Welt: Ein Journal (November 1975-März 1977) (Salzburg: Residenz, 1977); translated by Manheim as *The Weight of the World* (New York: Farrar, Straus & Giroux, 1984; London: Secker & Warburg, 1984);

Langsame Heimkehr: Erzählung (Frankfurt am Main: Suhrkamp, 1979); translated by Manheim as "The Long Way Around," in *Slow Homecoming* (New York: Farrar, Straus & Giroux, 1985);

Die Lehre der Sainte-Victoire (Frankfurt am Main: Suhrkamp, 1980); translated by Manheim as "The Lesson of Sainte Victoire," in *Slow Homecoming*;

Kindergeschichte (Frankfurt am Main: Suhrkamp, 1981); translated by Manheim as "Child's Story," in *Slow Homecoming*;

Über die Dörfer: Dramatisches Gedicht (Frankfurt am Main: Suhrkamp, 1981);

Die Geschichte des Bleistifts (Salzburg: Residenz, 1982);

Der Chinese des Schmerzes (Frankfurt am Main: Suhrkamp, 1983); translated by Manheim as *Across* (New York: Farrar, Straus & Giroux, 1986);

Phantasien der Wiederholung (Frankfurt am Main: Suhrkamp, 1983);

Gedicht an die Dauer (Frankfurt am Main: Suhrkamp, 1986);

Die Wiederholung (Frankfurt am Main: Suhrkamp, 1986); translated by Manheim as *Repetition* (New York: Farrar, Straus & Giroux, 1987);

Die Abwesenheit (Frankfurt am Main: Suhrkamp, 1987);

Nachmittag eines Schriftstellers (Salzburg: Residenz, 1987);

Der Himmel über Berlin, by Handke and Wim Wenders (Frankfurt am Main: Suhrkamp, 1987).

OTHER: "Das Umfallen der Kegel von einer bäuerlichen Kegelbahn," in *Der gewöhnliche Schrecken: Horrorgeschichten*, edited by Handke (Salzburg: Residenz, 1969), pp. 120-130;

Didi Petrikat, *Wiener Läden*, photos by Petrikat, texts by Handke (Munich & Vienna: Hanser, 1974);

Franz Nabl, *Charakter; Der Schwur des Martin Krist; Dokument: Frühe Erzählungen*, edited by Handke (Salzburg: Residenz, 1975);

Georges-Arthur Goldschmidt, *Der Spiegeltag: Roman*, translated by Handke (Frankfurt am Main: Suhrkamp, 1982);

Gustav Januš, *Gedichte 1962-1983*, translated by Handke (Frankfurt am Main: Suhrkamp, 1983).

Peter Handke is one of the most prolific and significant contributors to Austrian literature of the latter twentieth century. Controversy has beset this dramatist, novelist, essayist, poet, scriptwriter, and diarist from the beginning of his career: some critics hail him as an avant-garde genius while others dismiss him as a neurotic, narcissist, or charlatan. The problematic nature of Handke's oeuvre stems from its rigorously experimental and self-critical nature. His literary explorations question the integrity and value of liter-

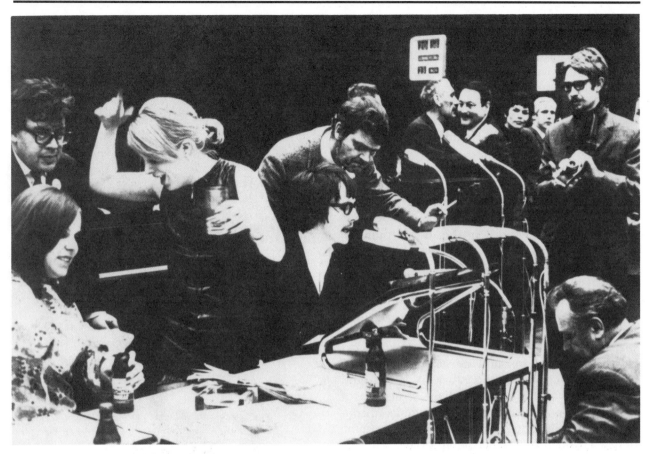

Handke (seated at lectern) giving a reading at the Second International Frankfurt Forum for Literature, 1967. H. C. Artmann is looking over Handke's shoulder; Erich Fried is at far left, behind the two women (photo: Erika Sulzer-Kleinmeier, Gleisweiler/Pfalz).

ature and of art in general, thereby raising questions about the mission, meaning, and ultimate value of his own works.

Handke was born on 6 December 1942 in Griffen, Austria. His father, a bank clerk, was married to someone other than Handke's mother; she entered into a marriage of convenience with Bruno Handke, a German army sergeant stationed in Austria. The family lived in Berlin with Handke's stepfather's parents from 1944 to 1948, then returned to Griffen. Handke was educated in a Jesuit seminary. From 1961 to 1965 he studied law at the University of Graz, where he became involved with the Grazer Gruppe (Graz Group), a literary organization. His first story, "Die Überschwemmung" (The Flood, 1964), was published in the group's journal *manuskripte;* it was republished, along with other early stories, in the collection *Begrüssung des Aufsichtrats* (Greeting the Board of Directors, 1967).

In 1966 Handke left Austria for Germany. That year he married Libgart Schwarz. For the next seven years he lived in Düsseldorf; in Ber-

lin, where his daughter Amina was born in 1969; and in Frankfurt am Main. It was during this period that he earned his reputation as an enfant terrible. The first and most notable Handke scandal occurred at the April 1966 conference of the writers' association Gruppe 47 in Princeton, New Jersey. On the last day Handke delivered a fierce invective in which he condemned what he termed empty descriptiveness used by his colleagues. He followed this display with an arch letter to the popular German magazine *Der Spiegel* implying that the inflammatory speech had been a ploy to insure his notice by that influential periodical. In 1967 he arrived late at the ceremony for the Gerhart Hauptmann award, and his acceptance speech was filled with caustic references to the recent acquittal of a policeman charged with manslaughter.

In 1966 and 1967 he published his first two novels. *Die Hornissen* (The Hornets, 1966) records the imperfect perceptions of a blind narrator who attempts to describe his experiences by relating them to those of a blind protagonist in a half-forgotten novel. *Der Hausierer* (The Peddler, 1967) is modeled after a typical murder mystery, but Handke reveals the essential emptiness of this type of novel by exposing the formulaic and mechanical nature of its construction. He later wrote about *Der Hausierer:* "Jemand kommt irgendwohin, wird hier Zeuge eines Mordes, wird verdächtigt, weil er (hier) fremd ist . . . kommt zu einem zweiten Mord dazu, wird verdächtigt, verhaftet, eingesperrt, freigelassen . . . entlarvt den *wahren* Mörder, und *alles* ist in Ordnung— Aber diese Geschichte habe ich nicht erfunden; es ist eine gefundene Geschichte. . . . In dem ich das Schema [des Krimis] prufte, es abstrahierte, mir seine unbewußten Regeln bewußt machte, hoffte ich, auch zu neuen Darstellungs- möglichkeiten meiner Wirklichkeit zu kommen" (Someone goes somewhere, witnesses a murder, becomes a suspect because he is a stranger [here], comes upon a second murder, becomes a suspect, is arrested, goes to jail, gets free, uncov- ers the *real* murderer and *everything* is in order— but I did not invent this story, it is a found story. . . . In so far as I tested the structure [of the mystery novel], abstracted it, made its uncon- scious rules conscious to myself, I hoped to come to new possibilities of descriptions of my own real- ity).

During the late 1960s Handke created his highly successful theatrical experiments, the "Sprechstücke" (speech plays). All five pieces rep- resent extreme and even gruesome exercises in the power of language. Profoundly antidramatic in the traditional sense, the "Sprechstücke" im- pose upon their audiences a sense of frustration while impressing them with their energy and ironic wit. *Publikumsbeschimpfung* (1966; translated as *Offending the Audience,* 1971) subjects the public to a monotonous four-man barrage of platitudes, followed by a symphonic effusion of theatrical, ra- cial, social, and religious insults; in *Weissagung* (1966; translated as *Prophecy,* 1970) four speakers pronounce tautological prophecies; the two char- acters in *Selbstbezichtigung* (1966; translated as *Self- Accusation,* 1971) utter a series of self-accusations; *Hilferufe* (1967; translated as *Calling for Help,* 1970) contains two warring choruses, one of which delivers disconnected commands and pleas to the resoundingly negative response of the other. In *Kaspar* (1968; translated, 1970), Handke's first full-length play and the most impor- tant of the "Sprechstücke," the protagonist is a masked, clownlike version of the autistic nineteenth-century foundling Kaspar Hauser.

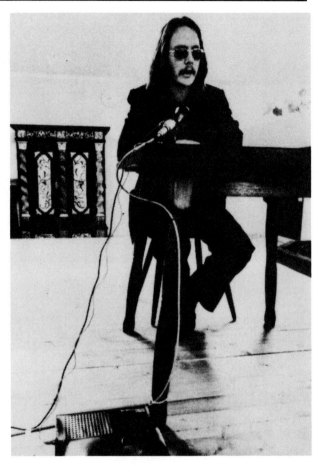

Handke reading from his work during the Rauriser Litera- ture Days, 1972 (Johann Barth, Salzburg)

This grotesque figure stumbles about an empty stage while merciless disembodied voices, the "Einsager" (prompters), teach him the language that will integrate him into society. His sociolinguistic education succeeds, but only at the price of complete self-fragmentation: Kaspar's entry into society by means of language robs him of his individuality, as the appearance of a multi- tude of identical Kaspars signifies.

In 1972 Handke received the Schiller Prize. That year he separated from his wife; in 1973, the year he received the Georg Büchner Prize, he moved with his daughter to the Paris suburb of Clamart. Since 1979 he has lived in Salzburg. While fiction was the focus of his creative ener- gies in the 1970s, Handke did not abandon other genres: he wrote a full-length drama, *Die Un- vernünftigen sterben aus* (The Unreasonable Ones Are Dying Out, 1973; translated as *They Are Dying Out,* 1975), which depicts a fateful soirée of successful capitalists, and a screenplay, *Falsche Bewegung* (False Move, 1975); he also published several collections of poems, essays, and radio plays. The narratives of the 1970s depict characters in the midst of psychological crises which are so private and so peculiar to their psyches that no one else is capable of understanding them; in fact, the others are for the most part oblivious to the existential agonies afflicting the protagonists. The main characters themselves fail to comprehend how their lives have gone so painfully awry, but they all experience the sudden and inexplicable urge to alter drastically existences that once seemed totally appropriate. Handke's work of the 1970s abandons the theoretical abstraction of the avant-garde "Sprechstücke" for the more specific and challenging psychological realm of the modern novel.

In the first of these narratives, the critically acclaimed *Die Angst des Tormanns beim Elfmeter* (1970; translated as *The Goalie's Anxiety at the Penalty Kick*, 1972), the former soccer goalie Josef Bloch erroneously believes that he has been fired from his job as a construction worker. In a desperate attempt to reestablish his shattered identity he murders a theater cashier with whom he has spent the night. This detective story in reverse deals primarily with the killer's subjective reactions to the crime. Although Bloch attempts to evade capture by the police, he also enjoys reading the reports of his pursuit in the newspapers; he revels in his criminal notoriety, which reminds him of the fame he once enjoyed as a professional athlete. Bloch is a deeply alienated character because he has lost the ability to connect the world around him with the words he has learned to describe that world. Handke suggests that Bloch's confusion as to the connection between words and objects may be the real motivation for his murder of the cashier and all of his other peculiar actions. Critics have seen the novel either as a parable of schizophrenia or as another of Handke's exercises in the power of language both to shape and distort reality.

In the following two works Handke demonstrated a previously unsuspected narrative skill and depth of emotion. *Der kurze Brief zum langen Abschied* (1972; translated as *Short Letter, Long Farewell*, 1974) parodies most of the themes of the traditional bildungsroman. Handke presents his reader with a journey deprived of any goal, a quest without an object, a love story in which love has died, and again, an inverted mystery—in this case, a murder tale in which the murder does not take place. The unnamed narrator, an Austrian writer, embarks on what proves to be a

remarkably unglamorous voyage as he flees across the United States from his estranged wife, who has left him a note that appears to be a threat against his life. Handke decelerates the standard fast-paced novelistic plot to almost a standstill, and his protagonist's actions are often comically mundane. Handke also disappoints the reader's expectations of a novel-like outcome: the hero neither becomes reconciled with his wife nor falls in love with someone else. He reaches no radically new self-understanding, and he appears at the end to be much the same person he was at the beginning. Yet the protagonist has grown through his experiences; as Jerome Klinkowitz and James Knowlton put it: "Finally in touch with the network of things, the narrator can escape himself and feel sympathy for others." Handke's understated narrative and rejection of a novelistic plot also suggest that the artist-protagonist learns that it is life, not art, which counts, and that art can find its inspiration only within the everydayness of real life. The novel gives convincing evidence of real life's unappreciated richness by offering a particularly impressive cast of the idiosyncratic characters who populate all of Handke's fiction: an unnamed St. Louis couple who both desire and resent visitors; the well-organized but remote Claire, who freezes vast quantities of soup so that she will have to cook as little as possible; Claire's daughter, Delta Benedictine, whose sense of order is so overdeveloped that she screams at the sight of anything awry or out of place, from an open car trunk to unevenly spaced telephone poles along the highway; and the motion picture director John Ford.

One of Handke's severest critics, Manfred Durzak, concedes that *Der kurze Brief zum langen Abschied* is a true literary accomplishment. The novel marks the author's desire to work innovatively within traditional genres and to revive the themes which have preoccupied European literature. The conflicts which dominate *Kaspar* and the other early work—individual versus society, power versus powerlessness, reason versus madness, language versus reality—remain in evidence but are joined with artistic concerns. From this point onward Handke addresses with increasing urgency the problems of mimesis and artistic communication: with what stylistic and structural innovations can the writer yield a more faithful report of reality?

This is precisely the dilemma that informs *Wunschloses Unglück* (1972; translated as *A Sorrow beyond Dreams*, 1975), Handke's record of the

Handke receiving the Georg Büchner Prize from Karl Krolow, president of the German Academy for Language and Poetry, 20 October 1973 (Süddeutscher Verlag München, Bilderdienst)

events leading to his mother's suicide in 1971. In an agonizing and eventually vain struggle to tell his mother's story in a way that will do justice to her, he paints a tragic portrait of an enthusiastic and vital individual who is gradually crushed by socioeconomic conditions. After introducing the death of his mother with a stark summary typical of a newspaper obituary, Handke frequently interrupts the narrative of her life with parenthetical expressions of concern as to how faithful such an account can be: "je mehr man fingiert, desto eher wird vielleicht die Geschichte auch für jemand andern interessant werden, weil man sich eher mit Formulierungen identifizieren kann als mit bloss berichteten Tatsachen" (the more fiction we put into a narrative, the more likely it is to interest others, because people identify more readily with formulations than with mere recorded facts). Reflecting the author's increasing anxiety as to the possibility of his project, the narrative gradually breaks down into fragmentary observations and lists of objects and events that were significant to Maria Handke. This narrative

deterioration aptly reflects the deterioration of her life, as she is gradually broken down by a society which has little regard for women. A spontaneous, romantic, and exuberant young woman, she was pressured into marriage with a man who was repulsive to her and found herself trapped in a life of rigidity and poverty from which there was no escape. Finally, suffering from a pain which no doctor could diagnose, she escaped from her unbearable existence through an overdose of sleeping pills. The reality of Maria Handke's personality and her son's most intimate, if not always positive, feelings for her frequently break through: "Mit ihrem Speichel reinigte sie den Kindern oft im Vorübergehen schnell Nasenlöcher und Ohren. Ich zückte immer zurück, der Speichelgeruch war mir unangenehm" (Often, as she passed by, she would quickly wipe out the children's ears and nostrils with her saliva. I always shrank back from the saliva smell). With these shamefaced admissions, Handke expresses the complexity of his relationship with his mother.

Cover for Handke's novel about an Austrian writer pursued across the United States by his wife, who wants to kill him

Similar experiments written during Handke's six-year sojourn in Paris include *Die Stunde der wahren Empfindung* (1975; translated as *A Moment of True Feeling*, 1977) and *Die linkshändige Frau* (1976; translated as *The Left-Handed Woman*, 1978). The former follows the manic behavior of Georg Keuschnig, an Austrian diplomat stationed in Paris. A dream in which he commits a murder convinces Keuschnig that his life has been a fraudulent and meaningless exercise; this discovery precipitates a series of increasingly outrageous attempts to experience his existence directly and honestly. Finally, in the moments before his intended suicide, he experiences a rush of empathy for the oblivious passersby in the Paris streets and abandons his plans for self-destruction. *Die*

linkshändige Frau may be seen as the complement to *Wunschloses Unglück*. Unlike Maria Handke, Marianne discovers a new life for herself and her son apart from her husband. Everyone else in the novel expects erratic behavior from her, since she is living on her own for the first time. Friends and colleagues constantly warn her against depression but actually look forward to her mental collapse. Yet unlike Handke's other protagonists of this period, Marianne remains surprisingly calm, finding a peace deep within herself that has nothing to do with the expectations, philosophies, and ideologies of others.

One of the most fascinating, although by no means the most accessible, of Handke's artistic experiments during the 1970s is his part narrative, part philosophical diary *Das Gewicht der Welt* (1977; translated as *The Weight of the World*, 1984), which covers seventeen months–November 1975 to March 1977–of his sojourn in Paris with his daughter. Through the potpourri of surrealistic pictures, snippets of dialogue, reactions to literature, and moments of feeling in *Das Gewicht der Welt*, Handke attempts to renew and sharpen his awareness of himself and of his surroundings. This reawakened vision will, he hopes, enable him to create a new literature that will revitalize society. According to Handke, modern society desperately needs such revitalization because it currently functions as a dehumanized and dehumanizing machine. Surprisingly, however, Handke maintains that the route to renewed social vitality does not lie in interaction with others but in each individual's development of a radically antisocial self-consciousness: "Der Mythos von Narziss: Ob nicht vielleicht gerade das lange, forschende Anschauen des eigenen Spiegelbilds (und im weiterem Sinn: der von einem verfertigten Sachen) die Kraft und Offenheit zu langem, unverwandtem, sich vertiefendem Anschauen andrer geben kann? (Der sterile, neuartige Narzissmus scheint mir die umgekehrte Haltung zu sein: das unverwandte, hysterisch *a priori* Teilnahme behauptende Anstarren ohne Erfahrung seiner selbst, unter Verleugnung des eigenen Ich)" (The myth of Narcissus: doesn't it seem possible that the long, inquiring contemplation of one's own mirror image [and in an extended sense, of the things one has made] prepares and equips one for long, steady, penetrating contemplation of others? [The sterile, modern kind of narcissism strikes me as just the opposite: one stares at others, hysterically proclaiming one's interest in them, while disavowing one's

Handke with his daughter Amina. Their life together in Paris from November 1975 to March 1977 is the subject of Handke's
Das Gewicht der Welt *(Hanns Hubmann, Ambach).*

own self]). *Das Gewicht der Welt* argues that the social and individual concerns of modern man interpenetrate each other; man needs isolation from society to become aware of and understand himself, so that he may then reaffirm and revitalize the connection between himself and others. Thus the individual's sensitivity to the outside world, which the institutions of contemporary society have weakened and threaten to obliterate, can only emerge from the deeply private experience of self-consciousness.

The three novels and dramatic poem of the "Langsame Heimkehr" (Slow Homecoming) tetralogy echo the credo of *Das Gewicht der Welt:* the individual must renew his perception of himself and the world to restore vitality to his own life and that of society. Handke demonstrates the urgency of this imperative by placing all of the protagonists in analogous predicaments: each has lost a crucial sensibility, thus incarnating the weakened consciousness which, according to Handke, dominates contemporary human experience. The tetralogy, however, places the process of percep-

tual revitalization under critical scrutiny, raising doubts as to its feasibility and its value. These doubts are especially evident in the first book, *Langsame Heimkehr* (1979; translated as "The Long Way Around," 1985), which follows the experiences of the expatriate Austrian geologist Valentin Sorger. Working contentedly in Alaska, Sorger suddenly loses his sense of space–the subjective, spontaneous feeling of being in a particular place. This loss prompts his roundabout journey back to his homeland. The ramifications of Sorger's perceptual loss are complex. The geologist undergoes considerable intellectual growth because of his deprivation, since his theoretical speculations on space take a new direction and eventually transcend the limitations of his discipline. Sorger dreams of writing not a scientific treatise but a poetic vision of personal geographies–small places which have special and subjective meaning for individuals. Moreover, Sorger's new focus paradoxically allows him to retrieve and even enhance his spatial sense, albeit briefly. This retrieval occurs during the hours when he prepares to leave each of the three geographical locations he inhabits during the story: Alaska, Los Angeles, and New York City. *Langsame Heimkehr* culminates in the hero's tragic recognition that his weakened sensibility reflects the predicament of the world at large: "Von jedem Eigennutz doch zu nichts als Geistesgegenwärtigkeit geläutert und nur noch heiß von Weltergänzungslust . . . wurde er da erst getroffen von der Erkenntnis eines unheilbaren Mangels, der weder in ihm persönlich gründete noch auf diese historische Epoche des in jedem Fall geliebten Planeten verwiesen konnte. Er wünschte sich ja in keine andere Zeit mehr–aber was er in der Jetztzeit, auch mit der reinsten, inständigsten Leidenschaftlichkeit, von der Welt erreichte und einzirkelte, war immer noch *viel zu wenig*" (Cleansed of all self-interest till nothing remained but presence of mind, desirous only of completing the world . . . he was struck by the consciousness of an incurable deficiency that was neither grounded in himself nor attributable to the present epoch of the earthly planet, which he loved in any case. He no longer wished himself in any other epoch–but that part of the world, which even with the purest, most fervent passion, he attained and staked out was still *far too little*). Sorger realizes that the poverty of his sensibilities can never be overcome because it stems from a global deprivation which is historically determined, unavoidable, and irremediable. Thus, for all his intellectual peculiarity (and occasional rhetorical pomposity), Handke's hero becomes a late-twentieth-century Everyman; Sorger's intuition of deficiency expresses a universal awareness of insufficiency of meaning on all levels of existence. Sorger exemplifies–sometimes comically–a typically late-twentieth-century malaise. He finds significance not in the positive but in the negative: not in arrivals but in departures, not in home but in exile, not in friends but in acquaintances and strangers, not in gains but in losses. The geologist refuses to resign himself to his sorrowful awareness of a universal poverty and decides to continue his slow journey home; as the story ends, he boards a plane for Europe. This final act suggests that Sorger will strive to transcend the boundaries of his own insufficiency and that of his historical moment, despite the possible futility of such an attempt; but the means by which he will carry out the creative project he has envisaged and carve out a fulfilling life for himself remain mysterious. The story's thematic emphasis

on deprivation thus finds stylistic fulfillment in an intentionally inadequate ending.

The other two narratives in the tetralogy attempt to resolve the deprivation problem by presenting cases where individuals reclaim their lost sensitivity by having their attention called to small, intimate, and previously unnoticed facets of experience. The writer in *Die Lehre der Sainte-Victoire* (1980; translated as "The Lesson of Sainte Victoire," 1985) has lost his sensitivity to color, although he retains the physical ability to perceive it. In an attempt to recapture the sensitivity to color he possessed as a child, the narrator repeatedly contemplates the Sainte Victoire, the mountain range which is the subject of many Cézanne paintings. The writer has his epiphany–a moment where color, words, and forms are synthesized into one harmonious intuition–not at the summit of the mountain but rather upon the discovery of a small crevice which he has not seen before. This experience follows a series of conversations with his friend D. D., a couturier who has been struggling with her own perceptual difficulties: she is trying to create the perfect coat which she can envision only when the fabric and pattern are not actually in front of her. This state of affairs suggests that the narrator's color sense owes its return not just to interaction with nature or with artistic depictions of nature but to meaningful dialogue with another human being.

The salvation of the self's awareness through connection to another person is the theme of *Kindergeschichte* (1981; translated as "Child's Story," 1985). The antisocial, order-obsessed narrator is at first threatened by the overwhelming presence of his daughter; but he soon learns to desire and value her companionship, while she in turn learns to seek a society of her own which does not include her father. During this process the narrator regains his capacity for wonder, and at the end of the story he is able to share his daughter's delight in observing the smallest details of existence. But the narrator's greatest admiration is reserved for the child herself–a mercurial creature of magical possibilities and secret powers who, he realizes only belatedly, has always been *his* teacher rather than the reverse. He gains on an emotional level what the writer in *Die Lehre der Sainte-Victoire* achieves aesthetically: a reborn and purified sensitivity to experience. But the solutions proposed by these narratives are provisional ones. The writer's newborn sensitivity represents only one brief triumph in a frustrating struggle for artistic expression. Similarly, the

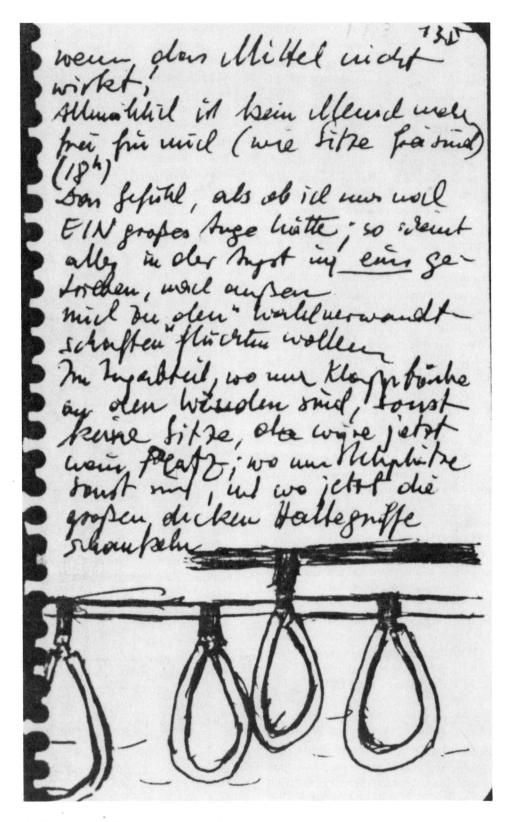

Page from the diary that was the basis for Das Gewicht der Welt *(photo: Barbara Klemm; from the cover of the novel)*

Handke (Austrian Institute)

value of the adult's tutelage to his child is qualified by the knowledge that someday she will grow up and he will lose his constant perceptual stimulus. Thus both narratives propose only the most idiosyncratic and fleeting solutions to the sense of deprivation presented in *Langsame Heimkehr*.

Über die Dörfer (Beyond the Villages, 1981) echoes Sorger's intuition of a universal deficiency in *Langsame Heimkehr* while it also addresses the problematic nature of the personal fulfillments described in *Die Lehre der Sainte-Victoire* and *Kindergeschichte*. The dramatic poem announces its synthetic mission in one of Handke's boldest artistic experiments to date: the plot–if one can call it that–has the static quality of a medieval pageant, yet the characters are stereotypically modern. Handke mixes dramatic, epic, and lyrical modes in the lengthy speeches of his characters, whose language ranges from realistic to vision-

ary. The tone wavers tantalizingly between tragedy and pastoral comedy, between ironic social criticism and a mystical futurist utopianism. Gregor, the main character, unites various features of the other "Langsame Heimkehr" protagonists: he is a university-educated eldest son who, like the order-obsessed adult in *Kindergeschichte*, has succeeded all too well in conquering his once strong empathic reactions to others in favor of anxiety-ridden strictness. Like the narrator of *Die Lehre der Sainte-Victoire* he has only one meaningful attachment: nature–in this case, his parents' country property. And like Sorger, Gregor intuits the human significance of geography: the fallen leaves in a park suggest to him the merging of all human beings. Because nature incarnates for him the common past and the future potentiality of mankind, Gregor fervently desires to protect the countryside from encroaching industrialization. He opposes the plans of his estranged younger siblings for their parents' property: Hans wants to live there with his family, while Sophie dreams of opening her own store. Yet he eventually turns the property over to his brother and sister, resigning himself to a bleak vision of all people everywhere as losers: "Und hier sitzt er schon, der kommende Verlierer. . . . Er wird ein Sklave sein wie sein Vater und sein Großvater, und er wird ohne Bedenken den nächsten Sklaven zeugen, der wiederum brav den Nachwuchssklaven in die Welt setzen wird. Nie wird ihm die Idee von irgendeiner weiterzugebenden Hinterlassenschaft kommen, gedächtnis- und orientierungslos wird er mit seinesgleichen in gleichwelchen Unterschlupf kriechen und in eine Himmelsrichtung den Kopf nur beim Kriegsspiel heben" (And here he sits now, the loser of the future. . . . He will be a slave just like his father and his grandfather, and without thinking he will create another slave, and that slave will bravely bring yet another enslaved generation into the world. The idea of passing down some kind of inheritance to his children will never occur to him. Without memory, without direction, he and those like him will crawl home into some hole in the ground. He will raise his head toward heaven only when he is fighting). Gregor extends Sorger's sense of deprivation into the future of mankind; he foresees the emergence of an automatized, perceptionless, literally thoughtless humanity, which crawls unaware through a world robbed of significance. Sorger's intuition of a world inhabited by people of impoverished sensibilities thus finds fulfillment in Gregor's vision of a world where man's perceptions are so numbed that he has lost the ability to recognize any deficiency. But Handke refuses the tragic conclusion toward which the work is moving. Nova, the spirit of the new age, intervenes; her poetic speech to the siblings and the other villagers validates both the sense of loss expressed in *Langsame Heimkehr* and the solutions proposed in the other two narratives: "Gerade in euren Verzweiflungsausbrüchen habt ihr vielleicht bemerkt, daß ihr gar nicht verzweifelt seid. Verzweifelt, wärt ihr schon tot. Man kann nicht aufgeben. . . . Es stimmt freilich, daß es in eurer Geschichte keinen einzigen stichhaltigen Trost gibt" (Perhaps you have noticed that even in your throes of despair you are not at all despairing. If you were, you would be dead already. You cannot give up. . . . Granted, it is true that there is no one lasting solace in your history). She proposes a temporary consolation which is a poetic

meshing of the sensibilities alluded to in the three other works: "Geht in der ausgestöpselten freien Ebene, als Nähe die Farben, als Ferne die Formen, die Farben leuchtend zu euren Füssen, die Formen die Zugkraft zu euren Häupten, und beides eure Beschützer" (Walk in the unstoppered free plains, colors nearby, forms far away, the colors glimmering at your feet, the forms, the force of attraction at your head, and both your protectors). Nova recommends nature as a creative intuition of form and color experienced from a naive, childlike perspective. *Über die Dörfer* closes with a community celebration, reinforcing the suggestion in *Die Lehre der Sainte-Victoire* and *Kindergeshichte* that perceptual renewal can occur only through interaction with other people. This scene also indicates that salvation through reawakened sensibility is possible not only for intellectuals or artists but for all kinds of people–salesgirls, construction workers, old and young.

But what if the quest for renewed perception leads to a no-man's-land where one's only sensibility is to one's utter lack thereof ? Such is the discovery of the classics teacher and amateur archaeologist in Handke's novel *Der Chinese des Schmerzes* (The Chinese of Pain, 1983; translated as *Across*, 1986). Andreas Loser's experiences do not lead him to an understanding of the hidden wealth of his emotions; instead he discovers only the darkest of drives–the desire to obliterate another human being. Having killed a graffitist who was spraying swastikas on trees, Loser at first believes that he has crossed into a new zone, bringing with it a new level of awareness; but he gradually comes to understand that by killing another he has only destroyed a vital part of himself. The new zone he now inhabits proves to be nothing but a hall of mirrors reflecting utter emptiness: "In der Mitte war nämlich nichts . . . oder in der Mitte war zwar etwas, aber nichts Liebes. . . . Oder die Mitte war der Ort der schwindelerregenden Sinnestäuschungen . . . oder die Mitte war ein Ort der Fälschungen. . . . Oder sie selbst, die Mitte, war gefälscht" (In the center there was nothing . . . or there was something in the center, but nothing pleasant. . . . Or the center was a place of staggering illusions . . . or the center was a place of disillusionment. . . . Or the center itself was falsified). The novel suggests that Loser's crisis could pave the way to a deeper self-understanding and a richer existence. At a card game the other players–a priest, a politician, a painter, and a pub owner–discuss Loser's pet archaeological interest, the history and meaning of thresholds. The priest indicates that negative experiences may be the necessary prerequisite to new and productive realizations: " 'Aber wo heuzutage ... die beseitigten Schwellen wiederfinden, wenn nicht in sich selbst? Durch unsere eigenen Wunden werden wir geheilt.' ... Jeder Schritt, jeder Blick, jede Gebärde sollte sich selber als einer möglichen Schwelle bewußt werden und das Verlorene auf diese Weise neu schaffen" ("But ... where nowadays are we to find the destroyed thresholds if not in ourselves? By our own wounds shall we be healed." ... Every step, every glance, every gesture ... should be aware of itself as a possible threshold and thus re-create what has been lost). Loser's crime represents one of these internal thresholds; his transgression provides him with the opportunity to admit his violent nature and in so doing to confront his connection to Austria's fascist past and to the violence inherent in all human beings. Through an admission of guilt, not just to the murder but to his part in a tradition of brutality, Loser could achieve self-knowledge and transcend the violence which drives human history. But he is unable to pass through the gateway his crime has created. Unable either to admit the murder to the authorities or to conquer his guilt, Handke's protagonist remains a prisoner of the threshold, a purgatorial gray zone. The only mode of action open to him is his present act of narration, as he tells his son his "threshold story."

The connection between personal and national identity implicit in *Der Chinese des Schmerzes* and the corresponding interdependence of the quest for renewed consciousness and the confrontation with history provide the focus for Handke's 1986 novel *Die Wiederholung* (translated as *Repetition*, 1987). The forty-five-year-old Austrian writer Filip Kobal looks back on a journey that he made at the age of twenty to Slovenia, which is now part of Yugoslavia. This memory in turn conjures up other memories of his childhood and of his older brother Gregor, who disappeared during World War II. Filip explains that although his family is Austrian, they and the whole village where they live are of Slovenian origin; German was not their native language, and their national roots lie not in the Austro-Hungarian Empire but in the short-lived Republic of Slovenia. Filip's trip represents an attempt to retrieve both his personal past and a larger national, linguistic, and cultural past that has been lost. This two-

pronged effort results in Filip's transformation from a solitary, silent seminarian into an Erzähler, an articulate teller of tales who lives by repeating and varying his own memories as well as the memories of others with whom he now feels solidarity because he has regained a sense of his own ancestry.

In his most personal work since *Wunschloses Unglück*, Handke escorts his reader through a day in the life of an unnamed writer in his moving story *Nachmittag eines Schriftstellers* (A Writer's Afternoon, 1987). The writer must remain alone, for this isolation is necessary to his work; yet he longs for nothing more than contact with others. Handke's writer is extremely successful; he receives impressive amounts of fan mail, which shows that his writing has made a significant impact. But in the emotional climax of the story he gives his manuscript to his translator and watches distractedly as it is borne out in a basket like a foundling Moses to be disseminated by the publisher, who is ironically compared to Pharaoh's daughter. Handke suggests that while the work of art may perform a prophetic function, the artist himself is left behind on this journey to salvation; like Moses, the writer will never see the promised land. At the end of the story the writer returns to his solitary home and prepares for bed. He had arisen in the morning afraid that he had lost forever the words he needs to work his craft; during the day he won them back, but he must face the same challenge tomorrow.

The conflict between an intense desire for contact with others and the will to retain an objective and aesthetic distance from them is the theme of the screenplay by Handke and Wim Wenders for Wenders's 1987 film *Der Himmel über Berlin* (Heaven over Berlin, published 1987; film released in English as *Wings of Desire*, 1988). The script goes beyond the concerns of the "Langsame Heimkehr" tetralogy, celebrating both the experience of the everyday and a distanced artistic perspective that makes the appreciation of the everyday possible. The opposition between the two angels–Damiel, who abjures his divine capabilities for the sensual pleasures of mortality, and Cassiel, who maintains his angelic distance although in so doing he deprives himself of any participation in human history–is not an either/or proposition. The film's resulting double vision represents an affirmation of the ability of the artist to live in both the angelic and the human spheres, to exist within and outside of history, to be a part of and yet remain separate from the human community. The artist enables the rest of mankind momentarily to exist in both worlds as well. The film ends not with the angels but with speeches by an aging male storyteller and a young female trapeze performer who proclaim both their solidarity with the rest of humanity and their allegiance to their own artistic visions. Handke and Wenders use the historically charged backdrop of Berlin to create a richly textured and profoundly idealistic parable. The film bears witness to the city's role in the rise of fascism, its ability to rise phoenixlike from the rubble and ignominy of the past, and its maintenance of a distinct identity despite its present division. The film suggests that it is in this Berlin filled with foreign guest workers and haunted by former SS men and Trümmerfrauen (women who live in the rubble of bombed-out buildings) that man might win a new sensibility with which to triumph over his dark collective past.

The simultaneously exalted, earthy, humorous, and serious paean to the human spirit suggests that Handke is entering yet another phase of artistic endeavor. Whatever critics may think of his most recent development in a metaphysical and mystical direction, he remains among the most powerful voices in postmodern literature.

References:

Heinz Ludwig Arnold, "Nicht Literatur machen, sondern als Schriftsteller leben: Gespräch mit Peter Handke," in *Als Schriftsteller leben: Gespräche mit Peter Handke, Franz Xaver Kroetz, Gerhard Zwerenz, Walter Jens, Peter Rühmkorf, Günter Grass,* edited by Arnold (Reinbek: Rowohlt, 1979), pp. 7-34;

Thomas F. Barry, "Sehnsucht nach einem Bezugssystem: The Existential Aestheticism of Peter Handke's Recent Fiction," *Neophilologus,* 2 (April 1984): 259-270;

Christoph Bartmann, *Suche nach Zusammenhang: Handkes Werk als Prozeß* (Vienna: Braumüller, 1984);

Russell E. Brown, "Peter Handke's *Die Angst des Tormanns beim Elfmeter,*" *Modern Language Studies,* 16, no. 3 (1986): 288-301;

Richard Critchfield, "From Abuse to Liberation: On Images of Women in Peter Handke's Writing of the Seventies," *Jahrbuch für Internationale Germanistik,* 14, no. 1 (1982): 27-36;

Manfred Durzak, *Peter Handke und die deutsche Gegenwartsliteratur* (Stuttgart: Kohlhammer, 1982);

Raimund Fellinger, ed., *Peter Handke* (Frankfurt am Main: Suhrkamp, 1985);

Norbert Gabriel, " 'Das Volk der Leser': Zum Dichtungsbegriff in Peter Handkes Tetralogie *Langsame Heimkehr,*" *Deutsche Vierteljahrschrift für Literaturwissenschaft und Geistesgeschichte,* 58, no. 3 (1984): 475-496;

Herbert Gamper, *Aber ich lebe nur von den Zwischenräumen: Ein Gespräch* (Zurich: Ammann, 1987);

Nicholas Hern, *Peter Handke: Theatre and Anti-Theatre* (London: Wolff, 1971; New York: Ungar, 1972);

Rainer Hoffmann, "Gelebtes als-ob und erarbeitete Zeit: Bemerkungen zu Peter Handkes *Das Gewicht der Welt,*" *Wirkendes Wort,* 29 (1979): 287-302;

Calvin N. Jones, "Learning to See, to Experience, to Write: Peter Handke's *Die Lehre der Sainte-Victoire* as Narrative," *Germanic Review,* 59, no. 4 (1984): 149-155;

Manfred Jurgensen, ed., *Handke: Ansätze, Analysen, Anmerkungen* (Bern & Munich: Francke, 1979);

Jerome Klinkowitz and James Knowlton, *Peter Handke and the Postmodern Transformation: The Goalie's Journey Home* (Columbia: University of Missouri Press, 1983);

Christian Linder, "Die Ausbeutung des Bewußtseins: Gespräch mit Peter Handke," in *Schreiben und Leben: Gespräche mit Jürgen Becker, Peter Handke, Walter Kewpowski, Wolfgang Koeppen, Günter Walraff, Dieter Wellershoff,* edited by Linder (Cologne: Kiepenheuer & Witsch, 1974), pp. 32-45;

Gerhard Melzer and Jale Tükel, eds., *Peter Handke: Die Arbeit am Glück* (Königstein: Athenäum, 1985);

David H. Miles, "Reality and the Two Realisms: Mimesis in Auerbach, Lukács and Handke," *Monatshefte,* 71 (1979): 371-378;

Manfred Mixner, *Peter Handke* (Kronberg: Athenäum, 1977);

Katharina Mommsen, "Peter Handke: *Das Gewicht der Welt:* Tagebuch als literarische Form," *Modern Austrian Literature,* 13, no. 1 (1980): 35-46;

Rainer Nägele, "Amerika als Fiktion und Wirklichkeit in Peter Handkes Roman *Der kurze Brief zum langen Abschied,*" in *Die USA und Deutschland: Wechselseitige Spiegelungen in der Literatur der Gegenwart,* edited by Wolfgang Paulsen (Bern: Francke, 1976), pp. 110-115;

Nägele and Renate Voris, *Peter Handke* (Munich: Beck, 1978);

Peter Pütz, *Peter Handke* (Frankfurt am Main: Suhrkamp, 1982);

Rolf Günter Renner, *Peter Handke* (Stuttgart: Metzler, 1985);

William H. Rey, "Provokation durch den Tod: Peter Handkes Erzählung 'Wunschloses Unglück' als Modell stilistischer Integration," *German Studies Review*, 1 (1978): 285-301;

Michael Scharang, ed., *Über Peter Handke* (Frankfurt am Main: Suhrkamp, 1972);

June Schlueter, *The Plays and Novels of Peter Handke* (Pittsburgh: University of Pittsburgh Press, 1981);

Schlueter and Ellis Finger, *Peter Handke: An Annotated Bibliography* (New York: Garland, 1982);

Gunther Sergooris, *Peter Handke und die Sprache* (Bonn: Bouvier, 1979);

Sergooris, "Der Realismus der entfremdeten Welt: Peter Handkes 'Der kurze Brief zum langen Abschied,'" *Acta Germanica*, 14 (1981): 157-174;

Ellen Summerfield, "Die Kamera als literarisches Mittel: Zu Peter Handkes *Die Angst des Tormanns beim Elfmeter*," *Modern Austrian Literature*, 12, no. 1 (1979): 95-112;

text + kritik, special Handke issues, 24 (October 1969); 24/24a (July 1971); 24/24a (September 1976);

Werner Thuswalder, *Sprach- und Gattungsexperiment bei Peter Handke: Praxis und Theorie* (Salzburg: Winter, 1976);

Johannes Vanderath, "Peter Handkes *Publikumsbeschimpfung:* Ende des aristotelischen Theaters?," *German Quarterly*, 43 (March 1970): 317-326;

Cecile Cazort Zorach, "The Artist as Joker in Peter Handke's *Langsame Heimkehr*," *Monatshefte*, 77, no. 2 (1985): 181-194.

Peter Henisch
(27 August 1943-   )

Ludwig M. Fischer
Willamette University

BOOKS: *Hamlet bleibt* (Frankfurt am Main: Fischer, 1971);

Vom Baronkarl: Peripheriegeschichten und andere Prosa (Frankfurt am Main: Fischer, 1972);

Die kleine Figur meines Vaters (Frankfurt am Main: Fischer, 1975; revised edition, Munich: Langen-Müller, 1980);

Wiener Fleisch und Blut (Vienna & Munich: Jugend und Volk, 1975);

Lumpazimoribundus: Antiposse mit Gesang (Eisenstadt: Roetezer / Vienna & Munich: Sessler, 1975);

Mir selbst auf der Spur; Hiob: Gedichte (Baden bei Wien: Grasl, 1977);

Der Mai ist vorbei: Roman (Frankfurt am Main: Fischer, 1978);

Die kleine Figur meines Vaters: Roman (Frankfurt am Main: Fischer, 1980);

Vagabundengeschichten (Munich & Vienna: Langen-Müller, 1980);

Hamlet, Fables and Other Poems, translated by Herman Salinger (Washington, D.C.: Charioteer Press, 1980);

Bali oder Swoboda steigt aus: Roman (Munich: Langen-Müller, 1981);

Zwischen allen Sesseln: Geschichten, Gedichte, Entwürfe, Notizen, Statements 1965-1982 (Vienna: Hannibal, 1982);

Hoffmanns Erzählungen (Munich: Nymphenburger Verlagshandlung, 1983);

Pepi Prehaska Prophet (Salzburg: Residenz, 1986);

Steins Paranoia (Salzburg: Residenz, 1988).

Many Austrian authors see social criticism as the main purpose of their literary endeavors. Often this dissatisfaction with current conditions, social structure, and politics finds expression in novels, plays, and poems filled with a peculiarly Austrian Weltschmerz, bitterness, irony, sarcasm, or cynicism. Protest combined with resignation–a nagging feeling that the world is out of joint together with a refusal to embrace new ideologies or advocate possible solutions–are attitudes the reader of Austrian literature will encounter again and again. Another major characteristic of Austrian works is the search for an understanding of the world from an individual perspective, a sense of meaning that has to be found within oneself.

Peter Henisch's work fits this description of Austrian qualities perfectly. This novelist and poet rejects post-World War II materialism and the consumer society on almost every page he writes. At the same time, he is uneasy about utopian strategies for improving the world. Instead, Henisch unmasks hypocrisy, refuses to participate in the pursuit of material wealth, and searches for the origins of his own suffering in a world where people are unable to live in harmony with themselves and others. Throughout his work, which is intensely autobiographical and quite frank about his personal life, Henisch holds up a mirror to his time, with all its distortions, deviations, missed opportunities, false hopes, fear, mistrust, manipulation, and exploitation. The need to understand the factors which brought about the pain, chaos, and confusion has been Henisch's subject matter from the beginning.

Henisch was born in Vienna on 27 August 1943. He spent his childhood in a partly destroyed house in a working-class neighborhood. The experience of being an outsider who has no place of his own, who looks in amazement and often in disgust at a world to which everyone else seems to be eager to adjust, developed in him in his early years. Music and literature were his passions in school; he showed no ambition to succeed in any professional career. After working briefly for a local newspaper, he entered the University of Vienna in 1963 to study history and philosophy; key philosophical influences on him during this period were Friedrich Nietzsche and Ernst Bloch. He was active in the student movement of the late 1960s. While working on a dissertation on eschatology and chiliasm in Marxism and in the theology of the twentieth century he read Shakespeare, Dostoyevski, and Camus. In 1969, when he received a contract from the S. Fischer publishing house for *Hamlet bleibt* (Ham-

Peter Henisch

let Remains, 1971; translated as "Hamlet," 1980), a collection of experimental prose and poetry on themes from the Shakespeare play, he left the university to devote himself to writing. Between 1969 and 1972 he wrote for journals, coedited the literary magazine *Wespennest*, and was involved in a commune. He received the Advancement Prize of the Austrian State Prize for Literature in 1971 and the Literature Prize of the Vienna Art Fund in 1972.

Henisch's early work abounds with abrupt changes in the narrative point of view and frequently contains linguistic experiments such as capitalization of entire words and sentences, repetition of words, several possible continuations of the narrative, and other devices through which he tries to fight against the limitations of lan-

guage. By the mid 1970s, however, he had adopted the language of everyday life as the appropriate vehicle for literary expression. As the form of his works returned to ordinary speech, the content moved to the periphery of society. He developed a strong interest in outsiders, hoboes, vagabonds, the outcasts of society, in the belief that "Es sind doch unsere Widerspräche, die in den Aussenseitern deutlich werden" (Our own contradictions become most evident in the outsider). Henisch tries to comprehend the world from the point where the insider meets the outsider; he says that he walks along the periphery of his society, just as one has to discover the coast of a country to get to know it.

In the volume *Vom Baronkarl* (Of Baronkarl, 1972) and the story *Lumpazimoribundus* (1975), based on Johann Nestroy's play *Der böse Geist Lumpazivagabundus* (The Evil Spirit Lumpazivagabundus, 1835), Henisch exposes the intolerance, bourgeois complacency, and restrictive norms of Vienna in the early 1970s. The inability of one of his characters to join the race toward material wealth is summed up in the words: "Und seine Muskeln sind weicher, seine Leber aber ist härter geworden" (And his muscles became softer but his liver harder). Disillusioned idealism leads to alcoholism, and the rebellious spirit of youthful protest turns into bitterness and resignation. In "Leo, sag ein Gedicht" (Leo, Tell a Poem), from *Vom Baronkarl*, even this resignation and helplessness are exploited. The hobo Leo discovers that his underprivileged status is of interest to university students looking for a proletarian subject on whom to test their socialist theories. Those who adjust to society and adopt the prescribed curriculum of career, marriage, and conformity suffer from this self-imposed stability; the character Scheck, for example, admits to himself that every time he comes home, he fails to find himself there. Leo has freed himself from those restrictions, but he lives off the charity of those who gave up their dreams in return for security and acceptability. The outsider rejects security to be free, but his freedom is the freedom of poverty, resignation, and hopelessness. Leo destroys his health through alcohol and is not interested in improving his condition. " 'Und verändern . . . verändern könnt ihr schon gar nichts' " ("Change . . . you can't change a thing"), he says. Henisch received the Prize of the Theodor Körner Foundation in 1973.

In *Die kleine Figur meines Vaters* (The Little Figure of My Father, 1975) Henisch conducts a dialogue with his dying father in an attempt to find out how a civilized country with a cultural heritage that includes Goethe, Mozart, Beethoven, and Einstein could have caused the Holocaust. Walter Henisch had been a successful photographer and war correspondent who was rewarded by the Nazis for showing them as victorious heroes. After the war he did not succeed in a civilian career and became an alcoholic. In his attempt to go beyond mere rejection and reach some degree of understanding, Henisch discovers that he has more in common with his father than he had realized. Walter Henisch had acted as an observer; like many Germans and Austrians who took refuge behind duty as an explanation for their compliance, he denies responsibility for the events he portrayed. Peter Henisch finds

himself taking a similar interest in his father's terminal illness: "Ich sehe Dein Alter, ich sehe Dein Krankheit, ich sehe Dein Verzweiflung, und finde das interessant. Ich notiere alles, was du sagst und tust, in meiner Erinnerung, unterstrütze mein Erinnerungsvermögen durch Tonband und Merkbuch" (I see your age, I see your illness, I see your desperation, and I find it interesting. I write down everything you say and support my memory with a tape recorder and a notebook). "Sein Tod war mir durch die ganzen anderthalb Jahre, während der ich an diesem Buch geschrieben gabe, *gegenwärtig*, ja bis zu einem gewissen Grad habe ich beim Schreiben dieses Buches mit seinem Tod spekuliert. Aber als er wirklich tot war, und der Jugoslawe vom Nebeubett aufstand, langsam herankem und leise fragte: *Kaputt?* Da hatte alles eine andere Dimension" (I was *aware* of his death during the eighteen months I worked on this book. I even speculated on his death to a certain degree while writing. But when he actually died and the guy from Yugoslavia in the bed next to him got up, slowly came closer, and asked quietly: *Kaputt?* then everything had new dimensions). He tries to understand his father without forgiving, accepting, or embracing his father's faults. Much had been written about the Third Reich from the analytical perspective of the detached historian; Henisch defends his personal approach in an unpublished 1981 interview: "Ein literarisches werk kann das, insofern es mit Menschenschicksalen zu tun hat, besser von der subjektiven und psychologischen Seite angehen. Das ist die Dimension, die ich erfassen konnte, die andere hätte ich nur zitieren können. Es geht ja nicht nur um den Faschismus als Phänomen das aussen liegt, sondern gerade in Hinblick auf die Entwicklung in der Zukunft um den Faschismus, den man sogar in relativ harmlos und sympathisch wirkenden Personen entdeckt. Dafür zu sensibilisieren halte ich für wichtig. Es bringt nicht viel, auf ein Phänomen in der Form hinzuweisen, daß man es von sich distanzieren kann. Dann sind die bösen Kapitalisten schuld. Und die sind nicht wir" (A literary work can approach a problem better from a subjective and psychological perspective because it deals with individual experiences. This was the dimension I could grasp, the others I could have only quoted from. The problem is not to explain fascism as an external general phenomenon but to deal with it as a developing characteristic trait which one can even see in relatively harmless and congenial people. I consider it important to make this a tangible perception. We do not gain much from the presentation of a phenomenon in a form from which we can easily dissociate ourselves. Then we arrive at the guilt of the mean capitalists, and they are someone else, not us). With this work Henisch anticipated a spate of "father books" which appeared in 1979 and 1980, after the 1979 film *Holocaust* sparked a renewed debate about the older generation's participation in the Nazi regime. Henisch received the Salzburg Literary Prize in 1976 and the Anton Wildgans Prize sponsored by Austrian industry in 1978; *Die kleine Figur meines Vaters* established him as a major author. The book was made into a film in 1979 by Jörg Eggers and Wolfgang Gluck; Henisch wrote the script. In 1980 Henisch published a second version to which he added four letters; he also reduced the use of dreams and omitted some highly impressionistic passages.

What was commissioned as a ten-page article about the student rebellion of the late 1960s for a conservative newspaper turned into the autobiographical novel *Der Mai ist vorbei* (May Is Gone, 1978). During four days in 1978 the journalist Paul Grünzweig relives his involvement in the student protest during May 1968 and attempts to evaluate the experience. In 1968 Grünzweig resisted the temptation to become part of a society whose values he felt were corrupt, but he was unwilling to sacrifice his idealism to an ideology determined to destroy the establishment. In 1978 he persists in his conviction that there was something right and worthwhile about the student protests, even though results did not meet the expectations of a young and hopeful generation. The issues addressed by the students are still unresolved.

Henisch's skepticism has often been denounced as too negative, as a voice of resignation; but Henisch sees his lack of optimism and the absence of positive models as a virtue. He said in his acceptance speech when he received the Anton Wildgans Prize: "Ich habe keine Lösungen, nicht einmal solche für meine eigenen Probleme und ich möchte auch nicht so tun, als ob ich sie hätte. Nichtsdestoweniger halte ich es für wichtig und richtig, immer wieder auf ungelöste Probleme und aufgelöste Widersprüche hinzuweisen. Ich weiss nicht, ob das zu ihrer Lösung beitragt, ich weiss auch nicht, ob manche von ihnen überhaupt zu lösen sind: aber ich fande es verlogen, darüber zu schweigen" (I don't have solutions. Yet I consider it important

and necessary to draw attention to unsolved contradictions. I don't know whether this contributes to solving them and I don't know whether some of them can be solved at all, but to ignore them I would consider dishonest).

Henisch uses his literary work as a means of self-clarification or self-therapy, a way to explore possibilities and to reflect on the motivations for his decisions. If he had continued with his university studies, he would have become a teacher; in the novel *Bali oder Swoboda steigt aus* (Bali; or, Swoboda Gets Out, 1981) he looks at the path he rejected. Swoboda is a Viennese geography teacher who studied the world so that he would not have to explore it. Now he has the nagging feeling of having missed out on life. He has to teach material he does not believe in; he has to represent a system against which he once rebelled. He identifies with his students and tries to be their friend rather than an oppressive "Professor Doktor." When the students respond to his liberal political views with cynicism and react to his nonauthoritarian style of teaching with apathy, Swoboda is hurt. A society characterized by material abundance and spiritual poverty, by an excess of wealth and a shortage of purpose, is rejected by a young generation which does not make an attempt to change it. Swoboda oversteps the limitations of proper conduct when he meets one of his female students in a tavern and plans to join a student rock band. He is almost relieved when his principal advises him to take an indefinite leave of absence. Swoboda, like many protagonists in Henisch's works, refuses to act until he is forced to do so by others. He sees his situation clearly without being able to arrive at a solution. He declares himself a failure: " 'Was hab ich den jungen Menschen anzubrieten, ausser Frust und Zweifeln? Welchen Weg soll ich ihnen weisen? Ich weiss ja selbst keinen Weg!' " ("What do I have to offer to these young people except my doubt and frustration? Which path should I teach them? I don't even know a way myself"). After consenting to his wife's request for a divorce Swoboda encounters alternative life-styles on a trip to Italy with his girlfriend, Jutta; but the new psychotherapies horrify Swoboda, who prefers resignation over primal screams.

In Henisch's next novel, *Hoffmanns Erzählungen* (Tales of Hoffmann, 1983), Professor Franz Kreisler is approached after a lecture in Berlin by a man named Kowalsky who introduces himself as the reincarnated eighteenth-century romantic writer E.T.A. Hoffmann. Kreisler, who has been preparing to write the definitive book about Hoffmann, now has the opportunity to experience the subject of his efforts in real life. But the presence of the mysterious Kowalsky-Hoffmann threatens his system of beliefs, for Kreisler lives in two conveniently separated realities. On the one side are the documented facts about the writer; on the other side there is his literary work. The task of a literary critic like Kreisler is to connect the two by evaluating the work of the author. But in this case the dead author does not wait to be explained; he explains himself. The division between historical facts and imagination has been suspended. Kreisler leaves his teaching post after his excursion into the realm of uncertainty.

Henisch sees his role as a writer as that of an observer rather than a partisan; thus his 1982 collection of short works and essays carries the title *Zwischen allen Sesseln* (Between All Chairs). Henisch remains skeptical toward all alliances, ideologies, and proposed solutions: "Die widersprüche kann man ja, glaub ich, entweder tragisch offen halten oder komisch. Ich mein, nicht aus boshafter Lust am Offenhalten, sondern weil viele von ihnen de facto noch nicht gelöst sind. Wenn man sie komisch offen hält, und das unter Beibehaltung einer gewissen menschlichen Hoffnung, naja das ist halt meine Idee von Ironie" (Contradictions, I believe, can be approached from the perspective of tragic or comical interpretation. I don't advocate an intentional manipulative effect to prevent resolutions, but simply the acceptance that many issues are indeed hitherto unresolved. If one leaves the contradictions unresolved and heals them from the perspective of the comic elements in them, while maintaining an attitude of hopefulness, then we have a definition of my understanding of irony).

Henisch's work has progressed from eso-teric formalism to subjective realism, from rebellious protest to a search for the causes of his personal conflicts and their relation to the problems of his society. What remains consistent in his work is solidarity with the outsider, critical compassion, ethical humanism, and an acute awareness of the role of the writer in bringing about social change.

References:

Otto F. Beer, "Ein falscher Baron und echte Vagabunden," *Die Welt*, 10 May 1980;

Gerald Froidevaux, "Ein Kramerladen zur Befriedigung linker Nostalgie," *Frankfurter Allgemeine Zeitung*, 8 December 1978;

Froidevaux, "Wo bleibt der Mai?," *Basler Zeitung*, 6 January 1979;

Peter Hoefer, "Die kleine Figur eines Sohnes," *Darmstädter Echo*, 5 May 1976;

Kurt Kahl, "Die Kamera als Schild eines traurigen Clowns," *Welt am Sonntag*, 2 November 1975;

B. Meier-Grobman, "Wiener Fleisch und Blut," *Südwest-Presse* (Ulm), 20 May 1976;

Jürgen Moeller, "Ballade vom kleinen Vater," *Münchner Merkur*, 15 November 1975;

Norbert Schachtsiek-Freitag, "Veteranen des Jahres '68," *Frankfurter Rundschau*, 9 April 1979;

Joachim Schondorff, "Der Baronkarl," *Münchner Merkur*, 11 February 1973;

Brigitte Schwaiger, "Wahr, aber betrübt," *Die Zeit*, 20 October 1978;

Joseph Strelka, "Eine Phänomenologie des Mitmachens: Zur frühen autobiographischen Erzählprosa von Peter Henisch," *Modern Austrian Literature*, 13, no. 1 (1981): 149-160;

Jürgen P. Wallman, "Vater und Sohn," *Tagesspiegel* (Berlin), 8 February 1976.

Ödön von Horváth

(9 December 1901-1 June 1938)

Horst Jarka

University of Montana

BOOKS: *Das Buch der Tänze* (Munich: Schahin, 1922);

Der ewige Spießer: Erbaulicher Roman in drei Teilen (Berlin: Propyläen, 1930);

Geschichten aus dem Wiener Wald: Volksstück in drei Teilen (Berlin: Propyläen, 1931); translated by Christopher Hampton as *Tales from the Vienna Woods* (London: Faber & Faber, 1977);

Italienische Nacht: Volksstück (Berlin: Propyläen, 1931);

Jugend ohne Gott: Roman (Amsterdam: De Lange, 1938); translated by R. Wills Thomas as "Youth without God," in *A Child of Our Time, Being Youth without God and A Child of Our Time* (London: Methuen, 1938); republished as *The Age of the Fish* (New York: Dial Press, 1939); German version, edited by Ian Huish (London: Harrap, 1974);

Ein Kind unserer Zeit: Roman (Amsterdam: De Lange, 1938); translated by Thomas as "A Child of Our Time," in *A Child of Our Time, Being Youth without God and A Child of Our Time;* republished as *A Child of Our Time* (New York: Dial Press, 1939);

Der jüngste Tag: Schauspiel in sieben Bildern (Emsdetten: Lechte, 1955);

Pompeji: Komödie eines Erdbebens in 6 Bildern (Munich: Sessler, 1960);

Unvollendet, edited by Franz Theodor Csokor (Graz: Stiasny, 1961);

Stücke, edited by Traugott Krischke (Hamburg: Rowohlt, 1961)–comprises *Italienische Nacht; Geschichten aus dem Wiener Wald; Kasmir und Karoline; Glaube Liebe Hoffnung; Die Unbekannte aus der Seine; Figaro läßt sich scheiden; Don Juan kommt aus dem Krieg,* translated by Hampton as *Don Juan Comes Back from the War* (London: Faber & Faber, 1978); *Der jüngste Tag; Pompeji;*

Zeitalter der Fische: Drei Romane und eine Erzählung (Vienna: Bergland, 1968)–comprises "Der ewige Spießer," "Jugend ohne Gott," "Ein Kind unserer Zeit," "Der Tod aus Tradition";

Rechts und links: Sportmärchen, edited by Walter Huder (Berlin: Berliner Handpresse, 1969);

Gesammelte Werke, edited by Huder, Krischke, and Dieter Hildebrandt, 4 volumes (Frankfurt am Main: Suhrkamp, 1970-1971; reprinted in 8 volumes, 1972);

Von Spießern, Kleinbürgern und Angestellten, edited by Krischke (Frankfurt am Main: Suhrkamp, 1971);

Glaube Liebe Hoffnung, edited by Krischke (Frankfurt am Main: Suhrkamp, 1973);

Sladek oder Die schwarze Armee: Historie in 3 Akten (11 Bildern), edited by Hildebrandt (Frankfurt am Main: Suhrkamp, 1974);

Italienische Nacht, edited by Krischke (Frankfurt am Main: Suhrkamp, 1974)–comprises *Italienische Nacht, Ein Wochenendspiel;*

Die stille Revolution: Kleine Prosa, edited by Krischke (Frankfurt am Main: Suhrkamp, 1975);

Die Geschichten der Agnes Pollinger: Volksstück in 3 Teilen, edited by Krischke (Eisenstadt: Edition Roetzer/Vienna & Munich: Sessler, 1975);

Ein Lesebuch, edited by Krischke (Frankfurt am Main: Suhrkamp, 1976);

Sechsunddreißig Stunden, edited by Krischke (Frankfurt am Main: Suhrkamp, 1979);

Gesammelte Werke: Kommentierte Werkausgabe in fünfzehn Bänden, edited by Krischke and Susanna Foral-Krischke, 14 volumes published (Frankfurt am Main: Suhrkamp, 1985-).

OTHER: "Ein Fräulein wird bekehrt," in *24 neue deutsche Erzähler,* edited by Hermann Kesten (Berlin: Kiepenheuer, 1929).

" 'Heimat?' Kenn ich nicht. Ich bin eine typisch alt-österreichisch-ungarische Mischung: magyarisch, kroatisch, deutsch, tschechisch–mein Name ist magyarisch, meine Muttersprache ist deutsch. Ich spreche weitaus am besten Deutsch, schreibe nunmehr nur Deutsch, gehöre also dem deutschen Kulturkreis an, dem deutschen Volke. Allerdings: der Begriff 'Vaterland,' national-

Ödön von Horváth

istisch gefälscht, ist mir fremd. Mein Vaterland ist das Volk.... Ich habe keine Heimat und leide natürlich nicht darunter, sondern freue mich meiner Heimatlosigkeit, denn sie befreit mich von einer unnötigen Sentimentalität" ("Home country?" I don't know any. I am a typically old Austro-Hungarian mixture: Hungarian, Croatian, German, Czech—my name is Hungarian, my mother tongue German. I speak German better than any other language, I write only in German, I belong to German culture, to the German people. But mind you: any nationalistically falsified concept of "fatherland" is alien to me. My fatherland is the people.... I have no homeland and naturally do not suffer as a result, but I rather

enjoy my homelessness because it spares me any unnecessary sentimentality). This statement, which Ödön von Horváth made in 1929, raises the question to what extent he may be called an Austrian writer. He was born on 9 December 1901 in Susak, a suburb of Fiume (now Rijeka, Yugoslavia), which at that time lay just within the southern border of the Austro-Hungarian Empire, to Dr. Edmund Josef von Horváth and Maria Hermine Prehnal von Horváth. Because his father was a diplomat, until 1918 the family led the nomadic existence characteristic of the imperial civil service; they moved to Belgrade, to Budapest, to Pressburg (now Bratislava, Czechoslovakia), and to Vienna. As a child Horváth experi-

Horváth's father, Dr. Edmund Josef von Horváth (Elisabeth von Horváth / Ödön von Horváth-Archiv)

enced the confusion brought about by the empire's disintegration. He once said: "Ich weine dem alten Österreich-Ungarn keine Träne nach. Was morsch ist, soll zusammenbrechen" (I don't shed a tear over old Austro-Hungary. What's rotten ought to collapse). Horváth lived longer in Germany than he did in Austria; but he called himself a German writer only because he wrote in German, not because he considered himself a German national. He was a Hungarian citizen all his life.

He seems to have adapted well to his surroundings; he was the Bavarian in Bavaria, the Austrian in Austria. His works are written in the languages of Bavaria and Austria, but his characters try to overcome their dialect by speaking the denaturalized language of modern German mass society. The most persuasive argument for calling him an Austrian author is his close kinship with the Austrian literary tradition: his social criticism, which is always language criticism, links him with the great Austrian satirists Johann Nestroy and Karl Kraus.

Horváth is known primarily as a playwright. Compared to his seventeen plays, his three novels and about three dozen short stories, comprising altogether about five hundred pages, are less impressive in quantity. But their moral depth and literary originality prove Horváth to be one of the most significant fiction writers of the early twentieth century. His critical detachment and intuitive psychological insight made him a perceptive analyst of central European society during the interwar period of economic, political, and spiritual instability. In his fiction, as in his best plays, he exposed the shoddy values, escape mechanisms, and aggressive tendencies of a society that would soon embrace fascism.

"Mein Leben beginnt mit der Kriegserklärung. . . . Der Weltkrieg verdunkelte unsere Jugend und wir haben wohl kaum Kindheitserinnerungen" (My life begins with the declaration of war. . . . The World War darkened our youth, and we hardly have any childhood memories), Horváth said. Frequent changes in schools did not favor smooth academic progress: when he was fourteen, his German was so poor that he had to repeat the class. He was not interested in school, and narrow-minded priests turned him against religion. The collapse of the monarchy awakened his political consciousness; he adored the revolutionary verse of the Hungarian poet Endre Ady. During the Communist regime of Béla Kun, Horváth's father was declared persona non grata, but after Admiral Horthy's counterrevolution in 1919 he was appointed the representative of the Hungarian government in Bavaria. In 1919 Horváth passed his school-leaving examination in Vienna, followed his family to Bavaria, and entered the University of Munich. He dropped out after four semesters and started writing.

The pantomime *Das Buch der Tänze* (The Book of Dances, 1922) proved to be a misapplication of Horváth's talents. His "Sportmärchen" (Sports Fairy Tales), which appeared in the widely read satirical magazine *Simplicissimus* and other periodicals from 1924 to 1926 and were collected as *Rechts und links* (Right and Left) in 1969, satirize the grotesqueness of the sports world in tones that vary from the playfully fantastic to the absurd. An avid mountain climber, Horváth tells of an ice-ax witch, of benevolent piton dwarfs, of pieces of equipment that rebel against neglect. Competition is carried to the point of absurdity: personified sports disciplines compete with each other (long jump against high

Horváth's mother, Maria Hermine Prehnal von Horváth (Elisabeth von Horváth / Ödön von Horváth-Archiv)

jump, for example), mountains vie with each other in degrees of difficulty for climbers. The tales are satires of sports fanaticism and specialization. In form they are related to the Munich nonsense verse of the period by Joachim Ringelnatz and Christian Morgenstern; in intention they are significant examples of the literary criticism of sports that became prominent in the 1920s.

In 1924 the Horváths bought a villa in Murnau, a small town south of Munich on the road to Garmisch-Partenkirchen, in one of the areas where alpine tourism began. To compete with the Bavarians' cable car up the Zugspitze, Germany's highest mountain, the Austrians built another one in 1926. Three workers died in the course of its construction, and the police had to settle a confrontation between labor and management. This conflict became the basis for Horváth's first successful play, *Die Bergbahn* (The Cable Car, published in Horváth's *Gesammelte Werke* [Collected Works], 1970), which premiered in Berlin in 1929. In this sociopolitical documentary Horváth grappled with the technique of the

Volksstück (a folk play–a play centering on the life of common people), the genre in which he was to create his most original dramas. His next play, *Zur schönen Aussicht* (Hotel Bella Vista, published in *Gesammelte Werke*, 1970), which premiered in Graz in 1969, is about a group of sleazy characters hiding out in cheap hotels. Its "heroine," Christine, prefigures the most memorable women characters in his novels and best plays: women who are the victims of men and of a society governed by male principles.

Horváth's interest in documentary drama was rekindled in 1926, when he did research in the Berlin archives of the German League of Human Rights. The case of a woman teacher who was fired by the Catholic school authorities in Bavaria because of Communist contacts served as the basis of his unfinished play *Der Fall E.* (The Case of E., published in *Gesammelte Werke*, 1971). While preparing documentation exposing the political bias of the judicial system, he came across records of the activities of a secret right-wing military organization which had taken the law into its own hands after the war, had murdered sixteen people, and was treated leniently in small-town courts away from the glare of publicity. Of the resulting play, *Sladek oder Die schwarze Armee* (Sladek; or, The Black Militia, 1974), which premiered in Berlin in 1929, Horváth said: "Sladek ist ein ausgesprochener Vertreter jener Jugend, jenes 'Jahrgangs 1902,' der in seiner Pubertät die 'große Zeit,' Krieg und Inflation, mitgemacht hat, ist der Typ des Traditionslosen, Entwurzelten ... der so zum Prototyp der Mitläufers wird.... Da ich die Hauptprobleme der Menschheit in erster Linie von sozialen Gesichtspunkten aus sehe, kam es mir bei meinem Sladek vor allem darauf an, die gesellschaftlichen Kräfte aufzuzeigen, aus denen dieser Typ entstanden ist" (Sladek is a true representative of the generation that, born in 1902, experienced during its puberty the "great time," war and inflation. He is the type of traditionless, rootless person ... who becomes the prototype of the fellow traveler.... Since I see the main problems of humanity from a social point of view, my intention in writing *Sladek* was to show the social forces that create this type of person).

Horváth's "social point of view" determined his first long work of fiction, *Sechsunddreißig Stunden* (Thirty-six Hours, 1979). Agnes Pollinger is Sladek's female counterpart: she, too, belongs to the lost generation that was born during the war, grew up in a hostile world of poverty,

Horváth (right) with his brother Lajos in 1905 (Elisabeth von Horváth / Ödön von Horváth-Archiv)

and faced a life without a future. But in contrast to Sladek, who overcomes his isolation in right-wing extremism, Agnes is apolitical. This poor working-class girl is a victim of the economic system and of male exploitation. Agnes's story is interwoven with a multitude of episodes and character sketches, miniatures of greed, vanity, hypocrisy, reactionary stupidity, naiveté, and meanness. In spite of the grim social panorama they convey, these hundred pages are extremely lively writing: exuberant, inventive, full of verbal and situational comedy. But the humor is always accompanied by bitterness over social injustice and the sadness of Agnes's miserable, lonely life. Hermann Kesten printed one of the chapters, "Ein Fräulein wird bekehrt" (Conversion of a Young Lady), in his anthology *24 neue deutsche Erzähler* (24 New German Prose Writers, 1929), but the novel was not published until 1979. Horváth used his advance from the publisher to

travel to the 1929 World Exposition in Barcelona.

Horváth's social perspective and awareness of the changes that the end of the war had brought about in the social structures of central Europe led him to sociological questions and insights. His grasp of essential sociological processes brought him close to the findings of scholars: in their study *Der neue Mittelstand* (The New Middle Class, 1926) Emil Lederer and Jakob Marschak had analyzed the dilemma of the middle class, a phenomenon with which Horváth deals in his novel *Der ewige Spießer* (The Eternal Philistine, 1930); Horváth's petit bourgeois characters could have been the subjects of Siegfried Kracauer's *Die Angestellten* (The White-Collar Workers, 1929-1930). The sociologists' abstractions gained flesh and blood in Horváth's stories and plays.

Der ewige Spießer is a masterpiece of making the banal hilariously entertaining. The first part

Bernd Spitzer as Sladek in a 1967 production of Horváth's play Sladek oder Die schwarze Armee *at the Ateliertheater am Naschmarkt, Vienna (Gretl Geiger, Vienna)*

describes the adventures of two chance traveling companions, both typical petit bourgeois, on their way to Spain: Alfons Kobler, a shady Munich car dealer, and Rudolf Schmitz, a second-rate Austro-Hungarian journalist. The dialogues between the self-made man who always combines the practical with the useful and the hack whose mind and newspaper articles are filled with the clichés of the pseudoeducated are the perfect satirical reflection of the modern mass mentality. Kobler, who is at the same time shrewd and gullible and, above all, convinced of his importance and irresistibility, expects to catch one of the wealthy women who, he has been told, are easy prey at world expositions. Kobler is an early prototype of the tourist rather than the traveler, of the person who experiences nothing but nevertheless returns home with the inflated ego of the world traveler. The journalist, who acts as his guide, feels superior without reason: the "sights" he picks out are restaurants and whorehouses. This first part is an antitravel book and anti-bildungsroman, a picaresque novel of stupidity. A host of passengers come and go as the journey progresses. Most of them are quarrelsome, aggressive, egotistical defenders of middle-class values and morality. Occasional omniscient-author remarks in support of the working class betray

Horváth's sympathies. Kobler returns from Spain a convinced Pan-European because the woman he had been chasing was reclaimed by her American fiancé—reason enough for Kobler to advocate a united Europe against foreign domination.

In the second part of the novel the tone changes drastically. Incorporating parts of *Sechsunddreißig Stunden* and changing the heroine's first name from Agnes to Anna, it tells the story of a simple office worker who loses her job in the Great Depression and is finally driven to sell herself. Horváth connects the two parts of the novel by making Anna the former girlfriend of Kobler; but the more essential link is the mentality of men like Kobler who consider women to be mere objects for their pleasure. Kobler's successor is Kastner, a peddler of pornography, who recommends Anna as a model to an "artist," who in turn passes her on to a friend to whom he owes forty marks. Anna, realizing that she is being traded like a commodity, becomes practical and demands money: "Sie nahm das Geld, als hätte sie nie darüber nachgedacht, daß man das nicht darf. Sie hatte wohl darüber nachgedacht, aber durch das Nachdenken wird die Ungerechtigkeit nicht anders, das Nachdenken tut nur weh. Es war ein Fünfmarkstück, und nun hatte sie keine Gefühle dabei, als wäre sie schon tot" (She took

Horváth (standing, second from left) at a masquerade party in Murnau, 1926 (Elisabeth von Horváth / Ödön von Horváth-Archiv)

the money as if it had never entered her mind that one must not do that. She had thought about it, but thinking does not make the injustice any more just; thinking about it only hurts. It was a five-mark piece, and now she had no feelings doing it, as if she were already dead).

In the third part of the novel, which also incorporates parts of *Sechsunddreißig Stunden,* the tone changes once more: Anna's life as a streetwalker is still bitter, but there is hope that she might return to a normal life. Reithofer, a decent man who is himself without a job or a future, is attracted to Anna and greatly disappointed when he finds out that she is a prostitute. It is not his love for her that leads him to help her find a respectable job but his sense of the solidarity of all poor people. Reithofer thinks: "Wenn sich alle Mistviecher helfen täten, ging es jedem Mistvieh besser, überhaupt sollten sich die Mistvieher mehr helfen, es ist doch direkt unanständig, wenn man einem nicht helfen tät, obwohl man könnt" (If all poor bastards helped each other, every poor bastard would be better off. Actually, all poor bastards ought to help each other more. It's downright indecent if one could help some-

one and doesn't do it). Anna "hatte ja bereits angefangen, nur an das Böse in der Welt zu glauben, aber nun erlebte sie ein Beispiel für das Vorhandensein des Gegenteils, zwar nur ein kleines Beispiel, aber doch ein Zeichen für die Möglichkeit menschlicher Kultur und Zivilisation" (had already begun to believe in nothing but the evil in this world, but now she experienced an example of the existence of the opposite, a small example to be sure, but still a sign of the possibility of human culture and civilization).

The novel, published by Propyläen in December 1930, was praised for the humor and satire of the first part; but Anna Pollinger's story apparently made no impression on the critics. Kesten wrote in *Die literarische Welt* (16 June 1931): "Horváth ist ein sehr witziger Erzähler, ein satirischer Beobachter der mittleren Gemeinheiten der mittleren Existenzen unserer mittleren Großstädte. Er erzählt innerhalb ganz einfacher Fabeln eine Fülle reizender, manchmal grotesker, scharf und treffend beobachteter, immer lustiger Anekdoten" (Horváth is a very witty storyteller, a satirical observer of the average meannesses of the average individuals in our average-sized cit-

Illustration by Lajos von Horváth for his brother's novel Der ewige Spießer

ies. Within simple plots he presents a wealth of charming, sometimes grotesque, always telling, always funny anecdotes). In a letter to Horváth he added: "Nichts von Thoma–überhaupt kein Vergleich (nicht einmal mit Aristophanes, Mark Twain, Don Quichote, Voltaire und Swift)" (Nothing of [the Bavarian humorist Ludwig] Thoma in it–beyond comparison [not even with Aristophanes, Mark Twain, Don Quixote, Voltaire, and Swift]). In his review in *Der Querschnitt* (December 1930) the Viennese satirist and cabaret author Anton Kuh called Horváth "ein amorphes Stück Natur, vulgär wie ein Noch-nicht-Literat, souverän wie ein Nicht-mehr-Literat; aus Elementarem und Dilettantischem gemengt. So könnte die Rohschrift eines großen satirischen Erzählers aussehen; aber auch die Reinschrift eines genialen Abenteurers, der sich für einen

Schriftsteller ausgibt" (An amorphous piece of nature; vulgar like one who has broken into the set of literati, sure of his gifts like one who left them behind him long ago: a mixture of elemental power and dilettantism. The rough draft by a great satirist might look like this–or the final version of an ingenious adventurer who poses as a writer). Such assessments show that the novel escaped classification: Horváth could not follow any literary trend but could only speak in his own unmistakable voice.

From 1931 to 1936 Horváth's work for the theater overshadowed his fiction. His most important contributions to twentieth-century German-language drama were his Volksstücke (folk plays). In the light of the social changes since the war, he redefined *Volk* as "vollendete oder verhinderte Kleinbürger" (established or would-be bourgeoisie). He felt that the traditional Volksstück could not reflect the life of the common man in industrial society: "Mit vollem Bewußtsein zerstöre ich nun das alte Volksstück, formal und ethisch–und versuche die neue Form des Volksstückes zu finden" (With full knowledge I am destroying the old folk play, its form as well as the ethics behind it, and I am trying to find the new form of the folk play), he said. Actually, the Volksstück before Horváth had not always been sentimental and idyllic; there is much social criticism in the plays of Nestroy, Thoma, Ludwig Anzengruber, and Marieluise Fleißer. Horváth's approach was most innovative in his dialogue, in which he aimed at a "Synthese von Realismus und Ironie" (synthesis of realism and irony). His characters speak what he called "Bildungsjargon" (cultivated jargon), a mixture of dialect, clichés, and misunderstood phrases from the language of academia, business, law, entertainment, and politics that reflects their loss of identity and spiritual impoverishment. Horváth had a fine ear for linguistic nuances that are at once funny and terrifying and that reveal conflicts between the conscious and subconscious mind. "Demaskierung des Bewußtseins" (To unmask consciousness) was his goal: by revealing the sterile, socially conditioned thoughts and feelings with which people hide their aggressions and selfish desires he hoped to increase his audience's self-awareness. His most successful plays were the Volksstücke in which he attacked "Dummheit und Lüge" (stupidity and deceit) and pleaded for reason and sincerity: *Italienische Nacht* (Italian Night, 1931), *Geschichten aus dem Wiener Wald* (1931; translated as *Tales from the Vienna Woods*, 1977), *Kasimir und Karoline*

Horváth circa 1931 (Elisabeth von Horváth / Ödön von Horváth-Archiv)

(premiered 1932; published in *Stücke* [Plays], 1961), *Glaube Liebe Hoffnung* (Faith Love Hope, premiered 1936; published in *Stücke*). The last three have been called the modern Everyman's tragedies of banality. All of these plays are set in the Great Depression, when unemployment rose to six million in Germany and to five hundred thousand (twenty-six percent of the work force) in Austria. Horváth's sympathies are with the oppressed–not only with the victims of capitalism but with women in a male-dominated society which takes out its aggressions and frustrations on them.

Ever since *Die Bergbahn* and *Sladek* reactionary critics had attacked Horváth as "eine Zierde des deutschen Kommunistenlagers" (a showpiece of the German Communist camp). *Italienische Nacht* hardly pacified them: the action in Horváth's most openly political play culminates in a clash between fascists and leftists in which the fascists are routed. A few months after the premiere reality almost duplicated the play: in Murnau fascists broke up a meeting of Social

Democrats, and at the trial Horváth testified on behalf of the latter. In 1931, on Carl Zuckmayer's recommendation, he received the Kleist Prize; overnight he became one of the best-known German dramatists. Rainer Schlösser, the Nazis' leading critic, ended his comment on the award: "Horváth [hat] deutschen Menschen nichts, aber auch gar nichts zu sagen" (Horváth [has] nothing to say to Germans, absolutely nothing). Critics like Schlösser, who had been a small but vociferous minority, dominated the German theater almost immediately after Hitler came to power on 30 January 1933. Horváth's *Glaube Liebe Hoffnung*, which had been accepted for performance in Berlin, was taken out of the schedule. In February 1933 Schlösser reminded readers of *Völkischer Beobachter*, the official Nazi government paper, of Horváth's *Italienische Nacht* and threatened: "Wird sich der Ödön noch wundern!" (Still, Ödön will be surprised!).

In March 1933 Horváth crossed the border into Austria. He kept his Berlin apartment because, like many others, he believed that Hiter's regime would not last. Later that year he returned to his parents' villa in Murnau, but after the villa was searched by storm troopers in his absence he went back to Austria. He joined Zuckmayer in Henndorf near Salzburg and later lived with Franz Theodor Csokor in Vienna. Late in 1933 he married the Berlin singer Marie Elsner, but they separated after a few weeks and were divorced in the fall of 1934.

Horváth's name did not appear on the official list of writers who were undesirables in Nazi Germany, but his plays were no longer performed there. He tried to avoid politics: he made no public political statements and declined Klaus Mann's invitation to contribute to *Die Sammlung*, a polemical journal of writers in exile. He was in Vienna during the uprising of workers against Austro-Fascism in February 1934 and was in Berlin when Hitler had Ernst Röhm and his associates liquidated in the summer of that year; neither of these dramatic political events was reflected in his letters or in his works. He did not want to break his ties with Germany; in comparison with Austria, where he was not well known, Germany–even under the new regime–seemed to offer better opportunities. But to work in Nazi Germany one had to make compromises. In June 1934 Horváth went so far as to offer the Nazis his cooperation, but the offer met with no response. The following month he joined the *Reichsverband deutscher Schriftsteller* (National Asso-

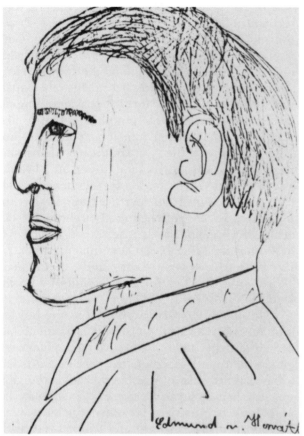

Self-portrait by Horváth (Elisabeth von Horváth / Ödön von Horváth-Archiv)

ciation of German Writers), to which writers had to belong if their works were to be published or performed. Apparently he never made any public use of his membership but wrote under pseudonyms and did some ghostwriting. After six months he stopped paying dues. The works he wrote in Berlin during 1934 were scripts for sentimental movies, and he later regretted writing them. In September 1935 he moved back to Vienna. The following year he visited his parents in Pöcking, a Bavarian village where they spent their summers after selling the Murnau villa. Shortly after his arrival the mayor informed him that he would not receive a visitor's permit. Germany was closed to him.

In Vienna Csokor introduced him to the salons of Alma Mahler Werfel and Berta Zuckerkandl, where he could mix with the cream of Austrian society, but Horváth's real milieu was at the opposite end of the social scale. Elegant restaurants bored him; he preferred to sit and write in cheap coffeehouses, the hangouts of whores, pimps, and petty racketeers. A performance of his extremely critical and realistic *Geschichten aus dem Wiener Wald* was unthinkable in Austro-Fascist Vienna; *Italienische Nacht* was performed in Vienna but in a small theater only. Nor did the plays he had written since 1932 win wide approval, although they marked a significant departure in dramatic style and proved his versatility. *Die Unbekannte aus der Seine* (The Unknown Girl from the Seine, published in *Stücke*), which combines exposure of petit bourgeois mentality with macabre and supernatural elements, was never performed in Horváth's lifetime. The premier of *Hin und Her* (Back and Forth, published in *Gesammelte Werke*, 1970), a farce about the conflict between an individual and an inhuman bureaucracy, was held in Zurich in 1934 and was virtually ignored by the critics. *Glaube Liebe Hoffnung,* which presents the same conflict in tragic terms, was performed in a small theater of the Viennese counterculture. *Himmelwärts* (Heavenward, published in *Gesammelte Werke,* 1970), a fairy-tale play similar to the conventional Volksstücke Horváth had rejected, was seen in a matinee performance only. *Ein Dorf ohne Männer* (A Village without Men, published in *Gesammelte Werke,* 1970), a charming romance about marital fidelity and good government, premiered in Prague. These plays indicate Horváth's withdrawal into a resigned, gentle humanism. Two plays written in 1937, however, give present-day relevance to traditional literary heroes: in *Figaro läßt sich scheiden* (Figaro Gets a Divorce, published in *Stücke*) problems of revolution and emigration are solved (to some critics, unsatisfactorily) by a plea for humaneness; *Don Juan kommt aus dem Krieg* (premiered in 1951; published in *Stücke*; translated as *Don Juan Comes Back from the War,* 1978) returns to the postwar atmosphere of disintegration and emphasizes the theme of guilt. The same theme is treated from a Christian perspective in the 1937 play *Der jüngste Tag* (Doomsday, 1955). Horváth's last play, *Pompeji: Komödie eines Erdbebens* (Pompeii: Comedy of an Earthquake, 1960), written in 1937, depicts the end of an inhuman, pagan order and the beginning of the Christian era of love and forgiveness.

In July 1937 Horváth left Vienna, rented a room in an old inn in Henndorf, and began writing furiously. Within six months two novels were finished. "Zum erstenmal habe ich den Menschen im faschistischen Staate geschildert" (For the first time I portrayed the individual in the fascist state), Horváth wrote about *Jugend ohne Gott* (1938; translated as "Youth without God," 1938).

Horváth in 1932 (Elisabeth von Horváth / Ödön von Horváth-Archiv)

The novel nowhere explicitly refers to Nazi Germany, but its allusions to Nazi propaganda are clear. The events take place three or four years after the inception of Nazi rule in Germany. Many passages in the novel have the directness of dialogue in a play, but they are all filtered through the mind of the protagonist, a teacher in a public school. The first-person narration, combined with journallike sections, letters, and interior monologue, effectively draws the reader into the consciousness of the central character. The book opens with a conflict between the teacher, who sees through the lies of fascism, and his students, who swear by them. A slight deviation from party doctrine—he calls negroes humans—antagonizes the class, which begins to spy on him. The students come to school with closed minds; their essays echo radio speeches. So that they may become the youth of the Führer, they

have been made into a youth without God. They herald a terrifying future. An older teacher tells the protagonist: " 'Es kommen kalte Zeiten, das Zeitalter der Fische. Da wird die Seele des Menschen unbeweglich wie das Antlitz eines Fisches' " ("Cold times are coming, the age of the fish. Then the soul of man becomes as immovable as the face of the fish"). To prepare the students for the war that they have been made to desire, they and their teachers are sent to a premilitary training camp. With the shift of scene the novel's scope widens: "Youth without God" no longer means just the boys; in a castle near the camp teenage girls are also conditioned for war duties. In a village a few miles away the closing of the sawmill has caused poverty and despair; the children of the unemployed workers do piecework while their adolescent siblings steal food from the surrounding farms. They, too, are a youth without God, callous and brutal. The misery of the exploited children raises the questions of social justice under capitalism and of divine justice. For the village priest such questions are irrelevant; human suffering is due to original sin. He tells the teacher: " 'Gott ist das Schrecklichste auf der Welt . . . Er straft. . . . Man darf Gott nicht vergessen, auch wenn wir nicht wissen, wofür er uns straft' " ("God is the most terrible thing on earth . . . He punishes. . . . One must never forget God even if we don't know what He is punishing us for"). The teacher cannot believe in original sin. " 'Dann glauben Sie auch nicht an Gott' " ("Then you don't believe in God"), the priest tells him. The religious theme dominates the rest of the book as Horváth skillfully casts the story of the teacher's gradual acceptance of God into the form of a detective novel. During a premilitary maneuver a boy is killed under mysterious circumstances. The investigation and courtroom scenes, the discovery of new evidence, and shifts in suspects provide the suspense of a thriller. But the moral issue centers on the teacher: by failing to perform an act that might have prevented the murder he shares in the guilt; yet he postpones his confession, struggling with his conscience, until he finally follows what he takes to be God's voice within him and recognizes that " 'Gott ist die Wahrheit' " ("God is the truth"). By admitting the truth the teacher does more than clear his own conscience. His example prompts others to confess and to defy the lies of the totalitarian state. In fact, the teacher's first defense of the truth, his correction of a student's racist disdain for blacks, had triggered, unknown to him, the first defiance among a few of his students. They formed a club called "Für Wahrheit und Gerechtigkeit" (For Truth and Justice) which meets secretly to read books forbidden by the regime. The club is instrumental in tracking down the murderer.

The teenage criminal killed for no other reason than that he wanted to see a human being die: "Geburt und Tod und alles, was dazwischen lag, wollte er genau wissen. Er wollte alle Geheimnisse ergründen, aber nur, um darüber stehen zu konnen–darüber mit seinem Hohn. Er kannte keine Schauer, denn seine Angst war nur Feigheit. Und seine Liebe zur Wirklichkeit war nur der Haß auf die Wahrheit" (Birth and death and everything in between he wanted to know exactly. He wanted to fathom all mysteries, but only in order to stand above them–above them with his scorn. He knew no awe, for his fear was only cowardice. And his love for reality was only his hatred for the truth). Horváth distinguishes between knowledge as a command of facts and knowledge that leads to understanding, between cold curiosity and desire for truth. Finally, even the young murderer who thought he was above morality cannot escape truth and kills himself. The teacher rejoices at the news of the murderer's suicide: "Ich fühle mich plötzlich wunderbar leicht, weil es keinen T [the murderer] mehr gibt. Einen weniger! Freue ich mich denn? Ja! ja, ich freue mich! Denn trotz aller eigenen Schuld an dem Bösen ist es herrlich, wenn ein Böser vernichtet wird" (I suddenly felt a wonderful sense of relief because T no longer exists. One less! Am I glad? Yes, yes, I am glad! For in spite of one's own guilty involvement with evil, it is splendid and magnificent when an evildoer is destroyed). Horváth implies that the individual's recognition of the power of truth will lead to resistance to fascism. The novel ends with the teacher, who has changed from a cautious opportunist to a free moral being with genuine love for others, losing his job and leaving Germany.

The novel was published in Holland by Allert de Lange, who printed many works of German writers in exile. It brought Horváth the wide recognition he had been denied since the early 1930s. Thomas Mann wrote to Zuckmayer that he considered it the best book of the year; Hermann Hesse recommended it to Alfred Kubin as a magnificent work "das quer durch den moralischen Weltzustand von heute [schneidet]" (that [cuts right through] the moral state of our world today). The best recommendation was provided by the Gestapo, who added the novel to the list of forbidden books because of its pacifist tendencies and ordered all copies that might have found their way into Germany to be confiscated. Within a short time the novel was translated into English, French, Danish, Dutch, Swedish, Serbo-Croatian, Polish, and Czech. In his review of the American edition in *Books* (5 March 1939) Alfred Kazin wrote: "One of the very few German novels I have read that masters the totalitarian state as a problem for the writer, and it solves the problem with so unusual an insight that it should become a primer for all writers who have realized that surface realism is no longer enough."

The other novel Horváth completed in Henndorf was *Ein Kind unserer Zeit* (1938; translated as "A Child of Our Time," 1939). The nameless central character is again an individual in a fascist state who is driven to an awareness of guilt and experiences a change of heart. But in contrast to the teacher in *Jugend ohne Gott* who rejects the fascist ideology, the protagonist in *Ein Kind unserer Zeit* is a soldier who takes the propaganda slogans to be the truth. Horváth explains the difference in the mentality of the two protagonists historically: whereas the teacher was raised with the humanist values of the pre-World War I era, the soldier was born during the war and knew nothing but the war's disastrous moral and economic aftermath. His mother died in the famine of 1918; because of a war injury his father, a waiter, can find work only in third-class restaurants. The army saves the son from unemployment, restores his self-respect, and frees him from living with his father, whom he despises.

The father-son conflict epitomizes the cases in fascist Germany where the fathers adhered to prefascist moral standards which in the eyes of the sons, who had been indoctrinated by the Nazi propaganda machine, were ridiculous, contemptible relics of a "weaker" era. The sons transferred their respect to substitute fathers, the leaders in the Nazi organizations, who in turn served the ultimate father figure: the Führer. In the novel the young soldier worships his captain. As in *Jugend ohne Gott*, the first-person narrative technique reveals the central character's consciousness: propaganda clichés have replaced thinking. The Bildungsjargon of Horváth's Volksstücke is replaced by fascist Parteijargon (party jargon), programmed modes of thought and speech that do not permit any individuality; the language is a direct reflection of the destruction of the individ-

First page of a letter from Horváth to his parents, dated 2 December 1934 (Elisabeth von Horváth / Ödön von Horváth-Archiv)

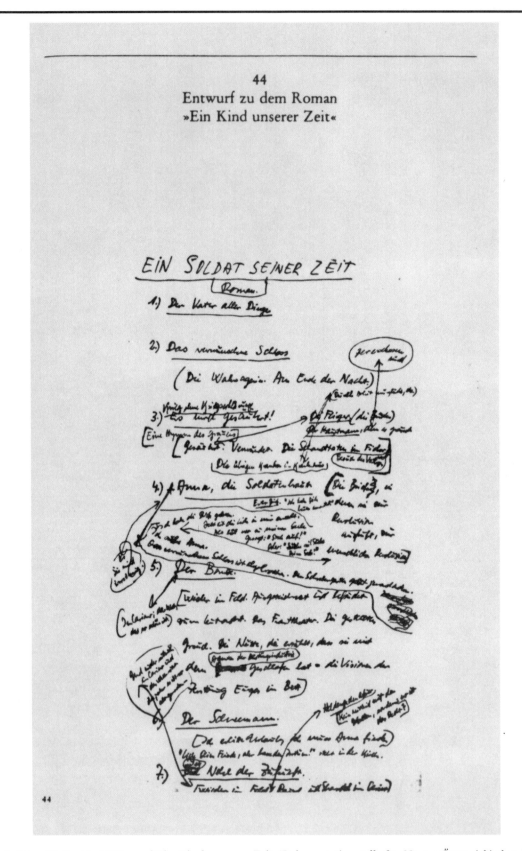

44
Entwurf zu dem Roman
»Ein Kind unserer Zeit«

Outline by Horváth for his 1938 novel Ein Kind unserer Zeit *(Dokumentationsstelle für Neuere Österreichischen Literatur)*

Horváth in 1938, the year of his death (Elisabeth von Horváth / Ödön von Horváth-Archiv)

ual by the military-fascist collective. A phrase repeated throughout the novel drives the point home: "Der einzelne zählt nichts" (The individual doesn't count).

The soldier volunteers for a military operation that subdues a neighboring country, and the war brings about his change of heart. It is not the suffering that he and the other soldiers inflict upon others that rouses his conscience, however; it is his own suffering that makes him see through the deception of the state. An act of selflessness begins the slow process of his awakening: he is wounded attempting to save his captain, and being no longer of use to the fatherland he is discharged and returns to the misery of unemployment. He learns that the captain deliberately walked into the enemy fire because, being a soldier of the old school, he could not tolerate the inhumanity of modern warfare in which defenseless women and children are murdered. The soldier begins to reassess his values. His initial disillusionment with the captain turns into understanding; the propaganda clichés begin to sound hollow. He remembers a girl whom he saw only

once but who had appeared to offer him the possibility of real love. He looks for her and discovers that she has lost her job and is in jail for having an abortion. The soldier tracks down the bookkeeper of the firm where the girl had been employed and reproaches him for not having opposed her firing. The bookkeeper replies that in business, as in war, the individual does not count. In these words the soldier hears his former self: "Was war ich für ein Lügner! Jawohl, ein feiger Lügner–denn wie bequem ist es doch, seine Untaten mit dem Vaterland zu verhüllen, als wäre das ein weißer Mantel der Unschuld! Als bliebe eine Untat kein Verbrechen, ob im Dienste des Vaterlands oder irgendeiner anderen Firma. . . . Für das Gute und für das Böse, da hat sich nur der einzelne zu verantworten und keinerlei Vaterland zwischen Himmel und Hölle" (What a liar I was! Yes, a cowardly liar–for it is so comfortable to cover up one's crimes with the fatherland, as if the fatherland were a white cloak of innocence! As if a crime did not remain a crime, whether committed in the service of the fatherland or in that of any other company. . . . For

207

good and evil only the individual has to take responsibility, no fatherland between heaven and hell can do that for him). But he concludes: "Es darf nicht sein daß der einzelne keine Rolle spielt ... und jeder, der das Gegenteil behauptet, gehört ausradiert" (No one must ever say again that the individual doesn't count–and anybody who does say it must be blotted out), and he kills the bookkeeper. The soldier has learned compassion, but he has not overcome the fascist mentality of aggression and violence. Unlike the teacher in *Jugend ohne Gott*, he is not given the chance of a new beginning; at the end of the novel he freezes to death in a blizzard–Horváth's metaphor for the coldness of the times. Shortly before he dies he recalls his childhood in an unheated room: "Es ist kalt, das bleibt meine erste Erinnerung" (It is cold, that remains my first memory). Inhuman conditions breed inhuman consequences. The novel ends with a plea to the younger generation not to judge the soldier too harshly: "Bedenk es doch: er wußt sich nicht anders zu helfen, er war eben ein Kind seiner Zeit" (Don't forget: he didn't know any better, he was just a child of his time).

The novel was published by de Lange in May 1938. The dust jacket quoted Stefan Zweig: "das realistische Bild der Nachkriegsgeneration. Ein Roman, der den Stempel echter Dichtung trägt. Ein Meisterwerk" (the realistic portrait of the generation that grew up after the war. A novel which bears the stamp of genuine art. A masterpiece). Franz Werfel wrote in a preface to a later edition: "Der Kleinbürger, wie ihn Horváth schildert, ist weniger der Angehörige einer Klasse als der dumpf-gebundene, dem Geist widerstrebende, als der schlechthin *verstockte* Mensch.... Auf dem verstockten Menschen, der um den Bestand der Lüge kämpft, beruht jede kollektive Teufelei. Mit ihm stehen und fallen die totalen Despotien. Von der Kälte seines Herzens geht der große Weltwinter aus" (The petit bourgeois as Horváth portrays him is less a member of a class than the primitively limited person who resists the spirit, the simply *obdurate* person.... The obdurate person who fights to keep the lie in power is the basis of all collective inhumanity. With him all totalitarian despotisms stand and fall. From the coldness of his heart spreads the great winter of the world). The novel appeared on the Nazi list of "schädliches und unerwünschtes Schrifttum" (harmful and undesirable literature) for December 1938. It was immediately translated into English, French, Spanish, and Chinese.

On 12 March 1938 German troops crossed the Austrian border. On 16 March Horváth left Vienna, and the restlessness of exile began. He spent two weeks in Budapest and three weeks with a friend in Toplitz-Schönau, Czechoslovakia; then he returned to Budapest and went on to Yugoslavia, Trieste, Venice, Milan, Brussels, and Amsterdam. He planned to settle near Geneva to work on another novel. On 28 May he arrived in Paris for talks with Armand Pierhal, the French translator of *Jugend ohne Gott* and *Ein Kind unserer Zeit*. On 1 June he was killed by a falling branch on the Champs-Elysées. Most of the Paris exile community attended the funeral; Joseph Roth, Werfel, Zuckmayer, Rudolf Leonhard, Paul Friedländer, and Manfred Georg spoke. The French literary world was represented by François Mauriac.

"Das Werk, das du uns zurückläßt, war die Skizze, der Entwurf, die geheime Planung zu einem größeren Werke von haftender Schönheit und Bedeutung, das dir zu schaffen nicht mehr erlaubt wurde" (The work that you left us was the sketch, the draft, the secret design for a greater work of lasting beauty and meaning, which you were not allowed to complete). These words, spoken by Zuckmayer at the graveside, were echoed by critics for years to come. Werfel judged the last two novels to be superior to anything else Horváth had ever written, but added: "Es wäre freilich ungehörig, ihnen den Rang vollendeter epischer Kunstwerke zubilligen zu wollen. Diesen Rang besitzen sie keineswegs" (It would be inappropriate, however, to grant them the rank of complete works of narrative art. They certainly do not belong in that category).

A reassessment of Horváth's literary craftsmanship came only after the first edition of his collected works in 1970-1971. Paradoxically, it was the politically conscious generation of the 1970s that discovered the artistry of his dialogues. The "sketchiness" for which his plays had been criticized was recognized as a highly original and innovative style. Horváth's plays became modern classics of the German theater, alongside those of Bertolt Brecht. His influence is most pronounced in the plays of Franz Xaver Kroetz, Martin Sperr, and Peter Turrini. The collected works also made it possible for the first time to assess the wealth of Horváth's fiction. Close analysis of the novels and their variants, of the short pieces, fragments, and unpublished manuscripts brought to light a dense fabric of recurring themes, situations, and types of characters. It became evident that the "light touch" and "spontaneity" of Horváth's prose works were the result of careful reworking of even the smallest phrases.

His two late novels are no longer regarded as the unfinished legacy of a writer of promise; they are recognized as highly original works in which psychological realism is combined with symbolic depth, social criticism with Christian humanism. Their political dimension has been reassessed. They are documents of anti-fascism and have retained their validity as analyses of the effects of propaganda on mass consciousness. With the perfection of the instruments of mass manipulation the problem that Horváth diagnosed so clearly has only grown worse.

Wilhelm Emrich said of Horváth's work: "Ob Horváths Werk einmal ins Bewußtsein der Öffentlichkeit eindringen wird, wir wissen es nicht. Aber die Antwort der Zukunft wird zugleich mit anderen Zeichen ein Gradmesser dafür sein, wieweit das Bewußtsein unserer sogenannten Kultur wächst oder noch bestialischer verdummt" (Whether Horváth's insights will one day be commonly shared by the rest of society, we do not know. But the answer to this question will be one indication of whether our so-called culture has increased in consciousness or whether it will deteriorate into even more bestial stupidity).

Biography:
Traugott Krischke, *Ödon von Horváth: Kind seiner Zeit* (Munich: Heyne, 1980).

References:
Alan F. Bance, "The Overcoming of the Collective: *Jugend ohne Gott* as Drama," *Publications of the Institute of Germanic Studies*, 43 (1989);

Kurt Bartsch, Uwe Baur, and Dietmar Goltschnigg, eds., *Horváth-Diskussion* (Kronberg: Scriptor, 1976);

Uwe Baur, "Horváth und die Sportbewegung der Zwanzigerjahre: Seine 'Sportmärchen' im Kontext der Münchner Nonsense-Dichtung," *Horváth Blätter*, 2 (1984): 75-96;

Wilhelm Emrich, "Die Dummheit oder das Gefühl der Unendlichkeit: Ödön von Horváths Kritik," in his *Geist und Widergeist: Wahrheit und Lüge der Literatur. Studien* (Frankfurt am Main & Bonn: Athenäum, 1965), pp. 185-196;

Reinhard Federmann, "Das Zeitalter der Fische: Ein Versuch über Ödön von Horváth," *Wort in der Zeit*, 6 (1962): 6-14;

Susanne Feigl, "Das Thema der menschlichen Wandlung in den Romanen Ödön von Horváths," Ph.D. dissertation, University of Vienna, 1970;

Riccardo Franchi, "Der Spießer und seine Sprache: Eine Untersuchung von Ödön von Horváths Werk," Ph.D. dissertation, University of Zurich, 1982;

Axel Fritz, *Ödön von Horváth als Kritiker seiner Zeit* (Munich: List, 1973);

Fritz, *Zeitthematik und Stilisierung in der erzählenden Prosa Ödön von Horváths (1901-1938)* (Aalborg: Aalborg Universitetsforlag, 1981);

Adolf Haslinger, "Ödön von Horváths 'Jugend ohne Gott' als Detektivroman: Ein Beitrag zur österreichischen Kriminalliteratur," in *Studien zur Literatur des 19. und 20. Jahrhunderts in Österreich: Festschrift für Alfred Doppler zum 69. Geburtstag*, edited by Johann Holzner, Michael Klein, and Wolfgang Wiesmüller (Innsbruck: 1981), pp. 197-204;

Dieter Hildebrandt, *Ödon von Horváth in Selbstzeugnissen und Bilddokumenten* (Reinbek: Rowohlt, 1975);

Hildebrandt and Traugott Krischke, eds., *Über Ödön von Horváth* (Frankfurt am Main: Suhrkamp, 1970);

Ian Huish, *Horváth: A Study* (London: Heinemann / Totowa, N.J.: Rowan & Littlefield, 1980);

Horst Jarka, "Horváth's Work in the United States," *Publications of the Institute of Germanic Studies*, 43 (1989);

Frank Kadrnoska, "Horvath und die Folgen? *Jugend ohne Gott* und die österreichische Vergangenheitsbewältigung fiktional–real," *Publications of the Institute of Germanic Studies*, 43 (1989);

Kadrnoska, "Die späten Romane Ödön von Horváths: Exilliteratur und Vergangenheitsbewältigung," *Österreich in Geschichte und Literatur*, 26 (1982): 81-109;

Jenö Krammer, "Ödön v. Horváths Romane," *Österreich in Geschichte und Literatur*, 13 (1969): 240-251;

Traugott Krischke, ed., *Horváths "Jugend ohne Gott": Materialien* (Frankfurt am Main: Suhrkamp, 1982);

Krischke, ed., *Materialien zu Ödön von Horváth* (Frankfurt am Main: Suhrkamp, 1970);

Krischke, ed., *Ödön von Horváth* (Frankfurt am Main: Suhrkamp, 1981);

Krischke and Hans F. Prokop, eds., *Ödön von Horváth: Leben und Werk in Dokumenten und Bildern* (Frankfurt am Main: Suhrkamp, 1972);

Wolfgang Lechner, *Mechanismus der Literaturrezeption in Österreich am Beispiel Ödön von Horváths* (Stuttgart: Akademischer Verlag Hans-Dieter Heinz, 1978);

Ian Loram, "Ödön von Horváth: An Appraisal," *Monatshefte*, 59 (Spring 1967): 19-34;

David R. Midgley, "Aetiology of the Banal: Horváth's Novel *Der ewige Spießer*," *Publications of the Institute of Germanic Studies*, 43 (1989);

Ödön von Horváth (1901-1938) (Nantes: Université de Nantes, 1982);

K. S. Parkes, "The Novels of Ödön von Horváth," *New German Studies*, 3 (1975): 81-97;

Jürgen Schröder, "Das Spätwerk Ödön von Horváths," *Sprachkunst*, 7, no. 1 (1976): 49-71;

Angelika Steets, *Die Prosawerke Ödön von Horváths: Versuch einer Bedeutungsanalyse* (Stuttgart: Akademischer Verlag Hans-Dieter Heinz, 1978);

Zsuzsa Szell, "Ödön von Horváth, ein Epiker seiner Zeit," *Literatur und Kritik*, 231/232 (February/March 1989): 11-28;

Ulrich Weisstein, "Ödön von Horváth: *A Child of Our Time*," *Monatshefte*, 3, no. 2 (1960): 343-352;

Benno von Wiese, "Ödön von Horváth," in his *Deutsche Dichter der Moderne* (Berlin: Schmidt, 1975), pp. 592-622;

Krishna Winston, "Ödön von Horváth: A Man for This Season," *Massachusetts Review*, 19 (Spring 1978): 169-180;

Viktor Žmegač, "Horváths Erzählkunst im europäischen Rahmen: Innovation und Tradition," *Literatur und Kritik*, 237/238 (1989).

Papers:

The Horváth Archive at the Academie of Arts, West Berlin, has Horváth's manuscripts, secondary literature, and reviews. Copies of these holdings are at the library of the University of Wisconsin, Madison, and at the University of Stockholm. A Horváth research center is being established at the Sessler Verlag, Vienna, which is to contain material not included in the Berlin archive. Some manuscripts are in the Franz Theodor Csokor estate at the Vienna City Library; the Manuscript Collection of the Austrian National Library, Vienna; the Schiller Archive at Marburg, West Germany; and the Munich City Library.

Franz Innerhofer
(2 May 1944-   )

Gerald A. Fetz
University of Montana

BOOKS: *Schöne Tage: Roman* (Salzburg: Residenz, 1974); translated by Anselm Hollo as *Beautiful Days* (New York: Urizen, 1976);
Schattseite: Roman (Salzburg: Residenz, 1975);
Innenansichten eines beginnenden Arbeitstages (Pfaffenweiler: Pfaffenweiler Presse, 1976);
Die großen Wörter: Roman (Salzburg: Residenz, 1977);
Der Emporkömmling: Erzählung (Salzburg: Residenz, 1982).

Franz Innerhofer stormed the literary scene in the German-speaking world with his highly acclaimed first novel, *Schöne Tage* (translated as *Beautiful Days*, 1976), in 1974. He was immediately awarded the Bremen Literature Prize, the Rauriser Literature Prize, and the Sandoz Prize and was regarded as one of the most important and exciting young authors writing in German.

Innerhofer was born on 2 May 1944 in the small Alpine village of Krimml, near Salzburg. He was the illegitimate child of Elise Bernhard, a farm girl, who put him in foster care for two years, then got married and raised him until he was six. At that point he was sent to live at the farm of his natural father, who no longer wanted to pay child support. For the next eleven years, by his own account, Innerhofer was subjected to brutality, incredibly hard work, exclusion from the family, and a childhood full of despair, self-hatred, desire for revenge, and failures at every turn. In 1961 he abruptly left the farm and used his skills as a hard worker and his knowledge of farm machinery to secure an apprenticeship in a blacksmith-machine shop in the nearby village of Uttendorf. During the three years of this apprenticeship his master's mother encouraged him to read and taught him to think critically and to expand his linguistic skills. His apprenticeship therefore turned out to be an informal introduction to the world of the mind, and Innerhofer set as his goal the formal entry into that world. When he completed the apprenticeship in 1964, he fled the rural environment for Salzburg. He found a job in a factory, where he discovered that the feeling of solidarity he had expected to find among the workers was sorely lacking. He also began to take evening classes to gain his Matura (diploma); in school, however, he found more pedantry than enlightenment. After struggling for two years to combine his fatiguing life as a factory worker with the demands of his schooling, Innerhofer took a job as a janitor in a dormitory so he might have more time and energy for learning. That move enabled him to graduate, and he was awarded a scholarship to the University of Salzburg. He became disillusioned with academic life, however, and left the university after six semesters.

Innerhofer wrote his first novel during a period of despair and thoughts of suicide. After reading *Wunschloses Unglück* (1972; translated as *A Sorrow beyond Dreams*, 1975), Peter Handke's work about his mother's suicide, however, he decided to try to sublimate his anger, depression, and confusion by writing about his past. The attempt was successful, at least temporarily, and his promising career as a writer was launched. The autobiographical *Schöne Tage* is a powerful story of a boy's desperate struggle to piece together an identity and liberate himself from the almost feudal bondage and terror of his father's farm. Noting the bitter irony of the novel's title— the days (and years) described are anything but beautiful—commentators have most frequently discussed the work in the context of the so-called Anti-Heimatroman. In the traditional Heimatroman, which was a popular literary genre in the nineteenth and first half of the twentieth centuries, the settings are usually small villages in the Alps, far from the "decadent" and threatening cities and the secular civilization that was seen to prevail there. These works tend to be pious and politically and socially conservative and to embody values that are rooted in the soil, home, family, church, village, and hard work. The "Blubo" (Blood and Soil) literature of the Nazi period took many of its cues from this

Franz Innerhofer

genre. The simple and often hard lives of the characters are idealized, as is the rural setting in general. This image of the Alpine countryside is still promoted in tourist brochures. In opposition to this sentimentalized image there has developed a sizable body of literature in Austria and Germany that offers a more realistic and critical picture. *Schöne Tage* is perhaps the most convincing and forceful of the Anti-Heimat novels.

The book is written in a simple, concrete style in which visual images predominate. Over the course of the eleven years covered by the novel, the protagonist, referred to only as Holl, comes to realize how closely language is associated with power; he is determined that he will "learn to talk" because he is convinced that language is the means to liberation. Innerhofer has said that *Schöne Tage* was written not only as a form of therapy for himself but also to give encouragement to others who had been similarly oppressed and had not attained the means to liberate themselves.

While *Schöne Tage* was almost unanimously praised by literary critics, it has remained controversial among the Austrian rural population. That the novel struck a responsive chord with many who had experienced life on the farm in a way similar to Holl was indicated by the hundreds of letters to newspapers, to Innerhofer's publishers, and to Innerhofer himself. Yet there were also protests against *Schöne Tage*, especially when it was made into a television film in 1980. From conservative farmers who saw the work as a vicious attack on their way of life came calls to ban the book and the film. Press conferences were called to refute the book's contents; at one of these press conferences Innerhofer's father claimed that the work did not correspond to reality in any way.

In *Schattseite* (Shade Side, 1975), the second novel in what would turn out to be a trilogy, Innerhofer portrays Holl as he somewhat clumsily but determinedly wades through three difficult years of an apprenticeship in a village ma-

Dust jacket for Innerhofer's autobiographical first novel, about a boy's struggle to free himself from his tyrannical father

chine shop. With the aid of Helene, his master's mother, Holl fights his way to a measure of intellectual independence, and at the end, fascinated by what he calls "the world of words," he decides to abandon the narrow confines of countryside and village to seek work in the city. As an indication of his growth toward a stronger sense of identity, Holl receives in this novel a first name: Franz. Also, while *Schöne Tage* had an anonymous third-person narrator, this novel is narrated in the first person by Holl himself. At first glance, *Schattseite* appears to be an almost classic bildungsroman: a young, inexperienced protagonist is taken under the wing of a wise older person, comes of age, and enters the realm of enlightened thinking. Yet at the end Holl is still innocent and naive, with visions of total liberation and complete faith in the ideals of education and enlightenment. His disappointment will be all the greater when that utopian illusion begins to fade.

In the final novel in the trilogy, *Die großen Wörter* (The Big Words, 1977), Holl is in Salzburg. There he is thrown back into a state of insecurity and confusion as he attempts to adjust to the complex city environment as a factory worker, then as a janitor and night-school student, and finally as a university student. When he achieves his goal of entering the university, the citadel of his revered "world of words," Holl realizes that he is still far from attaining the total freedom he had imagined would attend that achievement. At the end he faces the existential uncertainties, doubts, and anguish that characterize the late twentieth century. The style of this novel differs sharply from that of the preceding two: the concrete physical experiences which dominate those novels are abandoned in favor of conversation and interior monologues. And whereas the first two novels are chronological in their narration, *Die großen Wörter* shifts back and forth between time levels; one often has no clear idea of when a particular conversation is supposed to have taken place or when the protagonist had certain feelings or thoughts. The change is appropriate: Holl has moved from a milieu in *Schöne Tage* in which language was used only as a tool of power to one in *Schattseite* in which, although used for broader purposes, it was still viewed skeptically and therefore used sparingly, to one in which language is central. His feelings of inadequacy in this new milieu are reflected in a reversion to the third-person narration of the first novel: Holl is no longer competent to tell his own story. *Die großen Wörter* is set in the late 1960s, and even though student activism was quite subdued in Austria compared to West Germany, Holl and his acquaintances are zealous participants in the political, ideological, social, and cultural discussions of the time. Holl is lost and confused in most of these discussions as he struggles to reconcile his experiences with the ideals espoused by speakers representing various political viewpoints. Clichés and contradictions abound in these debates, a realistic reflection of much of the discourse of the student movement.

Once he becomes disillusioned with the academic enterprise Holl begins to be emotionally susceptible to the attraction of the simpler life he knew in the country and in the village; he even starts to romanticize the childhood that is so devastatingly described in *Schöne Tage*. At such moments Holl becomes anti-intellectual in the extreme and prefers to associate with auto mechanics, pimps, prostitutes, and neo-Nazis

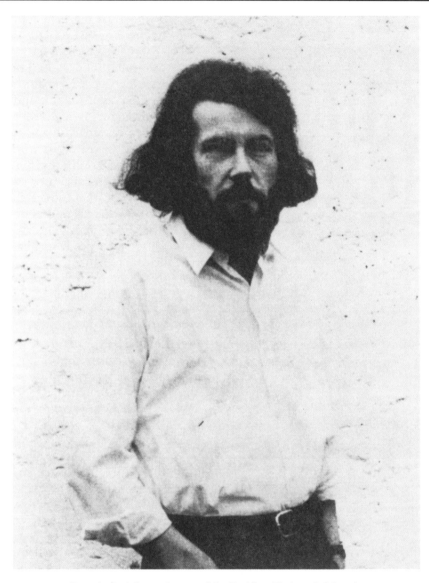

Innerhofer (photo courtesy of the Residenz Verlag, Salzburg)

rather than with his fellow students. Although Holl's intellectual sympathies clearly lie with the left, his emotional makeup and background make him vulnerable to appeals from the right. At the end of the novel he realizes that he cannot go back, yet his desire to go forward has been diminished by his disillusionment with the "world of words." On the final pages Holl begins his studies at the university, but the narrator indicates that his career as a student will be short-lived.

Reviews of *Die großen Wörter* were mixed: some critics found the portrayal of Holl's dilemma a convincing illustration of contemporary life; others said that when Innerhofer left the realm of the concrete and physical, his ability to master his material diminished sharply. The

third work is less able to stand as an independent novel than the first two, but the trilogy as a whole must be viewed as a remarkable literary achievement: both bildungsroman and anti-bildungsroman, it can even be read as an allegory of Western man's odyssey from the medieval farm to the nineteenth-century village and finally to the twentieth-century city. It clearly establishes Innerhofer as one of the most important contemporary fiction writers in German.

Following the appearance of *Die großen Wörter* in 1977, five years passed with no further publication by Innerhofer. There were rumors of problems with alcohol and depression, and some critics decided that Innerhofer had told his story with the trilogy and had nothing more to say. Fi-

Innerhofer at his desk (Residenz Verlag, Salzburg)

nally, Innerhofer published a fourth novel in 1982. *Der Emporkömmling* (The Parvenu) has individual passages that reflect his proven capabilities as a writer, but the overall concept of the work is unclear. The events and interior monologues which constitute the short novel are presented randomly, with little apparent logic or chronology. Though the work is obviously an extension of the trilogy, the protagonist is no longer Holl but Hans Peter Lambrecht. It seems that Innerhofer was trying to establish his independence from the trilogy but was unable to do so, in spite of the name change of the main character. As the work opens, Lambrecht's situation is identical to that of Holl at the end of *Die großen Wörter:* disillusioned with the "world of words," convinced that it is artificial at best, he has left the university to seek a job as a manual laborer in an effort, as he puts it, to "recapture" his hands and, thereby, his identity and self-respect. As a sign of his attitude

toward the world he is leaving, Lambrecht tries to sell the books he has accumulated during the previous several years; but he cannot bring himself to do so when the book dealer offers him a mere pittance for them. Lambrecht secures a job in a cement products factory near Munich, moves into the workers' barracks, and attempts to win both the confidence of his skeptical coworkers and his own self-confidence as a worker. Neither is attained with ease. The novel presents in anecdotal fashion descriptions of his life in the barracks; of his initially helpless attempts to regain his "hands"; of disjointed and mundane conversations with his coworkers, whom he tends to romanticize; and of a journey to the village in Austria where he grew up. Although he eventually gains the respect of his coworkers and regains confidence in his manual skills, he receives notification that he has won a prize for poetry and decides to return to the artificial world of words–

represented by a pseudointellectual groupie who flatters and attaches herself to him–and take up life as a writer in Salzburg.

Innerhofer has said that one of his intentions in *Der Emporkömmling* was to portray workers who could think critically. Several of the workers in the novel have political insights, but their mundane and narrow existences and interests, reflected in their conversation, contradict any notion that they are the critical thinkers Innerhofer claims they are. The muddled political and social thinking which was prevalent in *Die großen Wörter* is presented here as though it were profound.

Since *Die großen Wörter*, doubts have been raised about Innerhofer's ability to transcend the concrete realm and deal with the complexities of the "world of words." Like Holl in *Die großen Wörter* and Lambrecht in *Der Emporkömmling*, he seems to have been cut off from his roots and to be unable to put down new ones. The vacillation of his protagonists, their inability to integrate the world of the mind and that of "the hands," and their insistence on an either-or dichotomy reflect the dilemma that confronts Innerhofer as he seeks to come to terms with his past and present.

References:

Alexander Auer, "Nach Haudorf und anderswo hin," *Austriaca*, 7 (1978): 37-44;

Maria Luise Caputo-Mayr, "Überlieferung aus neuer Sicht: Zur jüngsten österreichischen Prosaliteratur," in *Perspectives and Personalities: Studies in Modern German Literature Honoring Claude Hill*, edited by Ralph Ley and others (Heidelberg: Winter, 1978), pp. 89-100;

Gerald A. Fetz, "Franz Innerhofer," in *Major Figures of Contemporary Austrian Literature*, edited by Donald G. Daviau (Bern: Lang, 1986), pp. 237-263;

Peter Frank, "Heimatromane von unten: Einige Gedanken zum Werk Franz Innerhofers," *Modern Austrian Literature*, 13, no. 1 (1980): 167-175;

Ulrich Greiner, "Franz Innerhofer," in his *Der Tod des Nachsommers* (Munich: Hanser, 1979), pp. 101-121;

Jürgen Koppensteiner, "Anti-Heimatliteratur: Ein Unterrichtsversuch mit Franz Innerhofers Roman 'Schöne Tage,'" *Unterrichtspraxis*, 14, no. 1 (1981): 9-19;

Koppensteiner, "Das Leben auf dem Lande: Zu den Anti-Heimatromanen österreichischer Gegenwartsautoren," in *Akten des VI. Internationalen Germanisten-Kongresses, Basel 1980* (Bern, Frankfurt am Main & New York: Lang, 1980), pp. 545-550;

Helmut Schink, "Vergewaltigung der Kindheit: Franz Innerhofers 'Schöne Tage,'" in his *Jugend als Krankheit?* (Linz: Oberösterreichischer Landesverlag, 1980), pp. 147-174.

Elfriede Jelinek

(20 October 1946-)

Frank W. Young
California State University, Los Angeles

BOOKS: *Lisas Schatten: 7 Gedichte* (Munich, Würzburg & Bern: Eilers, 1967);

wir sind lockvögel baby!: Roman (Reinbek: Rowohlt, 1970);

Michael: Ein Jugendbuch für die Infantilgesellschaft (Reinbek: Rowohlt, 1972);

Materialien zu Musiksoziologie, by Jelinek, Ferdinand Zellwecker, and Wilhelm Zobl (Vienna & Munich: Jugend und Volk, 1972);

Die Liebhaberinnen: Roman (Reinbek: Rowohlt, 1975); translated by Jorn K. Bramann as *The Brassiere Factory* (New York: Adler, 1987);

bukolit: hörroman (Vienna: Rhombus, 1979);

Die Ausgesperrten: Roman (Reinbek: Rowohlt, 1980);

Die endlose Unschuldigkeit: Prosa–Hörspiel–Essay (Schwifting: Schwiftinger Galerie-Verlag, 1980);

Ende: Gedichte von 1966-1968 (Munich: Schwiftinger Galerie-Verlag, 1980);

Was geschah, nachdem Nora ihren Mann verlassen hatte?: Acht Hörspiele, edited by Helga Geyer-Ryan (Munich: Deutscher Taschenbuch Verlag, 1982);

Die Klavierspielerin (Reinbek: Rowohlt, 1983); translated by Joachim Neugroschel as *The Piano Teacher* (New York: Weidenfeld & Nicolson, 1988);

Theaterstücke, edited by Uta Nyssen (Cologne: Prometh, 1984);

Oh Wildnis, oh Schutz vor ihr (Reinbek: Rowohlt, 1985);

Krankeit oder Moderne Frauen (Cologne: Prometh, 1987).

OTHER: "Statement" and "Untergang eines Tauchers," in *Grenzverschiebung: Neue Tendenzen in der deutschen Literatur der 60er Jahre*, edited by Renate Matthaei (Cologne & Berlin: Kiepenheuer & Witsch, 1970), pp. 215-218;

"Der fremde! störenfried der ruhe eines sommerabends der ruhe eines friedhofs," in *Der gewöhnliche Schrecken: Horrorgeschichten*, edited

Elfriede Jelinek (photo copyright © by Isolde Ohlbaum, Munich)

by Peter Handke (Munich: Deutscher Taschenbuch Verlag, 1971), pp. 135-147;

"Der brave Franz ist brav," in *Das Einhorn sagt zum Zweihorn: Schriftsteller schreiben für Kinder*, edited by Gert Loschitz and Gertraud Middelhauve (Cologne: Gertraud Middelhauve Verlag, 1974), pp. 126-135;

Thomas Pynchon, *V.: Roman*, translated by Dietrich Stössel and Wulf Teichmann, afterword by Jelinek (Reinbek: Rowohlt, 1976);

217

"Erschwerende Umstände oder kindlicher Bericht über einen Verwandten," in *Das Lächeln meines Großvaters und andere Familiengeschichten: erzählt von 47 deutschen Autoren*, edited by Wolfgang Weyrauch (Düsseldorf: Claassen, 1978), pp. 106-111;

"Wenn die sonne sinkt, ist für manche auch noch büroschluß," in *Und wenn du dann noch schreist . . . Deutsche Höspiele der 70er Jahre*, edited by Klaus Klöckner (Munich: Goldmann, 1980), pp. 151-176;

Pynchon, *Die Enden der Parabel–Gravity's Rainbow*, translated by Jelinek and Thomas Piltz (Reinbek: Rowohlt, 1982).

PERIODICAL PUBLICATIONS: "Elfriede Jelinek: 5 Gedichte," *protokolle* (Vienna), 68 (1968): 65-74;

"Offener Brief an Alfred Kolleritsch und Peter Handke," by Jelinek and Wilhelm Zobl, *manuskripte*, 27 (1969): 3-4;

"wir stecken einander unter der haut: konzept einer television des inneren raums," *protokolle* (Vienna), 70 (1970): 129-134;

"paula bei der rezeption eines buches, das auf dem lande spielt, und in dem sie die hauptrolle spielt," *manuskripte*, 50 (1975): 49-51;

"Der Überfluß ist kein Genuß," *Wespennest* (Vienna), 21 (1975): 62-70;

"kein licht am ende des tunnels–nachrichten über thomas pynchon," *manuskripte*, 51 (1976): 36-44;

"Von Natur aus sind . . . ," *Volkswille* (Klagenfurt), 11 November 1977;

"Was geschah, nachdem Nora ihren Mann verlassen hatte oder Stützen der Gesellschaft," *manuskripte*, 58 (1977/1978): 98-116;

"Der Mythos auf Glanzpaper," *Volksstimme* (Vienna), 28 July 1978;

"Ohne Angst in die Zukunft," *Volkswille* (Klagenfurt), 27 April 1979;

"Weil sie heimlich weinen muß, lacht sie über Zeitgenossen: Über Irmgard Keun," *die horen*, 25 (Winter 1980): 221-225;

"Das im Prinzip sinnlose Beschreiben von Landschaften," *manuskripte*, 69/70 (1980): 6-8;

"Für Elfriede Gerstel: Die Fünfziger Jahre," *Falter* (Vienna), 14 (20 April 1983): 13;

"Schamgrenzen? Die gewöhnliche Gewalt der weiblichen Hygiene," *Die Tageszeitung* (Berlin), 26 November 1983;

"Im Namen des Vaters," *Profil* (Vienna), 50 (12 December 1983): 52-53;

"Der Täter, der Opfer sein will," *Wiener* (Vienna), 48 (April 1984): 34-39.

The satirical-critical, Eastern European-Jewish strand in Austrian literature represented by Joseph Roth, Karl Kraus, Elias Canetti, and Ödön von Horváth persists in the work of Elfriede Jelinek. With those authors she shares mixed ethnic and cultural roots, a profound respect for language, and a commitment to using language to expose abuses of power. Because of the nontraditional aesthetic method she employs–her refusal to project herself into her characters' minds and her portrayal of the destructive impact of individualism on popular culture–her work remains the subject of intense controversy in the German-language press and is only gradually finding acceptance within the academic literary establishment.

Born in the Styrian town of Mürzzuschlag on 20 October 1946, Elfriede Jelinek grew up in Vienna. She was the late-born only child of a Rumanian-German, Catholic mother and a Czechoslovakian-Jewish father. Her mother, Olga Ilona Buchner Jelinek, a forceful, domineering woman from the Viennese upper-middle class, had risen to the position of personnel director at Siemens-Austria during World War II. Her father, Friedrich Jelinek, a chemical engineer, came from the Jewish proletariat and was an ardent social democrat. Diffident and unstable, he was unable to protect his daughter or himself from his wife's aggressiveness.

At her mother's insistence, Jelinek's education began in parochial school. The rigorous discipline of the convent was accompanied by after-school ballet and violin lessons. Concurrent enrollment at the Viennese Conservatory of Music accompanied her transfer from parochial to public school in the fifth grade. The double burden of demanding academic course work and intensive musical studies, which included piano, organ, viola, and composition, added to the stress caused by the tension between her parents. Toward the end of her secondary schooling her father was placed in a mental institution. Following her graduation with distinction from the Albertsgymnasium in 1964, the seventeen-year-old Jelinek suffered an emotional breakdown.

In the two years following her collapse Jelinek turned to writing, a preoccupation to which she largely attributes her recovery. She continued to write while studying art history and drama at the University of Vienna and completing her study of the organ at the conservatory. The first critical recognition and encouragement of her literary talent came in response to poetry she submitted to the Austrian Society for Literature in 1966. She received prizes for poetry and prose at the Twentieth Austrian Festival of Youth and Culture in Innsbruck in 1969.

The success of her first two published novels led to commissions to write radio plays for West German producers, and she received the Radio Play Award of the West German War Blind in 1973. Income from these plays allowed Jelinek to move to Berlin in 1972 and to reside for extended periods in Rome and Paris. She married Gottfried Heinrich Hungsberg, a West German information systems engineer, on 12 June 1974. That same year she joined the Austrian Communist party. She lives with her husband in Munich for a portion of each month and with her mother in Vienna for the remainder. She received the Literature Prize of the City of Bad Gandersheim in 1978.

When Jelinek was twenty-four *wir sind lockvögel baby!* (We're Decoys Baby!, 1970) appeared. The novel was heralded in Western Europe as a brilliant literary realization of the aesthetic principles of pop art. It was actually Jelinek's second novel; the first, *bukolit: hörroman* (Bukolit: A Radio Novel), had been completed in 1968 but was not published until 1979. In their application of the montage technique–mosaiclike composition, linguistic experimentation, and radical rejection of traditional aesthetic canons–these novels reflect the influence of the so-called Wiener Gruppe (Viennese Group). This circle of avant-garde writers–H. C. Artmann, Gerhard Rühm, Konrad Bayer, Oswald Wiener, and Friedrich Achleitner–collaborated from the mid 1950s to the mid 1960s.

Wir sind lockvögel baby! has neither plot nor characters in the traditional sense. A quartet of metamorphic Viennese proletarians surfaces periodically to mingle with figures from cartoons, comic books, advertisements, and adventure films, and with personalities made famous by the media. Allusions to Austrian economic and sociopolitical conditions recur as leitmotifs in fragmentary episodes involving media heroes. Discontinuity is the ordering principle; it is left to the reader to organize the kaleidoscopic play of images. The progressive social disintegration depicted culminates in John F. Kennedy's assassination, totalitarian rule, and nuclear annihilation.

The "decoys" in this phantasmagoria of contemporary commercial iconography are the consumers of popular culture: the mass media's uncritical audience, whose behavior and views are manipulated for profit by the power elite. Jelinek satirizes the myth of the benign moral order conveyed in the images of private detectives and sports heroes served up by the media. The book's revolutionary purpose is stated in the "Operating Instructions" prefacing the novel: "Sie brauchen das ganze nicht erst zu lesen wenn sie glauben zu keiner gegengewalt fähig zu sein" (If you believe yourself to be incapable of counterviolence, don't bother reading the book).

The student movement, which began while she was working on *wir sind lockvögel baby!* and in which she took an active part, opened Jelinek's eyes to the massive social ills perpetuated by the class to which she herself belonged; study of such critics as Roland Barthes, Theodor Adorno, and Marshall McLuhan followed. The process of what she views as her emancipation from bourgeois ideologies is documented in essays published in 1970 and 1971. "Die endlose Unschuldigkeit" (Endless Innocence) is especially valuable for an understanding of her development as a writer. Noting that the positive international critical response to *wir sind lockvögel baby!* came from members of the very power structure the book indicts, Jelinek accuses herself in this essay of having indulged her aesthetic tastes at the expense of communicating with those elements in Austrian society who were in a position to bring about fundamental social change.

The first major publication to follow this period of reflection and self-criticism was *Michael: Ein Jugendbuch für die Infantilgesellschaft* (Michael: A Young Person's Guide to Infantile Society, 1972). Using Freudian concepts, the novel portrays the inability of the consumers of commercial culture to resolve the Oedipal conflict with the societal father represented by the entertainment media. The story follows two sixteen-year-old girls during the first year of their apprenticeship in a coffee company. The thinking and behavior of the adolescents and their families are so dominated by the mass media that they cannot distinguish personal from electronically mediated experience. Unable to resolve the contradictions between the expectations raised by the world portrayed on television and hostility they encounter in the real world, they retreat into total passivity and dependency. *Michael* is a superbly wrought piece of experimental prose and a penetrating

Cover of Jelinek's 1980 novel based on an actual case of an honor student who killed and dismembered his mother, father, and sister

ing a skilled trade, Brigitte by marrying a man "with a future." Under the influence of her family and peers, Paula abandons the difficult path to independence in favor of that supreme good, love. Her marriage ultimately leads her to the very job on the production line in a brassiere factory from which Brigitte had escaped by marrying a skilled tradesman. Brigitte pays for her success—obtained through pregnancy in the nick of time—with a life of emotional atrophy. Both women are the victims of myths against which they are defenseless. Their fates are determined by the Olympians of business and industry, whose lives, as portrayed in popular magazines and television, provide the models the women struggle to emulate.

Feminists lauded *Die Liebhaberinnen* for its attack on a patriarchal society that forces women to seek their identity through men, thereby setting woman against woman and chaining them to a life of servility. Marxists recognized in it the portrayal of human relationships shaped by a dehumanizing economic system. Literary critics praised the author's keen powers of observation and brilliant command of language but objected to her acerbic, reductive, arbitrary treatment of her characters and the vulgarity and artificiality of the world she created, charges that have regularly greeted the performance or publication of her works. In fact, Jelinek treats her characters with the contempt she sees accorded the underprivileged in real life. The vehemence of her sarcasm is a measure of her compassion for the suffering of the human beings the characters represent.

In a manner reminiscent of socialist realism, she illustrates in the play *Was geschah, nachdem Nora ihren Mann verlassen hatte oder Stützen der Gesellschaften* (Whatever Happened to Nora after She Left Her Husband; or, The Pillars of Societies, radio version broadcast 1979, published 1982; stage version published 1977, premiered 1979), a sequel to Henrik Ibsen's *A Doll's House* (1879), how a small capitalist elite is able to control political and economic institutions and, through them, the destinies of the many. Nora, with effusive self-congratulation, frees herself from her upper-class role as a wife and mother to become a factory worker; she goes on to become the paramour of an industrial magnate and finally the shrewish wife of a shopkeeper. The "pillars of societies" in Jelinek's play are of two types: rebels in illusory pursuit of self-fulfillment like Nora, and laborers and shopkeepers who

novel of social criticism. It uses the principles of serial music, an Austrian tradition with which Jelinek was familiar as a musician and for which she has a particular affinity. The young author had acquired a style that satisfied her own aesthetic demands and, at the same time, communicated to readers not familiar with avant-garde literature.

Marriage and women's place in the work force are the main themes in *Die Liebhaberinnen* (The Lovers, 1975; translated as *The Brassiere Factory*, 1987), Jelinek's third and most widely read novel. The locale is the Alpine uplands of bucolic myth and flourishing tourism. Two women resolve to escape the cycle of dependency and deprivation in which they feel trapped: Paula by learn-

Jelinek (photo copyright © by Isolde Ohlbaum, Munich)

take fierce pride in their purported independence. By not using her newfound self-reliance to organize plant workers into an effective alliance, Nora chooses an individualistic rather than a cooperative approach to freeing her female coworkers from servitude. Her wan idealism leaves no trace in the lives of the women she vowed to emancipate. Nora walked out of her doll's house, but she remains the marionette of her bourgeois mentality. Thinking that they had in Jelinek a strong supportive voice, feminists were confounded by her treatment of such a prototypical emancipated woman as Ibsen's Nora; but memories of her mother's authoritarianism and cruelty precluded any sentimental or idealized portrayal of females. In response to questions about the feminist movement, Jelinek has consistently emphasized her belief in the primacy of economic over biological or cultural factors in governing relations between the sexes.

The consequences of an elitist mentality for young people maturing in a period of economic and political insecurity are explored in *Die Ausgesperrten* (The Excluded, 1980), a novel that gained a degree of notoriety through Franz Novotony's 1982 film version. The novel is set in the postwar recovery years of the 1950s, but the plot is based on a sensational 1965 case of an eighteen-year-old honor student at a Viennese college preparatory school who killed and dismembered his mother, father, and sister. Rainer Witkowski and his twin sister, Anna–the offspring of a former SS officer who is now a doorman and a severely abused former schoolteacher who is now a cleaning woman–try to escape their sordid home life by cultivating pretensions to genius, feigning contempt for their schoolmates' tastes and possessions, and committing senseless and increasingly violent criminal acts. The prospect of life apart from the hierarchy of the school, and the failure to attract the interest of an aristocratic classmate, shatter Rainer's narcissistic illusions. He commits his grisly act of self-assertion in pathetic imitation of Camus's Stranger.

The affinity between elitism and fascism postulated in *Die Ausgesperrten* takes broad historical dimensions in *Clara S.: Musikalische Tragödie* (Clara S.: Musical Tragedy, premiered 1982, published in *Theaterstücke* [Plays], 1984), Jelinek's first work conceived explicitly for the theater. Imagining a meeting between the German pianist Clara Wieck Schumann and the Italian writer, military hero, and cult figure Gabriele D'Annunzio, Jelinek explores male domination and women's self-destructive response to it from the perspective of an intelligent, sensitive artist. In search of money to finance treatment for her insane husband, the composer Robert Schumann, Clara comes to D'Annunzio's sumptuous villa near Gardone. She hopes to gain his favor by appealing to his respect for a fellow genius. D'Annunzio's lecherous and cynical assaults on her integrity as a woman, musician, wife, and mother force Clara to reflect on the circumstances that have brought her to Gardone. She gradually comes to understand that she has sacrificed her entire life and creative potential for the myth of male artistic genius, and that through this self-betrayal she has destroyed her husband and her children as well.

In *Clara S.* music functions as a metaphor for an ideology of individualism that invites total discipline of the self and totalitarian discipline of others. The most penetrating and poignant expression of the consequences of this ideology is the most critically acclaimed of Jelinek's books, the autobiographical *Die Klavierspielerin* (The Female Pianist, 1983; translated as *The Piano Teacher*, 1988). Erika Kohut, a thirty-year-old piano instructor at the Vienna Conservatory of Music, attracts the fleeting erotic interest of a student, Walter Klemmer. The desire for emotional fulfillment stirred by the young man's attention leads Erika into progressively more severe conflicts with her mother and with the patterns of repression and manipulation to which she has been subjected since childhood. Barred by discipline and contempt for the commonplace from indulging her reawakened sexual interests, Erika is driven to voyeurism. Having never experienced affection as a child, Erika can conceive of human intimacy only as relationships of power. Alternately humiliating Klemmer and debasing herself, she demands, as a final test of his love, that he subject her to sadomasochistic acts according to her instructions. Both offended and aroused by this chal-

lenge to his masculinity, Klemmer fails the paradoxical test–the real purpose of which was to see whether love would triumph over the will to dominate and prevent him from obeying her instructions–when he assaults and reviles her. Mother Kohut sacrificed Erika's childhood and youth for the sake of financial security and social status. The piano teacher's estrangement from her own sexuality and from her peers, and her inability to give and receive affection, are the results of a socialization process aimed at creating a dependent, alienated being whose behavior can be predicted and managed. "Vertrauen ist gut, Kontrolle ist besser!" (Trust is fine, but control is better!). The relationship of mother and daughter in *Die Klavierspielerin* is a metaphor for social relationships in a capitalist society. Only the delusion of being somehow superior separates the Kohuts' lot from that of the proletariat.

Burgtheater: Posse mit Gesang (Burgtheater: Satiric Comedy with Music, premiered 1985 published in *Theater-stücke*), depicts the private lives of some of the most venerated stars of this preeminent cultural institution. The verbal collage created by the characters' exchanges reveals the celebrities to be a coterie of shallow, racist, petty tyrants whose desire for personal aggrandizement transcends any other concern. The actors' success in representing their past collaboration with the Nazi regime as a form of political resistance is the crowning irony of the play. A storm of denunciation was unleashed in the Austrian press following the premiere in Bonn. Jelinek's links to the great Austrian satirical tradition of Johann Nestroy, Kraus, and Horváth are nowhere more apparent than in this indictment of venality among the cultural elite.

Jelinek has often spoken of her writing as an attempt to make apparent the economic and political structures that motivate people's values, attitudes, and behaviors. Socialization of youth to dependency, manipulation of popular tastes, and violence against women and children are dominant themes in her work. With few exceptions the settings and characters are unmistakably Austrian; the problems, however, are common to all industrialized societies.

Interviews:

Josef-Hermann Sauter, "Interviews mit Barbara Frischmuth, Elfriede Jelinek, Michael Scharang," *Weimarer Beiträge*, 6 (1981): 99-128;

Hilda Schmölzer, "Elfriede Jelinek: Ich funktioniere nur im Beschreiben von Wut," in her *Frau sein & schreiben: österreichische Schriftstelle-*

rinnen definieren sich selbst (Vienna: Österreichischer Bundesverlag, 1982), pp. 84-90;

Georg Biron, "Wahrscheinlich wäre ich ein Lustmörder: Ein Gespräch mit der Schriftstellerin Elfriede Jelinek," *Die Zeit*, 28 September 1984, pp. 47-48;

Jacqueline Vansant, "Gespräch mit Elfriede Jelinek," *Deutsche Bücher*, 15 (1985): 1-9;

Donna Hoffmeister, "Access Routes into Postmodernism: Interviews with Innerhofer, Jelinek, Rosei, and Wolfgruber," *Modern Austrian Literature*, 20, no. 2 (1987): 97-130.

References:

Alexander Bormann, " 'Von den Dingen, die sich in den Begriffen einnisten': Zur Stilform Elfriede Jelineks," in *Beiträge des Internationalen Kolloquiums: Frauenliteratur in Österreich von 1945 bis heute*, edited by Carine Kleiber and Erika Tunner (Bern, Frankfurt am Main & New York: Lang, 1986), pp. 27-54;

Rudolf Burger, "Dein böser Blick, Elfriede, " *Forum*, 30 (20 April 1983): 48-51;

Ria Endres, "Ein musikalisches Opfer," *Der Spiegel*, 37 (23 May 1983): 174-177;

Rüdiger Engerth, "Modelle und Mechanismen der Trivialliteratur," *Die Furche* (Vienna), 25 July 1970;

Georg Hensel, "Gehemmte weibliche Kunstproduktionen: *Clara S.*, eine 'musikalische Tragödie' von Elfriede Jelinek–Uraufführung in Bonn," *Frankfurter Allgemeine Zeitung*, 29 September 1982;

Joachim Kaiser, "Meine lieben jungen Freunde: Ein Jugendbuch für die Infantilgesellschaft," *Süddeutsche Zeitung*, 16 November 1972;

Marcelle Kempf, "Elfriede Jelinek ou la magie du verbe contre l'abêtissement et le conformisme," *Etudes allemandes et autrichiennes* (Nice), 33 (1977): 133-142;

Hans Christian Kosler, "Weit entfernt von den Menschen," *Süddeutsche Zeitung*, 21 May 1980;

Paul Kruntorad, "Was geschah, als Elfriede Jelinek Ibsen verließ: Uraufführung einer *Nora*-Projektion in Graz," *Theater heute* (November 1979);

Elke Kummer, "Glückliches Österreich, heirate," *Die Zeit*, 14 November 1975;

Tobe J. Levin, "Political Ideology and Aesthetics in Neo-Feminist German Fiction: Verena Stefan, Elfriede Jelinek, Margot Schroeder," Ph.D. dissertation, Cornell University, 1979;

Joachim Schmidt, "Das Karussell der Bosheiten: Wien in Bonn," *Frankfurter Allgemeine Zeitung*, 22 November 1985;

Peter Spycher, "Die Klavierspielerin," *World Literature Today*, 58 (Winter 1984): 92;

Jacqueline Vansant, *Against the Horizon: Feminism and Postwar Austrian Women Writers* (New York: Greenwood Press, 1988).

Gert F. Jonke

(8 February 1946-   )

Johannes W. Vazulik
North Dakota State University

BOOKS: *Geometrischer Heimatroman* (Frankfurt am Main: Suhrkamp, 1969); translated by Johannes W. Vazulik as "Geometric Regional Novel" in his "G. F. Jonke's *Geometrischer Heimatroman:* Translation and Critical Introduction," Ph.D. dissertation, Case Western Reserve University, 1974; excerpts translated by Vazulik, *Dimension*, 8, no. 1/2 (1975): 222-241;

Glashausbesichtigung (Frankfurt am Main: Suhrkamp, 1970);

Beginn einer Verzweiflung: Epiloge (Salzburg: Residenz, 1970);

Musikgeschichte (Berlin: Literarisches Colloquium, 1970);

Die Vermehrung der Leuchttürme (Frankfurt am Main: Suhrkamp, 1971);

Die Hinterhältigkeit der Windmaschinen oder Ein Schluck Gras löscht jeden Durst im Inland und im Ausland auch: Tragödie in drei Akten (Frankfurt am Main: Suhrkamp, 1972);

Die Magnetnadel zeigt nach Süden: Roman (Frankfurt am Main: Suhrkamp, 1972);

Im Inland und im Ausland auch: Prosa, Gedichte, Hörspiel, Theaterstück (Frankfurt am Main: Suhrkamp, 1974);

Schule der Geläufigkeit: Erzählung (Frankfurt am Main: Suhrkamp, 1977);

Der ferne Klang: Roman (Salzburg: Residenz, 1979);

Die erste Reise zum unerforschten Grund des stillen Horizonts: Von Glashäusern, Leuchttürmen, Windmaschinen und anderen Wahrzeichen der Gegend (Salzburg: Residenz, 1980);

Erwachen zum großen Schlafkrieg (Salzburg: Residenz, 1982);

Der Kopf des Georg Friedrich Händel (Salzburg: Residenz, 1988).

OTHER: *Weltbilder: 49 Beschreibungen*, edited by Jonke and Leo Navratil (Munich: Hanser, 1970).

Since making his successful literary debut at the age of twenty-three, Gert F. Jonke has established a place for himself as a significant contributor to German-language experimental literature. Early in his career he found support for his creative endeavors in the Forum Stadtpark Graz, the enclave of the avant-garde in Austria, which from the time of its founding in 1960 served as the breeding ground for a diversity of progressive literary and artistic talents. During the Forum Stadtpark's first decade, while official recognition and government stipends were being awarded to the establishment writers who congregated mainly in Vienna, the works of the Graz group began to be published in the Federal Republic of Germany and Switzerland. Jonke, whose first novel was published in Frankfurt am Main, shares in the general tendency of the Austrian experimentalists to seek out reality within language and to view the literary text as an autonomous structure, a linguistic entity that stands only for itself and represents no external reality. While he has also written poetry, plays, radio plays, and film scripts, Jonke's reputation rests primarily on his works of fiction. Their unique narrative construction, approaching the formal abstractness and lyrical intensity of musical compositions, provokes a critical awareness of the problematical interrelationships of language, reality, and art.

Much in Jonke's writing stems from his musical background. Gert Friedrich Jonke was born and reared in Klagenfurt in southern Austria, the son of a pianist. As a boy he studied the piano under his mother's tutelage. He began writing poetry at an early age, when he discovered the limitless possibilities of free verse. After serving in the Austrian Army he enrolled for several semesters in the School for Film and Television of the Academy for Music and Visual Arts in Vienna but left without graduating. He has been a free-lance writer since 1969. He has received many stipends and literary prizes, including the Advancement Prize of the Province of Carinthia in 1971, the Rising Generation Stipend for Litera-

Gert F. Jonke (Brigitte Friedrich, Cologne)

ture in 1973, and the Ingeborg Bachmann Prize in 1977. Jonke has lived for extended periods in Berlin and London and has traveled widely, including South America and the Orient in his itineraries.

Jonke has said that his writing is an attempt to reach a point at which a person can no longer be certain of his sanity. His work is suffused with skepticism toward everything that is ordinarily counted as real because of the deceptiveness of language. He wants to show that linguistic representations of reality are not reality, that language imposes patterns that distort rather than reflect what is real. His aim has been to extract the essence of the linguistic medium and to construct narratives whose significance lies primarily in their form. The result is provocative, highly original narratives in which a limited amount of material is worked and reworked in a multitude of variations in a way similar to a musical composition. Traditional considerations of plot and character are cast aside; events are related in a tentative and nonchronological manner, and the narrative typically proceeds in the subjunctive mood. Jonke

constantly interrupts the narrative thread with new strands of narration, ultimately producing a mazelike but–particularly in his later books–integrated construction. Ironically, even these painstakingly devised linguistic abstractions begin to appear as standing for something else, such as a satirical response to media platitudes or technical and bureaucratic jargon.

Conspicuously absent from Jonke's first published work of fiction, *Geometrischer Heimatroman* (1969; translated as "Geometric Regional Novel," 1974), are the romantically portrayed country folk, predictable melodramatic plot, and idyllic settings that typify the nineteenth-century Heimatroman. The characters in Jonke's work are caricatures; events develop in a seemingly arbitrary manner; and in the interest of objectivity things, people, and action are described in terms of their physical dimensions, using a mathematical vocabulary. The agrarian village depicted in the novel is a well-structured society in which each member's traditional role is carried out with an automatonlike precision; this precision is conveyed by the formularized repetition of trun-

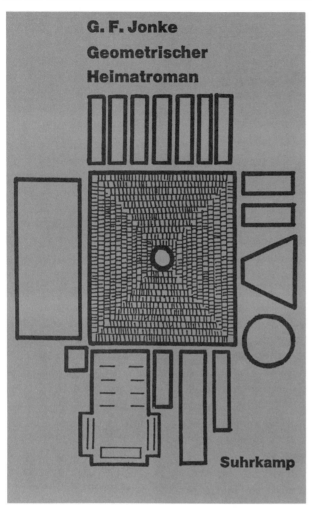

Cover of Jonke's first published work of fiction

power shifts to a nebulous and increasingly repressive authority. Under the pretext of protecting the citizens from bogeymen who hide behind trees, all the trees around the village square are cut down. A law is passed to monitor and control every activity in the region; simply to take a walk in the woods requires submission in duplicate of a lengthy document (six pages in the text) listing the vital–and nonvital–statistics not only of the petitioner but also of all near and distant relatives and acquaintances, as well as certain information that would be self-incriminating. The documents and verbal formulas dictating the course of life reflect the relationship of language to reality and the manner in which thinking and action are linguistically manipulated. The caption under a diagram of the village square says that in this community objects dictate patterns to people. Jonke shows his antipathy to patterned thinking and living by an obsession for equivocation that keeps the reader constantly engaged in deciphering the text's meaning.

The narrator of *Geometrischer Heimatroman* and an anonymous companion, who frequently contradicts the narrator's remarks, relate the story from a hiding place. Rather than providing a ready-made perspective on the events of the novel, the narrator tentatively offers a multitude of possible points of view. For example, the narrator's account of a performance in the town square by a tightrope walker is given in the subjunctive of indirect discourse, an untranslatable feature of the German language which indicates that the actions are being described at second hand. The passage includes fragments of the audience's comments on the show; their opinions differ markedly, essentially invalidating each other. The discrepancy in the assessments demonstrates that the relationship between what people say and what really happens is an arbitrary one. This point is made even more forcefully by the local art critic's comprehensive but blatantly subjective review of the show: its lofty treatment of and exaggerated praise for a carnival act and its exploitation of the event for political purposes show that language, instead of mirroring reality objectively, imposes particular values and attitudes on its users. The narrator's aloof and totally nonjudgmental reporting offers a strong contrast to the art critic's biased account but is no more informative. The pervasive uncertainty in the novel also derives from Jonke's experimentation with a variety of literary styles and narrative techniques and the novel's complicated structure, which

cated sentences and conversational fragments and by carefully calculated descriptions of bodily movements. Gradually the villagers' lives become even more restricted and their environment is radically changed by the advance of industrialization and bureaucratization. In the preindustrial state the village's most prominent figures are the teacher, mayor, and priest. The teacher, whose pedantic and moralistic lesson reads more like a litany than a lecture, is the prime inculcator of societal values, while the mayor and priest, preoccupied with observing ceremony and keeping records, are indifferent to social involvement. The other inhabitants possess a limited repertoire of behaviors which are either rooted in tradition or have been codified in some manner, and interspersed through the text are reproductions of the warning signs, official notices, and ordinances that shape their lives. As this community is confronted with technological development,

Jonke (foreground) in Berlin in 1972 with Gerald Bisinger (left) and H. C. Artmann (photo: Otto Breicha, Vienna)

mixes sketches of daily routine with fantastic dreamlike occurrences, diagrams, aphorisms, songs, historical records, and legal documents.

In his search for an adequate means of expression Jonke frequently uses a series of related or synonymous terms where a single word would ordinarily suffice; the implication is that in conventional usage individual words have lost their original force, which this method of accumulation is meant to restore. The goal of value-free narration accounts for his emphasis on the surface features and physical dimensions of things and his reliance on mathematical terminology to describe them: "Der Silhouettenrand der Bergkette im Norden des Dorfes hat die Form vierer Kurven, die ineinander übergehen: eine Sinuskurve, eine Cosinuskurve und eine Sinus und eine Cosinuskurve um je eindreiviertel Phasen verschoben" (The silhouetted edge of the mountain range north of the village has the shape of four curves that merge into one another: a sine curve, a cosine curve, and a sine and a cosine curve, each displaced by one and three-quarter phases).

The tentativeness permeating the book is part of a deliberate effort to expose all literary illusion to destructive scrutiny. This practice is irritating to the reader accustomed to suspending disbelief when reading fiction; but Jonke's keen insight, imagination, and wit enable him to annoy in a highly amusing way. The literary parodies, satirical sketches of bureaucrats and bourgeoisie, outrageously long compound nouns, preposterous logic, and legal gibberish keep the frightening implications of the contents in check.

In *Glashausbesichtigung* (Hothouse Tour, 1970) the notion that nothing can be perceived with total accuracy is reinforced by the depiction of objects as being in perpetual flux. The narrator's house is variously described as standing near a building site for future residential construction, next to a river, beside a canal, and by a bridge. It is said that the building site, which originated as rumor, only exists because it has been discussed for so long. Horribly and inexplicably building sites begin to multiply, burying each other and the entire landscape. The situation of the hothouse is similarly questionable. The narrator and a companion observing it disagree over its location. They watch people enter it but not re-appear, and they eventually enter it themselves, only to emerge having seen nothing. The book concludes with the narrator being trampled by the products of his own narration–a horde of ram-paging hothouses–illustrating the power of lan-guage to create or destroy reality. The main narra-tive is interrupted by the insertion of many short, stylistically varied narratives, each readable as a self-contained text unconnected to the sections preceding and following it. This seemingly hap-hazard organization spurs the reader to try to sys-tematize the components. Since the reader is free to reconstruct the text and establish networks of as-sociation or significance, he becomes a collabora-tor in creating the work. Whatever compulsion he feels to decipher a pattern gives further evi-dence of the manipulative power of language. The continual building and changing that occur on the landscape constituting the outer reality cor-respond to the writer's linguistically constructed inner reality. While the intertwining narrative threads and constantly shifting perspectives per-mit multiple interpretations, the absence of cer-tainty results in an overwhelming impression of something ominous and uncontrollable.

Jonke's characters allow themselves to be ac-complices in their own exploitation. In *Die Vermehrung der Leuchttürme* (Proliferation of Light-houses, 1971) they work overtime to build light-houses, even though the project is destroying their environment: the grass turns black, the sun is cut into pieces, and an epidemic of coughing breaks out. Lighthouse manufacturing becomes the basis for political alignment, but both the pro-lighthouse and antilighthouse parties are build-ing the beacons. Jonke's constant repetition of im-ages suggests a chronic and pervasive condition of social inertia and resignation.

In 1980 Jonke published *Die erste Reise zum unerforschten Grund des stillen Horizonts* (First Journey to the Unexplored Bottom of the Silent Horizon), which includes revised versions of *Geometrischer Heimatroman, Glashausbesichtigung,* and *Die Vermehrung der Leuchttürme,* plus several other pieces written over a span of fifteen years. "Die Hinterhältigkeit der Windmaschinen" (The Treachery of the Wind Machines), an unper-formed play rewritten in prose form, is about a theater rehearsal during which the actors and di-rector are threatened by winds emanating from thousands of huge concrete buttocks that house all of society's oppressive institutions. With zest-

Cover of Jonke's satirical novel about the art world

ful scatalogical humor Jonke ridicules the authori-tarian institutions and the individuals who seek refuge within them. The prose version of "Die Hinterhältigkeit der Windmaschinen" was later used as the basis for a dramatic presentation in Graz in which Jonke himself appeared.

In all of his works Jonke attempts to illumi-nate the danger in complacently accepting things as they seem to be or as one is told that they are. But while his early narratives create a sense of menace within a broad social context, his later works, beginning with *Schule der Geläufigkeit* (School of Dexterity, 1977), examine the threat in highly subjective terms through the sensations, thoughts, longings, and fantasies of the artist-narrators. The drive to comprehend reality is more urgent when the narrator recognizes that his own existence is at stake. Another develop-ment in Jonke's writing evident first in *Schule der Geläufigkeit* is the evolution of the episodic multiple narratives into an artfully textured, fuguelike whole: fanciful, satirical, and grotesque passages are woven into the narrative to produce a unified composition. The central question in these works is: where does art stand in relation to reality?

Two episodes in the life of a formerly productive and successful composer–a garden party for artists and their patrons and a visit by the composer to the music conservatory where he had been trained–constitute the action in *Schule der Geläufigkeit*. The first episode, subtitled "die gegenwart der erinnerung" (remembrance of the present), opens on a sinister note when the hosts, the photographer Diabelli and his sister Johanna, reveal to the narrator their intention to duplicate perfectly a party that had been held a year earlier and to capture the repetition in photographs identical to the ones taken then. Each of the artists in attendance is a failure in one way or another. Diabelli's plan to re-create the past is both hideous and ludicrous; for him the only legitimate experience is that which occurs in the isolation of the darkroom. Waldstein, the painter, lays claim to profound vision and insight beyond the grasp of ordinary people; his contemplation, waking or sleeping, is never to be disturbed. The poet Kalkbrenner is a fat, beer-guzzling exhibitionist. The composer-narrator is an ineffectual alcoholic, incapable of imposing order on the irrational world around him; his interpretation of events at the party is no more trustworthy than that of any of the other guests, and his lapses into fantasy and hallucination further obscure the novel's meaning.

If the artists are treated unsympathetically, so is their audience. The art patrons include several comically unattractive types: those who subordinate their personal inclinations to the views of imperious critics, those who insist on conventionalism in art, and those who pretend to be refined but are only capable of appreciating the obvious or sensational. That the most ardent patrons of the arts are an undertaker, a proctologist, and the architect of an insane asylum is a far from subtle indication of the precarious existence of the arts in society.

There is a positive side to Diabelli's scheme: were he to be successful in catching time in a loop as he proposes, he would have accomplished what all artists seek to achieve–to capture and hold a moment in which there is no degeneration or death. In the end, the question of whether Diabelli's project is good or evil is rendered moot by Jonke's habit of dashing expecta-

Cover of Jonke's story about a composer who can communicate with caryatids

tions. At the conclusion of the book's first part Diabelli and Johanna deny that they are going to reproduce the earlier party after all, just when the narrator is on the verge of coming to terms with, even relishing, the idea. The narrative that had been so scrupulously constructed is demolished, leaving the impression that all artistic experiments are exercises in futility. Both the narrator and the reader have been manipulated into believing that they were getting somewhere, only to find themselves back where they started.

The pressures that contributed to the composer-narrator's musical sterility and alcoholism are disclosed in the second part of the book, titled "gradus ad parnassum." In the attic of the music conservatory where the composer and his brother, who has become a piano mover, had studied, the brothers are reunited with their former professor, who is now the director of the school. The conversation of the three reveals that the narrator has always been at odds with the rest of society: the brother thinks that he should get a regular job, such as moving pianos; his mentor berates the narrator for excessive body movements while playing and advises him always to practice in front of a mirror; the public rejects his difficult compositions. The composer also suffers from an inability to penetrate beyond the mundane characteristics of his experience: he decries his sense organs as being capable of only superficial sensations and longs for direct contact with a universe that is constricted temporally, spatially, and logically. Jonke's inventive wordplays and coinages, insightful satire, inverted logic, and comically lavish treatment of trivial subjects such as the construction of piano crates are ample reward for the effort demanded to read the novel.

The composer reappears in *Der ferne Klang* (The Distant Sound, 1979). The title refers to the strange and elusive music that the composer hears and pursues throughout the book. The novel begins with the composer, in a state of semiconsciousness, carrying on a dialogue with himself concerning self-awareness. Fantastic images and musical ideas occur to him and remain after he awakens to find himself in a psychiatric clinic. He has no recollection of his own identity or of events leading up to his hospitalization but is told that he has tried to commit suicide. His medical file and a nurse with whom he apparently fell in love have disappeared. He escapes from the clinic and begins to search for the nurse, who may hold the key to his identity. While spending the night in an inn he hears rhythmic sounds coming from the next room which cause him to have an erotic dream; in the morning he discovers that the sounds were those of a woman dying. To elude the hospital authorities and search for his lover the composer joins an avant-garde theater troupe traveling by train. In the course of their travels the composer watches a tightrope walker who performs without a rope, walking in the air by the power of concentration. The theater director asks him to compose a violin piece using only the note D-sharp, and he tries to comply. Eventually the train returns him to the place where he got on, still without his lover and ignorant of his past. Later he arrives in a city where a tumultuous celebration is taking place. What at first looks like snow falling in the middle of summer is actually confetti made from shredded government documents captured in a revolution that has just occurred. By nightfall this euphoric scene has been transformed into a dismal repetition of the

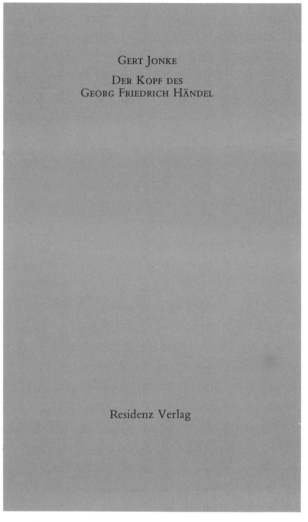

GERT JONKE
DER KOPF DES
GEORG FRIEDRICH HÄNDEL

Residenz Verlag

Title page for Jonke's story of the deathbed reflections of the composer

prerevolutionary condition of misery and oppression. Cause and effect, beginning and end continually flow into each other. The composer flees into the country, where he discovers that the magically beautiful sound that has attracted him throughout the story is the wind blowing through decaying cornstalks. It is the kind of music the composer yearns to produce, but it is impossible to write because it is intrinsic to nature and cannot be extracted. Ironically, nature only creates the music in the process of self-destruction. The book ends just as it began, with the semiconscious composer talking to himself about self-awareness.

If Jonke gives the impression of teetering on the brink of insanity in his writing, he has reached his goal of exploring the border region between sanity and madness. A similar compul-

Jonke (photo copyright © by Isolde Ohlbaum, Munich)

sion motivates the actress-writer in *Erwachen zum großen Schlafkrieg* (Awakening to the Great Sleep War, 1982). The narrator, Burgmüller, is a composer who calls himself an acoustical interior designer. He has the ability to hear with his eyes, a talent that enables him to communicate with the city's caryatids and telamones. These statues confide to him their utter ignorance of sleep, and he responds by conducting sleep seminars for them. Burgmüller and the telamones face similar fates: like them he has to balance a towering column on his head, except that his is a column of air rather than stone; and he too inhabits a world of continuous repetition. The caryatids and telamones could alter their circumstances by falling asleep, but that would cause the collapse of the city and would be an act of war.

Burgmüller becomes involved with an actress-writer whose ambition is to prove that the world exists merely as an invention: that is, by virtue of a convincing description. She wants to reduce reality to letters, words, and sentences, but such an undertaking requires an entirely new language and is fraught with danger. She runs the

risk of becoming so absorbed in her speculations that she will go insane. Nevertheless, not to pursue the project seems intolerable to her.

In the story *Der Kopf des Georg Friedrich Händel* (The Head of George Frederick Handel, 1988) the composer, on his deathbed, finds his memory jogged by a doctor's reference to the spa in Aachen; exactly twenty-two years earlier, Handel had gone there to recover from a stroke. He recalls the highs and lows of a long, prolific career: his early ambition to succeed Dietrich Buxtehude as the organist at Lübeck that was thwarted by his refusal to accept Buxtehude's condition that the new organist marry his daughter, his great success in Italy and then in England, his illness and the convalescence in Aachen, the decline in his popularity as tastes changed and the public became more attracted to works like John Gay's *Beggar's Opera*, and his triumphal resurgence with the composition and performance of the *Messiah*. Evidencing Jonke's affinity for musical forms, the book is characterized by thematic repetition and variation and by exploitation of the rhythmic and acoustic properties of language. Throughout are the comic elements that have come to be recognized as hallmarks of Jonke's work: linguistic drolleries, gigantic word clusters, and ironic twists (such as that which occurs at the massive celebration of the Peace of Aachen, where Handel conducts the musical accompaniment to a huge fireworks display: the fireworks cause a fire that results in members of the audience becoming the first victims of the peace). The tone and style of the narrative complement the depicted contradictions of Handel's life–hedonistic self-indulgence on the one hand and the prodigious output of ethereal music on the other.

Jonke is striving for a medium of expression that is so apt that it renders itself unnecessary. He alludes to this pursuit in his repeated references to the tightrope walker whose crowning achievement would be to perform without the rope. The conflict between an infinite artistic vision and the limitations of finite form is one that Jonke has been inclined to treat with humor and wit rather than with desperation. He is preoccupied with the question: does art mirror reality or does reality mirror art? It is in keeping with the inherent circularity of this question that for Jonke trains must always arrive at their point of departure.

References:

Maximilian Aue, "Natur und Geometrie: Eine Anmerkung zu Gert Friedrich Jonkes Roman *Geometrischer Heimatroman*," *Modern Language Notes*, 90 (October 1975): 696-702;

Thomas Beckermann, "Kalkül und Melancholie oder Die Vorstellung und die Wirklichkeit: Über Gert Jonke," in *Wie die Grazer auszogen, die Literatur zu erobern*, edited by Peter Laemmle and Jörg Drews (Munich: Edition text + kritik, 1975), pp. 200-220;

Maria Luise Caputo-Mayr, "Jonkes *Geometrischer Heimatroman*: Will er sich einen Jux machen?," *Modern Austrian Literature*, 15, no. 2 (1982): 57-63;

Martin Esslin, "Ein neuer Manierismus?: Randbemerkungen zu einigen Werken von Gert F. Jonke und Thomas Bernhard," *Modern Austrian Literature*, 13, no. 1 (1980): 111-128;

Ulrich Greiner, "Gert Jonke," in his *Der Tod des Nachsommers* (Munich: Hanser, 1979), pp. 123-136;

Hannes Rieser, "Die Grammatik des Dorfes," *Literatur und Kritik*, 49 (1970): 560-566;

Johannes W. Vazulik, "An Introduction to the Prose Narratives of Gert Jonke," in *Major Figures of Contemporary Austrian Literature*, edited by Donald G. Daviau (New York, Bern & Frankfurt am Main: Lang, 1987), pp. 293-311;

Vazulik, "G. F. Jonke's *Geometrischer Heimatroman*," *Modern Austrian Literature*, 10, no. 2 (1977): 1-7.

Alfred Kolleritsch
(16 February 1931-   )

Beth Bjorklund
University of Virginia

BOOKS: *erinnerter zorn* (Graz: Privately printed, 1972);
Die Pfirsichtöter: Seismographischer Roman (Salzburg: Residenz, 1972);
Die grüne Seite: Roman (Salzburg: Residenz, 1974);
Einübung in das Vermeidbare: Gedichte (Salzburg: Residenz, 1978);
Im Vorfeld der Augen: Gedichte (Salzburg: Residenz, 1982);
Absturz ins Glück: Gedichte (Salzburg: Residenz, 1983);
Gespräche im Heilbad: Verstreutes, Gesammeltes (Salzburg: Residenz, 1985);
Augenlust: Gedichte (Salzburg: Residenz, 1986).

OTHER: "Gekochte Innenwelt," in *Da nahm der Koch den Löffel: Ein kulinarisches Lesebuch,* edited by Gertrud Frank (Salzburg: Residenz, 1974), pp. 70-82;
"Gangaufsicht," in *Zwischenbilanz: Eine Anthologie österreichischer Gegenwartsliteratur,* edited by Walter Weiss and Sigrid Schmid (Salzburg: Residenz, 1976), pp. 77-79;
"Warum ich schreibe," in *Wie die Grazer auszogen, die Literatur zu erobern,* edited by Peter Laemmle and Jörg Drews (Munich: Deutscher Taschenbuch Verlag, 1979), pp. 85-87.

PERIODICAL PUBLICATIONS: "Wer der Mensch ist," "Das Sagen ist ein Herbeiholen," *protokolle,* 2 (1985): 81-85, 87-94.

Alfred Kolleritsch (photo copyright © by Isolde Ohlbaum, Munich)

If Alfred Kolleritsch was initially known as a catalyst of contemporary Austrian literature, he has since become one of its leading practitioners. His organizational and editorial accomplishments are truly remarkable, and his name has become virtually synonymous with Graz, the Forum Stadtpark, and the journal *manuskripte.* These activities delayed the publication of his own literary work, which began to appear in the 1970s, although some of it had originated ten years earlier. He has received many awards, including the Styrian Literature Prize in 1976 and the Petrarca Prize in 1978, confirming his status as a leading avant-garde writer.

Kolleritsch was born on 16 February 1931 in Brunnsee, in a southern, rural part of Styria. His father was a forester at a castle, a setting that figures prominently in Kolleritsch's first novel. He studied philosophy, history, and German literature at the University of Graz and received his doctorate in 1964 with a dissertation titled "Eigentlichkeit und Uneigentlichkeit in der Philosophie Martin Heideggers" (Authenticity and Inauthenticity in the Philosophy of Martin Heidegger). He has been a professor at a preparatory school in Graz since 1958, and since 1977 he has

233

also taught philosophy at the University of Graz. Although he plays a prominent role in the current literary scene, observers characterize him as a private, modest person who prefers to remain in the background.

Kolleritsch was one of the founding members of the Forum Stadtpark, the arts center in Graz, and has been its president since 1968. It opened in 1960 and has transformed the one-time smug, bourgeois provincial capital into a leading center of avant-garde art in Austria. The Forum Stadtpark serves as a workshop and exhibition hall for artists, musicians, and writers and sponsors an annual arts festival, "Steirischer Herbst" (Styrian Fall). The literary organ of the Forum Stadtpark, *manuskripte,* was also founded in 1960, with Kolleritsch as editor. Kolleritsch and his coeditor Günter Waldorf have made *manuskripte* one of the leading journals of contemporary literature in the German-speaking countries. In 1973 the so-called Grazer Gruppe (Graz Group), including Kolleritsch, was officially organized as the Grazer Autorenversammlung (Graz Authors' Association) in opposition to the more traditional P.E.N. Club in Vienna.

Kolleritsch's first major publication, *Die Pfirsichtöter: Seismographischer Roman* (The Peach Killers: Seismographic Novel, 1972), is an allegory on the structure of power. At the center of the work, set anachronistically sometime before World War I, is a feudal castle. The society is sharply divided into masters and servants, property owners and those without possessions. In lieu of a plot a series of ten loosely connected static tableaux portrays the relations between those above, who talk and eat, and those below, who only serve. The title derives from a scene in which the countess orders a peach tree to be chopped down as an arbitrary demonstration of power to the gardener who regarded it as his creation. In a parallel episode a member of the ruling class shoots a washerwoman's cat. The potential pathos of the topic is avoided by the stylized, mannered mode of narration, which precludes identification with the figures. Sexuality is portrayed as crippled and sterile, adding to the undercurrent of tension beneath the refined surface. Social relations are represented by the food that is eaten, and ritualistic descriptions are given of the hors d'oeuvres and the entrées, with elaborate recipes for preparation. Food becomes a fetish portrayed in grotesque images combined with metaphysical speculations on the nature of temporality. The servants do not eat; neither do they

Cover of the Graz literary magazine founded by Kolleritsch and other members of the Forum Stadtpark in 1960

speak or think, since language also belongs to the masters. The narrator never tells what any of the figures are feeling; he merely reports their actions, often in short sentences in the present tense. As the subtitle indicates, the work functions as a seismograph, registering movements below the surface. The novel stands as a strong statement of the author's opposition to the Hapsburg myth of bygone glory, which, Kolleritsch feels, leads to repressive traditionalism, authoritarian social structures, and uncritical acceptance of the status quo.

The novel *Die grüne Seite* (The Green Side, 1974) presents father-son relationships through three generations from the perspectives of the sons. Five episodes are used as a framework for discussion. The book opens with young Gottfried's father taking him to be photographed. The adolescent experiences an identity crisis in relation to the father and temporarily loses the ability to speak. The next chapter presents Gottfried's son Josef, who at a similar age is a sickly and speechless outsider among the other children. Subsequent scenes show Gottfried and

234

Alfred Kolleritsch
Gespräche im Heilbad

Residenz Verlag

Cover of Kolleritsch's 1985 collection of semi-auto-
biographical stories

Josef at the deaths of their fathers. In the middle chapter Gottfried is at a picnic in the country, discussing the "green side" of life–that elusive something that might be termed happiness or, more appropriately, the inner peace that is lacking in all three generations. The substance of the work is not the action, of which there is little, but the thoughts and conversations that surround the events. All three protagonists–Gottfried's father, Gottfried, and Josef–are introspective types who are inhibited in action and communication but read and think a great deal. They are plagued by anxiety and dissatisfaction. If the narrator identifies with anyone, it is with the sons in each generation, for whom the future exists as an open possibility–before it closes in on them. The image of the father remains indelibly imprinted on the son's mind for a lifetime; the son becomes a father in a vain attempt to escape from the status of being a son. The anxieties and insecurities, the sense of failure and resignation, are perpetuated. The characters constantly talk about change, particularly in regard to social, political, and economic issues, yet they are unable to effect change in their own lives, which remain static and unfulfilled.

Critics have often associated Kolleritsch with the movement in West Germany and Austria in the 1970s called "neue Subjektivität" (new subjectivity), as represented by Nicolas Born, Michael Krüger, and Peter Handke. This designation is, however, not entirely correct, for in essays such as "Wer der Mensch ist" (Who Man Is, 1985) Kolleritsch rails against the naive reduction of an individual into an "inner" and an "outer" self. *Die grüne Seite* could be considered a forerunner of the spate of "father" novels by Peter Härtling, Jutta Schutting, and Christoph Meckel that appeared around 1980; the absence of psychologizing in Kolleritsch's novel, however, sets it apart from other treatments of the topic. Both of Kolleritsch's novels bear some similarities to the popular subgenre of the later 1970s known as the "negativer Heimatroman" (negative regional novel); in contrast to the realistic and naturalistic works by Franz Innerhofer, Gernot Wolfgruber, and Michael Scharang, however, Kolleritsch's novels operate on an abstract philosophical and metaphorical level. Perhaps for that reason they did not attract wide attention.

After a small poetry collection published privately in 1972, Kolleritsch's first major volume of poetry, *Einübung in das Vermeidbare* (Exercise in the Avoidable, 1978), won the prestigious Petrarca Prize, catapulting the author to literary prominence. It was followed by three more volumes of poetry. In *Im Vorfeld der Augen* (In the Foreground of the Eyes, 1982) skepticism toward language emerges as a main theme: "Warum schaufelt und schaufelt man, / was das Auge aufwirft, / zurück in die Sätze / und sagt den Dingen die Litanei, / daß sie sind?" (Why do we shovel and shovel, / what the eye brings up, / back into the sentences / and say to the things the litany, / that they are?). Language criticism is even more intense in *Absturz ins Glück* (Fall into Happiness, 1983), with its logical paradoxes, apparent contradictions, double negations, and elaborations on what is *not* the case. There is reflection on the vast discrepancy between speech and what it is meant to signify: "Die schönen Wörter / erinnern uns an nichts" (The beautiful words /

Kolleritsch (photo: Brigitte Friedrich, Cologne)

remind us of nothing), the world remains "stumm mit unsren Wörtern" (mute with our words), and words become merely marks for "den Verlust des Bezeichneten" (the loss of the signified). The attempts to bring together word and thing resemble a dance around a hollow center; the goal recedes as one approaches, with the pursuit leading to an infinite regression. There are many parallels to poststructuralist thought on language and its limits. *Augenlust* (Eye Joy, 1986) continues some of the same themes but places more emphasis on temporality and mortality.

The collection *Gespräche im Heilbad* (Conversations at a Spa, 1985) consists of eight semiautobiographical prose pieces, several of which were published in journals and anthologies in the 1970s. Some of the themes from the novels recur. The pressure on a child to conform is treated in "Die Ebene" (The Plain), in which a schoolteacher forces a boy to learn to ski: "Sie hatte mich mit dem besten Schi um meine Freiheit gebracht" (She took away my freedom by giving me the best skis). In this piece Kolleritsch, who was seven years old at the time of the politi-

cal union of Austria with Germany in 1938, presents a chronicle of a physical education class under the Nazis, demonstrating the methods of indoctrination and brutalization. "Von der Unwahrheit der Wahrheit" (On the Untruth of Truth) shows the implications of the claims to certainty by those who believe that they are in possession of the truth; the results are inhuman discipline, absolute uniformity, suppression of individuality, and banishment of critical thought. The author speaks from experience when he discusses the Nazi movement in the ostensibly idyllic world of the farmers and artisans, and he concludes, "Das Übel liegt in der Herkunft der Macht" (The evil lies in the origins of power). The Nazis were defeated in 1945, but Kolleritsch finds that the authoritarian thought patterns and the willingness to accept political doctrines as absolute truth did not change. In "Die Gleichheit als Feind" (Uniformity as Enemy) he writes about the 1981 reunion of a former SS unit: not only has the older generation not changed but the group has been joined by many new members from the younger generation. In denouncing fascist activity Kolleritsch is well aware that he himself is taking an ideological stance with claims to authority; the only solution, he finds, is constant critical awareness on the part of each individual. It is thus disturbing to him when his own students repeat the clichés of liberalism and democracy, indicating that they, like the students during the Nazi period, have simply adopted an ideology without learning how to think. One of the artistically most successful pieces is "Das Einzelne und das Allgemeine" (The Particular and the General), a discussion between a man–presumably the author–and a woman who ironically comments that he talks like a book. This double perspective is vintage Kolleritsch; reality, in his view, is too multifaceted to be captured by any generalization, and the highest authority must be the independent and alert individual. In a letter to his baby son, "Brief an Julian" (Letter to Julian), he articulates his pedagogical theories and expresses the hope that he can avoid some of the errors portrayed in *Die grüne Seite*. The exercise of individuality is ultimately demonstrated in the delightful title piece, in which the author and his companions enjoy the sensuousness of the healing baths, the richness of human relations, and the stimulation of reading, thinking, and conversation.

Kolleritsch occupies an important place in contemporary literature between realism and idealism. What separates him from the latter is his mistrust of beautiful language, "die schönen Wörter"; what separates him from the former is his yearning for it. Whether in the sociopolitical criticism of the prose or the more individual experience of the poetry, his work is a philosophical enterprise. Some commentators say that it is too intellectual; others take the view that the days of naive, spontaneous literary creation are over and regard Kolleritsch's work as an intelligent, sensitive response to the state of the modern world.

References:

Wolfgang Bauer, "Rede auf Alfred Kolleritsch," in his *Die Sumpftänzer* (Cologne: Kiepenheuer & Witsch, 1978), pp. 376-379;

Beth Bjorklund, "Metaphors as Frescoes: Interview with Alfred Kolleritsch," *Literary Review*, 25 (Winter 1982): 263-267;

Peter Handke, "Der tiefe Atem: Rede zur Verleihung des Petrarca-Preises 1978 an Alfred Kolleritsch," in *Wie die Grazer auszogen, die Literatur zu erobern*, edited by Peter Laemmle and Jörg Drews (Munich: Deutscher Taschenbuch Verlag, 1979), pp. 78-83;

manuskripte, special Kolleritsch issue, edited by Helmut Eisendle and Klaus Hoffer (1981);

Manfred Mixner, "Alfred Kolleritsch," in *Kritisches Lexikon zur deutschsprachigen Gegenwartsliteratur*, edited by Heinz Ludwig Arnold (Munich: Edition text + kritik, 1978);

Urs Widmer, "Ferne Vergangenheit oder ferne Zukunft? Über die Romane von Alfred Kolleritsch," in *Wie die Grazer auszogen, die Literatur zu erobern*, pp. 71-77.

Alexander Lernet-Holenia

(21 October 1897-3 July 1976)

Hugo Schmidt

University of Colorado, Boulder

BOOKS: *Pastorale* (Vienna: Wiener Literarische Anstalt, 1921);

Kanzonnair (Leipzig: Insel, 1923);

Demetrius: Haupt- und Staatsaktion (Berlin: Fischer, 1926);

Ollapotrida: Komödie in zwei Akten (Berlin: Fischer, 1926);

Österreichische Komödie (Berlin: Fischer, 1927);

Das Geheimnis Sankt Michaels (Berlin: Fischer, 1927);

Parforce: Komödie (Berlin: Fischer, 1928);

Die nächtliche Hochzeit: Haupt- und Staatsaktion (Berlin: Fischer, 1929);

Die nächtliche Hochzeit: Roman (Berlin: Fischer, 1930);

Kavaliere: Komödie in drei Akten (Berlin: Fischer, 1931);

Die Abenteuer eines jungen Herrn in Polen: Roman (Berlin: Kiepenheuer, 1931); translated by Alan Harris as *A Young Gentleman in Poland* (London: Duckworth, 1933);

Die Lützowschen Reiter (Berlin: Kiepenheuer, 1932);

Ljubas Zobel: Roman (Berlin: Kiepenheuer, 1932); republished as *Die Frau im Zobel: Roman* (Munich: List, 1954);

Jo und der Herr zu Pferde: Roman (Berlin: Kiepenheuer, 1933);

Ich war Jack Mortimer: Roman (Berlin: Fischer, 1933);

Olympische Hymne (Vienna: Reichner, 1934);

Die Standarte: Roman (Berlin: Fischer, 1934); translated by Harris as *The Glory Is Departed* (New York & London: Harper, 1936); translation republished as *The Standard* (London & Toronto: Heinemann, 1936); German version republished as *Das Leben für Maria Isabella: Roman* (Frankfurt am Main: Ullstein, 1966);

Die Frau des Potiphar: Komödie (Berlin: Fischer, 1934);

Die goldene Horde: Gedichte und Szenen (Vienna: Reichner, 1935);

Die neue Atlantis: Erzählungen (Berlin: Fischer, 1935);

Alexander Lernet-Holenia (Bildarchiv der Österreichischen Nationalbibliothek)

Der Baron Bagge: Novelle (Berlin: Fischer, 1936); translated by Richard and Clara Winston as "Baron Bagge," in *Count Luna: Two Tales of the Real and the Unreal* (New York: Criterion Books, 1956), pp. 3-70; republished as *Count Luna & Baron Bagge* (London: Blond, 1960);

Der Herr von Paris: Eine Erzählung aus der Zeit der großen Revolution in Frankreich (Vienna: Reichner, 1936);

Die Auferstehung des Maltravers: Roman (Vienna: Reichner, 1936); translated by Joachim Neugroschel as *The Resurrection of Maltravers* (Hygiene, Colo.: Eridanos, 1989);

Der Mann im Hut: Roman (Berlin: Fischer, 1937);

Riviera: Roman (Berlin: Fischer, 1937);

Mona Lisa: Erzählung (Vienna: Höger, 1937); translated by Jane B. Greene as "Mona Lisa," in *German Stories and Tales*, edited by Robert Pick (New York: Knopf, 1954);

Glastüren (Berlin: Fischer, 1937);

Strahlenheim: Erzählung (Berlin: Fischer, 1938);

Ein Traum in Rot: Roman (Berlin: Fischer, 1939);

Mars im Widder: Roman (Berlin: Fischer, 1941; edition confiscated and destroyed; republished, Stockholm: Bermann-Fischer, 1947);

Beide Sizilien: Roman (Berlin: Suhrkamp, 1942);

Die Titanen: Gedichte (Vienna: Amandus, 1945);

Die Trophae, volume 1: *Gedichte*; volume 2: *Szenen: Saul; Alkestis; Lepanto* (Zurich: Pegasus, 1946);

Germanien (Stockholm: Bermann-Fischer, 1946);

Spangenberg: Erzählungen (Vienna: Bellaria, 1946);

Der siebenundzwanzigste November: Erzählungen (Vienna: Amandus, 1946);

Der 20. Juli: Erzählung (Vienna: Erasmus, 1947);

Spanische Komödie, in drei Akten (Vienna: Bermann-Fischer, 1948);

Der Graf von Saint-Germain: Roman (Zurich: Morgarten, 1948);

Das Feuer: Gedichte (Vienna: Erasmus, 1949);

Die Inseln unter dem Winde: Roman (Frankfurt am Main: Fischer, 1952);

Die Wege der Welt: Erzählungen (Vienna: Herold, 1952);

Die drei Federn: Erzählung (Graz, Vienna & Munich: Stiasny, 1953);

Der junge Moncada: Roman (Zurich: Rascher, 1954);

Das Finanzamt: Aufzeichnungen eines Geschädigten (Hamburg & Vienna: Zsolnay, 1955);

Der Graf Luna: Roman (Vienna: Zsolnay, 1955); translated by Greene as "Count Luna," in *Count Luna: Two Tales of the Real and the Unreal*, pp. 73-240;

Radetzky: Schauspiel in drei Akten (Frankfurt am Main: Fischer, 1956);

Das Goldkabinett: Roman, nach dem Italienischen des G. Montebachetta (Hamburg & Vienna: Zsolnay, 1957);

Die Schwäger des Königs: Schauspiel in drei Akten (Hamburg & Vienna: Zsolnay, 1958);

Die vertauschten Briefe: Roman (Hamburg & Vienna: Zsolnay, 1958);

Die wahre Manon (Hamburg & Vienna: Zsolnay, 1959);

Der wahre Werther (Hamburg & Vienna: Zsolnay, 1959);

Title page for Lernet-Holenia's novel about a young Austrian officer who is trapped behind Russian lines during World War I, disguises himself as a milkmaid, and becomes a hero

Mayerling: Erzählungen (Hamburg & Vienna: Zsolnay, 1960);

Prinz Eugen (Hamburg & Vienna: Zsolnay, 1960);

Naundorff (Hamburg & Vienna: Zsolnay, 1961);

Das Halsband der Königin (Hamburg & Vienna: Zsolnay, 1962);

Das Bad an der belgischen Küste (Vienna & Hamburg: Zsolnay, 1963);

Götter und Menschen (Vienna & Hamburg: Zsolnay, 1964);

Die weiße Dame: Roman (Vienna & Hamburg: Zsolnay, 1965);

Theater: Glastüren; Spanische Komödie; Die Thronprätendenten (Vienna & Hamburg: Zsolnay, 1965);

Pilatus: Ein Komplex (Vienna & Hamburg: Zsolnay, 1967);

Die Hexen: Roman (Vienna & Hamburg: Zsolnay, 1969);

Die Geheimnisse des Hauses Österreich: Roman einer Dynastie (Zurich: Flamberg, 1971);

Pendelschläge: Drei Erzählungen (Vienna: Zsolnay, 1972);

Konservatives Theater: Dramen (Vienna: Österreichische Verlagsanstalt, 1973).

OTHER: *Dies Büchlein sagt von hoher Minne,* translated by Lernet-Holenia (Vienna: Heidrich, 1922);

Saul, Die Neue Rundschau, 38 (February 1927): 182-198; translated anonymously in *Contemporary One-Act Plays,* edited by Percival Wilde (Boston: Little, Brown, 1936);

"Maresi," in *Maresi von Alexander Lernet-Holenia und andere Proben deutscher Prosa und Poesie,* edited by Lili Dircks and Sixten Wigardt (Stockholm: Fritze, 1936);

Greta Garbo: Ein Wunder in Bildern, introduction by Lernet-Holenia (Vienna: Höger, 1938); republished as *Greta Garbo: Ideal des Jahrhunderts* (Wiesbaden: Limes, 1956);

"Die heiligen drei Könige von Totenleben," in *Die heiligen drei Könige von Totenleben und andere Proben moderner und klassischer deutscher Prosa,* edited by Dircks and Wigardt (Stockholm: Fritze, 1940);

Alessandro Manzoni, *Die Verlobten,* translated by Lernet-Holenia (Zurich: Manesse, 1950);

Egle Marini, *Gedichte,* translated by Lernet-Holenia (Frankfurt am Main: Fischer, 1958);

Stanley Loomis, *Die Dubarry,* translated by Lernet-Holenia (Munich: Biederstein, 1960).

PERIODICAL PUBLICATION: "Adel und Gesellschaft in Österreich," *Der Monat,* 9 (February 1957): 33-43.

Critical evaluations of Alexander Lernet-Holenia teem with recurring clichés: he has been called the cavalier of the pen, the knightly poet, and the grandseigneur and the Lord Privy Seal of Austrian literature. These epithets imply conservatism, rejection of literary innovation, adherence to an antiquated system of values, and a rather gentlemanly attitude to the arts. While some of these characterizations contain some truth, they are superficial and do not capture the significance of Lernet-Holenia's literary achievement. It has also been said that his writings are uneven in quality, and it is true that his oeuvre

Title page for the novel in which Lernet-Holenia uses a mystery story to symbolize the passing of the old Austrian way of life

ranges from light entertainment to works of classical perfection and beauty; but the existence of such a spectrum does not mean that its lighter end is inferior. His lighter plays and novels offer sophisticated entertainment on a high level; in his more subtle works he creates his own poetical world. Without forsaking the elegant urbanity of his style he draws images and symbols that lead the reader to the frontiers of experience, especially the mysterious expanse that lies between life and death.

Alexander Lernet was born in Vienna on 21 October 1897 into a family of military officers; his ancestors came from Austria, Lorraine, and Spain. His father, Alexander Lernet, a lieutenant commander in the Austrian navy, left his wife, Sidonia, shortly after they were married, and the boy was adopted by the family of his mother; from then on he used the hyphenated name Lernet-Holenia. He was raised on the family's es-

Lernet-Holenia (right) with Reinhard Federmann, general secretary of the Austrian P.E.N. Club until his death in 1976. In 1972 Lernet-Holenia resigned from the presidency of the P.E.N. Club to protest the awarding of the Nobel Prize in Literature to Heinrich Böll (Österreichischer P.E.N. Club, Vienna).

tate, Schloß Wasserleonburg, in the province of Carinthia. After attending secondary school he enlisted in a cavalry regiment, serving on the eastern front during World War I. The Austrian cavalry, like the cavalries of other European nations, had become an anachronistic institution: still wearing their colorful uniforms and shakos, they made easy targets for Russian machine gunners. Lernet-Holenia's wartime experiences were to be central to his works. After the war he returned to Carinthia and began to write poetry. Although lambasted by the well-known critic Karl Kraus, he received the praise of such discerning readers as Rainer Maria Rilke and Hermann Bahr for his first volumes of poems. In the mid 1920s Lernet-Holenia turned to writing plays, becoming a successful author of social comedies; it was only after 1930 that he concentrated on short stories and novels. He traveled extensively, especially in the Americas, and stayed in South America for a long period. Several of his novels reflect his South American experiences.

He was drafted into the German army at the outbreak of World War II and fought in Po-

land. After being wounded he served briefly in the military film bureau in Berlin. His novel *Mars im Widder* (Mars under Aries, 1941), set before a background of the war against Poland, was confiscated by the Nazis. Lernet-Holenia spent the remaining war years at his country house in St. Wolfgang, near Salzburg. His plays were not performed, and few of his writings were published. In 1945 he married Eva Vollbach. After the war he divided his time mostly between Vienna and St. Wolfgang; his literary output included novels, essays, translations, and film scripts. He played a prominent role in Viennese society while ridiculing it in his writings. Although deeply rooted in the spiritual atmosphere of the Austrian monarchy, he attacked and exposed its myths. At the same time he opposed the literary avant-garde, and after being elected president of the Austrian P.E.N. Club in 1969, he prevented young writers whose works he considered offensive from joining. In 1972 he resigned the presidency to protest the award of the Nobel Prize in Literature to Heinrich Böll. He died four years later after a lengthy illness.

Lernet-Holenia received many awards: the Kleist Prize in 1926, the Goethe Prize of the City of Bremen in 1927, the Literature Prize of the City of Vienna in 1951, the Great Order of Merit of the Federal Republic of Austria in 1957, the Medal First Class for Science and Art of the Federal Republic of Austria in 1958, the Great Austrian State Prize for Literature in 1961, and the Adalbert Stifter Prize of the City of Linz in 1967.

The poems with which Lernet-Holenia began his literary career shortly after World War I show the influence of Rilke and Hugo von Hofmannsthal and have no affinity to the contemporaneous expressionist movement. The poems excel through a highly accomplished use of language and form and through their splendid imagery. They are of great formal beauty but are devoid of the creative intensity that lends the finest poems their unforgettable quality. The perfection of his prose style, with its sometimes lyrical quality, can be explained by his early preoccupation with difficult verse forms.

In 1925, when Lernet-Holenia began to write for the theater, he explained his reasons for doing so by pointing out that modern man is an activist; the art appropriate to him must be activist as well. The contemplative art of lyrical poetry is defunct, he believed. His plays and scenes of the next two years puzzled his critics; they could not decide into which of the available dramatic categories to place him. He wrote searching and subtle tragedies such as *Demetrius* (1926), *Alkestis* (premiered, 1926; published, 1946), and *Saul* (premiered, 1927; published, 1946; translated, 1936), as well as hilarious social comedies such as *Ollapotrida* (1926) and *Österreichische Komödie* (Austrian Comedy, 1927). Of his early plays, the serious ones have not been successful: *Demetrius* was produced once, *Alkestis* and *Saul* a few times, all in Leipzig; none was performed in Vienna. On the other hand, his early social comedies were popular with audiences. Their plots are inconsequential but cleverly woven, their dialogue is quick and witty, and the situations they present are irresistibly comic. When he received the Kleist Prize it was not clear whether he was being honored for his serious plays or his comedies; certainly the latter were better known to the public. Altogether he wrote eighteen light comedies, some of them as stage versions of his novels and one—*Das Goldkabinett* (The Golden Room, 1957)—as an adaptation from the Italian.

Lernet-Holenia was entering his mid thirties when he turned to fiction, the genre that was to dominate the rest of his career. He wrote two dozen novels and many short stories in a style that is urbane, elegant, polished, and brilliant, while at the same time possessing a charm that makes the reader feel that he is being taken on a fascinating journey by an able and pleasant guide. Many of his works are set in Austria just before, during, and after World War I; the end of the Austro-Hungarian monarchy in 1918, with its concomitant social upheaval, fascinated him. He wrote mostly about the social circles he knew best, aristocrats and military officers; his attitude toward this milieu is by no means uncritical, and it even became aggressive later in his life.

On the surface his first novel (other than a narrative version of one of his plays), *Die Abenteuer eines jungen Herrn in Polen* (The Adventures of a Young Gentleman in Poland, 1931; translated as *A Young Gentleman in Poland*, 1933), is a light and charming book, a classical war story of the "one man alone wins the war" variety. But on closer examination the novel reveals subtleties that give it a unique quality. During the summer of 1917 a young Austrian officer is trapped behind the Russian lines, disguises himself as a girl, is employed as a milkmaid on an estate, spies on the Russian staff officers quartered at the estate, and is finally rescued and celebrated as a hero. But he is unaware of his great deeds and is dumbfounded when he receives a high military honor. The novel is slightly ironic in tone and exposes military incompetence on both sides: commanders do little besides try to save face. Yet these observations are made not angrily but with humor. For example, early in the novel a German-Austrian cavalry attack is launched for no good reason, the commanding officers vie with each other both for greater glory and for the less dangerous positions, the soldiers die in droves, the survivors continue the attack partly out of a sense of duty and partly because their horses are out of control, the attack fails, and the commanders try to justify their order afterward. Absurdly, during the attack the division was under the command of an officer who did not realize that he was in charge; he had unknowingly moved into the position when the commanding general was killed. Chance determines the course of events, and a person's fate depends not on his own choice but on accidental circumstances.

Ljubas Zobel (Luba's Sable Coat, 1932) is another light novel with a profound impact. Like the preceding novel, it is set in Russia toward the end of World War I. Descriptions of the collaps-

Lernet-Holenia (Franz Hubmann, Vienna)

ing front line are interwoven with a love story in which a young Austrian officer rescues a Russian girl from marauders. Again there are scenes that demonstrate the futility of human efforts. One officer, suffering from influenza and trying to control his mutinous troops in a constant downpour, is seized by attacks of helpless rage and is finally killed in combat. In another scene an Austrian cavalry division meets a unit of Mongol horsemen. Uncertain whether they should regard each other as friend or enemy, the two columns ride side by side trying to decide what to do. When the Mongols abuse some civilian travelers, the two units engage in a ferocious battle. Lernet-Holenia's combat scenes are rendered more horrible by his dispassionate tone.

In *Die Standarte* (The Standard, 1934; translated as *The Glory Is Departed*, 1936), one of Lernet-Holenia's finest works, the junior officer of an Austrian regiment struggles against enormous difficulties to carry the regimental banner, hidden under his uniform, back to Vienna to return it to the emperor. But the empire has collapsed, and he arrives at the palace in time to witness the ignominious departure of the emperor. Wandering into a hall where several sergeants are burning stacks of banners in a fireplace, the officer throws his into the flames too.

The work usually regarded as Lernet-Holenia's masterpiece, *Der Baron Bagge* (1936; translated as "Baron Bagge," 1956), also takes place during the Russian campaign of World War I. But the story's theme is one that Lernet-Holenia was to return to again and again: the realm between life and death. During a reconnaissance mission in Hungary a captain insanely orders his cavalry squadron to attack a heavily defended bridge. While galloping across the bridge the protagonist, Bagge, feels that he has been hit by two pebbles. Miraculously, the attack succeeds; strangely, the squadron finds no further sign of the enemy. In a small town Bagge meets a young woman of unearthly beauty and temperament; within a few days they are married. As it advances the squadron has experiences that are more and more fantastic, but only Bagge seems to notice. Finally they approach a bridge that gleams metallically in the distance; drawing closer they find it to be made of gold. At this point Bagge realizes that he must be dreaming. Frantically, he pulls his horse aside, refusing to cross the bridge. He awakens to find himself lying on the bridge the squadron had tried to take. The "pebbles" he had felt were bullets; almost the entire squadron was killed. What Lernet-Holenia has described is what he calls the interval between dying and death. The rest of Bagge's life is changed by the other reality he experienced. If death is a dream, life may be one as well, he feels: "Zwischen den Träumen aber führten Brücken hin und wider, und wer könnte sagen, was Tod und was Leben sei oder wo der Raum und die Zeit zwischen beiden beginnen und wo sie enden!" (There are bridges built between the dreams, and who could say what is life and what is death or where the space and time between them begin and where they end!).

Another frequently recurring motif in Lernet-Holenia's fiction is the loss or exchange of identity, which is central to *Ich war Jack Mortimer* (I Was Jack Mortimer, 1933), *Ein Traum in Rot* (A Dream in Red, 1939), *Beide Sizilien* (The Two Sicilies, 1942), *Die Inseln unter dem Winde* (The Windward Islands, 1952), and *Die weiße Dame* (The White Lady, 1965). It plays a marginal role in other books and seems to have occupied Lernet-Holenia as much as the realm between life and death. A police inspector in *Beide Sizilien* may well express the author's views when he points out that people change so much during their lives that they seem to be playing the roles of others; Napoleon, for example, did not remain an insignificant artillery officer. Man's perpetual change, he concludes, is his only excuse for existing.

Mars im Widder was withheld from sale immediately upon its publication in 1941. The entire edition was hidden in a Leipzig warehouse by friends of Lernet-Holenia but was later destroyed in an air raid. The novel was republished in 1947. The protagonist, a former Austrian army officer drafted into the German forces at the outbreak of World War II, takes part in the fighting in Poland and is wounded twice, but his involvement with mysterious civilians, especially a woman of uncertain identity, overshadows the depiction of military operations. Supernatural experiences play a part, and the actual happenings around him do not command the protagonist's full attention. The book is anything but the type of war novel that would please the authorities of a totalitarian state, and its confiscation was no surprise.

In *Beide Sizilien* several former members of an imperial Austrian cavalry regiment named "Ferdinand der Erste, König beider Sizilien" (Ferdinand I, King of the Two Sicilies)–significantly, after a long vanished kingdom–come to the aid of their colonel, whose daughter has been implicated in the murder of one of their comrades. While investigating the crime and trying to exonerate the young lady, some of them, including the colonel, mysteriously disappear, die in strange accidents, or are wounded in duels. The murderer, whose true identity is a complex issue, is eventually discovered. The detective story, however, is not of central significance to the novel. What Lernet-Holenia is trying to convey is the feeling of a slow fading away, a gradual cessation of life. One character, mysteriously dying of no known medical cause, describes his sensations as he approaches the realm of the dead. The various deaths have an inexplicable interconnection; they are part of the symbolic ambience that characterizes the book. The funeral of one of the men is attended by an association of army veterans carrying an old flag. In describing the flag Lernet-Holenia sums up the transience and futility of worldly concerns: "Wenn die Falten sich rührten, blitzte der gestickte Adler in der Sonne. Er streckte seine Fänge nach Königreichen aus, die es längst nicht mehr gab" (When the cloth moved, the embroidered eagle gleamed in the sun. It reached with its talons for kingdoms that had long since ceased to exist).

With *Der Graf Luna* (1955; translated as "Count Luna," 1956) Lernet-Holenia turned to more recent and even current themes. The industrialist Alexander Jessiersky blames himself for the death of Count Luna in a concentration camp during the Hitler era, although Luna's incarceration happened against Jessiersky's will and only through his negligence. After the war, believing that Luna has survived and is trying to avenge himself, Jessiersky commits several murders in an effort to protect himself and his family. His plan to feign his own death fails, and he perishes while trying to find his way out of the catacombs under Rome. Hovering between life and death, he watches himself leave the catacombs and enter a wintry landscape, where a sleigh waits to take him to his ancestral estate in Poland. He is feted by his ancestors, but he is too tired to think of anything but lying down to rest.

In his later novels Lernet-Holenia mixed scant but amusing action with essayistic reflections. Both *Die weiße Dame* and *Die Hexen* (The Witches, 1969) deal with the fate of the crown jewels of the Austrian and Russian empires, some of which may have been taken illegally and sold by hastily departing members of the ruling houses. But it is the historical and political excursions that give these books their charm and interest. For example, in *Die Hexen* the Iron Curtain plays a role; Lernet-Holenia mentions another significant demarcation line, the Roman *limes*, which ran in a generally east-west direction through Central Europe and signified the boundary of the Roman Empire. Lernet-Holenia pinpoints the spot where the two borders would have intersected and brilliantly compares the situations in the various territories thus marked out.

Lernet-Holenia's historical knowledge was considerable and was not limited to the West. His novels, biographies, and essays show the extent of his research into lesser-known areas and periods. His essay "Adel und Gesellschaft in Österreich" (Nobility and Society in Austria, 1957) pokes fun at the pretense of noble ancestry and points out where one winds up, biologically speaking, when pursuing one's lineage too far back. The novel *Die vertauschten Briefe* (The Switched Letters, 1958) is a hilarious story of fraud in high society; it includes so many actual people and occurrences that it has been called a roman à clef. In *Pilatus: Ein Komplex* (Pilate: A Complex, 1967) he examines the question of the divinity of Christ against a rich background of ancient history and philosophy. In *Die Geheimnisse des Hauses Österreich: Roman einer Dynastie* (Secrets of the House of Austria: Novel of a Dynasty, 1971) he debunks with great relish some of the myths dear to many Austrians, including the sad story of Crown Prince Rudolph's suicide at Mayerling; the kindly old emperor Francis Joseph, who ruled over Austria for sixty-eight years and helplessly watched it collapse; the story of Austria's defeat at Königgrätz in 1866; and the fates of the archdukes and some of the illegitimate offspring of the ruling house. These fiction-alized essays raised the ire of the former aristocrats and monarchists who had always considered Lernet-Holenia one of their own.

In "Die Eroberung von Peru" (The Conquest of Peru), published in the collection *Götter und Menschen* (Gods and Men, 1964), he describes the smile on an excavated sculptured head of an Incan nobleman. It is a mild, imperious, somewhat empty smile, secure in the supremacy of an ancient culture. Even if such perfection is doomed, the enchanting smile endures. The vulgar ordinary world cannot reach it.

Lernet-Holenia's significance has to be seen in the context and tradition of Austrian letters in the late nineteenth and the early twentieth centuries. His language, which is of striking classical purity and great elegance, shows the influence of Rainer Marie Rilke and Hugo von Hofmannsthal; his narrative skill ranks him with Robert Musil and Heimito von Doderer. Despite the great variety of his themes, it is the collapse of the Austro-Hungarian monarchy at the end of World War I and the fate of its scions and servants in a new, baffling era that emerge as the pivotal points of his creative imagination. With a strong tendency toward the mysterious and the supernatural, he was especially fascinated with questions of identity and the threshold between life and death.

Letters:

Monologische Kunst–? Ein Briefwechsel zwischen Alexander Lernet-Holenia und Gottfried Benn (Wiesbaden: Limes, 1953).

References:

Friedrich Ackermann, "Alexander Lernet-Holenias Gedicht 'Der Bethlehemitische Kindermord,'" *Wirkendes Wort,* 11 (1961): 334-344;

Alexander Lernet-Holenia: Festschrift zum 70. Geburtstag des Dichters (Vienna: Zsolnay, 1967);

Armin Ayren, "Alexander Lernet-Holenia 70 Jahre," *Neue deutsche Hefte,* 14 (1967): 118-130;

Ayren, "Der Heilweg: Zu einem zentralen Motiv im erzählerischen Werk Alexander Lernet-Holenia," in Lernet-Holenia, *Der Mann im Hut* (Vienna: Zsolnay, 1976), pp. 289-300;

Ingeborg Brunkhorst, "Studien zu Alexander Lernet-Holenias Roman 'Die Standarte,'" Ph.D. dissertation, University of Stockholm, 1963;

Josef Halperin, "Alexander Lernet-Holenia," *Neue Rundschau*, 58 (1947): 456-465;

Eduard Hebra, "Alexander Lernet-Holenia," *Wort in der Zeit*, 1, no. 4 (1955): 193-199;

Franziska Müller-Widmer, *Alexander Lernet-Holenia: Grundzüge seines Prosawerkes dargestellt am Roman "Mars im Widder." Ein Beitrag zur neueren österreichischen Literaturgeschichte* (Bonn: Bouvier, 1980);

Peter Pott, *Alexander Lernet-Holenia: Gestalt, dramatisches Werk und Bühnengeschichte* (Vienna: Braumüller, 1972);

Harmut Scheible, "Suche nach Identität und Protest gegen Geschichte: Naturgeschichte der Snobs—Aufzeichnungen zu Alexander Lernet-Holenia," *Frankfurter Hefte*, 27 (1972): 275-283;

Hugo Schmidt, "Alexander Lernet-Holenia," in *Major Figures of Modern Austrian Literature*, edited by Donald G. Daviau (Riverside, Calif.: Ariande, 1988), pp. 285-313;

Wolfgang Schneditz, "Alexander Lernet Holenia [*sic*]," *Books Abroad*, 22 (Summer 1948): 229-232;

Hilde Spiel, "Alexander Lernet-Holenia," in her *In meinem Garten schlendernd: Essays* (Munich: Nymphenburger Verlagshandlung, 1981), pp. 91-105;

Eugen Turnherr, "Alexander Lernet-Holenia," in *Dichter zwischen den Zeiten: Festschrift für Rudolf Henz*, edited by Viktor Suchy (Vienna: Braumüller, 1977), pp. 250-254;

Heinz Wittmann, "Alexander Lernet-Holenia," in his *Gespräche mit Dichtern: Aufzeichnungen* (Vienna: Heimatland, 1976), pp. 88-116.

Papers:

Many of Alexander Lernet-Holenia's papers are in the Austrian National Library, Vienna.

Friederike Mayröcker

(20 December 1924-   )

Beth Bjorklund
University of Virginia

BOOKS: *Larifari: Ein konfuses Buch* (Vienna: Bergland, 1956);

Metaphorisch (Stuttgart: Walther, 1964);

Texte (Innsbruck: Allerheiligenpresse, 1966);

Tod durch Musen: Poetische Texte (Reinbek: Rowohlt, 1966);

Sägespäne für mein Herzbluten: 39 Gedichte (Berlin: Rainer, 1967); revised as *Sägespäne für mein Herzbluten und andere Gedichte* (Berlin: Rainer, 1973);

Minimonsters Traumlexikon: Texte in Prosa (Reinbek: Rowohlt, 1968);

Fantom Fan (Reinbek: Rowohlt, 1971);

Fünf Mann Menschen, by Mayröcker and Ernst Jandl (Neuwied & Darmstadt: Luchterhand, 1971);

Sinclair Sofokles der Baby-Saurier (Vienna & Munich: Jugend und Volk, 1971); translated by Renate Moore and Linda Hayward as *Sinclair Sophocles, the Baby Dinosaur* (New York: Random House, 1974);

Arie auf tönernen Füßen: Metaphysisches Theater (Neuwied & Darmstadt: Luchterhand, 1972);

Blaue Erleuchtungen: Erste Gedichte (Düsseldorf: Eremiten-Presse, 1973);

Je ein umwölkter Gipfel: Erzählung (Neuwied & Darmstadt: Luchterhand, 1973);

In langsamen Blitzen (Berlin: Literarisches Colloquium, 1974);

Augen wie Schaljapin bevor er starb (Dornbirn: Vorarlberger Verlagsanstalt, 1974);

Meine Träume, ein Flügelkleid (Düsseldorf: Eremiten-Presse, 1974);

Schriftungen oder Gerüchte aus dem Jenseits (Pfaffenweiler: Pfaffenweiler Presse, 1975);

Das Licht in der Landschaft (Frankfurt am Main: Suhrkamp, 1975);

Drei Hörspiele, by Mayröcker and Jandl (Vienna & Munich: Sessler, 1975);

Fast ein Frühling des Markus M. (Frankfurt am Main: Suhrkamp, 1976);

Rot ist unten (Vienna & Munich: Jugend und Volk, 1977);

Friederike Mayröcker

heisze hunde (Pfaffenweiler: Pfaffenweiler Presse, 1977);

Heiligenanstalt (Frankfurt am Main: Suhrkamp, 1978);

lütt'koch (Vienna: Herbstpresse, 1978);

Schwarmgesang: Szenen für die poetische Bühne (Berlin: Rainer, 1978);

Tochter der Bahn, published with *Der Ureinwohner*, by Klaus Rinke (Düsseldorf: Eremiten-Presse, 1979);

Ausgewählte Gedichte 1944-1978 (Frankfurt am Main: Suhrkamp, 1979);

Friederike Mayröcker: Ein Lesebuch, edited by Gisela Lindemann (Frankfurt am Main: Suhrkamp, 1979);

Pegas das Pferd (Salzburg: Neugebauer, 1980); translated as *Pegas the Horse* (London: Neugebauer, 1982);

Die Abschiede (Frankfurt am Main: Suhrkamp, 1980);

Schwarze Romanzen: Ein Gedichtzyklus (Pfaffenweiler: Pfaffenweiler Presse, 1981);

Treppen, by Mayröcker and Johann Kräftner (St. Pölten: Niederösterreichisches Pressehaus, 1981);

Bocca della Verita (Baden: Grasl, 1981);

Ich, der Rabe und der Mond: Ein Kinderbuch zum Lesen und Weiterzeichnen (Graz: Droschl, 1981);

Gute Nacht, guten Morgen: Gedichte 1978-1981 (Frankfurt am Main: Suhrkamp, 1982);

Magische Blätter (Frankfurt am Main: Suhrkamp, 1983);

Im Nervensaal, Himmel am zwölften Mai (Vienna: Herbstpresse, 1983);

Das Anheben der Arme bei Feuersglut, edited by Heinz F. Schafroth (Stuttgart: Reclam, 1984);

Kockodan Samota (Prague: Odeon, 1984);

Reise durch die Nacht (Frankfurt am Main: Suhrkamp, 1984);

Rosengarten (Pfaffenweiler: Pfaffenweiler Presse, 1984);

A travers les oeillets (Paris: muro torto, 1985);

Configurationen, by Mayröcker and Hubert Aratym (Vienna: Sonderzahl, 1985);

Das Herzzerreißende der Dinge (Frankfurt am Main: Suhrkamp, 1985);

Das Jahr Schnee (East Berlin: Volk & Welt, 1985);

Der Donner des Stillhaltens, by Mayröcker and Bodo Hell (Graz: Droschl, 1986);

Winterglück (Frankfurt am Main: Suhrkamp, 1986);

Blauer Streusand (Frankfurt am Main: Suhrkamp, 1987);

Magische Blätter II (Frankfurt am Main: Suhrkamp, 1987);

Mein Herz mein Zimmer mein Name (Frankfurt am Main: Suhrkamp, 1988).

OTHER: "Selbstdarstellung," in *Ein Gedicht und sein Autor*, edited by Walter Höllerer (Berlin: Literarisches Colloquium, 1967), pp. 362-371;

"Rede bei der Verleihung des Hörspielpreises der Kriegsblinden," *Frankfurter Allgemeine Zeitung*, 23 April 1969;

"Anmerkung zum Hörspiel," by Mayröcker and Ernst Jandl, in *Neues Hörspiel*, edited by Klaus Schöning (Frankfurt am Main: Suhrkamp, 1970), pp. 88-91;

"Traube," by Mayröcker, Jandl, and Heinz von Cramer, *protokolle*, 2 (1972): 163-181;

"Dada," *Sprache im technischen Zeitalter*, 55 (1975): 230-231;

Peter Pongratz, *Malerei, Zeichnungen, Graphik: Monographie mit einem Werkverzeichnis der Druckgraphik*, edited by Otto Breicha, texts by Mayröcker (Vienna & Munich: Jugend und Volk, 1975);

"Über meine Arbeit mich zu äußern," *protokolle*, 2 (1980): 45-49.

Friederike Mayröcker is one of the leading postwar writers in the German-speaking world. She has written more than forty books and many pieces for periodicals; these works include prose, poetry, and radio plays, as well as many unconventional hybrid forms. A striking feature of her works is the absence of a story in the conventional sense. Instead, she explores the possibilities of language when it is freed from the constraints of verisimilitude. Her work makes high demands on the reader and is often regarded as inaccessible; thus recognition was slow in coming. But her *Die Abschiede* (The Farewells, 1980) was on the best-seller list in West Germany; and she has won many important literary awards, including the Trakl Prize in 1977 and the Great Austrian State Prize in 1982.

Born in Vienna on 20 December 1924, Mayröcker continues to reside there. She began writing poetry at an early age, and her first published works appeared in the literary journal *Plan* shortly after World War II. Unlike many authors of her generation, Mayröcker does not refer to the war or subsequent sociopolitical events in these works, which are devoted to literary and aesthetic concerns. Her formal education culminated in the state examination in English in 1945, and from 1946 to 1967 she taught English at a secondary school in Vienna. Since 1969 she has been a free-lance writer. In 1954 she met the poet Ernst Jandl, with whom she has collaborated on various works. In the 1950s Mayröcker and Jandl were associated with the avant-garde Wiener Gruppe (Vienna Group); since 1973 they have been members of the Grazer Autor-

Mayröcker with her collaborator, the poet Ernst Jandl, in 1974 (photo: Gert Schlegel, Vienna)

enversammlung (Graz Authors' Association), a group founded in opposition to the more conservative P.E.N. Club in Vienna. She is also a member of the Academy of the Arts in West Berlin and since 1985 of the Academy of Language and Literature in Darmstadt. Mayröcker has traveled widely on reading tours throughout Europe, the United States, and the Soviet Union.

In Mayröcker's work memories, dreams, fantasies, perceptions, reflections, and feelings are brought together in a timeless amalgam. Reality is portrayed as discontinuous, nonchronological, and open-ended. Her writing creates reality rather than reproducing it, and language is both its medium and its content. Traditional metaphorical use of language gives way to innovative techniques, including montage, evocation, assemblage, permutation, dislocation, word chains, phrasal leitmotifs, juxtaposition, and repetition. The result is a network of associations in which all features of language–not only semantic meaning but also sounds, rhythms, and syntax– function as metaphor. Experimental literature is often seen as a generalized version of dada and surrealism; Mayröcker, however, is too individual

to be encompassed by any particular movement or manifesto. Her work has developed through a variety of styles, among which three main phases are discernible.

Her first major publication, *Tod durch Musen* (Death by the Muses, 1966), is a selection of her poetry from 1944 to 1965. Whereas the early poems reveal strong lyrical and imaginative qualities, the later ones demonstrate the objectivity, reduction, and precision that Mayröcker learned through contact with other experimental writers. Poetry of this sort requires participation by the reader; the more one brings to the poem the more meanings it will have.

The second period, beginning in the late 1960s and continuing through the early 1970s, is characterized by radical linguistic experimentation. Short prose texts present elements from pop culture, foreign languages, dialects, and jargon mixed with rhyming syllables and nonsense jingles. The texts are often accompanied by drawings or are themselves arranged in a graphic format. Explicit homage is paid to Gertrude Stein in "Tender Buttons für Selbstmörder" (Tender Buttons for Suicides) in *Fantom Fan* (1971), and the in-

Cover of Mayröcker's 1975 novel about a romantic triangle

fluence of e. e. cummings is also evident. *Arie auf tönernen Füßen: Metaphysisches Theater* (Aria on Feet of Clay: Metaphysical Theater, 1972) uses an assemblage of banalities and items from pornography, science fiction, detective stories, and comic strips. The short narrative or dialogue scenes include figures such as Maria Callas together with Snoopy, the Statue of Liberty brandishing a hand grenade, and Richard Wagner living in a commune with Lohengrin and other heros.

During this period Mayröcker began writing radio plays, some of them in collaboration with Jandl. Their award-winning *Fünf Mann Menschen* (Five Man Men, 1971) redefined the genre: gone are traditional dialogue and monologue; speech

takes on an entirely different function in combination with sound effects, and the script often resembles a musical score. Mayröcker's volume *Schwarmgesang: Szenen für die poetische Bühne* (Swarm Song: Scenes for the Poetic Stage, 1978) contains nine radio plays that explore the possibilities of stereophonic sound for the superimposition of speaking voices representing various views of reality. Mayröcker's plays are frequently performed on Austrian and German radio. She has also collaborated on a television film and has written several delightful children's books, some of which she illustrated herself.

Mayröcker's third period, dating from the early 1970s and extending to the present, contains major prose works which have won wide recognition. *Je ein umwölkter Gipfel* (Each a Cloud-covered Summit, 1973) consists of episodes loosely connected by structural relationships rather than by plot or continuity of characters. Dealing in part with Mayröcker's 1972 trip to the United States, the work consists of diverse experiences presented in fragmentary dialogue form. *Das Licht in der Landschaft* (The Light in the Landscape, 1975) represents a distillation of about 1,000 pages of manuscript to 140, achieving a compression comparable to that of poetry and resulting in a text that is extraordinarily rich in cross-references. Experiences from the recent and distant past are interspersed with conversations, letters, dreams, fantasies, and sensations, illuminating a vivid inner world. Only on rereading does one realize that the central theme is a triangular love affair; references to the initiation and dissolution of the affair are accompanied by reflections on the nature of human relationships.

In *Die Abschiede* the dominant metaphor is that of closure: evening, autumn, departure, desolation, decay, and death. The most apparent level is the dissolution of a love relationship; but the "story" is summarized in two prefatory statements, and the remaining 260 pages are devoted to the implications of the experience of endings. It is only through the eyes of the narrator, Marie, that the reader sees the female antagonist, Giselle, and the male protagonist, Valerian (suggestive of *vale*, the Latin for farewell). A motif will be initiated unobtrusively, recur in various contexts with added implications, reach a climax, then become dormant. It may, however, generate other motifs or may itself be reactivated in some other context.

Heiligenanstalt (Saints' Asylum, 1978) consists of fictionalized biographies of the composers

Mayröcker (photo: Renate von Mangoldt)

Chopin, Schumann, Bruckner, and Schubert, representing an exception to Mayröcker's usual interest in the visual arts. Conventional documentary forms are abandoned as the author presents a highly subjective interpretation of each character. *Gute Nacht, guten Morgen* (Good Night, Good Morning, 1982) consists of short poems that could be characterized as snapshots; readers find the work more accessible than Mayröcker's earlier poetry since the empirical context is generally specified. The movement toward a more realistic style is also evident in the prose work *Reise durch die Nacht* (Journey through the Night, 1984). The book deals with a train ride from Paris to Vienna, during which the protagonist records her observations, memories, fears, joys, and fantasies. Mayröcker's most recent book, *Mein Herz mein Zimmer mein Name* (My Heart My Room My Name, 1988), continues the autobiographical tendency evident in her fiction. The theme of writing is central, as the author comments on the very text that is being written. The self-portrayal deals mainly with feelings about personal relationships and with the fear that time to pursue her "obsession" (writing) is running out. Whether this tendency toward realism marks a fourth phase in Mayröcker's development remains to be seen. Mayröcker's prose works could be compared with the work of French novelist Nathalie Sarraute, with their interplay of dialogue, monologue, and preconscious "sub-conversations." They are part of a general development in modern fiction characterized by de-emphasis on plot and character and thematization of language and the writing process.

References:

Robert Acker, "Ernst Jandl and Friederike Mayröcker: A Study of Modulation and Crisis," *World Literature Today*, 55 (Autumn 1981): 597-602;

Beth Bjorklund, "The Austrian Avant-garde as Represented by Friederike Mayröcker," *poesis*, 5 (1984): 48-67;

Bjorklund, "The Modern Muse of Friederike Mayröcker's Literary Production," in *Major Figures of Contemporary Austrian Literature*, edited by Donald G. Daviau (New York, Bern & Frankfurt am Main: Lang, 1987), pp. 313-336;

Bjorklund, "Radical Transformation and Magical Synthesis: Interview with Friederike Mayröcker," *Literary Review*, 25 (1982): 222-228;

Ernst Jandl, "Ein neuer poetischer Raum: Zur Prosa Friederike Mayröckers," in *Views and Reviews of Modern German Literature: Festschrift for Adolf D. Klarmann*, edited by Karl S. Weimar (Munich: Delp, 1974), pp. 285-290;

jardin pour friederike mayröcker (Linz: Neue texte, 1978);

Lisa Kahn, "Ein Fall von Wahlverwandschaft: Kandinsky-Mayröcker," *Literatur und Kritik*, 142 (1980): 106-110;

Kahn, "Mayröckers Markus M.: Welt steter Wandlungen," *Literatur und Kritik*, 165/166 (1982): 73-78;

Kurt Klinger, "Poetische Phänomenologie: Friederike Mayröcker," in *Kindlers Literaturgeschichte der Gegenwart: Die zeitgenössische Literatur Österreichs*, edited by Hilde Spiel (Zurich: Kindler, 1976), pp. 436-441;

protokolle, special Mayröcker issue, 2 (1980);

Siegfried J. Schmidt, ed., *Friederike Mayröcker* (Frankfurt am Main: Suhrkamp, 1984);

Viktor Suchy, "Poesie und Poesis, dargestellt am Werke Friederike Mayröckers," in *Die andere Welt: Festschrift für Hellmuth Himmel*, edited by Kurt Bartsch and others (Bern: Francke, 1979), pp. 341-358;

text + kritik, special Mayröcker issue, 84 (1984).

Erika Mitterer

(30 March 1906-)

Catherine Hutter

BOOKS: *Dank des Lebens: Gedichte* (Frankfurt am Main: Rütten & Loening, 1930);

Charlotte Corday: Drama in vien Aufzügen (Berlin: Chronos, 1931);

Höhensonne (Stuttgart & Berlin: Deutsche Verlagsanstalt, 1933);

Gesang der Wandernden: Neue Gedichte (Leipzig: Staackmann, 1935);

Der Fürst der Welt: Roman (Hamburg: Schröder, 1940);

Begegnung im Süden: Erzählung (Hamburg: Schröder, 1941);

Die Seherin: Eine Erzählung (Hamburg: Schröder, 1942);

Wir sind allein: Ein Roman zwischen zwei Zeiten (Vienna: Luckmann, 1945);

Zwölf Gedichte: 1933-1945 (Vienna: Luckmann, 1946);

Die nackte Wahrheit: Roman (Innsbruck: Österreichische Verlagsanstalt, 1951);

Kleine Damengröße: Ein Roman im Schatten der Jugend (Vienna: Luckmann, 1953);

Wasser des Lebens: Roman (Vienna & Munich: Herold, 1953);

Gesammelte Gedichte (Vienna: Luckmann, 1956);

Tauschzentrale: Roman (Vienna: Luckmann, 1958);

Die Welt ist reich und voll Gefahr (Graz & Vienna: Stiasny, 1964);

Weihnacht der Einsamen: Erzählungen und Gedichte (Zurich: Arche, 1968);

Klopfsignale (Vienna & Munich: Jugend und Volk, 1970);

Entsühnung des Kain: Neue Gedichte (Einsiedeln: Johannes, 1974);

Alle unsere Spiele: Roman (Frankfurt am Main: Knecht, 1977); translated by Catherine Hutter as *All Our Games* (Columbia, S.C.: Camden House, 1988);

Das verhüllte Kreuz: Neue Gedichte (St. Pölten & Vienna: Niederösterreichisches Pressehaus, 1985).

Erika Mitterer is the dean of Austrian women writers. Born on 30 March 1906 in Vienna to Rudolf and Antonie Loeb Mitterer, she has spent practically all her life in Austria. From her father, an architect and civil servant whose passion was hunting, she inherited a love of nature and an inclination for sport. She is one of the few poets who has written verse on deerstalking, skiing, swimming (not until age sixty-five did she stop swimming across the Danube), and above all, hiking in the Vienna Woods and in the Austrian Alps. From Mitterer's mother, a painter, perhaps comes her fervent love of classical beauty in art.

Mitterer began at an early age to read the poetry of Johann Wolfgang von Goethe, Friedrich Schiller, Friedrich Hölderlin, Anton Wildgans, Hugo von Hofmannsthal, and Stefan George. She also began to write verse as a child. When she was eighteen she read Rainer Maria Rilke's *Die Sonette an Orpheus* (1923; translated as *Sonnets to Orpheus*, 1936), was deeply moved by it, and sent two of her poems to him. To Mitterer's surprise and joy, Rilke replied, also in verse. Their correspondence lasted almost until his death two years later. When she realized that he was seriously ill, she visited him in the Château de Muzot in November 1925. "Für Erika" of 24 August 1926 is one of his last known poems in German. She chose not to publish *Briefwechsel in Gedichten mit Erika Mitterer* (translated as *Correspondence in Verse with Erika Mitterer*, 1953) until 1950, after she had achieved fame on her own merit with a play, two volumes of poetry, three novellas, and four novels. The poetry collection *Dank des Lebens* (Gratitude of Life, 1930) received the Julius Reich Prize in 1930, and in 1948 she was awarded the Prize of the City of Vienna for Poetry.

Mitterer married the archivist Fritz Petrowsky on 23 August 1937; they have three children. At the time of her marriage she retired from her career as a social worker to devote herself to writing. She drew on her experience as a social worker in her first novella, *Höhensonne* (Violet Rays, 1933), in which a social worker from the city tells of the great change that took place within her after working in a mountain area.

Erika Mitterer (photo courtesy of Dr. Fritz Petrowsky)

Among her admirers and mentors in her early years were Stefan Zweig, Ernst Lissauer, Ina Seidel, Felix and Robert Braun, Theodor Kramer, and Hans Carossa. It was Carossa who found that even Mitterer's manner of speaking revealed "einen reinen Glanz der goldnen Welt, die Wien einmal gewesen" (the pure glow of the golden world which once was Vienna).

Until 1938 she was often invited to read in Austria and Germany, but these activities ended with the annexation of Austria by Nazi Germany. Her books, however, were never banned. In 1934 the publisher Staackmann did not dare to dis-

tribute her *Wir sind allein* (We Are Alone), even though it had already been printed, because she would not consent to changing the humane Jewish doctor into an "Aryan"; the novel, which deals with the problems of the young as they face the world, was published in 1945. Staackmann did publish her second volume of poetry, *Gesang der Wandernden* (Song of the Wanderers, 1935); the SS objected to a poem about Judas and had cynical things to say in their paper, *Das Schwarze Korps*, but they did not pursue the matter.

Mitterer spent seven years researching and writing the novel *Der Fürst der Welt* (The Prince

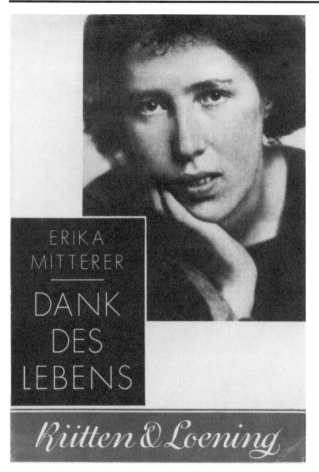

Cover of Mitterer's first book, a collection of poetry for which she won the Julius Reich Prize in 1930

of the World, 1940). It was her aim to show how evil can gain power in an apparently sane world; but owing to political conditions in Austria at the time she was writing, she set the story in the early sixteenth century. The novel offers an extraordinary tapestry of life in pre-Reformation Germany: the decline of the nobility, the rise of mercantile capitalism, the conflict of freethinking scholars and scientists with the Inquisition. At first no one seemed to notice the parallel with Hitler's Reich; the reviews were on the whole enthusiastic. Max Tau, however, who was living in exile in Norway, at once noticed the similarities to the Hitler regime and was instrumental in having the book republished by Aschehoug, where he was an editor. It sold eighteen thousand copies. Forty thousand copies were sold in Germany before the authorities caught on to the parallel, and there was suddenly no more paper for further printings. A paperback edition was published in Berlin in 1964, and the novel was reprinted in Vienna in 1988. It is justifiably a book

that does not die.

Der Fürst der Welt had a profound effect on Mitterer's life beyond the financial reward and esteem it brought her. When one has to invent dialogue between bishop and inquisitor and between bishop and abbot, one has to be familiar with their terminology; and if the protagonist is a nun, one has to understand life in a convent and has to be familiar with the writings of Thomas Aquinas and Saint Theresa of Avila. For seven years she devoted herself to such matters, but it was not until 1965, when her youngest child was to be confirmed, that she converted from Lutheranism to Catholicism. "Trotz all der Dogmen?" (In spite of the dogmas?), her Protestant aunt asked, horrified. "Gerade auch wegen der Dogmen" (Just because of the dogmas), Mitterer replied. She saw them as equivalent to the skeleton, a framework without which the body could not live.

Begegnung im Süden (Encounter in the South, 1941) is a complete change of pace from *Der Fürst der Welt*, a love story played against a background she loved–Greece. It is told in a muted ecstasy rarely encountered in fiction today.

According to Edwin Rollett, few women accept their femininity as wholeheartedly as does Mitterer. In her work one finds no trace of feminist aggression or resentment. For her, the child is a symbol of continuity from past to present. The novel *Kleine Damengröße* (Size-Petite, 1953) was written not only about but for young readers. In *Tauschzentrale* (Barter Center, 1958) a boy involves himself in the Hungarian uprising because he is disillusioned by what he feels are the priorities of his generation. In *Die nackte Wahrheit* (The Whole Truth, 1951) she writes: "Wenn man selbst ein Kind hat, ist das wohl anders. Da hat man nun ein für allemal Ja gesagt zum Leben und kann nicht zurück" (When one has a child oneself, I suppose things are different. Then one has said "yes" once and for all to life and there is no way back). This thought saves the heroine's life. In *Alle unsere Spiele* (1977; translated as *All Our Games*, 1988), when Helga finds out that rape has resulted in her pregnancy, she cries out, " 'Es soll nicht leben! Ich will es nicht!' " ("It shall not live! I don't want it to live!"); her ancient grandmother replies, " 'Es lebt aber schon' " ("But it is already alive"). *Alle unsere Spiele* deals with the Austria of 1938 to 1962 in a narrative that tells the story not from one side but from all sides. The heroine is a Viennese girl engaged to a German SS man; both are staunch believers in

Dust jacket for Mitterer's novel about young people facing life. Because of its sympathetic portrayal of a Jewish doctor, the original publisher did not dare to distribute it in 1934. The novel finally appeared in 1945.

Dust jacket for Mitterer's novel about romance in Greece

Dust jacket for Mitterer's novel written for and about young people

Dust jacket for Mitterer's novel about the 1956 Hungarian uprising

Mitterer in 1987 (photo by Dr. Fritz Petrowsky, Vienna)

Hitler. Her family, secretly engaged in resistance against Hitler, uses her as a shield, with the illusion that they can bring her over to their side before it is too late; but they fail. It is a book for those who want to know how the rise of Nazism could have occurred. *Alle unsere Spiele* was read in its entirety over the radio in Vienna and went into a second printing.

Mitterer has remonstrated against the permissiveness of the present day, especially when religious beliefs are defamed. In her poetry volume *Das verhüllte Kreuz* (The Veiled Cross, 1985) she writes that she feels "Fehl am Platz / unter den Verfechtern der Freiheit / aller Laster, weil diese / 'Privatsache' seien!" (Out of place / among the defenders of freedom / for all vices because / they are "private!"). She resigned from the

P.E.N. Club because it refused to condemn Herbert Achternbusch's film *Das Gespenst* (The Ghost, 1982), in which obscenity was joined with blasphemy against Christ. For the same reason she resigned from the Austrian Writers' League, of which she was an honorary member.

Mitterer received the Enrica von Handel-Mazzetti Prize in 1971, the Austrian Cross of Honor for Science and Art in 1975, and the Gold Medal of Honor of the City of Vienna in 1986. In February 1986 she received the Insignia of Honor for Science and Art, Austria's highest honor for scholars and artists. She ended her speech of thanks with the words: "Keiner wird sein Hiersein überdauern, der sich selber nicht die Treue hält" (No one will outlive his life on earth who is not true to himself). In his introduction of her at the ceremony, P.E.N. Club representative Roman Roček said: "So umfangreich ihr Lebenswerk auch ist, so hohe Auflagen ihr wichtigstes und gewichtigstes Buch, der Roman, 'Der Fürst der Welt,' auch erreicht hat: ihr Name wird von den Springfluten der Modeliteratur übertönt, überschrien. Und das ist bis zu einem gewissen Grad durchaus verständlich. Denn sie hat keine der Torheiten mitgemacht, schrieb nie Rilkischer als Rilke, zu einer Zeit, da dies zum Modediktat gehörte, verschrieb sich keinerlei Ismen, betrieb niemals irgendwelche Experimente, außer vielleicht jenem 'experimentum crucis,' gerade im Gegenwind den eigenen Weg zu suchen. . . . Sie ist den Weg zu den Wurzeln des Dichters und des Denkens gegangen. . . . Nie hat sie sich das Dichten leicht gemacht, nie das Spiel mit der Sprache gespielt; was aus ihr sprach, war eine härtere Wirklichkeit. . . . Ihre Gedichte, selbst die einfacheren, sangbaren haben etwas von der Alltagssprache an sich, ein Parlando, das man als dissonant empfunden haben mag. Wir ehren in der praktizierenden Katholikin den bekennenden Mut, die außerordentliche Kraft des Glaubens und verehren sie als eine der imaginationskräftigsten Dichterinnen unseres Landes seit Marie von Ebner-Eschenbach. . . . Heute wollen wir ihr versichern, daß sie eine der unsern geblieben ist: weil Freiheit ihr mehr war als leeres Stroh, weil Freiheit ihr stets verbunden blieb mit der Tat" (However extensive her oeuvre, however many editions her most impressive and important book, *Der Fürst der Welt*, may have gone into, her name has undoubtedly been drowned out by the spate of literature that is fashionable today. And this is to some extent understandable. Because she never went along with fashionable foolishness, never wrote more like Rilke than Rilke at a time when this was the thing to do, prescribed to no "isms," went in for no experimentation except perhaps the crucial experiment: to find her own way against the wind.... She chose the road to the roots of poetry and thought.... She never took lyricism lightly, never played games with language, wrote often with an almost harsh reality.... Even her less complex poems have the tone of everyday speech, a parlando which may have been misconstrued as dissonant. We respect in the practicing Catholic the avowed courage, the extraordinary strength of faith, and honor her as one of the most imaginative poets of our country since Marie von Ebner-Eschenbach.... Today we want to assure her that she has remained one of us: because for her freedom was more than empty straw, because for her freedom always remained bound to the act).

Letters:

Rainer Maria Rilke, *Briefwechsel in Gedichten mit Erika Mitterer 1924 bis 1926* (Wiesbaden: Insel, 1950); translated by N. K. Cruickshank as *Correspondence in Verse with Erika Mitterer* (London: Hogarth Press, 1953).

Bibliography:

Jorun B. Johns, "Erika Mitterer: Eine Bibliographie," *Modern Austrian Literature*, 19, no. 2 (1986): 77-95.

References:

Helene Henze, "Erika Mitterer," *Frankfurter Zeitung*, 22 December 1941;

Karl Humer, "Die Vorkriegsgeneration und ihre Stellungnahme zu den Zeitfragen," Ph.D. dissertation, University of Vienna, 1950, pp. 76-88;

Ernst Lissauer, "Die Lyrikerin Erika Mitterer," *Die Literatur*, 35 (May 1933): 476;

Joseph G. McVeigh, "Continuity as Problem and Promise: Erika Mitterer's Writings after 1945," *Modern Austrian Literature*, 12, no. 3 / 4 (1979): 113-126;

A. W. G. Randall, "Two German Women Poets," *Saturday Review of Literature*, 8 (15 August 1931): 58;

Ernst Rathgeber, "Frauen als Dichter," *Österreichische Blätter für freies Geistesleben* (November 1929): 39-42;

Roman Roček, "Dank an Erika Mitterer," *P.E.N.-Informationen*, 14 (1986): 12-15;

Edwin Rollett, "Erika Mitterer," *Wiener Zeitung*, 14 November 1953;

Werner Röttinger, "Aus dem Alltag des Lebens erhob sich ihr Schaffen," *Wiener Zeitung*, 25 March 1956;

Ernst Schönwiese, "Die österreichische Lyrik der Gegenwart," *Études Germaniques*, 13 (October-December 1958): 336;

Ina Seidel, "Höhensonne: Roman von Erika Mitterer," *Die Literatur*, 35 (May 1933): 476;

Paul Wimmer, "Gedichte von Erika Mitterer," *Wiener Zeitung*, 2 August 1985.

Peter Rosei
(17 June 1946-   )

Robert Acker
University of Montana

BOOKS: *Landstriche: Erzählungen* (Salzburg: Residenz, 1972);

Bei schwebendem Verfahren: Roman (Salzburg: Residenz, 1973);

Wege: Erzählungen (Salzburg: Residenz, 1974);

Klotz spricht mit seinem Anwalt (Munich: Lentz, 1975);

Entwurf für eine Welt ohne Menschen, Entwurf zu einer Reise ohne Ziel (Salzburg: Residenz, 1975);

Der Fluß der Gedanken durch den Kopf: Logbücher (Salzburg: Residenz, 1976);

Wer war Edgar Allen?: Roman (Salzburg: Residenz, 1977);

Von Hier nach Dort: Roman (Salzburg & Vienna: Residenz, 1978);

Nennt mich Tommy (Munich: Bertelsmann, 1978);

Alben (Erlangen & Munich: Renner, 1979);

Regentagstheorie: 59 Gedichte (Salzburg & Vienna: Residenz, 1979);

Das Lächeln des Jungen: 59 Gedichte (Salzburg & Vienna: Residenz, 1979);

Chronik der Versuche, ein Märchenerzähler zu werden (Weinheim & Basel: Beltz, 1979);

Das schnelle Glück: Roman (Salzburg & Vienna: Residenz, 1980);

Frühe Prosa (Salzburg & Vienna: Residenz, 1981);

Die Milchstraße: Sieben Bücher (Salzburg: Residenz, 1981);

Versuch, die Natur zu kritisieren: Essays (Salzburg: Residenz, 1982);

Reise ohne Ende: Aufzeichnungsbücher (Frankfurt am Main: Suhrkamp, 1983);

Mann & Frau (Salzburg: Residenz, 1984);

Komödie (Salzburg: Residenz, 1984);

15000 Seelen (Salzburg: Residenz, 1985);

Die Wolken (Salzburg: Residenz, 1986);

Der Aufstand (Salzburg: Residenz, 1987);

Unser Landschaftsbericht (Salzburg: Residenz, 1988).

OTHER: Gieselbert Hoke, *Gärten*, texts by Rosei and Margarethe Stolz (Vienna & Munich: Jugend und Volk, 1973).

Peter Rosei

Peter Rosei is emerging as one of the most important writers in contemporary Austrian letters. His works are reviewed regularly, and usually favorably, in major newspapers in Austria, Germany, and Switzerland. But Rosei's moderate form of experimentation and his sometimes bizarre, even morbid, themes have prevented him from achieving much success with the general reading public, even though many of his works have been published in West Germany in inexpensive paperback editions. This lack of interest can also perhaps be attributed to the deceptive nature of his writing: while on the surface Rosei's style appears to be straightforward and realistic, a closer examination reveals a complicated and iconoclastic Weltanschauung.

Born on 17 June 1946 in Vienna, Rosei studied law at the University of Vienna and received his doctorate in 1968. After completing his obligatory nine-month military service he worked as a secretary for the artist Ernst Fuchs. He soon became discouraged with the commercial aspects and crass consumerism of the art world and quit his job in 1971 to head a small textbook publishing house. This experience only made him more cynical about the culture industry, so in 1972 he moved to Bergheim, a small town near Salzburg, to devote himself to writing. Rosei adopted a simple life-style in Bergheim, renting a room in the attic of a farmhouse and keeping his purchases to a minimum. His most expensive possession was a motorcycle, on which he made extended trips. He had little contact with the villagers and was often seen taking long walks alone through the countryside. During this period he wrote at a steady pace, producing one or two works a year. He returned to Vienna in 1981.

From the essays in *Versuch, die Natur zu kritisieren* (Attempt to Criticize Nature, 1982) it emerges that Rosei rejects all scientific, mathematical, and logical approaches to the world as artificial systems that were invented in an attempt to control reality. They are illusions: man will never be able to rule nature, for nature follows its own course. People are powerless and have no relationship to objects or other human beings: they are isolated and autonomous individuals. All people seek certainty; all are on a perpetual journey, trying to discover the truth about their inner being. This attempt is futile as well, for the only certainty is death. Nevertheless, one must continue on this journey, for to act is better than to remain still; one must think other thoughts to avoid the thought of death. Instead of trying to control nature one should try to assimilate it, to make it part of oneself. The best way to interiorize nature is through a graphic and sensual description of it. This is the role of the artist, whose picture of the world must necessarily be a reflection of human consciousness, since man is part of nature. To encompass the world in all its manifold complexity is of course also an impossible task, but it is part of man's search for a meaningful self in a world devoid of reason and logic. An author can thus reach no rational conclusions, can give no message or interpretation. He can only register what he experiences by means of his senses. This sense experience is his "knowledge."

Rosei's novels reveal a progression from a concentration on the dark and negative aspects of life to a more positive position of relative happiness through the acceptance of fate. His early works contain graphic depictions of death, destruction, and threatening environments; the works of his middle period are preoccupied with the motif of the journey without a goal; his most recent works depict characters who obtain a modicum of peace and happiness by ceasing their attempts to have a dominating relationship to the world or to their fellow human beings.

Landstriche (Tracts of Land, 1972) and *Wege* (Ways, 1974) are collections of short stories which are parables of the human condition. They depict the devastating effect that hierarchal power structures have on human relationships. Where such power structures exist, there is no hope; one feels perpetually threatened by the brutality such structures engender. Death or blind obedience to arbitrary and senseless laws are the only alternatives, as is shown in his first novel, *Bei schwebendem Verfahren* (Pending Proceedings, 1973), written in imitation of Franz Kafka. In this novel competition, the urge to succeed, and the will to control the destinies of others are the prevalent values: all the characters are driven by brutality, sexual excess, greed, or madness. An all-encompassing law proposed by the president seeks to destroy all individual autonomy. The only time one senses a degree of individuality and independence among the characters is at the end of the novel, where revolt and anarchy break out and the chancellery explodes in flames.

Rosei's second phase began with *Entwurf für eine Welt ohne Menschen, Entwurf zu einer Reise ohne Ziel* (Plan for a World without People, Plan for a Trip without a Goal, 1975). The novel consists of two long parts. The first describes the narrator's trip through an imaginary landscape devoid of human beings; the objects of nature are, however, given human characteristics. In the second section a group of travelers journeys through another imaginary landscape toward a goal they will never reach. This landscape is populated by robbers, beggars, brutal shepherds, and stupid city dwellers. Rosei demonstrates the impossibility of interpersonal relationships in a world governed by the will for power and by the omnipresent specter of death. In both situations the individual must continue his journey through life, asking only the minimum and never giving up the search.

Rosei (center) with Helmut Eisendle (left) and H. C. Artmann in Höhnhart, 1977 (photo copyright © by Isolde Ohlbaum, Munich)

These philosophical speculations are continued in *Der Fluß der Gedanken durch den Kopf: Logbücher* (The Flow of Thoughts through the Head: Log Books, 1976), a collection of three short stories centering around literary personalities–the writers Antoine de Saint-Exupéry and Robert Louis Stevenson and the German folk hero Till Eulenspiegel. All three are seeking alternative worlds. Rosei employs diarylike entries and a collage of associations to probe the psychic condition of these men. All of the protagonists challenge death by exposing themselves to unique experiences. They are doomed to failure, but it is important that they make the attempt.

A journey of self-discovery forms the basis for Rosei's next two works. In *Wer war Edgar Allen?* (Who Was Edgar Allen?, 1977) the narrator is a medical student who goes to Venice to study art history but quickly succumbs to the excessive use of drugs and alcohol, seeking to find out more about the hidden side of his personality and to overcome his fears and doubts. *Von Hier nach Dort* (From Here to There, 1978) is the story of Karl, a young man who takes a motorcycle trip to the "North." He makes careful note of the landscape, both man-made and natural. He never remains long in any one place, has no memorable adventures, stays in cheap hotels, occasionally converses with strangers, has a casual af-

fair, and ends up back home. Only then does the reader discover that Karl is actually a drug dealer. After a successful deal he takes his new wealth, picks out a destination at random, and flies to the South to spend his time wandering about a large city. In the final scene Karl buys a horoscope from a vending machine; it tells him to forget his past sorrows since happiness will soon be his. The reader senses a conviction that a certain degree of contentment can be achieved by traveling alone, with no relationships or commitments: "Welch wunderbarer Wahnsinn ist das Allein-Sein" (What a wonderful madness is being alone), comments the narrator. Indifference and resignation can be overcome, if only for brief and fleeting moments, by maintaining constant movement.

In the novel *Das schnelle Glück* (Quick Happiness, 1980) a man tries to come to terms with the loss of his job. He finds himself plunged into feelings of hopelessness and despair bordering on madness; his normal order and harmony have been replaced by total emptiness. On one of his many trips through the city he meets his old school friend Bergmann, who lives without any kind of security: he has few possessions and supports himself with occasional jobs. Bergmann helps the protagonist overcome his crisis by forcing him to see, describe, and identify with exter-

Rosei (photo copyright © by Isolde Ohlbaum, Munich)

nal objects, bringing him to the existential awareness that there is no sense to life, nothing beyond surface reality. This recognition engenders a certain peace and calm, the "quick happiness" of the title. At the end of the novel the protagonist is beginning to support himself by working with Bergmann as a male prostitute. One could argue whether his turn to prostitution is a reversion to a consumer mentality of the worst kind or an act of freedom; it is, at least, a decisive action compared with his previous helpless floundering.

Die Milchstraße (The Milky Way, 1981) is perhaps Rosei's most difficult and, at more than three hundred pages, certainly his longest work to date. The protagonist, Ellis, is an outsider who travels around visiting his friends, who also exist on the fringes of society. These friends appear briefly, comment on their situations, and disappear. The characters have few relationships with each other; all of them are connected in some in-

definable way to the central character, just as the individual stars circle about a central mass in the Milky Way. There is no real bond between people, only occasional and superficial encounters in bars and restaurants. The characters cannot be called happy, for many suffer a great deal; but they have recognized that isolation brings them as close to happiness as it is possible to come.

A similar philosophy can be discerned in *Reise ohne Ende* (Trip without End, 1983), a compilation of aphorisms, short sketches, and observations. Rosei gives minute descriptions of the objects that surround him, and each object serves as a symbol for an aspect of his philosophy. Many of the pieces are veiled in ambiguity, but Rosei's central themes emerge: man's identity with nature, the never-ending search for an unattainable goal, the drug-induced state as a metaphor for the search for one's identity, the interior world as more significant than the exterior, and isolation as the only means of overcoming the awareness of death.

In 1984 Rosei began a cycle of six prose works on a central theme. *Mann & Frau* (Man & Wife, 1984) describes a failed marriage. After leaving his wife, Munrad longs for the companionship of a woman but sees that his only hope for happiness is in living without commitment. His wife, Susanne, also realizes that a new relationship will not bring happiness. She believes that she will find fulfillment in caring for her daughter, but the two become estranged. Susanne recognizes that one needs an indifferent attitude toward others, that being "next to one another" and not "with one another" is the key to survival.

In *Komödie* (Comedy, 1984) a lonely man adopts an orphan girl. He believes that controlling the girl's destiny will bring him happiness, and it does for a time. When the girl is sent to a boarding school, however, he suffers immensely until an old friend tells him that happiness is not achieved by control over others but by coexisting without bonds.

At first reading, the third novel in Rosei's cycle seems out of tune with the first two. In *15000 Seelen* (15,000 Souls, 1985) Klockmann, a traveling representative for a book of world records, has a series of fantastic experiences: a competition for continuous shaving with disposable razors, a gigantic line of ice skaters forming the figure eight who eventually cut through the ice and perish, a circus with orgiastic spectacles and a crazed audience, a man who has the largest meat collection in the world and plays chess by manipulating mountain climbers into squares on the side of a skyscraper, and the ruins of a modern city covered with corpses and the artifacts of a throw-away culture. The novel ends with the destruction of the world. Klockmann is, however, the typical Rosei hero—he lives alone, has no friends, travels a great deal, enjoys occasional meaningless sex, and earns his living from writing. The only characteristic that sets him apart is his search for stimulation in a world outside himself, a world gone mad. Rosei is showing what awaits the individual who does not live in isolation: chaos. Seen in this light the novel does form a unity with its predecessors.

In *Die Wolken* (The Clouds, 1986) Gobbo, a clothing store owner, has an affair with Eva, the wife of his friend Reinhard, a provincial judge. When Eva realizes that Gobbo is on the brink of financial ruin, she returns to Reinhard, who has been tending his garden with seeming indifference to the affair. Rosei shows that neither marriage nor extramarital adventures can bring happiness. Nor can religion: Gobbo and Eva visit a baroque church and view a painting of Christ, but the Savior's eyes fail to meet theirs.

Der Aufstand (The Rebellion, 1987) suggests a way out of the empty human condition. Herbert, a cynical and pessimistic economics professor, has a brief homosexual affair with a student, Mark. Herbert learns from Mark that a life of lethargy, hopelessness, and disillusion can be countered by having some sort of project, and he decides to join the student demonstrations that have begun at the school.

The short *Unser Landschaftsbericht* (Our Landscape Report, 1988) describes, metaphorically and in highly poetic language, the relationship between man and nature and summarizes the ideas of the five preceeding novels. Images of the flute and the lyre suggest that the poet, rejecting reason, is uniquely suited to design a modern concept of the world.

References:

Adriane Barth, "Reise ohne Ziel," *Der Spiegel*, 33 (28 August 1979): 184-188;

Alexander von Bormann, " 'Es ist, als wenn etwas wäre': Überlegungen zu Peter Roseis Prosa," in *Studien zur österreichischen Erzählliteratur der Gegenwart*, edited by Herbert Zeman (Amsterdam: Rodopi, 1982), pp. 156-188;

Richard Exner, "Stifter und die Folgen—Schreiben ohne Menschen, ohne Ziel? Reflexionen zu Peter Roseis Prosa," *Modern Austrian Literature*, 13, no. 1 (1980): 63-90;

Ulrich Greiner, "Peter Rosei," in his *Der Tod des Nachsommers* (Munich: Hanser, 1979), pp. 139-154;

Alfred von Schirnding, "Schreiben, weil Schweigen qualvoller ist: Über Peter Rosei," *Merkur*, 33, no. 7 (1979): 714-720;

Reinhardt Stumm, "Entwürfe für eine Welt ohne Menschen: Peter Roseis Romane und Erzählungen," *Die Zeit*, 14 October 1977.

Gerhard Roth
(24 June 1942-   )

Sigrid Bauschinger
University of Massachusetts

BOOKS: *die autobiographie des albert einstein: Roman* (Frankfurt am Main: Suhrkamp, 1972);

Der Ausbruch des Ersten Weltkriegs und andere Romane (Frankfurt am Main: Suhrkamp, 1972)–comprises "Künstel," "Der Ausbruch des Ersten Weltkriegs," "How to be a detective";

Der Wille zur Krankheit: Roman (Frankfurt am Main: Suhrkamp, 1973);

Lichtenberg (Frankfurt am Main: Verlag der Autoren, 1973);

Herr Mantel und Herr Hemd (Frankfurt am Main: Insel, 1974);

Der große Horizont: Roman (Frankfurt am Main: Suhrkamp, 1974);

Ein neuer Morgen: Roman (Frankfurt am Main: Suhrkamp, 1976);

Dämmerung (Frankfurt am Main: Fischer, 1977);

Winterreise (Frankfurt am Main: Fischer, 1978); translated by Joachim Neugroschl as *Winterreise* (New York: Farrar, Straus & Giroux, 1980);

Menschen, Bilder, Marionetten: Prosa, Kurzromane, Stücke (Frankfurt am Main: Fischer, 1979);

Der stille Ozean: Roman (Frankfurt am Main: Fischer, 1980);

Circus Saluti (Frankfurt am Main: Fischer, 1981);

Die schönen Bilder beim Trabrennen (Frankfurt am Main: Fischer, 1982);

Das Töten des Bussards (Graz: Droschl, 1982);

Lichtenberg; Sehnsucht; Dämmerung: Stücke (Frankfurt am Main: Fischer, 1983);

Landläufiger Tod: Roman (Frankfurt am Main: Fischer, 1984);

Dorfchronik zum "Landläufigen Tod" (Frankfurt am Main: Fischer, 1984);

Erinnerungen an die Menschheit (Graz: Droschl, 1985);

Die Vergessenen: Roman (Frankfurt am Main: Fischer, 1986);

Am Abgrund (Frankfurt am Main: Fischer, 1986);

Der Untersuchungsrichter (Frankfurt am Main: Fischer, 1988).

Gerhard Roth was recognized as a literary genius within the avant-garde group of Forum Stadtpark artists in Graz, the capital of the southeastern Austrian province of Styria, as soon as his first book was published in 1972. He was born in Graz on 24 June 1942, one of three sons of a physician from Transylvania; his mother came from a working-class background. Instead of completing his medical studies at the University of Graz, Roth joined the Graz Center for Statistics in 1966 and later became its manager. He began to write in 1967. Since 1978 he has been a free-lance writer, living in Graz and in a Styrian village. He is divorced and the father of two daughters and a son. He received the prize of the Southwestern Broadcasting System in 1978, a fellowship from the City of Hamburg in 1979, and the Alfred Döblin Prize in 1983.

Roth's first published book was *die autobiographie des albert einstein* (the autobiography of albert einstein, 1972), about a schizophrenic who believes himself to be Albert Einstein. He also suffers from perceptual hypersensitivity: he is unable to select from among his sensory impressions and is an obsessive observer of details. In the first part of the novel, einstein walks through the city following, observing, and imitating passersby. Soon he comes to believe that he is being observed by the authorities. In the second part he turns his attention inward and develops self-destructive impulses. He rebels against the limitations of his life and the conventions of thinking and writing. In the third part he tries to describe himself with scientific accuracy; as a mere object; but his illness and his body are the sources of more and more minute details, which, in the end, cannot be captured by language. The novel ends with an autopsy report on a male corpse.

In the same year Roth published *Der Ausbruch des Ersten Weltkriegs und andere Romane* (The Outbreak of the First World War and Other Novels). "Künstel," a fragment, has a protagonist similar to einstein. Künstel–his name is derived from the word *gekünstelt* (artificial)–is an obses-

Gerhard Roth (photo: Brigitte Friedrich, Cologne)

sive observer of himself and his surroundings. His observations–whether of his own body, which develops periodontal disease and athlete's foot, or of the wall of a men's room–are so detailed as to be irritating, and Künstel is finally driven to madness and the murder of his landlady. The title story tells nothing about the beginning of World War I; it is a surrealistic spy novel set in the early nineteenth century. Roth uses a montage technique, incorporating characters and passages from Joseph Roth's *Der stumme Prophet* (1966; translated as *The Silent Prophet*, 1980) and Giuseppe Tomaso di Lampedusa's *Il Gattoppardo* (1956; translated as *The Leopard*, 1960), as well as early surreal film techniques. Similar techniques are used in "How to be a detective," in which the protagonist, Kommissar Potter, behaves more like the criminal than the detective: he literally throws evidence out the window, and in the last of the sixty-nine installments he is shot dead before solving the case. The influence of surrealistic movies such as those of Salvador Dali and Luis Buñuel is evident.

In *Der Wille zur Krankheit* (The Will to Ill-

ness, 1973) a young man named Kalb, who seems to be a medical student, is another obsessive observer. He watches everything, even observing through a magnifying glass his thumb squashing a fly. Unlike einstein and Künstel, however, Kalb is not destroyed by his illness. Kalb imagines himself to be a detective when he sees a movie about a photographer who becomes entangled in a murder case; this episode is expanded to become the main plot in Roth's novel *Ein neuer Morgen* (A New Morning, 1976).

Between 1967 and 1973 Roth's language became more economical, realistic, and impressive. His experimental play *Lichtenberg* (1973) specifically treats language: power and language are identical, until a speechless and powerless object, a retarded young man, reveals his force by shooting the eloquent professor who has taunted him. With *Sehnsucht* (Desire, 1983) Roth leaves his experimental phase behind. An egocentric writer gradually talks himself into a crisis of guilt and hurt feelings. In *Dämmerung* (Dusk, 1977) the unpleasant family and employees of a mine director, assembled in the garden of a country inn after his funeral, are blown apart by an approaching thunderstorm.

In the spring of 1973 Roth made the first of four trips to America, visiting San Francisco, Los Angeles, Las Vegas, and New York. These cities provided the background for his next novel, *Der große Horizont* (The Great Horizon, 1974). After a painful divorce, the thirty-eight-year-old Viennese book dealer Daniel Haid, a poet and hypochondriac, travels to the United States to see friends. In San Francisco a young woman with whom Haid is spending the night dies in her sleep. He becomes convinced that the police are pursuing him. His paranoia drives him from Santa Monica to Las Vegas to New York City. Haid seems to attract hatred and is also obsessed by self-criticism. When he watches an epileptic having a seizure in San Francisco and does nothing to help him, Haid hates himself for it. A normal lifetime in New York City or San Francisco would include fewer repulsive scenes than this Viennese book dealer observes in a few days: he watches a black couple having intercourse in a Buick while passing his car, passersby do not reply to his questions, a desk clerk curses him, a drunk black man hits him, he is knocked down by a Filipino. He perceives a Times Square restaurant as "Gewimmel von prostatakranken Pensionisten, jüdischen Bankbeamten, geschlechtskranken Negern, Huren ... debilen Kindermädchen ... und abgetakelten Schauspielern" (crowds of retirees with prostate ailments, Jewish bank tellers, Negroes with venereal disease, prostitutes ... feebleminded nannies ... and run-down actors). Haid's reactions to others are actually projections of his feelings about himself. He cannot avoid situations in which his hatred is aroused. Roth does not prepare the reader for the novel's conclusion: as Haid is driving through a cemetery on Long Island, the view of the Manhattan skyline becomes a vision of paradise. The experience liberates him. He is now able to call San Francisco and learn that the dead woman had a heart ailment and that he had never been suspected of murdering her. The next morning Haid is in a sunny Washington Square watching a little boy. He recalls his own childhood and his grandfather, the only person he ever truly loved; this love makes him feel invulnerable.

Roth also incorporated his American impressions into *Ein neuer Morgen,* a more polished work than *Der große Horizont* but one which lacks the earlier novel's emotional strength. Weininger,

a thirty-three-year-old Austrian photographer working on a picture volume of New York, meets an American, Norman Dalton, and begins an affair with Dalton's girlfriend Patricia. Weininger realizes that Dalton is being followed; soon afterward he finds the pursuer's body in Dalton's slum apartment. The murdered man miraculously reappears at the Easter Parade, where he is killed by a private detective, who is then shot by a policeman. Before he dies, the detective hands Patricia an envelope containing plane tickets, and she and Weininger fly to meet Dalton on the Riviera. There he tells them his story. An average man whose real name is Robert Fin, Dalton had worked for thirty years at a bank in Minneapolis. Feeling exploited, he had begun an embezzling scheme, then had abandoned his wife and children. He had fled to Chicago and then to New York, pursued by a private detective and twin crooks determined to rob him of the embezzled money. The detective killed one of the twins in Dalton's room and the other at the Easter Parade. After telling his story, Dalton disappears in a department store in Nice. Patricia returns to New York, and the novel ends with Weininger looking out of his Cannes hotel room on a bright new morning.

Weininger represents the passive European observer, Dalton the American who acts and is the master of his fate. The weaker man tries to imitate the stronger: Weininger buys a shirt like Dalton's, falls in love with Dalton's girl, and develops an interest in the antique glass Dalton used to give Patricia. He takes his New York pictures in a detached manner; his volume will not be an original collection but a typical series of sightseeing pictures. This dispassionate recording of random observations characterizes his—and Roth's—way of looking at the world. Chance rules Weininger's fate, and Weininger prefers it that way. He wants his pictures to be accidental, just as Dalton and Patricia entered his life accidentally. Passive, photographic observation and description is the primary stylistic device of the book; the wildly improbable plot is merely a framework to link the descriptions, many of which are forceful and unforgettable.

In *Winterreise* (Winter Journey, 1978; translated as *Winterreise,* 1980) Nagl, a young teacher in an Austrian village, decides on the last day of the year to change his life completely. He abruptly ends his affair with a married woman and persuades Anna, a former lover, to go with him to Italy. They travel to Naples, Rome, and

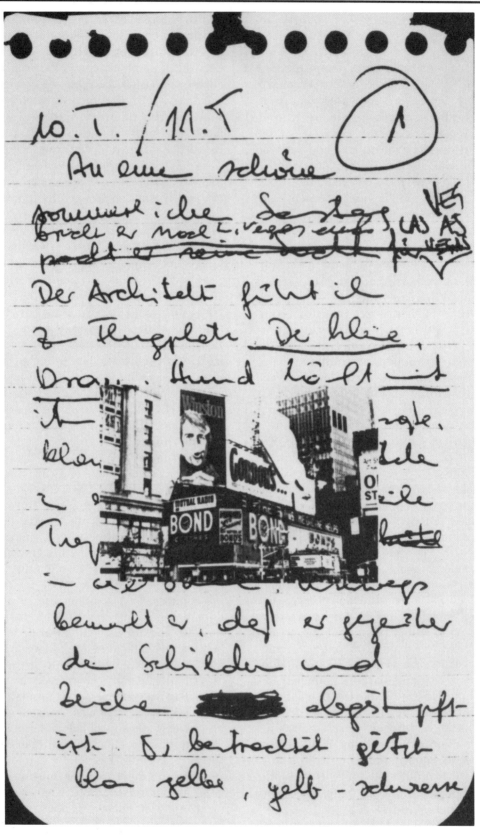

Notebook page and photograph from Roth's trip to the United States in 1973 (photo from manuscripte, *14, no. 50)*

Roth (photo copyright © by Isolde Ohlbaum, Munich)

Venice, where Anna leaves him. After a brief affair with an older woman he leaves for Fairbanks, Alaska. Like all of Roth's protagonists, Nagl is a driven man; he is a fugitive from an intolerably empty life. Images of death pervade his environment and his memory. To prove to himself that he is alive, Nagl engages in wild, desperate sex with Anna.

In *Der stille Ozean* (The Calm Ocean, 1980) the physician Dr. Ascher comes to a village in Styria to recover from the strain of a malpractice suit. He poses as a biologist who is convalescing from a severe illness. Ascher arrives in the village during hunting season. He does not hunt, but he goes along on several hunting expeditions. An outbreak of rabies results in even more hunting activity, as the villagers attempt to kill the infected animals. The hunting spreads from the animal to the human world when a farmer who kills three people is himself hunted down and turned over to the authorities. The villagers have a totally unsentimental relationship with nature; they are free of nostalgia, do not perceive

natural beauty, and have no sense of history. They tell Ascher about their harsh lives, and he gradually learns that the village society is a network of interdependence in which each person knows everything about everyone else; anonymity would be intolerable to them. It is for this reason that people always return to the village from the army, from prison, or from the insane asylum. Ascher, the observer, is increasingly drawn into this rural world; he finally decides to stay in the village as a country doctor.

In the short novel *Circus Saluti* (1981) a circus traveling through the southwestern Austrian countryside becomes a metaphor for the world at large. The director of Circus Saluti is a thoroughly evil man who exploits his animals, his workers, and his audience without a twinge of conscience. A young man who has lost his voice in an accident communicates with the circus director through messages scribbled on scraps of paper; the notes are cries of protest against the circus. The young mute represents the poet. The director sees in the mute a powerless person who cannot change anything with his writing. He offers to take the young man into his circus: "Mit Ihrem Schweigen und meinen Fragen können wir die Zuschauer zum Tränenlachen bringen" (With your silence and my questions we can make the audience cry with laughter). When the mute writes "Und am Ende?" (And in the end?) the director defines the poet's role by answering: "Am Ende behalten Sie recht. Was kümmert mich das?" (In the end you will be right. What do I care?).

After *Das Töten des Bussards* (The Killing of the Buzzard, 1982), which describes in twenty-one brief, violent episodes a series of killings committed by a creature that is apparently both man and bird, Roth continued the story of Franz Lindner, the young mute from *Circus Saluti*, in the eight-hundred-page novel *Landläufiger Tod* (Common Death, 1984). Lindner and a friend, a young law student, drive to the village depicted in *Der stille Ozean*. The director of the Circus Saluti sends an epileptic former policeman through the land as a herald of death; he walks silently and mechanically past the farms and through the villages, his white face a mask of death. Lindner's father and aunt relate innumerable accounts of death in their village. Dr. Ascher, who is now an alcoholic, complains of his miserable existence and tells of the many suicides he has witnessed; Ascher eventually takes his own life. In the second of the novel's six major parts Lindner is in an insane asylum. He passes the time by writing letters he never mails. He also writes surrealistic texts such as "Die Schöpfung" (The Creation), which consists of unconnected sentences such as "Die sprechenden Kometen beginnen sich langsam wie Pilze vom Aussehen kleiner Hunde zu verwandeln" (The talking comets slowly begin to change into mushrooms that look like small dogs). Another of Lindner's compositions, "Das Alter der Zeit" (The Age of Time), is a sequence of 679 consecutively numbered sentences of the same kind as those in "Die Schöpfung." The third part of the novel, titled "Mikrokosmus" (Microcosm), constitutes nearly half of the book. In a variety of narrative modes it relates the death of the owner of the village sawmill as told by his son, the experiences of older villagers, and technical aspects of rural life.

Death is the common theme of all these stories, which are recorded by Lindner. Amid these descriptions are many grotesque, dreamlike passages: birds talk, a knife changes into the skeleton of a bird, and radishes purr like cats. The longest narrative, "Das Verstummen des Jünglings im Feuerofen" (The Youth Falls Silent in the Fiery Furnace), is about Lindner's father, who was struck mute in 1918 when he witnessed war atrocities. Lindner asks: "Ja, aber wer wird uns die Geschichten erzählen, die als Erbgut unserer Vorfahren durch unsere Körper zirkulieren? . . . Um unseren Geist zu verwirren? Oder um uns zu erinnern, daß wir sterblich sind?" (Who will tell us stories that flow through our body as the inheritance from our ancestors? . . . [Did they give them to us] To make us insane? Or to remind us that we are mortal?). In book 4, "Aufbruch ins Unbekannte" (Departure into the Unknown), an undertaker's assistant experiences fantastic voyages into subterranean realms. Book 5 consists of sixty-six fairy tales created by asylum inmates; the tales are recorded by "the brothers Franz and Franz Lindner," showing that Lindner has a double personality even after his release.

Landläufiger Tod stretches the reader's endurance to its limits. The critic Fritz J. Raddatz accused Roth of treating topics of great import without adding anything significant to the understanding of them. Roth subsequently put together a hundred-page book, *Dorfchronik zum "Landläufigen Tod"* (Village Chronicle for "Common Death," 1984), as a "convergence" of the themes in the novel. It describes the day the village organ player died, indicating that she may have been the mother Lindner never knew. In fifty paragraphs the villagers' patterns of coexistence are displayed once more. "L." is sitting in a meadow counting the stamens of flowers. In the world of Gerhard Roth's fiction, such contentment is only possible in madness.

References:

Anne Louise Critchfield, "Austria Unmasked: The Problem of Identity . . . Prose of Bernhard, Handke, Innerhofer, and Roth," Ph.D. dissertation, University of Washington, 1985;

Elfriede Czurda, "Roths Sucht sich zu sehnen: Zur männlichen Selbstherrlichkeit in Gerhard Roths Theaterstück 'Sehnsucht,'" *Wespennest*, no. 44 (1981): 19-22;

Jörg Drews, "'Haid setzte die Brille wieder auf . . .': Über Gerhard Roths Bücher," in *Wie die Grazer auszogen, die Literatur zu erobern: Texte, Porträts, Analysen und Dokumente junger österreichischer Autoren*, edited by Drews and Peter Laemmle (Munich: Edition text + kritik, 1975);

Egon Gramer, "Lehrer in der Romanliteratur von 1978," *Diskussion Deutsch,* 11 (1980): 369-380;

Ulrich Greiner, *Der Tod des Nachsommers: Aufsätze, Porträts, Kritiken zur österreichischen Gegenwartsliteratur* (Munich: Hanser, 1979);

Peter Laemmle, "Die Ruhe auf dem Lande ist oft nur stille Wut: Zeitgenössische Autoren zum Thema: *Stadtflucht* heute," *Merkur,* 34 (1980): 938-945;

Gerhard Melzer, "Dieselben Dinge bringen langsam um: Die Reisemodelle in Peter Handkes 'Der kurze Brief zum langen Abschied' und Gerhard Roths 'Winterreise,'" in *Die andere Welt: Festschrift für Hellmuth Himmel zum 60. Geburtstag,* edited by Melzer, K. Bartsch, D. Goltschnigg, and W. Schober (Bern: Francke, 1979);

Heinz D. Osterle, "The Lost Utopia: New Images of America in German Literature," *German Quarterly,* 54 (1981): 427-446;

Fritz J. Raddatz, "Epische Geisterbahn: Gerhard Roths Roman *Landläufiger Tod* und *Dorfchronik* zu diesem Buch," *Die Zeit,* 16 November 1984, p. 23;

Jürgen Sang, *Fiktion und Aufklärung: Werkskizzen zu Andersch, Bernhard, Böll, Fichte, Frisch, Fröhlich, Grass, Handke, Härtling, Johnson, Lenz, Loetscher, Nossack, Roth, Walser, Wellershoff, Wohmann, Zwerenz* (Bern, Frankfurt am Main & Las Vegas: Lang, 1980);

Winfried Georg Sebald, *Die Beschreibung des Unglücks: Zur österreichischen Literatur von Stifter bis Handke* (Salzburg: Residenz, 1985);

Sebald, "In einer wildfremden Gegend: Zu Gerhard Roths Roman 'Landläufiger Tod,'" *manuskripte,* 26 (1986): 52-56;

Sebald, "Literarische Pornographie? Zur 'Winterreise' Gerhard Roths," *Merkur,* 38 (1984): 171-180.

Joseph Roth

(2 September 1894-27 May 1939)

Sidney Rosenfeld
Oberlin College

BOOKS: *Hotel Savoy: Ein Roman* (Berlin: Die Schmiede, 1924); translated by John Hoare in *Hotel Savoy; Fallmerayer the Stationmaster; The Bust of the Emperor* (Woodstock, N.Y.: Overlook Press, 1986);

Die Rebellion: Ein Roman (Berlin: Die Schmiede, 1924);

April: Die Geschichte einer Liebe (Berlin: Dietz, 1925);

Der blinde Spiegel: Ein kleiner Roman (Berlin: Dietz, 1925);

Juden auf Wanderschaft (Berlin: Die Schmiede, 1927);

Die Flucht ohne Ende: Ein Bericht (Munich: Wolff, 1927); translated by Ida Zeitlin as *Flight without End: A Report* (Garden City, N.Y.: Doubleday, Doran, 1930; London: Hutchinson, 1930); translated by David Le Vay and Beatrice Musgrave as *Flight without End* (London: Owen, 1977);

Zipper und sein Vater (Munich: Wolff, 1928);

Das Moskauer Jüdische Akademische Theater (Berlin: Die Schmiede, 1928);

Rechts und Links: Roman (Berlin: Kiepenheuer, 1929);

Hiob: Roman eines einfachen Mannes (Berlin: Kiepenheuer, 1930; New York: Ungar, 1945); translated by Dorothy Thompson as *Job: The Story of a Simple Man* (New York: Viking Press, 1931; London: Heinemann, 1932);

Panoptikum: Gestalten und Kulissen (Munich: Knorr & Hirth, 1930);

Radetzkymarsch: Roman (Berlin: Kiepenheuer, 1932; New York: Ungar, 1945); translated by Geoffrey Dunlop as *Radetzky March* (New York: Viking Press, 1932; London: Heinemann, 1934); translated by Eva Tucker as *The Radetzky March* (Woodstock, N.Y.: Overlook Press, 1974; London: Allen Lane, 1974);

Tarabas: Ein Gast auf dieser Erde: Roman (Amsterdam: Querido, 1934); translated anonymously as *Tarabas: A Guest on Earth* (New

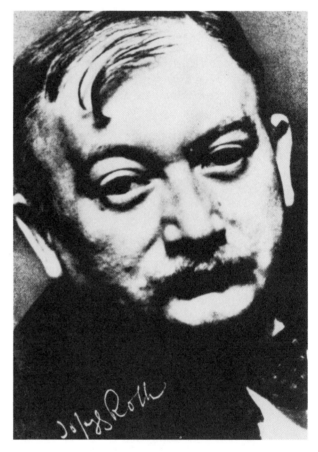

Joseph Roth (Bildarchiv der Österreichischen Nationalbibliothek)

York: Viking Press, 1934; London & Toronto: Heinemann, 1935);

Der Antichrist: Roman (Amsterdam: De Lange, 1934); translated by Moray Firth as *Antichrist* (New York: Viking Press, 1935; London & Toronto: Heinemann, 1935);

Beichte eines Mörders, erzählt in einer Nacht (Amsterdam: De Lange, 1936); translated by Desmond L. Vesey as *Confessions of a Murderer, Told in One Night* (London: Hale, 1938; Woodstock, N.Y.: Overlook Press, 1985);

Die hundert Tage: Roman (Amsterdam: De Lange, 1936); translated by Firth as *The Ballad of*

the Hundred Days (New York: Viking, 1936); translation republished as *The Story of the Hundred Days* (London: Heinemann, 1936);

Das falsche Gewicht: Die Geschichte eines Eichmeisters (Amsterdam: Querido, 1937); translated by Le Vay as *Weights and Measures* (London: Owen, 1982);

Die Kapuzinergruft: Roman (Bilthoven: De Gemeenschap, 1938; edited by A. F. Bance, London: Harrap, 1972); translated by Hoare as *The Emperor's Tomb* (London: Hogarth Press, 1984; Woodstock, N.Y.: Overlook Press, 1984);

Die Geschichte von der 1002. Nacht: Roman (Bilthoven: De Gemeenschap, 1939);

Die Legende vom heiligen Trinker (Amsterdam: De Lange, 1939); translated by E. B. Ashton as "The Legend of the Holy Drinker," in *Heart of Europe*, edited by Klaus Mann and Hermann Kesten (New York: Fischer, 1943);

Der Leviathan (Amsterdam: Querido, 1940);

Werke in drei Bänden, 3 volumes, edited by Kesten (Cologne & Berlin: Kiepenheuer & Witsch, 1956); enlarged as *Werke: Neue erweiterte Ausgabe in vier Bänden*, 4 volumes (Cologne: Kiepenheuer & Witsch, 1975-1976);

Zwischen Lemberg und Paris, edited by Ada Erhart (Graz & Vienna: Stiasny, 1961);

Romane, Erzählungen, Aufsätze (Cologne: Kiepenheuer & Witsch, 1964);

Der stumme Prophet: Roman (Cologne: Kiepenheuer & Witsch, 1966); translated by Le Vay as *The Silent Prophet* (London: Owen, 1979; Woodstock: Overlook Press, 1980);

Das Spinnennetz: Roman (Cologne & Berlin: Kiepenheuer & Witsch, 1967);

Die Büste des Kaisers: Kleine Prosa (Stuttgart: Reclam, 1969); title story translated as "The Bust of the Emperor" in *Hotel Savoy; Fallmerayer the Stationmaster; The Bust of the Emperor;*

Der neue Tag: Unbekannte politische Arbeiten 1919 bis 1927, Wien, Berlin, Moskau, edited by Ingeborg Sültemeyer (Cologne: Kiepenheuer & Witsch, 1970);

Perlefter: Die Geschichte eines Bürgers, edited by Friedemann Berger (Cologne: Kiepenheuer & Witsch, 1978);

Romane und Erzählungen (Cologne: Kiepenheuer & Witsch, 1982);

Berliner Saisonbericht: Reportagen und journalistische Arbeiten 1920-1939, edited by Klaus Westermann (Cologne: Kiepenheuer & Witsch, 1984).

Roth's mother, Maria Grübel Roth (David Bronsen, Joseph Roth: Eine Biographie, *1974)*

The Austrian novelist Joseph Roth was not yet forty-five years old when he died in French exile in 1939. Six years earlier, when he was at the peak of his literary success, his books had been outlawed and burned in Nazi Germany. From that time until his death his works were inaccessible to German readers. When the Third Reich collapsed in 1945, Roth was all but forgotten. The older generation may have still recalled him, at best, as the author of the novels *Hiob: Roman eines einfachen Mannes* (1930; translated as *Job: The Story of a Simple Man*, 1931) and *Radetzkymarsch* (1932; translated as *Radetzky March*, 1932); to the generation that had grown to adulthood during the Hitler years he was unknown. This situation changed radically in 1956, when Kiepenheuer & Witsch in Cologne published its three-volume edition of Roth's works. The rediscovered author was universally acknowledged as one of the most accomplished prose stylists in twentieth-century German literature, as a brilliant storyteller in the tradition of Gustave Flaubert, Stendhal, and–in certain of his later novels–Fyodor Dostoyevski and Nikolay Gogol. He was lauded, too, as a poetic chronicler of the lost worlds of both eastern European Jewry and Hapsburg Austria. In a review of the collected works Heinrich Böll praised Roth: "Daß sein Werk nun erscheint, ist nicht nur ein Akt der Gerechtigkeit, es füllt nicht nur eine Lücke in den meisten Bibliotheken; diese Ausgabe ist ein Geschenk, eine Überraschung, weil sie das Werk eines Dichters bietet, den man klassisch nennen kann" (That his works have now appeared is not only an act of justice, nor do they merely fill a gap in most libraries; this edition is a gift, a surprise, because it presents the work of an author whom one can call classical). By the time an enlarged edition of the collected works appeared in 1975-1976, Roth had indeed come to be regarded as one of the classical prose writers of twentieth-century German literature. English translations, both reissues of those from the 1930s and new ones, have introduced Roth to appreciative audiences in Great Britain and America.

The writer Hermann Kesten, Roth's intimate friend during his exile years and later the editor of his works, characterized Roth as a "Maskenspieler" (player of many roles). Roth suggested this view himself when he wrote in a letter of 1 October 1926 to the Frankfurt journalist and publisher Benno Reifenberg: "Ich bin ein Franzose aus dem Osten, ein Humanist, ein Rationalist mit Religion, ein Katholik mit jüdischem Gehirn, ein wirklicher Revolutionär" (I am a Frenchman from eastern Europe, a humanist, a rationalist with religion, a Catholic with a Jewish brain, a true revolutionary). The contradictory elements of Roth's personality at which this self-portrayal hints were pointedly, even grotesquely, underscored during his burial on 30 May 1939 at the Thiais Cemetery outside Paris. Among the many mourners, mainly émigrés and refugees from central Europe, was a group of Austrian legitimists delegated by the pretender to the throne, Otto von Hapsburg, who laid down a wreath dedicated to "the loyal defender of the monarchy." In angry reply the journalist Egon Erwin Kisch, representing the liberal Schutzverband deutscher Schriftsteller (Association for the Protection of the Rights of German Authors), stepped forth and threw a bouquet of

Friederike Reichler in 1922, the year of her marriage to Roth (David Bronsen, Joseph Roth: Eine Biographie, *1974*)

red carnations into the grave in the name of Roth's comrades from the Schutzverband. When an Austrian priest began the funeral ceremony, Roth's Jewish friends protested that a rabbi must be summoned to bury Roth according to Jewish rite. A Lithuanian-born Talmudist, the deceased writer's confidant in Paris, was too upset by the priest's presence to recite the kaddish. The scene–which might have been lifted from one of Roth's novels–attested to some of the intriguing riddles and paradoxes that stamped the author's life and helped to shape his literary work.

Moses Joseph Roth was born on 2 September 1894 in Brody (now in the Ukrainian Soviet Socialist Republic), an ethnically diverse town with a population of 17,500–two-thirds Jewish–in Galicia, the most easterly and most disparaged crown land of the Austro-Hungarian monarchy. He never knew his father, Nachum Roth, an unsuccessful trading agent who had gone insane while on a trip before Roth's birth and who died in 1910 in Poland. He was raised in the home of his maternal grandfather by his mother, Maria (known also as Miriam) Grübel Roth. He attended the Baron-Hirsch-Schule, a German-language elementary school run by the Brody Jewish community, from 1901 to 1905, and graduated with honors from the Imperial-Royal Crown-Prince Rudolf Gymnasium in 1913. After a semester at the University of Lemberg he entered the University of Vienna in 1914 to study German literature.

During his university years he published poems, short stories, and essays in the *Österreichs Illustrierte Zeitung*. In 1916 he left the university and enlisted in the army. While serving in the press corps in Galicia, he contributed feuilletons and poems to Vienna and Prague newspapers. After his discharge at war's end he made his way from Brody through the Carpathians and Hungary to Vienna, where he arrived in March 1919. His later claim that he had been held in Russia as a prisoner of war seems to be one of the many legends with which he embellished his biography.

For the next five years he wrote for socialist newspapers in Vienna, Prague, and Berlin. He was, however, not a political thinker; rather, he was a keen but impressionistic observer of the human condition who wrote in the conservative Viennese feuilleton tradition of Peter Altenberg and Alfred Polgar, both of whom he admired. Signing his articles in the Berlin paper *Vorwärts* "Der rote Joseph" (Red Joseph), he expressed sympathy for the disadvantaged but abstained from political activity on their behalf. In 1922 he married Friederike Reichler, a twenty-two-year-old Viennese woman.

Unlike his questionable "socialist engagement," with its romantic-poetic tendencies, Roth's opposition to National Socialism was informed by acute insight into the origins and workings of political criminality; and it was decisive and unswerving from the start. In his first novel, *Das Spinnennetz* (The Spider's Web, 1967), which was serialized in the Berlin *Arbeiter-Zeitung* in 1923, Theodor Lohse rises from lower middle-class origins through the ranks of the clandestine Fascist Right, to secret-police chief in the Weimar Republic. Benjamin Lenz, a Jewish eastern European anarchist, defeats Lohse in a clash of will and wit. Prophetically, Lenz says of Lohse: " 'Er wird Söhne zeugen, die wieder töten, Europäer, die Mörder sein werden, blutrünstig und feige, kriegerisch und national, blutige Kirchen-

besucher, Gläubige des europäischen Gottes, der Politik lenkte. Kinder wird Theodor zeugen, buntbebänderte Studenten. Schulen werden sie bevölkern und Kasernen' " ("He will produce sons, who will kill in turn. They will be Europeans, murderers, bloodthirsty and cowardly, warlike and nationalistic, bloody churchgoers, the faithful of the European God who guided politics. Theodor will produce children, dueling-fraternity students. They will populate schools and barracks").

In 1923 Roth joined the Berlin staff of the *Frankfurter Zeitung*, where his novel *Hotel Savoy* (1924, translated, 1986) first appeared. Gabriel Dan, the narrator of *Hotel Savoy*, making his way back to Vienna after three years as a prisoner of war in Siberia, takes a room in the hotel of the title. The city is unnamed but is recognizable as Lodz, Poland. Conditions in the hotel–where twenty-three of the novel's thirty short sections are fully or partly set–are intended to reflect the decay of the economic and social order after World War I. The hotel embodies a hierarchy of values based on wealth: the rich and respectable guests occupy the elegant lower floors while the top floors house a diverse group of downtrodden characters. But this microcosm does not really yield a universal model of social decay; rather, what is specifically portrayed in *Hotel Savoy* is the bleakness of *Jewish* existence in eastern Europe. The petty speculators, currency dealers, and owners of run-down factories are all Ostjuden (eastern Jews). Collectively, they symbolize the Luftmensch (trader without capital), who threatens to dissolve into nothingness as he struggles to give substance to an insecure existence. It is this world that Gabriel Dan describes most effectively and memorably. Henry Bloomfield, a philanthropic native son who made his fortune in America, returns to town, stirring hopes and schemes among the beggars and would-be entrepreneurs. Meanwhile, the town's exploited workers and unemployed veterans revolt against the order of wealth and privilege; the burning of the hotel is intended by Roth as a symbol of social conflagration.

In *Die Rebellion* (The Rebellion, 1924) Andreas Pum, a crippled war veteran, loses his faith in the justice of the state when his organ-grinder's license is revoked. At the end of the novel, as he is dying, Pum rebels against God in the name of a suffering humanity, thus rescuing his human dignity from the debasement to which his job as a toilet attendant had reduced him.

Letter from Roth to the writer René Schickele, 20 January 1930 (Verlag Kiepenheuer & Witsch, Cologne)

Dust jacket for Roth's updating of the story of Job (Verlag Kiepenheuer & Witsch, Cologne)

But the thrust of the novel remains pessimistic: exploitation and immorality are victorious in the end.

In the spring of 1925 Roth moved to Paris as cultural correspondent for the newspaper *Frankfurter Zeitung;* that fall a series of ten travel articles appeared there under the title "Im mittäglichen Frankreich" (France at Midday; republished in *Werke* [Works], 1975-1976). In 1926 the *Frankfurter Zeitung* sent him on a four-month journey through the Soviet Union. His travels resulted in seventeen articles, published in the paper between 14 September 1926 and 19 January 1927 under the title "Reise in Rußland" (Journey in Russia; republished in *Werke*). Each of these trips marks a decisive turning point in Roth's development. In southern France he discovered the vitality of the European historical and cultural tradition, in which he saw an intoxicating blend of ancient Mediterranean civilization and

medieval Catholicism. Like the nineteenth-century poet Heinrich Heine before him, he experienced France as a haven from the stifling social and political confines of bourgeois German society. In the Soviet Union, on the other hand, he discovered a spiritual and intellectual vacuity that, he thought, resulted from admiration for American material progress. He wrote in a letter of 26 September 1926: "Das Problem ist aber hier keineswegs ein politisches, sondern ein kulturelles, ein geistiges, ein religiöses, ein metaphysisches" (But the problem here is by no means political; rather it is cultural, spiritual, religious, metaphysical). The trips activated the cosmopolitan and conservative tendencies of his personality and marked the end of his sympathy for socialism.

In 1927 Roth traveled for three months in Albania, dispatching nine articles to the *Frankfurter Zeitung* under the title "Reise nach Albanien" (Journey to Albania; republished in *Werke*). That same year his long essay *Juden auf Wanderschaft* (Jews on Their Migrations) was published in Berlin. Written from intimate experience, it is an eloquent, impassioned defense of the Ostjuden in the "shtetl"–the mainly Jewish towns of eastern Europe–and in Vienna, Berlin, Paris, and Amsterdam. In the following year he went to Poland, where he wrote seven "Briefe aus Polen" (Letters from Poland; republished in *Werke*). By this time Roth had established a reputation among a broad readership as a lucid, original, and brilliant journalist.

Roth achieved his first success as a novelist in 1927 with *Die Flucht ohne Ende* (translated as *Flight without End,* 1930). This work, together with the two following novels, prompted some critics to view him as a prime exponent of the literary movement Neue Sachlichkeit (New Factualism). Born at the start of the 1920s in opposition to the excessive subjectivity of expressionism, Neue Sachlichkeit–for which the American writer Upton Sinclair provided a model–advocated the documentary, biographical, or autobiographical novel as the only adequate means of depicting current social problems. It dealt skeptically and ironically with World War I, industrialization and technology, reawakening militarism, fascism, social decay, and corruption. The preface of *Die Flucht ohne Ende* was widely considered a statement of the movement's aesthetic principles:

Im folgenden erzähle ich die Geschichte meines Freundes, Kameraden und Gesinnungs-

Second and third pages of the manuscript for Hiob *(David Bronsen,* Joseph Roth: Eine Biographie, *1974)*

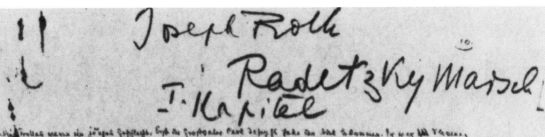

First page of the manuscript for Radetzkymarsch. *The heading is not in Roth's handwriting (Leo Baeck Institute, New York, and Kiepenheuer & Witsch).*

genossen Franz Tunda. Ich folge zum Teil seinen Aufzeichnungen, zum Teil seinen Erzählungen.

Ich habe nichts erfunden, nichts komponiert. Es handelt sich nicht mehr darum zu "dichten." Das Wichtigste ist das Beobachtete.

(In what follows I tell the story of my friend and comrade Franz Tunda, a man whose thinking I share. In part I am following his own notes, in part his oral accounts.

I have invented nothing, composed nothing. "Dreaming things up" is no longer what counts. Most important is what one has observed.)

In a 1930 article with the provocative title "Schluß mit der 'Neuen Sachlichkeit!'" (Enough of "New Factualism!," republished in *Werke*), Roth appeared to retract his own tenets. In reality, however, he was trying to clarify them, to define the possibilities of a literature of factualism. He rejects the claim of the writer to total objectivity and attacks the idea that factual depiction creates the only true literature. Facts, Roth maintains, must be shaped by language; observations must be filtered through a poetic temperament. His own novels of this period often reveal the kind of subjectivity that Neue Sachlichkeit opposed. Nonetheless, in their realism and themes they legitimately link Roth to the movement as it was represented by such outstanding exponents as Heinrich Mann, Alfred Döblin, Arnold Zweig, and Erich Kästner.

In *Die Flucht ohne Ende* Franz Tunda's "flight without end" leads him from a Siberian prisoner-of-war camp through European Russia, where he fights in the revolution as a Red Guard, back to Vienna, and on to Germany. Visiting his brother, an orchestra conductor in the Rhineland, he is disgusted by the pretense and spiritual emptiness of the bourgeoisie. At the conclusion of the novel he finds himself in the middle of Paris: "Er hatte keinen Beruf, keine Liebe, keine Lust, keine Hoffnung, keinen Ehrgeiz und nicht einmal Egoismus. So überflüssig wie er war niemand in der Welt" (He had no profession, no love, no desire, no hope, no ambition, and even no egoism. No one in the world was as superfluous as he).

The theme of *Zipper und sein Vater* (Zipper and His Father, 1928) is the homelessness of the generation that fought in the war in a world shaped by the values of its fathers. After failing at a career and at marriage, Arnold Zipper becomes a violin-playing clown on the vaudeville

stage. Like Franz Tunda, he is an outsider, a victim of society. Arnold's dull-witted younger brother, Cäsar, who lost a leg in the war, dies insane. In a "letter" appended to the novel Roth tells Zipper: "Dein Beruf ... ist symbolisch für unsere Generation der Heimgekehrten, die man verhindert zu spielen: eine Rolle, eine Handlung, eine Geige" (Your profession ... is symbolic of our generation of war returnees who are prevented from performing a role, a deed, a piece on the violin).

In *Rechts und Links* (Right and Left, 1929) Paul Bernheim dabbles in pacifist and revolutionary activities, but after his return from the war he strives after wealth and social status. He enters into a loveless marriage with the niece of an industrialist and becomes a puppet of her powerful uncle. Paul's brother Theodor joins the radical right but betrays his convictions by going to work for a Jewish-owned liberal newspaper. Theodor's patron, the Russian-Jewish financial adventurer Nikolai Brandeis, dominates the novel after he comes on the scene. The reader cannot help but conclude that Roth was uncertain of his theme and that the design of the novel had slipped from his hands.

His biographer David Bronsen concludes that by 1929 political disillusionment, financial and personal problems, and ill health worsened by excessive drinking had led Roth to a crisis of artistic doubt and self-alienation. The mental illness of his wife caused Roth agonies of guilt and despair; although there had been early signs of the schizophrenia that finally became severe in 1928, Roth blamed himself for her illness. Only once, for a short time in Berlin, had they had an apartment of their own; the rest of the time they lived in hotel rooms, and Roth had often left his oversensitive and shy wife alone while he traveled on journalistic assignments. It has also been suggested that his attempts to sophisticate the naive young woman may have hastened the onset of her illness. Roth was forced to commit her to a mental hospital in 1930; she was still institutionalized, in the Heil- und Pflegeanstalt für Geisteskranke, in Niedernhart, when she was killed by the Nazis ten years later. Roth's problems intensified steadily, and writing became torment. In July 1932 he wrote from Berlin to the author Annette Kolb: "Heute habe ich Unglück hinter und neben mir, graue Haare, eine kranke Leber und bin unheilbarer Alkoholiker" (Now misfortune is at my back and at my side; I have gray hair, a sick liver, and I am an incurable alco-

Roth (right) with Stefan Zweig in Ostend, Belgium, in 1936 (David Bronsen, Joseph Roth: Eine Biographie, *1974)*

holic). He believed that his suffering was a punishment sent by God.

Against the background of this personal misery Roth undertook the novel that was to found his reputation in twentieth-century German literature: *Hiob: Roman eines einfachen Mannes.* Its first lines make clear that Roth intended the Job of his story, the poor Russian-Jewish teacher Mendel Singer, to be a paradigmatic figure: "Er war fromm, gottesfürchtig und gewöhnlich, ein ganz alltäglicher Jude.... Er lehrte mit ehrlichem Eifer und ohne aufsehenerregendern Erfolg. Hunderttausende vor ihm hatten wie er gelebt und unterrichtet" (He was pious, God-fearing, and simple, a very ordinary Jew.... He taught with honest zeal and without conspicuous success. Hundreds of thousands of others had lived and taught as he did). Singer recognizes the tradition within which he lives. He says, as immigration to America draws near: "Hier war mein Großvater Lehrer; hier war mein Vater Lehrer, hier war ich ein Lehrer. Jetzt fahre ich nach Amerika" (My grandfather was a teacher here; my father was a teacher here; I was a teacher here. Now I'm going to America). The afflictions that strike Mendel Singer are universal, but Roth gives them a specifically Jewish cast. Mendel's daughter Mirjam indulges in trysts with "cossacks," as Mendel calls the soldiers of the nearby garrison with a contempt and dread born of the sorest Jewish experience. His son Jonas joins the Czar's army, thus moving beyond the pale of Jewish law. His oldest son, Schemarjah, has preceded the family to America, discarded the traditional orthodox garb of his people, and changed his name to Sam. Menuchim, the youngest son, a retarded cripple, is left behind in Russia. When Mendel's wife, Deborah, dies of a broken heart, Mendel grieves: "'Es ist nur schade, daß du keinen Sohn hinterlassen hast, ich selber muß das Totengebet sagen, ich werde aber bald sterben, und niemand wird uns beweinen'" ("It is a pity that you have left no son behind. I myself have to say the mourner's prayer. But soon I will die and there will be no one to mourn for us"). Since no son will remain to recite the Jewish mourner's prayer, the

last bond of Mendel's family with the Jewish people will be severed. The story culminates in the "miraculous" return of Menuchim, long presumed dead, renewing Mendel's faith in the continuity of life and the link between generations.

Contrary to the claim of some commentators, Roth's literary involvement with Jewish life and character did not begin with *Hiob* but with his first published book, *Hotel Savoy*. An episode toward the end of that novel hints that its author sought an answer to the precariousness and spiritual disorientation that stamp the lives of his figures. The narrator discovers that the real reason for the yearly return of the rich American Henry Bloomfield to his native Polish town is not to transact business, but—in the Jewish tradition—to visit the grave of his father, Jechiel Blumenfeld. Bloomfield's simple confession evokes a commentary from the narrator, Gabriel Dan: "Das Leben hängt so sichtbar mit dem Tod zusammen und das Lebendige mit seinen Toten. Es ist kein Ende da, kein Abbruch—immer Fortsetzung und

Anknüpfung" (Life is so visibly bound to death and the living with the deceased. There is no end here, no break—always continuation and linking). *Hotel Savoy* might have been a better novel had Roth pursued the Jewish theme, but he did not; and except for the noteworthy portrayal of Nikolai Brandeis in *Rechts und Links,* he all but abandoned the theme in the four novels that followed *Hotel Savoy.* When he returned to it in *Hiob,* it determined the content of the work and also a new style that departed radically from the demands of Neue Sachlichkeit. In keeping with its biblical source, *Hiob* introduces the lyrical tone that was to characterize much of Roth's later work.

If *Hiob* was Roth's tribute to his Jewish heritage, his next novel, *Radetzkymarsch,* was his profession of faith as an Austrian. In a letter of 28 October 1932 he declared: "Mein stärkstes Erlebnis war der Krieg und der Untergang meines Vaterlandes, des *einzigen,* das ich je besessen: der österreichisch-ungarischen Doppelmonarchie" (My most unforgettable experience was the war and the death of my fatherland, the *only one* that I have ever had: the Austro-Hungarian Dual Monarchy). The story of the young lieutenant Carl Joseph von Trotta reflects the decline and fall of Austria. For Trotta's grandfather, Austria was an all-embracing homeland, for whose salvation he risked his life at the Battle of Solferino. For his father, the quintessential Old Austrian civil servant, Austria exists, seemingly forever, as the sovereign realm of the emperor Franz Joseph; only when he realizes that the empire is threatened by the divisive forces of nationalism is his faith in Austria's vitality shaken. For Carl Joseph, Austria is no longer a reality in which he can find personal fulfillment. It exists only in nostalgic boyhood memories of the Radetzky March being played on Sundays by a military band and in the portrait of his grandfather, which tells of exploits that he cannot emulate.

Trotta's quest for a homeland that could be for him what the empire had been for his grandfather and even for his father leads him unknowingly to negate the supranational principle for which Austria historically stood: his request to be transferred to Slovenia, the home of his peasant ancestors, threatens to undo the assimilation of his family as Austrians that had been accomplished by his grandfather. Thus his father admonishes him: " 'Das Schicksal hat aus unserm Geschlecht von Grenzbauern Österreicher gemacht. Wir wollen es bleiben' " ("Fate has

Scene from a 1969 television film of Roth's Die Geschichte der 1002. Nacht, *directed by Peter Beauvais. Left to right: Trude Hajeck as Leni, Johanna Matz as Mizzi, and Helmut Qualtinger as Ignaz Trummer (Copyright © WDR/St. Börcsök).*

made Austrians of our family of border peasants. We want to remain Austrians"). Another character, Count Chojnicki, laments the loss of the Austrian idea of a supranational homeland: " 'Die Zeit will uns nicht mehr! Diese Zeit will sich erst selbständige Nationalstaaten schaffen! Man glaubt nicht mehr an Gott. Die neue Religion ist der Nationalismus. Die Völker gehn nicht mehr in die Kirchen. Sie gehn in nationale Vereine. Die Monarchie, unsere Monarchie, ist gegründet auf der Frömmigkeit, auf dem Glauben, daß Gott die Habsburger erwählt hat, über so und so viel christliche Völker zu regieren.... Der Kaiser von Österreich-Ungarn darf nicht von Gott verlassen werden. Nun aber hat ihn Gott

verlassen!' " ("The times no longer want us! The times want to create independent nation-states! People no longer believe in God. The new religion is nationalism. The peoples of the monarchy no longer go to church. They go to national clubs. The monarchy, our monarchy, is founded on piety: on the belief that God has chosen the Hapsburgs to rule over so and so many Christian peoples.... The Emperor of Austria-Hungary dare not be abandoned by God. But now God has abandoned him!"). Transferred to Galicia, which he chooses to think of as the "nördliche Schwester" (northern sister) of Slovenia, Trotta eventually leaves the army to live among the Ukrainian peasants. But he cannot regain the

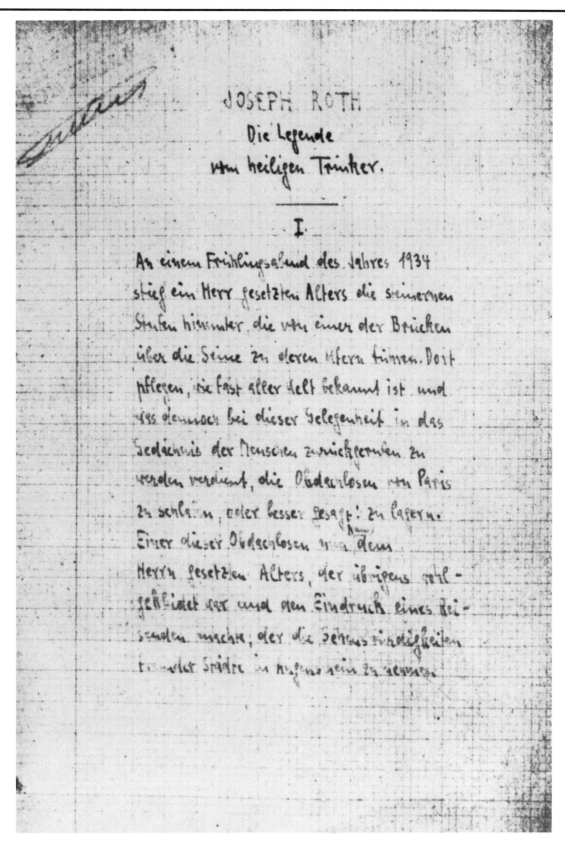

First page of the manuscript for Roth's novella Die Legende vom heiligen Trinker *(David Bronsen,* Joseph Roth: Eine Biographie, *1974)*

link with his family's past. At the outbreak of the World War I he returns to the army in the hope that he can recapture his grandfather's glory; instead, he is killed while fetching water for his men. His father dies in 1916 on the day of the emperor's burial. At the end the wise Dr. Skowronnek tells the mayor of the Trottas' provincial hometown: " 'Ich glaube, sie konnten beide Österreich nicht überleben' " ("I think that neither of them could survive Austria").

In his Vienna years from 1919 to 1923, when his sympathies still laid with the socialist movement, Roth strongly criticized the monarchy for its reactionary character; and the Austrian theme is altogether absent from the six novels that he published between 1923 and 1928. After his return to this theme in *Radetzkymarsch*, however, Roth's admiration for the monarchy became absolute veneration accompanied by unrealistic hopes for the restoration of the Hapsburgs to the throne. His passionate espousal of the Hapsburg cause was motivated by the increasing bleakness of his life, which led him to seek refuge from a hopeless present in an idealized past.

Hitler's ascent to power in 1933 cost Roth his German publishers and readers, and therewith his most vital source of income. On the morning of 30 January 1933 he left Berlin for exile in Paris. Although he would return to Vienna three times, his position in Austria was also untenable. In September 1934 he wrote to his friend, the author Stefan Zweig: "Die österreichischen Zeitungen behandeln mich als nicht existent–seit Hitler. Ich habe auch keine Freunde mehr in den Redaktionen" (The Austrian papers treat me as if I didn't exist–since Hitler. I also no longer have any friends in the editorial offices).

During his exile years Roth wrote anti-Nazi articles for exile journals in Paris, Brussels, and Prague, and his books were published in the Netherlands by Allert de Lange and Querido. But his income from these publications was small. He was constantly in debt, dependent on publishers' advances and loans from friends. He not only bore the burden of his wife's care but also helped to support the children of Andrea Manga Bell, his companion from 1931 to 1936. His favored domicile was a Paris hotel room, but he led a nomadic life that took him to Marseilles, Nice, Zurich, Amsterdam, Brussels, Ostend, and Salzburg. In 1933 and 1937 he traveled to Poland, the second time on a strenuous lecture tour at the invitation of the Polish P.E.N. Club. All the while he was tormented by guilt feelings, and

his health was growing steadily worse because of his drinking. Although he cultivated the air of an Imperial Austrian lieutenant (and falsely claimed to have been one), friends and colleagues were later to recall his often ravaged appearance. To Zweig he wrote pitifully in a letter of 12 November 1935: "es handelt sich für mich darum: *Nicht das Leben zu verlängern, sondern den unmittelbaren Tod zu verhindern.* . . . Ich versetze gewissermaßen die letzten 20 Jahre meines Lebens beim Alkohol, weil ich noch 7 oder 14 Tage Leben mir gewinnen muß" (what matters for me is this: *Not to extend my life, but to prevent my immediate death.* . . . In a sense, I am pawning the last 20 years of my life to alcohol, because I have to gain myself another one or two weeks to live).

Despite his agony, Roth continued to write. The essay *Der Antichrist* (1934; translated as *Antichrist,* 1935), which Roth called a novel, combines religious vision, political polemic, and cultural criticism in a rhapsodic damnation of the Antichrist in his twentieth-century embodiments: Nazism; communism; anti-Semitism; and technology, of which Hollywood was Roth's main example. Roth also condemned manifestations of the Antichrist among western European Jews, to whose materialism and assimilationist ambitions he opposed the traditional values of the Ostjuden, and within the Catholic church because of the Vatican's 1933 concordat with Hitler.

Der Antichrist is symptomatic of Roth's growing preoccupation with the religious themes of evil and righteousness, penance and forgiveness during his exile years. These themes are central to the four novels he published between 1934 and 1937. Nikolaus Tarabas, the protagonist of *Tarabas: Ein Gast auf dieser Erde* (1934; translated as *Tarabas: A Guest on Earth,* 1934), is–like Franz Tunda earlier–a man without a home or personal ties. But unlike the skeptical observer Tunda, Tarabas is a violent adventurer, a Czarist officer in World War I and the revolution. Now, however, it is peacetime, and he is assigned to organize a new regiment in Koropta, a tiny town in an unidentified republic. He is restless, insecure, and bored in the absence of violence. One of his soldiers incites the rest of Tarabas's men and the peasants who have come to town for the market to a pogrom against Koropta's Jews. Tormented by guilt for having failed to maintain order, Tarabas vents his frustration by ripping out the beard of Schemarjah, a frail Jew he chances to come upon after the pogrom. Recognizing this desecration as his real guilt, he becomes a hum-

Roth's grave in the Thiais Cemetery outside Paris (David Bronsen, Joseph Roth: Eine Biographie, *1974)*

ble wanderer. He finds peace only after he begs and receives forgiveness from Schemarjah, thereby fulfilling the prophecy of a gypsy at the start of the novel: "Sie werden sündigen und büßen–alles noch auf Erden" (You will sin and do penance–all in this life).

The story of Semjon Golubtschik, the narrator of *Beichte eines Mörders, erzählt in einer Nacht* (1936; translated as *Confessions of a Murderer, Told in One Night*, 1938), shares several noteworthy features with that of Nikolaus Tarabas. Both are set before World War I, partly in Russia. Just as Tarabas finds out that the New York barkeeper he had left for dead survived his murderous rage, Golubtschik discovers that he had not killed his mistress Lutetia and his half-brother the young Prince Krapotkin, whom he had found in an intimate embrace. And like Tarabas, Golubtschik only feels real remorse after he has claimed a Jewish victim: as a Czarist secret police agent in Paris, he betrays the Jewish revolutionary Chana Lea Rifkin, whose noble character had inspired him to love her. His overwhelming desire to rid himself of his laughable surname, which means "darling" or "sweetheart," and claim his birthright as the natural son of the elder Prince Krapotkin have made him "ein

hartgesottener Knecht der Hölle (a hard-boiled servant of hell). Unlike Tarabas, however, he experiences no redemption. After trying to atone for his crimes by risking his life in the war, he ends up in Paris as the henpecked husband of his former mistress, now an embittered hag.

Die hundert Tage (1936; translated as *The Ballad of the Hundred Days*, 1936) depicts the period from Napoleon's triumphant return from banishment to his defeat at Waterloo. Roth's Catholic tendencies, which were becoming ever more manifest, seem to have clouded his sense of narrative scale. The story of Napoleon's conversion from a demigod to a God-seeker who relinquishes his scepter for a cross is overwhelmed by the novel's panoramic historical setting, forcing Roth to resort to an overblown lyricism to lend epic quality to his protagonist's private fate. In his disappointment with the novel, Roth was in concurrence with its reception by the critics; but his self-criticism reflects the same religious leanings that contributed to the novel's weaknesses: he termed his project "gottlos" (impious) and said that the Antichrist had tempted him into undertaking it.

In *Das falsche Gewicht* (1937; translated as *Weights and Measures*, 1982) the Austrian weights inspector Anselm Eibenschütz, a former army man, is assigned to Zlotogrod, a Galician backwater. Despite his basically humane nature, he is unable to temper his rigid honesty with compassion for the town's indigent Jewish merchants, and they come to fear and detest him. His marriage is destroyed when his wife has his assistant's child. His moral fiber becomes corroded by lust for the sensuous gypsy Euphemia Nikitsch, and he degrades himself through drink and dissoluteness. In the end he is murdered by Nikitsch's former lover, the smuggler Jadlowker, whom Eibenschütz had contrived to send to prison so as to remove him as a rival. As he lies dying, Eibenschütz hallucinates that the Great Weights Inspector comes to test *his* "weights." Eibenschütz is astounded to hear the verdict: " 'Alle deine Gewichte sind falsch und alle sind dennoch richtig. Wir werden dich also nicht anzeigen. Wir glauben, daß alle deine Gewichte richtig sind' " ("All of your weights are false, and yet all of them are correct. Thus, we will not report you. We believe that all of your weights are correct"). This ending is ambiguous. Perhaps Eibenschütz's "false weights" were his descent into iniquity, but the novel suggests more strongly that this censure is aimed at his heartless severity in office. What, then, were the "correct weights" that merit him forgiveness in the great judgment? If they were his better human inclinations, it must be said that he never realized them.

In February 1938 Roth visited Vienna as an emissary of the legitimist supporters of Otto von Hapsburg. He planned to present Chancellor Kurt von Schuschnigg with a plan for averting the Anschluß (annexation of Austria by Nazi Germany) through a return to Hapsburg rule, but the Vienna police chief urged him to leave the country immediately. Three days later Austria became part of the Third Reich. In the following months Roth excoriated Hitler's Germany and pleaded the case of his lost homeland in public protests and impassioned articles for exile journals. He also returned to the Austrian theme in *Die Kapuzinergruft* (The Capuchin Crypt, 1938; translated as *The Emperor's Tomb*, 1984). Franz Ferdinand Trotta, an untitled cousin of Carl Joseph von Trotta of *Radetzkymarsch*, serves as an Austrian lieutenant in World War I, returns from imprisonment in a Russian prisoner-of-war camp to a society from which he feels estranged, marries a woman who leaves him for a lesbian lover and a career as a movie actress, and finally seeks refuge each evening in a Vienna coffeehouse as an "Exterritorialer . . . unter den Lebenden" (extraterritorial person . . . among the living). Like his

cousin Carl Joseph, he is unequal to the demands of society–in this case, postwar Viennese society–as well as to those of his family heritage. But whereas Carl Joseph's longing for the homeland that Austria cannot provide him defines his entire existence and radiates symbolic meaning for the most central concerns of the novel, Franz Ferdinand's search for a home is less profoundly motivated. Out of a vague feeling of homelessness, he seeks vainly for a sense of warmth or permanence. His desire to return to Sipolje, the family village in Slovenia, is merely a sentimental, romantic urge for something exotic. The critic Roland Wiegenstein pinpointed the problem when he said that Trotta is "loyal to the past because he is unable to accept the present"; the same statement could be made about Roth. At the end Trotta stands before the emperor's tomb–the Capuchin Crypt, from which the novel takes its title–and asks " 'Wohin soll ich jetzt, ein Trotta?' " ("Where can I go now, I, a Trotta?"). Roth's utopia proves once more to be not a vision of the future but a paradise lost forever.

By this time Roth's health was ruined; he had long suffered from liver disease, and in 1938 he had a heart attack. Yet he was able to write *Die Geschichte von der 1002. Nacht* (The Story of the Thousand-and-second Night, 1939), a novel that stands comparison with his finest works. Although *Die Geschichte von der 1002. Nacht* is set in the comparatively untroubled epoch just before the turn of the century, the darkness of the 1930s casts its shadow over the novel. The three principal figures–the ne'er-do-well cavalry captain Baron Taittinger, the aging madam Frau Matzner, and the gullible prostitute Mizzi Schinagl–receive unexpected rewards from a visit by the Shah of Persia to Frau Matzner's brothel. But their good fortune only confronts them with the emptiness of their existence. Deprived of their illusions, they become alienated and hopeless. After she leaves the security of the brothel, Mizzi is cast off by Taittinger, the father of her illegitimate son, and becomes the "Lieblingsfrau des Schas" (Favorite Wife of the Shah) in a sideshow. Frau Matzner also retires from her profession; consumed by her miserliness, she dies a fearful old woman. Taittinger is forced to withdraw from the army, his only real home, when his role in the Shah's visit to the brothel is revealed; unable to master the complexities of civilian life, he shoots himself. The novel exposes the moral lethargy, callousness, and self-deception that lay below the surface of gay Vienna.

In the spring of 1939 Roth ignored invitations to the United States from Eleanor Roosevelt and from Dorothy Thompson, the president of the American P.E.N. Club. He had given up hope and was waiting to die. His final work, the novella *Die Legende vom heiligen Trinker* (1939; translated as "The Legend of the Holy Drinker," 1943), is the story of the Paris tramp Andreas Kartak. After serving a prison term for murder and leading a dissipated life under the bridges of the Seine, Kartak, a coal miner from Polish Silesia, is set on the path of virtue through an unlikely series of "miracles"; but he succumbs repeatedly to temptation. He dies blissfully in the chapel of Ste Marie des Batignolles, believing that he has finally redeemed his vow to give two hundred francs as a tribute to Saint Thérèse de Lisieux; actually, however, he has given the money to an angelic-looking young girl named Thérèse. The narrator compassionately comments: "Gebe Gott uns allen, uns Trinkern, einen so leichten und so schönen Tod!" (May God grant all of us drinkers such an easy and beautiful death!).

Roth's death was neither easy nor beautiful. After learning that his friend, the dramatist Ernst Toller, had committed suicide in New York exile, he collapsed in the Café Tournon and was taken to the Hôpital Necker. On 27 May 1939, after four agonizing days of delirium tremens, he died of pneumonia.

Letters:

Joseph Roth: Briefe 1911-1939, edited by Hermann Kesten (Cologne & Berlin: Kiepenheuer & Witsch, 1970).

Biography:

David Bronsen, *Joseph Roth: Eine Biographie* (Cologne: Kiepenheuer & Witsch, 1974).

References:

Heinz Ludwig Arnold, ed., *Joseph Roth* (Munich: Edition text + kritik, 1974);

Heinrich Böll, "Die Trauer, die recht behielt: Leben und Work von Joseph Roth," *Deutsche Rundschau*, 6 (1957): 274-278;

David Bronsen, "Austrian versus Jew: The Torn Identity of Joseph Roth," in *Yearbook XVIII: Publications of the Leo Baeck Institute* (London: Secker & Warburg, 1973), pp. 219-226;

Bronsen, "The Jew in Search of a Fatherland: The Relationship of Joseph Roth to the Habsburg Monarchy," *Germanic Review*, 54 (Spring 1979): 54-61;

Bronsen, ed., *Joseph Roth und die Tradition* (Darmstadt: Agora, 1974);

Rudolf Koester, *Joseph Roth* (Berlin: Colloquium, 1982);

Hermann Linden, ed., *Joseph Roth: Leben und Werk, Ein Gedächtnisbuch* (Cologne: Kiepenheuer, 1949);

Claudio Margris, *Lontano da dove: Joseph Roth e la Tradizione Ebraico-Orientale* (Turin: Einaudi, 1971); translated by Jutta Prasse as *Weit von wo: Verlorene Welt des Ostjudentums* (Vienna: Europaverlag, 1974);

Helmuth Nürnberger, *Joseph Roth in Selbstzeugnissen und Bilddokumenten* (Reinbek: Rowohlt, 1981);

Günther Pflug, ed., *Joseph Roth, 1894-1939: Eine Ausstellung der Deutschen Bibliothek Frankfurt am Main*, second revised edition (Frankfurt am Main: Buchhändler-Vereinigung, 1979);

Marcel Reich-Ranicki, "Joseph Roths Flucht ins Märchen," in his *Nachprüfung: Aufsätze über deutsche Schriftsteller von gestern* (Munich: Piper, 1977), pp. 202-228;

Hartmut Scheible, *Joseph Roth, mit einem Essay über Gustav Flaubert* (Stuttgart: Kohlhammer, 1971);

Ingeborg Sültemeyer, *Das Frühwerk Joseph Roths: 1915-1926* (Vienna: Herder, 1976);

Frank Trommler, "Die österreichische Szene," in his *Roman und Wirklichkeit* (Stuttgart: Kohlhammer, 1966), pp. 50-67;

Roland Wiegenstein, "Die gerettete Welt des Joseph Roth," *Frankfurter Hefte*, 12 (1957): 581-586;

Cedric E. Williams, "Joseph Roth: A Time out of Joint," in his *The Broken Eagle: The Politics of Austrian Literature from Empire to Anschluss* (New York: Barnes & Noble, 1974), pp. 91-112.

Papers:

The Leo Baeck Institute, New York, houses an extensive Joseph Roth archive containing manuscripts, letters, and other materials.

George Saiko
(5 February 1892-23 December 1962)

Friedrich Achberger
University of Minnesota

BOOKS: *Auf dem Floß: Roman* (Zurich: Posen, 1948; revised edition, Hamburg: Von Schröder, 1954);

Der Mann im Schilf: Roman (Hamburg: Von Schröder, 1955; enlarged edition, Einsiedeln, Zurich & Cologne: Benziger, 1971);

Die dunkelste Nacht, edited by Ferdinand Wernigg (Graz & Vienna: Stiasny, 1961);

Giraffe unter Palmen: Geschichten vom Mittelmeer (Vienna: Deutsch, 1962)–comprises "Giraffe unter Palmen," "Das andere Leben," "Der feindliche Gott," "Die dunkelste Nacht," "Die Statue mit dem Gecko," "Die Geburt des Lammes," "Hafen der Venus," "Das offene Tor";

Der Opferblock (Vienna, Stuttgart & Basel: Deutsch, 1962)–comprises "In den Klauen des Doppeladlers" and "Die Badewanne";

Die erste und die letzte Erzählung (Vienna: Bergland, 1968)–comprises "Das letzte Ziel" and "Amelie auf dem Postament";

Erzählungen (Einsiedeln, Zurich & Cologne: Benziger, 1972);

Sämtliche Werke in fünf Bänden (Salzburg: Residenz, 1985).

OTHER: Georg Ebert, ed., *Der Zauberwald: Deutsche Märchen*, foreword by Saiko (Vienna: Verlag der Wiener Graphischen Werkstätte, 1922);

"Europa als Wunsch und Wirklichkeit," in *Lebendige Stadt: Literarischer Almanach der Stadt Wien* (Vienna: Amt für Kultur, Volksbildung und Schulverwaltung, 1960), pp. 11-18.

PERIODICAL PUBLICATIONS: "Das letzte Ziel," as Markus Saiko, *Der Brenner*, 15 (1913): 675-693;

"Die gnadenlose Stadt," *Die Muskete: Humoristische Wochenzeitung*, 458 (1914): 115-118;

"The Meaning of Cubism: 'Cubist' Drawings of the Sixteenth Century," translated by Ar-

George Saiko, 1962 (photo: Magdalena Saiko)

thur Oakey, *The Studio*, 100 (1930): 206-213;

"The Possibility of Symbolism in Modern Painting," translated by Oakey, *Creative Art*, 9 (1931): 467-474;

"The Tragic Position of Abstract Art," translated by Oakey, *The Studio*, 105 (1933): 43-48;

"Why Modern Art Is Primitive," translated by Oakey, *The Studio*, 108 (1934): 274-277;

"Zur Entstehung des modernen Landschaftsgefühls," *Die Schönen Künste*, 1 (1947): 20-25;

"Die Wirklichkeit hat doppelten Boden: Gedanken zum magischen Realismus in der Literatur," *Aktion*, 19 (1952): 80-82;

"Surrealismus und Realität: Aus den Prinzipien einer neuen Ästhetik," *Kontinente*, 11 / 12 (1955): 35-40;

"Zur Erneuerung des Romans," *Wiener Bücherbriefe*, 3 (1955): 1-3;

"Hinter dem Gesicht des Österreichers," *Comprendre: Société Européenne de Culture*, 17 / 18 (1957): 141-148;

"Die Rückkehr aus dem Unbewußten: Das Facit des Surrealismus," *Wort in der Zeit*, 5, no. 4 (1959): 15-18;

"Der Roman: heute und morgen," *Wort in der Zeit*, 9, no. 2 (1963): 37-40;

"Zur 'Entschlüsselung' der Symbolik in zwei Kurzgeschichten," *Literatur und Kritik*, 14 (1967): 213-215;

"Zur Situation der erzählenden Prosa," *Wiener Bücherbriefe*, 1 (1969): 1-5;

"Ein unveröffentlichtes Kapitel aus dem Roman *Der Mann im Schilf*," *protokolle*, 2 (1970): 148-152;

"Roman und Film: Die Formen unserer Weltinterpretation," *Literatur und Kritik*, 54 / 55 (1971): 271-282.

George Saiko's two novels and short stories contain a complex literary world in which examination of recent history is combined with exploration of the unconscious. Like Robert Musil, Hermann Broch, and Heimito von Doderer, Saiko deals with historic change in central Europe, especially the dissolution of the Austro-Hungarian Empire after World War I. Saiko's attempts to depict the totality of society can be compared to Musil's similar attempt in *Der Mann ohne Eigenschaften* (1930-1933, 1943; translated as *The Man without Qualities*, 1953-1960) or Doderer's in *Die Dämonen* (1956; translated as *The Demons*, 1961). Along with such modernist writers as Musil, James Joyce, Virginia Woolf, Broch, and William Faulkner, Saiko tries to expand the boundaries of the "sayable" far beyond the limits of the traditional novel. Saiko's works are Austrian in content but international in their experimental nature.

Georg Emmanuel Saikow was born on 5 February 1892 in Seestadtl, Bohemia (now Czechoslovakia). After deciding against a military career, he studied art history, archaeology, psychology, and philosophy at the University of Vienna. He spent much of the 1920s and 1930s abroad, mostly in Paris, studying modern art and publishing articles on the subject in British journals. An anglophile, he changed his first name to the English "George" and dropped the final *w* from his surname. He completed his first novel, *Auf dem Floß* (On the Raft, 1948), in 1938 or 1939; because the Nazis were in power in Germany and Austria, the book was not published until after World War II.

During the war Saiko was the curator of graphic arts at the Albertina in Vienna. He prevented the plunder of the museum's collection by giving fakes to Nazi officials and, after the liberation of Vienna, to Soviet officers. He resigned from the position in a dispute with the state which was not settled until 1951. He remained in retirement until his death. During the 1950s he published his second novel and several short stories. Two volumes of his short stories were published in 1962.

Saiko's first story, "Das letzte Ziel" (The Last Goal), was published in the journal *Der Brenner* in 1913. After receiving a modest promotion, the middle-aged civil servant Schneider revives his hope of becoming a father; but his plan, announced abruptly after years of poverty and self-denial, meets with incomprehension on the part of his wife. Schneider tramples her to death because she represents the prison he had built for himself. This early story reveals Saiko's skepticism toward the veneer of civilization and his belief in the Freudian concept of the self.

The novel *Auf dem Floß* is set on a large country estate in eastern Austria sometime after 1918. The indeterminacy of time and place contributes to the atmosphere of being adrift that is indicated by the title. The estate of Alexander, Prince Fenckh, serves as a would-be refuge where he attempts to live without interference from his older brother, Bishop Nico. Alexander is an anachronism: all titles of nobility had been abolished by the First Austrian Republic in April 1919, and his rule over his estate is generally ineffectual. He is torn between his lust for the sensual gypsy Marischka and his love for the countess Mary Tremblaye, who lives on the neighboring estate. When his houseguest Eugen woos Mary away from him, Alexander turns to her daughter, Gise. The novel also tells of the strange relationship between Alexander and his gigantic doorman, Joschko. Alexander's original intention is to draw Joschko into a symbiosis in which his own intelligence and Joschko's brawn will complement each other. When his brother

Saiko reading from his short-story collection Giraffe unter Palmen

pressures him to give up Marischka, Alexander marries her off to Joschko; in retaliation, Marischka poisons and finally suffocates Joschko. Alexander plans to have the doorman stuffed and to exhibit him in the great hall; but Marischka and her accomplice, Imre, sink the body in the swamp and flee. Finally, Alexander asserts his independence of his brother by announcing his plan to marry Gise. Saiko tries to grasp the human experience not only on the outer level of what happened but also on the subliminal level of feelings, associations, miscarried intentions, and repressions; the novel's main focus is on how actions are imbedded in a system of psychic events.

Auf dem Floß can also be read as an allegory dealing with the question of Austrian identity in a time of transition. Alexander represents an Austrian ruling elite cut off from its traditional purpose. The bishop, who abandoned a military career and abdicated his rights as the firstborn, symbolizes the Catholic church in Austria after 1918. The various ethnic groups in the novel–Hungarian, Slovak, gypsy, Austrian–suggest the problem of particularism resulting from the dissolution of the empire. Alexander's project of stuffing Joschko after his death may be read as a meta-

phor for the "Austrian Idea" that was propagated during and after the breakup of the empire in an attempt to reaffirm a multinational mission for Austria.

Saiko's second novel, *Der Mann im Schilf* (The Man in the Reeds), was published in an abridged version in 1955 and in a complete version in 1971. It focuses on the failed putsch of 25 July 1934 in which Austrian National Socialists assassinated Chancellor Engelbert Dollfuß but then were almost comically inept at linking up with the rest of Austria and with Nazi Germany. Saiko's choice of this incident does not allow for sharply defined issues and positions, for the differences between the authoritarian Dollfuß regime and the Fascists were less significant than their common negative views on democracy, socialism, and Jews. The British archaeologist Sir Gerald, his wife Loraine, and the Austrian Robert, on their way to London from an archaeological dig in Crete, stop off in Salzburg so that Robert can see his lover Hanna. The bungled Nazi putsch is witnessed by Robert and Hanna at a lakeside resort near Salzburg. After her reunion with Robert goes awry, Hanna conceives the project of rescuing a wounded fugitive who is hiding in the reeds that border the lake.

Dust jacket for the last of Saiko's books to be published during his life. It contains two stories.

Loraine and Gerald agree to transport the fugitive to safety rolled up in the sail of their boat, but Hanna is shot by the militia and the roll of sailcloth in her car is found to be empty. Far from advocating the irrationalism it depicts, the novel constitutes a scathing critique of the mentalities of the 1930s.

A group of stories collected in 1962 under the title *Giraffe unter Palmen* (Giraffe under Palm Trees) is linked by Italian themes. The title refers to the tattoo on the arm of Brogio, an Italian fisherman in the four-page title story. Brogio's terminally ill wife, Betta, has been clinging to life for weeks, and her friend Letizia has been caring for the household. The sexual attraction between Brogio and Letizia makes the neck of the giraffe on Brogio's muscular arm turn into a phallic sym-

bol in Letizia's eyes. Betta dies at the moment that she realizes their desire for each other. Saiko stages the conflict in "Giraffe unter Palmen" on two levels: that of conscious, conventional reality is sketched with a minimum of strokes, whereas that of subliminal, spontaneously perceived reality comes under detailed scrutiny. As Brogio washes himself the images on his body come to life, and Letizia reads their sign language. After Betta's funeral Letizia joins Brogio, with the approval of the community. In "Die Geburt des Lammes" (The Birth of the Lamb), another story in the collection, Paul and Gerda visit an ancient fertility temple on a sightseeing tour. Paul feels that it would be "inconvenient" for them to have a child; Gerda, who is pregnant without Paul's knowledge, begins to recognize her link to the symbols and reality of birth that surround her. As the two watch the birth of a lamb, Gerda realizes their incompatibility and, in a rage, almost pushes Paul over a cliff to his death. This story discredits conventional behavior–Paul is a caricature of smug rationality–by juxtaposing it with a rich realm of nonrationality: the realm of instinct, genius loci, myth. In "Das andere Leben" (The Other Life) the tourist Harold's desire to stay in the primitive fishing village he considers a paradise is met by scornful laughter from the local schoolteacher, who calls the village a prison. In characteristic fashion, this story develops contrasts but does not spell out a resolution.

The last story to appear during Saiko's lifetime was "Die Badewanne" (The Bathtub), published in the volume *Der Opferblock* (The Sacrificial Stone, 1962). The narrator, Rubiczka von Felsenwehr, vacationing in the late 1940s or early 1950s, reconstructs the story of a German army retreating through Russia in 1943. The army is commanded by a hedonistic general who desperately wants a bathtub so that he can persuade a woman to stay with him. A lieutenant, seeing a chance for promotion, "liberates" a tub in a foray that costs the lives of seventeen of his men and an equal number of Russians. Grotesque as this anecdote is in itself, it acquires its edge only in the barroom context of its retelling and in the prevailing attitude that nothing needs to be rethought. Years after World War II neither teller nor listeners see a need to change their views.

In the same year *Giraffe unter Palmen* and *Der Opferblock* were published, Saiko received his first major recognition, the Great Austrian State Prize. He died on 23 December 1962 in Rekawinkel, near Vienna.

References:

Ernst Alker, "George Saiko," *Schweizer Monatshefte*, 6 (1971): 443-446;

Alfred Doppler, *Wirklichkeit im Spiegel der Sprache: Aufsätze zur Literatur des 20. Jahrhunderts in Österreich* (Vienna: Europa, 1975), pp. 172-196;

Jeannie Ebner, "Hermann Broch und George Saiko," *Literatur und Kritik*, 54 / 55 (1971): 262-270;

Carol Lewis, "Search for Identity: Theme and Structure in George Saiko's *Auf dem Floß*," Ph.D. dissertation, Indiana University, 1977;

Christina Mayr, "Historisch-zeitkritische und psychoanalytische Dimensionen im Werk von George Saiko, unter besonderer Berücksichtigung seines Romans *Der Mann im Schilf*," Ph.D. dissertation, University of Innsbruck, 1978;

Janko von Musulin, "George Saiko," in *Schriftsteller der Gegenwart*, edited by Klaus Nonnemann (Olten: Walter, 1963), pp. 267-274;

Heinz Rieder, "George Saiko," in his *Österreichische Moderne: Studien zum Weltbild und Menschenbild in ihrer Epik und Lyrik* (Bonn: Bouvier, 1968), pp. 94-108;

Roman Roček, "Bewußtstein aus dem Konflikt: George Saiko," in his *Neue Akzente: Essays für Liebhaber der Literatur* (Vienna: Herold, 1984), pp. 163-173;

George C. Schoolfield, "Exercises in Brotherhood: The Recent Austrian Novel," *German Quarterly*, 26 (1953): 228;

Zsuzsa Széll, "George Saikos Wirklichkeit," *Literatur und Kritik*, 99 (1975): 553-561;

Cedric E. Williams, "George Saiko: Worlds within World," in *Modern Austrian Writing: Literature and Society after 1945*, edited by Alan Best and Hans Wolfschütz (London: Wolff, 1980), pp. 97-107.

Friedrich Torberg

(16 September 1908-10 November 1979)

Cornelius Schnauber
University of Southern California

BOOKS: *Der ewige Refrain: Lieder einer Alltagsliebe* (Vienna: Saturn, 1929);

Der Schüler Gerber hat absolviert: Roman (Vienna: Zsolnay, 1930); translated by F. A. Voight as *The Examination* (London: Chatto & Windus, 1932); German version revised as *Der Schüler Gerber: Roman* (Vienna: Zsolnay, 1954);

—und glauben, es wäre die Liebe: Roman unter jungen Menschen (Vienna: Zsolnay, 1932);

Die Mannschaft: Roman eines Sport-Lebens (Leipzig & Mährisch-Ostrau: Kittl, 1935);

Abschied: Roman einer ersten Liebe (Zurich: Humanitas, 1937);

Mein ist die Rache (Los Angeles: Pazifische Presse, 1943; Vienna: Bermann-Fischer, 1947);

Hier bin ich, mein Vater: Roman (Stockholm: Bermann-Fischer, 1948);

Die zweite Begegnung: Roman (Frankfurt am Main: Fischer, 1950);

Adenauer und die Intellektuellen (Cologne: Verlag Staat und Gesellschaft, 1957);

Lebenslied: Gedichte aus fünfundzwanzig Jahren (Munich: Langen-Müller, 1958);

PPP: Pamphlete, Parodien, Post Scripta (Munich: Langen-Müller, 1964);

Mit der Zeit, gegen die Zeit (Graz & Vienna: Stiasny, 1965);

Das fünfte Rad am Thespiskarren: Theaterkritiken, 2 volumes (Munich: Langen-Müller, 1966-1967);

Golems Wiederkehr und andere Erzählungen (Frankfurt am Main: Fischer, 1968);

Süßkind von Trimberg: Roman (Frankfurt am Main: Fischer, 1972);

Die Tante Jolesch oder Der Untergang des Abendlandes in Anekdoten (Munich: Langen-Müller, 1975);

Die Erben der Tante Jolesch (Munich: Langen-Müller, 1978);

Apropos: Nachgelassenes, Kritisches, Bleibendes (Munich & Vienna: Langen-Müller, 1981);

Auch das war Wien: Roman, edited by David Axmann and Marietta Torberg (Munich: Langen-Müller, 1984);

Friedrich Torberg (photo copyright © by Hilde Zemann, Munich)

Der letzte Ritt des Jockeys Matteo: Novelle aus dem Nachlaß, edited by Axmann and Marietta Torberg (Munich: Langen-Müller, 1985);

Auch Nichtraucher müssen sterben: Essays, Feuilletons, Notizen, Glossen (Munich: Langen-Müller, 1985).

OTHER: *Zehnjahrbuch 1938-1948*, edited by Torberg (Vienna & Stockholm: Bermann-Fischer, 1948);

Fritz von Herzmanovsky-Orlando, *Gesammelte Werke*, edited by Torberg, 4 volumes (Munich: Langen-Müller, 1958-1964);

Franz Mittler, *Gesammelte Schüttelreime*, edited by Torberg (Vienna: Gardena, 1969).

TRANSLATIONS: George Mikes, *Fernöstlicher Diwan: Eine Asienreise in achtzig Tagen* (Zurich: Diogenes, 1959);

Mikes, *Zwergstaaten für Anfänger: Liechtenstein, Monaco, San Marino, Andorra* (Zurich: Diogenes, 1959);

Ephraim Kishon, *Drehn Sie sich um, Frau Lot!: Satiren aus Israel* (Munich: Langen-Müller, 1962);

Kishon, *Arche Noah, Touristenklasse: Neue Satiren aus Israel* (Munich: Langen-Müller, 1963);

Kishon, *Der seekranke Walfisch oder Ein Israeli auf Reisen: Satiren* (Munich: Langen-Müller, 1965);

Kishon, *Wie unfair, David! und andere israelische Satiren* (Munich: Langen-Müller, 1967);

Kishon, *Pardon, wir haben gewonnen: Vom Sechstagekrieg bis zur Siegesparade 1 Jahr danach. Satiren* (Munich: Langen-Müller, 1968);

Kishon, *Beste Geschichten* (Berlin: Herbig, 1968);

Kishon, *Nicht so laut vor Jericho: Neue Satiren* (Munich: Langen-Müller, 1970);

Kishon, *Der Blaumilchkanal: Satirische Szenen* (Munich: Langen-Müller, 1971);

Kishon, *Kishons buntes Bilderbuch* (Munich: Langen-Müller, 1971);

Kishon, *Salomos Urteil–zweite Instanz: Neue Satiren* (Munich: Langen-Müller, 1972);

Kishon, *Kein Applaus für Podmanitzki: Satirisches* (Munich: Langen-Müller, 1973);

Kishon, *Kein Öl, Moses? Neue Satiren* (Munich: Langen-Müller, 1974);

Kishon, *Es war die Lerche: Ein heiteres Trauerspiel* (Frankfurt am Main: Fischer, 1975);

Kishon, *In Sachen Kain & Abel: Neue Satiren* (Munich: Langen-Müller, 1976);

Kishon, *Das große Kishon Karussell: Gesammelte Satiren* (Munich: Langen-Müller, 1978);

Kishon, *Kishon für Kenner: ABC der Heiterkeit*, edited by Brigitte Sinhuber-Erbacher, translated by Torberg (Munich: Langen-Müller, 1978);

Kishon, *Das Kamel im Nadelöhr: Neue Satiren*, translated by Torberg, Gerhard Bronner, and Immanuel Rosenne (Munich: Langen-Müller, 1982);

Kishon, *Bekenntnisse eines perfekten Ehemannes: Gesammelte Satiren*, translated by Torberg

and Bronner (Munich & Vienna: Langen-Müller, 1983).

For several decades Friedrich Torberg was a major figure in Austrian cultural life: controversial but always powerful; often hated, but–because of the incisiveness of his thinking and the consistency and integrity of his opinions–admired even by his enemies. He was also–to his disappointment–better known as one of Europe's leading critics of cultural politics and society than as a writer. This one-sided assessment is understandable: as an author Torberg is important and often underestimated; but as a critic he is fascinating, influential, and unique. He began to write parodies, pamphlets, and satirical essays in the late 1920s; the tone and the topics grew more serious during his exile in France and the United States. He developed these forms to a unique quality of style and trenchancy after he returned to Austria in 1951. Their only shortcoming–but one roundly criticized by his detractors–is that for the sake of an effective play on words Torberg sometimes abandons his objectivity and becomes polemical. Almost all of these works, however, no matter how topical, still make enjoyable reading, and they have been published in new editions since Torberg's death. Because of the continued success of this "short prose" there is a tendency to overlook the quality of his novels, novellas, and poems, some of which have also been republished since Torberg died.

Friedrich Kantor-Berg was born on 16 September 1908 in Vienna to Alfred Kantor and Therese Berg Kantor. In 1922 his family moved to Prague. In 1926 he published his first short stories in newspapers and magazines under the name Torberg, which became his legal name in 1930. He failed his final high school exam in 1927 and had to repeat the last year, an agony which led to his first novel, *Der Schüler Gerber hat absolviert* (The Pupil Gerber Has Graduated, 1930; translated as *The Examination*, 1932). Torberg describes the suffering of a pupil under the restrictive rules of an Austrian gymnasium and its oppressive teachers. This treatment leads to the protagonist's suicide, an act which was not uncommon among central European high school pupils at that time. The novel was an instant success, was translated into ten languages, and was filmed as recently as 1981.

Between 1928 and 1938 Torberg worked as a free-lance editor, reporter, and critic for newspapers and magazines in Prague, Leipzig, Berlin,

Cover of Torberg's novel about the love of a Jewish author and a gentile actress in Nazi-occupied Vienna

and Vienna. He published his first volume of poems, *Der ewige Refrain* (The Eternal Refrain), in 1929. After 1930 he divided his residence between Prague and Vienna. His next novel, *–und glauben, es wäre die Liebe* (–And They Believe It To Be Love, 1932), written in diary form, examines the relationships, emotions, and confrontation with the problems of the times of a group of young intellectuals.

A passionate soccer player, professional swimmer, and water polo player in Czechoslovakia between 1926 and 1932, Torberg describes in his next novel, *Die Mannschaft* (The Team, 1935), the struggle of Harry Baumeister to become a soccer player and his disappointment with the growing commercialism associated with the sport. Like Torberg, Baumeister switches to swimming and

water polo. Beneath these surface problems lies the never-ending conflict between the individual and the "team" or group in general.

In 1938 and 1939 Nazi Germany occupied Austria and Czechoslovakia, respectively; Torberg, a Jew, fled from Vienna to Paris via Prague and Zurich. During that period he was writing the novel *Auch das war Wien* (This Too Was Vienna), which was published posthumously in 1984. It was the basis for the Austrian film *38*, which received an Academy Award nomination for best foreign-language film in 1987. Martin, a Jewish author, falls in love with Karola, a gentile actress, and they move into an apartment in Vienna. But their dreams of a pleasant and romantic future are shattered by the Anschluß (annexation of Austria by Germany) in 1938. Karola

Torberg (left) with Reinhard Federmann, general secretary of the Austrian P.E.N. Club, in 1974

escapes; Martin is captured; and the historic streets of Vienna, which are vividly described by the homesick Torberg, are taken over by German and Austrian storm troopers.

In 1939 Torberg became a volunteer in the French army. In June 1940, after France surrendered, he escaped via Portugal to New York and then Los Angeles. Called one of the "ten outstanding Anti-Nazi writers" by the American P.E.N. Club, Torberg received a one-hundred-dollar-per-week contract to write film scripts for Warner Bros. Many exiled German and Austrian authors received such one-year contracts from the Hollywood studios, but only a few of them produced usable screenplays during the period of their contracts or as free-lance writers afterward. Torberg's only accepted script was written three years after his studio tenure: *Voice in the Wind* (1944), starring Francis Lederer, was an instant success and resulted in offers of new film contracts. But Torberg refused, and in 1944 he returned to New York. In December 1945 he married Marietta Bellak there.

Voice in the Wind is the story of a Czech pia-

nist who is arrested for playing the forbidden piano version of Bedřich Smetana's *Moldau*. He escapes while being transported to a concentration camp, but because of a head injury inflicted by the Gestapo during his interrogation, he suffers from amnesia and ends up doing odd jobs for an Italian criminal on the French island of Guadeloupe, where he finally dies. An adventurous escape via Lisbon, sinister gangsters in Lisbon and Guadeloupe, a love story, the protagonist's returning in flashbacks while he is playing the piano in Guadeloupe, and the sometimes lyrical and sometimes melodramatic dialogues give the film excitement, color, and atmosphere.

While living in Los Angeles, Torberg also wrote the novella *Mein ist die Rache* (Vengeance Is Mine, 1943), one of his best works of fiction. *Mein ist die Rache* is the story of the terrible suffering of eighty Jewish inmates in a German concentration camp under the sophisticated and sadistic brutality of its new commandant, Wagenseil, who rationalizes the Nazi program of genocide: " 'Die jüdische Weltverschwörung besteht darin, daß es

Torberg (right) with the Israeli author Ephraim Kishon, many of whose satires Torberg translated into German (photo: Hanns Hubmann, Ambach)

Juden gibt. Und sie wird so lange bestehen als es Juden gibt. Jeder Jude gehört ihr an, einfach dadurch, daß er Jude ist' " ("The Jewish world conspiracy has its origin in the simple fact that there are Jews. And the conspiracy will remain as long as there are Jews. Every Jew is part of it, simply because he is a Jew"). One of the inmates, acting without the agreement of the rest, kills the commandant and escapes. From then on he suffers under the uncertainty of what happened to the rest of the inmates in retaliation for his act: "Ich habe Rache genommen, und meine Rache wird gerächt. . . . Ich aber habe dem Herrn die Rache entwunden, und habe ihm nicht einmal das Opfer gebracht, das ihm gebührt" (I took revenge and my vengeance will be revenged. . . . I took away the vengeance from the Lord and did not give him the sacrifice which is his due). He did not sacrifice his life; instead, he escaped and let the others be sacrificed.

In the novel *Hier bin ich, mein Vater* (Here I Am, Father, 1948), which Torberg began in Los Angeles and finished in New York, Otto Maier becomes an informer for the Nazis in return for their promise to release his father from the Dachau concentration camp; he later discovers that they had murdered his father even before they made the offer. Tormented by guilt, he seeks advice from the religious teacher Bloch. Bloch asks Maier: " 'Frage dich, was geschehen wäre, wenn du deinem Vater wirklich das Leben gerettet hättest–auf solche Weise gerettet. Hättest du dann nicht durch alles ganz genauso hindurchzugehen gehabt? Oder durch Schlimmeres noch?' "

("Ask yourself what would have happened if indeed you had saved the life of your father with such methods. Would you not have suffered in your conscience in the same way? Or even more?"). Bloch concludes the discussion: " 'Ich kann dir nicht helfen. . . . Niemand kann das. Es hat niemand die Macht, dir zu helfen. Und es hat niemand das Recht, dich zu verurteilen. Jetzt geh!' " ("I cannot help you. . . . Nobody can. No one has the power to help you. And no one has the right to condemn you. Now, go!").

In *Die zweite Begegnung* (The Second Encounter, 1950) Torberg turns his attack from National Socialism to communism. Martin Dub, a Czech military officer who had escaped from the Nazis after they occupied his country, returns after the German defeats to find communism taking over Czechoslovakia: his "second encounter" with dictatorship. Dub tries to understand the attractiveness of communism for many people, especially intellectuals, in a series of meditations he writes in his notebook: "Es ist nicht schwer zu sehen, warum ein Hungernder, ein Bedürftiger, ein sozial Benachteiligter sich dem Kommunismus zuwendet und was er sich davon erhofft. Die steinerne Dummheit derer, die ihm den Zugang zum Besitz versperren, läßt ihm auf die Dauer keinen anderen Weg, und daß der Kommunismus seine Hoffnungen nicht erfüllen wird, kann ihm niemand beweisen" (It is not difficult to understand why someone who is starving or is socially discriminated against seeks hope in communism. The stupidity of those who bar his way to property gives him, in the long run, no other choice; and the fact that communism will not help him either, no one can prove to him in this situation). "Ursprünglich, und zweifellos mit Recht, hat der intellektuelle Kommunist seine Motive für moralisch gehalten–bis er eines Tages erfahren muß, daß sie nichts weiter sind als kleinbürgerliche Sentimentalitäten, deren er sich raschestens entledigen möge, weil sie die Revolution nicht fördern, sondern verhindern" (Originally and with justification the intellectual communist saw in his motives moral values, until he was forced to see that they are no better than petty bourgeois sentimentalities, of which he must rid himself as soon as possible, since they do not promote a revolution; on the contrary, they hinder it). "Man kann aus Menschenliebe zum Kommunismus kommen oder aus Menschenhaß" (You can become a communist out of love for mankind or out of hatred for it). Dub escapes from the communists as he had earlier fled from the Nazis.

Torberg returned to Vienna in 1951, retaining the American citizenship he had received in 1945. He worked for several newspapers and magazines in Austria and West Germany. In 1954 he founded the Austrian literary journal *Forum: Österreichische Monatsblätter für kulturelle Freiheit* (Forum: Austrian Monthly Magazine for Cultural Freedom), over which he presided until 1965. This publication became a powerful instrument which he used to promote or attack both new and established authors. He also continued to express his ideas in other journals and newspapers and at meetings of the P.E.N. Club, and he had great influence with the Austrian government. During the 1950s he prevented the plays of Bertolt Brecht from being performed in Austria because of Brecht's leftist political views and Soviet sympathies, even though, as he later declared in an essay, he always considered Brecht a great writer.

Torberg's literary work in Austria after 1951 was highlighted by his translation of the writings of the Jewish author Ephraim Kishon into German; his edition of the complete works of the Austrian author Fritz von Herzmanovsky-Orlando; and several original works: *Süßkind von Trimberg* (1972), *Die Tante Jolesch oder Der Untergang des Abendlandes in Anekdoten* (Aunt Jolesch; or, The Downfall of the Occident in Anecdotes, 1975), and *Die Erben der Tante Jolesch* (The Heirs of Aunt Jolesch, 1978).

In the novel *Süßkind von Trimberg*, Torberg not only portrays the life and death of the thirteenth-century German-Jewish minstrel with great sensitivity but also draws parallels to the predicament of the Jews and of many authors in the twentieth century. As a child Süßkind survives a pogrom in which his parents are killed, escapes with a monk, and earns his living in a variety of ways. Later, when he is admired and protected by the nobility, he is also welcomed by the Jewish communities in Germany. But after he loses the support of the nobility for criticizing their arbitrariness, he is also shunned by the Jews, who fear that affiliation with him will lead to reprisals against them. Süßkind lives and dies without a home, repudiated even by his own people. Torberg considered this novel his most important work, and it was the one into which he put his deepest feelings. Many critics, and especially other authors, recognized this personal commitment and praised the novel. Others, however, saying that Torberg's ambition was greater than his actual achievement, criticized the novel's con-

Friedrich Torberg and Joseph Strelka

ventional style and what they considered Torberg's unsuccessful attempt at reproducing archaic language. Nevertheless, *Süßkind von Trimberg* is a masterpiece, with a powerful story, tragic characters, lyrical and tender descriptions of love, even humor.

More successful with readers than *Süßkind von Trimberg* and most of his other novels were Torberg's two Tante Jolesch books. In anecdotes, episodes, quotations, and descriptions Torberg portrays eccentric individuals he remembers from his early years and from the Nazi period. These anecdotes reveal Torberg as a great master of wit and irony; they are amusing and melancholic, hilarious and tragic. Torberg believed that such strange individuals or freaks are not accepted in the modern world, and that their memory is worth preserving.

Torberg received the Julius Reich Prize in 1933; the Prize for Journalism of the City of Vienna in 1966; the Austrian Cross of Honor for Science and Art, First Degree, in 1968; the Commanders Cross of the Order of Merit of the Federal Republic of Germany in 1968; the Gold Medal of Honor of the City of Vienna in 1974; the Decoration of Honor for Science and Art in 1976; and the Grand National Prize of the Republic of Austria in 1979. He died in Vienna on 10 November 1979.

Letters:

In diesem Sinne: Briefe an Freunde und Zeitgenossen, edited by David Axmann and Marietta Torberg (Munich: Langen-Müller, 1981);

Kaffeehaus war überall: Briefwechsel mit Käuzen und Originalen, edited by Axmann and Marietta Torberg (Munich: Langen-Müller, 1982);

Pegasus im Joch: Briefwechsel mit Verlegern und Redakteuren, edited by Axmann and Marietta Torberg (Munich: Langen-Müller, 1983);

Liebste Freundin und Alma: Briefwechsel mit Alma Mahler-Werfel nebst einigen Briefen an Franz Werfel, edited by Axmann and Marietta Torberg (Munich: Langen-Müller, 1987);

Ein tolle, tolle Zeit: Briefe und Dokumente aus den Jahren 1938-1941, edited by Axmann and Marietta Torberg (Munich: Langen-Müller, 1989).

References:

Herbert Ahl, "Emigranten des Daseins: Friedrich Torberg," in his *Literarische Portraits* (Munich: Langen-Müller, 1962), pp. 93-100;

Herbert Eisenreich, "Friedrich Torberg," in *Handbuch der deutschen Gegenwartsliteratur*, volume 2 (Munich: Nymphenburger Verlagshaus, 1970), pp. 250-251;

Joachim Kaiser, "Friedrich Torberg," in his *Wie ich sie sah . . . und wie sie waren* (Munich: List, 1985), pp. 131-143;

Marcel Reich-Ranicki, "Denk ich an Torberg in der Nacht," in his *Literarisches Leben in Deutschland: Kommentare und Pamphlete* (Munich: Piper, 1964), pp. 142-145;

Reich-Ranicki, "Friedrich Torbergs Gleichnis," in his *Über Ruhestörer: Juden in der deutschen Literatur* (Munich: Piper, 1977), pp. 59-64;

Erwin Ringel, "Torbergs Schüler Gerber und seine Bedeutung für die moderne Selbstmordverhütung," in his *Die österreichische Seele* (Vienna: Böhlau, 1984), pp. 109-145;

Cornelius Schnauber, "Werk und Leben Friedrich Torbergs im amerikanischen Exil," *Literatur und Kritik*, 181/182 (1984): 60-67;

Rolf Schneider, "Die Wiener Institution Friedrich Torberg," *Musil-Forum*, 4 (1978): 309-314;

Ernst Schönwiese, "Die chassidische Seele singt: Der Lyriker Friedrich Torberg," in his *Literatur in Wien zwischen 1930 und 1980* (Vienna: Amalthea, 1980), pp. 159-165;

Manès Sperber, "Friedrich Torberg. Nachruf," *Jahrbuch der deutschen Akademie für Sprache und Dichtung* (1979): 115-118;

Joseph Strelka, "Friedrich Torberg," in *Deutsche Exilliteratur seit 1933*, volume 1: *Kalifornien*, edited by Strelka and John M. Spalek (Bern & Munich: Francke, 1976), pp. 616-632;

Strelka, ed., *Der Weg war schon das Ziel: Festschrift für Friedrich Torberg zum 70. Geburtstag* (Munich: Langen-Müller, 1978);

Hans Weigel, "Der Torberg," in his *Große Mücken, kleine Elefanten* (Zurich: Artemis, 1980), pp. 57-63;

Harry Zohn, "Friedrich Torberg," in his *Wiener Juden in der deutschen Literatur: Essays* (Tel Aviv: Edition Olamenu, 1964), pp. 101-105;

Zohn, " . . . ich bin ein Sohn der deutschen Sprache nur. . .," in his *Jüdisches Erbe in der österreichischen Literatur* (Vienna: Amalthea, 1986), pp. 164-177.

Papers:

The manuscripts for Friedrich Torberg's published works are in the Austrian National Library, Vienna; his unpublished papers are in the Vienna City Library.

Johannes Urzidil

(3 February 1896-2 November 1970)

Wolfgang D. Elfe
University of South Carolina

BOOKS: *Sturz der Verdammten: Gedichte* (Leipzig: Wolff, 1919);

Die Stimme: Gedichte (Berlin: Meyer, 1930);

Goethe in Böhmen (Vienna & Leipzig: Epstein, 1932; enlarged edition, Zurich & Stuttgart: Artemis, 1962);

Zeitgenössische Maler der Tschechen (Preßburg: Wawra, 1936);

Wenceslaus Hollar, der Kupferstecher des Barock, by Urzidil and Franz Sprinzels (Vienna & Leipzig: Passer, 1936); translated by Paul Selver as *Hollar: A Czech Emigré in England* (London: The Czechoslovak, 1942);

Der Trauermantel: Eine Erzählung aus Stifters Jugend (New York: Krause, 1945; Munich: Langen-Müller, 1955);

Über das Handwerk (Krefeld: Agis, 1954);

Die verlorene Geliebte (Munich & Vienna: Langen-Müller, 1956);

Die Memnonssäule: Gedichte (Vienna: Bergland, 1957);

Neujahrsrummel: Erzählungen (Stuttgart: Reclam, 1957);

Das Glück der Gegenwart: Goethes Amerikabild (Zurich & Stuttgart: Artemis, 1958);

Denkwürdigkeiten von Gibacht: Erzählung (Munich: Langen-Müller, 1958);

Das große Halleluja: Roman (Munich: Langen-Müller, 1959);

Prager Triptychon (Munich: Langen-Müller, 1960);

Geschenke des Lebens, edited by Ernst Schönwiese (Graz & Vienna: Stiasny, 1962);

Das Elefantenblatt: Erzählungen (Munich: Langen-Müller, 1962);

Amerika und die Antike (Zurich & Stuttgart: Artemis, 1964);

Entführung und sieben andere Ereignisse (Zurich & Stuttgart: Artemis, 1964);

Literatur als schöpferische Verantwortung (Zurich & Stuttgart: Artemis, 1965);

Prag als geistiger Ausgangspunkt: Ansprache zum 80sten Geburtstage von Erich von Kahler, gehalten im Leo Baeck Institut, New York am 21sten Oktober 1965 (New York, 1965); translated by

Johannes Urzidil (photo: Otto Breicha, Vienna)

Michael Lembeck as *The Living Contribution of Prague to Modern German Literature* (New York: Leo Baeck Institute, 1968);

Da geht Kafka (Zurich & Stuttgart: Artemis, 1965; enlarged edition, Munich: Deutscher Taschenbuch Verlag, 1966); translated by Harold A. Basilius as *There Goes Kafka* (Detroit: Wayne State University Press, 1968);

Prag—Glanz und Mystik einer Stadt (Krefeld: Scherpe, 1966);

Die erbeuteten Frauen: Sieben dramatische Geschichten (Zurich & Stuttgart: Artemis, 1966);

Bist du es, Ronald?: Erzählungen (Zurich & Stutt-
　　gart: Artemis, 1968);
*Väterliches aus Prag und Handwerkliches aus New
　　York* (Zurich: Artemis, 1969);
*Das Fortwirken der griechischen Antike in unsere Gegen-
　　wart: Vortrag, gehalten anläßlich des Symposions
　　zum Artemis-Jubiläum am 11. Oktober 1968 in
　　der Universität Zürich* (Zurich: Artemis,
　　1969);
Morgen fahr' ich heim: Böhmische Erzählungen (Mu-
　　nich: Langen-Müller, 1971);
Die letzte Tombola: Erzählungen (Zurich & Stutt-
　　gart: Artemis, 1971);
*Bekenntnisse eines Pedanten: Erzählungen und Essays
　　aus dem autobiographischen Nachlaß* (Zurich &
　　Munich: Artemis, 1972);
Die Rippe der Großmutter: Erzählungen, edited by
　　Dietrich Simon (Berlin: Volk und Welt,
　　1976).

OTHER: Karl Brand, *Das Vermächtnis eines Jüng-
　　lings*, edited by Urzidil (Vienna: Strache,
　　1921);
J. Papoucek, *Dr. Eduard Beneš: Sein Leben*, translat-
　　ed by Urzidil (Prague: Orbis, 1937);
Hilda Doolittle, *Avon: Ein Shakespearebuch*, translat-
　　ed by Urzidil (Berlin & Frankfurt am Main:
　　Suhrkamp, 1955).

Johannes Urzidil became widely known in
the 1950s as a writer of short stories; he also distinguished himself as a literary historian and critic
with publications on Goethe, Adalbert Stifter,
and Franz Kafka.

Urzidil was born in Prague in 1896 to Josef
Urzidil, a railroad official, and Elsa Metzeles
Urzidil, the daughter of a rabbi. Prague was still
part of the Austro-Hungarian Empire; it was a
multiethnic city with a sizable German-speaking
minority, to which the Urzidils belonged. The
death of his mother in 1900 and the remarriage
of his father three years later to a woman who
was less than an ideal stepmother had a trau-
matic effect on the young Urzidil.

From 1906 to 1914 Urzidil attended the
Humanistisches Gymnasium, a high school emphasizing the study of Greek and Latin and of the ancient Greek and Roman cultures. He then enrolled at the German University in Prague,
majoring in German and Slavic studies and art history. World War I interrupted his education
from 1916 to 1918, but Urzidil was able to fulfill
his military obligations in Prague rather than at
the front. During the war Urzidil, who had pub-

lished poems in the *Prager Tagblatt*, a German-
language newspaper in Prague, as early as 1913
under the pseudonym Hans Elmar, became acquainted with many other young Czech authors
writing in German. Among the writers with
whom he had regular contact at the Café Arco
were Kafka, Franz Werfel, Ernst Weiß, Max
Brod, Felix Weltsch, and Oskar Baum. Urzidil's
poems and stories were published in the journals
of the expressionist movement, notably *Die Aktion*
and *Der Mensch*. Kurt Wolff, the avant-garde publisher who had discovered many talented young
writers, published a volume of Urzidil's poems,
Sturz der Verdammten (The Fall of the Condemned), in 1919. His early poems and stories
are typical products of the expressionist movement with its characteristic rebellious spirit, the
emphasis on emotion, the rejection of authority
and of traditional literary forms, and extensive linguistic innovation.

Expressionism had run its course by about
1924, and Urzidil's own literary production slack-
ened. He worked as a correspondent for the Berlin newspaper *Börsen-Courier* and for a Berlin
news agency, Wolffs Telegraphisches Büro, and
from 1922 to 1933 he was press officer in the German embassy in Prague. His articles dealt with
Czech-German political and cultural relations,
the history and culture of Prague and Bohemia,
Czech art and literature, the German minority in
Czechoslovakia, and Goethe's stays at spas in Bohemia. In 1922 he married Gertrud Thieberger, a
Prague poet whose brother, a university professor, once gave Hebrew lessons to Kafka.

After the Nazis came to power in Germany
in 1933 Urzidil worked as Prague correspondent
for several Swiss newspapers and continued to
write for German-language publications in Czechoslovakia. In March 1939 the Nazis marched into
Czechoslovakia, putting the Urzidils in great
peril: Gertrud Urzidil was the daughter of a
rabbi; Urzidil's mother had been Jewish; while
working for the German embassy Urzidil had advocated peaceful coexistence among Czechs, Germans, and Austrians, a position that was clearly
at odds with the anti-Slavic, racist ideology of the
Nazis; as a Freemason he was a member of a society that was subjected to Nazi persecution; finally, Urzidil's strongly expressionistic early literary production was "degenerate" art according to
the Nazis. Urzidil and his wife escaped from
Prague at the end of June 1939. After a brief
stay in Italy they traveled by boat to Southamp-
ton, England, arriving on 2 August. Urzidil later

Urzidil's parents, Josef and Elsa Metzeles Urzidil (Leo Baeck Institute, New York)

gratefully acknowledged that getting out of Fascist Italy only weeks before the outbreak of World War II would not have been possible without the help of the English writer Bryher (pseudonym of Annie Winifred Ellerman). Bryher, who also helped other anti-Nazi exiles, supported the Urzidils financially during their eighteen-month stay in Viney Hall, a small village in Gloucestershire, and paid for their voyage to the United States in early 1941. After a tense crossing–the North Atlantic was the scene of intense submarine warfare at the time–Urzidil and his wife arrived in New York on 11 February on the Cunard-White Star Liner *Georgic*.

Urzidil worked as an American correspondent for two Czech exile papers in London, *Czechoslovak* and *Central European Observer*. The Czech papers ceased publication after the war, and Urzidil earned a modest living as a self-employed leather craftsman until 1951. Since he was able to work at home and never worked more than he had to, sufficient time was left for his writing. It was a life in which the big event well into the 1950s

was an almost annual vacation at "Twin Farms," the South Pomfret, Vermont, estate of the journalist Dorothy Thompson. Urzidil had met Thompson through an old friend from Prague, the painter and sculptor Maxim Kopf, who was Thompson's third husband. Urzidil and his wife became American citizens in 1946.

In 1950 the Urzidils were able to move from their small furnished apartment in a two-family house in Jackson Heights to a larger, unfurnished apartment in Kew Gardens. In April 1951 Urzidil's financial situation improved significantly when he was hired by the Austrian Division of the Voice of America as a scriptwriter and information specialist. But he was soon complaining in letters to friends that his work for the Voice of America was taking too much time away from his creative writing. He lost the position in 1953 because of pressure from Wisconsin senator Joseph McCarthy, who suspected Urzidil of communist sympathies.

In 1953 Urzidil traveled to Europe for the first time since coming to America. A major pur-

Urzidil and his wife, Gertrud Thieberger Urzidil (Leo Baeck Institute, New York)

Dust jackets for four of Urzidil's books

pose of the trip was to find a publisher in a German-speaking country. While in Munich Urzidil established contact with the Langen-Müller firm, which published *Die verlorene Geliebte* (The Lost Lover) in 1956. Urzidil's first major literary success, the book is a collection of eleven strongly autobiographical stories written for the most part in the first person and arranged in a chronological sequence that covers the time span from the protagonist's early childhood at the turn of the century to his exile in England from 1939 to 1941. The title refers to the loss of a girl or a woman, which occurs in several of the stories. On a symbolic level, the "lost lover" is Urzidil's homeland. In the last story of the volume, "Die Fremden" (The Strangers), Urzidil explicitly likens the community from which the exiles had been torn away to a lost lover. According to Urzidil, the continuing emotional ties to this "lost lover," the persistent though hopeless yearning to be reunited with it, constitute the tragedy of exile. This yearning for his lost homeland stimulated Urzidil's creative powers, a common phenomenon among exiled writers. In trying to save his own pre-exile existence from oblivion, Urzidil captures the Prague and Bohemia of his youth with such accuracy and pays so much loving attention to physical, sociopolitical, and cultural detail that many of the hundreds of thousands of Germans expelled from Czechoslovakia in 1945 saw their own lives immortalized in the tales. But the attraction of these stories stems not only from their nostalgic qualities: many of them have a symbolic meaning that transcends the particular events portrayed. The games the children play in the story "Spiele und Tränen" (Games and Tears), for example, are a reflection of the society in which they live. The growing animosity between two parts of a village in "Wo das Tal endet" (Where the Valley Ends) also signifies conflicts at an international level. The noticeable absence of dialogue in "Die Fremden," the only exile story in the volume, indicates the isolation of an exiled writer in an alien linguistic environment.

In his novel *Das große Halleluja* (The Great Hallelujah, 1959) Urzidil attempts to portray his adopted homeland, the United States, and to deal with the problems of life in the technological age. The novel has a highly episodic structure and many characters, but most of it revolves around the protagonist, Ellen Gaywood. Born on a farm in Vermont in the 1930s, Ellen loses her parents at an early age, becomes the servant and companion of a wealthy old lady in Salem, Massachusetts, moves to New York City after the death of her employer, works as a waitress while studying to become a nurse, finds employment in a New York hospital, marries a promising young scientist, and gives birth to her first child. Other characters include the exiled writer Joseph Weseritz and his wife Eva, modeled after Johannes and Gertrud Urzidil; the journalist Barnabe Nichols and her husband Alexander, based on Thompson and Kopf; and the exiled German dramatist Zeckendorff, modeled after Carl Zuckmayer. To the extent that the novel traces the growth of its protagonist from early childhood to maturity, it is a bildungsroman. But it also gives a panoramic view of rural, small-town, and metropolitan America. The main impression the reader gets is of a land obsessed by technology and characterized by vitality, restlessness, and mobility. In his use of montage techniques to capture the multitude of events that occur simultaneously in a metropolis, Urzidil seems to have been influenced by Alfred Döblin's *Berlin Alexanderplatz* (1929; translated as *Alexanderplatz, Berlin*, 1931) and John Dos Passos's *Manhattan Transfer* (1925). To capture the atmosphere of New York, Urzidil uses many English words and idiomatic expressions and then adds a German translation; often he creates loan-translations, thus inventing what seems to be a new German-American language that clashes with the stylistically refined and somewhat archaic German he uses for his comments and philosophical reflections. The novel represents a unique attempt on the part of an exiled German author to portray the United States with an open mind and to reconcile his prewar European, preindustrial, pronature outlook with the modern American technological age.

Urzidil never shared the feeling of cultural superiority that many educated Europeans had toward America; among anti-Nazi exiles such an attitude often developed as a reaction against the loss of social status they experienced in an environment in which their importance was not recognized. Urzidil never repeated the cliché *Kulturlosigkeit* (culturelessness) in reference to the United States. His close relationship with Thompson and her circle of friends allowed him to experience an urbane, cosmopolitan, educated America; in addition, his work for the Voice of America demanded cultural mediation between America and Europe. Urzidil studied American literature extensively and frequently referred to

Urzidil in 1964 (photo: Otto Breicha, Vienna; Bildarchiv der Österreichischen Nationalbibliothek)

Concord, Massachusetts, as the "American Weimar."

The three stories in *Prager Triptychon* (Prague Tryptich, 1960) take place in Prague before and during World War I. The young expressionist writers in Prague are portrayed with intimate knowledge and great authenticity in "Vermächtnis eines Jünglings" (Legacy of a Young Man). In each story a gifted young man–two of them writers–dies an untimely death. As was typical of many expressionist works, the protagonists of two of the stories, Helmuth Wellner in "Die Causa Wellner" (Wellner's Legal Case) and Kurt Weißenstein in "Weißenstein Karl," expe-

rience bitter conflict with their unfeeling, selfish, and authoritarian fathers.

In 1962, thirty years after its first publication, a greatly enlarged edition of Urzidil's *Goethe in Böhmen* (Goethe in Bohemia) was published. The book is a comprehensive study of Goethe's extensive stays in Bohemia. *Das Elefantenblatt* (The Drawing of the Elephant), also published in 1962, is a collection of fifteen stories, several of which had been published previously. Their settings vary: Prague and Bohemia, England, the United States, ancient Rome and Babylon. They also differ in their literary models: in "Zu den neun Teufeln" (The House of the Nine Devils), for example, the natural and the supernatural are joined in typically romantic fashion; "Traum eines Löwenbändigers" (Dream of a Lion Tamer), on the other hand, is reminiscent of Kafka. Urzidil focuses on the nondramatic life-giving and life-preserving forces of nature, a tendency that can be observed most clearly in "Der letzte Gast" (The Last Guest). Because of the senselessness of much that happens in the "big world," Urzidil tries to present a humane and well-ordered universe in which no crime, no transgression, no guilt is ever forgotten: in "Taubenfutter" (Pigeon Feed), "Ein alter Brief" (An Old Letter), and "Anekdote aus dem zweiten Punischen Krieg" (Anecdote from the Second Punic War) justice is always done sooner or later. Two stories deal with the development of artists, the seventeenth-century Czech engraver Václav Hollar in "Das Elefantenblatt" and the nineteenth-century Austrian writer Stifter in "Der Trauermantel" (The Mourning Cloak). Hollar is also the subject of a nonfiction study by Urzidil, published in 1936.

Urzidil's next book, *Entführung und sieben andere Ereignisse* (Abduction and Seven Other Events, 1964), consists of eight stories with contemporary American settings. In two stories an exile tries to find meaning for his life in the new country. The title figure of "Altheimer"–the name means "man from the old homeland"–travels across the American continent but does not find a new homeland. The same is true of the exiled writer Franz Lampenstein in "Der Tod und die Steuern" (Death and Taxes): his efforts at assimilation–he writes in English and anglicizes his name–ultimately fail. Most of the stories criticize modern technological society and its restlessness, noise, and rootlessness. Urzidil grieves over the destruction of nature: Altheimer, for example, is so upset that he decides to leave the city when a tree is cut down in front of his window to make room for a high-rise building. Urzidil likens skyscrapers to the Tower of Babel; when two young people get trapped in a stalled elevator of a skyscraper in "Im Aufzug" (In the Elevator), they see the breakdown as a warning by fate against technology. In the highly humorous "Kafkas Flucht" (Kafka's Escape) Kafka does not die in 1924 but secretly flees to America and lives a long and happy life as a family man and a gardener on Long Island–a life that contrasts tragically with Kafka's actual brief and tortured existence. In 1965 Urzidil combined several previously published essays on Kafka in the volume

Da geht Kafka (translated as *There Goes Kafka*, 1968).

Die erbeuteten Frauen (The Captured Women, 1966) contains seven stories with mostly typical Urzidil settings: contemporary America (mainly New York) and Prague and Bohemia before 1939. The highly comic title story, however, is about an episode in the Trojan War; the message of the story is strongly pacifist. Urzidil seems to have been troubled by everyday crime, especially in New York, and crime and punishment play a central role in "Die Herzogin von Albanera" (The Duchess of Albanera), "Der Stahlpalast" (The Palace of Steel), and "Bildnis eines Knaben" (Portrait of a Boy). In these stories the narrators somewhat desperately search for hidden meaning in the depressing events they relate. "Die Rippe meiner Großmutter" (My Grandmother's Rib), an antiwar story about World War I, is clearly influenced by the character Schwejk created by the Czech writer Jaroslav Hašek as well as by the scene in Thomas Mann's *Bekenntnisse des Hochstaplers Felix Krull* (1954; translated as *Confessions of Felix Krull, Confidence Man*, 1955), in which Felix simulates madness to avoid military service. In "Die erbeuteten Frauen" and especially in "Das Haus Colonna" (The House of Colonna) Urzidil's extensive knowledge of classical antiquity is evident. "Morgenroths Erbe" (Morgenroth's Inheritance) may be a critical self-examination by the author: it is the story of the owner of a horse-drawn merry-go-round with hand-carved figures who plays an accordion and tells the children stories rich in history and mythology. He refuses to keep up with modern technological developments in his business and ultimately goes bankrupt. Urzidil apparently sensed that his own existence in New York was anachronistic.

Bist du es, Ronald? (Is It You, Ronald?, 1968) is a collection of seven stories, four of them with a contemporary American setting, which do not present anything new in Urzidil's repertoire. The familiar topic of guilt and atonement is found in three stories, "Umwege durch Bingham Street" (Detour through Bingham Street), "Behelligungen eines Richters" (Troubles of a Judge), and "Meine Verehrung" (Your Honor). Urzidil rejects the notion that life is nothing but a chaotic multitude of unconnected incidents and that crimes or transgressions can be perpetrated with impunity. His belief that war is an evil which continuously produces new evil, even after it has ended, is effectively expressed in "Tausendfuß" (the name of a New York bum) and in the title story. "Morgen fahr' ich heim" (I'm Going Home Tomorrow) describes a wedding in rural Bohemia before World War I; it is an affirmation of simple village life in harmony with nature. This life is threatened by modern technology: one of the farm workers, who represents the essence of rustic strength, optimism, and vitality, is killed when a new farm machine is used for the first time. "Ein letztes Läuten" (A Final Ringing of the Bell) narrates the flight of a couple from Prague in 1939 and the events thereafter from the perspective of the couple's maid, who stays behind.

Urzidil received the Charles Veillon Prize in 1957, the Prize for Literature of the City of Cologne and the National Prize of Austria in 1964, and the Andreas Gryphius Prize in 1966. The president of Austria awarded him the title honorary professor in 1961, and in 1962 Urzidil became a member of the Academy for Language and Literature in Darmstadt. He made extensive European lecture tours in 1957, 1962, 1964, and 1968. He was on another such tour when he died in Rome on 2 November 1970 after a stroke. He is buried in that city. In 1971 two volumes of stories were published posthumously. *Morgen fahr' ich heim* is a collection of previously published works. *Die letzte Tombola* (The Last Tombola) contains five stories, three of which are set in the Prague and Bohemia of Urzidil's youth. The title story develops a favorite theme of Urzidil's: that there is a clear correlation between disorder and heartlessness in the small world and in the world at large. The narrator, a thirteen-year-old boy, learns that Mr. Pernold, his father's supervisor, has committed suicide because of his wife's infidelity. This experience profoundly affects the boy, revealing to him the chaotic and puzzling aspect of life. In an epilogue the narrator, who has just graduated from high school, sees Mrs. Pernold with her lover, an Austrian army officer. It is 28 July 1914, and a crowd gathers in front of a store where a bulletin has just been posted that war has been declared. The officer exclaims: "GOTT SEI DANK!" (THANK GOD!). "Die letzte Tombola" and "Von Odkolek zu Odradek" (From Odkolek to Odradek) give a familiar portrait of middle-class life in Prague at the turn of the century. "Die Frau mit den Handschuhen" (The Lady with the Gloves), a portrayal of rural, preindustrial life in Bohemia in the late nineteenth century, shows the influence of Stifter, who tried to find and present evidence of "das sanfte Gesetz" (the gentle law)–the positive, life-

sustaining forces in nature and human existence. "Das Gold von Caramablu" (The Gold of Caramablu) depicts the well-ordered life in harmony with nature of a Basque fishing village; the Spanish civil war–a frequent topic of anti-Nazi writers–destroys this world. "Die große Finsternis von New York" (The Great Darkness in New York) tells of the death of a boy during the blackout of 9 November 1965. The narrator, an exiled German writer, reflects about life in America. Many of Urzidil's favorite themes are taken up again, especially his criticism of the modern industrialized world, the yearning for one's lost homeland, and a growing feeling of alienation from the host country. In 1972 a volume of stories and essays from Urzidil's literary estate, *Bekenntnisse eines Pedanten* (Confessions of a Pedant), was published.

Urzidil rarely preaches. The tragic aspects of life, which are always present in his works, are often lightened by humor. Urzidil believed that the writer should be a therapist: he should try to make life more bearable for his readers. To writers who do the opposite he poses the provocative question in one of the essays in *Väterliches aus Prag und Handwerkliches aus New York* (About My Father in Prague and My Craft in New York, 1969): "Wozu schreibt ihr? Weshalb lebt ihr überhaupt? Auf welche Weise helft ihr anderen zu leben? Sterben können sie auch ohne euch" (Why do you write? Why do you live? In what way do you help others to live? They certainly can die without your help). Nature provides consolation in his stories: its life-giving and life-preserving qualities are emphasized, and in contrast to the vicissitudes of human life and history it represents a realm that is stable and inviolable. Urzidil writes for the most part in the tradition of the great realists of the nineteenth century. He is a gifted stylist who believes that a well-written sentence suggests a well-ordered, meaningful universe. The theoretical expression of the philosophy expressed in his works can be found in his *Literatur als schöpferische Verantwortung* (Literature as a Creative Responsibility, 1965): "Der Verzweiflung, der Ratlosigkeit, dem Selbstmord widerstrebt man nicht, indem man sorgfältig aufzeigt, wie ekel, flach und schal und unersprießlich das ganze Treiben doch sei, sondern indem man versucht, kraft des Absurden an das Leben zu glauben" (One does not escape from despair, helplessness, suicide by demonstrating with great diligence and accuracy how nauseating, shallow, stale and fruitless all our actions are, but by trying to believe in life by virtue of the absurd).

References:

Francoise Derré, "Johannes Urzidil, ein Meister der exakten Phantasie," *Modern Austrian Literature*, 5, no. 1/2 (1972): 45-57;

André von Gronicka, "Johannes Urzidils Leben und Werk," *Aufbau* (New York), 22 (3 February 1956): 10;

Christa Helling, *Johannes Urzidil und Prag: Versuch einer Interpretation* (Udine: Del Bianco industrie grafiche, 1981);

Peter Herren, *Beharren und Verwandeln: Eine Analyse von Grundzügen im Erzählwerk Johannes Urzidils* (Bern & Stuttgart: Haupt, 1981);

Johann Lachinger, Aldemar Schiffkorn, and Walter Zettl, eds., *Johannes Urzidil und der Prager Kreis: Vorträge des Johannes-Urzidil-Symposiums 1984* (Linz: Adalbert-Stifter-Institut, 1986);

Stella P. Rosenfeld, "Johannes Urzidil's Prague and Bohemian Stories: Major Aspects of Subject Matter and Theme," Ph.D. dissertation, Case Western Reserve University, 1976;

Ernst Schönwiese, "Der letzte große Erzähler der Prager Schule: Johannes Urzidil (1896-1970)," in his *Literatur in Wien zwischen 1930 und 1980* (Vienna & Munich: Amalthea, 1980), pp. 127-144;

Egon Schwarz, "Urzidil und Amerika," *German Quarterly*, 58 (Spring 1985): 223-237;

Richard Thieberger, "Johannes Urzidil (1896-1970)," in his *Gedanken über Dichter und Dichtungen: Essays aus fünf Jahrzehnten*, edited by Alain Faure, Yvon Flesch, and Armand Nivelle (Bern & Frankfurt am Main: Lang, 1982), pp. 227-252;

Gerhard Trapp, *Die Prosa Johannes Urzidils: Zum Verständnis eines literarischen Werdegangs vom Expressionismus zur Gegenwart* (Bern: Lang, 1967).

Papers:

Johannes Urzidil's papers are at the Leo Baeck Institute, New York City.

Martina Wied
(10 December 1882-25 January 1957)

Sylvia M. Patsch

BOOKS: *Bewegung: Gedichte* (Vienna: Strache, 1919);

Rauch über Sanct Florian oder Die Welt der Mißverständnisse: Roman (Vienna: Fromme, 1937);

Das Einhorn: Aus dem Tagebuch eines schottischen Malers in Italien (Vienna: Ullstein, 1948);

Kellingrath: Roman (Innsbruck: Österreichische Verlagsanstalt, 1950);

Das Krähennest: Begebnisse auf verschiedenen Ebenen (Vienna: Herold, 1951);

Die Geschichte des reichen Jünglings (Innsbruck: Österreichische Verlagsanstalt, 1952);

Brücken ins Sichtbare: Ausgewählte Gedichte 1912-1952 (Innsbruck: Österreichische Verlagsanstalt, 1952);

Der Ehering (Innsbruck: Österreichische Verlagsanstalt, 1954);

Das unvollendete Abenteuer: Eine Novelle (Vienna: Bergland, 1955).

OTHER: Emil Alphons Rheinhardt, *Die Botschaft: Neue Gedichte aus Österreich*, contributions by Wied (Vienna: Strache, 1920), pp. 302-304;

Wilhelm Cohn, *Chinese Painting*, translated by Wied (London: Phaidon Press, 1947);

"Sankt Stephan"/"Saint Stephen's," in *Austria in Poetry and History*, edited by Frederick Ungar, translated by Lowell A. Bangerter and others (New York: Ungar, 1984), pp. 196-197.

PERIODICAL PUBLICATIONS: "Romane der Lebensmitte," *Der Brenner*, 6 (1913): 696-702;

"Otto Stoessl der Erzähler," *Der Brenner*, 7 (1913-1914): 120-128;

"Das Ende des Bürgertums," *Arbeiter-Zeitung* (Vienna), 5 January 1921;

"Francis Thompson," *Zeitwende* (Hamburg), 1 (1925): 547-549;

"Neue Lyrik," *Zeitwende* (Hamburg), 1 (1925): 426-433;

Martina Wied (Bildarchiv der Österreichischen Nationalbibliothek)

"Das unruhige Herz," 11 installments, *Arbeiter-Zeitung* (Vienna), 11-21 May 1929;

"Dite," 5 installments, *Arbeiter-Zeitung* (Vienna), 11-15 September 1929;

"Der Türkisring," 14 installments, *Arbeiter-Zeitung* (Vienna), 17-30 January 1931;

"Das Venezianische Tuch," 3 installments, *Arbeiter-Zeitung* (Vienna), 22-24 March 1931;

"Das Asyl zum obdachlosen Geist," 106 installments, *Wiener Zeitung*, 25 February-17 June 1934;

"Die Legende des Heiligen von Canterbury in ihrer künstlerischen Spiegelung," *Wiener Zeitung*, 1 January 1936, pp. 1-2;

"Jeder hat sein Grundmotiv: Ein Selbstporträt," *Welt und Wort* (Tübingen), 8 (1953): 298-299.

There have been many historical and sociological investigations of the cultural life of Vienna at the turn of the twentieth century and of the decline and fall of the Austro-Hungarian Empire; Martina Wied portrays the same phenomena in her novels. Her early works belong to the cultural climate that produced Robert Musil's *Der Mann ohne Eigenschaften* (1931; translated as *The Man without Qualities*, 1965), Heimito von Doderer's *Die Strudlhofstiege* (1951; partially translated as "The Strudlhof Steps," 1974), and Hermann Broch's *Die Verzauberung* (1976; translated as *The Spell*, 1988). Eastern Europe plays an important part in her fiction, as it does in the work of Doderer, Karl Emil Franzos, Joseph Roth, Manès Sperber, and Robert Neumann. Her early fiction has some melodramatic traits—bloodshed, crime, suicides, and unexpected strokes of fate—but her work is invariably unsentimental and realistic and provides profound understanding of the political and sociological problems of her day. Although there is practically no discussion of her work by Austrian critics today, she was a literary figure of some eminence in the 1920s and 1930s and received literary prizes both for her fiction and for her poetry.

Wied was born Alexandrine Martina Augusta Schnabl in Vienna on 10 December 1882 to the poet Jenny Schnabl and the lawyer Dr. Joseph Schnabl. Their home was one of the many centers of cultural activity that were characteristic of fin-de-siècle Vienna. She attended elementary school from 1887 to 1891, grammar school from 1891 to 1899, and a teacher-training school from 1899 to 1902, and she studied art history, history, and modern literatures at the University of Vienna from 1906 to 1910. On 12 June 1910 she married the Vienna industrialist Siegmund Weisl. Their son Johann Georg, the "Hanno" to whom her novel *Das Krähennest* (The Crow's Nest, 1951) is dedicated, was born in 1911.

She had begun writing poetry as a schoolgirl, and some of her poems were published in literary magazines as early as 1912. In 1913 she began publishing pieces in the important Innsbruck periodical *Der Brenner*, and her lifelong friendship and voluminous correspondence with its founder, Ludwig von Ficker, dates from that

year. Her first volume of poems, *Bewegung* (Movement), appeared in 1919. Some of her early poems were published in *Die Botschaft: Neue Gedichte aus Österreich* (The Message: New Poetry from Austria, 1920); other contributors to this anthology of late expressionist verse included such distinguished writers as Stefan Zweig, Franz Werfel, Felix Braun, and Georg Trakl. *Brücken ins Sichtbare: Ausgewählte Gedichte 1912-1952* (Bridges into the Visible World: Selected Poems 1912-1952, 1952) is her only other book of verse. One group of these poems deals with her childhood in Vienna; another is addressed to writers she knew, many of whom are forgotten today. Some of her stories appeared in the Vienna *Arbeiter-Zeitung*: "Das unruhige Herz" (The Unquiet Heart) and "Dite" in 1929, and "Der Türkisring" (The Turquoise Ring) and "Das Venezianische Tuch" (The Venetian Shawl) in 1931. In 1934 the *Wiener Zeitung* published her first novel, "Das Asyl zum obdachlosen Geist" (The Asylum for the Homeless Spirit), in installments; the novel appeared in book form under the title *Kellingrath* in 1950. It had been written in 1925 and 1926.

She spent the years 1927 to 1929 in Poland with her husband, who was working as a consultant chemist in a Lodz textile firm; Lodz appears as the city "Dymno" (Polish for "smoke") in several of her works of fiction. Later she visited France, Britain, and Italy. After the death of her husband in 1930 she worked as a correspondent for literature and the arts for the *Frankfurter Zeitung* and contributed to the *Arbeiter-Zeitung*, the *Wiener Zeitung*, and the *Neue Freie Presse*. Although her publications had little to do with the political turmoil in Austria, her contributions to the socialist *Arbeiter-Zeitung* and *Neue Freie Presse* and the fact that she had Jewish ancestors made her position in Austria after the Anschluß (annexation of Austria by Nazi Germany) of 1938 precarious. In 1939 she left for France and went on to Scotland, where she taught German, French, and art history in several Catholic institutions. During her exile in Britain she concentrated on her novels. She made no contributions to the exile press, and she was unable to publish in her home country.

In several cases a connection can be noted between Wied's novels and short stories. For example, "Dite" reads like a chapter from the novel *Die Geschichte des reichen Jünglings* (The Story of the Wealthy Youth, 1952). Both are set in an industrial town where property, counted by the number of factory chimneys one owns, is the only consideration. Her thesis that such surroundings corrupt even the best people is exemplified both in the story and in the eight-hundred-page novel. And "Der Türkisring" actually appeared as the first chapter of *Die Geschichte des reichen Jünglings*. Her short novel *Das Einhorn* (The Unicorn, 1948) and her unpublished story "Jakobäa von Bayern" could be called biographies of marginal but interesting figures of history. "Das unruhige Herz" is an early version of the novel *Das unvollendete Abenteuer* (The Unfinished Adventure, 1955).

The main theme of *Kellingrath* is the question: where in the world is there "an asylum for the homeless spirit," for the expatriate, the exile, the refugee. Ironically, it is in the Vienna mental asylum to which his wife has him committed that John Kellingrath finds the peace that was denied him in his turbulent marriage. The depiction of the friendship and mutual trust between the psychiatrist-narrator and his patient shows Wied at her best. The catastrophic ending of the novel occurs during the influenza epidemic of 1918: Crown Prince Rudolf's servant, demented after his master's suicide, is admitted to the asylum even though its principal has given strict orders for quarantine, and the disease breaks out in the hospital. Skillfully woven into this panorama of fin-de-siècle Austria are the new ideas of Sigmund Freud, which are contrasted with the traditional religious beliefs of a neurotic, decadent society.

The novel *Rauch über Sanct Florian oder Die Welt der Mißverständnisse* (Smoke over Sanct Florian; or, The World of Misunderstandings, 1937), written between May 1933 and May 1936, deals with a summer week in 1931 in the imaginary Styrian village of Sanct Florian. The poet and philosopher Paul Ambros (modeled on Wied's friend, the dramatist Paul Ernst) has bought an old manor house from an impoverished nobleman; soon he becomes the center of the small cultivated community in the village. Among his friends is the violinist Corona Sonntag, who is preparing for a concert tour to the United States. When her lover arrives from Vienna, his apparent coldness shocks her, and she begins to believe in a gypsy soothsayer's prophecy that after a third disappointment she will die. She is killed in a fire that starts in the post office and spreads through the whole village. The patron saint of fire and flood, Saint Florian, did not save the village or its most promising inhabitant. Wied's later novels have similar motifs: a

love story with a disastrous ending; an atmosphere of impending doom; the apparently peaceful surface of rural life; the artist–musician, painter, or author–who cannot cope with life. She frequently places her characters in extreme situations in which they either prove themselves or fail. Her female figures are passionate lovers; even if they are doomed, their author supports their emotion and sacrifice, condemning aloofness and calculation.

Das Einhorn was begun in Edinburgh in April 1940 and completed in Glasgow in October of the same year. This historical novel about Scottish history–the unicorn is the heraldic emblem of Scotland–was Wied's first attempt at writing in the country of her refuge after she left Austria. The émigré who gets into trouble through no fault of his own was to be a recurrent theme in her work from this point on. The last of the Stuarts, Charles Edward, has taken refuge at the court of Grand Duke Leopold of Tuscany, second-eldest son of the empress Maria Theresa. Charles Edward and his wife, Louisa Stolberg, thirty years his junior and the daughter of an Austrian general, soon become the center of political intrigue. The narrator is a Scottish painter, Sir James Graham, who records his experiences and his views on art and literature in his diary. Graham observes the political life of his day, with all its plots and machinations, and in the end is himself assassinated. Wied displays a remarkable grasp of her subject and insight into her male characters.

Der Ehering (The Wedding Ring, 1954), written in Glasgow from October 1940 to January 1941, is a novel about Austrian society just before World War I; its characters are diplomats, aristocrats, and other figures prominent in fin-de-siècle Vienna. The protagonist is a young woman, the daughter of a fashionable painter, who loses her husband in a storm off the Dalmatian coast (the catastrophic ending of the marriage of a protagonist is a recurrent feature in Wied's novels). The wedding ring of the title implies that the same forces that bind people together make love and happiness impossible.

Wied began writing *Die Geschichte des reichen Jünglings* in Poland in 1928 and completed it in Glasgow in 1943; it was published on her seventieth birthday in 1952. The hero and narrator, the young Pole Adam Leontjew, comes under the influence of opposing political regimes at the Russian, German, and Polish schools he attends. After fighting against the Russians in the war of

1920-1922 he becomes involved in the dubious activities of secret agents, informers, and bankrupts among his fellow students at the University of Krakow. The character of Iwanow, Privatdozent (unsalaried lecturer) at the University of Heidelberg and author of a famous 1913 treatise on poetry whose "real" name is von Gjörffy, is a portrait of the Hungarian philosopher-critic Georg Lukács, whom Wied had met in Vienna. He casts a spell on Leontjew, who admires his integrity and intellect. Just when it has been arranged for Leontjew to work as Iwanow's secretary and accompany him to Vienna, Iwanow is arrested by his own comrades, who fear his individualist approach and his criticism of the party line. Leontjew abandons Marxism and adopts a Christian socialist outlook. As a member of the Polish army in Britain in World War II he tries to help his country win back its identity after the partitions, defeats, and occupations it suffered in the past. Wied describes the hardships, sufferings, vulnerability, and sense of unreality shared by all exiles. The refugees are flotsam and jetsam, stranded in a humiliating situation. At the end of the story the rich young man who has lost everything but his integrity is able to make a new start in Britain, and life begins to have meaning for him. The novel reveals the author's profound knowledge of Eastern European politics, economic conditions, and history. *Die Geschichte des reichen Jünglings* is Wied's most significant study of renunciation and disillusionment.

In *Das Krähennest*, finished in north Wales in 1948, Wied adopts the trend in modern fiction in which the author withholds information; thus this novel calls for a far greater degree of collaboration on the part of the reader than do her former works. For example, a personal relationship may be hinted at by a remark made by one of the characters, and only later in the story does the connection between the figures emerge. Even the country in which the novel is set cannot be identified with certainty: it could be any rural area which suffered air raids. Veiled allusions to a political killing and a suicide leave the reader to draw his own conclusions from partial information. Describing the difficulties of evacuating a big boarding school in the first chapter, "Die Flucht" (The Flight), Wied gives vivid impressions of civilian life during wartime. Before long the reader realizes that all the characters in the novel have been given names from the works of Shakespeare and other famous writers. News is received from the various theaters of war of the

deaths of former students: Antonius was killed in Libya, Hal in Crete, Jacques in Dieppe; Petruchio was drowned in the Atlantic, Horatio in the Pacific; Autolykus was burned to death in his plane over Burma. Wied is critical of the way refugees, including Austrians, behave: they either toady to their hosts with a complete lack of dignity or else behave as though they had lived in palaces and eaten off silver plates at home. *Krähennest* is an important antiwar novel.

Das unvollendete Abenteuer, a slightly revised and enlarged version of the 1929 story "Das unruhige Herz," describes the life and death of the Chevalier de Saint-Malo, a French nobleman who fights in the American Revolution and later in the Napoleonic Wars. In a key scene the chevalier, on a diplomatic mission from France to Vienna, meets a distant relative who has become the abbot of a convent in Moravia; for a moment he envies the latter's quiet and secluded life. This is a recurrent motif in Wied's works: the strong character stands at a crossroads where he is called upon to decide his future. Invariably, Wied has such characters choose an active and responsible life instead of the tranquillity of retirement.

Wied returned to Vienna in 1947. In 1952 she received the Austrian State Prize for Literature. She died on 25 January 1957. Her unpublished work includes radio plays, such as the mystery "Nikodemus," broadcast on Austrian Radio on 29 December 1952, and "Das fremde Haus" (The Strange House), broadcast on 15 May 1953, as well as theatrical plays and essays on literature. A book she had planned to write on the significance of motifs in literature was never finished, though she discussed her own motifs in the essay "Jeder hat sein Grundmotiv" (Every Writer Has His Main Motif, 1953). She says in this essay that although there was something of herself in many of her characters, none of them was a self-portrait.

Working as she did in Glasgow and later in north Wales, her isolation from London precluded her membership in any political group–nor would she have wished to join one. She played no part in the Free Austrian Movement or in the Free German League for Culture. This isolation may account for the rare mention of her name in studies of Austrians in exile. Critical comment on her work takes no account of her connection with Britain, although the impact of English on her style cannot be ignored. In spite of her interest in British history and literature, her work has remained unknown in Britain: there are no copies of her novels in the British Library and no translations of her novels into English, although her poem "Sankt Stephan" is included in the original and in English in the anthology *Austria in Poetry and History* (1984). She is likewise hardly known in German-speaking countries: her novels have long been out of print, and while there were notices of her seventieth birthday and obituaries at the time of her death, there were practically no commemorative articles on her one-hundredth birthday in 1982.

References:

Jesse Leroy Berry, "Martina Wied, Austrian Novelist, 1882-1957," Ph.D. dissertation, Vanderbilt University, 1966;

Felix Braun, "Nachruf auf Martina Wied," *Wort in der Zeit*, 3 (1957): 262-263;

Norbert Langer, Introduction to Wied's *Das Einhorn* (Graz: Stiasny, 1964), pp. 5-29;

Hubert Orlowski, "Martina Wied und Polen," in Orlowski, ed., *Österreichisch-polnische Nachbarschaft* (Uam Poznań: Naukowe Uniwersytetu im Adama Mickiewicza, 1979), pp. 117-125;

Sylvia M. Patsch, "Ein Fußbreit Boden—der vergessenen Österreicherin Martina Wied zum hundertsten Geburtstag," *Die Presse* (Vienna), 4 December 1982;

Patsch, *Österreichische Schriftsteller im Exil in Großbritannien* (Vienna: Brandstätter, 1985), pp. 155-162;

Patsch, *Österreichische Schriftsteller im Exil—Texte* (Vienna: Bradstätter, 1986), pp. 217-228, 306;

Patsch, "Und alles ist hier fremd"—Schreiben im Exil," *Deutsche Literatur von Frauen: Das 19. und 20. Jahrhundert*, edited by Gisela Brinker-Gabler (Munich: Beck, 1988), pp. 304-317;

Hans Friedrich Prokop, "Die Romane Martina Wieds," Ph.D dissertation, University of Vienna, 1971);

Viktor Suchy, "Martina Wied und die österreichische Literatur," *Die österreichische Furche* (Vienna), 25 March 1950, p. 3;

Hans Winter, "Martina Wied," *Wort in der Zeit*, 3 (1957): 257-261.

Papers:

There is a collection of Martina Wied's letters in the Brenner Archive at Innsbruck University; her literary estate is at the Dokumentationsstelle für neuere österreichische Literatur, Vienna.

Herbert Zand
(14 November 1923-14 July 1970)

Pamela S. Saur
Lamar University

BOOKS: *Die Sonnenstadt: Roman* (Linz, Vienna & Regensburg: Schönleitner, 1947);

Letzte Ausfahrt: Roman der Eingekesselten (Vienna & Munich: Donau, 1953); translated by C. M. Woodhouse as *The Last Sortie: The Story of the Cauldron* (London: Hart-Davis, 1955);

Die Glaskugel: Gedichte (Vienna & Munich: Donau, 1953);

Der Weg nach Hassi el emel (Vienna & Munich: Donau, 1956); translated by Norman Denny as *The Well of Hope* (London: Collins, 1957);

Erben des Feuers: Roman (Salzburg: Müller, 1961);

Kerne des paradiesischen Apfels: Aufzeichnungen, edited by Wolfgang Kraus (Vienna, Frankfurt am Main & Zurich: Europa, 1971);

Demosthenes spricht gegen die Brandung: Erzählungen, edited by Kraus (Vienna: Europa, 1972);

Aus zerschossenem Sonnengeflecht: Gedichte (Vienna, Munich & Zurich: Europa, 1973);

Träume im Spiegel: Essays, edited by Kraus (Vienna, Munich & Zurich: Europa, 1973).

OTHER: "Geschichte als Sinngebung der Gegenwart," in *Frank Thiess zum 75. Geburtstag: Mit Beiträgen von Ernst Alker, Walter Heynen und Herbert Zand* (Vienna & Hamburg: Zsolnay, 1965), pp. 56-72.

TRANSLATIONS: Henry Miller, *Das Lächeln am Fuße der Leiter: Roman* (Vienna & Munich: Donau, 1954);

Miller, *Symbole und Signale: Frühe Dokumente der literarischen Avantgarde*, edited by Wolfgang Kraus (Bremen: Lehünemann, 1961);

Lawrence Durrell, *Die schwarze Chronik: Roman* (Hamburg: Rowohlt, 1962);

Durrell, *Schwarze Oliven: Korfu-Insel der Phäaken*, translated by Zand and P. Bermbach (Hamburg: Rowohlt, 1963);

Durrell, *Leuchtende Orangen, Rhodos—Insel des Helios* (Hamburg: Rowohlt, 1964);

Anaïs Nin, *Tagebücher 1930-1934* (Hamburg: Rowohlt, 1966);

Herbert Zand (Bildarchiv der Österreichischen Nationalbibliothek)

Durrell and Miller, *Briefe* (Hamburg: Rowohlt, 1967);

Nin, *Tagebücher 1934-1939* (Hamburg: Wegner, 1967).

PERIODICAL PUBLICATION: "Aus dem Nachlaß: Romanfragmente und Briefe," *Literatur und Kritik*, 15 (May 1980): 198-248.

Herbert Zand, who was drafted into the German army and severely wounded on the eastern front during World War II, wrote a war novel and a novel on postwar Vienna, and many of his essays and stories explore the effects of Hitler and the war on Austria. Zand is a thoroughly Austrian writer, at home in both rural and urban environments. Born and raised on a farm, Zand reveals in his writings an appreciation of nature and a bond with the land that link him to the tradition of "Heimat" (regional) literature; but he transcended the sentimental and even fascist tendencies of some "Heimat" literature, using the land to express a humanistic existentialist position. Zand eventually died of his war wounds at the age of forty-six, having carried shrapnel in his body for twenty-five years; his grisly fate makes him a distressing symbol of a past that will not die. His early death cut his work short, but his books gained some recognition, including several literary prizes, during his lifetime. Although he is not considered a major author, the enduring literary merit and historical relevance of Zand's writings will ensure him a place in Austrian literary history.

Zand was born in the village of Knoppen bei Aussee on 14 November 1923, the only child of Adolf and Aloisia Zand, poor, uneducated Styrian farmers. Although he was raised in a home with scarcely any books and attended school for only eight years, he was fascinated by the stories told by his grandparents and enthralled by the books he encountered in school. He claimed that he never entered the world of literature but had always been at home in it. He published his first poem in a newspaper at age twelve. His German teacher, Hans Vlasics, introduced him to the work of some of the best-known German authors. Hermann Broch and Frank Thieß, both of whom lived at times in nearby Bad Aussee, encouraged Zand and critiqued his writing. Zand attended the elementary school in Knoppen from 1930 through 1934 and continued his schooling in Bad Aussee from 1934 through 1938, the year the Third Reich annexed Austria. In Bad Aussee, Zand met his future wife, Minnie (Mimi) Gutjahr.

In 1942 Zand was drafted into the German army, becoming a radio operator in the infantry. In July of that year he was sent to the eastern front; his unit had almost reached Moscow by New Year's Day. He was wounded during the German retreat in 1943. In 1944 he experienced the swamp warfare and the siege of Brest Litovsk that he later described in *Letzte Ausfahrt* (1953; translated as *The Last Sortie*, 1955). In 1945 he returned to Knoppen and began to write his first novel. The rest of his life was characterized by pro-

ductive literary activity along with an astonishing process of self-education in English, French, and Polish; much of his studying was done during long periods of hospitalization.

Zand's first novel, *Die Sonnenstadt* (The City of the Sun, 1947), concerns an aristocratic woman who turns her castle into a hotel after the war. After her death the hotel is taken over by her estranged son, a composer who has been living as a hermit on a nearby mountain. Along with several other artists he strives to create a new city and perhaps even a new religion on the site, where an ancient city with a temple to a sun goddess had once stood.

From 1950 through 1952 Zand was quite ill, but in 1953 he recovered his health and began a productive period. His marriage to Minnie Gutjahr took place on 16 June. The couple, who had no children, were happy together; his diaries tell of her support throughout his illness and of the poverty they endured. Both his parents and wife at first thought Zand should continue farming, but they accepted his choice of a literary career. After their marriage the couple moved to Vienna, where Zand went to work for the Donau publishing house.

Letzte Ausfahrt earned Zand his greatest public recognition: the book was translated into English, selected as a book of the month in Germany, and won the Austrian State Prize for Literature. Zand had intended never to write about war, but he found himself compelled to express its horrors and meaninglessness and to convey his belief that existentialist humanism offered a hopeful response. The novel alternately traces the advance of a company of German soldiers and portrays the claustrophobic life endured by the inhabitants of the besieged East German city of Mindenburg; the book ends with the Soviet flag flying triumphantly over the city. The company marches through a swamp, villages, and farms; trenches are dug and quickly fill with water; soldiers smoke and play the harmonica; people die; corpses are carried; a deserter is loaded onto a jeep; the sounds of shots, bombs, and explosions punctuate the narration. The characters' thoughts, conversations, and nightmares reveal their despair, deadened emotions, and sensations. Religion, morality, and idealism seem irrelevant in the face of death. War transforms young Ludwig Höhn from a sensitive, cultivated piano player into a crude, foul-mouthed killer driven by orders and by the fear of death. To save his comrades Höhn murders an officer; he

Zand's friend Wolfgang Kraus, who published Zand's collected writings after the author's death (Votava, Vienna)

is finally shot while trying to protect some young girls. In Mindenburg, Dr. Maja Vesalius takes morphine to endure the grim, endless work of treating the wounded. The general headquartered in Mindenburg emerges from his underground hideout plagued with guilt and is killed protecting some soldiers from a burning tank. Although the book emphasizes the dehumanization of war, it also portrays hope and freedom that existentialism cherishes as possible even in the midst of unspeakable guilt and suffering.

In 1953 Zand also published a volume of fifty-two poems, *Die Glaskugel* (The Glass Sphere); the title poem is about a princess's idealized plaything. The book celebrates the cycles of day and season and the beauties of weather and land, showing a melancholy acceptance of nature's harsh side and of mortality. Poems are narrated by a destructive storm, a tree, restless penned horses, a pavement witnessing a funeral procession, and a peaceful swamp unperturbed by the corpses of dead soldiers it holds. Zand won the Georg Trakl Prize in 1954.

Der Weg nach Hassi el emel (The Path to Hassi el emel, 1956; translated as *The Well of Hope*, 1957) is a compact, unified novella that effectively uses the theme of survival in the wilder-

ness to convey an existentialist affirmation of life and the will to survive. After his airplane crashes in the desert the pilot, Christopher Hall, displays heroic determination in following a trail that eventually leads him to a cave offering shelter from sun and sandstorm. In the end, Hall is reunited with his wife at the site of an ancient dry fountain, a symbol both of hope and of the threat of death in a hostile wilderness.

In 1957 Zand received the Prize of the City of Vienna and the Peter Rosegger Prize of Styria. In 1959 the owner of the Donau publishing house died, and the company went bankrupt. Zand attempted to rescue the firm, enduring for years a series of lawsuits related to its liquidation.

Always a rigorous self-critic, Zand is known to have burned in 1964 a novel first titled "Der eiserne Ofen" (The Iron Stove) and later "Ich ist ein anderer" (I Is Someone Else), and he left other manuscripts unpublished or unfinished. Extant in notebook form are the novel fragments "Therese Taufers" and "Der große Chor" (The Great Chorus). Zand had a contract with the Schönleitner publishing house for the latter book, but the company went bankrupt while he was revising it. Zand probably harbored some hope of discovery in the future, for he had agreed with Broch in a letter of 1950 that many works require an incubation period of twenty-five years before they find their rightful audience.

The last of Zand's books to appear during his lifetime was *Erben des Feuers* (Inheritors of Fire, 1961), for which he wrote at least eight drafts. The intricate plot, Vienna setting, and eccentric characters all contribute to the appeal of this engrossing mystery novel. On his way home around midnight the journalist Dr. Sasha Mallowan hears a shot. A few nights later he is attacked in his room and suffers a minor injury. The reader is then led through a labyrinth of interrelated narrative segments told from various perspectives. When the strands of the story are finally drawn together, it turns out that Mallowan's attacker was young Manfred Galland, whose mental disturbance was at least partly brought on by wartime trauma. He does not have to pay for his crimes, however, for his father, a prominent industrialist, takes care of everything and finds him a good position in his firm. Manfred's misdeeds, like those of Austria during World War II, are thus smoothed over with a veneer of prosperity. Attention is focused on the historical and sociological milieu of the story by the book's title, identifying the postwar generation as those who have inherited "fire," and by Mallowan's analysis of Vienna's class structure for a sociological monograph he intends to write.

Zand received a prize from the Theodor Körner Foundation in 1961 and the Anton Wildgans Prize of Austrian Industry in 1966. In 1968 he went to work for the literature division of the Austrian radio network.

During his last years Zand was hospitalized at various times in Ischl, Linz, and Vienna. Despite bouts of fever, pain, and kidney failure–he was an early dialysis patient–he continued to write creative pieces, keep a journal, and carry on a prodigious correspondence with both well-known writers and beginning authors. In 1970 he received a year's stipend from the Gerhard Fritsch Foundation for Austrian authors.

Three days before his death Zand wrote a moving poem of farewell, "Ich nehme Abschied" (I Take My Leave). On 14 July 1970 his kidneys failed; he died in the Wilhelminer Hospital in Vienna and was buried in the Maria Kumitz cemetery. In the three years following his death his friend Wolfgang Kraus brought out six volumes of Zand's work, much of it previously unpublished. *Kerne des paradiesischen Apfels* (The Core of

the Apple of Paradise, 1971) is a collection of essays, sketches, interviews, and diary entries. The longest piece, the autobiographical essay "Einsame Freiheit oder Landleben und Civilisation" (Lonely Freedom or Rural Life and Civilization), sketches the history of Zand's ancestors and presents vivid details of his childhood, ranging from the smells of different types of hay to memories of his family's first tractor and first radio. Eschewing romantic notions of "the farmer," Zand achieves a thoughtful blend of the positive and negative aspects of rural life. Particularly stunning are the portraits of his father and mother, awesome forces of nature thoroughly devoted to physical work. Despite his evident admiration for them, Zand asserts that they are guided by a philosophy of slavery, an attitude characterized by resignation, suspicion, the overvaluation of physical strength and labor, and a lack of interest in luxury, beauty, success, or even rest. Styrian farmers are isolated and wary of change, he says, more affected by a new tool than a new government; Hitler was able to placate farmers' fears of cultural change by enshrining familiar rural traditions. Asserting that farm life has no place for thought or reflection, Zand indicates that he diverged from his rural heritage because of his intellectual curiosity. He concludes by claiming that only those who work the land can really understand it, amending this statement to say that only those who *must* work the land develop a relationship with it that is not aesthetic but existential. The volume concludes with diary entries written during Zand's last two years, many during hospital stays. One notable passage is a succinct confession of faith in a meaningful universe and an affirmation that death is not final, although it may be for an individual creature. The last line of the volume is a tribute to his wife.

Demosthenes spricht gegen die Brandung (Demosthenes Orates against the Waves, 1972) includes *Der Weg nach Hassi el emel*; the other sixteen stories had never been published before, although several had been broadcast on the radio. Some of the stories are humorous or playful. Occasionally the surface realism is broken by the inclusion of hallucinations, incredible occurrences, or magical events. Although written with a light touch that prevents them from being deeply disturbing, the tales are haunted by a menacing undertone, a warning that life is fraught with danger and deception. The title story is centered around Demosthenes' brave decision to defy the conquering ruler, Philip of Macedonia, and traces his struggle to achieve the will to resist even if it means his death. In another story, "Ein verschwiegener Mensch" (A Quiet Man), the withdrawn Mr. Kormoran converses on the streetcar with a bookkeeper who died years ago; at the end a dazzling angel comes to fetch the bookkeeper home. In "Ein Engel für Hollywood" (An Angel for Hollywood) a young woman dreams of success as an actress but goes hungry in real life. In "Heimkehr im August" (Homecoming in August) a student visits her childhood home, which is now deserted; she relives memories of her childhood with mixed emotions, finally arriving at a renewed acceptance of her life. Another homecoming is experienced in "Mrs. Kossygian" by a woman who returns to Vienna after twenty-five years in America; she concludes that missed opportunities cannot be retrieved. In "Der Maler Quirini" (The Painter Quirini) a painter defeated by his inability to be satisfied with his own paintings—a condition suggestive of Zand's attitude toward his literary creations—magically disappears into one of the scenes he has painted. In the Kafkaesque "Überlegungen eines Boten" (Thoughts of a Messenger) a messenger thinks that he is himself a message from one unknown person to another.

The title essay of the 1973 volume *Träume im Spiegel* (Dreams in the Mirror) theorizes that artistic creations are daydreams controlled by the artist's conscious mind. The essay also discusses language, the faculty that evokes insight and turns chaos into order. Other topics treated in the twenty-six short essays include the hypocritical morality of the time, the growing power of public opinion and vulgar advertising, the social reception of literature, the questions of authenticity and realism posed by the nouveau roman, and the work and reception of several contemporary authors. An essay on whether there is a "crisis" in contemporary poetry opposes both conservatism and experimentalism when embraced for their own sakes. In "Ganz kleine Korrekturen" (Quite Minor Corrections) he broods on his power as an editor and on the accidental factors that determine the success or failure of authors. The essay reveals his sensitivity and suggests the existentialist idea that human interactions inevitably generate guilt.

Aus zerschossenem Sonnengeflecht (From a Shot-up Solar Plexus, 1973) contains poems written between 1949 and 1970, most of which had never before been published. Probably because Zand regarded his poetry as a personal means of expression, he took even less care to preserve it than he did his prose; Kraus found the poems on old envelopes and calendars or inserted carelessly in other manuscripts. Inventing his own rhythms, Zand alternates long lines and concentrated, sometimes aphoristic short ones. Only three poems are rhymed and strophic. Not particularly sophisticated or original in their use of language or creation of multilayered resonance, these straightforward poems draw the reader's attention to the emotions, images, and ideas that comprise their content. Many of the poems convey Zand's humble reverence for the cycles and laws of nature and his love of the land as a source of beauty, nurturance, and permanence. "Die alte Straße" (The Old Road) and "Der Pfeifer" (The Whistler), both written about a week before Zand's death, center on the road, one of Zand's favorite images symbolizing the human connection to the land: contemplation of familiar rural thoroughfares evokes both their permanence throughout seasons and years and their human history, recalling the soldiers, brides, churchgoers, farmers, and workers who have passed over them.

In 1980 fifty pages of material from Zand's literary estate appeared in the journal *Literatur und Kritik*. The fragmentary novel "Jester" consists of journal entries written by an Austrian film actor, Thomas W. Jester, and other passages narrated by an old friend whom Jester has asked to write his biography. The friend reflects bitterly on the subordinate, vicarious role he has played to the famous actor, a role that has at times almost caused him to doubt his own existence. The passages from Jester's journal contain his brooding meditations on the questionable worth of his own career as an actor, the elusiveness of happiness and the fickleness of fame, and his fear that acting has robbed him of a chance to develop a genuine identity; he considers a new career translating plays. Zand's existentialism is apparent in Jester's musings about suicide and his quest for meaning and authenticity through creative individual decisions. Another novel fragment, "Orpheus und Euridyke," reveals the thoughts and memories of a contemporary man and woman, given the classical Greek names Orpheus and Eurydice, as they visit during her brief release from a mental hospital.

Zand was a captivating storyteller who knew the appeal of suspense and adventure, mystery and romance. He drew sensitive psychological portraits of individuals facing such extreme physical challenges as war, violence, and abandonment in the wilderness or confronting the modern problem of finding meaning and identity in an apparently senseless universe. Zand's writings convey his fundamental vision of human beings drawing sustenance and a sense of permanence from the land, however bloodstained that land may be.

References:

Jan Chodera, "Die Erzählungen von Herbert Zand," *Studie Germanica Posnaniensia*, 5 (1976): 63-71;

Wolfgang Kraus, "Jahrmillionen der Ruhe: Herbert Zand und der Tod," in *Der Tod in Dichtung, Philosophie, und Kunst,* edited by Hans Helmut Jansen (Darmstadt: Steinkopff, 1978), pp. 243-246;

Kraus, "Das verdrängte Gewissen einer Generation: Gedanken über Herbert Zand," *Literatur und Kritik*, 6 (July 1971): 340-347;

Martin Kubaczek, "Zur Motivik in der Prosa Herbert Zands," *Die Rampe*, 2 (1982): 142-166;

Norbert Langer, "Herbert Zand," *Wort in der Zeit*, 6, no. 9 (1960): 13-17;

Joachim Müller, "Über Herbert Zand," *Literatur und Kritik*, 9 (May 1974): 229-241;

Klaus Podak, "Versuch über Herbert Zand," *Die Neue Rundschau*, 84 (1973): 545-550;

Hans Weigel, "Herbert Zand," in his *In Memoriam* (Graz: Styria, 1979), pp. 172-177.

Papers:

Herbert Zand's papers are at the Austrian National Library in Vienna.

Checklist of Further Readings

Adel, Kurt. *Aufbruch und Tradition: Einführung in die österreichische Literatur seit 1945*. Vienna: Braumüller, 1982.

Amann, Klaus. *Der Anschluß österreichischer Schriftsteller an das dritte Reich*. Frankfurt am Main: Athenäum, 1988.

Amann and Albert Berger, eds. *Österreichische Literatur der 30er Jahre: Ideologische Verhältnisse, institutionelle Voraussetzungen, Fallstudien*. Vienna: Böhlau, 1985.

Arnold, Heinz Ludwig, ed. *Kritisches Lexikon zur deutschsprachigen Gegenwartsliteratur*. Munich: Edition text kritik, 1978ff.

Aspetsberger, Friedbert. *Literarisches Leben im Austrofaschismus: Der Staatspreis*. Königstein: Hain, 1980.

Aspetsberger, ed. *Österreichische Literatur seit den zwanziger Jahren: Beiträge zu ihrer historisch-politischen Lokalisierung*. Vienna: Österreichischer Bundesverlag, 1979.

Aspetsberger, ed. *Staat und Gesellschaft in der modernen österreichischen Literatur*. Vienna: Österreichischer Bundesverlag, 1977.

Aspetsberger, ed. *Traditionen in der neueren österreichischen Literatur: Zehn Vorträge*, revised by Hermann Möcker. Vienna: Österreichischer Bundesverlag, 1980.

Bartsch, Kurt, Dietmar Goltschnigg, and Gerhard Melzer, eds. *Für und wider eine österreichische Literatur*. Königstein: Athenäum, 1982.

Best, Alan, and Hans Wolfschütz, eds. *Modern Austrian Writing: Literature and Society after 1945*. London: Wolff, 1980; Totowa, N.J.: Barnes & Noble, 1980.

Blauhut, Robert. *Österreichische Novellistik des 20. Jahrhunderts*. Vienna: Braumüller, 1966.

Branscombe, Peter, ed. *Austrian Life and Literature: Eight Essays, 1780-1938*. Edinburgh: Scottish Academic Press, 1978.

Breicha, Otto, and Gerhard Fritsch, eds. *Aufforderung zum Mißtrauen: Literatur, bildende Kunst, Musik in Österreich seit 1945*. Salzburg: Residenz, 1967.

Breicha and Reinhard Urbach, eds. *Österreich zum Beispiel: Literatur, bildende Kunst, Film und Musik seit 1968*. Salzburg & Vienna: Residenz, 1982.

Carr, Gilbert J., and Eda Sagarra, eds. *Irish Studies in Modern Austrian Literature: Proceedings of the 1. Irish Symposium in Austrian Studies, 19th-20th February 1982*. Dublin: Trinity College, 1982.

Closs, August. "Austria's Place in German Literature," in his *Medusa's Mirror*. London: Cresset, 1957, pp. 83-95.

Crankshaw, Edward. *The Habsburgs: Portrait of a Dynasty*. New York: Viking, 1971.

Daviau, Donald G., ed. *Major Figures of Contemporary Austrian Literature*. New York: Lang, 1987.

Daviau, ed. *Major Figures of Modern Austrian Literature*. Riverside, Cal.: Ariadne Press, 1988.

Demetz, Peter. *After the Fires: Recent Writing in the Germanies, Austria, and Switzerland*. New York: Harcourt Brace Jovanovich, 1986.

Dimension, special dual-language issue devoted to contemporary Austrian literature, edited by A. Leslie Willson, Ernst Jandl, and Hans F. Prokop, 8, nos. 1 and 2 (1975).

Doppler, Alfred. *Wirklichkeit im spiegel der Sprache: Aufsätze zur Literatur des 20. Jahrhunderts in Österreich*. Vienna: Europa, 1975.

Doppler and Aspetsberger, eds. *Erzähltechniken in der modernen österreichischen Literatur*. Vienna: Österreichischer Bundesverlag, 1976.

Giebisch, Hans, and Gustav Gugitz. *Bio-bibliographisches Literaturlexikon Österreichs, von den Anfängen bis zur Gegenwart*. Vienna: Hollinek, 1963.

Greiner, Ulrich. *Der Tod des Nachsommers: Aufsätze, Porträts, Kritiken zur österreichischen Gegenwartsliteratur*. Munich & Vienna: Hanser, 1979.

Gross, Ruth V. Plan *and the Austrian Rebirth: Portrait of a Journal*. Columbia, S.C.: Camden House, 1982.

Gross, Wilhelm, ed. *Moderne österreichische Novellisten: Mit einer Einleitung*, 2 volumes. Vienna: Österreichischer Bundesverlag, 1950.

Heger, Roland. *Der österreichische Roman des 20. Jahrhunderts*, 2 volumes. Vienna & Stuttgart: Braumüller, 1971-1972.

Holzner, Johann, Michael Klein, and Wolfgang Wiesmüller, eds. *Studien zur Literatur des 19. und 20. Jahrhunderts in Österreich: Festschrift für Alfred Doppler zum 60. Geburtstag*. Innsbruck: Innsbrucker Beiträge zur Kulturwissenschaft, 1981.

Janik, Allan, and Stephen Toulmin. *Wittgenstein's Vienna*. New York: Simon & Schuster, 1973.

Johnson, Lonnie. *Introducing Austria*. Riverside, Cal.: Ariadne Press, 1989.

Johnston, William M. *The Austrian Mind: An Intellectual and Social History, 1848-1938*. Berkeley: University of California Press, 1972.

Klein, Michael, and Sigurd Paul Scheichl, eds. *Thematisierung der Sprache in der österreichischen Literatur des 20. Jahrhunderts: Beiträge eines österreichischen-polnischen Germanistensymposiums*. Innsbruck: Institut für Germanistik der Universität Innsbruck, 1982.

Klinger, Kurt. "Die österreichische Nachkriegsliteratur," *Literatur und Kritik*, 63 (April 1972): 145-157.

Kreissler, Felix. *Von der Revolution zur Annexion: Österreich 1918 bis 1938*. Vienna, Frankfurt am Main & Zurich: Europa, 1970.

Luft, David S. *Robert Musil and the Crisis of European Culture 1880-1942*. Berkeley: University of California Press, 1980.

Magris, Claudio. *Der Habsburgische Mythos in der österreichischen Literatur*, translated by Madeleine von Pásztory. Salzburg: Müller, 1966.

Magris. *Der unauffindbare Sinn: Zur österreichischen Literatur des 20. Jahrhunderts*. Klagenfurt: Carinthia, 1978.

McGrath, William J. *Dionysian Art and Populist Politics in Austria*. New Haven: Yale University Press, 1974.

McVeigh, Joseph. *Kontinuität und Vergangenheitsbewältigung in der österreichischen Literatur nach 1945*. Vienna: Braumüller, 1988.

Modern Austrian Literature, special issue: "Perspectives on the Question of Austrian Literature," 17, no. 3/4 (1984).

Murdock, B. O., and M. G. Ward, eds. *Studies in Modern Austrian Literature: Eight Papers*. Glasgow: Scottish Papers in Germanic Studies, 1981.

Nagl, Johann Willibad, Jakob Zeidler, and Eduard Castle, eds. *Deutsch-österreichische Literaturgeschichte*, volume 4. Vienna: Fromme, 1937.

Opel, Adolf, ed. *Anthology of Modern Austrian Literature*. London: Wolff, 1981.

Patsch, Sylvia M. *Österreichische Schriftsteller im Exil in Großbritannien*. Vienna & Munich: Brandstätter, 1985.

Pauley, Bruce F. *Hitler and the Forgotten Nazis: A History of Austrian National Socialism*. Chapel Hill: University of North Carolina Press, 1981.

Paulsen, Wolfgang, ed. *Österreichische Gegenwart: Die moderne Literatur und ihr Verhältnis zur Tradition*. Bern & Munich: Francke, 1980.

Prokop, Hans F. "Österreichische literarische Zeitschriften 1945-1970," *Literatur und Kritik*, 50 (November 1970): 621-631.

Prokop. *Österreichisches Literaturhandbuch*. Vienna & Munich: Jugend und Volk, 1974.

Rabinbach, Anson, ed. *The Austrian Socialist Experiment: Social Democracy and Austromarxism, 1918-1934*. Boulder, Colo.: Westview Press, 1985.

Rollett, Edwin. *Österreichische Gegenwartsliteratur–Aufgabe, Lage, Forderung*. Vienna: Neues Österreich, 1946.

Ruiss, Gerhard, and Johannes A. Vyoral. *Dokumentation zur Situation junger österreichischer Autoren: Eine Bestandsaufnahme der gegenwärtigen österreichischen Literaturszene*. Vienna: Autorenkooperative, 1978.

Schmidt, Adalbert. *Dichtung und Dichter Österreichs im 19. und 20. Jahrhundert*, 2 volumes. Salzburg: Bergland, 1964.

Schnitzler, Heinrich. "Some Remarks on Austrian Literature," *Books Abroad*, 17 (Summer 1943): 215-221.

Schönwiese, Ernst. *Literatur in Wien zwischen 1930 und 1980.* Vienna & Munich: Amalthea, 1980.

Spalek, John M., Joseph Strelka, and S. H. Haurylchak. *Deutsche Exilliteratur seit 1933: Kalifornien*, 2 volumes. Bern: Francke, 1976.

Spiel, Hilde, ed. *Die zeitgenössische Literatur Österreichs.* Zurich & Munich: Kindler, 1976.

Steiner, Kurt, ed. *Modern Austria.* Palo Alto, Cal.: Society for the Promotion of Science and Scholarship, 1981.

Suchy, Viktor. *Literatur in Österreich von 1945-1970: Strömungen und Tendenzen.* Vienna: Dokumentationsstelle für neuere österreichische Literatur, 1971.

Ungar, Frederick, ed. *Handbook of Austrian Literature.* New York: Ungar, 1973.

Weber, Norbert. *Das gesellschaftlich Vermittelte der Romane österreichischer Schriftsteller seit 1970.* Frankfurt am Main & Bern: Lang, 1980.

Weinzierl, Ulrich, ed. *Österreicher im Exil: Frankreich 1938-1945. Eine Dokumentation.* Vienna: Österreichischer Bundesverlag, 1984.

Weinzierl, ed. *Österreichs Fall: Schriftsteller berichten vom Anschluß.* Vienna & Munich: Jugend und Volk, 1987.

Weyrer, Ursula. *"Das Silberboot": Eine österreichische Literaturzeitschrift (1935-36, 1946-52).* Innsbruck: Institut für Germanistik der Universität Innsbruck, 1984.

Williams, Cedric E. *The Broken Eagle: The Politics of Austrian Literature from Empire to Anschluss.* London: Elek, 1974.

Wischenbart, Rüdiger. *Literarischer Wiederaufbau in Österreich 1945-1949.* Königstein: Hain, 1983.

Zeman, Herbert, ed. *Studien zur österreichischen Erzählliteratur der Gegenwart.* Amsterdam: Editions Rodopi, 1982.

Contributors

Friedrich Achberger..*University of Minnesota*
Karen Achberger...*St. Olaf College*
Robert Acker ....*University of Montana*
Andrew W. Barker..*University of Edinburgh*
Sigrid Bauschinger..*University of Massachusetts*
Beth Bjorklund..*University of Virginia*
Donald G. Daviau ....*University of California, Riverside*
Steve Dowden..*Yale University*
Wolfgang D. Elfe ....*University of South Carolina*
Thomas H. Falk..*Michigan State University*
Gerald A. Fetz ....*University of Montana*
Ludwig Fischer...*Willamette University*
Jerry Glenn...*University of Cincinnati*
Stephanie Barbé Hammer................................*University of California, Riverside*
Catherine Hutter..*Hamden, Connecticut*
Horst Jarka...*University of Montana*
Jorun B. Johns.................................*California State University, San Bernardino*
Lynda J. King ....*Oregon State University*
Renate Latimer..*Auburn University*
Dagmar C. G. Lorenz...*Ohio State University*
Paul Michael Lützeler..*Washington University*
Joseph G. McVeigh ....*Smith College*
August Obermayer ....*University of Otago*
Peter Pabisch...*University of New Mexico*
Sylvia M. Patsch...*Vienna, Austria*
John Carson Pettey..*University of Nevada, Reno*
Sidney Rosenfeld..*Oberlin College*
Pamela S. Saur..*Lamar University*
Ernestine Schlant..*Montclair State College*
Hugo Schmidt...*University of Colorado, Boulder*
Cornelius Schnauber..*University of Southern California*
Johannes W. Vazulik ....*North Dakota State University*
Frank W. Young..*California State University, Los Angeles*

327

Cumulative Index

Dictionary of Literary Biography, Volumes 1-85
Dictionary of Literary Biography Yearbook, 1980-1988
Dictionary of Literary Biography Documentary Series, Volumes 1-6

Cumulative Index

DLB before number: *Dictionary of Literary Biography,* Volumes 1-85
Y before number: *Dictionary of Literary Biography Yearbook,* 1980-1988
DS before number: *Dictionary of Literary Biography Documentary Series,* Volumes 1-6

A

Abbey Press...DLB-49

The Abbey Theatre and Irish
  Drama, 1900-1945 ....DLB-10

Abbot, Willis J. 1863-1934 ....DLB-29

Abbott, Jacob 1803-1879 ....DLB-1

Abbott, Lyman 1835-1922 ....DLB-79

Abbott, Robert S. 1868-1940 ....DLB-29

Abelard-Schuman DLB-46

Abell, Arunah S. 1806-1888 ....DLB-43

Abercrombie, Lascelles 1881-1938 ....DLB-19

Abrams, M. H. 1912- DLB-67

Abse, Dannie 1923- DLB-27

Academy Chicago Publishers DLB-46

Ace Books DLB-46

Acorn, Milton 1923-1986 ....DLB-53

Acosta, Oscar Zeta 1935?- DLB-82

Actors Theatre of Louisville DLB-7

Adair, James 1709?-1783? DLB-30

Adame, Leonard 1947- DLB-82

Adamic, Louis 1898-1951.............................DLB-9

Adams, Alice 1926- Y-86

Adams, Brooks 1848-1927 ....DLB-47

Adams, Charles Francis, Jr. 1835-1915..............DLB-47

Adams, Douglas 1952- Y-83

Adams, Franklin P. 1881-1960 ....DLB-29

Adams, Henry 1838-1918.............................DLB-12, 47

Adams, Herbert Baxter 1850-1901 ....DLB-47

Adams, J. S. and C. [publishing house]..............DLB-49

Adams, James Truslow 1878-1949....................DLB-17

Adams, John 1735-1826................................DLB-31

Adams, John Quincy 1767-1848......................DLB-37

Adams, Léonie 1899-1988 ....DLB-48

Adams, Samuel 1722-1803...........................DLB-31, 43

Adams, William Taylor 1822-1897 ....DLB-42

Adcock, Fleur 1934- DLB-40

Ade, George 1866-1944 ....DLB-11, 25

Adeler, Max (see Clark, Charles Heber)

Advance Publishing Company DLB-49

AE 1867-1935 ....DLB-19

Aesthetic Poetry (1873), by Walter Pater...........DLB-35

Afro-American Literary Critics:
  An Introduction DLB-33

Agassiz, Jean Louis Rodolphe 1807-1873 ....DLB-1

Agee, James 1909-1955................................DLB-2, 26

Aichinger, Ilse 1921- DLB-85

Aiken, Conrad 1889-1973............................DLB-9, 45

Ainsworth, William Harrison 1805-1882 ....DLB-21

Aitken, Robert [publishing house]....................DLB-49

Akins, Zoë 1886-1958.................................DLB-26

Alain-Fournier 1886-1914............................DLB-65

Alba, Nanina 1915-1968..............................DLB-41

Albee, Edward 1928- DLB-7

Alcott, Amos Bronson 1799-1888 ....DLB-1

Alcott, Louisa May 1832-1888.................DLB-1, 42, 79

Alcott, William Andrus 1798-1859....................DLB-1

Alden, Henry Mills 1836-1919 ....DLB-79

Alden, Isabella 1841-1930............................DLB-42

Alden, John B. [publishing house] DLB-49

Alden, Beardsley and Company DLB-49

Aldington, Richard 1892-1962 ....DLB-20, 36

Aldis, Dorothy 1896-1966 ....DLB-22

Aldiss, Brian W. 1925- DLB-14

Aldrich, Thomas Bailey 1836-1907
  ....DLB-42, 71, 74, 79

Alexander, Charles Wesley
  [publishing house] DLB-49

Alexander, James 1691-1756 ....DLB-24

Alexander, Lloyd 1924- DLB-52

Alger, Horatio, Jr. 1832-1899.........................DLB-42

Algonquin Books of Chapel Hill.....................DLB-46

Algren, Nelson 1909-1981 ....DLB-9; Y-81, 82

Allan, Ted 1916- DLB-68

Alldritt, Keith 1935- DLB-14

Allen, Ethan 1738-1789 ....DLB-31

Allen, George 1808-1876 ....DLB-59

Allen, Grant 1848-1899...................................DLB-70

Allen, Henry W. 1912- Y-85

Allen, Hervey 1889-1949................................DLB-9, 45

Allen, James 1739-1808..................................DLB-31

Allen, James Lane 1849-1925 ....DLB-71

Allen, Jay Presson 1922- DLB-26

Allen, John, and Company DLB-49

Allen, Samuel W. 1917- DLB-41

Allen, Woody 1935- DLB-44

Allingham, Margery 1904-1966.......................DLB-77

Allingham, William 1824-1889........................DLB-35

Allison, W. L. [publishing house] DLB-49

Allott, Kenneth 1912-1973..............................DLB-20

Allston, Washington 1779-1843 ....DLB-1

Alsop, George 1636-post 1673..........................DLB-24

Alsop, Richard 1761-1815...............................DLB-37

Altemus, Henry, and Company.........................DLB-49

Altenberg, Peter 1885-1919 ....DLB-81

Alurista 1947- DLB-82

Alvarez, A. 1929- DLB-14, 40

Ambler, Eric 1909- DLB-77

*America: or, a Poem on the Settlement of the
    British Colonies* (1780?), by Timothy
    Dwight...DLB-37

American Conservatory Theatre DLB-7

American Fiction and the 1930s........................DLB-9

American Humor: A Historical Survey
    East and Northeast
    South and Southwest
    Midwest
    West...DLB-11

American News Company................................DLB-49

The American Poets' Corner: The First

Three Years (1983-1986)...............................Y-86

American Publishing Company DLB-49

American Stationers' Company.........................DLB-49

American Sunday-School Union DLB-49

American Temperance Union............................DLB-49

American Tract Society DLB-49

The American Writers Congress
    (9-12 October 1981) Y-81

The American Writers Congress: A Report
    on Continuing Business...............................Y-81

Ames, Fisher 1758-1808................................DLB-37

Ames, Mary Clemmer 1831-1884 ....DLB-23

Amini, Johari M. 1935- DLB-41

Amis, Kingsley 1922- DLB-15, 27

Amis, Martin 1949- DLB-14

Ammons, A. R. 1926- DLB-5

Amory, Thomas 1691?-1788............................DLB-39

Anaya, Rudolfo A. 1937- DLB-82

Andersch, Alfred 1914-1980............................DLB-69

Anderson, Margaret 1886-1973..........................DLB-4

Anderson, Maxwell 1888-1959..........................DLB-7

Anderson, Patrick 1915-1979...........................DLB-68

Anderson, Paul Y. 1893-1938...........................DLB-29

Anderson, Poul 1926- DLB-8

Anderson, Robert 1917- DLB-7

Anderson, Sherwood 1876-1941...........DLB-4, 9; DS-1

Andreas-Salomé, Lou 1861-1937.......................DLB-66

Andres, Stefan 1906-1970................................DLB-69

Andrews, Charles M. 1863-1943.......................DLB-17

Andrieux, Louis (see Aragon, Louis)

Andrian, Leopold von 1875-1951 ....DLB-81

Andrus, Silas, and Son DLB-49

Angell, James Burrill 1829-1916 ....DLB-64

Angelou, Maya 1928- DLB-38

The "Angry Young Men"...................................DLB-15

Anhalt, Edward 1914- DLB-26

Anners, Henry F. [publishing house].................DLB-49

Anthony, Piers 1934- DLB-8

Anthony Burgess's *99 Novels*: An Opinion Poll Y-84

Antin, Mary 1881-1949 ....Y-84

Antschel, Paul (see Celan, Paul)

Apodaca, Rudy S. 1939- DLB-82

Appleton, D., and Company DLB-49

Appleton-Century-Crofts DLB-46

Apple-wood Books DLB-46

Aquin, Hubert 1929-1977 ....DLB-53

Aragon, Louis 1897-1982 ....DLB-72

Arbor House Publishing Company DLB-46

Arcadia House DLB-46

Arce, Julio G. (see Ulica, Jorge)

Archer, William 1856-1924 ....DLB-10

Arden, John 1930- DLB-13

Arden of Faversham DLB-62

The Arena Publishing Company DLB-49

Arena Stage DLB-7

Arensberg, Ann 1937- Y-82

Arias, Ron 1941- DLB-82

Arland, Marcel 1899-1986 ....DLB-72

Arlen, Michael 1895-1956 ....DLB-36, 77

Armed Services Editions DLB-46

Arno Press DLB-46

Arnold, Edwin 1832-1904 ....DLB-35

Arnold, Matthew 1822-1888 ....DLB-32, 57

Arnold, Thomas 1795-1842 ....DLB-55

Arnow, Harriette Simpson 1908-1986 ....DLB-6

Arp, Bill (see Smith, Charles Henry)

Arthur, Timothy Shay 1809-1885 ....DLB-3, 42, 79

Artmann, H. C. 1921- DLB-85

As I See It, by Carolyn Cassady DLB-16

Asch, Nathan 1902-1964 ....DLB-4, 28

Ash, John 1948- DLB-40

Ashbery, John 1927- DLB-5; Y-81

Asher, Sandy 1942- Y-83

Ashton, Winifred (see Dane, Clemence)

Asimov, Isaac 1920- DLB-8

Atheneum Publishers DLB-46

Atherton, Gertrude 1857-1948 ....DLB-9, 78

Atkins, Josiah circa 1755-1781 ....DLB-31

Atkins, Russell 1926- DLB-41

The Atlantic Monthly Press DLB-46

Attaway, William 1911-1986 ....DLB-76

Atwood, Margaret 1939- DLB-53

Aubert, Alvin 1930- DLB-41

Aubin, Penelope 1685-circa 1731 ....DLB-39

Aubrey-Fletcher, Henry Lancelot (see Wade, Henry)

Auchincloss, Louis 1917- DLB-2; Y-80

Auden, W. H. 1907-1973 ....DLB-10, 20

Audio Art in America: A Personal
    Memoir Y-85

Auernheimer, Raoul 1876-1948 ....DLB-81

Austin, Alfred 1835-1913 ....DLB-35

Austin, Mary 1868-1934 ....DLB-9, 78

Austin, William 1778-1841 ....DLB-74

The Author's Apology for His Book
    (1684), by John Bunyan DLB-39

An Author's Response, by Ronald Sukenick Y-82

Authors and Newspapers Association DLB-46

Authors' Publishing Company DLB-49

Avalon Books DLB-46

Avendaño, Fausto 1941- DLB-82

Avison, Margaret 1918- DLB-53

Avon Books DLB-46

Ayckbourn, Alan 1939- DLB-13

Aymé, Marcel 1902-1967 ....DLB-72

Aytoun, William Edmondstoune 1813-1865 ......DLB-32

B

Babbitt, Irving 1865-1933 ....DLB-63

Babbitt, Natalie 1932- DLB-52

Babcock, John [publishing house] DLB-49

Bache, Benjamin Franklin 1769-1798 ....DLB-43

Bachmann, Ingeborg 1926-1973 ....DLB-85

Bacon, Delia 1811-1859 ....DLB-1

Bacon, Thomas circa 1700-1768 ....DLB-31

Badger, Richard G., and Company DLB-49

Bage, Robert 1728-1801 ....DLB-39

Bagehot, Walter 1826-1877 ....DLB-55

Bagnold, Enid 1889-1981 ....DLB-13

Bahr, Hermann 1863-1934 ....DLB-81

Bailey, Alfred Goldsworthy 1905- DLB-68

Bailey, Francis [publishing house] DLB-49

Bailey, H. C. 1878-1961 ....DLB-77

Bailey, Paul 1937- DLB-14

Bailey, Philip James 1816-1902.....................DLB-32

Baillie, Hugh 1890-1966 ....DLB-29

Bailyn, Bernard 1922- DLB-17

Bainbridge, Beryl 1933- DLB-14

Baird, Irene 1901-1981.............................DLB-68

The Baker and Taylor Company DLB-49

Baker, Houston A., Jr. 1943- DLB-67

Baker, Walter H., Company
("Baker's Plays")..................................DLB-49

Bald, Wambly 1902- DLB-4

Balderston, John 1889-1954 ....DLB-26

Baldwin, James 1924-1987 ....DLB-2, 7, 33; Y-87

Baldwin, Joseph Glover 1815-1864 ....DLB-3, 11

Ballantine Books...................................DLB-46

Ballard, J. G. 1930- DLB-14

Ballou, Maturin Murray 1820-1895...................DLB-79

Ballou, Robert O. [publishing house]...............DLB-46

Bambara, Toni Cade 1939- DLB-38

Bancroft, A. L., and Company DLB-49

Bancroft, George 1800-1891 ....DLB-1, 30, 59

Bancroft, Hubert Howe 1832-1918....................DLB-47

Bangs, John Kendrick 1862-1922...................DLB-11, 79

Banks, John circa 1653-1706 ....DLB-80

Bantam Books.......................................DLB-46

Banville, John 1945- DLB-14

Baraka, Amiri 1934- DLB-5, 7, 16, 38

Barber, John Warner 1798-1885 ....DLB-30

Barbour, Ralph Henry 1870-1944.....................DLB-22

Barbusse, Henri 1873-1935..........................DLB-65

Barclay, E. E., and Company DLB-49

Bardeen, C. W. [publishing house]..................DLB-49

Baring, Maurice 1874-1945..........................DLB-34

Barker, A. L. 1918- DLB-14

Barker, George 1913- DLB-20

Barker, Harley Granville 1877-1946 ....DLB-10

Barker, Howard 1946- DLB-13

Barker, James Nelson 1784-1858.....................DLB-37

Barker, Jane 1652-1727? DLB-39

Barks, Coleman 1937- DLB-5

Barlach, Ernst 1870-1938...........................DLB-56

Barlow, Joel 1754-1812 ....DLB-37

Barnard, John 1681-1770 ....DLB-24

Barnes, A. S., and Company.........................DLB-49

Barnes, Djuna 1892-1982 ....DLB-4, 9, 45

Barnes, Margaret Ayer 1886-1967 ....DLB-9

Barnes, Peter 1931- DLB-13

Barnes, William 1801-1886..........................DLB-32

Barnes and Noble Books.............................DLB-46

Barney, Natalie 1876-1972..........................DLB-4

Baron, Richard W., Publishing Company DLB-46

Barr, Robert 1850-1912 ....DLB-70

Barrax, Gerald William 1933- DLB-41

Barrie, James M. 1860-1937 ....DLB-10

Barrio, Raymond 1921- DLB-82

Barry, Philip 1896-1949............................DLB-7

Barse and Hopkins..................................DLB-46

Barstow, Stan 1928- DLB-14

Barth, John 1930- DLB-2

Barthelme, Donald 1931- DLB-2; Y-80

Barthelme, Frederick 1943- Y-85

Bartlett, John 1820-1905...........................DLB-1

Bartol, Cyrus Augustus 1813-1900...................DLB-1

Bartram, John 1699-1777 ....DLB-31

Bartram, William 1739-1823.........................DLB-37

Basic Books..DLB-46

Bass, T. J. 1932- Y-81

Bassett, John Spencer 1867-1928 ....DLB-17

Bassler, Thomas Joseph (see Bass, T. J.)

Bate, Walter Jackson 1918- DLB-67

Bates, Katharine Lee 1859-1929.....................DLB-71

Baum, L. Frank 1856-1919...........................DLB-22

Baum, Vicki 1888-1960..............................DLB-85

Baumbach, Jonathan 1933- Y-80

Bawden, Nina 1925- DLB-14

Bax, Clifford 1886-1962 ....DLB-10

Bayer, Eleanor (see Perry, Eleanor)

Bayer, Konrad 1932-1964 ....DLB-85

Bazin, Hervé 1911- DLB-83

Beach, Sylvia 1887-1962............................DLB-4

Beacon Press DLB-49

Beadle and Adams...................................DLB-49

Beagle, Peter S. 1939- Y-80

Beal, M. F. 1937- Y-81

Beale, Howard K. 1899-1959.....................DLB-17

Beard, Charles A. 1874-1948.....................DLB-17

A Beat Chronology: The First Twenty-five
    Years, 1944-1969 ....DLB-16

Beattie, Ann 1947- Y-82

Beauchemin, Yves 1941- DLB-60

Beaulieu, Victor-Lévy 1945- DLB-53

Beaumont, Francis circa 1584-1616
    and Fletcher, John 1579-1625 ....DLB-58

Beauvoir, Simone de 1908-1986..............Y-86, DLB-72

Becher, Ulrich 1910- DLB-69

Becker, Carl 1873-1945..........................DLB-17

Becker, Jurek 1937- DLB-75

Becker, Jürgen 1932- DLB-75

Beckett, Samuel 1906- DLB-13, 15

Beckford, William 1760-1844 ....DLB-39

Beckham, Barry 1944- DLB-33

Beecher, Catharine Esther 1800-1878.............DLB-1

Beecher, Henry Ward 1813-1887.................DLB-3, 43

Beer, George L. 1872-1920.....................DLB-47

Beer, Patricia 1919- DLB-40

Beerbohm, Max 1872-1956.....................DLB-34

Beer-Hofmann, Richard 1866-1945 ....DLB-81

Beers, Henry A. 1847-1926 ....DLB-71

Behan, Brendan 1923-1964 ....DLB-13

Behn, Aphra 1640?-1689........................DLB-39, 80

Behn, Harry 1898-1973 ....DLB-61

Behrman, S. N. 1893-1973 ....DLB-7, 44

Belasco, David 1853-1931 ....DLB-7

Belford, Clarke and Company...................DLB-49

Belitt, Ben 1911- DLB-5

Belknap, Jeremy 1744-1798.....................DLB-30, 37

Bell, James Madison 1826-1902.................DLB-50

Bell, Marvin 1937- DLB-5

Bell, Robert [publishing house] DLB-49

Bellamy, Edward 1850-1898 ....DLB-12

Bellamy, Joseph 1719-1790.....................DLB-31

Belloc, Hilaire 1870-1953 ....DLB-19

Bellow, Saul 1915- DLB-2, 28; Y-82; DS-3

Belmont Productions.............................DLB-46

Bemelmans, Ludwig 1898-1962.................DLB-22

Bemis, Samuel Flagg 1891-1973 ....DLB-17

Benchley, Robert 1889-1945.....................DLB-11

Benedictus, David 1938- DLB-14

Benedikt, Michael 1935- DLB-5

Benét, Stephen Vincent 1898-1943.................DLB-4, 48

Benét, William Rose 1886-1950.................DLB-45

Benford, Gregory 1941- Y-82

Benjamin, Park 1809-1864 ....DLB-3, 59, 73

Benn, Gottfried 1886-1956 ....DLB-56

Bennett, Arnold 1867-1931 ....DLB-10, 34

Bennett, Charles 1899- DLB-44

Bennett, Gwendolyn 1902- DLB-51

Bennett, Hal 1930- DLB-33

Bennett, James Gordon 1795-1872 ....DLB-43

Bennett, James Gordon, Jr. 1841-1918 ....DLB-23

Bennett, John 1865-1956 ....DLB-42

Benoit, Jacques 1941- DLB-60

Benson, Stella 1892-1933 ....DLB-36

Bentley, E. C. 1875-1956........................DLB-70

Benton, Robert 1932- and Newman,
    David 1937- DLB-44

Benziger Brothers.................................DLB-49

Beresford, Anne 1929- DLB-40

Berford, R. G., Company.........................DLB-49

Berg, Stephen 1934- DLB-5

Bergengruen, Werner 1892-1964 ....DLB-56

Berger, John 1926- DLB-14

Berger, Meyer 1898-1959 ....DLB-29

Berger, Thomas 1924- DLB-2; Y-80

Berkeley, Anthony 1893-1971 ....DLB-77

Berkeley, George 1685-1753.....................DLB-31

The Berkley Publishing Corporation DLB-46

Bernal, Vicente J. 1888-1915.....................DLB-82

Bernanos, Georges 1888-1948 ....DLB-72

Bernard, John 1756-1828 ....DLB-37

Bernhard, Thomas 1931-1989.....................DLB-85

Berrigan, Daniel 1921- DLB-5

Berrigan, Ted 1934-1983 ....DLB-5

Berry, Wendell 1934- DLB-5, 6

Berryman, John 1914-1972................................DLB-48

Bersianik, Louky 1930- DLB-60

Berton, Pierre 1920- DLB-68

Bessette, Gerard 1920- DLB-53

Bessie, Alvah 1904-1985..................................DLB-26

Bester, Alfred 1913- DLB-8

The Bestseller Lists: An Assessment Y-84

Betjeman, John 1906-1984 ....DLB-20; Y-84

Betts, Doris 1932- Y-82

Beveridge, Albert J. 1862-1927 ....DLB-17

Beverley, Robert circa 1673-1722................DLB-24, 30

Bichsel, Peter 1935- DLB-75

Biddle, Drexel [publishing house] DLB-49

Bidwell, Walter Hilliard 1798-1881 ....DLB-79

Bienek, Horst 1930- DLB-75

Bierbaum, Otto Julius 1865-1910 ....DLB-66

Bierce, Ambrose 1842-1914?......DLB-11, 12, 23, 71, 74

Biggle, Lloyd, Jr. 1923- DLB-8

Biglow, Hosea (see Lowell, James Russell)

Billings, Josh (see Shaw, Henry Wheeler)

Binding, Rudolf G. 1867-1938..........................DLB-66

Bingham, Caleb 1757-1817 ....DLB-42

Binyon, Laurence 1869-1943 ....DLB-19

Biographical Documents I....................................Y-84

Biographical Documents II Y-85

Bioren, John [publishing house].........................DLB-49

Bird, William 1888-1963 ....DLB-4

Bishop, Elizabeth 1911-1979............................DLB-5

Bishop, John Peale 1892-1944....................DLB-4, 9, 45

Bissett, Bill 1939- DLB-53

Black, David (D. M.) 1941- DLB-40

Black, Walter J. [publishing house] DLB-46

Black, Winifred 1863-1936 ....DLB-25

The Black Arts Movement, by Larry Neal........DLB-38

Black Theaters and Theater Organizations in
    America, 1961-1982: A Research List.........DLB-38

Black Theatre: A Forum [excerpts]....................DLB-38

Blackamore, Arthur 1679-? DLB-24, 39

Blackburn, Alexander L. 1929- Y-85

Blackburn, Paul 1926-1971....................DLB-16; Y-81

Blackburn, Thomas 1916-1977.........................DLB-27

Blackmore, R. D. 1825-1900 ....DLB-18

Blackmur, R. P. 1904-1965 ....DLB-63

Blackwood, Caroline 1931- DLB-14

Blair, Eric Arthur (see Orwell, George)

Blair, Francis Preston 1791-1876......................DLB-43

Blair, James circa 1655-1743............................DLB-24

Blair, John Durburrow 1759-1823 ....DLB-37

Blais, Marie-Claire 1939- DLB-53

Blaise, Clark 1940- DLB-53

Blake, Nicholas 1904-1972 ....DLB-77
    (see also Day Lewis, C.)

The Blakiston Company DLB-49

Blanchot, Maurice 1907- DLB-72

Bledsoe, Albert Taylor 1809-1877 ....DLB-3, 79

Blelock and Company DLB-49

Blish, James 1921-1975 ....DLB-8

Bliss, E., and E. White [publishing house].........DLB-49

Bloch, Robert 1917- DLB-44

Block, Rudolph (see Lessing, Bruno)

Bloom, Harold 1930- DLB-67

Bloomer, Amelia 1818-1894 ....DLB-79

Blume, Judy 1938- DLB-52

Blunck, Hans Friedrich 1888-1961....................DLB-66

Blunden, Edmund 1896-1974...........................DLB-20

Blunt, Wilfrid Scawen 1840-1922 ....DLB-19

Bly, Nellie (see Cochrane, Elizabeth)

Bly, Robert 1926- DLB-5

The Bobbs-Merrill Company DLB-46

Bobrowski, Johannes 1917-1965.......................DLB-75

Bodenheim, Maxwell 1892-1954 ....DLB-9, 45

Bodkin, M. McDonnell 1850-1933 ....DLB-70

Bodmershof, Imma von 1895-1982....................DLB-85

Bodsworth, Fred 1918- DLB-68

Boehm, Sydney 1908- DLB-44

Boer, Charles 1939- DLB-5

Bogan, Louise 1897-1970.................................DLB-45

Bogarde, Dirk 1921- DLB-14

Boland, Eavan 1944- DLB-40

Böll, Heinrich 1917-1985.........................Y-85, DLB-69

Bolling, Robert 1738-1775 ....DLB-31

Bolt, Carol 1941- DLB-60

Bolt, Robert 1924- DLB-13

Bolton, Herbert E. 1870-1953 ....DLB-17

Bond, Edward 1934- DLB-13

Boni, Albert and Charles [publishing house].....DLB-46

Boni and Liveright DLB-46

Robert Bonner's Sons.......................................DLB-49

Bontemps, Arna 1902-1973 ....DLB-48, 51

The Book League of America DLB-46

Book Reviewing in America: I Y-87

Book Reviewing in America: II Y-88

Book Supply Company DLB-49

The Booker Prize
  Address by Anthony Thwaite, Chairman
    of the Booker Prize Judges
  Comments from Former Booker Prize
    Winners Y-86

Boorstin, Daniel J. 1914- DLB-17

Booth, Mary L. 1831-1889...............................DLB-79

Booth, Philip 1925- Y-82

Booth, Wayne C. 1921- DLB-67

Borchardt, Rudolf 1877-1945.........................DLB-66

Borchert, Wolfgang 1921-1947 ....DLB-69

Borges, Jorge Luis 1899-1986.........................Y-86

Borrow, George 1803-1881..........................DLB-21, 55

Bosco, Henri 1888-1976...................................DLB-72

Bosco, Monique 1927- DLB-53

Botta, Anne C. Lynch 1815-1891 ....DLB-3

Bottomley, Gordon 1874-1948.........................DLB-10

Bottoms, David 1949- Y-83

Bottrall, Ronald 1906- DLB-20

Boucher, Anthony 1911-1968..........................DLB-8

Boucher, Jonathan 1738-1804 ....DLB-31

Bourjaily, Vance Nye 1922- DLB-2

Bourne, Edward Gaylord 1860-1908.................DLB-47

Bourne, Randolph 1886-1918...........................DLB-63

Bousquet, Joë 1897-1950 ....DLB-72

Bova, Ben 1932- Y-81

Bove, Emmanuel 1898-1945 ....DLB-72

Bovard, Oliver K. 1872-1945 ....DLB-25

Bowen, Elizabeth 1899-1973 ....DLB-15

Bowen, Francis 1811-1890..........................DLB-1, 59

Bowen, John 1924- DLB-13

Bowen-Merrill Company...................................DLB-49

Bowering, George 1935- DLB-53

Bowers, Claude G. 1878-1958..........................DLB-17

Bowers, Edgar 1924- DLB-5

Bowles, Paul 1910- DLB-5, 6

Bowles, Samuel III 1826-1878..........................DLB-43

Bowman, Louise Morey 1882-1944 ....DLB-68

Boyd, James 1888-1944....................................DLB-9

Boyd, John 1919- DLB-8

Boyd, Thomas 1898-1935 ....DLB-9

Boyesen, Hjalmar Hjorth 1848-1895 ....DLB-12, 71

Boyle, Kay 1902- DLB-4, 9, 48

Boyle, Roger, Earl of Orrery
  1621-1679 ....DLB-80

Boyle, T. Coraghessan 1948- Y-86

Brackenbury, Alison 1953- DLB-40

Brackenridge, Hugh Henry 1748-1816........DLB-11, 37

Brackett, Charles 1892-1969 ....DLB-26

Brackett, Leigh 1915-1978 ....DLB-8, 26

Bradburn, John [publishing house] DLB-49

Bradbury, Malcolm 1932- DLB-14

Bradbury, Ray 1920- DLB-2, 8

Braddon, Mary Elizabeth 1835-1915............DLB-18, 70

Bradford, Andrew 1686-1742......................DLB-43, 73

Bradford, Gamaliel 1863-1932..........................DLB-17

Bradford, John 1749-1830 ....DLB-43

Bradford, William 1590-1657 ....DLB-24, 30

Bradford, William III 1719-1791 ....DLB-43, 73

Bradlaugh, Charles 1833-1891..........................DLB-57

Bradley, David 1950- DLB-33

Bradley, Ira, and Company...............................DLB-49

Bradley, J. W., and Company DLB-49

Bradley, Marion Zimmer 1930- DLB-8

Bradley, William Aspenwall 1878-1939...............DLB-4

Bradstreet, Anne 1612 or 1613-1672 ....DLB-24

Brady, Frederic A. [publishing house] DLB-49

Bragg, Melvyn 1939- DLB-14

Brainard, Charles H. [publishing house]...........DLB-49

Braine, John 1922-1986 ....DLB-15; Y-86

Braithwaite, William Stanley
  1878-1962 ....DLB-50, 54

Bramah, Ernest 1868-1942................DLB-70

Branagan, Thomas 1774-1843.............DLB-37

Branch, William Blackwell 1927- DLB-76

Branden Press................................DLB-46

Brault, Jacques 1933- DLB-53

Braun, Volker 1939- DLB-75

Brautigan, Richard 1935-1984 ....DLB-2, 5; Y-80, 84

Braxton, Joanne M. 1950- DLB-41

Bray, Thomas 1656-1730 ....DLB-24

Braziller, George [publishing house] DLB-46

The Bread Loaf Writers' Conference 1983............Y-84

The Break-Up of the Novel (1922),
        by John Middleton Murry...........DLB-36

Breasted, James Henry 1865-1935.........DLB-47

Brecht, Bertolt 1898-1956................DLB-56

Bredel, Willi 1901-1964.................DLB-56

Bremser, Bonnie 1939- DLB-16

Bremser, Ray 1934- DLB-16

Brentano, Bernard von 1901-1964.........DLB-56

Brentano's.................................DLB-49

Brenton, Howard 1942- DLB-13

Breton, André 1896-1966..................DLB-65

Brewer, Warren and Putnam................DLB-46

Brewster, Elizabeth 1922- DLB-60

Bridgers, Sue Ellen 1942- DLB-52

Bridges, Robert 1844-1930................DLB-19

Bridie, James 1888-1951..................DLB-10

Briggs, Charles Frederick 1804-1877 ......DLB-3

Brighouse, Harold 1882-1958..............DLB-10

Brimmer, B. J., Company DLB-46

Brinnin, John Malcolm 1916- DLB-48

Brisbane, Albert 1809-1890................DLB-3

Brisbane, Arthur 1864-1936...............DLB-25

Broadway Publishing Company DLB-46

Broch, Hermann 1886-1951.................DLB-85

Brochu, André 1942- DLB-53

Brock, Edwin 1927- DLB-40

Brod, Max 1884-1968......................DLB-81

Brodhead, John R. 1814-1873 ....DLB-30

Brome, Richard circa 1590-1652 ....DLB-58

Bromfield, Louis 1896-1956 ....DLB-4, 9

Broner, E. M. 1930- DLB-28

Brontë, Anne 1820-1849...................DLB-21

Brontë, Charlotte 1816-1855..............DLB-21

Brontë, Emily 1818-1848 ....DLB-21, 32

Brooke, Frances 1724-1789................DLB-39

Brooke, Henry 1703?-1783 ....DLB-39

Brooke, Rupert 1887-1915.................DLB-19

Brooke-Rose, Christine 1926- DLB-14

Brookner, Anita 1928- Y-87

Brooks, Charles Timothy 1813-1883 ....DLB-1

Brooks, Cleanth 1906- DLB-63

Brooks, Gwendolyn 1917- DLB-5, 76

Brooks, Jeremy 1926- DLB-14

Brooks, Mel 1926- DLB-26

Brooks, Noah 1830-1903...................DLB-42

Brooks, Richard 1912- DLB-44

Brooks, Van Wyck 1886-1963...........DLB-45, 63

Brophy, Brigid 1929- DLB-14

Brossard, Chandler 1922- DLB-16

Brossard, Nicole 1943- DLB-53

Brother Antoninus (see Everson, William)

Brougham, John 1810-1880.................DLB-11

Broughton, James 1913- DLB-5

Broughton, Rhoda 1840-1920...............DLB-18

Broun, Heywood 1888-1939 ....DLB-29

Brown, Alice 1856-1948 ....DLB-78

Brown, Bob 1886-1959.................DLB-4, 45

Brown, Cecil 1943- DLB-33

Brown, Charles Brockden 1771-1810.....DLB-37, 59, 73

Brown, Christy 1932-1981.................DLB-14

Brown, Dee 1908- Y-80

Browne, Francis Fisher 1843-1913 ....DLB-79

Brown, Frank London 1927-1962 ....DLB-76

Brown, Fredric 1906-1972 ....DLB-8

Brown, George Mackay 1921- DLB-14, 27

Brown, Harry 1917-1986 ....DLB-26

Brown, Marcia 1918- DLB-61

Brown, Margaret Wise 1910-1952 ....DLB-22

Brown, Oliver Madox 1855-1874...........DLB-21

Brown, Sterling 1901-1989 ....DLB-48, 51, 63

Brown, T. E. 1830-1897...................DLB-35

Brown, William Hill 1765-1793 ....DLB-37

Brown, William Wells 1814-1884..................DLB-3, 50

Browne, Charles Farrar 1834-1867.....................DLB-11

Browne, Michael Dennis 1940- DLB-40

Browne, Wynyard 1911-1964..............................DLB-13

Brownell, W. C. 1851-1928 ....DLB-71

Browning, Elizabeth Barrett 1806-1861 ....DLB-32

Browning, Robert 1812-1889 ....DLB-32

Brownjohn, Allan 1931- DLB-40

Brownson, Orestes Augustus
    1803-1876.......................................DLB-1, 59, 73

Bruce, Charles 1906-1971 ....DLB-68

Bruce, Leo 1903-1979 ....DLB-77

Bruce, Philip Alexander 1856-1933...................DLB-47

Bruce Humphries [publishing house] DLB-46

Bruce-Novoa, Juan 1944- DLB-82

Bruckman, Clyde 1894-1955..............................DLB-26

Brundage, John Herbert (see Herbert, John)

Bryant, William Cullen 1794-1878...........DLB-3, 43, 59

Buchan, John 1875-1940.............................DLB-34, 70

Buchanan, Robert 1841-1901 ....DLB-18, 35

Buchman, Sidney 1902-1975 ....DLB-26

Buck, Pearl S. 1892-1973 ....DLB-9

Buckingham, Joseph Tinker 1779-1861 and
    Buckingham, Edwin 1810-1833..................DLB-73

Buckler, Ernest 1908-1984.................................DLB-68

Buckley, William F., Jr. 1925- Y-80

Buckminster, Joseph Stevens 1784-1812............DLB-37

Buckner, Robert 1906- DLB-26

Budd, Thomas ?-1698...DLB-24

Budrys, A. J. 1931- DLB-8

Buechner, Frederick 1926- Y-80

Buell, John 1927- DLB-53

Buffum, Job [publishing house].........................DLB-49

Bukowski, Charles 1920- DLB-5

Bullins, Ed 1935- DLB-7, 38

Bulwer-Lytton, Edward (also Edward Bulwer)
    1803-1873 ....DLB-21

Bumpus, Jerry 1937- Y-81

Bunce and Brother DLB-49

Bunner, H. C. 1855-1896 ....DLB-78, 79

Bunting, Basil 1900-1985 ....DLB-20

Bunyan, John 1628-1688.....................................DLB-39

Burch, Robert 1925- DLB-52

Burciaga, José Antonio 1940- DLB-82

Burgess, Anthony 1917- DLB-14

Burgess, Gelett 1866-1951 ....DLB-11

Burgess, John W. 1844-1931................................DLB-47

Burgess, Thornton W. 1874-1965 ....DLB-22

Burgess, Stringer and Company........................DLB-49

Burk, John Daly circa 1772-1808.....................DLB-37

Burke, Kenneth 1897- DLB-45, 63

Burlingame, Edward Livermore 1848-1922.......DLB-79

Burnett, Frances Hodgson 1849-1924................DLB-42

Burnett, W. R. 1899-1982 ....DLB-9

Burney, Fanny 1752-1840 ....DLB-39

Burns, Alan 1929- DLB-14

Burns, John Horne 1916-1953..............................Y-85

Burnshaw, Stanley 1906- DLB-48

Burr, C. Chauncey 1815?-1883.........................DLB-79

Burroughs, Edgar Rice 1875-1950 ....DLB-8

Burroughs, John 1837-1921................................DLB-64

Burroughs, Margaret T. G. 1917- DLB-41

Burroughs, William S., Jr. 1947-1981 ....DLB-16

Burroughs, William Seward 1914-
    ....DLB-2, 8, 16; Y-81

Burroway, Janet 1936- DLB-6

Burt, A. L., and Company DLB-49

Burton, Miles (see Rhode, John)

Burton, Richard F. 1821-1890 ....DLB-55

Burton, Virginia Lee 1909-1968.......................DLB-22

Burton, William Evans 1804-1860.....................DLB-73

Busch, Frederick 1941- DLB-6

Busch, Niven 1903- DLB-44

Butler, E. H., and Company DLB-49

Butler, Juan 1942-1981 ....DLB-53

Butler, Octavia E. 1947- DLB-33

Butler, Samuel 1835-1902...........................DLB-18, 57

Butor, Michel 1926- DLB-83

Butterworth, Hezekiah 1839-1905.....................DLB-42

B. V. (see Thomson, James)

Byars, Betsy 1928- DLB-52

Byatt, A. S. 1936- DLB-14

Byles, Mather 1707-1788................................DLB-24

Bynner, Witter 1881-1968................................DLB-54

Byrd, William II 1674-1744 ....DLB-24

Byrne, John Keyes (see Leonard, Hugh)

C

Cabell, James Branch 1879-1958 ....DLB-9, 78

Cable, George Washington 1844-1925 ....DLB-12, 74

Cahan, Abraham 1860-1951....................DLB-9, 25, 28

Cain, George 1943- DLB-33

Caldwell, Ben 1937- DLB-38

Caldwell, Erskine 1903-1987................................DLB-9

Caldwell, H. M., Company................................DLB-49

Calhoun, John C. 1782-1850 ....DLB-3

Calisher, Hortense 1911- DLB-2

Callaghan, Morley 1903-................................DLB-68

Callaloo..Y-87

A Call to Letters and an Invitation
    to the Electric Chair,
    by Siegfried Mandel................................DLB-75

Calmer, Edgar 1907-................................DLB-4

Calverley, C. S. 1831-1884 ....DLB-35

Calvert, George Henry 1803-1889 ....DLB-1, 64

Cambridge Press................................DLB-49

Cameron, Eleanor 1912-................................DLB-52

Camm, John 1718-1778 ....DLB-31

Campbell, Gabrielle Margaret Vere
    (see Shearing, Joseph)

Campbell, James Edwin 1867-1896....................DLB-50

Campbell, John 1653-1728................................DLB-43

Campbell, John W., Jr. 1910-1971 ....DLB-8

Campbell, Roy 1901-1957................................DLB-20

Campion, Thomas 1567-1620................................DLB-58

Camus, Albert 1913-1960................................DLB-72

Candelaria, Cordelia 1943- DLB-82

Candelaria, Nash 1928- DLB-82

Candour in English Fiction (1890),
    by Thomas Hardy DLB-18

Canetti, Elias 1905- DLB-85

Cannan, Gilbert 1884-1955................................DLB-10

Cannell, Kathleen 1891-1974................................DLB-4

Cannell, Skipwith 1887-1957 ....DLB-45

Cantwell, Robert 1908-1978................................DLB-9

Cape, Jonathan, and Harrison Smith
    [publishing house] DLB-46

Capen, Joseph 1658-1725 ....DLB-24

Capote, Truman 1924-1984................DLB-2; Y-80, 84

Cardinal, Marie 1929- DLB-83

Carey, Henry circa 1687-1689-1743 ....DLB-84

Carey, M., and Company DLB-49

Carey, Mathew 1760-1839 ....DLB-37, 73

Carey and Hart................................DLB-49

Carlell, Lodowick 1602-1675 ....DLB-58

Carleton, G. W. [publishing house] DLB-49

Carossa, Hans 1878-1956................................DLB-66

Carr, Emily 1871-1945................................DLB-68

Carrier, Roch 1937- DLB-53

Carlyle, Jane Welsh 1801-1866 ....DLB-55

Carlyle, Thomas 1795-1881 ....DLB-55

Carpenter, Stephen Cullen ?-1820?................DLB-73

Carroll, Gladys Hasty 1904- DLB-9

Carroll, John 1735-1815................................DLB-37

Carroll, Lewis 1832-1898 ....DLB-18

Carroll, Paul 1927- DLB-16

Carroll, Paul Vincent 1900-1968 ....DLB-10

Carroll and Graf Publishers DLB-46

Carruth, Hayden 1921- DLB-5

Carryl, Charles E. 1841-1920................................DLB-42

Carswell, Catherine 1879-1946 ....DLB-36

Carter, Angela 1940- DLB-14

Carter, Henry (see Leslie, Frank)

Carter, Landon 1710-1778................................DLB-31

Carter, Lin 1930- Y-81

Carter, Robert, and Brothers................................DLB-49

Carter and Hendee................................DLB-49

Caruthers, William Alexander 1802-1846............DLB-3

Carver, Jonathan 1710-1780................................DLB-31

Carver, Raymond 1938-1988 ....Y-84, 88

Cary, Joyce 1888-1957................................DLB-15

Casey, Juanita 1925- DLB-14

Casey, Michael 1947- DLB-5

Cassady, Carolyn 1923- DLB-16

Cassady, Neal 1926-1968................................DLB-16

Cassell Publishing Company DLB-49

Cassill, R. V. 1919- DLB-6

Castlemon, Harry (see Fosdick, Charles Austin)

Caswall, Edward 1814-1878 ....DLB-32

Cather, Willa 1873-1947................DLB-9, 54, 78; DS-1

Catherwood, Mary Hartwell 1847-1902.............DLB-78

Catton, Bruce 1899-1978................................DLB-17

Causley, Charles 1917- DLB-27

Caute, David 1936- DLB-14

Cawein, Madison 1865-1914 ....DLB-54

The Caxton Printers, Limited.........................DLB-46

Cayrol, Jean 1911- DLB-83

Celan, Paul 1920-1970....................................DLB-69

Céline, Louis-Ferdinand 1894-1961 ....DLB-72

Center for the Book Research Y-84

Centlivre, Susanna 1669?-1723.......................DLB-84

The Century Company DLB-49

Cervantes, Lorna Dee 1954- DLB-82

Chacón, Eusebio 1869-1948.............................DLB-82

Chacón, Felipe Maximiliano
      1873-?..DLB-82

Challans, Eileen Mary (see Renault, Mary)

Chalmers, George 1742-1825............................DLB-30

Chamberlain, Samuel S. 1851-1916..................DLB-25

Chamberland, Paul 1939- DLB-60

Chamberlin, William Henry 1897-1969 ....DLB-29

Chambers, Charles Haddon 1860-1921 ....DLB-10

Chandler, Harry 1864-1944.............................DLB-29

Chandler, Raymond 1888-1959 ....DS-6

Channing, Edward 1856-1931 ....DLB-17

Channing, Edward Tyrrell 1790-1856 ....DLB-1, 59

Channing, William Ellery 1780-1842 ....DLB-1, 59

Channing, William Ellery II 1817-1901..............DLB-1

Channing, William Henry 1810-1884 ....DLB-1, 59

Chaplin, Charlie 1889-1977 ....DLB-44

Chapman, George 1559 or 1560-1634 ....DLB-62

Chappell, Fred 1936- DLB-6

Charbonneau, Robert 1911-1967 ....DLB-68

Charles, Gerda 1914- DLB-14

Charles, William [publishing house]..................DLB-49

The Charles Wood Affair:
      A Playwright Revived Y-83

Charlotte Forten: Pages from her Diary............DLB-50

Charteris, Leslie 1907- DLB-77

Charyn, Jerome 1937- Y-83

Chase, Borden 1900-1971.................................DLB-26

Chase-Riboud, Barbara 1936- DLB-33

Chauncy, Charles 1705-1787 ....DLB-24

Chávez, Fray Angélico 1910- DLB-82

Chayefsky, Paddy 1923-1981...............DLB-7, 44; Y-81

Cheever, Ezekiel 1615-1708............................DLB-24

Cheever, George Barrell 1807-1890.................DLB-59

Cheever, John 1912-1982 ....DLB-2; Y-80, 82

Cheever, Susan 1943- Y-82

Chelsea House DLB-46

Cheney, Ednah Dow (Littlehale) 1824-1904 ....DLB-1

Cherry, Kelly 1940 ....Y-83

Cherryh, C. J. 1942- Y-80

Chesnutt, Charles Waddell 1858-1932...DLB-12, 50, 78

Chester, George Randolph 1869-1924 ....DLB-78

Chesterton, G. K. 1874-1936............DLB-10, 19, 34, 70

Cheyney, Edward P. 1861-1947........................DLB-47

Chicano History...DLB-82

Chicano Language..DLB-82

Child, Francis James 1825-1896 ....DLB-1, 64

Child, Lydia Maria 1802-1880......................DLB-1, 74

Child, Philip 1898-1978 ....DLB-68

Childers, Erskine 1870-1922............................DLB-70

Children's Book Awards and Prizes DLB-61

Childress, Alice 1920- DLB-7, 38

Childs, George W. 1829-1894...........................DLB-23

Chilton Book Company....................................DLB-46

Chittenden, Hiram Martin 1858-1917...............DLB-47

Chivers, Thomas Holley 1809-1858 ....DLB-3

Chopin, Kate 1850-1904 ....DLB-12, 78

Choquette, Adrienne 1915-1973.......................DLB-68

Choquette, Robert 1905- DLB-68

The Christian Publishing Company DLB-49

Christie, Agatha 1890-1976 ....DLB-13, 77

Church, Benjamin 1734-1778...........................DLB-31

Church, Francis Pharcellus 1839-1906................DLB-79

Church, William Conant 1836-1917..................DLB-79

Churchill, Caryl 1938- DLB-13

Ciardi, John 1916-1986.....................DLB-5; Y-86

Cibber, Colley 1671-1757..........................DLB-84

City Lights Books DLB-46

Cixous, Hélène 1937- DLB-83

Clapper, Raymond 1892-1944 ....DLB-29

Clare, John 1793-1864 ....DLB-55

Clark, Alfred Alexander Gordon (see Hare, Cyril)

Clark, Ann Nolan 1896- DLB-52

Clark, C. M., Publishing Company..................DLB-46

Clark, Catherine Anthony 1892-1977 ....DLB-68

Clark, Charles Heber 1841-1915 ....DLB-11

Clark, Davis Wasgatt 1812-1871 ....DLB-79

Clark, Eleanor 1913- DLB-6

Clark, Lewis Gaylord 1808-1873 ....DLB-3, 64, 73

Clark, Walter Van Tilburg 1909-1971...............DLB-9

Clarke, Austin 1896-1974 ....DLB-10, 20

Clarke, Austin C. 1934- DLB-53

Clarke, Gillian 1937- DLB-40

Clarke, James Freeman 1810-1888...............DLB-1, 59

Clarke, Rebecca Sophia 1833-1906..................DLB-42

Clarke, Robert, and Company DLB-49

Clausen, Andy 1943- DLB-16

Claxton, Remsen and Haffelfinger..................DLB-49

Clay, Cassius Marcellus 1810-1903 ....DLB-43

Cleary, Beverly 1916- DLB-52

Cleaver, Vera 1919-   and
    Cleaver, Bill 1920-1981.......................DLB-52

Cleland, John 1710-1789...........................DLB-39

Clemens, Samuel Langhorne
    1835-1910.....................DLB-11, 12, 23, 64, 74

Clement, Hal 1922-................................DLB-8

Clemo, Jack 1916- DLB-27

Clifton, Lucille 1936- DLB-5, 41

Clode, Edward J. [publishing house]...............DLB-46

Clough, Arthur Hugh 1819-1861.....................DLB-32

Cloutier, Cécile 1930-............................DLB-60

Coates, Robert M. 1897-1973 ....DLB-4, 9

Coatsworth, Elizabeth 1893- DLB-22

Cobb, Jr., Charles E. 1943- DLB-41

Cobb, Frank I. 1869-1923..........................DLB-25

Cobb, Irvin S. 1876-1944......................DLB-11, 25

Cobbett, William 1762-1835 ....DLB-43

Cochran, Thomas C. 1902- DLB-17

Cochrane, Elizabeth 1867-1922 ....DLB-25

Cockerill, John A. 1845-1896......................DLB-23

Cocteau, Jean 1889-1963...........................DLB-65

Coffee, Lenore J. 1900?-1984......................DLB-44

Coffin, Robert P. Tristram 1892-1955 ....DLB-45

Cogswell, Fred 1917- DLB-60

Cogswell, Mason Fitch 1761-1830 ....DLB-37

Cohen, Arthur A. 1928-1986........................DLB-28

Cohen, Leonard 1934- DLB-53

Cohen, Matt 1942- DLB-53

Colden, Cadwallader 1688-1776.................DLB-24, 30

Cole, Barry 1936- DLB-14

Colegate, Isabel 1931- DLB-14

Coleman, Emily Holmes 1899-1974 ....DLB-4

Coleridge, Mary 1861-1907.........................DLB-19

Colette 1873-1954.................................DLB-65

Colette, Sidonie Gabrielle (see Colette)

Collier, John 1901-1980 ....DLB-77

Collier, P. F. [publishing house] DLB-49

Collin and Small DLB-49

Collins, Isaac [publishing house] DLB-49

Collins, Mortimer 1827-1876...................DLB-21, 35

Collins, Wilkie 1824-1889.....................DLB-18, 70

Collyer, Mary 1716?-1763? DLB-39

Colman, Benjamin 1673-1747........................DLB-24

Colman, S. [publishing house] DLB-49

Colombo, John Robert 1936- DLB-53

Colter, Cyrus 1910- DLB-33

Colum, Padraic 1881-1972..........................DLB-19

Colwin, Laurie 1944- Y-80

Comden, Betty 1919-   and Green,
    Adolph 1918- DLB-44

The Comic Tradition Continued
    [in the British Novel]........................DLB-15

Commager, Henry Steele 1902- DLB-17

The Commercialization of the Image of

Revolt, by Kenneth Rexroth DLB-16

Community and Commentators: Black
    Theatre and Its Critics DLB-38

Compton-Burnett, Ivy 1884?-1969 ....DLB-36

Conference on Modern Biography.........................Y-85

Congreve, William 1670-1729 ....DLB-39, 84

Conkey, W. B., Company....................................DLB-49

Connell, Evan S., Jr. 1924- DLB-2; Y-81

Connelly, Marc 1890-1980.......................DLB-7; Y-80

Connolly, James B. 1868-1957...........................DLB-78

Connor, Tony 1930- DLB-40

Conquest, Robert 1917- DLB-27

Conrad, John, and Company................................DLB-49

Conrad, Joseph 1857-1924 ....DLB-10, 34

Conroy, Jack 1899- Y-81

Conroy, Pat 1945- DLB-6

The Consolidation of Opinion: Critical
    Responses to the Modernists DLB-36

Constantine, David 1944- DLB-40

Contempo Caravan: Kites in a Windstorm Y-85

A Contemporary Flourescence of Chicano
    Literature Y-84

The Continental Publishing Company DLB-49

A Conversation with Chaim Potok........................Y-84

Conversations with Publishers I: An Interview
    with Patrick O'Connor...............................Y-84

The Conversion of an Unpolitical Man,
    by W. H. Bruford DLB-66

Conway, Moncure Daniel 1832-1907....................DLB-1

Cook, David C., Publishing Company DLB-49

Cook, Ebenezer circa 1667-circa 1732................DLB-24

Cook, Michael 1933- DLB-53

Cooke, George Willis 1848-1923 ....DLB-71

Cooke, Increase, and Company..........................DLB-49

Cooke, John Esten 1830-1886............................DLB-3

Cooke, Philip Pendleton 1816-1850 ....DLB-3, 59

Cooke, Rose Terry 1827-1892 ....DLB-12, 74

Coolbrith, Ina 1841-1928..................................DLB-54

Coolidge, George [publishing house] DLB-49

Coolidge, Susan (see Woolsey, Sarah Chauncy)

Cooper, Giles 1918-1966...................................DLB-13

Cooper, James Fenimore 1789-1851....................DLB-3

Cooper, Kent 1880-1965....................................DLB-29

Coover, Robert 1932- DLB-2; Y-81

Copeland and Day..DLB-49

Coppel, Alfred 1921- Y-83

Coppola, Francis Ford 1939- DLB-44

Corcoran, Barbara 1911- DLB-52

Corelli, Marie 1855-1924 ....DLB-34

Corle, Edwin 1906-1956.......................................Y-85

Corman, Cid 1924- DLB-5

Cormier, Robert 1925- DLB-52

Corn, Alfred 1943- Y-80

Cornish, Sam 1935- DLB-41

Corpi, Lucha 1945- DLB-82

Corrington, John William 1932- DLB-6

Corrothers, James D. 1869-1917 ....DLB-50

Corso, Gregory 1930- DLB-5, 16

Cortez, Jayne 1936- DLB-41

Corvo, Baron (see Rolfe, Frederick William)

Cory, William Johnson 1823-1892......................DLB-35

Cosmopolitan Book Corporation.......................DLB-46

Costain, Thomas B. 1885-1965............................DLB-9

Cotter, Joseph Seamon, Sr.
    1861-1949 ....DLB-50

Cotter, Joseph Seamon, Jr.
    1895-1919 ....DLB-50

Cotton, John 1584-1652 ....DLB-24

Coulter, John 1888-1980....................................DLB-68

Cournos, John 1881-1966 ....DLB-54

Coventry, Francis 1725-1754 ....DLB-39

Coverly, N. [publishing house] DLB-49

Covici-Friede..DLB-46

Coward, Noel 1899-1973 ....DLB-10

Coward, McCann and Geoghegan.....................DLB-46

Cowles, Gardner 1861-1946...............................DLB-29

Cowley, Malcolm 1898-1989.................DLB-4, 48; Y-81

Cox, A. B. (see Berkeley, Anthony)

Cox, Palmer 1840-1924 ....DLB-42

Coxe, Louis 1918- DLB-5

Coxe, Tench 1755-1824......................................DLB-37

Cozzens, James Gould 1903-1978 ....DLB-9; Y-84; DS-2

Craddock, Charles Egbert (see Murfree, Mary N.)

Cradock, Thomas 1718-1770 ....DLB-31

Craig, Daniel H. 1811-1895 ....DLB-43

Craik, Dinah Maria 1826-1887 ....DLB-35

Cranch, Christopher Pearse 1813-1892..........DLB-1, 42

Crane, Hart 1899-1932 ....DLB-4, 48

Crane, R. S. 1886-1967 ....DLB-63

Crane, Stephen 1871-1900 ....DLB-12, 54, 78

Crapsey, Adelaide 1878-1914 ....DLB-54

Craven, Avery 1885-1980...................................DLB-17

Crawford, Charles 1752-circa 1815 ....DLB-31

Crawford, F. Marion 1854-1909.........................DLB-71

Crawley, Alan 1887-1975 ....DLB-68

Crayon, Geoffrey (see Irving, Washington)

Creasey, John 1908-1973 ....DLB-77

Creative Age Press..DLB-46

Creel, George 1876-1953 ....DLB-25

Creeley, Robert 1926- DLB-5, 16

Creelman, James 1859-1915 ....DLB-23

Cregan, David 1931- DLB-13

Crèvecoeur, Michel Guillaume Jean de
    1735-1813 ....DLB-37

Crews, Harry 1935- DLB-6

Crichton, Michael 1942- Y-81

A Crisis of Culture: The Changing Role
    of Religion in the New Republic DLB-37

Cristofer, Michael 1946- DLB-7

"The Critic as Artist" (1891), by Oscar Wilde....DLB-57

Criticism In Relation To Novels (1863),
    by G. H. Lewes DLB-21

Crockett, David (Davy) 1786-1836.................DLB-3, 11

Croft-Cooke, Rupert (see Bruce, Leo)

Crofts, Freeman Wills 1879-1957 ....DLB-77

Croly, Jane Cunningham 1829-1901 ....DLB-23

Crosby, Caresse 1892-1970 ....DLB-48

Crosby, Caresse 1892-1970 and Crosby,
    Harry 1898-1929 ....DLB-4

Crosby, Harry 1898-1929 ....DLB-48

Crossley-Holland, Kevin 1941- DLB-40

Crothers, Rachel 1878-1958..............................DLB-7

Crowell, Thomas Y., Company..........................DLB-49

Crowley, John 1942- Y-82

Crowley, Mart 1935- DLB-7

Crown Publishers...DLB-46

Crowne, John 1641-1712 ....DLB-80

Croy, Homer 1883-1965 ....DLB-4

Crumley, James 1939- Y-84

Cruz, Victor Hernández 1949- DLB-41

Csokor, Franz Theodor 1885-1969 ....DLB-81

Cullen, Countee 1903-1946.....................DLB-4, 48, 51

Culler, Jonathan D. 1944- DLB-67

The Cult of Biography
    Excerpts from the Second Folio Debate:
      "Biographies are generally a disease of
      English Literature"–Germaine Greer,
      Victoria Glendinning, Auberon Waugh,
      and Richard Holmes..........................Y-86

Cummings, E. E. 1894-1962 ....DLB-4, 48

Cummings, Ray 1887-1957 ....DLB-8

Cummings and Hilliard DLB-49

Cummins, Maria Susanna 1827-1866.................DLB-42

Cuney, Waring 1906-1976...................................DLB-51

Cuney-Hare, Maude 1874-1936.........................DLB-52

Cunningham, J. V. 1911- DLB-5

Cunningham, Peter F. [publishing house]..........DLB-49

Cuomo, George 1929- Y-80

Cupples and Leon DLB-46

Cupples, Upham and Company.........................DLB-49

Cuppy, Will 1884-1949 ....DLB-11

Currie, Mary Montgomerie Lamb Singleton,
    Lady Currie (see Fane, Violet)

Curti, Merle E. 1897- DLB-17

Curtis, George William 1824-1892.................DLB-1, 43

D

D. M. Thomas: The Plagiarism Controversy Y-82

Dabit, Eugène 1898-1936 ....DLB-65

Daborne, Robert circa 1580-1628......................DLB-58

Daggett, Rollin M. 1831-1901 ....DLB-79

Dahlberg, Edward 1900-1977 ....DLB-48

Dale, Peter 1938- DLB-40

Dall, Caroline Wells (Healey) 1822-1912..............DLB-1

Dallas, E. S. 1828-1879......................................DLB-55

The Dallas Theater Center DLB-7

D'Alton, Louis 1900-1951 ....DLB-10

Daly, T. A. 1871-1948........................DLB-11

Damon, S. Foster 1893-1971 ....DLB-45

Damrell, William S. [publishing house]............DLB-49

Dana, Charles A. 1819-1897..........DLB-3, 23

Dana, Richard Henry, Jr. 1815-1882 ....DLB-1

Dandridge, Ray Garfield DLB-51

Dane, Clemence 1887-1965...............DLB-10

Danforth, John 1660-1730 ....DLB-24

Danforth, Samuel I 1626-1674 ....DLB-24

Danforth, Samuel II 1666-1727.........DLB-24

Dangerous Years: London Theater, 1939-1945 ....DLB-10

Daniel, John M. 1825-1865 ....DLB-43

Daniel, Samuel 1562 or 1563-1619................DLB-62

Daniells, Roy 1902-1979.....................DLB-68

Daniels, Josephus 1862-1948 ....DLB-29

Danner, Margaret Esse 1915- DLB-41

Darwin, Charles 1809-1882.................DLB-57

Daryush, Elizabeth 1887-1977 ....DLB-20

Dashwood, Edmée Elizabeth Monica de la Pasture (see Delafield, E. M.)

d'Aulaire, Edgar Parin 1898- and d'Aulaire, Ingri 1904- DLB-22

Davenant, Sir William 1606-1668.....DLB-58

Davenport, Robert ?-? DLB-58

Daves, Delmer 1904-1977 ....DLB-26

Davey, Frank 1940- DLB-53

Davidson, Avram 1923- DLB-8

Davidson, Donald 1893-1968.............DLB-45

Davidson, John 1857-1909 ....DLB-19

Davidson, Lionel 1922- DLB-14

Davie, Donald 1922- DLB-27

Davies, Robertson 1913- DLB-68

Davies, Samuel 1723-1761..................DLB-31

Davies, W. H. 1871-1940....................DLB-19

Daviot, Gordon 1896?-1952 ....DLB-10
(see also Tey, Josephine)

Davis, Charles A. 1795-1867...............DLB-11

Davis, Clyde Brion 1894-1962.............DLB-9

Davis, Dick 1945- DLB-40

Davis, Frank Marshall 1905-? DLB-51

Davis, H. L. 1894-1960.......................DLB-9

Davis, John 1774-1854 ....DLB-37

Davis, Margaret Thomson 1926- DLB-14

Davis, Ossie 1917- DLB-7, 38

Davis, Rebecca Harding 1831-1910 ....DLB-74

Davis, Richard Harding 1864-1916 ....DLB-12, 23, 78, 79

Davis, Samuel Cole 1764-1809............DLB-37

Davison, Peter 1928- DLB-5

Davys, Mary 1674-1732......................DLB-39

DAW Books DLB-46

Dawson, William 1704-1752................DLB-31

Day, Benjamin Henry 1810-1889 ....DLB-43

Day, Clarence 1874-1935 ....DLB-11

Day, Dorothy 1897-1980 ....DLB-29

Day, John circa 1574-circa 1640 ....DLB-62

Day, The John, Company DLB-46

Day Lewis, C. 1904-1972.............DLB-15, 20
(see also Blake, Nicholas)

Day, Mahlon [publishing house] DLB-49

Day, Thomas 1748-1789 ....DLB-39

Deacon, William Arthur 1890-1977 ....DLB-68

Deal, Borden 1922-1985 ....DLB-6

de Angeli, Marguerite 1889-1987.....................DLB-22

De Bow, James Dunwoody Brownson 1820-1867 ....DLB-3, 79

de Bruyn, Günter 1926- DLB-75

de Camp, L. Sprague 1907- DLB-8

The Decay of Lying (1889), by Oscar Wilde [excerpt]............DLB-18

Dedication, *Ferdinand Count Fathom* (1753), by Tobias Smollett DLB-39

Dedication, *Lasselia* (1723), by Eliza Haywood [excerpt] DLB-39

Dedication, *The History of Pompey the Little* (1751), by Francis Coventry DLB-39

Dedication, *The Wanderer* (1814), by Fanny Burney DLB-39

Defense of *Amelia* (1752), by Henry Fielding.....DLB-39

Defoe, Daniel 1660-1731....................DLB-39

de Fontaińe, Felix Gregory 1834-1896 ....DLB-43

De Forest, John William 1826-1906....................DLB-12

de Graff, Robert 1895-1981 ....Y-81

DeJong, Meindert 1906- DLB-52

Dekker, Thomas circa 1572-1632 ....DLB-62

Delafield, E. M. 1890-1943 ....DLB-34

de la Mare, Walter 1873-1956...........................DLB-19

Deland, Margaret 1857-1945 ....DLB-78

Delaney, Shelagh 1939- DLB-13

Delany, Martin Robinson 1812-1885 ....DLB-50

Delany, Samuel R. 1942- DLB-8, 33

de la Roche, Mazo 1879-1961 ....DLB-68

Delbanco, Nicholas 1942- DLB-6

De León, Nephtalí 1945- DLB-82

Delgado, Abelardo Barrientos 1931- DLB-82

DeLillo, Don 1936- DLB-6

Dell, Floyd 1887-1969 ....DLB-9

Dell Publishing Company..................................DLB-46

delle Grazie, Marie Eugene 1864-1931 ....DLB-81

del Rey, Lester 1915- DLB-8

de Man, Paul 1919-1983 ....DLB-67

Demby, William 1922- DLB-33

Deming, Philander 1829-1915 ....DLB-74

Demorest, William Jennings 1822-1895 ....DLB-79

Denham, Sir John 1615-1669 ....DLB-58

Denison, T. S., and Company............................DLB-49

Dennie, Joseph 1768-1812...............DLB-37, 43, 59, 73

Dennis, Nigel 1912- DLB-13, 15

Dent, Tom 1932- DLB-38

Denton, Daniel circa 1626-1703........................DLB-24

DePaola, Tomie 1934- DLB-61

Derby, George Horatio 1823-1861 ....DLB-11

Derby, J. C., and Company................................DLB-49

Derby and Miller DLB-49

Derleth, August 1909-1971 ....DLB-9

The Derrydale Press..DLB-46

Desbiens, Jean-Paul 1927- DLB-53

des Forêts, Louis-René 1918- DLB-83

DesRochers, Alfred 1901-1978 ....DLB-68

Desrosiers, Léo-Paul 1896-1967 ....DLB-68

Destouches, Louis-Ferdinand (see Céline,
    Louis-Ferdinand)

De Tabley, Lord 1835-1895 ....DLB-35

Deutsch, Babette 1895-1982 ....DLB-45

Deveaux, Alexis 1948- DLB-38

The Development of Lighting in the Staging
    of Drama, 1900-1945 [in Great Britain]......DLB-10

de Vere, Aubrey 1814-1902 ....DLB-35

The Devin-Adair Company................................DLB-46

De Voto, Bernard 1897-1955 ....DLB-9

De Vries, Peter 1910- DLB-6; Y-82

Dewdney, Christopher 1951- DLB-60

Dewdney, Selwyn 1909-1979 ....DLB-68

DeWitt, Robert M., Publisher DLB-49

DeWolfe, Fiske and Company............................DLB-49

de Young, M. H. 1849-1925 ....DLB-25

The Dial Press...DLB-46

Diamond, I. A. L. 1920-1988 ....DLB-26

Di Cicco, Pier Giorgio 1949- DLB-60

Dick, Philip K. 1928- DLB-8

Dick and Fitzgerald DLB-49

Dickens, Charles 1812-1870...................DLB-21, 55, 70

Dickey, James 1923- DLB-5; Y-82

Dickey, William 1928- DLB-5

Dickinson, Emily 1830-1886 ....DLB-1

Dickinson, John 1732-1808 ....DLB-31

Dickinson, Jonathan 1688-1747 ....DLB-24

Dickinson, Patric 1914- DLB-27

Dickson, Gordon R. 1923- DLB-8

Didion, Joan 1934- DLB-2; Y-81, 86

Di Donato, Pietro 1911- DLB-9

Dillard, Annie 1945- Y-80

Dillard, R. H. W. 1937- DLB-5

Dillingham, Charles T., Company......................DLB-49

The G. W. Dillingham Company........................DLB-49

Dintenfass, Mark 1941- Y-84

Diogenes, Jr. (see Brougham, John)

DiPrima, Diane 1934- DLB-5, 16

Disch, Thomas M. 1940- DLB-8

Disney, Walt 1901-1966....................................DLB-22

Disraeli, Benjamin 1804-1881................DLB-21, 55

Ditzen, Rudolf (see Fallada, Hans)

Dix, Dorothea Lynde 1802-1887 ....DLB-1

Dix, Dorothy (see Gilmer, Elizabeth Meriwether)

Dix, Edwards and Company DLB-49

Dixon, Paige (see Corcoran, Barbara)

Dixon, Richard Watson 1833-1900 ....DLB-19

Dobell, Sydney 1824-1874...............................DLB-32

Döblin, Alfred 1878-1957 ....DLB-66

Dobson, Austin 1840-1921 ....DLB-35

Doctorow, E. L. 1931- DLB-2, 28; Y-80

Dodd, William E. 1869-1940 ....DLB-17

Dodd, Mead and Company................................DLB-49

Doderer, Heimito von 1896-1968....................DLB-85

Dodge, B. W., and Company.............................DLB-46

Dodge, Mary Mapes 1831?-1905 ....DLB-42, 79

Dodge Publishing Company DLB-49

Dodgson, Charles Lutwidge (see Carroll, Lewis)

Dodson, Owen 1914-1983 ....DLB-76

Doesticks, Q. K. Philander, P. B. (see Thomson,
    Mortimer)

Donahoe, Patrick [publishing house]..................DLB-49

Donald, David H. 1920- DLB-17

Donleavy, J. P. 1926- DLB-6

Donnadieu, Marguerite (see Duras, Marguerite)

Donnelley, R. R., and Sons Company DLB-49

Donnelly, Ignatius 1831-1901..........................DLB-12

Donohue and Henneberry DLB-49

Doolady, M. [publishing house]..........................DLB-49

Dooley, Ebon (see Ebon)

Doolittle, Hilda 1886-1961............................DLB-4, 45

Dor, Milo 1923- DLB-85

Doran, George H., Company............................DLB-46

Dorgelès, Roland 1886-1973 ....DLB-65

Dorn, Edward 1929- DLB-5

Dorr, Rheta Childe 1866-1948 ....DLB-25

Dorst, Tankred 1925- DLB-75

Dos Passos, John 1896-1970 ....DLB-4, 9; DS-1

Doubleday and Company................................DLB-49

Doughty, Charles M. 1843-1926..................DLB-19, 57

Douglas, Keith 1920-1944...............................DLB-27

Douglas, Norman 1868-1952 ....DLB-34

Douglass, Frederick 1817?-1895.........DLB-1, 43, 50, 79

Douglass, William circa 1691-1752....................DLB-24

Dover Publications......................................DLB-46

Dowden, Edward 1843-1913...............................DLB-35

Downing, J., Major (see Davis, Charles A.)

Downing, Major Jack (see Smith, Seba)

Dowson, Ernest 1867-1900.................................DLB-19

Doxey, William [publishing house].....................DLB-49

Doyle, Sir Arthur Conan 1859-1930 ....DLB-18, 70

Doyle, Kirby 1932- DLB-16

Drabble, Margaret 1939- DLB-14

Drach, Albert 1902- DLB-85

The Dramatic Publishing Company DLB-49

Dramatists Play Service.................................DLB-46

Draper, John W. 1811-1882..............................DLB-30

Draper, Lyman C. 1815-1891 ....DLB-30

Dreiser, Theodore 1871-1945 ....DLB-9, 12; DS-1

Drewitz, Ingeborg 1923-1986 ....DLB-75

Drieu La Rochelle, Pierre 1893-1945.................DLB-72

Drinkwater, John 1882-1937 ....DLB-10, 19

The Drue Heinz Literature Prize
    Excerpt from "Excerpts from a Report
        of the Commission," in David
        Bosworth's *The Death of Descartes*
    An Interview with David Bosworth.................Y-82

Dryden, John 1631-1700....................................DLB-80

Duane, William 1760-1835................................DLB-43

Dubé, Marcel 1930- DLB-53

Dubé, Rodolphe (see Hertel, François)

Du Bois, W. E. B. 1868-1963.......................DLB-47, 50

Du Bois, William Pène 1916- DLB-61

Ducharme, Réjean 1941- DLB-60

Duell, Sloan and Pearce DLB-46

Duffield and Green DLB-46

Duffy, Maureen 1933- DLB-14

Dugan, Alan 1923- DLB-5

Duhamel, Georges 1884-1966...........................DLB-65

Dukes, Ashley 1885-1959 ....DLB-10

Dumas, Henry 1934-1968 ....DLB-41

Dunbar, Paul Laurence 1872-1906 ....DLB-50, 54, 78

Duncan, Robert 1919-1988 ....DLB-5, 16

Duncan, Ronald 1914-1982...............................DLB-13

Dunigan, Edward, and Brother DLB-49

Dunlap, John 1747-1812 ....DLB-43

Dunlap, William 1766-1839...................DLB-30, 37, 59

Dunn, Douglas 1942- DLB-40

Dunne, Finley Peter 1867-1936 ....DLB-11, 23

Dunne, John Gregory 1932- Y-80

Dunne, Philip 1908- DLB-26

Dunning, Ralph Cheever 1878-1930 ....DLB-4

Dunning, William A. 1857-1922 ....DLB-17

Plunkett, Edward John Moreton Drax,
    Lord Dunsany 1878-1957 ....DLB-10, 77

Durand, Lucile (see Bersianik, Louky)

Duranty, Walter 1884-1957..............................DLB-29

Duras, Marguerite 1914- DLB-83

Durfey, Thomas 1653-1723 ....DLB-80

Durrell, Lawrence 1912- DLB-15, 27

Durrell, William [publishing house].................DLB-49

Dürrenmatt, Friedrich 1921- DLB-69

Dutton, E. P., and Company.............................DLB-49

Duvoisin, Roger 1904-1980..............................DLB-61

Duyckinck, Evert Augustus 1816-1878 ....DLB-3, 64

Duyckinck, George L. 1823-1863 ....DLB-3

Duyckinck and Company DLB-49

Dwight, John Sullivan 1813-1893 ....DLB-1

Dwight, Timothy 1752-1817 ....DLB-37

Dyer, Charles 1928- DLB-13

Dylan, Bob 1941- DLB-16

E

Eager, Edward 1911-1964.................................DLB-22

Earle, James H., and Company DLB-49

Early American Book Illustration,
    by Sinclair Hamilton DLB-49

Eastlake, William 1917- DLB-6

Eastman, Carol ?- DLB-44

Eberhart, Richard 1904- DLB-48

Ebner, Jeannie 1918- DLB-85

Ebner-Eschenbach, Marie von
    1830-1916 ....DLB-81

Ebon 1942- DLB-41

Ecco Press...DLB-46

Edes, Benjamin 1732-1803................................DLB-43

Edgar, David 1948- DLB-13

The Editor Publishing Company.......................DLB-49

Edmonds, Randolph 1900- DLB-51

Edmonds, Walter D. 1903- DLB-9

Edschmid, Kasimir 1890-1966 ....DLB-56

Edwards, Jonathan 1703-1758 ....DLB-24

Edwards, Jonathan, Jr. 1745-1801.....................DLB-37

Edwards, Junius 1929- DLB-33

Edwards, Richard 1524-1566 ....DLB-62

Effinger, George Alec 1947- DLB-8

Eggleston, Edward 1837-1902 ....DLB-12

Ehrenstein, Albert 1886-1950...........................DLB-81

Eich, Günter 1907-1972 ....DLB-69

1873 Publishers' Catalogues..............................DLB-49

Eighteenth-Century Aesthetic Theories............DLB-31

Eighteenth-Century Philosophical
    Background DLB-31

Eigner, Larry 1927- DLB-5

Eisenreich, Herbert 1925-1986.........................DLB-85

Eisner, Kurt 1867-1919.....................................DLB-66

Eklund, Gordon 1945- Y-83

Elder, Lonne III 1931- DLB-7, 38, 44

Elder, Paul, and Company.................................DLB-49

Elements of Rhetoric (1828; revised, 1846),
    by Richard Whately [excerpt] DLB-57

Eliot, George 1819-1880 ....DLB-21, 35, 55

Eliot, John 1604-1690.......................................DLB-24

Eliot, T. S. 1888-1965 ....DLB-7, 10, 45, 63

Elizondo, Sergio 1930- DLB-82

Elkin, Stanley 1930- DLB-2, 28; Y-80

Elles, Dora Amy (see Wentworth, Patricia)

Ellet, Elizabeth F. 1818?-1877...........................DLB-30

Elliott, George 1923- DLB-68

Elliott, Janice 1931- DLB-14

Elliott, William 1788-1863 ....DLB-3

Elliott, Thomes and Talbot DLB-49

Ellis, Edward S. 1840-1916 ....DLB-42

The George H. Ellis Company DLB-49

Ellison, Harlan 1934- DLB-8

Ellison, Ralph 1914- DLB-2, 76

Ellmann, Richard 1918-1987 ....Y-87

The Elmer Holmes Bobst Awards
    in Arts and Letters Y-87

Emanuel, James Andrew 1921- DLB-41

Emerson, Ralph Waldo 1803-1882...........DLB-1, 59, 73

Emerson, William 1769-1811..............................DLB-37

Empson, William 1906-1984.............................DLB-20

The End of English Stage Censorship,
　　1945-1968 ....DLB-13

Ende, Michael 1929- DLB-75

Engel, Marian 1933-1985 ....DLB-53

Engle, Paul 1908- DLB-48

English Composition and Rhetoric (1866),
　　by Alexander Bain [excerpt].......................DLB-57

The English Renaissance of Art (1908),
　　by Oscar Wilde DLB-35

Enright, D. J. 1920- DLB-27

Enright, Elizabeth 1909-1968 ....DLB-22

L'Envoi (1882), by Oscar Wilde DLB-35

Epps, Bernard 1936- DLB-53

Epstein, Julius 1909-　and
　　Epstein, Philip 1909-1952 ....DLB-26

Equiano, Olaudah circa 1745-1797 ....DLB-37, 50

Ernst, Paul 1866-1933 ....DLB-66

Erskine, John 1879-1951....................................DLB-9

Ervine, St. John Greer 1883-1971 ....DLB-10

Eshleman, Clayton 1935- DLB-5

Ess Ess Publishing Company............................DLB-49

Essay on Chatterton (1842),
　　by Robert Browning DLB-32

Estes, Eleanor 1906-1988 ....DLB-22

Estes and Lauriat..DLB-49

Etherege, George 1636-circa 1692.....................DLB-80

Ets, Marie Hall 1893- DLB-22

Eudora Welty: Eye of the Storyteller......................Y-87

Eugene O'Neill Memorial Theater Center...........DLB-7

Eugene O'Neill's Letters: A Review........................Y-88

Evans, Donald 1884-1921.................................DLB-54

Evans, George Henry 1805-1856.......................DLB-43

Evans, M., and Company DLB-46

Evans, Mari 1923- DLB-41

Evans, Mary Ann (see Eliot, George)

Evans, Nathaniel 1742-1767.............................DLB-31

Evans, Sebastian 1830-1909 ....DLB-35

Everett, Alexander Hill 1790-1847....................DLB-59

Everett, Edward 1794-1865 ....DLB-1, 59

Everson, William 1912- DLB-5, 16

Every Man His Own Poet; or, The
　　Inspired Singer's Recipe Book (1877),
　　by W. H. Mallock DLB-35

Ewart, Gavin 1916- DLB-40

Ewing, Juliana Horatia 1841-1885....................DLB-21

Exley, Frederick 1929- Y-81

Experiment in the Novel (1929),
　　by John D. Beresford DLB-36

F

"F. Scott Fitzgerald: St. Paul's Native Son
　　and Distinguished American Writer":
　　University of Minnesota Conference,
　　29-31 October 1982...Y-82

Faber, Frederick William 1814-1863 ....DLB-32

Fair, Ronald L. 1932- DLB-33

Fairfax, Beatrice (see Manning, Marie)

Fairlie, Gerard 1899-1983 ....DLB-77

Fallada, Hans 1893-1947 ....DLB-56

Fancher, Betsy 1928- Y-83

Fane, Violet 1843-1905....................................DLB-35

Fantasy Press Publishers DLB-46

Fante, John 1909-1983..Y-83

Farber, Norma 1909-1984................................DLB-61

Farigoule, Louis (see Romains, Jules)

Farley, Walter 1920- DLB-22

Farmer, Philip José 1918- DLB-8

Farquhar, George circa 1677-1707 ....DLB-84

Farquharson, Martha (see Finley, Martha)

Farrar and Rinehart...DLB-46

Farrar, Straus and Giroux.................................DLB-46

Farrell, James T. 1904-1979 ....DLB-4, 9; DS-2

Farrell, J. G. 1935-1979....................................DLB-14

Fast, Howard 1914- DLB-9

Faulkner, William 1897-1962
　　.................................DLB-9, 11, 44; DS-2; Y-86

Fauset, Jessie Redmon 1882-1961 ....DLB-51

Faust, Irvin 1924- DLB-2, 28; Y-80

Fawcett Books DLB-46

Fearing, Kenneth 1902-1961 ....DLB-9

Federal Writers' Project.....................................DLB-46

Federman, Raymond 1928- Y-80

Feiffer, Jules 1929- DLB-7, 44

Feinberg, Charles E. 1899-1988...........................Y-88

Feinstein, Elaine 1930- DLB-14, 40

Fell, Frederick, Publishers.................................DLB-46

Fels, Ludwig 1946- DLB-75

Felton, Cornelius Conway 1807-1862 ....DLB-1

Fennario, David 1947- DLB-60

Fenno, John 1751-1798..................................DLB-43

Fenno, R. F., and Company.............................DLB-49

Fenton, James 1949- DLB-40

Ferber, Edna 1885-1968 ....DLB-9, 28

Ferdinand, Vallery III (see Salaam, Kalamu ya)

Ferguson, Sir Samuel 1810-1886 ....DLB-32

Ferguson, William Scott 1875-1954 ....DLB-47

Ferlinghetti, Lawrence 1919- DLB-5, 16

Fern, Fanny (see Parton, Sara
    Payson Willis)

Ferret, E., and Company...................................DLB-49

Ferrini, Vincent 1913- DLB-48

Ferron, Jacques 1921-1985.................................DLB-60

Ferron, Madeleine 1922- DLB-53

Fetridge and Company.....................................DLB-49

Feuchtwanger, Lion 1884-1958 ....DLB-66

Ficke, Arthur Davison 1883-1945...................DLB-54

Fiction Best-Sellers, 1910-1945............................DLB-9

Fiction into Film, 1928-1975: A List of Movies
    Based on the Works of Authors in
    British Novelists, 1930-1959...........................DLB-15

Fiedler, Leslie A. 1917- DLB-28, 67

Field, Eugene 1850-1895 ....DLB-23, 42

Field, Nathan 1587-1619 or 1620 ....DLB-58

Field, Rachel 1894-1942 ....DLB-9, 22

A Field Guide to Recent Schools of
    American Poetry.......................................Y-86

Fielding, Henry 1707-1754.................DLB-39, 84

Fielding, Sarah 1710-1768 ....DLB-39

Fields, James Thomas 1817-1881 ....DLB-1

Fields, Julia 1938-.........................DLB-41

Fields, W. C. 1880-1946....................................DLB-44

Fields, Osgood and Company............................DLB-49

Fifty Penguin Years...Y-85

Figes, Eva 1932- DLB-14

Filson, John circa 1753-1788..............................DLB-37

Findley, Timothy 1930- DLB-53

Finlay, Ian Hamilton 1925- DLB-40

Finley, Martha 1828-1909 ....DLB-42

Finney, Jack 1911- DLB-8

Finney, Walter Braden (see Finney, Jack)

Firbank, Ronald 1886-1926...............................DLB-36

Firmin, Giles 1615-1697 ....DLB-24

First Strauss "Livings" Awarded to Cynthia
    Ozick and Raymond Carver
    An Interview with Cynthia Ozick
    An Interview with Raymond Carver Y-83

Fish, Stanley 1938- DLB-67

Fisher, Clay (see Allen, Henry W.)

Fisher, Dorothy Canfield 1879-1958 ....DLB-9

Fisher, Leonard Everett 1924- DLB-61

Fisher, Roy 1930- DLB-40

Fisher, Rudolph 1897-1934...............................DLB-51

Fisher, Sydney George 1856-1927 ....DLB-47

Fisher, Vardis 1895-1968 ....DLB-9

Fiske, John 1608-1677 ....DLB-24

Fiske, John 1842-1901 ....DLB-47, 64

Fitch, Thomas circa 1700-1774...........................DLB-31

Fitch, William Clyde 1865-1909.........................DLB-7

FitzGerald, Edward 1809-1883 ....DLB-32

Fitzgerald, F. Scott 1896-1940......DLB-4, 9; Y-81; DS-1

Fitzgerald, Penelope 1916- DLB-14

Fitzgerald, Robert 1910-1985.............................Y-80

Fitzgerald, Thomas 1819-1891 ....DLB-23

Fitzgerald, Zelda Sayre 1900-1948.....................Y-84

Fitzhugh, Louise 1928-1974...............................DLB-52

Fitzhugh, William circa 1651-1701 ....DLB-24

Flanagan, Thomas 1923- Y-80

Flanner, Hildegarde 1899-1987.........................DLB-48

Flanner, Janet 1892-1978..................................DLB-4

Flavin, Martin 1883-1967.................................DLB-9

Flecker, James Elroy 1884-1915 ....DLB-10, 19

Fleeson, Doris 1901-1970..................................DLB-29

Fleidser, Marieluise 1901-1974............................DLB-56

The Fleshly School of Poetry and Other
  Phenomena of the Day (1872), by Robert
  Buchanan...DLB-35

The Fleshly School of Poetry: Mr. D. G.
  Rossetti (1871), by Thomas Maitland
  (Robert Buchanan)...DLB-35

Fletcher, J. S. 1863-1935.................................DLB-70

Fletcher, John (see Beaumont, Francis)

Fletcher, John Gould 1886-1950....................DLB-4, 45

Flieg, Helmut (see Heym, Stefan)

Flint, F. S. 1885-1960.....................................DLB-19

Flint, Timothy 1780-1840 ....DLB-73

Follen, Eliza Lee (Cabot) 1787-1860...............DLB-1

Follett, Ken 1949- Y-81

Follett Publishing Company............................DLB-46

Folsom, John West [publishing house]...............DLB-49

Foote, Horton 1916- DLB-26

Foote, Shelby 1916- DLB-2, 17

Forbes, Calvin 1945- DLB-41

Forbes, Ester 1891-1967..................................DLB-22

Forbes and Company DLB-49

Force, Peter 1790-1868....................................DLB-30

Forché, Carolyn 1950- DLB-5

Ford, Charles Henri 1913- DLB-4, 48

Ford, Corey 1902-1969 ....DLB-11

Ford, Ford Madox 1873-1939 ....DLB-34

Ford, J. B., and Company.................................DLB-49

Ford, Jesse Hill 1928- DLB-6

Ford, John 1586-?...DLB-58

Ford, Worthington C. 1858-1941.......................DLB-47

Fords, Howard, and Hulbert DLB-49

Foreman, Carl 1914-1984................................DLB-26

Forester, Frank (see Herbert, Henry William)

Fornés, María Irene 1930- DLB-7

Forrest, Leon 1937- DLB-33

Forster, E. M. 1879-1970.................................DLB-34

Forten, Charlotte L. 1837-1914 ....DLB-50

Fortune, T. Thomas 1856-1928.........................DLB-23

Fosdick, Charles Austin 1842-1915....................DLB-42

Foster, Genevieve 1893-1979 ....DLB-61

Foster, Hannah Webster 1758-1840....................DLB-37

Foster, John 1648-1681 ....DLB-24

Foster, Michael 1904-1956................................DLB-9

Four Essays on the Beat Generation,
  by John Clellon Holmes...............................DLB-16

Four Seas Company...DLB-46

Four Winds Press..DLB-46

Fournier, Henri Alban (see Alain-Fournier)

Fowler and Wells Company..............................DLB-49

Fowles, John 1926- DLB-14

Fox, John, Jr. 1862 or 1863-1919 ....DLB-9

Fox, Paula 1923- DLB-52

Fox, Richard K. [publishing house] DLB-49

Fox, Richard Kyle 1846-1922...........................DLB-79

Fox, William Price 1926- DLB-2; Y-81

Fraenkel, Michael 1896-1957 ....DLB-4

France, Richard 1938- DLB-7

Francis, C. S. [publishing house] DLB-49

Francis, Convers 1795-1863.............................DLB-1

Francke, Kuno 1855-1930.................................DLB-71

Frank, Leonhard 1882-1961 ....DLB-56

Frank, Melvin (see Panama, Norman)

Frank, Waldo 1889-1967................................DLB-9, 63

Franken, Rose 1895?-1988 ....Y-84

Franklin, Benjamin 1706-1790...............DLB-24, 43, 73

Franklin, James 1697-1735 ....DLB-43

Franklin Library DLB-46

Frantz, Ralph Jules 1902-1979..........................DLB-4

Fraser, G. S. 1915-1980....................................DLB-27

Frayn, Michael 1933- DLB-13, 14

Frederic, Harold 1856-1898 ....DLB-12, 23

Freeman, Douglas Southall 1886-1953...............DLB-17

Freeman, Legh Richmond 1842-1915.................DLB-23

Freeman, Mary E. Wilkins 1852-1930..........DLB-12, 78

Freeman, R. Austin 1862-1943 ....DLB-70

French, Alice 1850-1934 ....DLB-74

French, David 1939- DLB-53

French, James [publishing house].......................DLB-49

French, Samuel [publishing house] DLB-49

Freneau, Philip 1752-1832.........................DLB-37, 43

Fried, Erich 1921-1988.....................................DLB-85

Friedman, Bruce Jay 1930- DLB-2, 28

Friel, Brian 1929- DLB-13

Friend, Krebs 1895?-1967? DLB-4

Fries, Fritz Rudolf 1935- DLB-75

Fringe and Alternative Theater
    in Great Britain............................DLB-13

Frisch, Max 1911- DLB-69

Frischmuth, Barbara 1941- DLB-85

Fritz, Jean 1915- DLB-52

Frost, Robert 1874-1963 ....DLB-54

Frothingham, Octavius Brooks 1822-1895 ....DLB-1

Froude, James Anthony 1818-1894............DLB-18, 57

Fry, Christopher 1907- DLB-13

Frye, Northrop 1912- DLB-67, 68

Fuchs, Daniel 1909- DLB-9, 26, 28

The Fugitives and the Agrarians:
    The First Exhibition Y-85

Fuller, Charles H., Jr. 1939- DLB-38

Fuller, Henry Blake 1857-1929 ....DLB-12

Fuller, John 1937- DLB-40

Fuller, Roy 1912- DLB-15, 20

Fuller, Samuel 1912- DLB-26

Fuller, Sarah Margaret, Marchesa
    D'Ossoli 1810-1850 ....DLB-1, 59, 73

Fulton, Len 1934- Y-86

Fulton, Robin 1937- DLB-40

Furman, Laura 1945- Y-86

Furness, Horace Howard 1833-1912................DLB-64

Furness, William Henry 1802-1896................DLB-1

Furthman, Jules 1888-1966 ....DLB-26

The Future of the Novel (1899),
    by Henry James............................DLB-18

G

Gaddis, William 1922- DLB-2

Gág, Wanda 1893-1946..........................DLB-22

Gagnon, Madeleine 1938- DLB-60

Gaine, Hugh 1726-1807.........................DLB-43

Gaine, Hugh [publishing house]................DLB-49

Gaines, Ernest J. 1933- DLB-2, 33; Y-80

Gaiser, Gerd 1908-1976 ....DLB-69

Galaxy Science Fiction Novels.................DLB-46

Gale, Zona 1874-1938 ....DLB-9, 78

Gallagher, William Davis 1808-1894 ....DLB-73

Gallant, Mavis 1922- DLB-53

Gallico, Paul 1897-1976.......................DLB-9

Galsworthy, John 1867-1933 ....DLB-10, 34

Galvin, Brendan 1938- DLB-5

Gambit.......................................DLB-46

Gammer Gurton's Needle......................DLB-62

Gannett, Frank E. 1876-1957...................DLB-29

García, Lionel G. 1935- DLB-82

Gardam, Jane 1928- DLB-14

Garden, Alexander circa 1685-1756.............DLB-31

Gardner, John 1933-1982 ....DLB-2; Y-82

Garis, Howard R. 1873-1962 ....DLB-22

Garland, Hamlin 1860-1940 ....DLB-12, 71, 78

Garneau, Michel 1939- DLB-53

Garner, Hugh 1913-1979........................DLB-68

Garnett, David 1892-1981 ....DLB-34

Garraty, John A. 1920- DLB-17

Garrett, George 1929- DLB-2, 5; Y-83

Garrick, David 1717-1779......................DLB-84

Garrison, William Lloyd 1805-1879.............DLB-1, 43

Gary, Romain 1914-1980 ....DLB-83

Gascoyne, David 1916- DLB-20

Gaskell, Elizabeth Cleghorn 1810-1865.........DLB-21

Gass, William Howard 1924- DLB-2

Gates, Doris 1901- DLB-22

Gates, Henry Louis, Jr. 1950- DLB-67

Gates, Lewis E. 1860-1924 ....DLB-71

Gay, Ebenezer 1696-1787.......................DLB-24

Gay, John 1685-1732...........................DLB-84

The Gay Science (1866),
    by E. S. Dallas [excerpt]..................DLB-21

Gayarré, Charles E. A. 1805-1895 ....DLB-30

Gaylord, Charles [publishing house]...........DLB-49

Geddes, Gary 1940- DLB-60

Geddes, Virgil 1897- DLB-4

Geis, Bernard, Associates DLB-46

Geisel, Theodor Seuss 1904- DLB-61

Gelber, Jack 1932- DLB-7

Gellhorn, Martha 1908- Y-82

Gems, Pam 1925- DLB-13

A General Idea of the College of Mirania (1753),
    by William Smith [excerpts].........................DLB-31

Genet, Jean 1910-1986 ....Y-86, DLB-72

Genevoix, Maurice 1890-1980 ....DLB-65

Genovese, Eugene D. 1930- DLB-17

Gent, Peter 1942- Y-82

George, Henry 1839-1897.................................DLB-23

George, Jean Craighead 1919- DLB-52

Gerhardie, William 1895-1977...........................DLB-36

Germanophilism, by Hans Kohn DLB-66

Gernsback, Hugo 1884-1967...............................DLB-8

Gerould, Katharine Fullerton 1879-1944..........DLB-78

Gerrish, Samuel [publishing house]....................DLB-49

Gerrold, David 1944- DLB-8

Geston, Mark S. 1946- DLB-8

Gibbon, Lewis Grassic (see Mitchell, James Leslie)

Gibbons, Floyd 1887-1939 ....DLB-25

Gibbons, William ?-?.......................................DLB-73

Gibson, Graeme 1934- DLB-53

Gibson, Wilfrid 1878-1962................................DLB-19

Gibson, William 1914- DLB-7

Gide, André 1869-1951....................................DLB-65

Giguère, Diane 1937- DLB-53

Giguère, Roland 1929- DLB-60

Gilbert, Anthony 1899-1973 ....DLB-77

Gilder, Jeannette L. 1849-1916.........................DLB-79

Gilder, Richard Watson 1844-1909 ....DLB-64, 79

Gildersleeve, Basil 1831-1924 ....DLB-71

Giles, Henry 1809-1882 ....DLB-64

Gill, William F., Company DLB-49

Gillespie, A. Lincoln, Jr. 1895-1950 ....DLB-4

Gilliam, Florence ?-?..DLB-4

Gilliatt, Penelope 1932- DLB-14

Gillott, Jacky 1939-1980 ....DLB-14

Gilman, Caroline H. 1794-1888 ....DLB-3, 73

Gilman, W. and J. [publishing house]................DLB-49

Gilmer, Elizabeth Meriwether 1861-1951 ....DLB-29

Gilmer, Francis Walker 1790-1826 ....DLB-37

Gilroy, Frank D. 1925- DLB-7

Ginsberg, Allen 1926- DLB-5, 16

Ginzkey, Franz Karl 1871-1963 ....DLB-81

Giono, Jean 1895-1970......................................DLB-72

Giovanni, Nikki 1943- DLB-5, 41

Gipson, Lawrence Henry 1880-1971 ....DLB-17

Giraudoux, Jean 1882-1944 ....DLB-65

Gissing, George 1857-1903 ....DLB-18

Gladstone, William Ewart 1809-1898 ....DLB-57

Glaeser, Ernst 1902-1963 ....DLB-69

Glanville, Brian 1931- DLB-15

Glapthorne, Henry 1610-1643? DLB-58

Glasgow, Ellen 1873-1945..............................DLB-9, 12

Glaspell, Susan 1876-1948........................DLB-7, 9, 78

Glass, Montague 1877-1934 ....DLB-11

Glassco, John 1909-1981 ....DLB-68

Glauser, Friedrich 1896-1938 ....DLB-56

F. Gleason's Publishing Hall DLB-49

Glück, Louise 1943- DLB-5

Godbout, Jacques 1933- DLB-53

Goddard, Morrill 1865-1937 ....DLB-25

Goddard, William 1740-1817 ....DLB-43

Godey, Louis A. 1804-1878 ....DLB-73

Godey and McMichael.....................................DLB-49

Godfrey, Dave 1938- DLB-60

Godfrey, Thomas 1736-1763 ....DLB-31

Godine, David R., Publisher DLB-46

Godkin, E. L. 1831-1902...................................DLB-79

Godwin, Gail 1937- DLB-6

Godwin, Parke 1816-1904...........................DLB-3, 64

Godwin, William 1756-1836 ....DLB-39

Goes, Albrecht 1908- DLB-69

Goffe, Thomas circa 1592-1629.........................DLB-58

Goffstein, M. B. 1940- DLB-61

Gogarty, Oliver St. John 1878-1957 ....DLB-15, 19

Goines, Donald 1937-1974...............................DLB-33

Gold, Herbert 1924- DLB-2; Y-81

Gold, Michael 1893-1967 ....DLB-9, 28

Goldberg, Dick 1947- DLB-7

Golding, William 1911- DLB-15

Goldman, William 1931- DLB-44

Goldsmith, Oliver 1730 or 1731-1774...............DLB-39

Goldsmith Publishing Company DLB-46

Gomme, Laurence James
[publishing house] DLB-46

González-T., César A. 1931- DLB-82

The Goodman Theatre.....................DLB-7

Goodrich, Frances 1891-1984 and
Hackett, Albert 1900- DLB-26

Goodrich, S. G. [publishing house] DLB-49

Goodrich, Samuel Griswold 1793-1860 ...DLB-1, 42, 73

Goodspeed, C. E., and Company DLB-49

Goodwin, Stephen 1943- Y-82

Gookin, Daniel 1612-1687 ....DLB-24

Gordon, Caroline 1895-1981.................DLB-4, 9; Y-81

Gordon, Giles 1940- DLB-14

Gordon, Mary 1949- DLB-6; Y-81

Gordone, Charles 1925- DLB-7

Gorey, Edward 1925- DLB-61

Gosse, Edmund 1849-1928 ....DLB-57

Gould, Wallace 1882-1940 ....DLB-54

Goyen, William 1915-1983...................DLB-2; Y-83

Gracq, Julien 1910- DLB-83

Grady, Henry W. 1850-1889...................DLB-23

Graf, Oskar Maria 1894-1967...................DLB-56

Graham, George Rex 1813-1894 ....DLB-73

Graham, Lorenz 1902- DLB-76

Graham, Shirley 1896-1977 ....DLB-76

Graham, W. S. 1918- DLB-20

Graham, William H. [publishing house] DLB-49

Graham, Winston 1910- DLB-77

Grahame, Kenneth 1859-1932...................DLB-34

Gramatky, Hardie 1907-1979 ....DLB-22

Granich, Irwin (see Gold, Michael)

Grant, Harry J. 1881-1963...................DLB-29

Grant, James Edward 1905-1966...................DLB-26

Grass, Günter 1927- DLB-75

Grasty, Charles H. 1863-1924...................DLB-25

Grau, Shirley Ann 1929- DLB-2

Graves, John 1920- Y-83

Graves, Richard 1715-1804 ....DLB-39

Graves, Robert 1895-1985 ....DLB-20; Y-85

Gray, Asa 1810-1888 ....DLB-1

Gray, David 1838-1861...................DLB-32

Gray, Simon 1936- DLB-13

Grayson, William J. 1788-1863...................DLB-3, 64

The Great War and the Theater, 1914-1918
[Great Britain]...................DLB-10

Greeley, Horace 1811-1872 ....DLB-3, 43

Green, Adolph (see Comden, Betty)

Green, Duff 1791-1875 ....DLB-43

Green, Gerald 1922- DLB-28

Green, Henry 1905-1973 ....DLB-15

Green, Jonas 1712-1767 ....DLB-31

Green, Joseph 1706-1780...................DLB-31

Green, Julien 1900- DLB-4, 72

Green, Paul 1894-1981 ....DLB-7, 9; Y-81

Green, T. and S. [publishing house] DLB-49

Green, Timothy [publishing house]...................DLB-49

Greenberg: Publisher DLB-46

Green Tiger Press...................DLB-46

Greene, Asa 1789-1838 ....DLB-11

Greene, Benjamin H. [publishing house]...........DLB-49

Greene, Graham 1904- DLB-13, 15, 77; Y-85

Greene, Robert 1558-1592 ....DLB-62

Greenhow, Robert 1800-1854...................DLB-30

Greenough, Horatio 1805-1852...................DLB-1

Greenwell, Dora 1821-1882 ....DLB-35

Greenwillow Books...................DLB-46

Greenwood, Grace (see Lippincott, Sara Jane Clarke)

Greenwood, Walter 1903-1974 ....DLB-10

Greer, Ben 1948- DLB-6

Greg, W. R. 1809-1881...................DLB-55

Gregg Press...................DLB-46

Persse, Isabella Augusta,
Lady Gregory 1852-1932 ....DLB-10

Gregory, Horace 1898-1982...................DLB-48

Greville, Fulke, First Lord Brooke
1554-1628 ....DLB-62

Grey, Zane 1872-1939 ....DLB-9

Grieve, C. M. (see MacDiarmid, Hugh)

Griffith, Elizabeth 1727?-1793...................DLB-39

Griffiths, Trevor 1935- DLB-13

Griggs, S. C., and Company...................DLB-49

Griggs, Sutton Elbert 1872-1930 ....DLB-50

Grignon, Claude-Henri 1894-1976......................DLB-68

Grigson, Geoffrey 1905- DLB-27

Grimké, Angelina Weld 1880-1958...............DLB-50, 54

Grimm, Hans 1875-1959.................................DLB-66

Griswold, Rufus Wilmot 1815-1857 ....DLB-3, 59

Gross, Milt 1895-1953 ....DLB-11

Grosset and Dunlap...DLB-49

Grossman Publishers DLB-46

Groulx, Lionel 1878-1967 ....DLB-68

Grove Press..DLB-46

Grubb, Davis 1919-1980.................................DLB-6

Gruelle, Johnny 1880-1938.............................DLB-22

Guare, John 1938- DLB-7

Guest, Barbara 1920- DLB-5

Guèvremont, Germaine 1893-1968 ....DLB-68

Guilloux, Louis 1899-1980..............................DLB-72

Guiney, Louise Imogen 1861-1920..................DLB-54

Guiterman, Arthur 1871-1943.........................DLB-11

Gunn, Bill 1934- DLB-38

Gunn, James E. 1923- DLB-8

Gunn, Neil M. 1891-1973 ....DLB-15

Gunn, Thom 1929- DLB-27

Gunnars, Kristjana 1948- DLB-60

Gurik, Robert 1932- DLB-60

Gütersloh, Albert Paris 1887-1973 ....DLB-81

Guthrie, A. B., Jr. 1901- DLB-6

Guthrie, Ramon 1896-1973.............................DLB-4

The Guthrie Theater..DLB-7

Guy, Ray 1939- DLB-60

Guy, Rosa 1925- DLB-33

Gwynne, Erskine 1898-1948 ....DLB-4

Gysin, Brion 1916- DLB-16

H

H. D. (see Doolittle, Hilda)

Hackett, Albert (see Goodrich, Frances)

Hagelstange, Rudolf 1912-1984......................DLB-69

Haggard, H. Rider 1856-1925 ....DLB-70

Hailey, Arthur 1920- Y-82

Haines, John 1924- DLB-5

Hake, Thomas Gordon 1809-1895 ....DLB-32

Haldeman, Joe 1943- DLB-8

Haldeman-Julius Company..............................DLB-46

Hale, E. J., and Son..DLB-49

Hale, Edward Everett 1822-1909 ....DLB-1, 42, 74

Hale, Leo Thomas (see Ebon)

Hale, Lucretia Peabody 1820-1900....................DLB-42

Hale, Nancy 1908-1988 ....Y-80, 88

Hale, Sarah Josepha (Buell) 1788-1879 ...DLB-1, 42, 73

Haley, Alex 1921- DLB-38

Haliburton, Thomas Chandler 1796-1865.........DLB-11

Hall, Donald 1928- DLB-5

Hall, James 1793-1868 ....DLB-73, 74

Hall, Samuel [publishing house]......................DLB-49

Hallam, Arthur Henry 1811-1833.....................DLB-32

Halleck, Fitz-Greene 1790-1867 ....DLB-3

Hallmark Editions DLB-46

Halper, Albert 1904-1984................................DLB-9

Halstead, Murat 1829-1908.............................DLB-23

Hamburger, Michael 1924- DLB-27

Hamilton, Alexander 1712-1756 ....DLB-31

Hamilton, Alexander 1755?-1804.....................DLB-37

Hamilton, Cicely 1872-1952............................DLB-10

Hamilton, Edmond 1904-1977 ....DLB-8

Hamilton, Gail (see Corcoran, Barbara)

Hamilton, Ian 1938- DLB-40

Hamilton, Patrick 1904-1962 ....DLB-10

Hamilton, Virginia 1936- DLB-33, 52

Hammett, Dashiell 1894-1961 ....DS-6

Hammon, Jupiter 1711-died between
    1790 and 1806.....................................DLB-31, 50

Hammond, John ?-1663....................................DLB-24

Hamner, Earl 1923- DLB-6

Hampton, Christopher 1946- DLB-13

Handel-Mazzetti, Enrica von
    1871-1955 ....DLB-81

Handke, Peter 1942- DLB-85

Handlin, Oscar 1915- DLB-17

Hankin, St. John 1869-1909 ....DLB-10

Hanley, Clifford 1922- DLB-14

Hannah, Barry 1942- DLB-6

Hannay, James 1827-1873................................DLB-21

Hansberry, Lorraine 1930-1965...................DLB-7, 38

Harcourt Brace Jovanovich..........................DLB-46

Hardwick, Elizabeth 1916-.............................DLB-6

Hardy, Thomas 1840-1928.......................DLB-18, 19

Hare, Cyril 1900-1958...................................DLB-77

Hare, David 1947-.......................................DLB-13

Hargrove, Marion 1919-..............................DLB-11

Harlow, Robert 1923-..................................DLB-60

Harness, Charles L. 1915-..............................DLB-8

Harper, Fletcher 1806-1877...........................DLB-79

Harper, Frances Ellen Watkins
    1825-1911...DLB-50

Harper, Michael S. 1938-...............................DLB-41

Harper and Brothers.......................................DLB-49

Harris, Benjamin ?-circa 1720...................DLB-42, 43

Harris, George Washington 1814-1869..........DLB-3, 11

Harris, Joel Chandler 1848-1908.....DLB-11, 23, 42, 78

Harris, Mark 1922-..................................DLB-2; Y-80

Harrison, Charles Yale 1898-1954...................DLB-68

Harrison, Frederic 1831-1923.........................DLB-57

Harrison, Harry 1925-..................................DLB-8

Harrison, James P., Company..........................DLB-49

Harrison, Jim 1937-......................................Y-82

Harrison, Paul Carter 1936-............................DLB-38

Harrison, Tony 1937-...................................DLB-40

Harrisse, Henry 1829-1910.............................DLB-47

Harsent, David 1942-...................................DLB-40

Hart, Albert Bushnell 1854-1943.....................DLB-17

Hart, Moss 1904-1961......................................DLB-7

Hart, Oliver 1723-1795..................................DLB-31

Harte, Bret 1836-1902...................DLB-12, 64, 74, 79

Hartlaub, Felix 1913-1945.............................DLB-56

Hartley, L. P. 1895-1972................................DLB-15

Hartley, Marsden 1877-1943...........................DLB-54

Härtling, Peter 1933-...................................DLB-75

Hartman, Geoffrey H. 1929-...........................DLB-67

Hartmann, Sadakichi 1867-1944......................DLB-54

Harwood, Lee 1939-.....................................DLB-40

Harwood, Ronald 1934-................................DLB-13

Haskins, Charles Homer 1870-1937..................DLB-47

The Hatch-Billops Collection.........................DLB-76

A Haughty and Proud Generation (1922),
    by Ford Madox Hueffer.............................DLB-36

Hauptmann, Carl 1858-1921.........................DLB-66

Hauptmann, Gerhart 1862-1946......................DLB-66

Hauser, Marianne 1910-..................................Y-83

Hawker, Robert Stephen 1803-1875.................DLB-32

Hawkes, John 1925-.............................DLB-2, 7; Y-80

Hawkins, Walter Everette 1883-?.....................DLB-50

Hawthorne, Nathaniel 1804-1864.................DLB-1, 74

Hay, John 1838-1905.................................DLB-12, 47

Hayden, Robert 1913-1980..........................DLB-5, 76

Hayes, John Michael 1919-............................DLB-26

Hayne, Paul Hamilton 1830-1886............DLB-3, 64, 79

Haywood, Eliza 1693?-1756...........................DLB-39

Hazard, Willis P. [publishing house]................DLB-49

Hazzard, Shirley 1931-...................................Y-82

Headley, Joel T. 1813-1897............................DLB-30

Heaney, Seamus 1939-..................................DLB-40

Heard, Nathan C. 1936-...............................DLB-33

Hearn, Lafcadio 1850-1904.........................DLB-12, 78

Hearst, William Randolph 1863-1951...............DLB-25

Heath, Catherine 1924-.................................DLB-14

Heath-Stubbs, John 1918-..............................DLB-27

Hébert, Anne 1916-.....................................DLB-68

Hébert, Jacques 1923-..................................DLB-53

Hecht, Anthony 1923-....................................DLB-5

Hecht, Ben 1894-1964.................DLB-7, 9, 25, 26, 28

Hecker, Isaac Thomas 1819-1888......................DLB-1

Hedge, Frederic Henry 1805-1890.................DLB-1, 59

Heidish, Marcy 1947-.....................................Y-82

Heinlein, Robert A. 1907-...............................DLB-8

Heinrich, Willi 1920-...................................DLB-75

Hei;denbüttel 1921-....................................DLB-75

Heller, Joseph 1923-...........................DLB-2, 28; Y-80

Hellman, Lillian 1906-1984.......................DLB-7; Y-84

Helprin, Mark 1947-.....................................Y-85

Helwig, David 1938-....................................DLB-60

Hemingway, Ernest
    1899-1961.....................DLB-4, 9; Y-81, 87; DS-1

Hemingway: Twenty-Five Years Later................Y-85

Hemphill, Paul 1936- Y-87

Henchman, Daniel 1689-1761 ....DLB-24

Henderson, Alice Corbin 1881-1949 ....DLB-54

Henderson, David 1942- DLB-41

Henderson, George Wylie 1904- DLB-51

Henderson, Zenna 1917- DLB-8

Henisch, Peter 1943- DLB-85

Henley, Beth 1952- Y-86

Henley, William Ernest 1849-1903 ....DLB-19

Henry, Buck 1930- DLB-26

Henry, Marguerite 1902- DLB-22

Henry, Robert Selph 1889-1970 ....DLB-17

Henry, Will (see Allen, Henry W.)

Henschke, Alfred (see Klabund)

Henty, G. A. 1832-1902 ....DLB-18

Hentz, Caroline Lee 1800-1856 ....DLB-3

Herbert, Alan Patrick 1890-1971 ....DLB-10

Herbert, Frank 1920-1986 ....DLB-8

Herbert, Henry William 1807-1858 ....DLB-3, 73

Herbert, John 1926- DLB-53

Herbst, Josephine 1892-1969 ....DLB-9

Herburger, Günter 1932- DLB-75

Hercules, Frank E. M. 1917- DLB-33

Herder, B., Book Company DLB-49

Hergesheimer, Joseph 1880-1954 ....DLB-9

Heritage Press DLB-46

Hermlin, Stephan 1915- DLB-69

Hernton, Calvin C. 1932- DLB-38

"The Hero as Man of Letters: Johnson,
     Rousseau, Burns" (1841), by Thomas
     Carlyle [excerpt] DLB-57

The Hero as Poet. Dante; Shakspeare (1841),
     by Thomas Carlyle DLB-32

Herrick, E. R., and Company DLB-49

Herrick, Robert 1868-1938 ....DLB-9, 12, 78

Herrick, William 1915- Y-83

Herrmann, John 1900-1959 ....DLB-4

Hersey, John 1914- DLB-6

Hertel, François 1905-1985 ....DLB-68

Hervé-Bazin, Jean Pierre Marie (see Bazin, Hervé)

Herzog, Emile Salomon Wilhelm (see Maurois, André)

Hesse, Hermann 1877-1962 ....DLB-66

Hewat, Alexander circa 1743-circa 1824 ....DLB-30

Hewitt, John 1907- DLB-27

Hewlett, Maurice 1861-1923 ....DLB-34

Heyen, William 1940- DLB-5

Heyer, Georgette 1902-1974 ....DLB-77

Heym, Stefan 1913- DLB-69

Heyward, Dorothy 1890-1961 and
     Heyward, DuBose 1885-1940 ....DLB-7

Heyward, DuBose 1885-1940 ....DLB-7, 9, 45

Heywood, Thomas 1573 or 1574-1641 ....DLB-62

Hiebert, Paul 1892-1987 ....DLB-68

Higgins, Aidan 1927- DLB-14

Higgins, Colin 1941-1988 ....DLB-26

Higgins, George V. 1939- DLB-2; Y-81

Higginson, Thomas Wentworth 1823-1911 ...DLB-1, 64

Highwater, Jamake 1942?- DLB-52; Y-85

Hildesheimer, Wolfgang 1916- DLB-69

Hildreth, Richard 1807-1865 ....DLB-1, 30, 59

Hill, Aaron 1685-1750 ....DLB-84

Hill, Geoffrey 1932- DLB-40

Hill, George M., Company DLB-49

Hill, "Sir" John 1714?-1775 ....DLB-39

Hill, Lawrence, and Company, Publishers DLB-46

Hill, Leslie 1880-1960 ....DLB-51

Hill, Susan 1942- DLB-14

Hill, Walter 1942- DLB-44

Hill and Wang DLB-46

Hilliard, Gray and Company DLB-49

Hillyer, Robert 1895-1961 ....DLB-54

Hilton, James 1900-1954 ....DLB-34, 77

Hilton and Company DLB-49

Himes, Chester 1909-1984 ....DLB-2, 76

Hine, Daryl 1936- DLB-60

Hinojosa-Smith, Rolando 1929- DLB-82

The History of the Adventures of Joseph Andrews
     (1742), by Henry Fielding [excerpt] DLB-39

Hirsch, E. D., Jr. 1928- DLB-67

Hoagland, Edward 1932- DLB-6

Hoagland, Everett H. III 1942- DLB-41

Hoban, Russell 1925- DLB-52

Hobsbaum, Philip 1932- DLB-40

Hobson, Laura Z. 1900- DLB-28

Hochman, Sandra 1936- DLB-5

Hodgins, Jack 1938- DLB-60

Hodgman, Helen 1945- DLB-14

Hodgson, Ralph 1871-1962 ....DLB-19

Hodgson, William Hope 1877-1918 ....DLB-70

Hoffenstein, Samuel 1890-1947 ....DLB-11

Hoffman, Charles Fenno 1806-1884 ....DLB-3

Hoffman, Daniel 1923- DLB-5

Hofmann, Michael 1957- DLB-40

Hofmannsthal, Hugo von 1874-1929 ....DLB-81

Hofstadter, Richard 1916-1970 ....DLB-17

Hogan, Desmond 1950- DLB-14

Hogan and Thompson DLB-49

Hohl, Ludwig 1904-1980 ....DLB-56

Holbrook, David 1923- DLB-14, 40

Holcroft, Thomas 1745-1809 ....DLB-39

Holden, Molly 1927-1981 ....DLB-40

Holiday House DLB-46

Holland, Norman N. 1927- DLB-67

Hollander, John 1929- DLB-5

Holley, Marietta 1836-1926 ....DLB-11

Hollingsworth, Margaret 1940- DLB-60

Hollo, Anselm 1934- DLB-40

Holloway, John 1920- DLB-27

Holloway House Publishing Company DLB-46

Holme, Constance 1880-1955 ....DLB-34

Holmes, Oliver Wendell 1809-1894 ....DLB-1

Holmes, John Clellon 1926-1988 ....DLB-16

Holst, Hermann E. von 1841-1904 ....DLB-47

Holt, Henry, and Company DLB-49

Holt, John 1721-1784 ....DLB-43

Holt, Rinehart and Winston DLB-46

Holthusen, Hans Egon 1913- DLB-69

Home, Henry, Lord Kames 1696-1782 ....DLB-31

Home, John 1722-1808 ....DLB-84

Home Publishing Company DLB-49

Home, William Douglas 1912- DLB-13

Homes, Geoffrey (see Mainwaring, Daniel)

Honig, Edwin 1919- DLB-5

Hood, Hugh 1928- DLB-53

Hooker, Jeremy 1941- DLB-40

Hooker, Thomas 1586-1647 ....DLB-24

Hooper, Johnson Jones 1815-1862 ....DLB-3, 11

Hopkins, Gerard Manley 1844-1889 ....DLB-35, 57

Hopkins, John H., and Son DLB-46

Hopkins, Lemuel 1750-1801 ....DLB-37

Hopkins, Pauline Elizabeth 1859-1930 ....DLB-50

Hopkins, Samuel 1721-1803 ....DLB-31

Hopkinson, Francis 1737-1791 ....DLB-31

Horgan, Paul 1903- Y-85

Horizon Press..................................DLB-46

Horne, Frank 1899-1974.....................DLB-51

Horne, Richard Henry (Hengist) 1802
    or 1803-1884................................DLB-32

Hornung, E. W. 1866-1921..................DLB-70

Horovitz, Israel 1939- DLB-7

Horton, George Moses 1797?-1883? DLB-50

Horváth, Ödön von 1901-1938............DLB-85

Horwood, Harold 1923- DLB-60

Hosford, E. and E. [publishing house]..........DLB-49

Hotchkiss and Company DLB-49

Hough, Emerson 1857-1923................DLB-9

Houghton Mifflin Company DLB-49

Houghton, Stanley 1881-1913 ....DLB-10

Housman, A. E. 1859-1936................DLB-19

Housman, Laurence 1865-1959...........DLB-10

Hovey, Richard 1864-1900..................DLB-54

Howard, Maureen 1930- Y-83

Howard, Richard 1929- DLB-5

Howard, Roy W. 1883-1964...............DLB-29

Howard, Sidney 1891-1939.................DLB-7, 26

Howe, E. W. 1853-1937 ....DLB-12, 25

Howe, Henry 1816-1893 ....DLB-30

Howe, Irving 1920- DLB-67

Howe, Julia Ward 1819-1910..............DLB-1

Howell, Clark, Sr. 1863-1936.............DLB-25

Howell, Evan P. 1839-1905.................DLB-23

Howell, Soskin and Company..............DLB-46

Howells, William Dean 1837-1920...DLB-12, 64, 74, 79

Hoyem, Andrew 1935- DLB-5

de Hoyos, Angela 1940- DLB-82

Hoyt, Henry [publishing house] DLB-49

Hubbard, Kin 1868-1930 ....DLB-11

Hubbard, William circa 1621-1704 ....DLB-24

Huch, Friedrich 1873-1913 ....DLB-66

Huch, Ricarda 1864-1947 ....DLB-66

Huck at 100: How Old Is
    Huckleberry Finn? Y-85

Hudson, Henry Norman 1814-1886 ....DLB-64

Hudson and Goodwin DLB-49

Huebsch, B. W. [publishing house] DLB-46

Hughes, David 1930- DLB-14

Hughes, John 1677-1720 ....DLB-84

Hughes, Langston 1902-1967..............DLB-4, 7, 48, 51

Hughes, Richard 1900-1976 ....DLB-15

Hughes, Ted 1930- DLB-40

Hughes, Thomas 1822-1896 ....DLB-18

Hugo, Richard 1923-1982............................DLB-5

Hugo Awards and Nebula Awards.....................DLB-8

Hull, Richard 1896-1973............................DLB-77

Hulme, T. E. 1883-1917 ....DLB-19

Hume, Fergus 1859-1932 ....DLB-70

Humorous Book Illustration.........................DLB-11

Humphrey, William 1924- DLB-6

Humphreys, David 1752-1818.........................DLB-37

Humphreys, Emyr 1919- DLB-15

Huncke, Herbert 1915- DLB-16

Huneker, James Gibbons 1857-1921 ....DLB-71

Hunt, Irene 1907- DLB-52

Hunt, William Gibbes 1791-1833 ....DLB-73

Hunter, Evan 1926- Y-82

Hunter, Jim 1939- DLB-14

Hunter, Kristin 1931- DLB-33

Hunter, N. C. 1908-1971 ....DLB-10

Hurd and Houghton.................................DLB-49

Hurst and Company.................................DLB-49

Hurston, Zora Neale 1891-1960 ....DLB-51

Huston, John 1906- DLB-26

Hutcheson, Francis 1694-1746.......................DLB-31

Hutchinson, Thomas 1711-1780 ....DLB-30, 31

Hutton, Richard Holt 1826-1897.....................DLB-57

Huxley, Aldous 1894-1963..............................DLB-36

Huxley, Elspeth Josceline
    1907- DLB-77

Huxley, T. H. 1825-1895 ....DLB-57

Hyman, Trina Schart 1939- DLB-61

I

The Iconography of Science-Fiction Art.............DLB-8

Ignatow, David 1914- DLB-5

Iles, Francis (see Berkeley, Anthony)

Imbs, Bravig 1904-1946 ....DLB-4

Inchbald, Elizabeth 1753-1821 ....DLB-39

Inge, William 1913-1973............................DLB-7

Ingelow, Jean 1820-1897............................DLB-35

The Ingersoll Prizes Y-84

Ingraham, Joseph Holt 1809-1860 ....DLB-3

Inman, John 1805-1850 ....DLB-73

Innerhofer, Franz 1944- DLB-85

International Publishers Company DLB-46

An Interview with Peter S. Prescott.................Y-86

An Interview with Tom Jenks........................Y-86

Introduction to Paul Laurence Dunbar,
    Lyrics of Lowly Life (1896),
    by William Dean Howells.........................DLB-50

Introductory Essay: *Letters of Percy Bysshe
    Shelley* (1852), by Robert Browning DLB-32

Introductory Letters from the Second Edition
    of *Pamela* (1741), by Samuel Richardson.....DLB-39

Irving, John 1942- DLB-6; Y-82

Irving, Washington
    1783-1859 ....DLB-3, 11, 30, 59, 73, 74

Irwin, Grace 1907- DLB-68

Irwin, Will 1873-1948 ....DLB-25

Isherwood, Christopher 1904-1986.........DLB-15; Y-86

The Island Trees Case: A Symposium on School
        Library Censorship
    An Interview with Judith Krug
    An Interview with Phyllis Schlafly
    An Interview with Edward B. Jenkinson
    An Interview with Lamarr Mooneyham
    An Interview with Harriet Bernstein Y-82

Ivers, M. J., and Company..............................DLB-49

J

Jackmon, Marvin E. (see Marvin X)

Jackson, Angela 1951- DLB-41

Jackson, Helen Hunt 1830-1885 ....DLB-42, 47

Jackson, Laura Riding 1901- DLB-48

Jackson, Shirley 1919-1965 ....DLB-6

Jacob, Piers Anthony Dillingham (see Anthony, Piers)

Jacobs, George W., and Company DLB-49

Jacobson, Dan 1929- DLB-14

Jahnn, Hans Henny 1894-1959 ....DLB-56

Jakes, John 1932- Y-83

James, Henry 1843-1916 ....DLB-12, 71, 74

James, John circa 1633-1729 ....DLB-24

James Joyce Centenary: Dublin, 1982 ....Y-82

James Joyce Conference Y-85

James, U. P. [publishing house] DLB-49

Jameson, Fredric 1934- DLB-67

Jameson, J. Franklin 1859-1937 ....DLB-17

Jameson, Storm 1891-1986 ....DLB-36

Jarrell, Randall 1914-1965 ....DLB-48, 52

Jasmin, Claude 1930- DLB-60

Jay, John 1745-1829 ....DLB-31

Jeffers, Lance 1919-1985 ....DLB-41

Jeffers, Robinson 1887-1962 ....DLB-45

Jefferson, Thomas 1743-1826 ....DLB-31

Jelinek, Elfriede 1946- DLB-85

Jellicoe, Ann 1927- DLB-13

Jenkins, Robin 1912- DLB-14

Jenkins, William Fitzgerald (see Leinster, Murray)

Jennings, Elizabeth 1926- DLB-27

Jens, Walter 1923- DLB-69

Jensen, Merrill 1905-1980 ....DLB-17

Jerome, Jerome K. 1859-1927 ....DLB-10, 34

Jesse, F. Tennyson 1888-1958 ....DLB-77

Jewett, John P., and Company DLB-49

Jewett, Sarah Orne 1849-1909 ....DLB-12, 74

The Jewish Publication Society DLB-49

Jewsbury, Geraldine 1812-1880 ....DLB-21

Joans, Ted 1928- DLB-16, 41

John Edward Bruce: Three Documents.............DLB-50

John O'Hara's Pottsville Journalism........................Y-88

John Steinbeck Research Center.............................Y-85

John Webster: The Melbourne Manuscript............Y-86

Johnson, B. S. 1933-1973.............................DLB-14, 40

Johnson, Benjamin [publishing house]..............DLB-49

Johnson, Benjamin, Jacob, and Robert [publishing house]...........................DLB-49

Johnson, Charles 1679-1748 ....DLB-84

Johnson, Charles R. 1948- DLB-33

Johnson, Charles S. 1893-1956 ....DLB-51

Johnson, Diane 1934- Y-80

Johnson, Edward 1598-1672............................DLB-24

Johnson, Fenton 1888-1958 ....DLB-45, 50

Johnson, Georgia Douglas 1886-1966 ....DLB-51

Johnson, Gerald W. 1890-1980..........................DLB-29

Johnson, Helene 1907- DLB-51

Johnson, Jacob, and Company...........................DLB-49

Johnson, James Weldon 1871-1938 ....DLB-51

Johnson, Lionel 1867-1902 ....DLB-19

Johnson, Nunnally 1897-1977 ....DLB-26

Johnson, Owen 1878-1952 ....Y-87

Johnson, Pamela Hansford 1912- DLB-15

Johnson, Samuel 1696-1772.............................DLB-24

Johnson, Samuel 1709-1784.............................DLB-39

Johnson, Samuel 1822-1882.................................DLB-1

Johnson, Uwe 1934-1984 ....DLB-75

Johnston, Annie Fellows 1863-1931...................DLB-42

Johnston, Basil H. 1929- DLB-60

Johnston, Denis 1901-1984 ....DLB-10

Johnston, Jennifer 1930- DLB-14

Johnston, Mary 1870-1936...................................DLB-9

Johnston, Richard Malcolm 1822-1898 ....DLB-74

Johnstone, Charles 1719?-1800? DLB-39

Jolas, Eugene 1894-1952.............................DLB-4, 45

Jones, Charles C., Jr. 1831-1893.......................DLB-30

Jones, D. G. 1929- DLB-53

Jones, David 1895-1974....................................DLB-20

Jones, Ebenezer 1820-1860 ....DLB-32

Jones, Ernest 1819-1868...................................DLB-32

Jones, Gayl 1949- DLB-33

Jones, Glyn 1905- DLB-15

Jones, Gwyn 1907- DLB-15

Jones, Henry Arthur 1851-1929.......................DLB-10

Jones, Hugh circa 1692-1760............................DLB-24

Jones, James 1921-1977...............................DLB-2

Jones, LeRoi (see Baraka, Amiri)

Jones, Lewis 1897-1939 ....DLB-15

Jones, Major Joseph (see Thompson, William Tappan)

Jones, Preston 1936-1979.................................DLB-7

Jones, William Alfred 1817-1900 ....DLB-59

Jones's Publishing House DLB-49

Jong, Erica 1942- DLB-2, 5, 28

Jonke, Gert F. 1946- DLB-85

Jonson, Ben 1572?-1637...............................DLB-62

Jordan, June 1936- DLB-38

Joseph, Jenny 1932- DLB-40

Josephson, Matthew 1899-1978 ....DLB-4

Josiah Allen's Wife (see Holley, Marietta)

Josipovici, Gabriel 1940- DLB-14

Josselyn, John ?-1675...............................DLB-24

Joyaux, Philippe (see Sollers, Philippe)

Joyce, Adrien (see Eastman, Carol)

Joyce, James 1882-1941 ....DLB-10, 19, 36

Judd, Orange, Publishing Company.................DLB-49

Judd, Sylvester 1813-1853............................DLB-1

June, Jennie (see Croly, Jane Cunningham)

Jünger, Ernst 1895- DLB-56

Justice, Donald 1925- Y-83

K

Kacew, Romain (see Gary, Romain)

Kafka, Franz 1883-1924 ....DLB-81

Kalechofsky, Roberta 1931- DLB-28

Kaler, James Otis 1848-1912............................DLB-12

Kandel, Lenore 1932- DLB-16

Kanin, Garson 1912- DLB-7

Kant, Hermann 1926- DLB-75

Kantor, Mackinlay 1904-1977 ....DLB-9

Kaplan, Johanna 1942- DLB-28

Kasack, Hermann 1896-1966............................DLB-69

Kaschnitz, Marie Luise 1901-1974.....................DLB-69

Kästner, Erich 1899-1974.................................DLB-56

Kattan, Naïm 1928- DLB-53

Katz, Steve 1935- Y-83

Kauffman, Janet 1945- Y-86

Kaufman, Bob 1925- DLB-16, 41

Kaufman, George S. 1889-1961............................DLB-7

Kavanagh, Patrick 1904-1967 ....DLB-15, 20

Kavanagh, P. J. 1931- DLB-40

Kaye-Smith, Sheila 1887-1956 ....DLB-36

Kazin, Alfred 1915- DLB-67

Keane, John B. 1928- DLB-13

Keats, Ezra Jack 1916-1983............................DLB-61

Keble, John 1792-1866.................................DLB-32, 55

Keeble, John 1944- Y-83

Keeffe, Barrie 1945- DLB-13

Keeley, James 1867-1934 ....DLB-25

W. B. Keen, Cooke and Company.....................DLB-49

Keillor, Garrison 1942- Y-87

Keller, Gary D. 1943- DLB-82

Kelley, Edith Summers 1884-1956 ....DLB-9

Kelley, William Melvin 1937- DLB-33

Kellogg, Ansel Nash 1832-1886.......................DLB-23

Kellogg, Steven 1941- DLB-61

Kelly, George 1887-1974.................................DLB-7

Kelly, Piet and Company DLB-49

Kelly, Robert 1935- DLB-5

Kemble, Fanny 1809-1893.................................DLB-32

Kemelman, Harry 1908- DLB-28

Kempowski, Walter 1929- DLB-75

Kendall, Claude [publishing company] DLB-46

Kendell, George 1809-1867 ....DLB-43

Kenedy, P. J., and Sons.................................DLB-49

Kennedy, Adrienne 1931- DLB-38

Kennedy, John Pendleton 1795-1870...................DLB-3

Kennedy, Margaret 1896-1967 ....DLB-36

Kennedy, William 1928- Y-85

Kennedy, X. J. 1929- DLB-5

Kennelly, Brendan 1936- DLB-40

Kenner, Hugh 1923- DLB-67

Kennerley, Mitchell [publishing house].............DLB-46

Kent, Frank R. 1877-1958.......................DLB-29

Keppler and Schwartzmann......................DLB-49

Kerouac, Jack 1922-1969......................DLB-2, 16; DS-3

Kerouac, Jan 1952- DLB-16

Kerr, Charles H., and Company.......................DLB-49

Kerr, Orpheus C. (see Newell, Robert Henry)

Kesey, Ken 1935- DLB-2, 16

Kessel, Joseph 1898-1979.................DLB-72

Kessel, Martin 1901- DLB-56

Kesten, Hermann 1900- DLB-56

Keun, Irmgard 1905-1982 ....DLB-69

Key and Biddle.......................DLB-49

Keyserling, Eduard von 1855-1918 ....DLB-66

Kiely, Benedict 1919- DLB-15

Kiggins and Kellogg.......................DLB-49

Kiley, Jed 1889-1962 ....DLB-4

Killens, John Oliver 1916- DLB-33

Killigrew, Thomas 1612-1683.................DLB-58

Kilmer, Joyce 1886-1918.................DLB-45

King, Clarence 1842-1901.................DLB-12

King, Florence 1936 ....Y-85

King, Francis 1923- DLB-15

King, Grace 1852-1932 ....DLB-12, 78

King, Solomon [publishing house].................DLB-49

King, Stephen 1947- Y-80

King, Woodie, Jr. 1937- DLB-38

Kinglake, Alexander William 1809-1891...........DLB-55

Kingsley, Charles 1819-1875.................DLB-21, 32

Kingsley, Henry 1830-1876.................DLB-21

Kingsley, Sidney 1906- DLB-7

Kingston, Maxine Hong 1940- Y-80

Kinnell, Galway 1927- DLB-5; Y-87

Kinsella, Thomas 1928- DLB-27

Kipling, Rudyard 1865-1936 ....DLB-19, 34

Kirk, John Foster 1824-1904.................DLB-79

Kirkconnell, Watson 1895-1977.................DLB-68

Kirkland, Caroline M. 1801-1864 ....DLB-3, 73, 74

Kirkland, Joseph 1830-1893 ....DLB-12

Kirkup, James 1918- DLB-27

Kirsch, Sarah 1935- DLB-75

Kirst, Hans Hellmut 1914- DLB-69

Kitchin, C. H. B. 1895-1967 ....DLB-77

Kizer, Carolyn 1925- DLB-5

Klabund 1890-1928 ....DLB-66

Klappert, Peter 1942- DLB-5

Klass, Philip (see Tenn, William)

Klein, A. M. 1909-1972 ....DLB-68

Kluge, Alexander 1932- DLB-75

Knapp, Samuel Lorenzo 1783-1838 ....DLB-59

Knickerbocker, Diedrich (see Irving, Washington)

Knight, Damon 1922- DLB-8

Knight, Etheridge 1931- DLB-41

Knight, John S. 1894-1981...............DLB-29

Knight, Sarah Kemble 1666-1727...............DLB-24

Knister, Raymond 1899-1932 ....DLB-68

Knoblock, Edward 1874-1945...............DLB-10

Knopf, Alfred A. 1892-1984 ....Y-84

Knopf, Alfred A. [publishing house]...............DLB-46

Knowles, John 1926- DLB-6

Knox, Frank 1874-1944 ....DLB-29

Knox, John Armoy 1850-1906...............DLB-23

Knox, Ronald Arbuthnott 1888-1957...............DLB-77

Kober, Arthur 1900-1975 ....DLB-11

Koch, Howard 1902- DLB-26

Koch, Kenneth 1925- DLB-5

Koenigsberg, Moses 1879-1945 ....DLB-25

Koeppen, Wolfgang 1906- DLB-69

Koestler, Arthur 1905-1983 ....Y-83

Kolb, Annette 1870-1967 ....DLB-66

Kolbenheyer, Erwin Guido 1878-1962...............DLB-66

Kolleritsch, Alfred 1931- DLB-85

Kolodny, Annette 1941- DLB-67

Komroff, Manuel 1890-1974 ....DLB-4

Konigsburg, E. L. 1930- DLB-52

Kopit, Arthur 1937- DLB-7

Kops, Bernard 1926?- DLB-13

Kornbluth, C. M. 1923-1958...............DLB-8

Kosinski, Jerzy 1933- DLB-2; Y-82

Kraf, Elaine 1946- Y-81

Krasna, Norman 1909-1984...............DLB-26

Krauss, Ruth 1911- DLB-52

Kreuder, Ernst 1903-1972 ....DLB-69

Kreymborg, Alfred 1883-1966 ....DLB-4, 54

Krieger, Murray 1923- DLB-67

Krim, Seymour 1922- DLB-16

Krock, Arthur 1886-1974 ....DLB-29

Kroetsch, Robert 1927- DLB-53

Krutch, Joseph Wood 1893-1970 ....DLB-63

Kubin, Alfred 1877-1959 ....DLB-81

Kubrick, Stanley 1928- DLB-26

Kumin, Maxine 1925- DLB-5

Kunnert, Günter 1929- DLB-75

Kunitz, Stanley 1905- DLB-48

Kunjufu, Johari M. (see Amini, Johari M.)

Kunze, Reiner 1933- DLB-75

Kupferberg, Tuli 1923- DLB-16

Kurz, Isolde 1853-1944 ....DLB-66

Kusenberg, Kurt 1904-1983 ....DLB-69

Kuttner, Henry 1915-1958........................DLB-8

Kyd, Thomas 1558-1594 ....DLB-62

Kyger, Joanne 1934- DLB-16

Kyne, Peter B. 1880-1957 ....DLB-78

L

Laberge, Albert 1871-1960 ....DLB-68

Laberge, Marie 1950- DLB-60

Lacretelle, Jacques de 1888-1985 ....DLB-65

Ladd, Joseph Brown 1764-1786 ....DLB-37

La Farge, Oliver 1901-1963......................DLB-9

Lafferty, R. A. 1914- DLB-8

Laird, Carobeth 1895- Y-82

Laird and Lee DLB-49

Lalonde, Michèle 1937- DLB-60

Lamantia, Philip 1927- DLB-16

Lambert, Betty 1933-1983 ....DLB-60

L'Amour, Louis 1908?- Y-80

Lamson, Wolffe and Company DLB-49

Lancer Books..DLB-46

Landesman, Jay 1919- and
    Landesman, Fran 1927- DLB-16

Lane, Charles 1800-1870.............................DLB-1

The John Lane Company DLB-49

Lane, M. Travis 1934- DLB-60

Lane, Patrick 1939- DLB-53

Lane, Pinkie Gordon 1923- DLB-41

Laney, Al 1896- DLB-4

Langevin, André 1927- DLB-60

Langgässer, Elisabeth 1899-1950 ....DLB-69

Lanham, Edwin 1904-1979.........................DLB-4

Lanier, Sidney 1842-1881 ....DLB-64

Lardner, Ring 1885-1933......................DLB-11, 25

Lardner, Ring, Jr. 1915- DLB-26

Lardner 100: Ring Lardner
    Centennial Symposium....................................Y-85

Larkin, Philip 1922-1985 ....DLB-27

La Rocque, Gilbert 1943-1984 ....DLB-60

Laroque de Roquebrune, Robert
    (see Roquebrune, Robert de)

Larrick, Nancy 1910- DLB-61

Larsen, Nella 1893-1964 ....DLB-51

Lasker-Schüler, Else 1869-1945 ....DLB-66

Lathrop, Dorothy P. 1891-1980.................DLB-22

Lathrop, George Parsons 1851-1898 ....DLB-71

Lathrop, John, Jr. 1772-1820 ....DLB-37

Latimore, Jewel Christine McLawler (see Amini,
    Johari M.)

Laughlin, James 1914- DLB-48

Laumer, Keith 1925- DLB-8

Laurence, Margaret 1926-1987..................DLB-53

Laurents, Arthur 1918- DLB-26

Laurie, Annie (see Black, Winifred)

Lavin, Mary 1912- DLB-15

Lawless, Anthony (see MacDonald, Philip)

Lawrence, David 1888-1973.......................DLB-29

Lawrence, D. H. 1885-1930.................DLB-10, 19, 36

Lawson, John ?-1711 ....DLB-24

Lawson, Robert 1892-1957 ....DLB-22

Lawson, Victor F. 1850-1925 ....DLB-25

Lea, Henry Charles 1825-1909 ....DLB-47

Lea, Tom 1907- DLB-6

Leacock, John 1729-1802 ....DLB-31

Lear, Edward 1812-1888......................DLB-32

Leary, Timothy 1920- DLB-16

Leary, W. A., and Company DLB-49

Léautaud, Paul 1872-1956 ....DLB-65

Leavitt and Allen...............................DLB-49

Lécavelé, Roland (see Dorgelès, Roland)

Lechlitner, Ruth 1901- DLB-48

Leclerc, Félix 1914- DLB-60

Le Clézio, J. M. G. 1940- DLB-83

Lectures on Rhetoric and Belles Lettres (1783),
    by Hugh Blair [excerpts].............DLB-31

Leder, Rudolf (see Hermlin, Stephan)

Lederer, Charles 1910-1976................DLB-26

Ledwidge, Francis 1887-1917 ....DLB-20

Lee, Dennis 1939- DLB-53

Lee, Don L. (see Madhubuti, Haki R.)

Lee, George W. 1894-1976 ....DLB-51

Lee, Harper 1926- DLB-6

Lee, Harriet (1757-1851) and
    Lee, Sophia (1750-1824) DLB-39

Lee, Laurie 1914- DLB-27

Lee, Nathaniel circa 1645 - 1692 ....DLB-80

Lee, Vernon 1856-1935 ....DLB-57

Lee and Shepard DLB-49

Le Fanu, Joseph Sheridan 1814-1873 ....DLB-21, 70

Leffland, Ella 1931- Y-84

le Fort, Gertrud von 1876-1971 ....DLB-66

Le Gallienne, Richard 1866-1947 ....DLB-4

Legaré, Hugh Swinton 1797-1843 ....DLB-3, 59, 73

Legaré, James M. 1823-1859 ....DLB-3

Le Guin, Ursula K. 1929- DLB-8, 52

Lehman, Ernest 1920- DLB-44

Lehmann, John 1907- DLB-27

Lehmann, Rosamond 1901- DLB-15

Lehmann, Wilhelm 1882-1968 ....DLB-56

Leiber, Fritz 1910- DLB-8

Leinster, Murray 1896-1975 ....DLB-8

Leitch, Maurice 1933- DLB-14

Leland, Charles G. 1824-1903 ....DLB-11

L'Engle, Madeleine 1918- DLB-52

Lennart, Isobel 1915-1971 ....DLB-44

Lennox, Charlotte 1729 or 1730-1804 ....DLB-39

Lenski, Lois 1893-1974 ....DLB-22

Lenz, Hermann 1913- DLB-69

Lenz, Siegfried 1926- DLB-75

Leonard, Hugh 1926- DLB-13

Leonard, William Ellery 1876-1944 ....DLB-54

Le Queux, William 1864-1927.............DLB-70

Lerner, Max 1902- DLB-29

Lernet-Holenia, Alexander 1897-1976..............DLB-85

LeSieg, Theo. (see Geisel, Theodor Seuss)

Leslie, Frank 1821-1880......................DLB-43, 79

The Frank Leslie Publishing House DLB-49

Lessing, Bruno 1870-1940...................DLB-28

Lessing, Doris 1919- DLB-15; Y-85

Lettau, Reinhard 1929- DLB-75

Letter to [Samuel] Richardson on *Clarissa*
    (1748), by Henry Fielding............DLB-39

Lever, Charles 1806-1872 ....DLB-21

Levertov, Denise 1923- DLB-5

Levi, Peter 1931- DLB-40

Levien, Sonya 1888-1960 ....DLB-44

Levin, Meyer 1905-1981 ....DLB-9, 28; Y-81

Levine, Philip 1928- DLB-5

Levy, Benn Wolfe 1900-1973................DLB-13; Y-81

Lewes, George Henry 1817-1878 ....DLB-55

Lewis, Alfred H. 1857-1914................DLB-25

Lewis, Alun 1915-1944.......................DLB-20

Lewis, C. Day (see Day Lewis, C.)

Lewis, Charles B. 1842-1924................DLB-11

Lewis, C. S. 1898-1963 ....DLB-15

Lewis, Henry Clay 1825-1850 ....DLB-3

Lewis, Janet 1899- Y-87

Lewis, Matthew Gregory 1775-1818 ....DLB-39

Lewis, Richard circa 1700-1734 ....DLB-24

Lewis, Sinclair 1885-1951 ....DLB-9; DS-1

Lewis, Wyndham 1882-1957.................DLB-15

Lewisohn, Ludwig 1882-1955................DLB-4, 9, 28

The Library of America DLB-46

The Licensing Act of 1737....................DLB-84

Liebling, A. J. 1904-1963 ....DLB-4

Lieutenant Murray (see Ballou, Maturin Murray)

Lilar, Françoise (see Mallet-Joris, Françoise)

Lillo, George 1691-1739......................DLB-84

Lilly, Wait and Company DLB-49

Limited Editions Club DLB-46

Lincoln and Edmands DLB-49

Lindsay, Jack 1900- Y-84

Lindsay, Vachel 1879-1931......................DLB-54

Linebarger, Paul Myron Anthony (see
    Smith, Cordwainer)

Link, Arthur S. 1920- DLB-17

Linn, John Blair 1777-1804 ....DLB-37

Linton, Eliza Lynn 1822-1898......................DLB-18

Linton, William James 1812-1897 ....DLB-32

Lion Books......................DLB-46

Lionni, Leo 1910- DLB-61

Lippincott, J. B., Company DLB-49

Lippincott, Sara Jane Clarke 1823-1904............DLB-43

Lippmann, Walter 1889-1974 ....DLB-29

Lipton, Lawrence 1898-1975 ....DLB-16

Literary Documents: William Faulkner
    and the People-to-People Program Y-86

Literary Documents II: *Library Journal*–
    Statements and Questionnaires from
    First Novelists......................Y-87

Literary Effects of World War II
    [British novel] DLB-15

Literary Prizes [British] DLB-15

Literary Research Archives: The Humanities
    Research Center, University of Texas............Y-82

Literary Research Archives II: Berg
    Collection of English and American Literature
    of the New York Public Library......................Y-83

Literary Research Archives III:
    The Lilly Library......................Y-84

Literary Research Archives IV:
    The John Carter Brown Library......................Y-85

Literary Research Archives V:
    Kent State Special Collections......................Y-86

Literary Research Archives VI: The Modern
    Literary Manuscripts Collection in the
    Special Collections of the Washington
    University Libraries Y-87

"Literary Style" (1857), by William

Forsyth [excerpt]......................DLB-57

Literatura Chicanesca:
    The View From Without......................DLB-82

Literature at Nurse, or Circulating Morals (1885),
    by George Moore DLB-18

Littell, Eliakim 1797-1870......................DLB-79

Littell, Robert S. 1831-1896......................DLB-79

Little, Brown and Company......................DLB-49

Littlewood, Joan 1914- DLB-13

Lively, Penelope 1933- DLB-14

Livesay, Dorothy 1909- DLB-68

Livings, Henry 1929- DLB-13

Livingston, Anne Howe 1763-1841 ....DLB-37

Livingston, Myra Cohn 1926- DLB-61

Livingston, William 1723-1790 ....DLB-31

Lizárraga, Sylvia S. 1925- DLB-82

Llewellyn, Richard 1906-1983 ....DLB-15

Lobel, Arnold 1933- DLB-61

Lochridge, Betsy Hopkins (see Fancher, Betsy)

Locke, David Ross 1833-1888......................DLB-11, 23

Locke, John 1632-1704......................DLB-31

Locke, Richard Adams 1800-1871......................DLB-43

Locker-Lampson, Frederick 1821-1895............DLB-35

Lockridge, Ross, Jr. 1914-1948......................Y-80

Locrine and *Selimus*......................DLB-62

Lodge, David 1935- DLB-14

Lodge, George Cabot 1873-1909......................DLB-54

Lodge, Henry Cabot 1850-1924 ....DLB-47

Loeb, Harold 1891-1974 ....DLB-4

Logan, James 1674-1751 ....DLB-24

Logan, John 1923- DLB-5

Logue, Christopher 1926- DLB-27

London, Jack 1876-1916......................DLB-8, 12, 78

Long, H., and Brother DLB-49

Long, Haniel 1888-1956......................DLB-45

Longfellow, Henry Wadsworth 1807-1882 ....DLB-1, 59

Longfellow, Samuel 1819-1892......................DLB-1

Longley, Michael 1939- DLB-40

Longmans, Green and Company......................DLB-49

Longstreet, Augustus Baldwin
    1790-1870......................DLB-3, 11, 74

Longworth, D. [publishing house] DLB-49

Lonsdale, Frederick 1881-1954..........................DLB-10

A Look at the Contemporary Black Theatre
    Movement DLB-38

Loos, Anita 1893-1981.......................DLB-11, 26; Y-81

Lopate, Phillip 1943- Y-80

López, Diana (see Isabella, Ríos)

The Lord Chamberlain's Office and Stage
    Censorship in England................................DLB-10

Lorde, Audre 1934- DLB-41

Loring, A. K. [publishing house].......................DLB-49

Loring and Mussey....................................DLB-46

Lossing, Benson J. 1813-1891.........................DLB-30

Lothar, Ernst 1890-1974 ....DLB-81

Lothrop, D., and Company...............................DLB-49

Lothrop, Harriet M. 1844-1924.......................DLB-42

The Lounger, no. 20 (1785), by Henry
    Mackenzie...DLB-39

Lounsbury, Thomas R. 1838-1915 ....DLB-71

Lovell, John W., Company...............................DLB-49

Lovell, Coryell and Company DLB-49

Lovingood, Sut (see Harris, George Washington)

Low, Samuel 1765-? DLB-37

Lowell, Amy 1874-1925....................................DLB-54

Lowell, James Russell 1819-1891 ....DLB-1, 11, 64, 79

Lowell, Robert 1917-1977 ....DLB-5

Lowenfels, Walter 1897-1976............................DLB-4

Lowndes, Marie Belloc 1868-1947.....................DLB-70

Lowry, Lois 1937- DLB-52

Lowry, Malcolm 1909-1957..............................DLB-15

Lowther, Pat 1935-1975 ....DLB-53

Loy, Mina 1882-1966 ....DLB-4, 54

Lucas, Fielding, Jr. [publishing house]..............DLB-49

Luce, John W., and Company DLB-46

Lucie-Smith, Edward 1933- DLB-40

Ludlum, Robert 1927- Y-82

Ludwig, Jack 1922- DLB-60

Luke, Peter 1919- DLB-13

The F. M. Lupton Publishing Company DLB-49

Lurie, Alison 1926- DLB-2

Lyly, John circa 1554-1606 ....DLB-62

Lyon, Matthew 1749-1822................................DLB-43

Lytle, Andrew 1902- DLB-6

Lytton, Edward (see Bulwer-Lytton, Edward)

Lytton, Edward Robert Bulwer 1831-1891 ....DLB-32

M

Maass, Joachim 1901-1972 ....DLB-69

Mabie, Hamilton Wright 1845-1916...................DLB-71

Mac A'Ghobhainn, Iain (see Smith, Iain Crichton)

MacArthur, Charles 1895-1956................DLB-7, 25, 44

Macaulay, David 1945- DLB-61

Macaulay, Rose 1881-1958 ....DLB-36

Macaulay, Thomas Babington 1800-1859 ....DLB-32, 55

Macaulay Company DLB-46

MacBeth, George 1932- DLB-40

MacCaig, Norman 1910- DLB-27

MacDiarmid, Hugh 1892-1978 ....DLB-20

MacDonald, George 1824-1905 ....DLB-18

MacDonald, John D. 1916-1986 ....DLB-8; Y-86

MacDonald, Philip 1899?-1980 ....DLB-77

Macdonald, Ross (see Millar, Kenneth)

MacEwen, Gwendolyn 1941- DLB-53

Macfadden, Bernarr 1868-1955..........................DLB-25

Machen, Arthur Llewelyn Jones 1863-1947.......DLB-36

MacInnes, Colin 1914-1976 ....DLB-14

MacKaye, Percy 1875-1956 ....DLB-54

Macken, Walter 1915-1967................................DLB-13

Mackenzie, Compton 1883-1972........................DLB-34

Mackenzie, Henry 1745-1831 ....DLB-39

Mackey, William Wellington 1937- DLB-38

Mackintosh, Elizabeth (see Tey, Josephine)

MacLean, Katherine Anne 1925- DLB-8

MacLeish, Archibald 1892-1982.......DLB-4, 7, 45; Y-82

MacLennan, Hugh 1907- DLB-68

MacLeod, Alistair 1936- DLB-60

Macleod, Norman 1906- DLB-4

The Macmillan Company...................................DLB-49

MacNamara, Brinsley 1890-1963 ....DLB-10

MacNeice, Louis 1907-1963 ....DLB-10, 20

Macpherson, Jay 1931- DLB-53

Macpherson, Jeanie 1884-1946..........................DLB-44

Macrae Smith Company.....................................DLB-46

Macy-Masius...DLB-46

Madden, David 1933- DLB-6

Maddow, Ben 1909- DLB-44

Madgett, Naomi Long 1923- DLB-76

Madhubuti, Haki R. 1942-................DLB-5, 41

Madison, James 1751-1836 ....DLB-37

Mahan, Alfred Thayer 1840-1914.................DLB-47

Maheux-Forcier, Louise 1929- DLB-60

Mahin, John Lee 1902-1984 ....DLB-44

Mahon, Derek 1941- DLB-40

Mailer, Norman 1923-
          ....DLB-2, 16, 28; Y-80, 83; DS-3

Maillet, Adrienne 1885-1963 ....DLB-68

Maillet, Antonine 1929- DLB-60

Main Selections of the Book-of-the-Month Club,
    1926-1945 ....DLB-9

Main Trends in Twentieth-Century
    Book Clubs DLB-46

Mainwaring, Daniel 1902-1977 ....DLB-44

Major, André 1942- DLB-60

Major, Clarence 1936- DLB-33

Major, Kevin 1949- DLB-60

Major Books...DLB-46

Makemie, Francis circa 1658-1708.................DLB-24

The Making of a People,
    by J. M. Ritchie.....................................DLB-66

Malamud, Bernard 1914-1986 ....DLB-2, 28; Y-80, 86

Malleson, Lucy Beatrice (see Gilbert, Anthony)

Mallet-Joris, Françoise 1930- DLB-83

Mallock, W. H. 1849-1923 ....DLB-18, 57

Malone, Dumas 1892-1986..........................DLB-17

Malraux, André 1901-1976..........................DLB-72

Malzberg, Barry N. 1939- DLB-8

Mamet, David 1947- DLB-7

Mandel, Eli 1922- DLB-53

Mandiargues, André Pieyre de 1909- DLB-83

Manfred, Frederick 1912- DLB-6

Mangan, Sherry 1904-1961 ....DLB-4

Mankiewicz, Herman 1897-1953 ....DLB-26

Mankiewicz, Joseph L. 1909- DLB-44

Mankowitz, Wolf 1924- DLB-15

Manley, Delarivière 1672?-1724 ....DLB-39, 80

Mann, Abby 1927- DLB-44

Mann, Heinrich 1871-1950 ....DLB-66

Mann, Horace 1796-1859............................DLB-1

Mann, Klaus 1906-1949 ....DLB-56

Mann, Thomas 1875-1955 ....DLB-66

Manning, Marie 1873?-1945 ....DLB-29

Manning and Loring DLB-49

Mano, D. Keith 1942- DLB-6

Manor Books DLB-46

March, William 1893-1954............................DLB-9

Marchessault, Jovette 1938- DLB-60

Marcus, Frank 1928- DLB-13

Marek, Richard, Books.................................DLB-46

Marion, Frances 1886-1973..........................DLB-44

Marius, Richard C. 1933- Y-85

The Mark Taper Forum.................................DLB-7

Markfield, Wallace 1926- DLB-2, 28

Markham, Edwin 1852-1940.........................DLB-54

Markle, Fletcher 1921- DLB-68

Marlatt, Daphne 1942- DLB-60

Marlowe, Christopher 1564-1593 ....DLB-62

Marmion, Shakerley 1603-1639 ....DLB-58

Marquand, John P. 1893-1960.......................DLB-9

Marquis, Don 1878-1937.............................DLB-11, 25

Marriott, Anne 1913- DLB-68

Marryat, Frederick 1792-1848 ....DLB-21

Marsh, George Perkins 1801-1882 ....DLB-1, 64

Marsh, James 1794-1842..............................DLB-1, 59

Marsh, Capen, Lyon and Webb DLB-49

Marsh, Ngaio 1899-1982.............................DLB-77

Marshall, Edward 1932- DLB-16

Marshall, James 1942- DLB-61

Marshall, Paule 1929- DLB-33

Marshall, Tom 1938- DLB-60

Marston, John 1576-1634.............................DLB-58

Marston, Philip Bourke 1850-1887................DLB-35

Martens, Kurt 1870-1945 ....DLB-66

Martien, William S. [publishing house]..........DLB-49

Martin, Abe (see Hubbard, Kin)

Martin, Claire 1914- DLB-60

Martin du Gard, Roger 1881-1958.................DLB-65

Martineau, Harriet 1802-1876......................DLB-21, 55

Martínez, Max 1943- DLB-82

Martyn, Edward 1859-1923 ....DLB-10

Marvin X 1944- DLB-38

Marzials, Theo 1850-1920................................DLB-35

Masefield, John 1878-1967 ....DLB-10, 19

Mason, A. E. W. 1865-1948 ....DLB-70

Mason, Bobbie Ann 1940- Y-87

Mason Brothers..DLB-49

Massey, Gerald 1828-1907 ....DLB-32

Massinger, Philip 1583-1640 ....DLB-58

Masters, Edgar Lee 1868-1950 ....DLB-54

Mather, Cotton 1663-1728............................DLB-24, 30

Mather, Increase 1639-1723 ....DLB-24

Mather, Richard 1596-1669 ....DLB-24

Matheson, Richard 1926- DLB-8, 44

Matheus, John F. 1887- DLB-51

Mathews, Cornelius 1817?-1889 ....DLB-3, 64

Mathias, Roland 1915- DLB-27

Mathis, June 1892-1927 ....DLB-44

Mathis, Sharon Bell 1937- DLB-33

Matthews, Brander 1852-1929......................DLB-71, 78

Matthews, Jack 1925- DLB-6

Matthews, William 1942- DLB-5

Matthiessen, F. O. 1902-1950 ....DLB-63

Matthiessen, Peter 1927- DLB-6

Maugham, W. Somerset 1874-1965 ....DLB-10, 36, 77

Mauriac, Claude 1914- DLB-83

Mauriac, François 1885-1970...........................DLB-65

Maurice, Frederick Denison 1805-1872 ....DLB-55

Maurois, André 1885-1967 ....DLB-65

Maury, James 1718-1769..................................DLB-31

Mavor, Elizabeth 1927- DLB-14

Mavor, Osborne Henry (see Bridie, James)

Maxwell, H. [publishing house] DLB-49

Maxwell, William 1908- Y-80

May, Elaine 1932- DLB-44

May, Thomas 1595 or 1596-1650 ....DLB-58

Mayer, Mercer 1943- DLB-61

Mayer, O. B. 1818-1891 ....DLB-3

Mayes, Wendell 1919- DLB-26

Mayfield, Julian 1928-1984.......................DLB-33; Y-84

Mayhew, Henry 1812-1887...........................DLB-18, 55

Mayhew, Jonathan 1720-1766...........................DLB-31

Mayne, Seymour 1944- DLB-60

Mayor, Flora Macdonald 1872-1932....................DLB-36

Mayröcker, Friederike 1924- DLB-85

Mazursky, Paul 1930- DLB-44

McAlmon, Robert 1896-1956 ....DLB-4, 45

McBride, Robert M., and Company DLB-46

McCaffrey, Anne 1926- DLB-8

McCarthy, Cormac 1933- DLB-6

McCarthy, Mary 1912- DLB-2; Y-81

McCay, Winsor 1871-1934 ....DLB-22

McClatchy, C. K. 1858-1936 ....DLB-25

McClellan, George Marion 1860-1934 ....DLB-50

McCloskey, Robert 1914- DLB-22

McClure, Joanna 1930- DLB-16

McClure, Michael 1932- DLB-16

McClure, Phillips and Company........................DLB-46

McClurg, A. C., and Company DLB-49

McCluskey, John A., Jr. 1944- DLB-33

McCollum, Michael A. 1946...............................Y-87

McCord, David 1897- DLB-61

McCorkle, Jill 1958- Y-87

McCorkle, Samuel Eusebius 1746-1811 ....DLB-37

McCormick, Anne O'Hare 1880-1954................DLB-29

McCormick, Robert R. 1880-1955 ....DLB-29

McCoy, Horace 1897-1955...................................DLB-9

McCullagh, Joseph B. 1842-1896 ....DLB-23

McCullers, Carson 1917-1967.......................DLB-2, 7

McDonald, Forrest 1927- DLB-17

McDougall, Colin 1917-1984 ....DLB-68

McDowell, Obolensky DLB-46

McEwan, Ian 1948- DLB-14

McFadden, David 1940- DLB-60

McGahern, John 1934- DLB-14

McGeehan, W. O. 1879-1933.............................DLB-25

McGill, Ralph 1898-1969 ....DLB-29

McGinley, Phyllis 1905-1978......................DLB-11, 48

McGirt, James E. 1874-1930 ....DLB-50

McGough, Roger 1937- DLB-40

McGraw-Hill DLB-46

McGuane, Thomas 1939- DLB-2; Y-80

McGuckian, Medbh 1950- DLB-40

McGuffey, William Holmes 1800-1873 ....DLB-42

McIlvanney, William 1936- DLB-14

McIntyre, O. O. 1884-1938..........................DLB-25

McKay, Claude 1889-1948......................DLB-4, 45, 51

The David McKay Company........................DLB-49

McKean, William V. 1820-1903.......................DLB-23

McKinley, Robin 1952- DLB-52

McLaren, Floris Clark 1904-1978.......................DLB-68

McLaverty, Michael 1907- DLB-15

McLean, John R. 1848-1916 ....DLB-23

McLean, William L. 1852-1931..........................DLB-25

McLoughlin Brothers DLB-49

McMaster, John Bach 1852-1932......................DLB-47

McMurtry, Larry 1936- DLB-2; Y-80, 87

McNally, Terrence 1939- DLB-7

McNeil, Florence 1937- DLB-60

McNeile, Herman Cyril 1888-1937 ....DLB-77

McPherson, James Alan 1943- DLB-38

McPherson, Sandra 1943- Y-86

McWhirter, George 1939- DLB-60

Mead, Matthew 1924- DLB-40

Mead, Taylor ?- DLB-16

Medill, Joseph 1823-1899 ....DLB-43

Medoff, Mark 1940- DLB-7

Meek, Alexander Beaufort 1814-1865 ....DLB-3

Meinke, Peter 1932- DLB-5

Melançon, Robert 1947- DLB-60

Mell, Max 1882-1971..........................DLB-81

Meltzer, David 1937- DLB-16

Meltzer, Milton 1915- DLB-61

Melville, Herman 1819-1891 ....DLB-3, 74

Memoirs of Life and Literature (1920),
    by W. H. Mallock [excerpt]........................DLB-57

Mencken, H. L. 1880-1956 ....DLB-11, 29, 63

Méndez M., Miguel 1930- DLB-82

Mercer, Cecil William (see Yates, Dornford)

Mercer, David 1928-1980..........................DLB-13

Mercer, John 1704-1768 ....DLB-31

Meredith, George 1828-1909..................DLB-18, 35, 57

Meredith, Owen (see Lytton, Edward Robert Bulwer)

Meredith, William 1919- DLB-5

Meriwether, Louise 1923- DLB-33

Merriam, Eve 1916- DLB-61

The Merriam Company DLB-49

Merrill, James 1926- DLB-5; Y-85

Merrill and Baker........................DLB-49

The Mershon Company DLB-49

Merton, Thomas 1915-1968 ....DLB-48; Y-81

Merwin, W. S. 1927- DLB-5

Messner, Julian [publishing house]........................DLB-46

Metcalf, J. [publishing house] DLB-49

Metcalf, John 1938- DLB-60

The Methodist Book Concern DLB-49

Mew, Charlotte 1869-1928..........................DLB-19

Mewshaw, Michael 1943- Y-80

Meyer, E. Y. 1946- DLB-75

Meyer, Eugene 1875-1959 ....DLB-29

Meynell, Alice 1847-1922..........................DLB-19

Meyrink, Gustav 1868-1932 ....DLB-81

Micheaux, Oscar 1884-1951..........................DLB-50

Micheline, Jack 1929- DLB-16

Michener, James A. 1907?- DLB-6

Micklejohn, George circa 1717-1818 ....DLB-31

Middleton, Christopher 1926- DLB-40

Middleton, Stanley 1919- DLB-14

Middleton, Thomas 1580-1627..........................DLB-58

Miegel, Agnes 1879-1964..........................DLB-56

Miles, Josephine 1911-1985 ....DLB-48

Milius, John 1944- DLB-44

Mill, John Stuart 1806-1873 ....DLB-55

Millar, Kenneth 1915-1983 ....DLB-2; Y-83; DS-6

Millay, Edna St. Vincent 1892-1950 ....DLB-45

Miller, Arthur 1915- DLB-7

Miller, Caroline 1903- DLB-9

Miller, Eugene Ethelbert 1950- DLB-41

Miller, Henry 1891-1980 ....DLB-4, 9; Y-80

Miller, J. Hillis 1928- DLB-67

Miller, James [publishing house] DLB-49

Miller, Jason 1939- DLB-7

Miller, May 1899- DLB-41

Miller, Perry 1905-1963 ....DLB-17, 63

Miller, Walter M., Jr. 1923- DLB-8

Miller, Webb 1892-1940 ....DLB-29

Millhauser, Steven 1943- DLB-2

Millican, Arthenia J. Bates 1920- DLB-38

Milne, A. A. 1882-1956................................DLB-10, 77

Milner, Ron 1938- DLB-38

Milnes, Richard Monckton (Lord Houghton)
    1809-1885 ....DLB-32

Minton, Balch and Company.............................DLB-46

Miron, Gaston 1928- DLB-60

Mitchel, Jonathan 1624-1668 ....DLB-24

Mitchell, Adrian 1932- DLB-40

Mitchell, Donald Grant 1822-1908 ....DLB-1

Mitchell, Gladys 1901-1983................................DLB-77

Mitchell, James Leslie 1901-1935........................DLB-15

Mitchell, John (see Slater, Patrick)

Mitchell, John Ames 1845-1918.........................DLB-79

Mitchell, Julian 1935- DLB-14

Mitchell, Ken 1940- DLB-60

Mitchell, Langdon 1862-1935 ....DLB-7

Mitchell, Loften 1919- DLB-38

Mitchell, Margaret 1900-1949.............................DLB-9

Mitterer, Erika 1906- DLB-85

Modern Age Books DLB-46

"Modern English Prose" (1876),
    by George Saintsbury DLB-57

The Modern Language Association of America
    Celebrates Its Centennial Y-84

The Modern Library DLB-46

Modern Novelists–Great and Small (1855), by
    Margaret Oliphant.......................................DLB-21

"Modern Style" (1857), by Cockburn
    Thomson [excerpt]......................................DLB-57

The Modernists (1932), by Joseph Warren
    Beach..DLB-36

Modiano, Patrick 1945- DLB-83

Moffat, Yard and Company DLB-46

Monkhouse, Allan 1858-1936 ....DLB-10

Monro, Harold 1879-1932 ....DLB-19

Monroe, Harriet 1860-1936...............................DLB-54

Monsarrat, Nicholas 1910-1979 ....DLB-15

Montague, John 1929- DLB-40

Montgomery, John 1919- DLB-16

Montgomery, Marion 1925- DLB-6

Montherlant, Henry de 1896-1972....................DLB-72

Moody, Joshua circa 1633-1697..........................DLB-24

Moody, William Vaughn 1869-1910..............DLB-7, 54

Moorcock, Michael 1939- DLB-14

Moore, Catherine L. 1911- DLB-8

Moore, Clement Clarke 1779-1863....................DLB-42

Moore, George 1852-1933......................DLB-10, 18, 57

Moore, Marianne 1887-1972 ....DLB-45

Moore, T. Sturge 1870-1944 ....DLB-19

Moore, Ward 1903-1978 ....DLB-8

Moore, Wilstach, Keys and Company DLB-49

The Moorland-Spingarn
    Research Center DLB-76

Moraga, Cherríe 1952- DLB-82

Morales, Alejandro 1944- DLB-82

Morency, Pierre 1942- DLB-60

Morgan, Berry 1919- DLB-6

Morgan, Charles 1894-1958................................DLB-34

Morgan, Edmund S. 1916- DLB-17

Morgan, Edwin 1920- DLB-27

Morgner, Irmtraud 1933- DLB-75

Morison, Samuel Eliot 1887-1976......................DLB-17

Morley, Christopher 1890-1957...........................DLB-9

Morley, John 1838-1923................................DLB-57

Morris, George Pope 1802-1864........................DLB-73

Morris, Lewis 1833-1907 ....DLB-35

Morris, Richard B. 1904- DLB-17

Morris, William 1834-1896....................DLB-18, 35, 57

Morris, Willie 1934- Y-80

Morris, Wright 1910- DLB-2; Y-81

Morrison, Arthur 1863-1945 ....DLB-70

Morrison, Toni 1931- DLB-6, 33; Y-81

Morrow, William, and Company DLB-46

Morse, James Herbert 1841-1923......................DLB-71

Morse, Jedidiah 1761-1826 ....DLB-37

Morse, John T., Jr. 1840-1937...........................DLB-47

Mortimer, John 1923- DLB-13

Morton, John P., and Company DLB-49

Morton, Nathaniel 1613-1685 ....DLB-24

Morton, Sarah Wentworth 1759-1846 ....DLB-37

Morton, Thomas circa 1579-circa 1647 ....DLB-24

Mosley, Nicholas 1923- DLB-14

Moss, Arthur 1889-1969 ....DLB-4

Moss, Howard 1922- DLB-5

The Most Powerful Book Review in America
    [*New York Times Book Review*] Y-82

Motion, Andrew 1952- DLB-40

Motley, John Lothrop 1814-1877 ....DLB-1, 30, 59

Motley, Willard 1909-1965.................................DLB-76

Motteux, Peter Anthony 1663-1718 ....DLB-80

Mottram, R. H. 1883-1971.................................DLB-36

Mouré, Erin 1955- DLB-60

Movies from Books, 1920-1974 ....DLB-9

Mowat, Farley 1921- DLB-68

Mowrer, Edgar Ansel 1892-1977.......................DLB-29

Mowrer, Paul Scott 1887-1971 ....DLB-29

Mucedorus...DLB-62

Muhajir, El (see Marvin X)

Muhajir, Nazzam Al Fitnah (see Marvin X)

Muir, Edwin 1887-1959......................................DLB-20

Muir, Helen 1937- DLB-14

Mukherjee, Bharati 1940- DLB-60

Muldoon, Paul 1951- DLB-40

Mumford, Lewis 1895- DLB-63

Munby, Arthur Joseph 1828-1910......................DLB-35

Munday, Anthony 1560-1633 ....DLB-62

Munford, Robert circa 1737-1783 ....DLB-31

Munro, Alice 1931- DLB-53

Munro, George [publishing house].....................DLB-49

Munro, H. H. 1870-1916 ....DLB-34

Munro, Norman L. [publishing house] DLB-49

Munroe, James, and Company DLB-49

Munroe, Kirk 1850-1930 ....DLB-42

Munroe and Francis DLB-49

Munsell, Joel [publishing house].........................DLB-49

Munsey, Frank A. 1854-1925..............................DLB-25

Munsey, Frank A., and Company.......................DLB-49

Murdoch, Iris 1919- DLB-14

Murfree, Mary N. 1850-1922 ....DLB-12, 74

Muro, Amado 1915-1971....................................DLB-82

Murphy, Beatrice M. 1908- DLB-76

Murphy, John, and Company............................DLB-49

Murphy, Richard 1927- DLB-40

Murray, Albert L. 1916- DLB-38

Murray, Gilbert 1866-1957 ....DLB-10

Murray, Judith Sargent 1751-1820....................DLB-37

Murray, Pauli 1910-1985...................................DLB-41

Muschg, Adolf 1934- DLB-75

Musil, Robert 1880-1942....................................DLB-81

Mussey, Benjamin B., and Company.................DLB-49

Myers, Gustavus 1872-1942 ....DLB-47

Myers, L. H. 1881-1944 ....DLB-15

Myers, Walter Dean 1937- DLB-33

N

Nabbes, Thomas circa 1605-1641 ....DLB-58

Nabl, Franz 1883-1974......................................DLB-81

Nabokov, Vladimir 1899-1977 ....DLB-2; Y-80; DS-3

Nabokov Festival at Cornell...................................Y-83

Nafis and Cornish..DLB-49

Naipaul, Shiva 1945-1985......................................Y-85

Naipaul, V. S. 1932- Y-85

Nancrede, Joseph [publishing house].................DLB-49

Nasby, Petroleum Vesuvius (see Locke, David Ross)

Nash, Ogden 1902-1971.....................................DLB-11

Nathan, Robert 1894-1985..................................DLB-9

The National Jewish Book Awards.........................Y-85

The National Theatre and the Royal Shakespeare
    Company: The National Companies...........DLB-13

Naughton, Bill 1910- DLB-13

Neagoe, Peter 1881-1960 ....DLB-4

Neal, John 1793-1876 ....DLB-1, 59

Neal, Joseph C. 1807-1847.................................DLB-11

Neal, Larry 1937-1981 ....DLB-38

The Neale Publishing Company DLB-49

Neely, F. Tennyson [publishing house] DLB-49

"The Negro as a Writer," by
    G. M. McClellan DLB-50

"Negro Poets and Their Poetry," by
  Wallace Thurman DLB-50

Neihardt, John G. 1881-1973 ....DLB-9, 54

Nelson, Alice Moore Dunbar
  1875-1935 ....DLB-50

Nelson, Thomas, and Sons....................DLB-49

Nelson, William Rockhill 1841-1915 ....DLB-23

Nemerov, Howard 1920- DLB-5, 6; Y-83

Ness, Evaline 1911-1986....................................DLB-61

Neugeboren, Jay 1938- DLB-28

Neumann, Alfred 1895-1952 ....DLB-56

Nevins, Allan 1890-1971 ....DLB-17

The New American Library.............................DLB-46

New Directions Publishing Corporation............DLB-46

A New Edition of *Huck Finn* Y-85

New Forces at Work in the American Theatre:
  1915-1925 ....DLB-7

New Literary Periodicals: A Report
  for 1987.....................................Y-87

New Literary Periodicals: A Report
  for 1988.....................................Y-88

The New *Ulysses* Y-84

The New Variorum Shakespeare............................Y-85

A New Voice: The Center for the Book's First
  Five Years Y-83

The New Wave [Science Fiction] DLB-8

Newbolt, Henry 1862-1938................................DLB-19

Newbound, Bernard Slade (see Slade, Bernard)

Newby, P. H. 1918- DLB-15

Newcomb, Charles King 1820-1894 ....DLB-1

Newell, Peter 1862-1924 ....DLB-42

Newell, Robert Henry 1836-1901.....................DLB-11

Newman, David (see Benton, Robert)

Newman, Frances 1883-1928 ....Y-80

Newman, John Henry 1801-1890 ....DLB-18, 32, 55

Newman, Mark [publishing house]....................DLB-49

Newsome, Effie Lee 1885-1979 ....DLB-76

Newspaper Syndication of American Humor....DLB-11

Nichol, B. P. 1944- DLB-53

Nichols, Dudley 1895-1960 ....DLB-26

Nichols, John 1940- Y-82

Nichols, Mary Sargeant (Neal) Gove
  1810-1884 ....DLB-1

Nichols, Peter 1927- DLB-13

Nichols, Roy F. 1896-1973 ....DLB-17

Nichols, Ruth 1948- DLB-60

Nicholson, Norman 1914- DLB-27

Ní Chuilleanáin, Eiléan 1942- DLB-40

Nicol, Eric 1919- DLB-68

Nicolay, John G. 1832-1901 and
  Hay, John 1838-1905 ....DLB-47

Niebuhr, Reinhold 1892-1971 ....DLB-17

Niedecker, Lorine 1903-1970 ....DLB-48

Nieman, Lucius W. 1857-1935...........................DLB-25

Niggli, Josefina 1910- Y-80

Niles, Hezekiah 1777-1839 ....DLB-43

Nims, John Frederick 1913- DLB-5

Nin, Anaïs 1903-1977....................................DLB-2, 4

1985: The Year of the Mystery:
  A Symposium....................................Y-85

Nissenson, Hugh 1933- DLB-28

Niven, Larry 1938- DLB-8

Nizan, Paul 1905-1940 ....DLB-72

Nobel Peace Prize
  The 1986 Nobel Peace Prize
    Nobel Lecture 1986: Hope, Despair
    and Memory
    Tributes from Abraham Bernstein,
      Norman Lamm, and John R. Silber Y-86

The Nobel Prize and Literary
  Politics...................................Y-88

Nobel Prize in Literature
  The 1982 Nobel Prize in Literature
    Announcement by the Swedish Academy
      of the Nobel Prize
    Nobel Lecture 1982: The Solitude of Latin
      America
    Excerpt from *One Hundred Years
      of Solitude*
    The Magical World of Macondo
    A Tribute to Gabriel García Márquez Y-82
  The 1983 Nobel Prize in Literature
    Announcement by the Swedish
      Academy
    Nobel Lecture 1983
    The Stature of William Golding...............Y-83
  The 1984 Nobel Prize in Literature
    Announcement by the Swedish
      Academy

Jaroslav Seifert Through the Eyes of the
  English-Speaking Reader
    Three Poems by Jaroslav Seifert Y-84

The 1985 Nobel Prize in Literature
  Announcement by the Swedish
  Academy
    Nobel Lecture 1985 ....Y-85

The 1986 Nobel Prize in Literature
  Nobel Lecture 1986: This Past Must
    Address Its Present Y-86

The 1987 Nobel Prize in Literature
  Nobel Lecture 1987 ....Y-87

The 1988 Nobel Prize in Literature
  Nobel Lecture 1988 ....Y-88

Noel, Roden 1834-1894 ....DLB-35

Nolan, William F. 1928- DLB-8

Noland, C. F. M. 1810?-1858 ....DLB-11

Noonday Press DLB-46

Noone, John 1936- DLB-14

Nordhoff, Charles 1887-1947 ....DLB-9

Norman, Marsha 1947- Y-84

Norris, Charles G. 1881-1945 ....DLB-9

Norris, Frank 1870-1902 ....DLB-12

Norris, Leslie 1921- DLB-27

Norse, Harold 1916- DLB-16

North Point Press DLB-46

Norton, Alice Mary (see Norton, Andre)

Norton, Andre 1912- DLB-8, 52

Norton, Andrews 1786-1853 ....DLB-1

Norton, Caroline 1808-1877 ....DLB-21

Norton, Charles Eliot 1827-1908 ....DLB-1, 64

Norton, John 1606-1663 ....DLB-24

Norton, Thomas (see Sackville, Thomas)

Norton, W. W., and Company DLB-46

Nossack, Hans Erich 1901-1977 ....DLB-69

A Note on Technique (1926), by Elizabeth
  A. Drew [excerpts] DLB-36

Nourse, Alan E. 1928- DLB-8

The Novel in [Robert Browning's] "The Ring
  and the Book" (1912), by Henry James DLB-32

The Novel of Impressionism,
  by Jethro Bithell DLB-66

Novel-Reading: *The Works of Charles Dickens,
  The Works of W. Makepeace Thackeray* (1879),
  by Anthony Trollope DLB-21

The Novels of Dorothy Richardson (1918), by
  May Sinclair DLB-36

Novels with a Purpose (1864),
  by Justin M'Carthy DLB-21

Nowlan, Alden 1933-1983 ....DLB-53

Noyes, Alfred 1880-1958 ....DLB-20

Noyes, Crosby S. 1825-1908 ....DLB-23

Noyes, Nicholas 1647-1717 ....DLB-24

Noyes, Theodore W. 1858-1946 ....DLB-29

Nugent, Frank 1908-1965 ....DLB-44

Nye, Edgar Wilson (Bill) 1850-1896 ....DLB-11, 23

Nye, Robert 1939- DLB-14

O

Oakes, Urian circa 1631-1681 ....DLB-24

Oates, Joyce Carol 1938- DLB-2, 5; Y-81

Oberholtzer, Ellis Paxson 1868-1936 ....DLB-47

O'Brien, Edna 1932- DLB-14

O'Brien, Fitz-James 1828-1862 ....DLB-74

O'Brien, Kate 1897-1974 ....DLB-15

O'Brien, Tim 1946- Y-80

O'Casey, Sean 1880-1964 ....DLB-10

Ochs, Adolph S. 1858-1935 ....DLB-25

O'Connor, Flannery 1925-1964 ....DLB-2; Y-80

O'Dell, Scott 1903- DLB-52

Odell, Jonathan 1737-1818 ....DLB-31

Odets, Clifford 1906-1963 ....DLB-7, 26

O'Faolain, Julia 1932- DLB-14

O'Faolain, Sean 1900- DLB-15

O'Flaherty, Liam 1896-1984 ....DLB-36; Y-84

Off Broadway and Off-Off-Broadway DLB-7

Off-Loop Theatres DLB-7

Offord, Carl Ruthven 1910- DLB-76

Ogilvie, J. S., and Company DLB-49

O'Grady, Desmond 1935- DLB-40

O'Hagan, Howard 1902-1982 ....DLB-68

O'Hara, Frank 1926-1966 ....DLB-5, 16

O'Hara, John 1905-1970 ....DLB-9; DS-2

O. Henry (see Porter, William Sydney)

Old Franklin Publishing House DLB-49

Older, Fremont 1856-1935 ....DLB-25

Oliphant, Laurence 1829?-1888........................DLB-18

Oliphant, Margaret 1828-1897 ....DLB-18

Oliver, Chad 1928- DLB-8

Oliver, Mary 1935- DLB-5

Ollier, Claude 1922- DLB-83

Olsen, Tillie 1913?- DLB-28; Y-80

Olson, Charles 1910-1970............................DLB-5, 16

Olson, Elder 1909- DLB-48, 63

On Art in Fiction (1838), by
    Edward Bulwer..DLB-21

On Learning to Write...Y-88

On Some of the Characteristics of Modern
    Poetry and On the Lyrical Poems of Alfred
    Tennyson (1831), by Arthur Henry
    Hallam DLB-32

"On Style in English Prose" (1898), by Frederic
    Harrison..DLB-57

"On Style in Literature: Its Technical Elements"
    (1885), by Robert Louis Stevenson..............DLB-57

"On the Writing of Essays" (1862),
    by Alexander Smith......................................DLB-57

Ondaatje, Michael 1943- DLB-60

O'Neill, Eugene 1888-1953 ....DLB-7

Oppen, George 1908-1984..............................DLB-5

Oppenheim, E. Phillips 1866-1946...................DLB-70

Oppenheim, James 1882-1932.........................DLB-28

Oppenheimer, Joel 1930- DLB-5

Optic, Oliver (see Adams, William Taylor)

Orczy, Emma, Baroness 1865-1947...................DLB-70

Orlovitz, Gil 1918-1973...............................DLB-2, 5

Orlovsky, Peter 1933- DLB-16

Ormond, John 1923- DLB-27

Ornitz, Samuel 1890-1957 ....DLB-28, 44

Orton, Joe 1933-1967....................................DLB-13

Orwell, George 1903-1950.............................DLB-15

The Orwell Year Y-84

Osbon, B. S. 1827-1912..................................DLB-43

Osborne, John 1929- DLB-13

Osgood, Herbert L. 1855-1918........................DLB-47

Osgood, James R., and Company.....................DLB-49

O'Shaughnessy, Arthur 1844-1881...................DLB-35

O'Shea, Patrick [publishing house]....................DLB-49

Oswald, Eleazer 1755-1795 ....DLB-43

Otero, Miguel Antonio 1859-1944 ....DLB-82

Otis, James (see Kaler, James Otis)

Otis, James, Jr. 1725-1783 ....DLB-31

Otis, Broaders and Company...........................DLB-49

Ottendorfer, Oswald 1826-1900 ....DLB-23

Otway, Thomas 1652-1685 ....DLB-80

Ouellette, Fernand 1930- DLB-60

Ouida 1839-1908..DLB-18

Outing Publishing Company DLB-46

Outlaw Days, by Joyce Johnson.........................DLB-16

The Overlook Press...DLB-46

Overview of U.S. Book Publishing, 1910-1945....DLB-9

Owen, Guy 1925- DLB-5

Owen, John [publishing house].........................DLB-49

Owen, Wilfred 1893-1918...............................DLB-20

Owsley, Frank L. 1890-1956 ....DLB-17

Ozick, Cynthia 1928- DLB-28; Y-82

P

Pack, Robert 1929- DLB-5

Packaging Papa: *The Garden of Eden* Y-86

Padell Publishing Company DLB-46

Padgett, Ron 1942- DLB-5

Page, L. C., and Company DLB-49

Page, P. K. 1916- DLB-68

Page, Thomas Nelson 1853-1922 ....DLB-12, 78

Page, Walter Hines 1855-1918........................DLB-71

Paget, Violet (see Lee, Vernon)

Pain, Philip ?-circa 1666.................................DLB-24

Paine, Robert Treat, Jr. 1773-1811 ....DLB-37

Paine, Thomas 1737-1809 ....DLB-31, 43, 73

Paley, Grace 1922- DLB-28

Palfrey, John Gorham 1796-1881..................DLB-1, 30

Palgrave, Francis Turner 1824-1897 ....DLB-35

Paltock, Robert 1697-1767.............................DLB-39

Panama, Norman 1914-   and
    Frank, Melvin 1913-1988 ....DLB-26

Pangborn, Edgar 1909-1976 ....DLB-8

"Panic Among the Philistines": A Postscript,
An Interview with Bryan Griffin Y-81

Panneton, Philippe (see Ringuet)

Panshin, Alexei 1940- DLB-8

Pansy (see Alden, Isabella)

Pantheon Books DLB-46

Paperback Library DLB-46

Paperback Science Fiction DLB-8

Paquet, Alfons 1881-1944 ....DLB-66

Paradis, Suzanne 1936- DLB-53

Parents' Magazine Press DLB-46

Parisian Theater, Fall 1984: Toward
A New Baroque Y-85

Parizeau, Alice 1930- DLB-60

Parke, John 1754-1789 ....DLB-31

Parker, Dorothy 1893-1967 ....DLB-11, 45

Parker, James 1714-1770 ....DLB-43

Parker, Theodore 1810-1860 ....DLB-1

Parkman, Francis, Jr. 1823-1893 ....DLB-1, 30

Parks, Gordon 1912- DLB-33

Parks, William 1698-1750 ....DLB-43

Parks, William [publishing house] DLB-49

Parley, Peter (see Goodrich, Samuel Griswold)

Parrington, Vernon L. 1871-1929 ....DLB-17, 63

Parton, James 1822-1891 ....DLB-30

Parton, Sara Payson Willis 1811-1872..........DLB-43, 74

Pastan, Linda 1932- DLB-5

Pastorius, Francis Daniel 1651-circa 1720 ....DLB-24

Patchen, Kenneth 1911-1972.....................DLB-16, 48

Pater, Walter 1839-1894...................................DLB-57

Paterson, Katherine 1932- DLB-52

Patmore, Coventry 1823-1896 ....DLB-35

Paton, Joseph Noel 1821-1901..........................DLB-35

Patrick, John 1906- DLB-7

Pattee, Fred Lewis 1863-1950..........................DLB-71

Pattern and Paradigm: History as
Design, by Judith Ryan DLB-75

Patterson, Eleanor Medill 1881-1948 ....DLB-29

Patterson, Joseph Medill 1879-1946.............DLB-29

Pattillo, Henry 1726-1801................................DLB-37

Paul, Elliot 1891-1958 ....DLB-4

Paul, Peter, Book Company DLB-49

Paulding, James Kirke 1778-1860 ....DLB-3, 59, 74

Paulin, Tom 1949- DLB-40

Pauper, Peter, Press...DLB-46

Paxton, John 1911-1985 ....DLB-44

Payn, James 1830-1898....................................DLB-18

Payne, John 1842-1916.....................................DLB-35

Payne, John Howard 1791-1852 ....DLB-37

Payson and Clarke DLB-46

Peabody, Elizabeth Palmer 1804-1894.................DLB-1

Peabody, Elizabeth Palmer [publishing
house]..DLB-49

Peabody, Oliver William Bourn 1799-1848 ....DLB-59

Peachtree Publishers, Limited..........................DLB-46

Pead, Deuel ?-1727 ....DLB-24

Peake, Mervyn 1911-1968 ....DLB-15

Pearson, H. B. [publishing house] DLB-49

Peck, George W. 1840-1916........................DLB-23, 42

Peck, H. C., and Theo. Bliss [publishing
house]..DLB-49

Peck, Harry Thurston 1856-1914 ....DLB-71

Peele, George 1556-1596..................................DLB-62

Pellegrini and Cudahy.......................................DLB-46

Pemberton, Sir Max 1863-1950 ....DLB-70

Penguin Books DLB-46

Penn Publishing Company DLB-49

Penn, William 1644-1718 ....DLB-24

Penner, Jonathan 1940- Y-83

Pennington, Lee 1939- Y-82

Percy, Walker 1916- DLB-2; Y-80

Perec, Georges 1936-1982.................................DLB-83

Perelman, S. J. 1904-1979............................DLB-11, 44

Periodicals of the Beat Generation DLB-16

Perkins, Eugene 1932- DLB-41

Perkoff, Stuart Z. 1930-1974............................DLB-16

Permabooks..DLB-46

Perry, Bliss 1860-1954......................................DLB-71

Perry, Eleanor 1915-1981.................................DLB-44

"Personal Style" (1890), by John Addington
Symonds...DLB-57

Perutz, Leo 1882-1957......................................DLB-81

Peter, Laurence J. 1919- DLB-53

Peterkin, Julia 1880-1961.................................DLB-9

Petersham, Maud 1889-1971 and
      Petersham, Miska 1888-1960 ....DLB-22

Peterson, Charles Jacobs 1819-1887 ....DLB-79

Peterson, Louis 1922- DLB-76

Peterson, T. B., and Brothers DLB-49

Petry, Ann 1908- DLB-76

Pharr, Robert Deane 1916- DLB-33

Phelps, Elizabeth Stuart 1844-1911 ....DLB-74

Philippe, Charles-Louis 1874-1909....................DLB-65

Phillips, David Graham 1867-1911...............DLB-9, 12

Phillips, Jayne Anne 1952- Y-80

Phillips, Stephen 1864-1915..............................DLB-10

Phillips, Ulrich B. 1877-1934..............................DLB-17

Phillips, Willard 1784-1873...............................DLB-59

Phillips, Sampson and Company DLB-49

Phillpotts, Eden 1862-1960..........................DLB-10, 70

Philosophical Library....................................DLB-46

"The Philosophy of Style" (1852), by
      Herbert Spencer...DLB-57

Phinney, Elihu [publishing house].....................DLB-49

Phoenix, John (see Derby, George Horatio)

PHYLON (Fourth Quarter, 1950),
      The Negro in Literature:
      The Current Scene....................................DLB-76

Pickard, Tom 1946- DLB-40

Pictorial Printing Company............................DLB-49

Pike, Albert 1809-1891.................................DLB-74

Pilon, Jean-Guy 1930- DLB-60

Pinckney, Josephine 1895-1957 ....DLB-6

Pinero, Arthur Wing 1855-1934.........................DLB-10

Pinget, Robert 1919- DLB-83

Pinnacle Books...DLB-46

Pinsky, Robert 1940- Y-82

Pinter, Harold 1930- DLB-13

Piontek, Heinz 1925- DLB-75

Piper, H. Beam 1904-1964 ....DLB-8

Piper, Watty DLB-22

Pisar, Samuel 1929- Y-83

Pitkin, Timothy 1766-1847 ....DLB-30

The Pitt Poetry Series: Poetry

Publishing Today Y-85

Pitter, Ruth 1897- DLB-20

Pix, Mary 1666-1709 ....DLB-80

The Place of Realism in Fiction (1895), by
      George Gissing...DLB-18

Plante, David 1940- Y-83

Plath, Sylvia 1932-1963 ....DLB-5, 6

Platt and Munk Company DLB-46

Playboy Press...DLB-46

Plays, Playwrights, and Playgoers......................DLB-84

Playwrights and Professors, by Tom
      Stoppard DLB-13

Playwrights on the Theater DLB-80

Plenzdorf, Ulrich 1934- DLB-75

Plessen, Elizabeth 1944- DLB-75

Plievier, Theodor 1892-1955 ....DLB-69

Plomer, William 1903-1973................................DLB-20

Plumly, Stanley 1939- DLB-5

Plumpp, Sterling D. 1940- DLB-41

Plunkett, James 1920- DLB-14

Plymell, Charles 1935- DLB-16

Pocket Books...DLB-46

Poe, Edgar Allan 1809-1849...............DLB-3, 59, 73, 74

Poe, James 1921-1980.....................................DLB-44

The Poet Laureate of the United States
      Statements from Former Consultants
      in Poetry...Y-86

Pohl, Frederik 1919- DLB-8

Poirier, Louis (see Gracq, Julien)

Poliakoff, Stephen 1952- DLB-13

Polite, Carlene Hatcher 1932- DLB-33

Pollard, Edward A. 1832-1872............................DLB-30

Pollard, Percival 1869-1911 ....DLB-71

Pollard and Moss DLB-49

Pollock, Sharon 1936- DLB-60

Polonsky, Abraham 1910- DLB-26

Poole, Ernest 1880-1950....................................DLB-9

Poore, Benjamin Perley 1820-1887.....................DLB-23

Popular Library...DLB-46

Porlock, Martin (see MacDonald, Philip)

Porter, Eleanor H. 1868-1920.............................DLB-9

Porter, Henry ?-? DLB-62

Porter, Katherine Anne 1890-1980........DLB-4, 9; Y-80

Porter, Peter 1929- DLB-40

Porter, William Sydney 1862-1910........DLB-12, 78, 79

Porter, William T. 1809-1858.......................DLB-3, 43

Porter and Coates DLB-49

Portis, Charles 1933- DLB-6

Poston, Ted 1906-1974......................................DLB-51

Postscript to [the Third Edition of] *Clarissa*
(1751), by Samuel Richardson DLB-39

Potok, Chaim 1929- DLB-28; Y-84

Potter, David M. 1910-1971 ....DLB-17

Potter, John E., and Company DLB-49

Pottle, Frederick A. 1897-1987 ....Y-87

Poulin, Jacques 1937- DLB-60

Pound, Ezra 1885-1972......................DLB-4, 45, 63

Powell, Anthony 1905- DLB-15

Pownall, David 1938- DLB-14

Powys, John Cowper 1872-1963 ....DLB-15

Powys, T. F. 1875-1953 ....DLB-36

The Practice of Biography: An Interview with
Stanley Weintraub...Y-82

The Practice of Biography II: An Interview with
B. L. Reid...Y-83

The Practice of Biography III: An Interview with
Humphrey Carpenter Y-84

The Practice of Biography IV: An Interview with
William Manchester..Y-85

The Practice of Biography V: An Interview with
Justin Kaplan Y-86

The Practice of Biography VI: An Interview with
David Herbert Donald Y-87

Praeger Publishers...DLB-46

Pratt, Samuel Jackson 1749-1814 ....DLB-39

Preface to *Alwyn* (1780), by Thomas
Holcroft..DLB-39

Preface to *Colonel Jack* (1722), by Daniel
Defoe...DLB-39

Preface to *Evelina* (1778), by Fanny Burney.......DLB-39

Preface to *Ferdinand Count Fathom* (1753), by
Tobias Smollett DLB-39

Preface to *Incognita* (1692), by William
Congreve..DLB-39

Preface to *Joseph Andrews* (1742), by
Henry Fielding DLB-39

Preface to *Moll Flanders* (1722), by Daniel
Defoe...DLB-39

Preface to *Poems* (1853), by Matthew
Arnold...DLB-32

Preface to *Robinson Crusoe* (1719), by Daniel
Defoe...DLB-39

Preface to *Roderick Random* (1748), by Tobias
Smollett...DLB-39

Preface to *Roxana* (1724), by Daniel Defoe DLB-39

Preface to *St. Leon* (1799),
by William Godwin...DLB-39

Preface to Sarah Fielding's *Familiar Letters*
(1747), by Henry Fielding [excerpt].............DLB-39

Preface to Sarah Fielding's *The Adventures of
David Simple* (1744), by Henry Fielding.......DLB-39

Preface to *The Cry* (1754), by Sarah Fielding DLB-39

Preface to *The Delicate Distress* (1769), by
Elizabeth Griffin...DLB-39

Preface to *The Disguis'd Prince* (1733), by Eliza
Haywood [excerpt] DLB-39

Preface to *The Farther Adventures of Robinson
Crusoe* (1719), by Daniel Defoe DLB-39

Preface to the First Edition of *Pamela* (1740), by
Samuel Richardson...DLB-39

Preface to the First Edition of *The Castle of
Otranto* (1764), by Horace Walpole..............DLB-39

Preface to *The History of Romances* (1715), by
Pierre Daniel Huet [excerpts]........................DLB-39

Preface to *The Life of Charlotta du Pont* (1723),
by Penelope Aubin DLB-39

Preface to *The Old English Baron* (1778), by
Clara Reeve...DLB-39

Preface to the Second Edition of *The Castle of
Otranto* (1765), by Horace Walpole..............DLB-39

Preface to *The Secret History, of Queen Zarah, and
the Zarazians* (1705), by Delarivière
Manley...DLB-39

Preface to the Third Edition of *Clarissa* (1751),
by Samuel Richardson [excerpt]..................DLB-39

Preface to *The Works of Mrs. Davys* (1725), by
Mary Davys...DLB-39

Preface to Volume 1 of *Clarissa* (1747), by
Samuel Richardson...DLB-39

Preface to Volume 3 of *Clarissa* (1748), by
Samuel Richardson...DLB-39

Préfontaine, Yves 1937- DLB-53

Prelutsky, Jack 1940- DLB-61

Premisses, by Michael Hamburger DLB-66

Prentice, George D. 1802-1870.........................DLB-43

Prentice-Hall DLB-46

Prescott, William Hickling 1796-1859......DLB-1, 30, 59

The Present State of the English Novel (1892),
    by George Saintsbury DLB-18

Preston, Thomas 1537-1598 ....DLB-62

Price, Reynolds 1933- DLB-2

Price, Richard 1949- Y-81

Priest, Christopher 1943- DLB-14

Priestley, J. B. 1894-1984 ....DLB-10, 34, 77; Y-84

Prime, Benjamin Young 1733-1791 ....DLB-31

Prince, F. T. 1912- DLB-20

Prince, Thomas 1687-1758 ....DLB-24

The Principles of Success in Literature (1865), by
    George Henry Lewes [excerpt]...................DLB-57

Pritchett, V. S. 1900- DLB-15

Procter, Adelaide Anne 1825-1864 ....DLB-32

The Progress of Romance (1785), by Clara Reeve
    [excerpt].......................................DLB-39

Prokosch, Frederic 1906- DLB-48

The Proletarian Novel...............................DLB-9

Propper, Dan 1937- DLB-16

The Prospect of Peace (1778), by Joel Barlow DLB-37

Proud, Robert 1728-1813...........................DLB-30

Proust, Marcel 1871-1922 ....DLB-65

Prynne, J. H. 1936- DLB-40

Przybyszewski, Stanislaw 1868-1927 ....DLB-66

The Public Lending Right in America
    Statement by Sen. Charles McC. Mathias, Jr.
    PLR and the Meaning of Literary Property
    Statements on PLR by American Writers.........Y-83

The Public Lending Right in the United Kingdom
    Public Lending Right: The First Year in the
      United Kingdom Y-83

The Publication of English Renaissance
    Plays DLB-62

Publications and Social Movements
    [Transcendentalism] DLB-1

Publishers and Agents: The Columbia
    Connection...................................Y-87

Publishing Fiction at LSU Press............................Y-87

Pugin, A. Welby 1812-1852................................DLB-55

Pulitzer, Joseph 1847-1911 ....DLB-23

Pulitzer, Joseph, Jr. 1885-1955 ....DLB-29

Pulitzer Prizes for the Novel, 1917-1945 ....DLB-9

Purdy, James 1923- DLB-2

Pusey, Edward Bouverie 1800-1882..................DLB-55

Putnam, George Palmer 1814-1872 ....DLB-3, 79

Putnam, Samuel 1892-1950 ....DLB-4

G. P. Putnam's Sons DLB-49

Puzo, Mario 1920- DLB-6

Pyle, Ernie 1900-1945 ....DLB-29

Pyle, Howard 1853-1911 ....DLB-42

Pym, Barbara 1913-1980 ....DLB-14; Y-87

Pynchon, Thomas 1937- DLB-2

Pyramid Books......................................DLB-46

Pyrnelle, Louise-Clarke 1850-1907.....................DLB-42

Q

Quad, M. (see Lewis, Charles B.)

The Queen City Publishing House....................DLB-49

Queneau, Raymond 1903-1976 ....DLB-72

The Question of American Copyright
    in the Nineteenth Century
      Headnote
      Preface, by George Haven Putnam
      The Evolution of Copyright, by Brander
        Matthews
      Summary of Copyright Legislation in the
        United States, by R. R. Bowker
      Analysis of the Provisions of the Copyright
        Law of 1891, by George Haven Putnam
      The Contest for International Copyright,
        by George Haven Putnam
      Cheap Books and Good Books,
        by Brander Matthews...................DLB-49

Quin, Ann 1936-1973.......................................DLB-14

Quincy, Samuel of Georgia ?-? DLB-31

Quincy, Samuel of Massachusetts 1734-1789.....DLB-31

Quintana, Leroy V. 1944- DLB-82

Quist, Harlin, Books...DLB-46

Quoirez, Françoise (see Sagan, Françoise)

R

Rabe, David 1940- DLB-7

Radcliffe, Ann 1764-1823 ....DLB-39

Raddall, Thomas 1903- DLB-68

Radiguet, Raymond 1903-1923...........................DLB-65

Radványi, Netty Reiling (see Seghers, Anna)

Raine, Craig 1944- DLB-40

Raine, Kathleen 1908- DLB-20

Ralph, Julian 1853-1903....................................DLB-23

Ralph Waldo Emerson in 1982 ....Y-82

Rambler, no. 4 (1750), by Samuel Johnson
    [excerpt]...DLB-39

Ramée, Marie Louise de la (see Ouida)

Ramsay, David 1749-1815 ....DLB-30

Rand, Avery and Company..................................DLB-49

Rand McNally and Company...............................DLB-49

Randall, Dudley 1914- DLB-41

Randall, Henry S. 1811-1876..............................DLB-30

Randall, James G. 1881-1953..............................DLB-17

The Randall Jarrell Symposium: A Small
    Collection of Randall Jarrells
    Excerpts From Papers Delivered at
        the Randall Jarrell Symposium Y-86

Randolph, Anson D. F. [publishing house]........DLB-49

Randolph, Thomas 1605-1635............................DLB-58

Random House...DLB-46

Ranlet, Henry [publishing house]......................DLB-49

Ransom, John Crowe 1888-1974 ....DLB-45, 63

Raphael, Frederic 1931- DLB-14

Raphaelson, Samson 1896-1983..........................DLB-44

Raskin, Ellen 1928-1984....................................DLB-52

Rattigan, Terence 1911-1977 ....DLB-13

Rawlings, Marjorie Kinnan 1896-1953..........DLB-9, 22

Raworth, Tom 1938- DLB-40

Ray, David 1932- DLB-5

Ray, Henrietta Cordelia 1849-1916....................DLB-50

Raymond, Henry J. 1820-1869....................DLB-43, 79

Raymond Chandler Centenary Tributes
    from Michael Avallone, James Elroy, Joe Gores,
    and William F. Nolan.......................................Y-88

Reach, Angus 1821-1856.....................................DLB-70

Read, Herbert 1893-1968 ....DLB-20

Read, Opie 1852-1939..DLB-23

Read, Piers Paul 1941- DLB-14

Reade, Charles 1814-1884..................................DLB-21

Reader's Digest Condensed Books DLB-46

Reading, Peter 1946- DLB-40

Reaney, James 1926- DLB-68

Rechy, John 1934- Y-82

Redding, J. Saunders 1906-1988.................DLB-63, 76

Redfield, J. S. [publishing house].......................DLB-49

Redgrove, Peter 1932- DLB-40

Redmon, Anne 1943- Y-86

Redmond, Eugene B. 1937- DLB-41

Redpath, James [publishing house] DLB-49

Reed, Henry 1808-1854 ....DLB-59

Reed, Henry 1914- DLB-27

Reed, Ishmael 1938- DLB-2, 5, 33

Reed, Sampson 1800-1880..................................DLB-1

Reese, Lizette Woodworth 1856-1935 ....DLB-54

Reese, Thomas 1742-1796 ....DLB-37

Reeve, Clara 1729-1807.....................................DLB-39

Regnery, Henry, Company DLB-46

Reid, Alastair 1926- DLB-27

Reid, Christopher 1949- DLB-40

Reid, Helen Rogers 1882-1970..........................DLB-29

Reid, James ?-? DLB-31

Reid, Mayne 1818-1883.....................................DLB-21

Reid, Thomas 1710-1796 ....DLB-31

Reid, Whitelaw 1837-1912 ....DLB-23

Reilly and Lee Publishing Company DLB-46

Reimann, Brigitte 1933-1973 ....DLB-75

Reisch, Walter 1903-1983..................................DLB-44

Remarque, Erich Maria 1898-1970....................DLB-56

"Re-meeting of Old Friends": The Jack Kerouac
    Conference...Y-82

Remington, Frederic 1861-1909 ....DLB-12

Renaud, Jacques 1943- DLB-60

Renault, Mary 1905-1983 ....Y-83

Representative Men and Women: A Historical
    Perspective on the British Novel,

1930-1960 ....DLB-15

(Re-)Publishing Orwell Y-86

Reuter, Gabriele 1859-1941 ....DLB-66

Revell, Fleming H., Company.....................DLB-49

Reventlow, Franziska Gräfin zu
    1871-1918 ....DLB-66

Review of [Samuel Richardson's] *Clarissa* (1748),
    by Henry Fielding DLB-39

The Revolt (1937), by Mary
    Colum [excerpts] DLB-36

Rexroth, Kenneth 1905-1982 ....DLB-16, 48; Y-82

Rey, H. A. 1898-1977...................................DLB-22

Reynal and Hitchcock DLB-46

Reynolds, G. W. M. 1814-1879 ....DLB-21

Reynolds, Mack 1917- DLB-8

Reznikoff, Charles 1894-1976.....................DLB-28, 45

"Rhetoric" (1828; revised, 1859), by
    Thomas de Quincey [excerpt] DLB-57

Rhett, Robert Barnwell 1800-1876...............DLB-43

Rhode, John 1884-1964 ....DLB-77

Rhodes, James Ford 1848-1927 ....DLB-47

Rhys, Jean 1890-1979 ....DLB-36

Ricardou, Jean 1932- DLB-83

Rice, Elmer 1892-1967................................DLB-4, 7

Rice, Grantland 1880-1954 ....DLB-29

Rich, Adrienne 1929- DLB-5, 67

Richards, David Adams 1950- DLB-53

Richards, George circa 1760-1814.............DLB-37

Richards, I. A. 1893-1979 ....DLB-27

Richards, Laura E. 1850-1943 ....DLB-42

Richards, William Carey 1818-1892 ....DLB-73

Richardson, Charles F. 1851-1913.............DLB-71

Richardson, Dorothy M. 1873-1957 ....DLB-36

Richardson, Jack 1935- DLB-7

Richardson, Samuel 1689-1761.................DLB-39

Richardson, Willis 1889-1977 ....DLB-51

Richler, Mordecai 1931- DLB-53

Richter, Conrad 1890-1968........................DLB-9

Richter, Hans Werner 1908- DLB-69

Rickword, Edgell 1898-1982 ....DLB-20

Riddell, John (see Ford, Corey)

Ridge, Lola 1873-1941 ....DLB-54

Ridler, Anne 1912- DLB-27

Riffaterre, Michael 1924- DLB-67

Riis, Jacob 1849-1914 ....DLB-23

Riker, John C. [publishing house] DLB-49

Riley, John 1938-1978................................DLB-40

Rilke, Rainer Maria 1875-1926 ....DLB-81

Rinehart and Company DLB-46

Ringuet 1895-1960 ....DLB-68

Rinser, Luise 1911- DLB-69

Ríos, Isabella 1948- DLB-82

Ripley, Arthur 1895-1961 ....DLB-44

Ripley, George 1802-1880 ....DLB-1, 64, 73

The Rising Glory of America: Three Poems DLB-37

The Rising Glory of America: Written in 1771
    (1786), by Hugh Henry Brackenridge and
    Philip Freneau DLB-37

Riskin, Robert 1897-1955............................DLB-26

Risse, Heinz 1898- DLB-69

Ritchie, Anna Mowatt 1819-1870 ....DLB-3

Ritchie, Anne Thackeray 1837-1919 ....DLB-18

Ritchie, Thomas 1778-1854 ....DLB-43

Rites of Passage [on William Saroyan]................Y-83

The Ritz Paris Hemingway Award.................Y-85

Rivera, Tomás 1935-1984...........................DLB-82

Rivers, Conrad Kent 1933-1968 ....DLB-41

Riverside Press...DLB-49

Rivington, James circa 1724-1802..............DLB-43

Rivkin, Allen 1903- DLB-26

Robbe-Grillet, Alain 1922- DLB-83

Robbins, Tom 1936- Y-80

Roberts, Elizabeth Madox 1881-1941............DLB-9, 54

Roberts, Kenneth 1885-1957 ....DLB-9

Roberts Brothers..DLB-49

Robertson, A. M., and Company.................DLB-49

Robinson, Casey 1903-1979 ....DLB-44

Robinson, Edwin Arlington 1869-1935 ....DLB-54

Robinson, James Harvey 1863-1936..............DLB-47

Robinson, Lennox 1886-1958 ....DLB-10

Robinson, Mabel Louise 1874-1962................DLB-22

Robinson, Therese 1797-1870 ....DLB-59

Roblès, Emmanuel 1914- DLB-83

Rodgers, Carolyn M. 1945- DLB-41

Rodgers, W. R. 1909-1969 ....DLB-20

Rodriguez, Richard 1944- DLB-82

Roethke, Theodore 1908-1963 ....DLB-5

Rogers, Will 1879-1935 ....DLB-11

Rohmer, Sax 1883-1959 ....DLB-70

Roiphe, Anne 1935- Y-80

Rojas, Arnold R. 1896-1988 ....DLB-82

Rolfe, Frederick William 1860-1913 ....DLB-34

Rolland, Romain 1866-1944 ....DLB-65

Rolvaag, O. E. 1876-1931 ....DLB-9

Romains, Jules 1885-1972 ....DLB-65

Roman, A., and Company DLB-49

Romero, Orlando 1945- DLB-82

Roosevelt, Theodore 1858-1919 ....DLB-47

Root, Waverley 1903-1982 ....DLB-4

Roquebrune, Robert de 1889-1978 ....DLB-68

Rose, Reginald 1920- DLB-26

Rosei, Peter 1946- DLB-85

Rosen, Norma 1925- DLB-28

Rosenberg, Isaac 1890-1918 ....DLB-20

Rosenfeld, Isaac 1918-1956 ....DLB-28

Rosenthal, M. L. 1917- DLB-5

Ross, Leonard Q. (see Rosten, Leo)

Rossen, Robert 1908-1966 ....DLB-26

Rossetti, Christina 1830-1894 ....DLB-35

Rossetti, Dante Gabriel 1828-1882 ....DLB-35

Rossner, Judith 1935- DLB-6

Rosten, Leo 1908- DLB-11

Roth, Gerhard 1942- DLB-85

Roth, Henry 1906?- DLB-28

Roth, Joseph 1894-1939 ....DLB-85

Roth, Philip 1933- DLB-2, 28; Y-82

Rothenberg, Jerome 1931- DLB-5

Rowe, Elizabeth 1674-1737 ....DLB-39

Rowe, Nicholas 1674-1718 ....DLB-84

Rowlandson, Mary circa 1635-circa 1678 ....DLB-24

Rowley, William circa 1585-1626 ....DLB-58

Rowson, Susanna Haswell circa 1762-1824 ....DLB-37

Roy, Gabrielle 1909-1983 ....DLB-68

Roy, Jules 1907- DLB-83

The Royal Court Theatre and the English
    Stage Company DLB-13

The Royal Court Theatre and the New
    Drama DLB-10

The Royal Shakespeare Company
    at the Swan Y-88

Royall, Anne 1769-1854 ....DLB-43

The Roycroft Printing Shop DLB-49

Rubens, Bernice 1928- DLB-14

Rudd and Carleton DLB-49

Rudkin, David 1936- DLB-13

Ruffin, Josephine St. Pierre 1842-1924 ....DLB-79

Ruggles, Henry Joseph 1813-1906 ....DLB-64

Rukeyser, Muriel 1913-1980 ....DLB-48

Rule, Jane 1931- DLB-60

Rumaker, Michael 1932- DLB-16

Rumens, Carol 1944- DLB-40

Runyon, Damon 1880-1946 ....DLB-11

Rush, Benjamin 1746-1813 ....DLB-37

Ruskin, John 1819-1900 ....DLB-55

Russ, Joanna 1937- DLB-8

Russell, B. B., and Company DLB-49

Russell, Benjamin 1761-1845 ....DLB-43

Russell, Charles Edward 1860-1941 ....DLB-25

Russell, George William (see AE)

Russell, R. H., and Son DLB-49

Rutherford, Mark 1831-1913 ....DLB-18

Ryan, Michael 1946- Y-82

Ryan, Oscar 1904- DLB-68

Ryga, George 1932- DLB-60

Ryskind, Morrie 1895-1985 ....DLB-26

S

The Saalfield Publishing Company DLB-46

Saberhagen, Fred 1930- DLB-8

Sackler, Howard 1929-1982 ....DLB-7

Sackville, Thomas 1536-1608
    and Norton, Thomas 1532-1584 ....DLB-62

Sackville-West, V. 1892-1962 ....DLB-34

Sadlier, D. and J., and Company DLB-49

Saffin, John circa 1626-1710 ....DLB-24

Sagan, Françoise 1935- DLB-83

Sage, Robert 1899-1962 ....DLB-4

Sagel, Jim 1947- DLB-82

Sahkomaapii, Piitai (see Highwater, Jamake)

Sahl, Hans 1902- DLB-69

Said, Edward W. 1935- DLB-67

Saiko, George 1892-1962 ....DLB-85

St. Johns, Adela Rogers 1894-1988 ....DLB-29

St. Martin's Press DLB-46

Saint-Exupéry, Antoine de 1900-1944 ....DLB-72

Saint Pierre, Michel de 1916-1987 ....DLB-83

Saintsbury, George 1845-1933 ....DLB-57

Saki (see Munro, H. H.)

Salaam, Kalamu ya 1947- DLB-38

Salas, Floyd 1931- DLB-82

Salemson, Harold J. 1910-1988 ....DLB-4

Salinas, Luis Omar 1937- DLB-82

Salinger, J. D. 1919- DLB-2

Salt, Waldo 1914- DLB-44

Sampson, Richard Henry (see Hull, Richard)

Sanborn, Franklin Benjamin 1831-1917 ....DLB-1

Sánchez, Ricardo 1941- DLB-82

Sanchez, Sonia 1934- DLB-41

Sandburg, Carl 1878-1967 ....DLB-17, 54

Sanders, Ed 1939- DLB-16

Sandoz, Mari 1896-1966 ....DLB-9

Sandys, George 1578-1644 ....DLB-24

Santayana, George 1863-1952 ....DLB-54, 71

Santmyer, Helen Hooven 1895-1986 ....Y-84

Sapper (see McNeile, Herman Cyril)

Sargent, Pamela 1948- DLB-8

Saroyan, William 1908-1981 ....DLB-7, 9; Y-81

Sarraute, Nathalie 1900- DLB-83

Sarrazin, Albertine 1937-1967 ....DLB-83

Sarton, May 1912- DLB-48; Y-81

Sartre, Jean-Paul 1905-1980 ....DLB-72

Sassoon, Siegfried 1886-1967 ....DLB-20

Saturday Review Press DLB-46

Saunders, James 1925- DLB-13

Saunders, John Monk 1897-1940 ....DLB-26

Savage, James 1784-1873 ....DLB-30

Savage, Marmion W. 1803?-1872 ....DLB-21

Savard, Félix-Antoine 1896-1982 ....DLB-68

Sawyer, Ruth 1880-1970 ....DLB-22

Sayers, Dorothy L. 1893-1957 ....DLB-10, 36, 77

Sayles, John Thomas 1950- DLB-44

Scannell, Vernon 1922- DLB-27

Scarry, Richard 1919- DLB-61

Schaeffer, Albrecht 1885-1950 ....DLB-66

Schaeffer, Susan Fromberg 1941- DLB-28

Schaper, Edzard 1908-1984 ....DLB-69

Scharf, J. Thomas 1843-1898 ....DLB-47

Schickele, René 1883-1940 ....DLB-66

Schlesinger, Arthur M., Jr. 1917- DLB-17

Schlumberger, Jean 1877-1968 ....DLB-65

Schmid, Eduard Hermann Wilhelm
       (see Edschmid, Kasimir)

Schmidt, Arno 1914-1979 ....DLB-69

Schmidt, Michael 1947- DLB-40

Schmitz, James H. 1911- DLB-8

Schnitzler, Arthur 1862-1931 ....DLB-81

Schnurre, Wolfdietrich 1920- DLB-69

Schocken Books DLB-46

The Schomburg Center for Research
       in Black Culture DLB-76

Schouler, James 1839-1920 ....DLB-47

Schrader, Paul 1946- DLB-44

Schreiner, Olive 1855-1920 ....DLB-18

Schroeder, Andreas 1946- DLB-53

Schulberg, Budd 1914- DLB-6, 26, 28; Y-81

Schulte, F. J., and Company DLB-49

Schurz, Carl 1829-1906 ....DLB-23

Schuyler, George S. 1895-1977 ....DLB-29, 51

Schuyler, James 1923- DLB-5

Schwartz, Delmore 1913-1966 ....DLB-28, 48

Schwartz, Jonathan 1938- Y-82

Science Fantasy DLB-8

Science-Fiction Fandom and Conventions DLB-8

Science-Fiction Fanzines: The Time Binders DLB-8

Science-Fiction Films DLB-8

Science Fiction Writers of America and the
       Nebula Awards DLB-8

Scott, Evelyn 1893-1963 ....DLB-9, 48

Scott, Harvey W. 1838-1910 ....DLB-23

Scott, Paul 1920-1978 ....DLB-14

Scott, Sarah 1723-1795......................................DLB-39

Scott, Tom 1918- DLB-27

Scott, William Bell 1811-1890............................DLB-32

Scott, William R. [publishing house] DLB-46

Scott-Heron, Gil 1949- DLB-41

Charles Scribner's Sons DLB-49

Scripps, E. W. 1854-1926 ....DLB-25

Scudder, Horace Elisha 1838-1902 ....DLB-42, 71

Scudder, Vida Dutton 1861-1954 ....DLB-71

Scupham, Peter 1933- DLB-40

Seabrook, William 1886-1945 ....DLB-4

Seabury, Samuel 1729-1796...............................DLB-31

Sears, Edward I. 1819?-1876 ....DLB-79

Sears Publishing Company..................................DLB-46

Seaton, George 1911-1979 ....DLB-44

Seaton, William Winston 1785-1866...................DLB-43

Sedgwick, Arthur George 1844-1915 ....DLB-64

Sedgwick, Catharine Maria 1789-1867..........DLB-1, 74

Seeger, Alan 1888-1916 ....DLB-45

Segal, Erich 1937- Y-86

Seghers, Anna 1900-1983 ....DLB-69

Seid, Ruth (see Sinclair, Jo)

Seidel, Frederick Lewis 1936- Y-84

Seidel, Ina 1885-1974...DLB-56

Séjour, Victor 1817-1874 ....DLB-50

Séjour Marcou et Ferrand,
    Juan Victor (see Séjour, Victor)

Selby, Hubert, Jr. 1928- DLB-2

Selden, George 1929- DLB-52

Selected English-Language Little Magazines and
    Newspapers [France, 1920-1939] DLB-4

Selected Humorous Magazines (1820-1950) DLB-11

Selected Science-Fiction Magazines and
    Anthologies...DLB-8

Seligman, Edwin R. A. 1861-1939 ....DLB-47

Seltzer, Chester E. (see Muro, Amado)

Seltzer, Thomas [publishing house]...................DLB-46

Sendak, Maurice 1928- DLB-61

Sensation Novels (1863), by H. L. Manse..........DLB-21

Seredy, Kate 1899-1975 ....DLB-22

Serling, Rod 1924-1975......................................DLB-26

Settle, Mary Lee 1918- DLB-6

Seuss, Dr. (see Geisel, Theodor Seuss)

Sewall, Joseph 1688-1769...................................DLB-24

Sewell, Samuel 1652-1730..................................DLB-24

Sex, Class, Politics, and Religion [in the British
    Novel, 1930-1959] DLB-15

Sexton, Anne 1928-1974.......................................DLB-5

Shaara, Michael 1929-1988 ....Y-83

Shadwell, Thomas 1641?-1692 ....DLB-80

Shaffer, Anthony 1926- DLB-13

Shaffer, Peter 1926- DLB-13

Shairp, Mordaunt 1887-1939.............................DLB-10

Shakespeare, William 1564-1616 ....DLB-62

Shange, Ntozake 1948- DLB-38

Shapiro, Karl 1913- DLB-48

Sharon Publications DLB-46

Sharpe, Tom 1928- DLB-14

Shaw, Bernard 1856-1950...........................DLB-10, 57

Shaw, Henry Wheeler 1818-1885 ....DLB-11

Shaw, Irwin 1913-1984 ....DLB-6; Y-84

Shaw, Robert 1927-1978 ....DLB-13, 14

Shay, Frank [publishing house]..........................DLB-46

Shea, John Gilmary 1824-1892 ....DLB-30

Shearing, Joseph 1886-1952...............................DLB-70

Shebbeare, John 1709-1788 ....DLB-39

Sheckley, Robert 1928- DLB-8

Shedd, William G. T. 1820-1894 ....DLB-64

Sheed, Wilfred 1930- DLB-6

Sheed and Ward...DLB-46

Sheldon, Alice B. (see Tiptree, James, Jr.)

Sheldon, Edward 1886-1946...............................DLB-7

Sheldon and Company...DLB-49

Shepard, Sam 1943- DLB-7

Shepard, Thomas I 1604 or 1605-1649 ....DLB-24

Shepard, Thomas II 1635-1677..........................DLB-24

Shepard, Clark and Brown DLB-49

Sheridan, Frances 1724-1766........................DLB-39, 84

Sherriff, R. C. 1896-1975...................................DLB-10

Sherwood, Robert 1896-1955 ....DLB-7, 26

Shiels, George 1886-1949..............................DLB-10

Shillaber, B.[enjamin] P.[enhallow]
    1814-1890 ....DLB-1, 11

Shine, Ted 1931- DLB-38

Shirer, William L. 1904- DLB-4

Shirley, James 1596-1666 ....DLB-58

Shockley, Ann Allen 1927- DLB-33

Shorthouse, Joseph Henry 1834-1903..............DLB-18

Showalter, Elaine 1941- DLB-67

Shulevitz, Uri 1935- DLB-61

Shulman, Max 1919-1988 ....DLB-11

Shute, Henry A. 1856-1943 ....DLB-9

Shuttle, Penelope 1947- DLB-14, 40

Sidney, Margaret (see Lothrop, Harriet M.)

Sidney's Press...DLB-49

Siegfried Loraine Sassoon: A Centenary Essay
    Tributes from Vivien F. Clarke and
      Michael Thorpe Y-86

Sierra Club Books.......................................DLB-49

Sigourney, Lydia Howard (Huntley)
    1791-1865 ....DLB-1, 42, 73

Silkin, Jon 1930- DLB-27

Silliphant, Stirling 1918- DLB-26

Sillitoe, Alan 1928- DLB-14

Silman, Roberta 1934- DLB-28

Silverberg, Robert 1935- DLB-8

Simak, Clifford D. 1904-1988 ....DLB-8

Simcox, George Augustus 1841-1905...............DLB-35

Simenon, Georges 1903- DLB-72

Simmel, Johannes Mario 1924- DLB-69

Simmons, Herbert Alfred 1930- DLB-33

Simmons, James 1933- DLB-40

Simms, William Gilmore 1806-
    1870..DLB-3, 30, 59, 73

Simon, Claude 1913- DLB-83

Simon, Neil 1927- DLB-7

Simon and Schuster.....................................DLB-46

Simons, Katherine Drayton Mayrant 1890-1969.....Y-83

Simpson, Helen 1897-1940 ....DLB-77

Simpson, Louis 1923- DLB-5

Simpson, N. F. 1919- DLB-13

Sims, George R. 1847-1922.........................DLB-35, 70

Sinclair, Andrew 1935- DLB-14

Sinclair, Jo 1913- DLB-28

Sinclair Lewis Centennial Conference Y-85

Sinclair, May 1863-1946 ....DLB-36

Sinclair, Upton 1878-1968...........................DLB-9

Sinclair, Upton [publishing house] DLB-46

Singer, Isaac Bashevis 1904- DLB-6, 28, 52

Singmaster, Elsie 1879-1958 ....DLB-9

Siodmak, Curt 1902- DLB-44

Sissman, L. E. 1928-1976 ....DLB-5

Sisson, C. H. 1914- DLB-27

Sitwell, Edith 1887-1964 ....DLB-20

Skelton, Robin 1925- DLB-27, 53

Skinner, John Stuart 1788-1851 ....DLB-73

Skipsey, Joseph 1832-1903...........................DLB-35

Slade, Bernard 1930- DLB-53

Slater, Patrick 1880-1951 ....DLB-68

Slavitt, David 1935- DLB-5, 6

A Slender Thread of Hope: The Kennedy
    Center Black Theatre Project DLB-38

Slick, Sam (see Haliburton, Thomas Chandler)

Sloane, William, Associates DLB-46

Small, Maynard and Company DLB-49

Small Presses in Great Britain and Ireland,
    1960-1985 ....DLB-40

Small Presses I: Jargon Society Y-84

Small Presses II: The Spirit That
    Moves Us Press Y-85

Small Presses III: Pushcart Press......................Y-87

Smiles, Samuel 1812-1904............................DLB-55

Smith, Alexander 1829-1867 ....DLB-32, 55

Smith, Betty 1896-1972 ....Y-82

Smith, Carol Sturm 1938- Y-81

Smith, Charles Henry 1826-1903 ....DLB-11

Smith, Charlotte 1749-1806 ....DLB-39

Smith, Cordwainer 1913-1966 ....DLB-8

Smith, Dave 1942- DLB-5

Smith, Dodie 1896- DLB-10

Smith, Doris Buchanan 1934- DLB-52

Smith, E. E. 1890-1965................................DLB-8

Smith, Elihu Hubbard 1771-1798......................DLB-37

Smith, Elizabeth Oakes (Prince) 1806-1893 ....DLB-1

Smith, George O. 1911-1981 ....DLB-8

Smith, H. Allen 1907-1976..........................DLB-11, 29

Smith, Harrison, and Robert Haas
    [publishing house] DLB-46

Smith, Iain Crichten 1928- DLB-40

Smith, J. Allen 1860-1924................................DLB-47

Smith, J. Stilman, and Company DLB-49

Smith, John 1580-1631 ....DLB-24, 30

Smith, Josiah 1704-1781.................................DLB-24

Smith, Ken 1938- DLB-40

Smith, Lee 1944- Y-83

Smith, Mark 1935- Y-82

Smith, Michael 1698-circa 1771 ....DLB-31

Smith, Red 1905-1982.....................................DLB-29

Smith, Roswell 1829-1892................................DLB-79

Smith, Samuel Harrison 1772-1845....................DLB-43

Smith, Samuel Stanhope 1751-1819...................DLB-37

Smith, Seba 1792-1868..................................DLB-1, 11

Smith, Stevie 1902-1971 ....DLB-20

Smith, Sydney Goodsir 1915-1975 ....DLB-27

Smith, W. B., and Company DLB-49

Smith, William 1727-1803...............................DLB-31

Smith, William 1728-1793...............................DLB-30

Smith, William Gardner 1927-1974...................DLB-76

Smith, William Jay 1918- DLB-5

Smollett, Tobias 1721-1771.............................DLB-39

Snellings, Rolland (see Touré, Askia Muhammad)

Snodgrass, W. D. 1926- DLB-5

Snow, C. P. 1905-1980 ....DLB-15, 77

Snyder, Gary 1930- DLB-5, 16

Sobiloff, Hy 1912-1970 ....DLB-48

The Society for Textual Scholarship
    and *TEXT*...Y-87

Solano, Solita 1888-1975 ....DLB-4

Sollers, Philippe 1936- DLB-83

Solomon, Carl 1928- DLB-16

Solway, David 1941- DLB-53

Solzhenitsyn and America Y-85

Sontag, Susan 1933- DLB-2, 67

Sorrentino, Gilbert 1929- DLB-5; Y-80

Soto, Gary 1952- DLB-82

Sources for the Study of Tudor
    and Stuart Drama.......................................DLB-62

Southerland, Ellease 1943- DLB-33

Southern, Terry 1924- DLB-2

Southern Writers Between the Wars DLB-9

Southerne, Thomas 1659-1746........................DLB-80

Spark, Muriel 1918- DLB-15

Sparks, Jared 1789-1866 ....DLB-1, 30

Sparshott, Francis 1926- DLB-60

Späth, Gerold 1939- DLB-75

Spellman, A. B. 1935- DLB-41

Spencer, Anne 1882-1975..........................DLB-51, 54

Spencer, Elizabeth 1921- DLB-6

Spencer, Herbert 1820-1903...........................DLB-57

Spencer, Scott 1945- Y-86

Spender, Stephen 1909-.................................DLB-20

Spicer, Jack 1925-1965 ....DLB-5, 16

Spielberg, Peter 1929- Y-81

Spier, Peter 1927- DLB-61

Spinrad, Norman 1940- DLB-8

Spofford, Harriet Prescott 1835-1921...............DLB-74

Squibob (see Derby, George Horatio)

Stafford, Jean 1915-1979 ....DLB-2

Stafford, William 1914- DLB-5

Stage Censorship: "The Rejected Statement"
    (1911), by Bernard Shaw [excerpts] DLB-10

Stallings, Laurence 1894-1968.......................DLB-7, 44

Stallworthy, Jon 1935- DLB-40

Stampp, Kenneth M. 1912- DLB-17

Stanford, Ann 1916- DLB-5

Stanton, Elizabeth Cady 1815-1902...................DLB-79

Stanton, Frank L. 1857-1927...........................DLB-25

Stapledon, Olaf 1886-1950.............................DLB-15

Star Spangled Banner Office............................DLB-49

Starkweather, David 1935- DLB-7

Statements on the Art of Poetry DLB-54

Steadman, Mark 1930- DLB-6

The Stealthy School of Criticism (1871), by
    Dante Gabriel Rossetti...............................DLB-35

Stearns, Harold E. 1891-1943.............................DLB-4

Stedman, Edmund Clarence 1833-1908.............DLB-64

Steele, Max 1922- Y-80

Steele, Richard 1672-1729.................................DLB-84

Steere, Richard circa 1643-1721 ....DLB-24

Stegner, Wallace 1909- DLB-9

Stehr, Hermann 1864-1940 ....DLB-66

Steig, William 1907- DLB-61

Stein, Gertrude 1874-1946.........................DLB-4, 54

Stein, Leo 1872-1947......................................DLB-4

Stein and Day Publishers.................................DLB-46

Steinbeck, John 1902-1968....................DLB-7, 9; DS-2

Steiner, George 1929- DLB-67

Stephen, Leslie 1832-1904 ....DLB-57

Stephens, Alexander H. 1812-1883.................DLB-47

Stephens, Ann 1810-1886.........................DLB-3, 73

Stephens, Charles Asbury 1844?-1931 ....DLB-42

Stephens, James 1882?-1950.........................DLB-19

Sterling, George 1869-1926 ....DLB-54

Sterling, James 1701-1763..............................DLB-24

Stern, Richard 1928- Y-87

Stern, Stewart 1922- DLB-26

Sterne, Laurence 1713-1768 ....DLB-39

Sternheim, Carl 1878-1942 ....DLB-56

Stevens, Wallace 1879-1955 ....DLB-54

Stevenson, Anne 1933- DLB-40

Stevenson, Robert Louis 1850-1894.............DLB-18, 57

Stewart, Donald Ogden 1894-1980.........DLB-4, 11, 26

Stewart, Dugald 1753-1828 ....DLB-31

Stewart, George R. 1895-1980 ....DLB-8

Stewart and Kidd Company..............................DLB-46

Stickney, Trumbull 1874-1904 ....DLB-54

Stiles, Ezra 1727-1795 ....DLB-31

Still, James 1906- DLB-9

Stith, William 1707-1755...............................DLB-31

Stockton, Frank R. 1834-1902 ....DLB-42, 74

Stoddard, Ashbel [publishing house] DLB-49

Stoddard, Richard Henry 1825-1903............DLB-3, 64

Stoddard, Solomon 1643-1729 ....DLB-24

Stoker, Bram 1847-1912................................DLB-36, 70

Stokes, Frederick A., Company DLB-49

Stokes, Thomas L. 1898-1958.........................DLB-29

Stone, Herbert S., and Company DLB-49

Stone, Lucy 1818-1893..................................DLB-79

Stone, Melville 1848-1929.............................DLB-25

Stone, Samuel 1602-1663..............................DLB-24

Stone and Kimball..DLB-49

Stoppard, Tom 1937- DLB-13; Y-85

Storey, Anthony 1928- DLB-14

Storey, David 1933- DLB-13, 14

Story, Thomas circa 1670-1742 ....DLB-31

Story, William Wetmore 1819-1895.....................DLB-1

Storytelling: A Contemporary Renaissance.............Y-84

Stoughton, William 1631-1701 ....DLB-24

Stowe, Harriet Beecher 1811-1896 ....DLB-1, 12, 42, 74

Stowe, Leland 1899- DLB-29

Strand, Mark 1934- DLB-5

Stratemeyer, Edward 1862-1930....................DLB-42

Stratton and Barnard DLB-49

Straub, Peter 1943- Y-84

Street, Cecil John Charles (see Rhode, John)

Street and Smith...DLB-49

Streeter, Edward 1891-1976 ....DLB-11

Stribling, T. S. 1881-1965 ....DLB-9

Stringer and Townsend DLB-49

Strittmatter, Erwin 1912- DLB-69

Strother, David Hunter 1816-1888.....................DLB-3

Stuart, Jesse 1906-1984.........................DLB-9, 48; Y-84

Stuart, Lyle [publishing house] DLB-46

Stubbs, Harry Clement (see Clement, Hal)

The Study of Poetry (1880), by Matthew
    Arnold..DLB-35

Sturgeon, Theodore 1918-1985 ....DLB-8; Y-85

Sturges, Preston 1898-1959............................DLB-26

"Style" (1840; revised, 1859), by Thomas
    de Quincey [excerpt].................................DLB-57

"Style" (1888), by Walter Pater DLB-57

Style (1897), by Walter Raleigh [excerpt]............DLB-57

"Style" (1877), by T. H. Wright [excerpt].........DLB-57

"Le Style c'est l'homme" (1892),
    by W. H. Mallock DLB-57

Styron, William 1925- DLB-2; Y-80

Suárez, Mario 1925- DLB-82

Such, Peter 1939- DLB-60

Suckling, Sir John 1609-1642 ....DLB-58

Suckow, Ruth 1892-1960..........................DLB-9

Suggs, Simon (see Hooper, Johnson Jones)

Sukenick, Ronald 1932- Y-81

Suknaski, Andrew 1942- DLB-53

Sullivan, C. Gardner 1886-1965 ....DLB-26

Sullivan, Frank 1892-1976 ....DLB-11

Summers, Hollis 1916- DLB-6

Sumner, Henry A. [publishing house] DLB-49

Surtees, Robert Smith 1803-1864 ....DLB-21

A Survey of Poetry
    Anthologies, 1879-1960 ....DLB-54

Surveys of the Year's Biography
    A Transit of Poets and Others: American
        Biography in 1982 ....Y-82
    The Year in Literary Biography Y-83
    The Year in Literary Biography Y-84
    The Year in Literary Biography Y-85
    The Year in Literary Biography Y-86
    The Year in Literary Biography Y-87
    The Year in Literary Biography Y-88

Surveys of the Year's Book Publishing
    The Year in Book Publishing................Y-86

Surveys of the Year's Drama
    The Year in Drama...............................Y-82
    The Year in Drama...............................Y-83
    The Year in Drama...............................Y-84
    The Year in Drama...............................Y-85
    The Year in Drama...............................Y-87
    The Year in Drama...............................Y-88

Surveys of the Year's Fiction
    The Year's Work in Fiction: A Survey..............Y-82
    The Year in Fiction: A Biased View................Y-83
    The Year in Fiction...............................Y-84
    The Year in Fiction...............................Y-85
    The Year in Fiction...............................Y-86
    The Year in the Novel..........................Y-87
    The Year in Short Stories......................Y-87
    The Year in the Novel..........................Y-88
    The Year in Short Stories......................Y-88

Surveys of the Year's Poetry
    The Year's Work in American Poetry..............Y-82
    The Year in Poetry Y-83
    The Year in Poetry Y-84
    The Year in Poetry Y-85
    The Year in Poetry Y-86

The Year in Poetry Y-87
The Year in Poetry Y-88

Sutherland, John 1919-1956.....................DLB-68

Sutro, Alfred 1863-1933 ....DLB-10

Swados, Harvey 1920-1972 ....DLB-2

Swain, Charles 1801-1874 ....DLB-32

Swallow Press.......................................DLB-46

Swenson, May 1919- DLB-5

Swerling, Jo 1897- DLB-44

Swift, Jonathan 1667-1745 ....DLB-39

Swinburne, A. C. 1837-1909.................DLB-35, 57

Swinnerton, Frank 1884-1982...................DLB-34

Swisshelm, Jane Grey 1815-1884 ....DLB-43

Swope, Herbert Bayard 1882-1958 ....DLB-25

Swords, T. and J., and Company DLB-49

Swords, Thomas 1763-1843 and
    Swords, James ?-1844................................DLB-73

Symonds, John Addington 1840-1893 ....DLB-57

Symons, Arthur 1865-1945 ....DLB-19, 57

Symons, Scott 1933- DLB-53

Synge, John Millington 1871-1909.............DLB-10, 19

T

Tafolla, Carmen 1951- DLB-82

Taggard, Genevieve 1894-1948..................DLB-45

Tait, J. Selwin, and Sons..........................DLB-49

Talvj or Talvi (see Robinson, Therese)

Taradash, Daniel 1913- DLB-44

Tarbell, Ida M. 1857-1944 ....DLB-47

Tarkington, Booth 1869-1946....................DLB-9

Tashlin, Frank 1913-1972 ....DLB-44

Tate, Allen 1899-1979............................DLB-4, 45, 63

Tate, James 1943- DLB-5

Tate, Nahum circa 1652-1715....................DLB-80

Taylor, Bayard 1825-1878.........................DLB-3

Taylor, Bert Leston 1866-1921 ....DLB-25

Taylor, Charles H. 1846-1921....................DLB-25

Taylor, Edward circa 1642-1729.................DLB-24

Taylor, Henry 1942- DLB-5

Taylor, Sir Henry 1800-1886 ....DLB-32

Taylor, Mildred D. ?- DLB-52

Taylor, Peter 1917- Y-81

Taylor, William, and Company DLB-49

Taylor-Made Shakespeare? Or Is
    "Shall I Die?" the Long-Lost Text
    of Bottom's Dream?................................Y-85

Teasdale, Sara 1884-1933 ....DLB-45

The Tea-Table (1725), by Eliza Haywood
    [excerpt] DLB-39

Tenn, William 1919- DLB-8

Tennant, Emma 1937- DLB-14

Tenney, Tabitha Gilman 1762-1837 ....DLB-37

Tennyson, Alfred 1809-1892 ....DLB-32

Tennyson, Frederick 1807-1898 ....DLB-32

Terhune, Albert Payson 1872-1942 ....DLB-9

Terry, Megan 1932- DLB-7

Terson, Peter 1932- DLB-13

Tesich, Steve 1943- Y-83

Tey, Josephine 1896?-1952 ....DLB-77

Thacher, James 1754-1844 ....DLB-37

Thackeray, William Makepeace
    1811-1863 ....DLB-21, 55

Thanet, Octave (see French, Alice)

The Theater in Shakespeare's Time DLB-62

The Theatre Guild DLB-7

Thério, Adrien 1925- DLB-53

Theroux, Paul 1941- DLB-2

Thoma, Ludwig 1867-1921 ....DLB-66

Thoma, Richard 1902- DLB-4

Thomas, Audrey 1935- DLB-60

Thomas, D. M. 1935- DLB-40

Thomas, Dylan 1914-1953 ....DLB-13, 20

Thomas, Edward 1878-1917 ....DLB-19

Thomas, Gwyn 1913-1981 ....DLB-15

Thomas, Isaiah 1750-1831 ....DLB-43, 73

Thomas, Isaiah [publishing house] DLB-49

Thomas, John 1900-1932 ....DLB-4

Thomas, Joyce Carol 1938- DLB-33

Thomas, Lorenzo 1944- DLB-41

Thomas, R. S. 1915- DLB-27

Thompson, Dorothy 1893-1961 ....DLB-29

Thompson, Francis 1859-1907 ....DLB-19

Thompson, George Selden (see Selden, George)

Thompson, John 1938-1976 ....DLB-60

Thompson, John R. 1823-1873 ....DLB-3, 73

Thompson, Maurice 1844-1901 ....DLB-71, 74

Thompson, Ruth Plumly 1891-1976 ....DLB-22

Thompson, William Tappan 1812-1882 ....DLB-3, 11

Thomson, James 1834-1882 ....DLB-35

Thomson, Mortimer 1831-1875 ....DLB-11

Thoreau, Henry David 1817-1862 ....DLB-1

Thorpe, Thomas Bangs 1815-1878 ....DLB-3, 11

Thoughts on Poetry and Its Varieties (1833),
    by John Stuart Mill...............................DLB-32

Thurber, James 1894-1961 ....DLB-4, 11, 22

Thurman, Wallace 1902-1934 ....DLB-51

Thwaite, Anthony 1930- DLB-40

Thwaites, Reuben Gold 1853-1913 ....DLB-47

Ticknor, George 1791-1871 ....DLB-1, 59

Ticknor and Fields DLB-49

Ticknor and Fields (revived) DLB-46

Tietjens, Eunice 1884-1944 ....DLB-54

Tilton, J. E., and Company DLB-49

Time and Western Man (1927), by Wyndham
    Lewis [excerpts] DLB-36

Time-Life Books DLB-46

Times Books DLB-46

Timothy, Peter circa 1725-1782 ....DLB-43

Timrod, Henry 1828-1867........................DLB-3

Tiptree, James, Jr. 1915- DLB-8

Titus, Edward William 1870-1952 ....DLB-4

Toklas, Alice B. 1877-1967 ....DLB-4

Tolkien, J. R. R. 1892-1973 ....DLB-15

Tolson, Melvin B. 1898-1966 ....DLB-48, 76

Tom Jones (1749), by Henry
    Fielding [excerpt] DLB-39

Tomlinson, Charles 1927- DLB-40

Tomlinson, Henry Major 1873-1958 ....DLB-36

Tompkins, Abel [publishing house] DLB-49

Tompson, Benjamin 1642-1714 ....DLB-24

Tonks, Rosemary 1932- DLB-14

Toole, John Kennedy 1937-1969 ....Y-81

Toomer, Jean 1894-1967 ....DLB-45, 51

Tor Books DLB-46

Torberg, Friedrich 1908-1979 ....DLB-85

Torrence, Ridgely 1874-1950...........................DLB-54

Toth, Susan Allen 1940- Y-86

Tough-Guy Literature DLB-9

Touré, Askia Muhammad 1938- DLB-41

Tourgée, Albion W. 1838-1905.......................DLB-79

Tourneur, Cyril circa 1580-1626 ....DLB-58

Tournier, Michel 1924- DLB-83

Tousey, Frank [publishing house].....................DLB-49

Tower Publications...DLB-46

Towne, Benjamin circa 1740-1793....................DLB-43

Towne, Robert 1936- DLB-44

Tracy, Honor 1913- DLB-15

The Transatlantic Publishing Company DLB-49

Transcendentalists, American DS-5

Traven, B. 1882? or 1890?-1969?.................DLB-9, 56

Travers, Ben 1886-1980 ....DLB-10

Tremain, Rose 1943- DLB-14

Tremblay, Michel 1942- DLB-60

Trends in Twentieth-Century
    Mass Market Publishing DLB-46

Trent, William P. 1862-1939............................DLB-47

Trescot, William Henry 1822-1898...................DLB-30

Trevor, William 1928- DLB-14

Trilling, Lionel 1905-1975 ....DLB-28, 63

Triolet, Elsa 1896-1970....................................DLB-72

Tripp, John 1927- DLB-40

Trocchi, Alexander 1925- DLB-15

Trollope, Anthony 1815-1882 ....DLB-21, 57

Trollope, Frances 1779-1863 ....DLB-21

Troop, Elizabeth 1931- DLB-14

Trotter, Catharine 1679-1749 ....DLB-84

Trotti, Lamar 1898-1952 ....DLB-44

Trottier, Pierre 1925- DLB-60

Troupe, Quincy Thomas, Jr. 1943- DLB-41

Trow, John F., and Company DLB-49

Trumbo, Dalton 1905-1976 ....DLB-26

Trumbull, Benjamin 1735-1820........................DLB-30

Trumbull, John 1750-1831................................DLB-31

T. S. Eliot Centennial Y-88

Tucholsky, Kurt 1890-1935...............................DLB-56

Tucker, George 1775-1861 ....DLB-3, 30

Tucker, Nathaniel Beverley 1784-1851 ....DLB-3

Tucker, St. George 1752-1827 ....DLB-37

Tuckerman, Henry Theodore 1813-1871 ....DLB-64

Tunis, John R. 1889-1975 ....DLB-22

Tuohy, Frank 1925- DLB-14

Tupper, Martin F. 1810-1889 ....DLB-32

Turbyfill, Mark 1896- DLB-45

Turco, Lewis 1934- Y-84

Turnbull, Gael 1928- DLB-40

Turner, Charles (Tennyson) 1808-1879.............DLB-32

Turner, Frederick 1943- DLB-40

Turner, Frederick Jackson 1861-1932.............DLB-17

Turner, Joseph Addison 1826-1868 ....DLB-79

Turpin, Waters Edward 1910-1968 ....DLB-51

Twain, Mark (see Clemens, Samuel Langhorne)

The 'Twenties and Berlin,
    by Alex Natan...DLB-66

Tyler, Anne 1941- DLB-6; Y-82

Tyler, Moses Coit 1835-1900 ....DLB-47, 64

Tyler, Royall 1757-1826 ....DLB-37

Tylor, Edward Burnett 1832-1917....................DLB-57

U

Udall, Nicholas 1504-1556................................DLB-62

Uhse, Bodo 1904-1963......................................DLB-69

Ulibarrí, Sabine R. 1919- DLB-82

Ulica, Jorge 1870-1926......................................DLB-82

Under the Microscope (1872), by A. C.
    Swinburne...DLB-35

United States Book Company DLB-49

Universal Publishing and Distributing
    Corporation DLB-46

The University of Iowa Writers'
    Workshop Golden Jubilee Y-86

"The Unknown Public" (1858), by
    Wilkie Collins [excerpt]..............................DLB-57

Unruh, Fritz von 1885-1970 ....DLB-56

Upchurch, Boyd B. (see Boyd, John)

Updike, John 1932- DLB-2, 5; Y-80, 82; DS-3

Upton, Charles 1948- DLB-16

Upward, Allen 1863-1926 ....DLB-36

Urista, Alberto Baltazar (see Alurista)

Urzidil, Johannes 1896-1976 ....DLB-85

Ustinov, Peter 1921- DLB-13

V

Vail, Laurence 1891-1968 ....DLB-4

Vailland, Roger 1907-1965 ....DLB-83

Vajda, Ernest 1887-1954 ....DLB-44

Valgardson, W. D. 1939- DLB-60

Van Allsburg, Chris 1949- DLB-61

Van Anda, Carr 1864-1945 ....DLB-25

Vanbrugh, Sir John 1664-1726 ....DLB-80

Vance, Jack 1916?- DLB-8

Van Doren, Mark 1894-1972 ....DLB-45

van Druten, John 1901-1957 ....DLB-10

Van Duyn, Mona 1921- DLB-5

Van Dyke, Henry 1852-1933 ....DLB-71

Van Dyke, Henry 1928- DLB-33

Vane, Sutton 1888-1963 ....DLB-10

Vanguard Press DLB-46

van Itallie, Jean-Claude 1936- DLB-7

Vann, Robert L. 1879-1940 ....DLB-29

Van Rensselaer, Mariana Griswold
    1851-1934 ....DLB-47

Van Rensselaer, Mrs. Schuyler (see Van
    Rensselaer, Mariana Griswold)

Van Vechten, Carl 1880-1964 ....DLB-4, 9

van Vogt, A. E. 1912- DLB-8

Varley, John 1947- Y-81

Vassa, Gustavus (see Equiano, Olaudah)

Vega, Janine Pommy 1942- DLB-16

Veiller, Anthony 1903-1965 ....DLB-44

Venegas, Daniel ?-? DLB-82

Verplanck, Gulian C. 1786-1870 ....DLB-59

Very, Jones 1813-1880 ....DLB-1

Vian, Boris 1920-1959 ....DLB-72

Vickers, Roy 1888?-1965 ....DLB-77

Victoria 1819-1901 ....DLB-55

Vidal, Gore 1925- DLB-6

Viebig, Clara 1860-1952 ....DLB-66

Viereck, George Sylvester 1884-1962 ....DLB-54

Viereck, Peter 1916- DLB-5

Viewpoint: Politics and Performance, by David
    Edgar DLB-13

Vigneault, Gilles 1928- DLB-60

The Viking Press DLB-46

Villanueva, Tino 1941- DLB-82

Villard, Henry 1835-1900 ....DLB-23

Villard, Oswald Garrison 1872-1949 ....DLB-25

Villarreal, José Antonio 1924- DLB-82

Villemaire, Yolande 1949- DLB-60

Villiers, George, Second Duke
    of Buckingham 1628-1687 ....DLB-80

Viorst, Judith ?- DLB-52

Volkoff, Vladimir 1932- DLB-83

Volland, P. F., Company DLB-46

von der Grün, Max 1926- DLB-75

Vonnegut, Kurt 1922- DLB-2, 8; Y-80; DS-3

Vroman, Mary Elizabeth circa 1924-1967 ....DLB-33

W

Waddington, Miriam 1917- DLB-68

Wade, Henry 1887-1969 ....DLB-77

Wagoner, David 1926- DLB-5

Wah, Fred 1939- DLB-60

Wain, John 1925- DLB-15, 27

Wainwright, Jeffrey 1944- DLB-40

Waite, Peirce and Company DLB-49

Wakoski, Diane 1937- DLB-5

Walck, Henry Z. DLB-46

Walcott, Derek 1930- Y-81

Waldman, Anne 1945- DLB-16

Walker, Alice 1944- DLB-6, 33

Walker, George F. 1947- DLB-60

Walker, Joseph A. 1935- DLB-38

Walker, Margaret 1915- DLB-76

Walker, Ted 1934- DLB-40

Walker and Company DLB-49

Walker, Evans and Cogswell Company DLB-49

Walker, John Brisben 1847-1931 ....DLB-79

Wallace, Edgar 1875-1932.................................DLB-70

Wallant, Edward Lewis 1926-1962 ....DLB-2, 28

Walpole, Horace 1717-1797..............................DLB-39

Walpole, Hugh 1884-1941 ....DLB-34

Walrond, Eric 1898-1966 ....DLB-51

Walser, Martin 1927- DLB-75

Walser, Robert 1878-1956.................................DLB-66

Walsh, Ernest 1895-1926..............................DLB-4, 45

Walsh, Robert 1784-1859 ....DLB-59

Wambaugh, Joseph 1937- DLB-6; Y-83

Ward, Artemus (see Browne, Charles Farrar)

Ward, Arthur Henry Sarsfield
    (see Rohmer, Sax)

Ward, Douglas Turner 1930- DLB-7, 38

Ward, Lynd 1905-1985.......................................DLB-22

Ward, Mrs. Humphry 1851-1920 ....DLB-18

Ward, Nathaniel circa 1578-1652 ....DLB-24

Ward, Theodore 1902-1983...............................DLB-76

Ware, William 1797-1852...................................DLB-1

Warne, Frederick, and Company.......................DLB-49

Warner, Charles Dudley 1829-1900 ....DLB-64

Warner, Rex 1905- DLB-15

Warner, Susan Bogert 1819-1885...................DLB-3, 42

Warner, Sylvia Townsend 1893-1978 ....DLB-34

Warner Books DLB-46

Warren, John Byrne Leicester (see De Tabley, Lord)

Warren, Lella 1899-1982 ....Y-83

Warren, Mercy Otis 1728-1814............................DLB-31

Warren, Robert Penn 1905- DLB-2, 48; Y-80

Washington, George 1732-1799...........................DLB-31

Wassermann, Jakob 1873-1934 ....DLB-66

Wasson, David Atwood 1823-1887 ....DLB-1

Waterhouse, Keith 1929- DLB-13, 15

Waterman, Andrew 1940- DLB-40

Waters, Frank 1902- Y-86

Watkins, Tobias 1780-1855 ....DLB-73

Watkins, Vernon 1906-1967 ....DLB-20

Watmough, David 1926- DLB-53

Watson, Sheila 1909- DLB-60

Watson, Wilfred 1911- DLB-60

Watt, W. J., and Company DLB-46

Watterson, Henry 1840-1921 ....DLB-25

Watts, Alan 1915-1973 ....DLB-16

Watts, Franklin [publishing house].....................DLB-46

Waugh, Auberon 1939- DLB-14

Waugh, Evelyn 1903-1966.................................DLB-15

Way and Williams..DLB-49

Wayman, Tom 1945- DLB-53

Weatherly, Tom 1942- DLB-41

Webb, Frank J. ?-? DLB-50

Webb, James Watson 1802-1884 ....DLB-43

Webb, Mary 1881-1927......................................DLB-34

Webb, Phyllis 1927- DLB-53

Webb, Walter Prescott 1888-1963 ....DLB-17

Webster, Augusta 1837-1894 ....DLB-35

Webster, Charles L., and Company DLB-49

Webster, John 1579 or 1580-1634?.....................DLB-58

Webster, Noah 1758-1843 ....DLB-1, 37, 42, 43, 73

Weems, Mason Locke 1759-1825............DLB-30, 37, 42

Weidman, Jerome 1913- DLB-28

Weinbaum, Stanley Grauman 1902-1935 ....DLB-8

Weisenborn, Günther 1902-1969.......................DLB-69

Weiß, Ernst 1882-1940 ....DLB-81

Weiss, John 1818-1879 ....DLB-1

Weiss, Peter 1916-1982 ....DLB-69

Weiss, Theodore 1916- DLB-5

Welch, Lew 1926-1971? DLB-16

Weldon, Fay 1931- DLB-14

Wellek, René 1903- DLB-63

Wells, Carolyn 1862-1942..................................DLB-11

Wells, Charles Jeremiah circa 1800-1879 ....DLB-32

Wells, H. G. 1866-1946 ....DLB-34, 70

Wells, Robert 1947- DLB-40

Wells-Barnett, Ida B. 1862-1931........................DLB-23

Welty, Eudora 1909- DLB-2; Y-87

Wendell, Barrett 1855-1921 ....DLB-71

Wentworth, Patricia 1878-1961 ....DLB-77

Werfel, Franz 1890-1945...................................DLB-81

The Werner Company..DLB-49

Wersba, Barbara 1932- DLB-52

Wescott, Glenway 1901- DLB-4, 9

Wesker, Arnold 1932- DLB-13

Wesley, Richard 1945- DLB-38

Wessels, A., and Company DLB-46

West, Anthony 1914-1988 ....DLB-15

West, Dorothy 1907- DLB-76

West, Jessamyn 1902-1984 ....DLB-6; Y-84

West, Mae 1892-1980.......................................DLB-44

West, Nathanael 1903-1940 ....DLB-4, 9, 28

West, Paul 1930- DLB-14

West, Rebecca 1892-1983 ....DLB-36; Y-83

West and Johnson DLB-49

Western Publishing Company DLB-46

Wetherell, Elizabeth (see Warner, Susan Bogert)

Whalen, Philip 1923- DLB-16

Wharton, Edith 1862-1937 ....DLB-4, 9, 12, 78

Wharton, William 1920s?- Y-80

What's Really Wrong With Bestseller Lists Y-84

Wheatley, Dennis Yates 1897-1977 ....DLB-77

Wheatley, Phillis circa 1754-1784 ....DLB-31, 50

Wheeler, Charles Stearns 1816-1843...................DLB-1

Wheeler, Monroe 1900-1988 ....DLB-4

Wheelock, John Hall 1886-1978......................DLB-45

Wheelwright, John circa 1592-1679 ....DLB-24

Wheelwright, J. B. 1897-1940 ....DLB-45

Whetstone, Colonel Pete (see Noland, C. F. M.)

Whipple, Edwin Percy 1819-1886 ....DLB-1, 64

Whitaker, Alexander 1585-1617........................DLB-24

Whitaker, Daniel K. 1801-1881 ....DLB-73

Whitcher, Frances Miriam 1814-1852 ....DLB-11

White, Andrew 1579-1656 ....DLB-24

White, Andrew Dickson 1832-1918....................DLB-47

White, E. B. 1899-1985 ....DLB-11, 22

White, Edgar B. 1947- DLB-38

White, Ethel Lina 1887-1944 ....DLB-77

White, Horace 1834-1916 ....DLB-23

White, Richard Grant 1821-1885......................DLB-64

White, Walter 1893-1955.................................DLB-51

White, William, and Company...........................DLB-49

White, William Allen 1868-1944 ....DLB-9, 25

White, William Anthony Parker (see Boucher, Anthony)

White, William Hale (see Rutherford, Mark)

Whitechurch, Victor L. 1868-1933 ....DLB-70

Whitehead, James 1936- Y-81

Whitehead, William 1715-1785.........................DLB-84

Whitfield, James Monroe 1822-1871 ....DLB-50

Whiting, John 1917-1963 ....DLB-13

Whiting, Samuel 1597-1679..............................DLB-24

Whitlock, Brand 1869-1934 ....DLB-12

Whitman, Albert, and Company DLB-46

Whitman, Albery Allson 1851-1901 ....DLB-50

Whitman, Sarah Helen (Power) 1803-1878..........DLB-1

Whitman, Walt 1819-1892 ....DLB-3, 64

Whitman Publishing Company DLB-46

Whittemore, Reed 1919- DLB-5

Whittier, John Greenleaf 1807-1892 ....DLB-1

Whittlesey House...DLB-46

Wideman, John Edgar 1941- DLB-33

Wiebe, Rudy 1934- DLB-60

Wiechert, Ernst 1887-1950...............................DLB-56

Wied, Martina 1882-1957.................................DLB-85

Wieners, John 1934- DLB-16

Wier, Ester 1910- DLB-52

Wiesel, Elie 1928- DLB-83; Y-87

Wiggin, Kate Douglas 1856-1923 ....DLB-42

Wigglesworth, Michael 1631-1705.....................DLB-24

Wilbur, Richard 1921- DLB-5

Wild, Peter 1940- DLB-5

Wilde, Oscar 1854-1900 ....DLB-10, 19, 34, 57

Wilde, Richard Henry 1789-1847 ....DLB-3, 59

Wilde, W. A., Company DLB-49

Wilder, Billy 1906- DLB-26

Wilder, Laura Ingalls 1867-1957.......................DLB-22

Wilder, Thornton 1897-1975 ....DLB-4, 7, 9

Wiley, Bell Irvin 1906-1980..............................DLB-17

Wiley, John, and Sons DLB-49

Wilhelm, Kate 1928- DLB-8

Wilkes, George 1817-1885 ....DLB-79

Wilkinson, Sylvia 1940- Y-86

Wilkinson, William Cleaver 1833-1920 ....DLB-71

Willard, L. [publishing house] DLB-49

Willard, Nancy 1936- DLB-5, 52

Willard, Samuel 1640-1707 ....DLB-24

Williams, A., and Company DLB-49

Williams, C. K. 1936- DLB-5

Williams, Chancellor 1905- DLB-76

Williams, Emlyn 1905- DLB-10, 77

Williams, Garth 1912- DLB-22

Williams, George Washington 1849-1891 ....DLB-47

Williams, Heathcote 1941- DLB-13

Williams, Hugo 1942- DLB-40

Williams, Isaac 1802-1865 ....DLB-32

Williams, Joan 1928- DLB-6

Williams, John A. 1925- DLB-2, 33

Williams, John E. 1922- DLB-6

Williams, Jonathan 1929- DLB-5

Williams, Raymond 1921- DLB-14

Williams, Roger circa 1603-1683 ....DLB-24

Williams, Samm-Art 1946- DLB-38

Williams, Sherley Anne 1944- DLB-41

Williams, T. Harry 1909-1979 ....DLB-17

Williams, Tennessee 1911-1983 ....DLB-7; Y-83; DS-4

Williams, Valentine 1883-1946 ....DLB-77

Williams, William Appleman 1921- DLB-17

Williams, William Carlos 1883-1963 ....DLB-4, 16, 54

Williams, Wirt 1921- DLB-6

Williams Brothers DLB-49

Williamson, Jack 1908- DLB-8

Willingham, Calder Baynard, Jr. 1922- DLB-2, 44

Willis, Nathaniel Parker 1806-1867 ...DLB-3, 59, 73, 74

Wilmer, Clive 1945- DLB-40

Wilson, A. N. 1950- DLB-14

Wilson, Angus 1913- DLB-15

Wilson, Arthur 1595-1652 ....DLB-58

Wilson, Augusta Jane Evans 1835-1909 ....DLB-42

Wilson, Colin 1931- DLB-14

Wilson, Edmund 1895-1972 ....DLB-63

Wilson, Ethel 1888-1980 ....DLB-68

Wilson, Harriet E. Adams 1828?-1863? DLB-50

Wilson, Harry Leon 1867-1939 ....DLB-9

Wilson, John 1588-1667 ....DLB-24

Wilson, Lanford 1937- DLB-7

Wilson, Margaret 1882-1973 ....DLB-9

Wilson, Michael 1914-1978 ....DLB-44

Wilson, Woodrow 1856-1924 ....DLB-47

Wimsatt, William K., Jr. 1907-1975 ....DLB-63

Winchell, Walter 1897-1972 ....DLB-29

Winchester, J. [publishing house] DLB-49

Windham, Donald 1920- DLB-6

Winsor, Justin 1831-1897 ....DLB-47

John C. Winston Company DLB-49

Winters, Yvor 1900-1968 ....DLB-48

Winthrop, John 1588-1649 ....DLB-24, 30

Winthrop, John, Jr. 1606-1676 ....DLB-24

Wirt, William 1772-1834 ....DLB-37

Wise, John 1652-1725 ....DLB-24

Wisner, George 1812-1849 ....DLB-43

Wister, Owen 1860-1938 ....DLB-9, 78

Witherspoon, John 1723-1794 ....DLB-31

Wittig, Monique 1935- DLB-83

Wodehouse, P. G. 1881-1975 ....DLB-34

Wohmann, Gabriele 1932- DLB-75

Woiwode, Larry 1941- DLB-6

Wolcott, Roger 1679-1767 ....DLB-24

Wolf, Christa 1929- DLB-75

Wolfe, Gene 1931- DLB-8

Wolfe, Thomas 1900-1938 ....DLB-9; DS-2; Y-85

Wollstonecraft, Mary 1759-1797 ....DLB-39

Wondratschek, Wolf 1943- DLB-75

Wood, Benjamin 1820-1900 ....DLB-23

Wood, Charles 1932- DLB-13

Wood, Mrs. Henry 1814-1887 ....DLB-18

Wood, Samuel [publishing house] DLB-49

Wood, William ?-? DLB-24

Woodberry, George Edward 1855-1930 ....DLB-71

Woodbridge, Benjamin 1622-1684 ....DLB-24

Woodhull, Victoria C. 1838-1927 ....DLB-79

Woodmason, Charles circa 1720-? DLB-31

Woodson, Carter G. 1875-1950 ....DLB-17

Woodward, C. Vann 1908- DLB-17

Woolf, David (see Maddow, Ben)

Woolf, Virginia 1882-1941 ....DLB-36

Woollcott, Alexander 1887-1943 ....DLB-29

Woolman, John 1720-1772 ....DLB-31

Woolner, Thomas 1825-1892 ....DLB-35

Woolsey, Sarah Chauncy 1835-1905 ....DLB-42

Woolson, Constance Fenimore 1840-1894 ....DLB-12, 74

Worcester, Joseph Emerson 1784-1865 ....DLB-1

The Works of the Rev. John Witherspoon
    (1800-1801) [excerpts] DLB-31

A World Chronology of Important Science
    Fiction Works (1818-1979) DLB-8

World Publishing Company DLB-46

Worthington, R., and Company.........................DLB-49

Wouk, Herman 1915- Y-82

Wright, Charles 1935- Y-82

Wright, Charles Stevenson 1932- DLB-33

Wright, Frances 1795-1852 ....DLB-73

Wright, Harold Bell 1872-1944 ....DLB-9

Wright, James 1927-1980 ....DLB-5

Wright, Jay 1935- DLB-41

Wright, Louis B. 1899-1984 ....DLB-17

Wright, Richard 1908-1960 ....DS-2, DLB-76

Wright, Richard B. 1937- DLB-53

Wright, Sarah Elizabeth 1928- DLB-33

Writers and Politics: 1871-1918,
    by Ronald Gray...DLB-66

Writers' Forum..Y-85

Writing for the Theatre, by Harold Pinter DLB-13

Wycherley, William 1641-1715 ....DLB-80

Wylie, Elinor 1885-1928.............................DLB-9, 45

Wylie, Philip 1902-1971 ....DLB-9

Y

Yates, Dornford 1885-1960 ....DLB-77

Yates, J. Michael 1938- DLB-60

Yates, Richard 1926- DLB-2; Y-81

Yeats, William Butler 1865-1939 ....DLB-10, 19

Yep, Laurence 1948- DLB-52

Yerby, Frank 1916- DLB-76

Yezierska, Anzia 1885-1970...............................DLB-28

Yolen, Jane 1939- DLB-52

Yonge, Charlotte Mary 1823-1901 ....DLB-18

A Yorkshire Tragedy DLB-58

Yoseloff, Thomas [publishing house] DLB-46

Young, Al 1939- DLB-33

Young, Stark 1881-1963 ....DLB-9

Young, Waldeman 1880-1938 ....DLB-26

Young, William [publishing house]....................DLB-49

Yourcenar, Marguerite 1903-1987...........DLB-72; Y-88

"You've Never Had It So Good," Gusted by
    "Winds of Change": British Fiction in the
    1950s, 1960s, and After DLB-14

Z

Zamora, Bernice 1938- DLB-82

Zand, Herbert 1923-1970 ....DLB-85

Zangwill, Israel 1864-1926..................................DLB-10

Zebra Books DLB-46

Zebrowski, George 1945- DLB-8

Zech, Paul 1881-1946 ....DLB-56

Zelazny, Roger 1937- DLB-8

Zenger, John Peter 1697-1746 ....DLB-24, 43

Zieber, G. B., and Company DLB-49

Zieroth, Dale 1946- DLB-60

Zimmer, Paul 1934- DLB-5

Zindel, Paul 1936- DLB-7, 52

Zolotow, Charlotte 1915- DLB-52

Zubly, John Joachim 1724-1781......................DLB-31

Zu-Bolton II, Ahmos 1936- DLB-41

Zuckmayer, Carl 1896-1977 ....DLB-56

Zukofsky, Louis 1904-1978 ....DLB-5

zur Mühlen, Hermynia 1883-1951 ....DLB-56

Zweig, Arnold 1887-1968...................................DLB-66

Zweig, Stefan 1881-1942 ....DLB-81

(Continued from front endsheets)

71: *American Literary Critics and Scholars, 1880-1900,* edited by John W. Rathbun and Monica M. Grecu (1988)

72: *French Novelists, 1930-1960,* edited by Catharine Savage Brosman (1988)

73: *American Magazine Journalists, 1741-1850,* edited by Sam G. Riley (1988)

74: *American Short-Story Writers Before 1880,* edited by Bobby Ellen Kimbel, with the assistance of William E. Grant (1988)

75: *Contemporary German Fiction Writers,* Second Series, edited by Wolfgang D. Elfe and James Hardin (1988)

76: *Afro-American Writers, 1940-1955,* edited by Trudier Harris (1988)

77: *British Mystery Writers, 1920-1939,* edited by Bernard Benstock and Thomas F. Staley (1988)

78: *American Short-Story Writers, 1880-1910,* edited by Bobby Ellen Kimbel, with the assistance of William E. Grant (1988)

79: *American Magazine Journalists, 1850-1900,* edited by Sam G. Riley (1988)

80: *Restoration and Eighteenth-Century Dramatists,* First Series, edited by Paula R. Backscheider (1989)

81: *Austrian Fiction Writers, 1875-1913,* edited by James Hardin and Donald G. Daviau (1989)

82: *Chicano Writers,* First Series, edited by Francisco A. Lomelí and Carl R. Shirley (1989)

83: *French Novelists Since 1960,* edited by Catharine Savage Brosman (1989)

84: *Restoration and Eighteenth-Century Dramatists,* Second Series, edited by Paula R. Backscheider (1989)

85: *Austrian Fiction Writers After 1914,* edited by James Hardin and Donald G. Daviau (1989)

Documentary Series

1: *Sherwood Anderson, Willa Cather, John Dos Passos, Theodore Dreiser, F. Scott Fitzgerald, Ernest Hemingway, Sinclair Lewis,* edited by Margaret A. Van Antwerp (1982)

2: *James Gould Cozzens, James T. Farrell, William Faulkner, John O'Hara, John Steinbeck, Thomas Wolfe, Richard Wright,* edited by Margaret A. Van Antwerp (1982)

3: *Saul Bellow, Jack Kerouac, Norman Mailer, Vladimir Nabokov, John Updike, Kurt Vonnegut,* edited by Mary Bruccoli (1983)

4: *Tennessee Williams,* edited by Margaret A. Van Antwerp and Sally Johns (1984)

5: *American Transcendentalists,* edited by Joel Myerson (1988)

6: *Hardboiled Mystery Writers,* edited by Matthew J. Bruccoli and Richard Layman (1988)

Yearbooks

1980, edited by Karen L. Rood, Jean W. Ross, and Richard Ziegfeld (1981)

1981, edited by Karen L. Rood, Jean W. Ross, and Richard Ziegfeld (1982)

1982, edited by Richard Ziegfeld; associate editors: Jean W. Ross and Lynne C. Zeigler (1983)

1983, edited by Mary Bruccoli and Jean W. Ross; associate editor: Richard Ziegfeld (1984)

1984, edited by Jean W. Ross (1985)

1985, edited by Jean W. Ross (1986)

1986, edited by J. M. Brook (1987)